Macroeconomics For Today

Enhanced and Customized for the Economists at Hudson Valley Community College

EIGHTH EDITION

Irvin B. Tucker

CENGAGE
Learning·

Australia • Brazil • Japan • Korea • Mexico • Singapore • Spain • United Kingdom • United States

CENGAGE
Learning®

Macroeconomics For Today, Enhanced and Customized for the Economists at Hudson Valley Community College, 8E

Macroeconomics for Today, 8th Edition
Irvin B. Tucker

© 2014 Cengage Learning. All rights reserved.

The New Humanities Reader, 5th Edition
Richard E. Miller, Kurt Spellmeyer

© 2015 Cengage Learning. All rights reserved.

Macroeconomics, 11th Edition
Roger A. Arnold

© 2014 Cengage Learning. All rights reserved.

Economics of Natural Disasters
Bill Boyes, Mike Melvin

© 2006 Cengage Learning. All rights reserved.

Senior Manager, Student Engagement:
Linda deStefano

Manager, Student Engagement:
Julie Dierig

Marketing Manager:
Rachael Kloos

Manager, Premedia:
Kim Fry

Manager, Intellectual Property Project Manager:
Brian Methe

Senior Manager, Production:
Donna M. Brown

Manager, Production:
Terri Daley

For product information and technology assistance, contact us at
Cengage Learning Customer & Sales Support, 1-800-354-9706

For permission to use material from this text or product,
submit all requests online at **cengage.com/permissions**
Further permissions questions can be emailed to
permissionrequest@cengage.com

This book contains select works from existing Cengage Learning resources and was produced by Cengage Learning Custom Solutions for collegiate use. As such, those adopting and/or contributing to this work are responsible for editorial content accuracy, continuity and completeness.

Compilation © 2014 Cengage Learning

ISBN: 978-1-305-29306-9

WCN: 01-100-101

Cengage Learning
20 Channel Center Street
Boston, MA 02210
USA

Cengage Learning is a leading provider of customized learning solutions with office locations around the globe, including Singapore, the United Kingdom, Australia, Mexico, Brazil, and Japan. Locate your local office at:
international.cengage.com/region.

Cengage Learning products are represented in Canada by Nelson Education, Ltd.
For your lifelong learning solutions, visit **www.cengage.com/custom.**
Visit our corporate website at **www.cengage.com.**

Printed in: United States of America

Brief Contents

Text with a Mission

The purpose of *Economics for Today*, eighth edition, is to teach, in an engaging style, the basic operations of the U.S. economy to students who will take a two-term economics course. Rather than taking an encyclopedic approach to economic concepts, *Economics for Today* focuses on the most important tool in economics—supply and demand analysis—and applies it to clearly explained real-world economic issues.

Every effort has been made to ensure that *Economics for Today* is the most "student-friendly" text on the market. This text was written because so many other economics textbooks expose students to a confusing array of analyses that force students to memorize facts to pass the course. Instead, *Economics for Today* presents a straightforward and unbiased approach that effectively teaches the application of basic economic principles. After reading this text, students should be able to say "now that economics stuff in the news makes sense."

How It Fits Together

This text presents the core principles of microeconomics, macroeconomics, and international economics. The first 14 chapters introduce the logic of economic analysis and develop the core of microeconomic analysis. Here students learn the role of demand and supply in determining prices in competitive versus monopolistic markets. This part of the book explores issues such as minimum wage laws, rent control, and pollution. The next 13 chapters develop the macroeconomics part of the text. Using the modern yet simple aggregate demand and aggregate supply model, the text explains measurement of and changes in price level, national output, and employment in the economy. The study of macroeconomics also includes how the supply of and demand for money influence the economy. Finally, this text concludes with three chapters devoted entirely to global issues. For example, students will learn how the supply of and demand for currencies determine exchange rates and what the complications of a strong or a weak dollar are.

Text Flexibility

The full version of *Economics for Today* is easily adapted to an instructor's preference for the sequencing of microeconomics and macroeconomics topics. This text can be used in a macroeconomic-microeconomic sequence by teaching the first four chapters and then Parts 5 through 7. Microeconomics is then covered in Parts 2 through 4. Finally, the course can be completed using Part 8, consisting of three chapters devoted to international economics.

An important design of this text is that it accommodates the two camps for teaching principles of macroeconomics: (1) those who cover both the Keynesian Cross and AD/AS models and (2) those who skip the Keynesian model and cover only the AD/AS model. For instructors who prefer the former model sequence, *Economics for Today* moves smoothly in Chapters 18 and 19 (8 and 9) from the Keynesian model (based on the Great Depression) to the AD/AS model in

Chapter 20 (10). For instructors using the latter approach, this text is written so that they can skip the Keynesian model in Chapters 18 and 19 (8 and 9) and proceed from Chapter 17 (7) to Chapter 20 (10) without losing any content. For example, the spending multiplier is covered in both the Keynesian and AD/AS model chapters.

For instructors who want to teach the self-correcting AD/AS model, they can emphasize the appendixes to Chapters 20 (10) and 26 (16). Instructors who choose not to cover this model can skip these appendixes. In short, *Economics for Today* provides more comprehensive and flexible coverage of macroeconomics models than is available in other texts. Also, a customized text might meet your needs. If so, contact your Cengage South Western sales representative for information.

How Not to Study Economics

To some students, studying economics is a little frightening because many chapters are full of graphs. Students often make the mistake of preparing for tests by trying to memorize the lines of graphs. When their graded tests are returned, students using this strategy may wonder what happened. The answer is that they should have learned the economic concepts *first;* then they would have understood the graphs as *illustrations* of the underlying concepts. Stated simply, superficial cramming for economics quizzes does not work.

For students who are anxious about using graphs, the appendix to Chapter 1 provides a brief review of graphical analysis. In addition, *The Graphing Workshop* on the Tucker Web site and the *Study Guide* contain step-by-step features on how to interpret graphs.

Changes to the Eighth Edition

The basic layout of the eighth edition remains the same. The following changes have been made:

- Chapter 1 recognizes that students taking introductory college-level economics courses are considering their major. One reason to select economics is that the average starting salary for an undergraduate economics major is higher compared to many other majors. To aid in their decision, current average starting salary figures for selected majors have been updated.
- Chapter 12 on income distribution, poverty, and discrimination has been updated with the latest figures on family income distribution and poverty rates. In addition, the feature article on fair pay for females has been updated. This feature generates great interest for students.
- Chapter 14 on environmental economics is one of today's highly controversial issues. This chapter has been updated and a new concept of sustainability added.
- Chapter 16 (6) on business cycles and unemployment includes updated business cycles and unemployment data. A new section on globalization discusses the differences between outsourcing and offshoring.
- Chapter 17 (7) on inflation updates data on inflation, including a global comparison of annual inflation rates. In addition, the Checkpoint titled "What Is

the Real Price of Gasoline?" provides an application for adjusting the price of gasoline for inflation over time. In addition, students enjoy learning how Babe Ruth's 1932 salary is converted into today's dollars.

- Chapter 18 (8) on the Keynesian model now ends with a discussion of the investment function. Instead of the aggregate expenditures function being introduced here with only consumption and investment components, the aggregate expenditure model is presented after all components $(C + I + G + (X - M))$ are explained in Chapter 19 (9) on the Keynesian model in action. The complete aggregate expenditures model is now presented in a new Exhibit 2 in Chapter 19 (9). The objective is to make these two chapters more equal in length and provide a smoother progression in the development of the model.
- Chapter 21 (11) on fiscal policy uses realism as its hallmark by explaining the stimulus package and the spending multiplier process with real-world updated numbers.
- Chapter 22 (12) on the public sector highlights the important current issue of the changing economic character of the United States with global comparisons to other countries. Here, for example, updated data and exhibits trace the growth of U.S. government expenditures and taxes since the Great Depression. In addition, global comparison of spending and taxation exhibits have been revised.
- Chapter 23 (13) on federal deficits, surpluses, and the national debt focuses on the current "hot button" issue of federal deficits and the national debt by using updated data and exhibits. This chapter includes global comparisons of the deficit and national debt as a percentage of GDP.
- Chapter 24 (14) on money and the Federal Reserve System has updated money supply figures and Exhibit 4 showing the current listing of the ten top U.S. banks by asset size.
- Chapter 26 (16) on monetary policy has been updated using actual data in the model that link changes in the money supply and changes in the aggregate demand curve required to restore the economy to full employment. Student interest is enhanced by Exhibit 9 that compares monetary policy during the Great Depression to monetary policy during the current Great Recession.
- Each of the final three chapters of the text, the international chapters, has been updated. For example, the chapter on international trade and finance explains the recent U.S. balance of trade. The difference between absolute advantage and comparative advantage has been rewritten, with the discussion of absolute advantage now preceding the explanation of comparative advantage. The chapter on economies in transition contrasts privatization in Cuba, Russia, and China to recent nationalization in the United States. And the chapter on growth and the less-developed countries presents updated data used to explain, for example, the link between economic freedom and quality-of-life indicators.
- The lecture PowerPoint® slides have been updated and revised by the author.
- Each chapter includes a new sample quiz with new free corresponding tutorial quizzes that explain the answers on the Tucker Web site.

- New questions have been written by the author and added to the test bank.
- New Appendix D presents U.S. Gross Domestic Product and Related Statistics.
- With the growth in eReader usage among students, this edition features a new numbering system for major headings that we recommend instructors use instead of page numbers when creating assignments. For more information or to purchase an eReader for *Economics for Today,* please visit www.cengage brain.com.

Alternate Versions of the Book

For instructors who want to spend different amounts of time on their courses and offer different topics of this text:

- *Economics for Today.* This complete version of the book contains all 30 chapters. It is designed for two-semester introductory courses that cover both microeconomics and macroeconomics.
- *Microeconomics for Today.* This version contains 17 chapters and is designed for one-semester courses in introductory microeconomics.
- *Macroeconomics for Today.* This version contains 20 chapters and is designed for one-semester courses in introductory macroeconomics.
- *Survey of Economics for Today.* This version of the book contains 23 chapters. It is designed for one-semester courses that cover the basics of both microeconomics and macroeconomics.

The accompanying table shows which chapters are included in each book.

Instructors who want more information about these alternative versions should contact their local Cengage South-Western representative or visit www.cengage brain.com.

Motivational Pedagogical Features

Economics for Today strives to motivate and advance the boundaries of pedagogy with the following features:

PART OPENERS

Each part begins with a statement of the overall mission of the chapters in the part. In addition, there is a nutshell introduction of each chapter in relation to the part's learning objective.

CHAPTER PREVIEWS

Each chapter begins with a preview designed to pique student interest and reinforce how the chapter fits into the overall scheme of the book. Each preview appeals to students' "Sherlock Holmes" impulses by posing several economics puzzles that can be solved by understanding the material presented in the chapter.

MARGIN DEFINITIONS AND FLASHCARDS

Key concepts introduced in the chapter are highlighted in bold type and then defined with the definitions again in the margins. Therefore, this feature serves as a quick reference. Key terms are also defined on the Tucker Web site with a Flash-card feature that is useful for learning terms.

YOU'RE THE ECONOMIST

Each chapter includes boxed inserts that provide the acid test of "relevance to everyday life." This feature gives students an opportunity to encounter timely, real-world extensions of economic theory. For example, students read about Fred Smith as he writes an economics term paper explaining his plan to create FedEx. To ensure that students waste no time figuring out which concepts apply to the article, applicable concepts are listed after each title. Many of these boxed features include quotes from newspaper articles over a period of years, demonstrating that economic concepts remain relevant over time.

CONCLUSION STATEMENTS

Throughout the chapters, highlighted conclusion statements of key concepts appear at the end of sections and tie together the material just presented. Students will be able to see quickly whether they understand the main points of the section. A summary of these conclusion statements is provided at the end of each chapter.

GLOBAL ECONOMICS

Today's economic environment is global. *Economics for Today* carefully integrates international topics throughout the text and presents the material using a highly readable and accessible approach designed for students with no training in international economics. All sections of the text that present global economics are identified by a special global icon in the margin and in the Global Economics boxes. In addition, the final three chapters of the book are devoted entirely to international economics.

ANALYZE THE ISSUE

This feature follows each *You're the Economist* and *Global Economics* feature and asks specific questions that require students to test their knowledge of how the material in the boxed insert is relevant to the applicable concept. So that these questions can be used in classroom discussions or homework assignments, answers are provided in the *Instructor's Manual* rather than the text.

CHECKPOINT

Watch for these! Who said learning economics can't be fun? This feature is a unique approach to generating interest and critical thinking. These questions spark students to check their progress through challenging economics puzzles in gamelike style. Students enjoy thinking through and answering the questions then checking the answers at the end of the chapter. Students who answer correctly earn the satisfaction of knowing they have mastered the concepts.

ILLUSTRATIONS

Attractive large graphical presentations with grid lines and real-world numbers are essential for any successful economics textbook. Each exhibit has been carefully analyzed to ensure that the key concepts stand out clearly. Brief descriptions are included with graphs to provide guidance as students study the graphs. When actual data are used, the Web site reference is provided so that students can easily locate the data source.

CAUSATION CHAINS GAME

This will be one of your favorites. The highly successful causation chains are included under many graphs throughout the text. This pedagogical device helps students visualize complex economic relationships in terms of simple box diagrams that illustrate how one change causes another change. Each exhibit having a causation chain in the text is included in the Animated Causation Chains game on the Tucker Web site. This game makes it fun to learn. Arrange the blocks correctly and hear the cheers.

KEY CONCEPTS

Key concepts introduced in the chapters are listed at the end of each chapter and on the Tucker Web site. As a study aid, students can use the key concepts as flashcards to test their knowledge. First state the definition and then click on the term to check for correctness.

VISUAL SUMMARIES

Each chapter ends with a brief point-by-point summary of the key concepts. Many of these summarized points include miniaturized versions of the important graphs and causation chains that illustrate key concepts. These are intended to serve as visual reminders for students as they finish the chapters and are useful in reviewing and studying for quizzes and exams.

STUDY QUESTIONS AND PROBLEMS

The end-of-chapter questions and problems offer a variety of levels ranging from straightforward recall to deeply thought-provoking applications. The answers to odd-numbered questions and problems are in the back of the text. This feature gives students immediate feedback without requiring the instructor to check their work.

END-OF-CHAPTER SAMPLE QUIZZES

A great help before quizzes. Many instructors test students using multiple-choice questions. For this reason, the final section of each chapter provides the type of multiple-choice questions given in the instructor's Test Bank. The answers to all of these questions are given in the back of the text. In addition, students may visit the Tucker Web site and answer the questions in the online sample quizzes for free. In addition, students can email themselves and/or their instructor the quiz results with a list of correct and incorrect answers. The Web site is a tutorial because it provides explanations for why answers are correct.

PART ROAD MAP

This feature concludes each part and includes review questions listed by chapter from the previous part. To reinforce the concepts, each set of questions relates to the interactive causation chain game. Click on the Tucker Web site and make learning fun by listening to the cheers when correct and the jeers for a wrong answer. Answers to the questions are in the back of the text.

INTERACTIVE QUIZZES

In addition to the end-of-chapter sample quizzes, additional multiple-choice questions written by the author are available on the Tucker CourseMate Web site. Each quiz contains multiple questions like those found on a typical exam. Feedback is included for each answer so that students know instantly why they answered correctly or incorrectly. In addition, students can email themselves and/or their instructor the quiz results with a listi of correct and incorrect answers. Between this feature and the end-of-chapter sample quizzes, students are well prepared for tests.

ONLINE EXERCISES

These exercises for each chapter are designed to spark student excitement about researching on the Internet by asking them to access online economic data and then answer questions related to the content of the chapter. All Internet exercises are on the Tucker CourseMate site with direct links to the addresses so that students do not have the tedious and error-prone task of entering long Web site addresses.

LEARNING OBJECTIVES

Learning objectives link sections in the text and steps to achieve learning objectives. The steps include reference to "Ask the Instructor Video Clips" and the "Graphing Workshop" that are available through CourseMate on the Tucker Web site.

A Supplements Package Designed for Success

To access additional course materials for *Economics for Today,* [including Course-Mate], please visit www.cengagebrain.com. At the CengageBrain.com home page, search for the ISBN of your title (from the back cover of your book) using the search box at the top of the page. This will take you to the product page where these resources can be found. Or visit the Tucker Web site, www.cengage.com/economics/tucker. For additional information, contact your Cengage South-Western sales representative.

Instructor Resources
APLIA™

Aplia™, www.aplia.com, has joined forces with Cengage South-Western, the leading publisher for principles of economics and finance, to create the Aplia Integrated Textbook Solution. More students are currently using an Aplia™ product for principles of economics than those who are using all other Web-based learning programs combined. Because the homework in Aplia™ is automatically graded, you can assign homework more frequently to ensure that students are putting forth their full effort and getting the most out of your class.

INSTRUCTOR'S MANUAL

This manual, prepared by Douglas Copeland of Johnson County Community College, provides valuable course assistance to instructors. It includes chapter outlines, instructional objectives, critical-thinking/group discussion questions, hints for effective teaching, answers to the Analyze the Issue questions, answers to even-numbered questions and problems, summary quizzes with answers, and classroom games.

Instructor's Manual ISBN: 9781133562368

TEST BANK

Too often, Test Banks are not written by the author and the questions do not really fit the text. Not so here. This Test Bank was prepared by the text author to match the text. The Test Bank includes over 7,000 multiple-choice, true/false, and short essay questions arranged in the order presented in the chapter and grouped with concept headings that make it easy to select questions. Most questions have been thoroughly tested in the classroom by the author and are classified by topic and degree of difficulty.

Test Bank ISBN: 9781285184395 (Macroeconomics split), 9781285184401 (Microeconomics split), or on the IRCD: 9781285074269

EXAMVIEW®

ExamView® Computerized Testing Software contains all of the questions in the printed Test Bank. ExamView® is easy-to-use test creation software that is compatible with both Microsoft Windows® and Apple Macintosh®. You can add or edit questions, instructions, and answers; select questions by previewing them on the screen; or select questions randomly or by number. You can also create and administer quizzes online, whether over the Internet, a local area network (LAN), or a wide area network (WAN).

ExamView® available on Instructor's Resource CD: ISBN: 9781285074269

POWERPOINT® LECTURE SLIDES

This state-of-the-art slide presentation written and prepared by the text author provides you with visual support in the classroom for each chapter. Lecture slides contain vivid automated highlights of important concepts and exhibits. You can edit the PowerPoint® presentations or create your own exciting in-class presentations. These slides are available on the Instructor's Resource CD (9781285074269) as well as the Tucker Web site.

POWERPOINT® EXHIBIT SLIDES

These slides contain the exhibits, charts, and tables from the text. You can easily incorporate them into your own PowerPoint® presentations by downloading them from the Instructor's Resource CD (9781285074269) as well as the Tucker Web site.

INSTRUCTOR'S RESOURCE CD

Get quick access to all instructor ancillaries from your desktop. This easy-to-use CD lets you review, edit, and copy exactly what you need in the format you want. This supplement contains the *Instructor's Manual*, Test Bank, ExamView® Testing software, and PowerPoint® presentation slides.

IRCD ISBN: 9781285074269

Student Resources
THE TUCKER COURSEMATE WEB SITE

Available for purchase, the CourseMate Web site (www.cengagebrain.com) features a content-rich, robust set of interactive learning, study, and exam preparation tools to support the textbook. CourseMate includes an integrated eBook, interactive teaching and learning tools, quizzes, flashcards, videos, and more. It also includes Engagement Tracer, a first-of-its kind resource that monitors student engagement in the course.

Following are some of the CourseMate features that have been specifically developed with the student in mind:

- **Study Guide.** *The Study Guide*, available on the Cengage CourseMate site, is recommended for each student using the text. It is perhaps the best way to prepare for quizzes. The *Study Guide* was prepared by the text author to prepare students before they take tests in class. The *Study Guide* contains student-friendly features such as "Chapter in a Nutshell," key concepts review, learning objectives, fill-in-the-blank questions, step-by-step interpretation of the graph boxes, multiple-choice questions, true/false questions, and crossword puzzles.

  Study Guide ISBN: 9781285184371 (CourseMate ISBN)

- **News Videos.** This supplement consists of high-interest clips from current news events as well as historic raw footage going back 40 years. Perfect to use as discussion starters or to enrich your lectures and spark interest in the material in the text, these brief videos provide students with a new lens through which to view the past and present, one that will greatly enhance their knowledge and understanding of significant events and open up new dimension in learning. Clips are drawn from such programs as *World News Tonight, Good Morning America, This Week, PrimeTime Live, 20/20,* and *Nightline,* as well as numerous British Movietone News collections. Your Cengage South-Western representative will be happy to provide a complete list of the videos and policies addressed.

- **The Graphing Workshop.** The Graphing Workshop is a one-stop learning resource for help in mastering the language of graphs, one of the more difficult aspects of an economics course for many students. It enables students to explore important economic concepts through a unique learning system made up of tutorials; interactive drawing tools; and exercises that teach how to interpret, reproduce, and explain graphs.

- **Ask the Instructor Video Clips.** Via streaming video, difficult concepts are explained and illustrated. These video clips are extremely helpful review and clarification tools if a student has trouble understanding an in-class lecture or is a visual learner.

For Students and Instructors
CENGAGE LEARNING'S GLOBAL ECONOMIC WATCH

Lessons from real life right now

The credit collapse. Tumbling markets. Bailouts and bankruptcies. Surging unemployment. Political debate. Today's financial turmoil transforms academic theory into intense real-life challenges that affect every family and business sector, making it one of the most teachable moments in modern history.

Cengage Learning's Global Economic Watch helps instructors bring these pivotal current events into the classroom through a powerful, continuously updated online suite of content, discussion forums, testing tools, and more.

The Watch, a first-of-its kind resource, stimulates discussion and understanding of the global downturn with easy-to-integrate teaching solutions:

- A content-rich blog of breaking news, expert analysis, and commentary updated multiple times daily, in addition to links to other blogs
- A powerful real-time database of hundreds of relevant and vetted journal, newspaper, and periodical articles; videos; and podcasts updated four times every day
- A thorough overview and timeline of events leading up to the global economic crisis
- Discussion and testing content, PowerPoint® slides on key topics, sample syllabi, and other teaching resources
- Instructor and student forums for sharing questions, ideas, and opinions

History is happening now. Bring it into your classroom. For more information on how you can enrich your course with The Watch, please visit www.cengage.com/thewatch.

TUCKER WEB SITE

The Tucker Web site at www.cengage.com/economics/tucker provides open access to PowerPoint® chapter review slides, flashcards, animated causation chains, tutorials for the text's end-of-chapter sample quizzes, and other downloadable teaching and learning resources.

Acknowledgments

A deep debt of gratitude is owed to the reviewers for their expert assistance. All comments and suggestions were carefully evaluated and served to improve the final product. To each of the reviewers of all eight editions, I give my sincerest thanks.

Special Thanks

My appreciation goes to Steve Scoble, Acquisitions Editor for Cengage South-Western. My thanks also to Clara Goosman, Developmental Editor; Darrell Frye, Content Project Manager; Elizabeth Beiting-Lipps, Editorial Assistant; and Iyssa Harbatkin, Marketing Coordinator who put all the pieces of the puzzle together and brought their creative talent to this text. I especially wish to express my deepest appreciation to Douglas Copeland of Johnson County Community College for preparing the *Instructor's Manual*. I am also grateful to John Carey and Robin LeFevre for their skillful marketing. Finally, I give my sincere thanks for a job well done to the entire team at Cengage South-Western.

Introduction to Economics

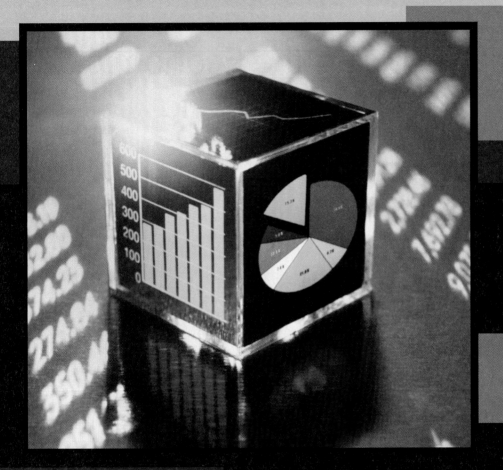

part 1

The first two chapters introduce you to a foundation of economic knowledge vital to understanding the other chapters in the text. In these introductory chapters, you will begin to learn a valuable reasoning approach to solving economics puzzles that economists call "the economic way of thinking." Part 1 develops the cornerstone of this type of logical analysis by presenting basic economic models that explain such important topics as scarcity, opportunity cost, production possibilities, and economic growth.

chapter 1

Introducing the Economic Way of Thinking

Welcome to an exciting and useful subject economists call "the economic way of thinking." As you learn this reasoning technique, it will become infectious. You will discover that the world is full of economics problems requiring more powerful tools than just common sense. As you master the methods explained in this book, you will appreciate economics as a valuable reasoning approach to solving economics puzzles. Stated differently, the economic way of thinking is important because it provides a logical framework for organizing your thoughts and understanding an economic issue or event. Just to give a sneak preview, in later chapters, you will study the perils of government price fixing for gasoline and health care. You will also find out why colleges and universities charge students different tuitions for the same education. You will investigate whether you should worry if the federal government fails to balance its budget.

You will learn that the island of Yap uses large stones with holes in the center as money. In the final chapter, you will study why some countries grow rich while others remain poor and less developed. And the list of fascinating and relevant topics continues throughout each chapter. As you read these pages, your efforts will be rewarded by an understanding of just how economic theories and policies affect our daily lives—past, present, and future.

Chapter 1 acquaints you with the foundation of the economic way of thinking. The first building blocks joined are the concepts of scarcity and choice. The next building blocks are the steps in the model-building process that economists use to study the choices people make. Then we look at some pitfalls of economic reasoning and explain why economists might disagree with one another. The chapter concludes with a discussion of why you may want to be an economics major.

In this chapter, you will learn to solve these economics puzzles:

- Can you prove there is no person worth a trillion dollars?
- Why would you purchase more Coca-Cola when the price increases?
- How can we explain the relationship between the Super Bowl winner and changes in the stock market?

1-1 The Problem of Scarcity

Our world is a finite place where people, both individually and collectively, face the problem of scarcity. Scarcity is the condition in which human wants are forever greater than the available supply of time, goods, and resources. Because of scarcity, it is impossible to satisfy every desire. Pause for a moment to list some of your unsatisfied wants. Perhaps you would like a big home, gourmet meals, designer clothes, clean air, better health care, shelter for the homeless, and more leisure time. Unfortunately, nature does not offer the Garden of Eden, where every desire is fulfilled. Instead, there are always limits on the economy's ability to satisfy unlimited wants. Alas, scarcity is pervasive, so "You can't have it all."

You may think your scarcity problem would disappear if you were rich, but wealth does not solve the problem. No matter how affluent an individual is, the wish list continues to grow. We are familiar with the "rich and famous" who never seem to have enough. Although they live well, they still desire finer homes, faster planes, and larger yachts. In short, the condition of scarcity means all individuals, whether rich or poor, are dissatisfied with their material well-being and would like more. What is true for individuals also applies to society. Even Uncle Sam can't escape the problem of scarcity because the federal government never has enough money to spend for the poor, education, highways, police, national defense, Social Security, and all the other programs it wishes to fund.

Scarcity is a fact of life throughout the world. In much of South America, Africa, and Asia, the problem of scarcity is often life-threatening. On the other hand, North America, Western Europe, and some parts of Asia have achieved substantial economic growth and development. Although life is much less grueling in the more developed countries, the problem of scarcity still exists because individuals and countries never have as much of all the goods and services as they would like to have.

> **CONCLUSION:** *The problem of scarcity and choice are basic economic problems faced by every society.*

1-2 Scarce Resources and Production

Because of the economic problem of scarcity, no society has enough resources to produce all the goods and services necessary to satisfy all human wants. Resources are the basic categories of inputs used to produce goods and services. Resources are also called *factors of production*. Economists divide resources into three categories: *land*, *labor*, and *capital* (see Exhibit 1).

Scarcity

The condition in which human wants are forever greater than the available supply of time, goods, and resources.

Resources

The basic categories of inputs used to produce goods and services. Resources are also called *factors of production*. Economists divide resources into three categories: land, labor, and capital.

EXHIBIT 1	Three Categories of Resources

Resources are the basic categories of inputs organized by entrepreneurship (a special type of labor) to produce goods and services. Economists divide resources into the three categories of land, labor, and capital.

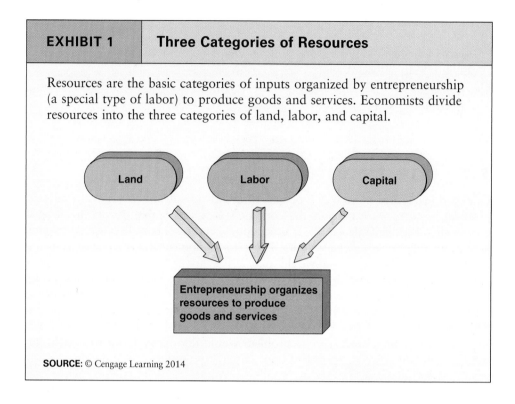

SOURCE: © Cengage Learning 2014

1-2a LAND

Land

Any natural resource provided by nature that is used to produce a good or service.

Land is a shorthand expression for any natural resource provided by nature that is used to produce a good or service. *Land* includes those resources that are gifts of nature available for use in the production process. Farming, building factories, and constructing oil refineries would be impossible without land. Land includes anything natural above or below the ground, such as forests, gold, diamonds, oil, coal, wind, and the ocean. Two broad categories of natural resources are *renewable resources* and *nonrenewable resources*. Renewable resources are basic inputs that nature can automatically replace. Examples include lakes, crops, and clean air. Nonrenewable resources are basic inputs that nature cannot automatically replace. There is only so much coal, oil, and natural gas in the world. If these fossil fuels disappear, we must use substitutes.

1-2b LABOR

Labor

The mental and physical capacity of workers to produce goods and services.

Entrepreneurship

The creative ability of individuals to seek profits by taking risks and combining resources to produce innovative products.

Labor is the mental and physical capacity of workers to produce goods and services. The services of farmers, assembly-line workers, lawyers, professional football players, and economists are all *labor*. The labor resource is measured both by the number of people available for work and by the skills or quality of workers. One reason nations differ in their ability to produce is that human characteristics, such as the education, experience, health, and motivation of workers, differ among nations.

Entrepreneurship is a special type of labor. Entrepreneurship is the creative ability of individuals to seek profits by taking risks and combining resources to produce innovative products. An *entrepreneur* is a motivated person who seeks profits by undertaking such risky activities as starting new businesses, creating new products, or inventing new ways of accomplishing tasks. Entrepreneurship is a scarce human resource because relatively few people are willing or able to innovate and make decisions involving greater-than-normal chances for failure. An important benefit of entrepreneurship is that it creates a growing economy.

Entrepreneurs are the agents of change who bring material progress to society. The birth of the Levi Strauss Company is a classic entrepreneurial success story. In 1853, at the age of 24, Levi Strauss, who was born in Bavaria, sailed from New York to join the California Gold Rush. His intent was not to dig for gold, but to sell cloth. By the time he arrived in San Francisco, he had sold most of his cloth to other people on the ship. The only cloth he had left was a roll of canvas for tents and covered wagons. On the dock, he met a miner who wanted sturdy pants that would last while digging for gold, so Levi made a pair from the canvas. Later, a customer gave Levi the idea of using little copper rivets to strengthen the seams. Presto! Strauss knew a good thing when he saw it, so he hired workers, built factories, and became one of the largest pants makers in the world. As a reward for taking business risks, organizing production, and introducing a product, the Levi Strauss Company earned profits, and Strauss became rich and famous.

1-2c CAPITAL

Capital is a human-made good used to produce other goods and services. Capital includes the physical plants, machinery, and equipment used to produce other goods. Capital goods are human-made goods that do not directly satisfy human wants. Before the Industrial Revolution, *capital* meant a tool, such as a hoe, an axe, or a bow and arrow. In those days, these items served as capital to build a house or provide food for the dinner table. Today, capital also consists of factories, office buildings, warehouses, robots, trucks, roads, and distribution facilities. College buildings, the printing presses used to produce this textbook, and iPhones are also examples of capital. The term *capital* as it is used in the study of economics can be confusing. Economists know that capital in everyday conversations means money or the money value of paper assets, such as stocks, bonds, or a deed to a house. This is actually *financial* capital. In the study of economics, capital does not refer to money assets. Capital in economics means a factor of production, such as a factory or machinery. Stated simply, you must pay special attention to this point: Money is not capital and is therefore not a resource. Instead, money is used to purchase land, labor, or capital.

Capital
A human-made good used to produce other goods and services.

> **CONCLUSION:** *Money by itself does not produce goods and services; instead, it is only a means of buying capital.*

1-3 Economics: The Study of Scarcity and Choice

The perpetual problem of scarcity forcing people to make choices is the basis for the definition of economics. Economics is the study of how society chooses to allocate its scarce resources to the production of goods and services to satisfy

Economics
The study of how society chooses to allocate its scarce resources to the production of goods and services to satisfy unlimited wants.

unlimited wants. You may be surprised by this definition. People often think economics means studying supply and demand, the stock market, money, and banking. In fact, there are many ways one could define *economics*, but economists accept the definition given here because it includes the link between *scarcity* and *choices*.

Society makes two kinds of choices: economy-wide, or macro choices, and individual, or micro, choices. The prefixes *macro* and *micro* come from the Greek words meaning "large" and "small," respectively. Reflecting the macro and micro perspectives, economics consists of two main branches: *macroeconomics* and *microeconomics*.

1-3a MACROECONOMICS

Macroeconomics

The branch of economics that studies decision making for the economy as a whole.

The old saying "Looking at the forest rather than the trees" describes macroeconomics. Macroeconomics is the branch of economics that studies decision making for the economy as a whole. Macroeconomics applies an overview perspective to an economy by examining economy-wide variables, such as inflation, unemployment, growth of the economy, the money supply, and the national incomes of developing countries. Macroeconomic decision making considers such "big picture" policies as the effect that federal tax cuts will have on unemployment and the effect that changing the money supply will have on prices.

1-3b MICROECONOMICS

Microeconomics

The branch of economics that studies decision making by a single individual, household, firm, industry, or level of government.

Examining individual trees, leaves, and pieces of bark, rather than surveying the forest, illustrates microeconomics. Microeconomics is the branch of economics that studies decision making by a single individual, household, firm, industry, or level of government. Microeconomics applies a microscope to study specific parts of an economy, as one would examine cells in the body. The focus is on small economic units, such as economic decisions of particular groups of consumers and businesses. An example of microeconomic analysis would be to study economic units involved in the market for ostrich eggs. Will suppliers decide to supply more, less, or the same quantity of ostrich eggs to the market in response to price changes? Will individual consumers of these eggs decide to buy more, less, or the same quantity at a new price?

We have described macroeconomics and microeconomics as two separate branches, but they are related. Because the overall economy is the sum, or aggregation, of its parts, micro changes affect the macro economy, and macro changes produce micro changes.

1-4 The Methodology of Economics

As used by other disciplines, such as criminology, biology, chemistry, and physics, economists employ a step-by-step procedure for solving problems by identifying the problem, developing a model, gathering data, and testing whether the data are consistent with the theory. Based on this analysis, economists formulate a conclusion. Exhibit 2 summarizes the model-building process.

EXHIBIT 2	The Steps in the Model-Building Process

The first step in developing a model is to identify the problem. The second step is to select the critical variables necessary to formulate a model that explains the problem under study. Eliminating other variables that complicate the analysis requires simplifying assumptions. In the third step, the researcher collects data and tests the model. If the evidence supports the model, the conclusion is to accept the model. If the evidence doesn't support the model, the model is rejected.

Identify the problem

Develop a model based on simplified assumptions

Collect data, test the model, and formulate a conclusion

SOURCE: © Cengage Learning 2014

1-4a PROBLEM IDENTIFICATION

The first step in applying the economic method is to define the issue. Suppose an economist wishes to investigate the microeconomic problem of why U.S. motorists cut back on gasoline consumption in a given year from, for example, 400 million gallons per day in May to 300 million gallons per day in December.

1-4b MODEL DEVELOPMENT

The second step in our hypothetical example toward finding an explanation is for the economist to build a model. A model is a simplified description of reality used to understand and predict the relationship between variables. The terms *model* and *theory* are interchangeable. A model emphasizes only those variables that

Model

A simplified description of reality used to understand and predict the relationship between variables.

A map is a model because it is an abstraction from reality.

Scott Rothstein/
iStockphoto.com

are most important to explaining an event. As Albert Einstein said, "Theories should be as simple as possible, but not more so." The purpose of a model is to construct an abstraction from real-world complexities and make events understandable. Consider a model airplane that is placed in a wind tunnel to test the aerodynamics of a new design. For this purpose, the model must represent only the shapes of the wings and fuselage, but it does not need to include tiny seats, electrical wiring, or other interior design details. A highway map is another example. To find the best route to drive between two distant cities, you do not want extraneous information on the location of all roads, streets, potholes, telephone lines, trees, stoplights, schools, hospitals, and firehouses. This would be too much detail, and the complexity would make it difficult to choose the best route.

To be useful, a model requires simplified assumptions. Someone must decide, for example, whether a map will include only symbols for the major highways or the details of hiking trails through mountains. In our gasoline consumption example, several variables might be related to the quantity of gasoline consumed, including consumer incomes, the prices of substitutes for gasoline, the price of gasoline, the fuel economy of cars, and weather conditions. Because a theory focuses only on the main or critical variables, the economist must be a "Sherlock Holmes" and use a keen sense of observation to form a model. Using his or her expertise, the economist must select the variables that are related to gasoline consumption and reject variables that have only a slight or no relationship to gasoline consumption. In this simple case, the economist removes the cloud of complexity by formulating the theory that increases in the price of gasoline *cause* the quantity of gasoline consumed to decrease during the time period.

1-4c TESTING A THEORY

An economic model can be stated as a verbal argument, numerical table, graph, or mathematical equation. You will soon discover that a major part of this book is devoted to building and using economic models. The purpose of an economic model is to *forecast* or *predict* the results of various changes in variables. Note that the appendix to this chapter provides a review of graphical analysis. An economic theory can be expressed in the form "If *A*, then *B*, other things held constant." An economic model is useful only if it yields accurate predictions. When the evidence is consistent with the theory that *A* causes outcome *B*, there is confidence in the theory's validity. When the evidence is inconsistent with the theory that *A* causes outcome *B*, the researcher rejects this theory.

In the third step, the economist gathers data to test the theory that if the price of gasoline rises, then gasoline purchases fall—all other relevant factors held constant. Suppose the investigation reveals that the price of gasoline rose sharply between May and December of the given year. The data are therefore consistent with the theory that the quantity of gasoline consumed per month falls when its price rises, assuming no other relevant factors change. Thus, the conclusion is that the theory is valid if, for example, consumer incomes or population size does not change at the same time that gasoline prices rise.

✓ CHECKPOINT

Can You Prove There Is No Trillion-Dollar Person?

Suppose a theory says that no U.S. citizen is worth $1 trillion. You decide to test this theory and send researchers to all corners of the nation to check financial records to see whether someone qualifies by owning assets valued at $1 trillion or more. After years of checking, the researchers return and report that not a single person is worth at least $1 trillion. Do you conclude that the evidence proves the theory? Explain.

1-5 Hazards of the Economic Way of Thinking

Models help us understand and predict the impact of changes in economic variables. A model is an important tool in the economist's toolkit, but it must be handled with care. The economic way of thinking seeks to avoid reasoning mistakes. Two of the most common pitfalls to clear thinking are (1) failing to understand the *ceteris paribus assumption* and (2) confusing *association* and *causation*.

1-5a THE CETERIS PARIBUS ASSUMPTION

As you work through a model, try to think of a host of relevant variables assumed to be "standing still," or "held constant." Ceteris paribus is a Latin phrase that means while certain variables change, "all other things remain unchanged." In short, the ceteris paribus assumption allows us to isolate or focus attention on selected variables. In the gasoline example discussed earlier, a key simplifying assumption of the model is that changes in consumer incomes and certain other variables do not occur and complicate the analysis. The ceteris paribus assumption holds everything else constant, and therefore allows us to concentrate on the relationship between two key variables: changes in the price of gasoline and the quantity of gasoline purchased per month.

> **Ceteris paribus**
>
> A Latin phrase that means while certain variables change, "all other things remain unchanged"

Now suppose an economist examines a model explaining the relationship between the price and quantity purchased of Coca-Cola. The theory is "If the price increases, then the quantity of Coca-Cola purchased decreases, ceteris paribus." Now assume you observe that the price of Coca-Cola increased one summer and some people actually bought more, not less. Based on this real-world observation, you declare the theory is incorrect. Think again! The economist responds that this is a reasoning pitfall because the model is valid based on the assumption of ceteris paribus, and your observation gives us no reason to reject the model. The reason the model appeared flawed is because another factor, a sharp rise in the temperature, *caused* people to buy more Coca-Cola in spite of its higher price. If the temperature and all other factors are held constant as the price of Coca-Cola rises, then people will indeed buy less Coca-Cola, as the model predicts.

> **CONCLUSION:** *A theory cannot be tested legitimately unless its ceteris paribus assumption is satisfied.*

1-5b ASSOCIATION VERSUS CAUSATION

Another common error in reasoning is confusing *association* (or correlation) and *causation* between variables. Stated differently, you err when you read more into a relationship between variables than is actually there. A model is valid only when a cause-and-effect relationship is stable or dependable over time, rather than being an association that occurs by chance and eventually disappears. Suppose a witch doctor performs a voodoo dance during three different months and stock market prices skyrocket during each of these months. The voodoo dance is *associated* with the increase in stock prices, but this does not mean the dance *caused* the event. Even though there is a statistical relationship between these two variables in a number of observations, eventually the voodoo dance will be performed, and stock prices will fall or remain unchanged. The reason is that there is no true systematic economic relationship between voodoo dances and stock prices.

Further investigation may reveal that stock prices actually responded to changes in interest rates during the months that the voodoo dances were performed. Changes in interest rates affect borrowing and, in turn, profits and stock prices. In contrast, there is no real economic relationship between voodoo dances and stock prices, and, therefore, the voodoo model is not valid.

> **CONCLUSION:** *The fact that one event follows another does not necessarily mean that the first event caused the second event.*

✔ CHECKPOINT

Should Nebraska State Join a Big-Time Athletic Conference?
Nebraska State (a mythical university) stood by while Penn State, Florida State, the University of Miami, and the University of South Carolina joined big-time athletic conferences. Now Nebraska State officials are pondering whether to remain independent or to pursue membership in a conference noted for high-quality football and basketball programs. An editorial in the newspaper advocates joining and cites a study showing that universities belonging to major athletic conferences have higher graduation rates than nonmembers. Because educating its students is the number one goal of Nebraska State, will this evidence persuade Nebraska State officials to join a big-time conference? Why or why not?

Throughout this book, you will study economic models or theories that include variables linked by stable cause-and-effect relationships. For example, the theory that a change in the price of a good *causes* a change in the quantity purchased is a valid microeconomic model. The theory that a change in the money supply *causes* a change in interest rates is an example of a valid macroeconomic model. The You're the Economist gives some amusing examples of the "association means causation" reasoning pitfall.

Mops and Brooms, the Boston Snow Index, the Super Bowl, and Other Economic Indicators

Applicable Concept: association versus causation

Although the Commerce Department, the Wharton School, the Federal Reserve Board, and other organizations publish economic forecasts and data on key economic indicators, they are not without armchair competition. For example, the chief executive of Standex International Corporation, Daniel E. Hogan, reported that his company can predict economic downturns and recoveries from sales reports of its National Metal Industries subsidiary in Springfield, Massachusetts. National makes metal parts for about 300 U.S. manufacturers of mops and brooms. A drop in National's sales always precedes a proportional fall in consumer spending. The company's sales always pick up slightly before consumer spending does.[1]

The Boston Snow Index (BSI) is the brainchild of a vice president of a New York securities firm. It predicts a rising economy for the next year if there is snow on the ground in Boston on Christmas Day. The BSI predicted correctly about 73 percent of the time over a 30-year period. However, its creator, David L. Upshaw, did not take it too seriously and views it as a spoof of other forecasters' methods.

Greeting card sales are another tried and true indicator, according to a vice president of American Greetings. Before a recession sets in, sales of higher-priced greeting cards rise. It seems that people substitute the cards for gifts, and since there is no gift, the card must be fancier.

A Super Bowl win by an NFC team predicts that in the following December, the stock market will be higher than the year before. A win by an old AFL team predicts a dip in the stock market.

Several other less well-known indicators have also been proposed. For example, one economist suggested that the surliness of waiters is a countercyclical indicator. If they are nice, expect that bad times are coming, but if they are rude, expect an upturn. Waiters, on the other hand, counter that a fall in the average tip usually precedes a downturn in the economy.

Finally, Anthony Chan, chief economist for Bank One Investment Advisors, studied marriage trends

LUCY NICHOLSON/Reuters/Landov

over a 34-year period. He discovered that when the number of marriages increases, the economy rises significantly, and a slowdown in marriages is followed by a decline in the economy. Chan explains that there is usually about a one-year lag between a change in the marriage rate and the economy.[2]

Analyze the Issue

Which of the above indicators are examples of causation? Explain.

1. "Economic Indicators, Turtles, Butterflies, Monks, and Waiters," *The Wall Street Journal*, Aug. 27, 1979, pp. 1, 16.
2. Sandra Block, "Worried? Look at Wedding Bell Indicator," *The Charlotte Observer*, Apr. 15, 1995, p. 8A.

Source: © Cengage Learning 2014

I. Tucker

1-6 Why Do Economists Disagree?

Why might one economist say a clean environment should be our most important priority and another economist say economic growth should be our most important goal? If economists share the economic way of thinking and carefully avoid reasoning pitfalls, then why do they disagree? Why are economists known for giving advice by saying, "On the one hand, if you do this, then *A* results, and on the other hand, doing this causes result *B*?" In fact, President Harry Truman once jokingly exclaimed, "Find me an economist with only one hand." George Bernard Shaw offered another famous line in the same vein: "If you took all the economists in the world and laid them end to end, they would never reach a conclusion." These famous quotes imply that economists should agree, but the quotes ignore the fact that physicists, doctors, business executives, lawyers, and other professionals often disagree.

Economists may appear to disagree more than other professionals partly because it is more interesting to report disagreements than agreements. Actually, economists agree on a wide range of issues. Many economists, for example, agree on free trade among nations, the elimination of farm subsidies and rent ceilings, government deficit spending to recover from a recession, and many other issues. When disagreements do exist, the reason can often be explained by the difference between *positive economics* and *normative economics*.

1-6a POSITIVE ECONOMICS

Positive economics

An analysis limited to statements that are verifiable.

Positive economics deals with facts and therefore addresses "what is" or "verifiable" questions. Positive economics is an analysis limited to statements that are verifiable. Positive statements can be proven either true or false. Often a positive statement is expressed: "If *A*, then *B*." For example, if the national unemployment rate rises to 9 percent, then teenage unemployment exceeds 80 percent. This is a positive "if-then" prediction, which may or may not be correct. Accuracy is not the criterion for a statement to be positive. The key consideration is whether the statement is *testable* and not whether it is true or false. Suppose the data show that when the nation's overall unemployment rate is close to 9 percent, the unemployment rate for teenagers never reaches 80 percent. For example, the overall unemployment rate was 9.3 percent in 2011, and the rate for teenagers was 24.3 percent—far short of 80 percent. Based on the facts, we would conclude that this positive statement is false.

Now we can explain one reason why economists' forecasts can diverge. The statement "If event *A* occurs, then event *B* follows" can be thought of as a *conditional* positive statement. For example, two economists may agree that if the federal government cuts spending by 10 percent this year, prices will fall about 2 percent next year. However, their predictions about the fall in prices may differ because one economist assumes Congress will not cut spending, while the other economist assumes Congress will cut spending by 10 percent.

> **CONCLUSION:** *Economists' forecasts can differ because using the same methodology, economists can agree that event A causes event B, but disagree over the assumption that event A will occur.*

Does the Minimum Wage Really Help the Working Poor?

Applicable Concepts: *positive and normative analyses*

Minimum wages exist in more than 100 countries. In 1938, Congress enacted the federal Fair Labor Standards Act, commonly known as the "minimum-wage law." Today, a minimum wage worker who works full-time still earns a deplorably low annual income. One approach to help the working poor earn a living wage might be to raise the minimum wage.

The dilemma for Congress is that a higher minimum wage for the employed is enacted at the expense of jobs for unskilled workers. Opponents forecast that the increased labor cost from a large minimum wage hike would jeopardize hundreds of thousands of unskilled jobs. For example, employers may opt to purchase more capital and less expensive labor. The fear of such sizable job losses forces Congress to perform a difficult balancing act to ensure that a minimum wage increase is large enough to help the working poor, but not so large as to threaten their jobs.

Some politicians claim that raising the minimum wage is a way to help the working poor without cost to taxpayers. Others believe the cost is hidden in inflation and lost employment opportunities for marginal workers, such as teenagers, the elderly, and minorities. One study by economists, for example, examined 60 years of data and concluded that minimum wage increases resulted in reduced employment and hours of work for low-skilled workers.[1]

Another problem with raising the minimum wage to aid the working poor is that minimum wage is a blunt weapon for redistributing wealth. Studies show that only a small percentage of minimum wage earners are full-time workers whose family income falls below the poverty line. This means that most increases in the minimum wage go to workers who are not poor. For example, many minimum wage workers are students living at home or workers whose spouse earns a much higher income. To help only the working poor, some economists argue that the government should target only those people who need assistance, rather than using the "shotgun" approach of raising the minimum wage.

Supporters of raising the minimum wage are not convinced by these arguments. They say it is outrageous that a worker can work full-time and still live in poverty. Moreover, people on this side of the debate believe that opponents exaggerate the dangers to the economy from a higher minimum wage. For example, one could argue that a higher minimum wage will force employers to upgrade the skills and productivity of their workers. Increasing the minimum wage may therefore be a win-win proposition rather than a win-lose proposition. Finally, across the United States, 32 states and numerous localities have implemented minimum wage laws. At least 17 states recently raised the minimum wage or are considering doing so in 2012, the most in at least six years. The Republican presidential candidate Mitt Romney and President Obama

support automatic federal minimum wage increases to keep up with inflation. Note that we return to this issue in Chapter 4 as an application of supply and demand analysis.

Analyze the Issue

1. Identify two positive and two normative statements given above concerning raising the minimum wage. List other minimum wage arguments not discussed in this You're the Economist, and classify them as either positive or normative economics.

2. Give a positive and a normative argument why a business leader would oppose raising the minimum wage. Give a positive and a normative argument why a labor leader would favor raising the minimum wage.

3. Explain your position on this issue. Identify positive and normative reasons for your decision. Are there alternative ways to aid the working poor? Explain.

---

1. David Neumark and William Wascher, *Minimum Wages*, Cambridge, MA: *The MIT Press*, 2008.

Source: © Cengage Learning 2014

1-6b NORMATIVE ECONOMICS

Normative economics

An analysis based on value judgment.

Instead of using objective statements, an argument can be phrased subjectively. Normative economics attempts to determine "what should be." Normative economics is an analysis based on value judgments. Normative statements express an individual or collective opinion on a subject and cannot be proven by facts to be true or false. Certain words or phrases, such as *good*, *bad*, *need*, *should*, and *ought to*, tell us clearly that we have entered the realm of normative economics.

The point here is that people wearing "different-colored glasses" see the same facts differently. Each of us has individual subjective preferences that we apply to a particular subject. An animal rights activist says that no one *should* purchase a fur coat. Or one senator argues, "We *ought to* ensure that every teenager who wants a job has one." Another senator counters by saying, "Maintaining the purchasing power of the dollar is *more important* than teenage unemployment."

> **CONCLUSION:** *When opinions or points of view are not based on facts, they are scientifically untestable.*

When considering a debate, make sure to separate the arguments into their positive and normative components. This distinction allows you to determine whether you are choosing a course of action based on factual evidence or on opinion. The material presented in this textbook, like most of economics, takes pains to stay within the boundaries of positive economic analysis. In our everyday lives, however, politicians, business executives, relatives, and friends use mostly normative statements to discuss economic issues. Economists also may associate themselves with a political position and use normative arguments for or against some economic policy. When using value judgments, an economist's normative arguments may have no greater validity than those of other people. Biases or preconceptions can cloud an economist's thinking about deficit spending or whether to increase taxes on gasoline. Like beginning economics students, economists are human.

1-7 Careers in Economics

The author of this text entered college more years ago than I would like to admit. In those days, economics was not taught in high school, so I knew nothing of the subject. Like many students taking this course, I was uncertain about which major to pursue, but selected electrical engineering because I was an amateur radio operator and enjoyed building radio receivers and transmitters. My engineering curriculum required a course in economics. I signed up thinking that "econ is boring." Instead, it was an eye-opening experience that inspired me to change my major to economics and pursue an economics teaching career.

The study of economics has attracted a number of well-known people. For example, The Rolling Stones' Mick Jagger attended the London School of Economics, and other famous people who majored in economics include former Supreme Court Justice Sandra Day O'Connor, and three former presidents—George H. W. Bush, Ronald Reagan, and Gerald Ford.

An economics major can choose many career paths. Most economics majors work for business firms. Because economists are trained in analyzing financial matters, they find good jobs in management, sales, or as a market analyst interpreting economic conditions relevant to a firm's market. For those with an undergraduate degree, private-sector job opportunities exist in banking, securities brokering, management consulting, computer and data processing firms, the power industry, market research, finance, health care, and many other industries. Other economics majors work for government agencies and in colleges and universities.

Government economists work for federal, state, and local governments. For example, a government economist might compile and report national statistics for economic growth or work on projects such as how to improve indexes to measure trends in consumer prices. Economists in academe not only enjoy the challenge of teaching economics, but also have great freedom in selecting research projects.

Studying economics is also an essential preparation for other careers. Those preparing for law school, for example, find economics an excellent major because of its emphasis on a logical approach to problem solving. Economics is also great preparation for an MBA. In fact, students majoring in any field will benefit throughout their lives from learning how to apply the economic way of thinking to analyze real-world economic issues.

Finally, economics majors shine in salary offers upon graduation. Exhibit 3 shows average yearly salary offers for bachelor's degree candidates for April 2011.

EXHIBIT 3	Average Yearly Salary Offers for Selected Majors
Undergraduate Major	**Average Offer, April 2011**
Computer science	$63,017
Electrical engineering	60,646
Computer engineering	60,112
Nursing	55,774
Mathematics	55,300
Economics	54,634
Management information systems	54,372
Accounting	50,316
Liberal arts and sciences	50,313
Political sciences	48,129
Business administration	46,832
Marketing	44,432
Psychology	40,611
Environmental science	40,093
Criminal justice	38,741
Foreign languages	37,743
Sociology	37,464
Animal Science	34,324
Visual and performing arts	32,371
Journalism	31,591
Social work	31,397

SOURCE: National Association of Colleges and Employers, *Salary Survey*, Spring 2011.

Key Concepts

Scarcity
Resources
Land
Labor
Entrepreneurship

Capital
Economics
Macroeconomics
Microeconomics
Model

Ceteris paribus
Positive economics
Normative economics

Summary

- **Scarcity** is the fundamental economic problem that human wants exceed the availability of time, goods, and resources. Individuals and society therefore can never have everything they desire.
- **Resources** are factors of production classified as land, labor, and capital. Entrepreneurship is a special type of labor. An entrepreneur seeks profits by taking risks and combining resources to produce innovative products.
- **Economics** is the study of how individuals and society choose to allocate scarce resources to satisfy unlimited wants. Faced with unlimited wants and scarce resources, we must make choices among alternatives.

SOURCE: © Cengage Learning 2014

- **Macroeconomics** applies an economy-wide perspective that focuses on such issues as inflation, unemployment, and the growth rate of the economy.
- **Microeconomics** examines individual decision-making units within an economy, such as a

consumer's response to changes in the price of coffee and the reasons for changes in the market price of personal computers.

- **Models** are simplified descriptions of reality used to understand and predict economic events. An economic model can be stated verbally or in a table, a graph, or an equation. If the event is not consistent with the model, the model is rejected.

- **Ceteris paribus** holds "all other factors unchanged" that might affect a particular relationship. If this assumption is violated, a model cannot be tested. Another reasoning pitfall is to think that *association* means *causation*.
- Use of positive versus normative economic analysis is a major reason for disagreements among economists. **Positive economics** uses testable statements. Often a positive argument is expressed as an *if-then* statement. **Normative economics** is based on value judgments or opinions and uses words such as *good, bad, ought to,* and *should.*

Summary of Conclusion Statements

- The problem of scarcity and choice are basic economic problems faced by every society.

- Money by itself does not produce goods and services; instead, it is only a means of buying capital.

- A theory cannot be tested legitimately unless its ceteris paribus assumption is satisfied.
- The fact that one event follows another does not necessarily mean that the first event caused the second event.
- Economists' forecasts can differ because using the same methodology, economists can agree that event A causes event B, but disagree over the assumption that event A will occur.
- When opinions or points of view are not based on facts, they are scientifically untestable.

Study Questions and Problems

1. Explain why both nations with high living standards and nations with low living standards face the problem of scarcity. If you won $1 million in a lottery, would you escape the scarcity problem?

2. Why isn't money considered capital in economics?

3. Explain the difference between macroeconomics and microeconomics. Give examples of the areas of concern to each branch of economics.

4. Which of the following are microeconomic issues? Which are macroeconomic issues?
   a. How will an increase in the price of Coca-Cola affect the quantity of Pepsi-Cola sold?
   b. What will cause the nation's inflation rate to fall?
   c. How does a quota on textile imports affect the textile industry?
   d. Does a large federal budget deficit reduce the rate of unemployment in the economy?

5. Explain why it is important for an economic model to be an abstraction from the real world.

6. Explain the importance of the ceteris paribus assumption for an economic model.

7. Suppose Congress cuts spending for the military, and then unemployment rises in the U.S. defense industry. Is there causation in this situation, or are we observing an association between events?

8. Analyze the positive versus normative arguments in the following case. What statements of positive economics are used to support requiring air bags? What normative reasoning is used?

Should the Government Require Air Bags?

Air bag advocates say air bags will save lives and the government should require them in all cars. Air bags add an estimated $600 to the cost of a car, compared to about $100 for a set of regular seat belts. Opponents argue that air bags are electronic devices subject to failure and have produced injuries and death. For example, air bags have killed both adults and children whose heads were within the inflation zone at the time of deployment. Opponents therefore believe the government should leave the decision of whether to spend an extra $600 or so for an air bag to the consumer. The role of the government should be limited to providing information on the risks of having versus not having air bags.

For Online Exercises, go the Tucker Web site at www.cengage.com/economics/tucker.

✓ CHECKPOINT ANSWERS

Can You Prove There Is No Trillion-Dollar Person?

How can researchers ever be certain they have found all the rich people in the United States? There is always the possibility that somewhere there is a person who qualifies. If the researchers had found one, you could have rejected the theory. Because they did not, you cannot reject the theory. If you said that the evidence can support, but never prove the theory, **YOU ARE CORRECT.**

Should Nebraska State Join a Big-Time Athletic Conference?

Suppose universities that belong to big-time athletic conferences do indeed have higher graduation rates than nonmembers. This is not the only possible explanation for the statistical correlation (or association) between the graduation rate and membership in a big-time athletic conference. A more plausible explanation is that improving academic variables, such as tuition, quality of faculty, and student-faculty ratios, and not athletic conference membership, increase the graduation rate. If you said correlation, does not mean causation, and therefore Nebraska State officials will not necessarily accept the graduation rate evidence, **YOU ARE CORRECT.**

Sample Quiz

For an explanation of the correct answers, visit the Tucker Web site at www.cengage.com/economics/tucker.

1. Which of the following illustrates the concept of scarcity?
   a. More clean air is wanted than is available in large polluted metropolitan areas such as Mexico City.
   b. There is usually more than one use of your "free" time in the evening.
   c. There are many competing uses for the annual budget of your city, county, or state.
   d. All of the above are correct.

2. Which of the following are factors of production?
   a. The outputs generated by the production process transforming land, labor, and capital into goods and services
   b. Resources restricted to the land, such as natural resources that are unimproved by human economic activity

   c. Land (natural resources), labor (human capital, entrepreneurship), and capital (constructed inputs such as factories).
   d. Just labor and capital in industrialized countries, where natural resources are no longer used to produce goods and services

3. Which of the following is *not* an example of a capital input?
   a. A person's skills and abilities, which can be employed to produce valuable goods and services
   b. Factories and offices where goods and services are produced
   c. Tools and equipment
   d. Computers used by a company to record inventory, sales, and payroll

Sample Quiz *continued*

4. Which of the following is the best definition of economics?
   a. Economics is the study of how to manage corporations to generate the greatest return on shareholder investment.
   b. Economics is the study of how to manage city and county government to generate the greatest good to its citizens.
   c. Economics is the study of how society chooses to allocate its scarce resources.
   d. Economics is the study of how to track revenues and costs in a business.

5. Which of the following *best* illustrates the application of the model-building process to economics?
   a. On a Sunday morning talk show, two economists with differing political agendas argue about the best way to solve the Social Security problem.
   b. A labor economist notices that unemployment tends to be higher among teenagers than more experienced workers, develops a model, and gathers data to test the hypotheses in the model.
   c. A Ph.D. student in economics makes up data on the lumber market and develops a model for his dissertation that seems to be consistent with the data.
   d. Economists come to believe that some economic models are true simply because prominent leading economists say they are true.

6. Which of the following represents causality rather than association?
   a. In years that fashion dictates wider lapels on men's jackets, the stock market grows by at least 5 percent.
   b. Interest rates are higher in years ending with a 1 or a 6.
   c. Unemployment falls when the AFC champion wins the Super Bowl.
   d. Quantity demanded goes up when price falls because lower prices increase consumer purchasing power and because some consumers of substitute goods switch.

7. Which of the following describes the ceteris paribus assumption?
   a. If we increase the price of a good, reduce consumer income, and lower the price of substitutes and if quantity demanded is observed to fall, we know that the price increase caused the decline in quantity demanded.
   b. If the federal government increases government spending and the Federal Reserve Bank lowers interest rates, we know that the increase in government spending caused unemployment to fall.
   c. If a company reduces its labor costs, negotiates lower materials costs from its vendors, and advertises, we know that the reduced labor costs are why the company's profits are higher.
   d. If we decrease the price of a good and observe that there is an increase in the quantity demanded, holding all other factors that influence this relationship constant.

8. The condition of scarcity
   a. cannot be eliminated.
   b. prevails in poor economies.
   c. prevails in rich economies.
   d. all of the above are correct.

9. Which of the following *best* describes an entrepreneur?
   a. A person who works as an office clerk at a major corporation
   b. A person who combines the factors of production to produce innovative products
   c. A special type of capital
   d. Wealthy individuals who provide savings that stimulates the economy

10. Which of the following is *true* about renewable natural resources?
    a. They are a type of land resource (for example, oil, coal, and natural gas) that has a fixed stock.
    b. They are a type of capital resource (for example, irrigation networks and wastewater treatment plants) that utilize water.
    c. They are a type of capital resource (for example, air filtration systems in buildings)

Sample Quiz *continued*

that renew and refresh polluted air from the outside.

d. They are a type of land resource (for example, forests, rangelands, and marine fisheries) that naturally regenerate and thus can tolerate a sustained harvest but can be depleted from excessive harvest.

11. Because of scarcity,
    a. it is impossible to satisfy every desire and choices must be made.
    b. the available supply of time, goods, and resources is greater than human wants.
    c. every desire is fulfilled.
    d. there are no limits on the economy's ability to satisfy unlimited wants.

12. Which of the following represents positive economics?
    a. Policy A is fair.
    b. Outcome B is the best objective to achieve.
    c. If policy A is followed, then outcome B results.
    d. All of the above are positive economic analyses.

13. Which of the following is the last step in the model-building process?
    a. Collect data and test the model.
    b. Develop a model based on simplified assumptions.
    c. Identify the problem.
    d. Formulate an assumption.

14. Which of the following is *not* a type of economic analysis?
    a. Positive
    b. Resources
    c. Normative
    d. None of the above

15. Which word indicates that an economist is using positive economics?

a. Good
b. Bad
c. If-then
d. Should

16. Which of the following would eliminate scarcity as an economic problem?
    a. Moderation of people's competitive instincts
    b. Discovery of new, sufficiently large energy reserves
    c. Resumption of steady productivity growth
    d. None of the above is correct

17. Which resource is *not* an example of capital?
    a. Equipment
    b. Machinery
    c. Physical plants
    d. Stocks and bonds

18. Which of the following is the second step in the model-building process?
    a. Collect data and test the model.
    b. Develop a model based on simplified assumptions.
    c. Identify the problem.
    d. Include all possible variables that affect the model.

19. Which of the following is a type of economic analysis?
    a. Positive
    b. Resources
    c. Association
    d. None of the above is correct.

20. Which of the following careers could result from majoring in economics?
    a. Management
    b. Banking
    c. Government
    d. All of the above is correct.

Applying Graphs to Economics

Economists are famous for their use of graphs. The reason is that "a picture is worth a thousand words." Graphs are used throughout this text to present economics models. By drawing a line, you can use a two-dimensional illustration to analyze the effects of a change in one variable on another. You could describe the same information using other model forms, such as verbal statements, tables, or equations, but a graph is the simplest way to present and understand the relationship between economic variables.

Don't be worried that graphs will "throw you for a loop." Relax! This appendix explains all of the basic graphical language you will need. The following illustrates the simplest use of graphs for economic analysis.

A-1 A Direct Relationship

Basic economic analysis typically concerns the relationship between two variables, both having positive values. Hence, we can confine our graphs to the upper-right (northeast) quadrant of the coordinate number system. In Exhibit A-1, notice that the scales on the horizontal axis (*x*-axis) and the vertical axis (*y*-axis) do not necessarily measure the same numerical values.

The horizontal axis in Exhibit A-1 measures annual income, and the vertical axis shows the amount spent per year for a personal computer (PC). In the absence of any established traditions, we could decide to measure income on the vertical axis and expenditure on the horizontal axis. The intersection of the horizontal and vertical axes is the *origin*—and the point at which both income and expenditure are zero. In Exhibit A-1, each point is a coordinate that matches the dollar value of income and the corresponding expenditure for a PC. For example, point *A* on the graph shows that people with an annual income of $10,000 spent $1,000 per year for a PC. Other incomes are associated with different expenditure levels. For example, at $30,000 per year (point *C*), $3,000 will be spent annually for a PC.

The straight line in Exhibit A-1 allows us to determine the direction of change in PC expenditure as annual income changes. This relationship is *positive* because PC expenditure, measured along the vertical axis, and annual income, measured along the horizontal axis, move in the same direction. PC expenditure increases as annual income increases. As income declines, so does the amount spent on a PC. Thus, the straight line representing the relationship between income and PC expenditure is a direct relationship. A direct relationship is a positive association between two variables. When one variable increases, the other variable increases, and when one variable decreases, the other variable decreases. In short, both variables change in the *same* direction.

Finally, an important point to remember: A two-variable graph, like any model, isolates the relationship between two variables and holds all other variables

Direct relationship

A positive association between two variables. When one variable increases, the other variable increases, and when one variable decreases, the other variable decreases.

EXHIBIT A-1 | A Direct Relationship between Variables

The line with a positive slope shows that the expenditure per year for a personal computer has a direct relationship to annual income, ceteris paribus. As annual income increases along the horizontal axis, the amount spent on a PC also increases, as measured by the vertical axis. Along the line, each 10-unit increase in annual income results in a 1-unit increase in expenditure for a PC. Because the slope is constant along a straight line, we can measure the same slope between any two points. Between points B and C or between points A and D, the slope $= \Delta Y / \Delta X = +3/+30 = +1/+10 = 1/10$.

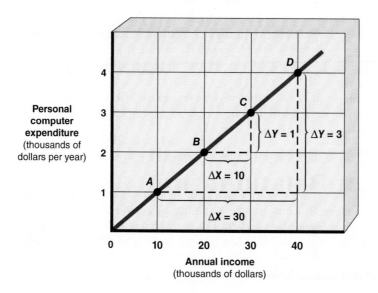

Expenditure for a Personal Computer at Different Annual Incomes

Point	Personal computer expenditure (thousands of dollars per year)	Annual income (thousands of dollars)
A	$1	$10
B	2	20
C	3	30
D	4	40

SOURCE: © Cengage Learning 2014

constant under the ceteris paribus assumption. In Exhibit A-1, for example, factors such as the prices of PCs and education are held constant by assumption. In Chapter 3, you will learn that allowing variables not shown in the graph to change can shift the position of the curve.

A-2 An Inverse Relationship

Now consider the relationship between the price of compact discs (CDs) and the quantity consumers will buy per year, shown in Exhibit A-2. These data indicate a *negative* relationship between the price and quantity variables. When the price is low, consumers purchase a greater quantity of CDs than when the price is high.

In Exhibit A-2, there is an inverse relationship between the price per CD and the quantity consumers buy. An inverse relationship is a negative association between two variables. When one variable increases, the other variable decreases, and when one variable decreases, the other variable increases. Stated simply, the variables move in *opposite* directions.

The line drawn in Exhibit A-2 is an inverse relationship. By long-established tradition, economists put price on the vertical axis and quantity on the horizontal axis. In Chapter 3, we will study in more detail the relationship between price and quantity called the *law of demand*.

In addition to observing the inverse relationship (slope), you must interpret the *intercept* at point *A* in the exhibit. The intercept in this case means that at a price of $25 no consumer is willing to buy a single CD.

Inverse relationship

A negative association between two variables. When one variable increases, the other variable decreases, and when one variable decreases, the other variable increases.

A-3 The Slope of a Straight Line

Plotting numbers provides a clear visual expression of the relationship between two variables, but it is also important to know how much one variable changes as another variable changes. To find out, we calculate the slope. The slope is the ratio of the change in the variable on the vertical axis (the rise or fall) to the change in the variable on the horizontal axis (the run). Algebraically, if Y is on the vertical axis and X is on the horizontal axis, the slope is expressed as follows (the delta symbol, Δ, means "change in"):

Slope

The ratio of the change in the variable on the vertical axis (the rise or fall) to the change in the variable on the horizontal axis (the run).

$$\text{Slope} = \frac{\text{rise}}{\text{run}} = \frac{\text{change in vertical axis}}{\text{change in horizontal axis}} = \frac{\Delta Y}{\Delta X}$$

Consider the slope between points *B* and *C* in Exhibit A-1. The change in expenditure for a PC, Y, is equal to $+1$ (from $2,000 to $3,000 per year), and the change in annual income, X, is equal to $+10$ (from $20,000 to $30,000 per year). The slope is therefore $+1/+10$. The sign is positive because computer expenditure is directly, or positively, related to annual income. The steeper the line, the greater the slope because the ratio of ΔY to ΔX rises. Conversely, the flatter the line, the smaller the slope. Exhibit A-1 also illustrates that the slope of a straight line is constant. That is, the slope between any two points along the line, such as between points *A* and *D*, is equal to $+3/+30 = 1/10$.

What does the slope of 1/10 mean? It tells you that a $1,000 increase (decrease) in PC expenditure each year occurs for each $10,000 increase (decrease) in annual income. The line plotted in Exhibit A-1 has a *positive slope,* and we describe the line as "upward-sloping."

On the other hand, the line in Exhibit A-2 has a *negative slope.* The change in Y between points *C* and *D* is equal to -5 (from $15 down to $10), and the change in X is equal to $+25$ (from 50 million up to 75 million CDs purchased

EXHIBIT A-2	An Inverse Relationship between Variables

The line with a negative slope shows an inverse relationship between the price per compact disc and the quantity of CDs consumers purchase, ceteris paribus. As the price of a CD rises, the quantity of CDs purchased falls. A lower price for CDs is associated with more CDs purchased by consumers. Along the line, with each $5 decrease in the price of CDs, consumers increase the quantity purchased by 25 units. The slope $= \Delta Y/\Delta X = -5/+25 = -1/5$.

The Quantity of Compact Discs Consumers Purchase at Different Prices

Point	Price per compact disc	Quantity of compact discs purchased (millions per year)
A	$25	0
B	20	25
C	15	50
D	10	75
E	5	100

SOURCE: © Cengage Learning 2014

per year). The slope is therefore $-5/+25 = -1/5$, and this line is described as "downward-sloping."

What does this slope of $-1/5$ mean? It means that raising (lowering) the price per CD by $1 decreases (increases) the quantity of CDs purchased by 5 million per year.

Suppose we calculate the slope between any two points on a flat line—for example, points *B* and *C* in Exhibit A-3. In this case, there is no change in *Y* (expenditure for toothpaste) as *X* (annual income) increases. Consumers spend $20 per year on toothpaste regardless of annual income. It follows that $\Delta Y = 0$ for any ΔX, so the slope is equal to 0. The two variables along a flat line (horizontal or vertical) have an *independent relationship*. An independent relationship is a zero association between two variables. When one variable changes, the other variable remains unchanged.

Independent relationship

A zero association between two variables. When one variable changes, the other variable remains unchanged.

EXHIBIT A-3	An Independent Relationship between Variables

The flat line with a zero slope shows that the expenditure per year for toothpaste is unrelated to annual income. As annual income increases along the horizontal axis, the amount spent each year for toothpaste remains unchanged at 20 units. If annual income increases 10 units, the corresponding change in expenditure is zero. The slope $= \Delta Y/\Delta X = 0/+10 = 0$.

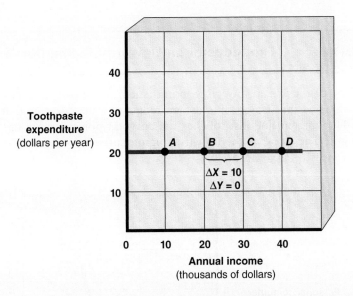

Expenditure for Toothpaste at Different Annual Incomes		
Point	Toothpaste expenditure (dollars per year)	Annual income (thousands of dollars)
A	$20	$10
B	20	20
C	20	30
D	20	40

SOURCE: © Cengage Learning 2014

A-4 The Slope of a Curve

The slope of a curve changes from one point to another. Suppose the relationship between the expenditure for a PC per year and annual income is not a straight line, but an upward-sloping curve, as drawn in Exhibit A-4. This means that the slope of the curve is *positive* as we move along the curve. To calculate the slope of a given point on the curve requires two steps. For example, at point *A*, the first step is to draw a tangent line that just touches the curve at this point without crossing it. The second step is to determine the slope of the tangent line. In Exhibit A-4, the slope of the tangent line, and therefore the slope of the curve at point *A*, is $+2/+30 = 1/15$. What does this slope of 1/15 mean? It means that at point *A*, there will be a $1,000 increase (decrease) in PC expenditure each year for each $15,000 increase (decrease) in annual income.

Now consider that the relationship between the price per CD and the quantity demanded by consumers per year is the downward-sloping curve shown in Exhibit A-5. In this case, the slope of the curve is *negative* as we move along the curve. To calculate the slope at point *A*, draw a line tangent to the curve at point *A*. Thus, the slope of the curve at point *A* is $-10/+50 = -1/+5 = -1/5$.

EXHIBIT A-4	The Slope of an Upward-Sloping Curve

The slope of a curve at any given point, such as point *A*, is equal to the slope of the straight line drawn tangent to the curve at that point. The tangent line just touches the curve at point *A* without crossing it. The slope of the upward-sloping curve at point *A* is $+2/+30 = +1/+15 = 1/15$.

EXHIBIT A-5	The Slope of a Downward-Sloping Curve

In this exhibit, the negative slope changes as one moves from point to point along the curve. The slope at any given point, such as point A, can be determined by the slope of the straight line tangent to that point. The slope of the downward-sloping curve at point A is $-10/+50 = -1/+5 = -1/5$.

SOURCE: © Cengage Learning 2014

A-5 A Three-Variable Relationship in One Graph

The two-variable relationships drawn so far conform to a two-dimensional flat piece of paper. For example, the vertical axis measures the price per CD variable and the horizontal axis measures the quantity of CDs purchased variable. All other factors, such as consumer income, that may affect the relationship between the price and quantity variables are held constant by the ceteris paribus assumption. But reality is frequently not so accommodating. Often a model must take into account the impact of changes in a third variable (consumer income) drawn on a two-dimensional piece of graph paper.

Economists' favorite method of depicting a three-variable relationship is shown in Exhibit A-6. As explained earlier, the cause-and-effect relationship between price and quantity of CDs determines the downward-sloping curve. A change in the price per CD causes a movement downward along either of the two separate curves. As the price falls, consumers increase the quantity of CDs demanded. The location of each curve on the graph, however, depends on the annual income of consumers. As the annual income variable increases from $30,000 to $60,000 and consumers can afford to pay more, the price-quantity

EXHIBIT A-6	Changes in Price, Quantity, and Income in Two Dimensions

Economists use a multicurve graph to represent a three-variable relationship in a two-dimensional graph. A decrease in the price per CD causes a movement downward along each curve. As the annual income of consumers rises, there is a shift rightward in the position of the demand curve.

SOURCE: © Cengage Learning 2014

demanded curve shifts rightward. Conversely, as the annual income variable decreases and consumers have less to spend, the price-quantity demanded curve shifts leftward.

This is an extremely important concept that you must understand: Throughout this book, you must distinguish between *movements along* and *shifts in* a curve. Here's how to tell the difference. A change in one of the variables shown on either of the coordinate axes of the graph causes *movement along* a curve. On the other hand, a change in a variable not shown on one of the coordinate axes of the graph causes a *shift in* a curve's position on the graph.

CONCLUSION: *A shift in a curve occurs only when the ceteris paribus assumption is relaxed and a third variable not shown on either axis of the graph is allowed to change.*

A-6 A Helpful Study Hint for Using Graphs

To some students, studying economics is a little frightening because many chapters are full of graphs. An often-repeated mistake is to prepare for tests by trying to memorize the lines of graphs. When their graded tests are returned, the students using this strategy will probably exclaim, "What happened?" The answer is that if you learn the economic concepts first, you will understand the graphs as illustrations of these underlying concepts. Stated simply, superficial cramming for economics quizzes does not work. For students who are anxious about using graphs, in addition to the brief review of graphical analysis in this appendix, the Graphing Workshop on the EconCentral link of the Tucker Web site and the Study Guide contain step-by-step features on how to interpret graphs.

Key Concepts

Direct relationship
Inverse relationship

Slope
Independent relationship

Summary

- **Graphs** provide a means to clearly show economic relationships in two-dimensional space. Economic analysis is often concerned with two variables confined to the upper-right (northeast) quadrant of the coordinate number system.
- A **direct relationship** occurs when two variables change in the *same* direction.

Direct Relationship

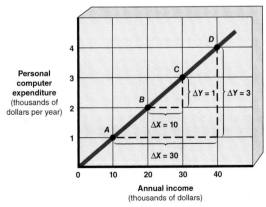

SOURCE: © Cengage Learning 2014

- An **inverse relationship** occurs when two variables change in *opposite* directions.

Inverse Relationship

SOURCE: © Cengage Learning 2014

- An **independent relationship** occurs when two variables are unrelated.

Independent Relationship

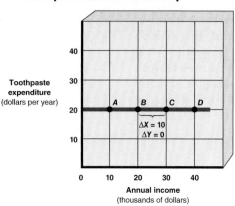

- **Slope** is the ratio of the vertical change (the rise or fall) to the horizontal change (the run). The slope of an *upward-sloping* line is *positive*, and the slope of a *downward-sloping* line is *negative*.

Positive Slope of an Upward-Sloping Curve

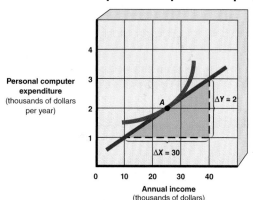

Negative Slope of a Downward-Sloping Curve

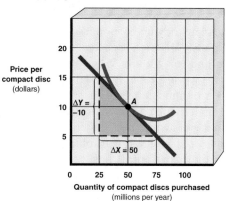

- A **three-variable relationship** is depicted by a graph showing a shift in a curve when the ceteris paribus assumption is relaxed and a third variable (such as annual income) not on either axis of the graph is allowed to change.

Three-Variable Relationship

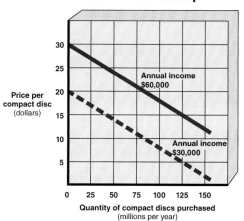

Summary of Conclusion Statement

- A shift in a curve occurs only when the ceteris paribus assumption is relaxed and a third variable not shown on either axis of the graph is allowed to change.

Study Questions and Problems

1. Draw a graph without specific data for the expected relationship between the following variables:
   a. The probability of living and age
   b. Annual income and years of education
   c. Inches of snow and sales of bathing suits
   d. Number of football games won and the athletic budget

In each case, state whether the expected relationship is *direct* or *inverse*. Explain an additional factor that would be included in the *ceteris paribus* assumption because it might change and influence your theory.

2. Assume that a research firm collects survey sales data that reveal the relationship between the possible selling prices of hamburgers and the quantity of hamburgers consumers would purchase per year at alternative prices. The report states that if the price of a hamburger is $4, 20,000 will be bought. However, at a price of $3, 40,000 hamburgers will be bought. At $2, 60,000 hamburgers will be bought, and at $1, 80,000 hamburgers will be purchased.

Based on these data, describe the relevant relationship between the price of a hamburger and the quantity consumers are willing to purchase, using a verbal statement, a numerical table, and a graph. Which model do you prefer? Why?

Sample Quiz

For an explanation of the correct answers, visit the Tucker Web site at www.cengage.com/economics/tucker.

1. What is used to illustrate an independent relationship between two variables?
   a. An upward-sloping curve
   b. A downward-sloping curve
   c. A hill-shaped curve
   d. A horizontal or vertical line

2. Which of the following pairs is *most* likely to exhibit an inverse relationship?
   a. The amount of time you study and your grade point average
   b. People's annual income and their expenditure on personal computers
   c. Baseball players' salaries and their batting averages
   d. The price of a concert and the number of tickets that people purchase

3. According to Exhibit A-7, what is the relationship between the price per pizza and the quantity of pizzas purchased?
   a. Direct
   b. Inverse
   c. Complex
   d. Independent

4. What is the slope of the line shown in Exhibit A-7?
   a. −1
   b. −1/2
   c. −1/4
   d. 0

5. Which of the following would cause a leftward shift in the relationship shown in Exhibit A-7?
   a. A fall in household incomes
   b. A fall in the price of pizza
   c. A fall in the quantity of pizza that people want to purchase
   d. All of the above would shift the line in the graph

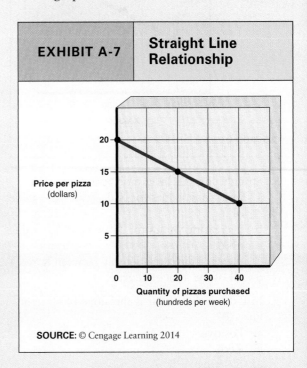

EXHIBIT A-7   Straight Line Relationship

SOURCE: © Cengage Learning 2014

Sample Quiz *continued*

6. Suppose two variables are directly related. If one variable rises, the other variable
   a. also rises.
   b. falls.
   c. remains unchanged.
   d. reacts unpredictably.

7. When an inverse relationship is graphed, the resulting line or curve is
   a. horizontal.
   b. vertical.
   c. upward-sloping.
   d. downward-sloping.

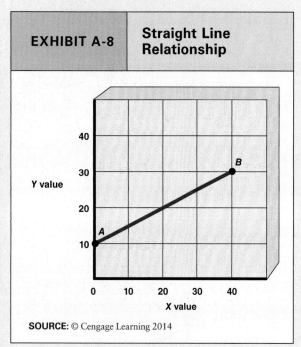

EXHIBIT A-8 **Straight Line Relationship**

SOURCE: © Cengage Learning 2014

8. Straight line AB in Exhibit A-8 shows that
   a. increasing values for X decreases the values of Y.
   b. decreasing values for X increases the values of Y.
   c. there is a direct relationship between X and Y.
   d. all of the above are true.

9. In Exhibit A-8, what is the slope of straight line AB?
   a. Positive
   b. Zero
   c. Negative
   d. Variable

10. In Exhibit A-8, what is the slope of straight line AB?
    a. 1
    b. 5
    c. 1/2
    d. −1

11. As shown in Exhibit A-8, the slope of straight line AB
    a. decreases with increases in X.
    b. increases with increases in X.
    c. increases with decreases in X.
    d. remains constant with changes in X.

12. In Exhibit A-8, as X increases along the horizontal axis, the Y values increase. What is the relationship between the X and Y variables?
    a. Direct
    b. Inverse
    c. Independent
    d. Variable

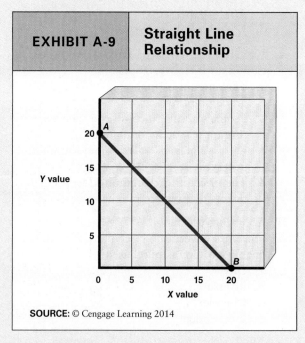

EXHIBIT A-9 **Straight Line Relationship**

SOURCE: © Cengage Learning 2014

13. In Exhibit A-9, as X increases along the horizontal axis, the Y values decrease. What is the relationship between the X and Y variables?
    a. Direct
    b. Inverse
    c. Independent
    d. Variable

Sample Quiz *continued*

14. Straight line AB in Exhibit A-9 shows that
    a. increasing values for X reduces the value of Y.
    b. decreasing values for X increases the value of Y.
    c. there is an inverse relationship between X and Y.
    d. all of the above are true.

15. As shown in Exhibit A-9, the slope of straight line AB
    a. decreases with increases in X.
    b. increases with increases in X.
    c. increases with decreases in X.
    d. remains constant with changes in X.

16. In Exhibit A-9, what is the slope for straight line AB?
    a. 3
    b. 1
    c. −1
    d. −5

17. In Exhibit A-9, what is the slope of straight line AB?
    a. Positive
    b. Zero
    c. Negative
    d. Variable

18. In Exhibit A-10, as X increases along the horizontal axis, corresponding to points A–D on the line, the Y values remain unchanged at 20 units. What is the relationship between the X and Y variables?
    a. Direct
    b. Inverse
    c. Independent
    d. Undefined

19. In Exhibit A-10, what is the slope of straight line A–D?
    a. Greater than 1
    b. Equal to 1
    c. Less than 1
    d. Zero

EXHIBIT A-11   Multicurve Graph

SOURCE: © Cengage Learning 2014

20. Exhibit A-11 represents a three-variable relationship. As the annual income of consumers falls from $50,000 (line A) to $30,000 (line B), the result is a(n)
    a. upward movement along each curve.
    b. downward movement along each curve.
    c. leftward shift in curve A to curve B.
    d. rightward shift in curve A to curve B.

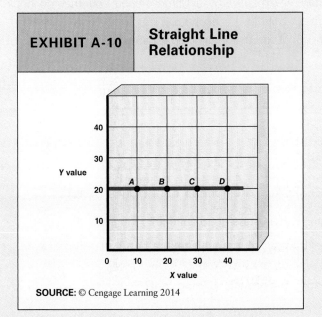

EXHIBIT A-10   Straight Line Relationship

SOURCE: © Cengage Learning 2014

chapter 2

Production Possibilities, Opportunity Cost, and Economic Growth

This chapter continues building on the foundation laid in the preceding chapter. Having learned that *scarcity* forces *choices*, here you will study the choices people make in more detail. This chapter begins by examining the three basic choices: *What, How,* and *For Whom* to produce. The process of answering these basic questions introduces two other key building blocks in the economic way of thinking: *opportunity cost* and *marginal analysis*. Once you understand these important concepts stated in words, it will be easier to interpret our first formal economic model, the *production*

possibilities curve. This model illustrates how economists use graphs as a powerful tool to supplement words and develop an understanding of basic economic principles. You will discover that the production possibilities model teaches many of the most important concepts in economics, including scarcity, the law of increasing opportunity costs, efficiency, investment, and economic growth. For example, the chapter concludes by using the production possibilities curve to explain why underdeveloped countries do not achieve economic growth and thereby improve their standard of living.

In this chapter, you will learn to solve these economics puzzles:

- Why do so few rock stars and movie stars go to college?
- Why would you spend an extra hour reading this text rather than going to a movie or sleeping?
- Why are investment and economic growth so important?
- What does a war on terrorism really mean?

2-1 Three Fundamental Economic Questions

Because of the problem of scarcity, whether rich or poor, every nation must answer the same three fundamental economic questions: (1) *What* products will be produced? (2) *How* will they be produced? (3) *For Whom* will they be produced? Later, the chapter on economies in transition introduces various types of economic systems and describes how each deals with these three economic choices.

2-1a WHAT TO PRODUCE?

The *What* question requires an economy to decide the mix and quantity of goods and services it will produce. Should society devote its limited resources to producing more health care and fewer military goods? Should society produce more iPods and fewer CDs? Should more capital goods be produced instead of consumer goods, or should small hybrid cars and fewer SUVs be produced? The problem of scarcity restricts our ability to produce everything we want during a given period, so the choice to produce "more" of one good requires producing "less" of another good. In the United States, consumer sovereignty answers the *What* question. In Cuba and North Korea, for example, the government and not the consumer answers this question.

2-1b HOW TO PRODUCE?

After deciding which products to make, the second question for society to decide is *how* to mix technology and scarce resources in order to produce these goods. For instance, a towel can be sewn primarily by hand (labor), partially by hand and partially by machine (labor and capital), or primarily by machine (capital). In short, the *How* question asks whether a production technique will be more or less capital-intensive. The *How* question also concerns choices among resources for production. Should electricity be produced from oil, solar power, or nuclear power?

Education plays an important role in answering the *How* question. Education improves the ability of workers to perform their work. Variation in the quality and quantity of education among nations is one reason economies differ in their capacities to apply resources and technology to answer the *How* question. For example, the United States is striving to catch up with Japan in the use of robotics. Answering the question *How do we improve our robotics?* requires engineers and employees with the proper training in the installation and operation of robots.

2-1c FOR WHOM TO PRODUCE?

Once the *What* and *How* questions are resolved, the third question is *For Whom*. Among all those desiring the produced goods, who actually receives them? This question concerns how the economic pie is divided. Who is fed well? Who drives a Mercedes? Who receives organ transplants? Should economics professors earn a salary of $1 million a year and others pay higher taxes to support economists? The *For Whom* question means that society must have a method to decide who will be "rich and famous" and who will be "poor and unknown." Chapter 10 returns to the *For Whom* question and discusses it in more detail.

2-2 Opportunity Cost

Because of scarcity, the three basic questions cannot be answered without sacrifice or cost. But what does the term *cost* really mean? The common response would be to say that the purchase price is the cost. A movie ticket *costs* $8, or a shirt *costs* $50. Applying the economic way of thinking, however, *cost* is defined differently. A well-known phrase from Nobel Prize-winning economist Milton Friedman says, "There is no such thing as a free lunch." This expression captures the links among the concepts of scarcity, choice, and cost. Because of scarcity, people must make choices, and each choice incurs a cost (sacrifice). Once one option is chosen, another option is given up. The money you spend on a movie ticket cannot also buy a Blu-ray. A business may purchase a new textile machine to manufacture towels, but this same money cannot be used to buy a new recreation facility for employees.

The Blu-ray and recreation facility examples illustrate that the true cost of these decisions is the opportunity cost of a choice, not the purchase price. Opportunity cost is the best alternative sacrificed for a chosen alternative. Stated differently, it is the cost of not choosing the next best alternative. This principle states that some highly valued opportunity must be forgone in all economic decisions. The actual good or use of time given up for the chosen good or use of time measures the opportunity cost. We may omit the word *opportunity* before the word *cost*, but the concept remains the same. Exhibit 1 illustrates the causation chain linking scarcity, choice, and opportunity cost.

Examples are endless, but let's consider a few. Suppose your economics professor decides to become a rock star in the Rolling in Dough band. Now all his or

Opportunity cost

The best alternative sacrificed for a chosen alternative.

EXHIBIT 1	The Links between Scarcity, Choice, and Opportunity Cost

Scarcity means that no society has enough resources to produce all the goods and services necessary to satisfy all human wants. As a result, society is always confronted with the problem of making choices. This concept is captured in Milton Friedman's famous phrase, "There is no such thing as a free lunch." This means that each decision has a sacrifice in terms of an alternative not chosen.

Scarcity → Choice → Opportunity cost

SOURCE: © Cengage Learning 2014

her working hours are devoted to creating hit music, and the opportunity cost is the educational services no longer provided. Now a personal example: The opportunity cost of dating a famous model or movie star (name your favorite) might be the loss of your current girlfriend or boyfriend. Opportunity cost also applies to national economic decisions. Suppose the federal government decides to spend tax revenues on a space station. The opportunity cost depends on the next best program *not* funded. Assume roads and bridges are the highest-valued projects not built as a result of the decision to construct the space station. Then the opportunity cost of the decision to devote resources to the space station is the forgone roads and bridges and not the money actually spent to build the space station.

To personalize the relationship between time and opportunity cost, ask yourself what you would be doing if you were not reading this book. Your answer might be watching television or sleeping. If sleeping is your choice, the opportunity cost of studying this text is the sleep you sacrifice. Rock stars and movie stars, on the other hand, must forfeit a large amount of income to attend college. Now you know why you see so few of these stars in class.

Decisions often involve sacrifice of *both* goods and time. Suppose you decide to see a movie at a theater located 15 minutes from campus. If you had not spent the money at the movie theater, you could have purchased a Blu-ray and watched a movie at home. And the time spent traveling to and from the movie and sitting through it could have been devoted to studying for your economics exam. The opportunity cost of the movie consists of giving up (1) a Blu-ray and (2) study time needed to score higher on the economics exam.

2-3 Marginal Analysis

At the heart of many important decision-making techniques used throughout this text is marginal analysis. Marginal analysis examines the effects of additions to or subtractions from a current situation. This is a very valuable tool in the economic-way-of-thinking toolkit because it considers the "marginal" effects of change. The rational decision maker decides on an option only if the marginal benefit exceeds the marginal cost. For example, you must decide how to use your scarce time. Should you devote an extra hour to reading this book, going to a movie, watching television, texting, or sleeping? Which of your many options do you choose? The answer depends on marginal analysis. If you decide the benefit of a higher grade in economics exceeds the opportunity cost of, say, sleep, then you allocate the extra hour to studying economics. Excellent choice!

Businesses use marginal analysis. Hotels, for example, rent space to student groups for dances and other events. Assume you are the hotel manager and a student group offers to pay $400 to use the ballroom for a party. To decide whether to accept the offer requires marginal analysis. The marginal benefit of renting otherwise vacant space is $400, and the marginal cost is $300 for extra electricity and cleaning services. Since the marginal benefit exceeds the marginal cost, the manager sensibly accepts the offer.

Similarly, farmers use marginal analysis. For example, a farmer must decide whether to add fertilizer when planting corn. Using marginal analysis, the farmer estimates that the corn revenue yield will be about $75 per acre without fertilizer and about $100 per acre using fertilizer. If the cost of fertilizer is $20 per acre,

Marginal analysis

An examination of the effects of additions to or subtractions from a current situation.

marginal analysis tells the farmer to fertilize. The addition of fertilizer will increase profit by $5 per acre because fertilizing adds $25 to the value of each acre at a cost of $20 per acre.

Marginal analysis is an important concept when the government considers changes in various programs. For example, as demonstrated in the next section, it is useful to know that an increase in the production of military goods will result in an opportunity cost of fewer consumer goods produced.

2-4 The Production Possibilities Curve

The economic problem of scarcity means that society's capacity to produce combinations of goods is constrained by its limited resources. This condition can be represented in a model called the production possibilities curve. The production possibilities curve shows the maximum combinations of two outputs that an economy can produce in a given period of time with its available resources and technology. Three basic assumptions underlie the production possibilities curve model:

Production possibilities curve

A curve that shows the maximum combinations of two outputs an economy can produce in a given period of time with its available resources and technology.

1. **Fixed Resources.** The quantities and qualities of all resource inputs remain unchanged during the time period. But the "rules of the game" do allow an economy to shift any resource from the production of one output to the production of another output. For example, an economy might shift workers from producing consumer goods to producing capital goods. Although the number of workers remains unchanged, this transfer of labor will produce fewer consumer goods and more capital goods.
2. **Fully Employed Resources.** The economy operates with all its factors of production fully employed and producing the greatest output possible without waste or mismanagement.
3. **Technology Unchanged.** Holding existing technology fixed creates limits, or constraints, on the amounts and types of goods any economy can produce. Technology is the body of knowledge applied to how goods are produced.

Technology

The body of knowledge applied to how goods are produced.

Exhibit 2 shows a hypothetical economy that has the capacity to manufacture any combination of military goods ("guns") and consumer goods ("butter") per year along its production possibilities curve (PPC), including points A, B, C, and D. For example, if this economy uses all its resources to make military goods, it can produce a *maximum* of 160 billion units of military goods and zero units of consumer goods (combination A). Another possibility is for the economy to use all its resources to produce a *maximum* of 100 billion units of consumer goods and zero units of military goods (point D). Between the extremes of points A and D lie other production possibilities for combinations of military and consumer goods. If combination B is chosen, the economy will produce 140 billion units of military goods and 40 billion units of consumer goods. Another possibility (point C) is to produce 80 billion units of military goods and 80 billion units of consumer goods.

What happens if the economy does not use all its resources to their capacity? For example, some workers may not find work, or plants and equipment may be idle for any number of reasons. The result is that our hypothetical economy fails to reach any of the combinations along the PPC. In Exhibit 2, point U illustrates an *inefficient* output level for any economy operating without all its resources fully employed. At point U, our model economy is producing 80 billion units of military

EXHIBIT 2	The Production Possibilities Curve for Military Goods and Consumer Goods

All points along the production possibilities curve (*PPC*) are maximum possible combinations of military goods and consumer goods. One possibility, point *A*, would be to produce 160 billion units of military goods and zero units of consumer goods each year. At the other extreme, point *D*, the economy uses all its resources to produce 100 billion units of consumer goods and zero units of military goods each year. Points *B* and *C* are obtained by using some resources to produce each of the two outputs. If the economy fails to utilize its resources fully, the result is the inefficient point *U*. Point *Z* lies beyond the economy's present production capabilities and is unattainable.

Production Possibilities Schedule for Military and Consumer Goods per Year

Output	Production possibilities			
(billions of units per year)	A	B	C	D
Military goods	160	140	80	0
Consumer goods	0	40	80	100

SOURCE: © Cengage Learning 2014

goods and 40 billion units of consumer goods per year. Such an economy is under-producing because it could satisfy more of society's wants if it were producing at some point along the *PPC*.

Even if an economy fully employs all its resources, it is impossible to produce certain output quantities. Any point outside the production possibilities curve is *un-attainable* because it is beyond the economy's present production capabilities. Point Z, for example, represents an unattainable output of 140 billion units of military goods and 80 billion units of consumer goods. Society would prefer this combination to any combination along, or inside, the *PPC*, but the economy cannot reach this point with its existing resources and technology.

> **CONCLUSION:** *Scarcity limits an economy to points on or below its production possibilities curve.*

Because all the points along the curve are *maximum* output levels with the given resources and technology, they are all called *efficient* points. A movement between any two efficient points on the curve means that *more* of one product is produced only by producing *less* of the other product. In Exhibit 2, moving from point A to point B produces 40 billion additional units of consumer goods per year, but only at a cost of sacrificing 20 billion units of military goods. Thus, a movement between any two efficient points graphically illustrates that "There is no such thing as a free lunch."

> **CONCLUSION:** *The production possibilities curve consists of all efficient output combinations at which an economy can produce more of one good only by producing less of the other good.*

2-5 The Law of Increasing Opportunity Costs

Why is the production possibilities curve shaped the way it is? Exhibit 3 will help us answer this question. It presents a production possibilities curve for a hypothetical economy that must choose between producing tanks and producing sailboats. Consider expanding the production of sailboats in 20,000-unit increments. Moving from point A to point B, the *opportunity cost* is 10,000 tanks; between point B and point C, the *opportunity cost* is 20,000 tanks; and the *opportunity cost* of producing at point D, rather than point C, is 50,000 tanks.

Law of increasing opportunity costs

The principle that the opportunity cost increases as production of one output expands.

Exhibit 3 illustrates the law of increasing opportunity costs, which states that the opportunity cost increases as production of one output expands. Holding the stock of resources and technology constant (ceteris paribus), the law of increasing opportunity costs causes the production possibilities curve to display a *bowed-out* shape.

Why must our hypothetical economy sacrifice larger and larger amounts of tank output in order to produce each additional 20,000 sailboats? The reason is that all workers are not equally suited to producing one good compared to another good.

EXHIBIT 3 The Law of Increasing Opportunity Costs

A hypothetical economy produces equal increments of 20,000 sailboats per year as we move from point *A* through point *D* on the production possibilities curve (*PPC*). If the economy moves from point *A* to point *B*, the opportunity cost of 20,000 sailboats is a reduction in tank output of 10,000 per year. This opportunity cost rises to 20,000 tanks if the economy moves from point *B* to point *C*. Finally, production at point *D*, rather than point *C*, results in an opportunity cost of 50,000 tanks per year. The opportunity cost rises because workers are not equally suited to making tanks and sailboats.

Production Possibilities Schedule for Tanks and Sailboats per Year

Output (thousands per year)	Production possibilities			
	A	B	C	D
Tanks	80	70	50	0
Sailboats	0	20	40	60

Expanding the output of sailboats requires the use of workers who are less suited to producing sailboats than producing tanks. Suppose our hypothetical economy produces no sailboats (point *A*) and then decides to produce them. At first, the least-skilled tank workers are transferred to making sailboats, and 10,000 tanks are sacrificed at point *B*. As the economy moves from point *B* to point *C*, more highly skilled tank makers become sailboat makers, and the opportunity cost rises to 20,000 tanks. Finally, the economy can decide to move from point *C* to point *D*, and the opportunity cost increases even more—to 50,000 tanks. Now the remaining tank workers, who are superb tank makers, but poor sailboat makers, must adapt to the techniques of sailboat production.

Finally, it should be noted that the production possibilities curve model could assume that resources can be substituted and the opportunity cost remains constant. In this case, the production possibilities curve would be a straight line, which is the model employed in the chapter on international trade and finance.

> **CONCLUSION:** *The lack of interchangeability between workers is the cause of increasing opportunity costs and the bowed-out shape of the production possibilities curve.*

2-6 Sources of Economic Growth

Economic growth

The ability of an economy to produce greater levels of output, represented by an outward shift of its production possibilities curve.

The economy's production capacity is not permanently fixed. If either the resource base increases or technology advances, the economy experiences economic growth, and the production possibilities curve shifts outward. Economic growth is the ability of an economy to produce greater levels of output, represented by an outward shift of its production possibilities curve. Exhibit 4 illustrates the importance of an outward shift. (Note the causation chain, which is often used in this text to focus on a model's cause-and-effect relationship.) At point *A* on PPC_1, a hypothetical full-employment economy produces 40,000 computers and 200 million pizzas per year. If the curve shifts outward to the new curve PPC_2, the economy can expand its full-employment output options. One option is to produce at point *B* and increase computer output to 70,000 per year. Another possibility is to increase pizza output to 400 million per year. Yet another choice is to produce more of both at some point between points *B* and *C*.

2-6a CHANGES IN RESOURCES

One way to accelerate economic growth is to gain additional resources. Any increase in resources, for example, more natural resources, a baby boom, or more factories will shift the production possibilities curve outward. In Exhibit 4, assume curve PPC_1 represents Japan's production possibilities for clothing and food in a given year. Suddenly, Japan discovers within its borders new sources of labor and other resources. As a result of the new resources, Japan will have an expanded capacity to produce any combination along an expanded curve, such as curve PPC_2.

Reductions in resources will cause the production possibilities curve to shift inward. Assume curve PPC_2 describes Japan's economy before World War II and the destruction of its factors of production during the war caused

EXHIBIT 4	An Outward Shift of the Production Possibilities Curve for Computers and Pizzas

The economy begins with the capacity to produce combinations along the first production possibilities curve PPC_1. Growth in the resource base or technological advances can shift the production possibilities curve outward from PPC_1 to PPC_2. Points along PPC_2 represent new production possibilities that were previously impossible. This outward shift permits the economy to produce greater quantities of output. Instead of producing combination A, the economy can produce, for example, more computers at point B or more pizzas at point C. If the economy produces at a point between B and C, more of both pizzas and computers can be produced, compared to point A.

CAUSATION CHAIN

Increase in resources or technological advances → Economic growth

Japan's curve to shift leftward to curve PPC_1. Over the years, Japan trained its workforce, built new factories and equipment, and used new technology to shift its curve outward and surpass its original production capacity at curve PPC_2.

2-6b TECHNOLOGICAL CHANGE

Another way to achieve economic growth is through research and development of new technologies. The knowledge of how to transform a stone into a wheel vastly improved the prehistoric standard of living. Technological change also makes it possible to shift the production possibilities curve outward by producing more from the same resources base. One source of technological change is *invention*. Computer chips, satellites, and the Internet are all examples of technological advances resulting from the use of science and engineering knowledge.

Technological change also results from the innovations of entrepreneurship, introduced in the previous chapter. Innovation involves creating and developing new products or productive processes. Seeking profits, entrepreneurs create new, better, or less expensive products. This requires organizing an improved mix of resources, which expands the production possibilities curve.

One entrepreneur, Henry Ford, changed auto industry technology by pioneering the use of the assembly line for making cars. Another entrepreneur, Chester Carlson, a law student, became so frustrated copying documents that he worked on his own to develop photocopying. After years of disappointment, a small firm named Xerox Corporation accepted Carlson's invention and transformed a good idea into a revolutionary product. These and a myriad of other business success stories illustrate that entrepreneurs are important because they transform their new ideas into production and practical use. Throughout history, technological advances have fostered economic growth by increasing our nation's productive power. Today, the Internet and computers are "new" technologies, but railroads, electricity, and automobiles, for example, were also "new" technologies in their time.

✓ CHECKPOINT

What Does a War on Terrorism Really Mean?

With the disappearance of the former Soviet Union and the end of the Cold War, the United States became the world's only superpower and no longer engaged in an intense competition to build up its military. As a result, in the 1990s, Congress and the White House had the opportunity to reduce the military's share of the budget and spend more funds for nondefense goods. This situation was referred to as the "peace dividend." Now consider that the need to combat terrorism diverts resources back to military and security output. Does the peace dividend or a reversal to more military spending represent a possible shift of the production possibilities curve or a movement along it?

FedEx Wasn't an Overnight Success

Applicable Concept: entrepreneurship

Frederick W. Smith is a classic entrepreneurial success story. Young Fred went to Yale University, had a good new idea, secured venture capital, worked like crazy, and made a fortune, and the Smithsonian Institution rendered its ultimate accolade. It snapped up an early Federal Express jet for its collection, displaying it for a time in the National Air and Space Museum in Washington, D.C., not far from the Wright brothers' first airplane.

Smith's saga began with a college economics term paper that spelled out a nationwide overnight parcel delivery system that would be guaranteed to "absolutely, positively" beat the pants off the U.S. Postal Service. People, he said, would pay much more if their packages arrived at their destination the next morning. To accomplish his plan, planes would converge nightly on Memphis, Tennessee, carrying packages accepted at any location throughout the nation. Smith chose

this city for its central U.S. location and because its airport has little bad weather to cause landing delays. In the morning hours, all items would be unloaded, sorted, and rerouted to other airports, where vans would battle rush-hour traffic to make deliveries before the noon deadline.

Smith's college term paper only got a C grade. Perhaps the professor thought the idea was too risky, and lots of others certainly agreed. In 1969, after college and a tour as a Marine pilot in Vietnam, the 24-year-old Smith began pitching his parcel delivery plan to mostly skeptical financiers. Nevertheless, with $4 million of his family's money, he persuaded a few venture capitalists to put up $80 million. At the time, this was the largest venture capital package ever assembled. In 1973, delivery service began with 33 jets connecting 25 cities, but on the first night, only 86 packages showed up.

It was years before Smith looked like a genius. The company posted a $27 million loss the first

year; turned the corner in 1976; and then took off, helped by a 1981 decision to add letters to its basic package delivery service. Today, Smith's basic strategy hasn't changed, but the scale of the operation has exploded. FedEx is the world's largest express transportation company serving over 200 countries.

Analyze the Issue

Draw a production possibilities curve for an economy producing only pizzas and computers. Explain how Fred Smith and other entrepreneurs affect the curve.

Source: © Cengage Learning 2014

2-7 Present Investment and the Future Production Possibilities Curve

When the decision for an economy involves choosing between capital goods and consumer goods, the output combination for the present period can determine future production capacity.

Exhibit 5 compares two countries producing different combinations of capital and consumer goods. Part (a) shows the production possibilities curve for the low-investment economy of Alpha. This economy was producing combination A in 2000, which is an output of C_a of consumer goods and an output of K_a of capital goods per year. Let's assume K_a is just enough capital output to replace the capital being worn out each year (depreciation). As a result, Alpha fails to accumulate the net gain of

| EXHIBIT 5 | Alpha's and Beta's Present and Future Production Possibilities Curves |

In part (a), each year Alpha produces only enough capital (K_a) to replace existing capital that has worn out. Without greater capital and assuming other resources remain fixed, Alpha is unable to shift its production possibilities curve outward. In part (b), each year Beta produces K_b capital, which is more than the amount required to replenish its depreciated capital. In 2010, this expanded capital provides Beta with the extra production capacity to shift its production possibilities curve to the right (outward). If Beta chooses point B on its curve, it has the production capacity to increase the amount of consumer goods from C_b to C_c without producing fewer capital goods.

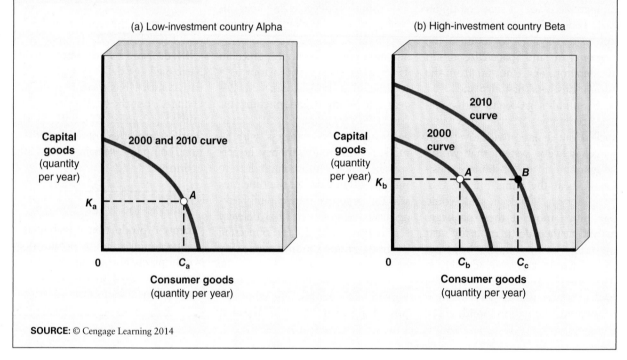

SOURCE: © Cengage Learning 2014

factories and equipment required to expand its production possibilities curve outward in future years.[1] Why wouldn't Alpha simply move up along its production curve by shifting more resources to capital goods production? The problem is that sacrificing consumer goods for capital formation causes the standard of living to fall.

Comparing Alpha to Beta illustrates the importance of being able to do more than just replace worn-out capital. Beta operated in 2000 at point A in part (b), which is an output of C_b of consumer goods and K_b of capital goods. Assuming K_b is more than enough to replenish worn-out capital, Beta is a high-investment economy, adding to its capital stock and creating extra production capacity. This process of accumulating capital *(capital formation)* is investment. Investment is the accumulation of capital, such as factories, machines, and inventories, used to produce goods and services. Newly built factories and machines in the present provide an economy

Investment

The accumulation of capital, such as factories, machines, and inventories used to produce goods and services.

---

[1]Recall from the appendix to Chapter 1 that a third variable can affect the variables measured on the vertical and horizontal axes. In this case, the third variable is the quantity of capital worn out per year.

How Does Public Capital Affect a Nation's Curve?
Applicable Concept: economic growth

The discussion of low-investment country Alpha versus high-investment country Beta explained that sacrificing production of consumer goods for an increase in capital goods output can result in economic growth and a higher standard of living. Stated differently, there was a long-run benefit from the accumulation of capital that offset the short-run opportunity cost in terms of consumer goods. Here the analysis was in terms of investment in private capital such as factories, machines, and inventories. However, public or government capital can also influence the production of both capital goods and consumption goods. For example, the government provides infrastructure such as roads, schools, bridges, ports, dams, and sanitation that makes the accumulation process for private capital more efficient, and in turn, an economy grows at a greater rate.

Using data from 21 high-investment countries, a recent study by economists investigated how government investment policy affected the productivity of new private capital goods.[1] Countries included in the research were, for example, Canada, Japan, New Zealand, Spain, and the United States. A key finding was that a 1 percent increase in public investment increased the productivity of private investment by 27 percent. As a result, public capital caused the stock of private capital to rise more quickly over time.

Finally, economic growth and development is a major goal of countries throughout the world, and there are numerous factors that cause some countries to experience greater economic growth compared to other countries. Note that this topic is discussed in more depth in the last chapter of the text.

Analyze the Issue
Construct a production possibilities curve for a hypothetical country. Put public capital goods per year on the vertical axis and consumer goods per year on the horizontal axis. Not shown directly in your graph, assume that this country produces just enough private capital per year to replace its depreciated capital. Assume further that this country is without public capital and is operating at point *A*, where consumer goods are at a maximum. Based on the above research and using a production possibilities curve, show and explain what happens to this country's private capital, production possibilities curve, and standard of living if it increases its output of public capital.

1. Stuart Fowler and Bichaka Fayissa, "Public Capital Spending Shocks and the Price of Investment: Evidence from a Panel of Countries," The 2007 Missouri Economics Conference.

Source: © Cengage Learning 2014

with the capacity to expand its production options in the future. For example, the outward shift of its curve allows Beta to produce C_c consumer goods at point *B* in 2010. This means Beta will be able to improve its standard of living by producing $C_c - C_b$ extra consumer goods, while Alpha's standard of living remains unchanged because the production of consumer goods remains unchanged.

CONCLUSION: *A nation can accelerate economic growth by increasing its production of capital goods in excess of the capital being worn out in the production process.*

Key Concepts

What, How, and *For Whom* questions	Production possibilities curve	Economic growth
Opportunity cost	Technology	Investment
Marginal analysis	Law of increasing opportunity costs	

Summary

- **Three fundamental economic questions** facing any economy are *What, How*, and *For Whom* to produce goods. The *What* question asks exactly which goods are to be produced and in what quantities. The *How* question requires society to decide the resource mix used to produce goods. The *For Whom* problem concerns the division of output among society's citizens.

- **Opportunity cost** is the best alternative forgone for a chosen option. This means no decision can be made without cost.

SOURCE: © Cengage Learning 2014

- **Marginal analysis** examines the impact of changes from a current situation and is a technique used extensively in economics. The basic approach is to compare the additional benefits of a change with the additional costs of the change.

- A **production possibilities curve** illustrates an economy's capacity to produce goods, subject to the constraint of scarcity. The production possibilities curve is a graph of the maximum possible combinations of two outputs that can be produced in a given period of time, subject to three conditions: (1) All resources are fully employed. (2) The resource base is not allowed to vary during the time period. (3) **Technology**, which is the body of knowledge applied to the production of goods, remains constant. **Inefficient** production occurs at any point inside the production possibilities curve. All points along the curve are **efficient** points because each point represents a maximum output possibility.

Production Possibilities Curve

SOURCE: © Cengage Learning 2014

- The **law of increasing opportunity costs** states that the opportunity cost increases as the production of an output expands. The explanation for this law is that the suitability of resources declines sharply as greater amounts are transferred from producing one output to producing another output.

- **Economic growth** is represented by the production possibilities curve shifting outward as the result of an increase in resources or an advance in technology.

Economic Growth

CAUSATION CHAIN

Increase in resources or technological advances → Economic growth

SOURCE: © Cengage Learning 2014

- **Investment** means that an economy is producing and accumulating capital. Investment consists of factories, machines, and inventories (capital) produced in the present that are used to shift the production possibilities curve outward in the future.

Summary of Conclusion Statements

- Scarcity limits an economy to points on or below its production possibilities curve.
- The production possibilities curve consists of all efficient output combinations at which an economy can produce more of one good only by producing less of the other good.

- The lack of perfect interchangeability between workers is the cause of increasing opportunity costs and the bowed-out shape of the production possibilities curve.
- A nation can accelerate economic growth by increasing its production of capital goods in excess of the capital being worn out in the production process.

Study Questions and Problems

1. Explain why scarcity forces individuals and society to incur opportunity costs. Give specific examples.

2. Suppose a retailer promotes its store by advertising a drawing for a "free car." Is this car *free* because the winner pays *zero* for it?

3. Explain verbally the statement "There is no such thing as a free lunch" in relation to scarce resources.

4. Which of the following decisions has the greater opportunity cost? Why?
   a. A decision to use an undeveloped lot in Tokyo's financial district for an apartment building.
   b. A decision to use a square mile in the desert for a gas station.

5. Attending college is expensive, time-consuming, and requires effort. So why do people decide to attend college?

6. The following is a set of hypothetical production possibilities for a nation.

Combination	Automobiles (thousands)	Beef (thousands of tons)
A	0	10
B	2	9
C	4	7
D	6	4
E	8	0

a. Plot these production possibilities data. What is the opportunity cost of the first 2,000 automobiles produced? Between which points is the opportunity cost per thousand automobiles highest? Between which points is the opportunity cost per thousand tons of beef highest?

b. Label a point *F* inside the curve. Why is this an inefficient point? Label a point *G* outside the curve. Why is this point unattainable? Why are points *A* through *E* all efficient points?

c. Does this production possibilities curve reflect the law of increasing opportunity costs? Explain.

d. What assumptions could be changed to shift the production possibilities curve?

7. The following table shows the production possibilities for pies and flower boxes. Fill in the opportunity cost (pies forgone) of producing the first through the fifth flower box.

Combination	Pies	Flower boxes	Opportunity cost
A	30	0	_____
B	26	1	_____
C	21	2	_____
D	15	3	_____
E	8	4	_____
F	0	5	_____

8. Why does a production possibilities curve have a bowed-out shape?

9. Interpret the phrases "There is no such thing as a free lunch" and "A free lunch is possible" in terms of the production possibilities curve.

10. Suppose, unfortunately, your mathematics and economics professors have decided to give tests two days from now and you can spend a total of only 12 hours studying for both exams. After some thought, you conclude that dividing your study time equally between each subject will give you an expected grade of C in each course. For each additional three hours of study time for one of the subjects, your grade will increase one letter for that subject, and your grade will fall one letter for the other subject.

a. Construct a table for the production possibilities and corresponding number of hours of study in this case.

b. Plot these production possibilities data in a graph.

c. Does this production possibilities curve reflect the law of increasing opportunity costs? Explain.

11. Draw a production possibilities curve for a hypothetical economy producing capital goods and consumer goods. Suppose a major technological breakthrough occurs in the capital goods industry and the new technology is widely adopted only in this industry. Draw the new production possibilities curve. Now assume that a technological advance occurs in consumer goods production, but not in capital goods production. Draw the new production possibilities curve.

12. The present choice between investing in capital goods and producing consumer goods now affects the ability of an economy to produce in the future. Explain.

✓ CHECKPOINT ANSWERS

What Does a War on Terrorism Really Mean?

A "peace dividend" suggests resources are allocated away from military production and used for greater nonmilitary production. The war on terrorism arguably shifts resources in the opposite direction. If you said that this phrase represents a movement along the production possibilities curve, **YOU ARE CORRECT.**

Sample Quiz

For an explanation of the correct answers, visit the Tucker Web site at www.cengage.com/economics/tucker.

1. Which of the following *best* describes the three fundamental economic questions?
   a. What to produce, when to produce, and where to produce
   b. What time to produce, what place to produce, and how to produce
   c. What to produce, when to produce, and for whom to produce
   d. What to produce, how to produce, and for whom to produce

2. Suppose the alternative uses of an hour of your time in the evening, ranked from best to worst, are (1) study economics, (2) watch two half-hour sitcoms, (3) play video games, and (4) jog around town. You can choose only one activity. What is the opportunity cost of studying economics for one hour given this information?
   a. Jogging around town
   b. Watching two half-hour TV sitcoms
   c. Playing video games
   d. The sum of watching two half-hour TV sitcoms, playing pool, and doing your laundry

3. Which word or phrase *best* completes the following sentence? Marginal analysis means evaluating _____ changes from a current situation.
   a. positive or negative
   b. infinite
   c. no
   d. maximum

4. Which of the following is an example of an organization using marginal analysis?
   a. A hotel manager calculating the average cost per guest for the past year
   b. A farmer hoping for rain
   c. A government official considering the effect an increase in military goods production will have on the production of consumer goods
   d. A businessperson calculating economic profits

5. A production possibilities curve shows the various combinations of two outputs that
   a. consumers would like to consume.
   b. producers would like to produce.
   c. an economy can produce.
   d. an economy should produce.

6. A production possibilities curve is drawn based on which of the following assumptions?
   a. Resources are fixed and fully employed, and technology advances at the rate of growth of the economy overall.
   b. Resources such as nonrenewable resources will decline, but labor remains fully employed and technology is unchanged.
   c. Resources can vary; most resources experience times of unemployment; and technology advances, particularly during wartime.

Sample Quiz *continued*

d. Resources such as labor and capital will grow and are fully employed, and technology is unchanged.

e. None of the above answers is correct.

7. If an economy can produce various combinations of food and shelter along a production possibilities curve (PPC), then if we increase the production of shelter along the PPC, which of the following is *true*?

a. We also increase the production of food.

b. We must decrease the production of food. This forgone food production represents the opportunity cost of the increase in shelter.

c. We cannot change the production of food.

d. The concept of opportunity cost does not apply along PPC.

8. An economy can produce various combinations of food and shelter along a production possibilities curve (PPC). We first increase the production of shelter along the PPC. If we then continue to shift more and more production to shelter, which of the following will *most* likely happen to the opportunity cost of a unit of shelter?

a. Opportunity cost will increase because as more and more shelter is produced, labor and capital that is highly productive at producing food is being shifted to shelter production, and so more and more food is being given up to produce a unit of shelter.

b. Opportunity cost is the amount of labor (but not capital) that is used to produce the extra shelter.

c. Opportunity cost must stay constant if we are to stay on the production possibilities curve (PPC).

d. Opportunity cost includes all options given up to produce shelter.

9. An economy can produce various combinations of food and shelter along a production possibilities curve (PPC). Suppose a technological innovation resulted in a new, higher-yielding crop that generated more bushels of grain for a given set of land, labor, and capital resources. If this innovation did not affect the productivity of shelter production, which of the following would be *true*?

a. The PPC will shift outward equally along both axes of the graph.

b. The PPC will rotate inward along the food axis, but will not shift on the shelter axis.

c. The PPC will rotate outward along the food axis, but will not shift on the shelter axis.

d. The PPC will not change.

10. If a production possibilities curve (PPC) has capital on the vertical axis and consumer goods on the horizontal axis, which of the following is true?

a. There is a trade-off between emphasizing the production of capital today to benefit people today versus emphasizing the production of consumer goods today that will generate benefits in the future.

b. Greater emphasis on the production of capital today leads to future inward shifts in the PPC, thus decreasing the wealth of people in the future.

c. Greater emphasis on the production of consumer goods today leads to greater outward shifts in the PPC, thus increasing the wealth of people in the future.

d. Greater emphasis on the production of capital today leads to greater outward shifts in the PPC, thus increasing the wealth of people in the future.

11. Which of the following reasons could explain why an economy would be operating inside its production possibilities curve (PPC)?

a. Because shrinking population has reduced the number of productive workers in the economy

b. Because technological innovations have increased the productivity of labor and capital

c. Because damage to natural resources, such as damage caused by deforestation leading to erosion of topsoil, has shrunk the land resource

d. Because of unemployment or underemployment of labor, perhaps due to discrimination against employing workers of a certain race or gender

Sample Quiz *continued*

12. Combinations of goods outside the production possibilities curve (PPC) have which of the following characteristics?
    a. They are attainable today only if we employ all unemployed or underemployed resources.
    b. They are not attainable given our existing stock of resources and technology.
    c. They imply that some resources, such as labor, are unemployed or underemployed.
    d. None of the above answers is correct.

13. Suppose an economy can produce various combinations of fish and bread. If more people with strong fishing skills became employed in this economy, how would the production possibilities curve (PPC) change?
    a. The PPC would shift outward on the fish axis, but would not change on the bread axis.
    b. The PPC would shift outward equally along both the fish and bread axes.
    c. The PPC would shift inward on the bread axis, but would not change on the fish axis.
    d. The PPC would shift inward equally along both the fish and bread axes.

14. Three different economies have made choices about the production of capital goods. Which of the following is *most* likely to produce the greatest growth in the production possibilities curve (PPC)?
    a. Capital goods produced at the exact rate needed to replace worn-out capital.
    b. Greater production of capital goods than what is needed to replace worn-out capital.
    c. Less production of capital goods than what is needed to replace worn-out capital.
    d. More production of consumption goods that replace worn-out capital.

15. In the study of economics, investment means
    a. the accumulation of capital that is used to produce goods and services.
    b. owning stocks and bonds.

    c. the principle that the opportunity cost increases as the production of one output expands.
    d. the effect of stock prices on the production possibilities curve.

16. Which of the following is *not* one of the three fundamental economic questions?
    a. What happens when you add to or subtract from a current situation?
    b. For whom to produce?
    c. How to produce?
    d. What to produce?

17. Opportunity cost
    a. represents the best alternative sacrificed for a chosen alternative.
    b. has no relationship to the various alternatives that must be given up when a choice is made in the context of scarcity.
    c. represents the worst alternative sacrificed for a chosen alternative.
    d. represents all alternatives not chosen.

18. Which words best complete the following sentence? A rational decision maker always chooses the option for which marginal benefit is _____ marginal cost.
    a. less than
    b. equal to
    c. unrelated to
    d. more than

19. The principle that the opportunity cost increases as the production of one output expands is the
    a. law of increasing opportunity costs.
    b. law of demand.
    c. law of supply.
    d. law of increasing returns to scale.

20. The ability of an economy to produce greater levels of output per time period is called
    a. positive economics.
    b. negative economics.
    c. economic growth.
    d. the law of specialization.

This road map feature helps you tie together material in the part as you travel the Economic Way of Thinking Highway. The following are review questions listed by chapter from the previous part. The key concept in each question is given for emphasis, and each question or set of questions concludes with an interactive game to reinforce the concepts. Click on the Tucker Web site at www.cengage.com/economics/tucker, select the chapter, and play the visual causation chain game designed to make learning fun. Enjoy the cheers when correct and suffer the jeers if you miss. The correct answers to the multiple choice questions are given in Appendix C of the text.

CHAPTER **1**. INTRODUCING THE ECONOMIC WAY OF THINKING

1. **Key Concept: Scarcity**
   Economists believe that scarcity forces everyone to
   a. satisfy all wants.
   b. abandon consumer sovereignty.
   c. lie about their wants.
   d. create unlimited resources.
   e. make choices.

2. **Key Concept: Economics**
   The subject of economics is primarily the study of
   a. the government decision-making process.
   b. how to operate a business successfully.
   c. decision making because of the problem of scarcity.
   d. how to make money in the stock market.

   Causation Chain Game
   The Relationship between Scarcity and Decision Making

3. **Key Concept: Model**
   When building a model, an economist must
   a. adjust for exceptional situations.
   b. provide a complete description of reality.
   c. make simplifying assumptions.
   d. develop a set of behavioral equations.

4. **Key Concept: Ceteris paribus**
   If the price of a textbook rises and students purchase fewer textbooks, an economic model can show a cause-and-effect relationship only if which of the following conditions holds?

a. Students' incomes fall.
b. Tuition decreases.
c. The number of students increases.
d. Everything else is constant.
e. The bookstore no longer accepts used book trade-ins.

5. **Key Concept: Association versus causation**
   Someone notices that sunspot activity is high just prior to recessions and concludes that sunspots cause recessions. This person has
   a. confused association and causation.
   b. misunderstood the ceteris paribus assumption.
   c. used normative economics to answer a positive question.
   d. built an untestable model.

 Causation Chain Game
The Steps in the Model-Building Process—Exhibit 2

CHAPTER 2. PRODUCTION POSSIBILITIES, OPPORTUNITY COST, AND ECONOMIC GROWTH

6. **Key Concept: Production possibilities curve**
   Which of the following is *not* true about a production possibilities curve? The curve
   a. indicates the combinations of goods and services that can be produced with a given technology.
   b. indicates the efficient production points.
   c. indicates the nonefficient production points.
   d. indicates the feasible (attainable) and nonfeasible production points.
   e. indicates which production point will be chosen.

7. **Key Concept: Production possibilities curve**
   Which of the following is *true* about the production possibilities curve when a technological progress occurs?
   a. Shifts inward to the left
   b. Becomes flatter at one end and steeper at the other end
   c. Becomes steeper
   d. Shifts outward to the right
   e. Does not change

8. **Key Concept: Shifting the production possibilities curve**
   An outward shift of an economy's production possibilities curve is caused by
   a. entrepreneurship.
   b. an increase in labor.
   c. an advance in technology.
   d. all of the above.

9. **Key Concept: Shifting the production possibilities curve**
   Which would be *least* likely to cause the production possibilities curve to shift to the right?
   a. An increase in the labor force
   b. Improved methods of production
   c. An increase in the education and training of the labor force
   d. A decrease in unemployment

10. **Key Concept: Investment**
    A nation can accelerate its economic growth by
    a. reducing the number of immigrants allowed into the country.
    b. adding to its stock of capital.
    c. printing more money.
    d. imposing tariffs and quotas on imported goods.

Causation Chain Game
Economic Growth and Technology—Exhibit 4

Microeconomic Fundamentals

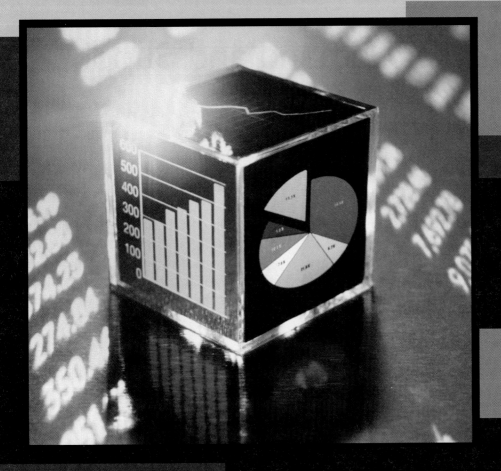

part 2

I n your study of the microeconomy, the chapters in Part 2 build on
the basic concepts you learned in Part 1. Chapters 3 and 4 explain
the market demand and supply model, which has a wide range of
real-world applications. Part 2 concludes with an extension of the concepts of demand and supply, useful in analyzing health care markets.

chapter 3

Market Demand and Supply

A cornerstone of the U.S. economy is the use of markets to answer the basic economic questions discussed in the previous chapter. Consider baseball cards, Blu-rays, physical fitness, gasoline, soft drinks, and sneakers. In a *market economy*, each is bought and sold by individuals coming together as buyers and sellers in markets. This chapter is extremely important because it introduces basic supply and demand analysis. This technique will prove to be valuable because it is applicable to a multitude of real-world choices of buyers and sellers facing the problem of scarcity. For example, the Global

Economics feature asks you to consider the highly controversial issue of international trade in human organs.

Demand represents the choice-making behavior of consumers, while supply represents the choices of producers. The chapter begins by looking closely at demand and then supply. Finally, it combines these forces to see how prices and quantities are determined in the marketplace. Market demand and supply analysis is the basic tool of microeconomic analysis.

In this chapter, you will learn to solve these economics puzzles:

- What is the difference between a "change in quantity demanded" and a "change in demand"?

- Can Congress repeal the law of supply to control oil prices?

- Does the price system eliminate scarcity?

3-1 The Law of Demand

Economics might be referred to as "graphs and laughs" because economists are so fond of using graphs to illustrate demand, supply, and many other economic concepts. Unfortunately, some students taking economics courses say they miss the laughs.

Exhibit 1 reveals an important "law" in economics called the law of demand. The law of demand states there is an inverse relationship between the price of a good and the quantity buyers are willing to purchase in a defined time period, ceteris paribus. The law of demand makes good sense. At a "sale," consumers buy more when the price of merchandise is cut.

Law of demand

The principle that there is an inverse relationship between the price of a good and the quantity buyers are willing to purchase in a defined time period, ceteris paribus.

EXHIBIT 1	An Individual Buyer's Demand Curve for Blu-rays

Bob's demand curve shows how many Blu-rays he is willing to purchase at different possible prices. As the price of Blu-rays declines, the quantity demanded increases, and Bob purchases more Blu-rays. The inverse relationship between price and quantity demanded conforms to the law of demand.

An Individual Buyer's Demand Schedule for Blu-rays

Point	Price per Blu-ray	Quantity demanded (per year)
A	$20	4
B	15	6
C	10	10
D	5	16

SOURCE: © Cengage Learning 2014

In Exhibit 1, the *demand curve* is formed by the line connecting the possible price and quantity purchased responses of an individual consumer. The demand curve therefore allows you to find the quantity demanded by a buyer at any possible selling price by moving along the curve. For example, Bob, a sophomore at Marketplace College, enjoys watching Blu-ray movies. Bob's demand curve shows that at a price of $15 per Blu-ray, his quantity demanded is 6 Blu-rays purchased annually (point *B*). At the lower price of $10, Bob's quantity demanded increases to 10 Blu-rays per year (point *C*). Following this procedure, other price and quantity possibilities for Bob are read along the demand curve.

Note that until we know the actual price determined by both demand and supply, we do not know how many Blu-rays Bob will actually purchase annually. The demand curve is simply a summary of Bob's buying intentions. Once we know the market price, a quick look at the demand curve tells us how many Blu-rays Bob will buy.

Demand

A curve or schedule showing the various quantities of product consumers are willing to purchase at possible prices during a specified period of time, ceteris paribus.

> **CONCLUSION:** *Demand is a curve or schedule showing the various quantities of a product consumers are willing to purchase at possible prices during a specified period of time, ceteris paribus.*

3-1a MARKET DEMAND

To make the transition from an *individual* demand curve to a *market* demand curve, we total, or sum, the individual demand schedules. Suppose the owner of ZapMart, a small retail chain of stores serving a few states, tries to decide what to charge for Blu-rays and hires a consumer research firm. For simplicity, we assume Fred and Mary are the only two buyers in ZapMart's market, and they are sent a questionnaire that asks how many Blu-rays each would be willing to purchase at several possible prices. Exhibit 2 reports their price-quantity demanded responses in tabular and graphical form.

The market demand curve, D_{total}, in Exhibit 2 is derived by summing *horizontally* the two individual demand curves, D_1 and D_2, for each possible price. At a price of $20, for example, we sum Fred's 2 Blu-rays demanded per year and Mary's 1 Blu-ray demanded per year to find that the total quantity demanded at $20 is 3 Blu-rays per year. Repeating the same process for other prices generates the market demand curve, D_{total}. For example, at a price of $5, the total quantity demanded is 12 Blu-rays.

3-2 The Distinction between Changes in Quantity Demanded and Changes in Demand

Price is not the only variable that determines how much of a good or service consumers will buy. Recall from Exhibit A-6 of Appendix 1 that the price and quantity variables in our model are subject to the ceteris paribus assumption. If we relax this assumption and allow other variables held constant to change, a variety

---

EXHIBIT 2 — The Market Demand Curve for Blu-rays

Individual demand curves differ for consumers Fred and Mary. Assuming they are the only buyers in the market, the market demand curve, D_{total}, is derived by summing horizontally the individual demand curves, D_1 and D_2.

Market Demand Schedule for Blu-rays				
	Quantity Demanded per Year			
Price per Blu-ray	**Fred**	**+**	**Mary**	**= Total Demand**
$25	1		0	1
20	2		1	3
15	3		3	6
10	4		5	9
5	5		7	12

SOURCE: © Cengage Learning 2014

---

of factors can influence the position of the demand curve. Because these factors are not the price of the good itself, these variables are called *nonprice determinants,* or simply, *demand shifters.* The major nonprice determinants include (1) the number of buyers; (2) tastes and preferences; (3) income; (4) expectations of future changes in prices, income, and availability of goods; and (5) prices of related goods.

Before discussing these nonprice determinants of demand, we must pause to explain an important and possibly confusing distinction in terminology. We have been referring to a change in quantity demanded, which results solely from a change in the price. A change in quantity demanded is a movement between points along a stationary demand curve, ceteris paribus. In Exhibit 3(a), at the price of $15, the quantity demanded is 20 million Blu-rays per year. This is shown as

Change in quantity demanded

A movement between points along a stationary demand curve, ceteris paribus.

| EXHIBIT 3 | Movement along a Demand Curve versus a Shift in Demand |

Part (a) shows the demand curve, D, for Blu-rays per year. If the price is $15 at point A, the quantity demanded by consumers is 20 million Blu-rays. If the price decreases to $10 at point B, the quantity demanded increases from 20 million to 30 million Blu-rays.

Part (b) illustrates an increase in demand. A change in some nonprice determinant can cause an increase in demand from D_1 to D_2. At a price of $15 on D_1 (point A), 20 million Blu-rays is the quantity demanded per year. At this price on D_2 (point B), the quantity demanded increases to 30 million.

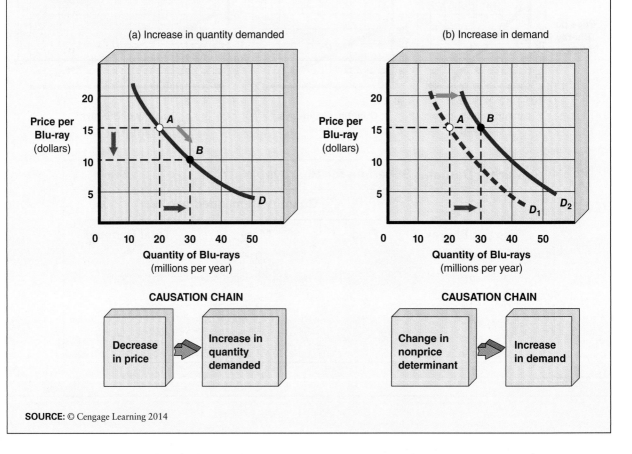

SOURCE: © Cengage Learning 2014

point A on the demand curve, D. At a lower price of, say, $10, the quantity demanded increases to 30 million Blu-rays per year, shown as point B. Verbally, we describe the impact of the price decrease as an increase in the quantity demanded of 10 million Blu-rays per year. We show this relationship on the demand curve as a movement down along the curve from point A to point B.

CONCLUSION: *Under the law of demand, any decrease in price along the vertical axis will cause an increase in quantity demanded, measured along the horizontal axis.*

A change in demand is an increase (rightward shift) or a decrease (leftward shift) in the quantity demanded at each possible price. If ceteris paribus no longer applies and if one of the five nonprice factors changes, the location of the demand curve shifts.

> **CONCLUSION:** *Changes in nonprice determinants can produce only a shift in the demand curve and not a movement along the demand curve, which is caused by a change in the price.*

Comparing parts (a) and (b) of Exhibit 3 is helpful in distinguishing between a change in quantity demanded and a change in demand. In part (b), suppose the market demand curve for Blu-rays is initially at D_1 and there is a shift to the right (an increase in demand) from D_1 to D_2. This means that at *all* possible prices, consumers wish to purchase a larger quantity than before the shift occurred. At \$15 per Blu-ray, for example, 30 million Blu-rays (point *B*) will be purchased each year, rather than 20 million Blu-rays (point *A*).

Now suppose a change in some nonprice factor causes demand curve D_1 to shift leftward (a decrease in demand). The interpretation in this case is that at *all* possible prices, consumers will buy a smaller quantity than before the shift occurred.

Exhibit 4 summarizes the terminology for the effects of changes in price and nonprice determinants on the demand curve.

3-3 Nonprice Determinants of Demand

Distinguishing between a change in quantity demanded and a change in demand requires some patience and practice. The following discussion of specific changes in nonprice factors, or demand shifters, will clarify how each nonprice variable affects demand.

3-3a NUMBER OF BUYERS

Look back at Exhibit 2 and imagine the impact of adding more individual demand curves to the individual demand curves of Fred and Mary. At all possible prices, there is extra quantity demanded by the new customers, and the market demand curve for Blu-rays shifts rightward (an increase in demand). Population growth therefore tends to increase the number of buyers, which shifts the market demand curve for a good or service rightward. Conversely, a population decline shifts most market demand curves leftward (a decrease in demand).

The number of buyers can be specified to include both foreign and domestic buyers. Suppose the market demand curve D_1 in Exhibit 3(b) is for Blu-rays purchased in the United States by customers at home and abroad. Also assume Japan

Change in demand

An increase or a decrease in the quantity demanded at each possible price. An increase in demand is a rightward shift in the entire demand curve. A decrease in demand is a leftward shift in the entire demand curve.

EXHIBIT 4	**Terminology for Changes in Price and Nonprice Determinants of Demand**

Caution! It is important to distinguish between a change in quantity demanded, which is a movement along a demand curve (D_1) caused by a change in price, and a change in demand, which is a shift in the demand curve. An increase in demand (shift to D_2) or a decrease in demand (shift to D_3) is not caused by a change in price. Instead, a shift is caused by a change in one of the nonprice determinants.

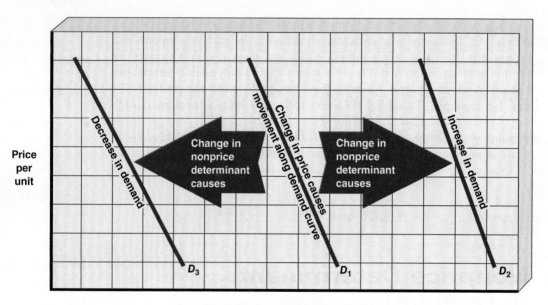

Quantity of good or service per unit of time

Change	Effect	Terminology
Price increases	Upward movement along the demand curve	Decrease in the quantity demanded
Price decreases	Downward movement along the demand curve	Increase in the quantity demanded
Nonprice determinant	Leftward or rightward shift in the demand curve	Decrease or increase in demand

SOURCE: © Cengage Learning 2014

restricts the import of Blu-rays into Japan. What would be the effect of Japan removing this trade restriction? The answer is that the demand curve shifts rightward from D_1 to D_2 when Japanese consumers add their individual demand curves to the U.S. market demand for Blu-rays.

3-3b TASTES AND PREFERENCES

A favorable or unfavorable change in consumer tastes or preferences means more or less of a product is demanded at each possible price. Fads, fashions, advertising, and new products can influence consumer preferences to buy a particular good or service. Beanie Babies, for example, became the rage in the 1990s, and the demand curve for these products shifted to the right. When people tire of a product, the demand curve will shift leftward. The physical fitness trend has increased the demand for health clubs and exercise equipment. On the other hand, have you noticed many stores selling hula hoops? Advertising can also influence consumers' taste for a product. As a result, consumers are more likely to buy more at every price, and the demand curve for the product will shift to the right. Concern for global climate change has increased the demand for hybrid cars and recycling.

3-3c INCOME

Most students are all too familiar with how changes in income affect demand. There are two possible categories for the relationship between changes in income and changes in demand: (1) normal goods and (2) inferior goods.

A normal good is any good for which there is a direct relationship between changes in income and its demand curve. For many goods and services, an increase in income causes buyers to purchase more at any possible price. As buyers receive higher incomes, the demand curve shifts rightward for such *normal goods* as cars, steaks, vintage wine, cleaning services, and Blu-rays. A decline in income has the opposite effect, and the demand curve shifts leftward.

An inferior good is any good for which there is an inverse relationship between changes in income and its demand curve. A rise in income can result in reduced purchases of a good or service at any possible price. This might happen with such *inferior goods* as generic brands, Spam, discount clothes, and used cars. Instead of buying these inferior goods, higher incomes allow consumers to buy brand-name products, steaks, designer clothes, or new cars. Conversely, a fall in income causes the demand curve for inferior goods to shift rightward.

Normal good
Any good for which there is a direct relationship between changes in income and its demand curve.

Inferior good
Any good for which there is an inverse relationship between changes in income and its demand curve.

3-3d EXPECTATIONS OF BUYERS

What is the effect on demand in the present when consumers anticipate future changes in prices, incomes, or availability? What happens when a war breaks out in the Middle East? Expectations that there will be a shortage of gasoline induce consumers to say "fill 'er up" at every opportunity, and demand increases. Suppose students learn that the prices of the textbooks for several courses they plan to take next semester will double soon. Their likely response is to buy now, which causes an increase in the demand curve for these textbooks. Another example is a change in the weather, which can indirectly cause expectations to shift demand for some products. Suppose severe weather destroys a substantial portion of the peach crop. Consumers reason that the reduction in available supply will soon drive up prices, and they dash to stock up before it is too late. This change in expectations causes the demand curve for peaches to increase. Prior to Hurricane Katrina hitting New Orleans, sales of batteries and flashlights soared.

3-3e PRICES OF RELATED GOODS

Possibly the most confusing nonprice factor is the influence of other prices on the demand for a particular good or service. The term *nonprice* seems to forbid any shift in demand resulting from a change in the price of *any* product. This confusion exists when one fails to distinguish between changes in quantity demanded and changes in demand. Remember that ceteris paribus holds all prices of other goods constant. Therefore, movement along a demand curve occurs solely in response to changes in the price of a product, that is, its "own" price. When we draw the demand curve for Coca-Cola, for example, we assume that the prices of Pepsi-Cola and other colas remain unchanged. What happens if we relax the ceteris paribus assumption and the price of Pepsi rises? Many Pepsi buyers switch to Coca-Cola, and the demand curve for Coca-Cola shifts rightward (an increase in demand). Coca-Cola and Pepsi-Cola are one type of related goods called substitute goods. A substitute good competes with another good for consumer purchases. As a result, there is a direct relationship between a price change for one good and the demand for its "competitor" good. Other examples of substitutes include margarine and butter, domestic cars and foreign cars, and Blu-rays and Internet movie downloads.

Blu-rays and Blu-ray players illustrate a second type of related goods called complementary goods. A complementary good is jointly consumed with another good. As a result, there is an inverse relationship between a price change for one good and the demand for its "go together" good. Although buying a Blu-ray and buying a Blu-ray player can be separate decisions, these two purchases are related. The more Blu-ray players consumers buy, the greater the demand for Blu-rays. What happens when the price of Blu-ray players falls sharply? The market demand curve for Blu-rays shifts rightward (an increase in demand) because new owners of players add their individual demand curves to those of people already owning players and buying Blu-rays. Conversely, a sharp rise in the price of deskjet printers would decrease the demand for ink cartridges.

Exhibit 5 summarizes the relationship between changes in the nonprice determinants of demand and the demand curve, accompanied by examples for each type of nonprice factor change.

Substitute good

A good that competes with another good for consumer purchases. As a result, there is a direct relationship between a price change for one good and the demand for its "competitor" good.

Complementary good

A good that is jointly consumed with another good. As a result, there is an inverse relationship between a price change for one good and the demand for its "go together" good.

✔ CHECKPOINT

Can Gasoline Become an Exception to the Law of Demand?

Suppose war in the Middle East threatened oil supplies, and gasoline prices began rising. Consumers feared future oil shortages, so they rushed to fill up their gas tanks. In this case, as the price of gas increased, consumers bought more, not less. Is this an exception to the law of demand?

EXHIBIT 5	Summary of the Impact of Changes in Nonprice Determinants of Demand on the Demand Curve		
Nonprice Determinant of Demand	Relationship to Changes in Demand Curve	Shift in the Demand Curve	Examples
1. Number of buyers	Direct		• Immigration from Mexico increases the demand for Mexican food products in grocery stores.
			• A decline in the birthrate reduces the demand for baby clothes.
2. Tastes and preferences	Direct		• For no apparent reason, consumers want Beanie Babies and demand increases.
			• After a while, the fad dies and demand declines.
3. Income			• Consumers' incomes increase, and the demand for steaks increases.
a. Normal goods	Direct		
			• A decline in income decreases the demand for air travel.
b. Inferior goods	Inverse		• Consumers' incomes increase, and the demand for hamburger decreases.
			• A decline in income increases the demand for bus service.

Continued

Continued from previous page

Nonprice Determinant of Demand	Relationship to Changes in Demand Curve	Shift in the Demand Curve	Examples
4. Expectations of buyers	Direct		• Consumers expect that gasoline will be in short supply next month and that prices will rise sharply. Consequently, consumers fill the tanks in their cars this month, and there is an increase in demand for gasoline.
			• Months later, consumers expect the price of gasoline to fall soon, and the demand for gasoline decreases.
5. Prices of related Goods			• A reduction in the price of tea decreases the demand for coffee.
a. Substitute goods	Direct		• An increase in the price of airfares causes higher demand for bus transportation.
b. Complementary goods	Inverse		• A decline in the price of cellular service increases the demand for cell phones.
			• A higher price for peanut butter decreases the demand for jelly.

SOURCE: © Cengage Learning 2014

3-4 The Law of Supply

Law of supply

The principle that there is a direct relationship between the price of a good and the quantity sellers are willing to offer for sale in a defined time period, ceteris paribus.

In everyday conversations, the term *supply* refers to a specific quantity. A "limited supply" of golf clubs at a sporting goods store means there are only so many clubs for sale and that's all. This interpretation of supply is *not* the economist's definition. To economists, supply is the relationship between ranges of possible prices and quantities supplied, which is stated as the law of supply. The law of supply states there is a direct relationship between the price of a good and the quantity sellers are willing to offer for sale in a defined time period, ceteris paribus. Interpreting the individual *supply curve* for ZapMart shown in Exhibit 6 is basically the same

EXHIBIT 6 | An Individual Seller's Supply Curve for Blu-rays

The supply curve for an individual seller, such as ZapMart, shows the quantity of Blu-rays offered for sale at different possible prices. As the price of Blu-rays rises, a retail store has an incentive to increase the quantity of Blu-rays supplied per year. The direct relationship between price and quantity supplied conforms to the law of supply.

An Individual Seller's Supply Schedule for Blu-rays

Point	Price per Blu-ray	Quantity supplied (thousands per year)
A	$20	50
B	15	45
C	10	35
D	5	20

SOURCE: © Cengage Learning 2014

as interpreting Bob's demand curve shown in Exhibit 1. Each point on the curve represents a quantity supplied (measured along the horizontal axis) at a particular price (measured along the vertical axis). For example, at a price of $10 per Blu-ray (point C), the quantity supplied by the seller, ZapMart, is 35,000 Blu-rays per year. At the higher price of $15, the quantity supplied increases to 45,000 Blu-rays per year (point B).

Supply
A curve or schedule showing the various quantities of a product sellers are willing to produce and offer for sale at possible prices during a specified period of time, ceteris paribus.

CONCLUSION: *Supply is a curve or schedule showing the various quantities of a product sellers are willing to produce and offer for sale at possible prices during a specified period of time, ceteris paribus.*

Why are sellers willing to sell more at a higher price? Suppose Farmer Brown is trying to decide whether to devote more of his land, labor, and barn space to the production of soybeans. Recall from Chapter 2 the production possibilities curve and the concept of increasing opportunity cost developed in Exhibit 3. If Farmer Brown devotes few of his resources to producing soybeans, the opportunity cost of, say, producing milk is small. But increasing soybean production means a higher opportunity cost, measured by the quantity of milk not produced. The logical question is: What would induce Farmer Brown to produce more soybeans for sale and overcome the higher opportunity cost of producing less milk? You guessed it! There must be the *incentive* of a higher price for soybeans.

CONCLUSION: *Only at a higher price will it be profitable for sellers to incur the higher opportunity cost associated with producing and supplying a larger quantity.*

✓ CHECKPOINT

Can the Law of Supply Be Repealed for the Oil Market?

The United States experienced two oil shocks during the 1970s in the aftermath of Middle East tensions. Congress said no to high oil prices by passing a law prohibiting prices above a legal limit. Supporters of such price controls said this was a way to ensure adequate supply without allowing oil producers to earn excess profits. Did price controls increase, decrease, or have no effect on U.S. oil production during the 1970s?

3-4a MARKET SUPPLY

To construct a *market* supply curve, we follow the same procedure used to derive a market demand curve. That is, we *horizontally* sum all the quantities supplied at various prices that might prevail in the market.

Let's assume that Entertain City and High Vibes are the only two firms selling Blu-rays in a given market. As you can see in Exhibit 7, the market supply curve, S_{total}, slopes upward to the right. At a price of $25, Entertain City will supply 25,000 Blu-rays per year, and High Vibes will supply 35,000 Blu-rays per year. Thus, summing the two individual supply curves, S_1 and S_2, *horizontally*, the total of 60,000 Blu-rays is plotted at this price on the market supply curve, S_{total}. Similar calculations at other prices along the price axis generate a market supply curve, telling us the total amount of Blu-rays these businesses offer for sale at different selling prices.

EXHIBIT 7 | The Market Supply Curve for Blu-rays

Entertain City and High Vibes are two businesses selling Blu-rays. If these are the only two firms in the Blu-ray market, the market supply curve, S_{total}, can be derived by summing horizontally the individual supply curves, S_1 and S_2.

The Market Supply Schedule for Blu-rays			
	Quantity supplied (thousands per year)		
Price per Blu-ray	Entertain City +	High Vibes =	Total Supply
$25	25	35	60
20	20	30	50
15	15	25	40
10	10	20	30
5	5	15	20

SOURCE: © Cengage Learning 2014

3-5 The Distinction between Changes in Quantity Supplied and Changes in Supply

As in demand theory, the price of a product is not the only factor that influences how much sellers offer for sale. Once we relax the ceteris paribus assumption, there are six principal *nonprice determinants* (also called *supply shifters)* that can shift the supply curve's position: (1) the number of sellers, (2) technology, (3) resource prices, (4) taxes and subsidies, (5) expectations, and (6) prices of other goods. We will discuss these nonprice determinants in more detail momentarily,

72   PART 2   MICROECONOMIC FUNDAMENTALS

Change in quantity supplied

A movement between points along a stationary supply curve, ceteris paribus.

Change in supply

An increase or a decrease in the quantity supplied at each possible price. An increase in supply is a rightward shift in the entire supply curve. A decrease in supply is a leftward shift in the entire supply curve.

but first we must distinguish between a change in quantity supplied and a change in supply.

A change in quantity supplied is a movement between points along a stationary supply curve, ceteris paribus. In Exhibit 8(a), at the price of $10, the quantity supplied is 30 million Blu-rays per year (point *A*). At the higher price of $15, sellers offer a larger "quantity supplied" of 40 million Blu-rays per year (point *B*). Economists describe the effect of the rise in price as an increase in the quantity supplied of 10 million Blu-rays per year.

> **CONCLUSION:** *Under the law of supply, any increase in price along the vertical axis will cause an increase in the quantity supplied, measured along the horizontal axis.*

A change in supply is an increase (rightward shift) or a decrease (leftward shift) in the quantity supplied at each possible price. If ceteris paribus no longer applies and if one of the six nonprice factors changes, the impact is to alter the supply curve's location.

> **CONCLUSION:** *Changes in nonprice determinants can produce only a shift in the supply curve and not a movement along the supply curve.*

In Exhibit 8(b), the rightward shift (an increase in supply) from S_1 to S_2 means that at all possible prices, sellers offer a greater quantity for sale. At $15 per Blu-ray, for instance, sellers provide 40 million for sale annually (point *B*), rather than 30 million (point *A*).

Another case is that some nonprice factor changes and causes a leftward shift (a decrease in supply) from supply curve S_1. As a result, a smaller quantity will be offered for sale at any price.

Exhibit 9 summarizes the terminology for the effects of changes in price and nonprice determinants on the supply curve.

3-6 Nonprice Determinants of Supply

Now we turn to how each of the six basic nonprice factors affects supply.

3-6a NUMBER OF SELLERS

What happens when a severe drought destroys wheat or a frost ruins the orange crop? The damaging effect of the weather may force orange growers out of business, and supply decreases. When the government eases restrictions on hunting alligators, the number of alligator hunters increases, and the supply curve for alligator meat and skins increases. Internationally, the United States may decide to lower trade barriers on textile imports, and this action increases supply by allowing new

EXHIBIT 8	Movement along a Supply Curve versus a Shift in Supply

Part (a) presents the market supply curve, S, for Blu-rays per year. If the price is $10 at point A, the quantity supplied by firms will be 30 million Blu-rays. If the price increases to $15 at point B, the quantity supplied will increase from 30 million to 40 million Blu-rays.

Part (b) illustrates an increase in supply. A change in some nonprice determinant can cause an increase in supply from S_1 to S_2. At a price of $15 on S_1 (point A), the quantity supplied per year is 30 million Blu-rays. At this same price on S_2 (point B), the quantity supplied increases to 40 million.

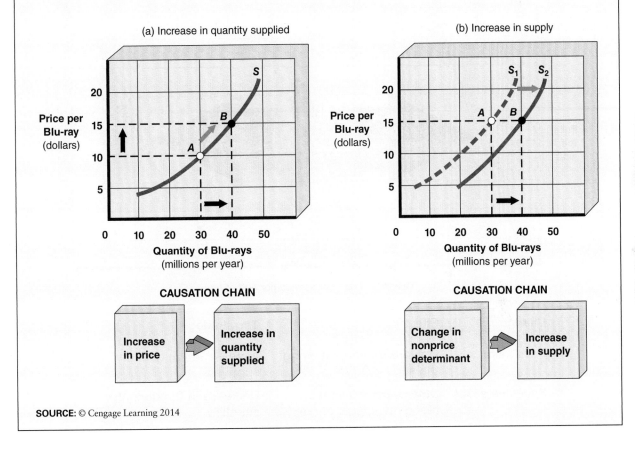

SOURCE: © Cengage Learning 2014

foreign firms to add their individual supply curves to the U.S. market supply curve for textiles. Conversely, higher U.S. trade barriers on textile imports shift the U.S. market supply curve for textiles leftward.

3-6b TECHNOLOGY

Never has society experienced such an explosion of new production techniques. Throughout the world, new and more efficient technology is making it possible to manufacture more products at any possible selling price. New, more powerful personal computers (PCs) reduce production costs and increase the supply of all sorts of goods and services. For example, computers are now milking cows. Computers

| EXHIBIT 9 | Terminology for Changes in Price and Nonprice Determinants of Supply |

Caution! As with demand curves, you must distinguish between a change in quantity supplied, which is a movement along a supply curve (S_1) in response to a change in price, and a shift in the supply curve. An increase in supply (shift to S_2) or a decrease in supply occurs (shift to S_3) is caused by a change in some nonprice determinant and not by a change in the price.

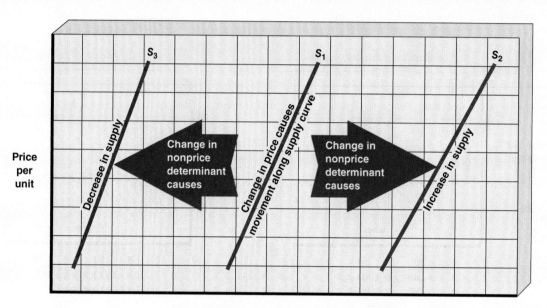

Quantity of good or service per unit of time

Change	Effect	Terminology
Price increases	Upward movement along the supply curve	Increase in the quantity supplied
Price decreases	Downward movement along the supply curve	Decrease in the quantity supplied
Nonprice determinant	Leftward or rightward shift in the supply curve	Decrease or increase in supply

SOURCE: © Cengage Learning 2014

admit the cows into the milking area and then activate lasers to guide milking cups into place. Dairy farmers no longer must wake up at 5:30 a.m., and cows get milked whenever they wish, day or night. As this technology spreads across the United States, it will be possible to offer more milk for sale at each possible price, and the entire supply curve for milk shifts to the right.

3-6c RESOURCE PRICES

Natural resources, labor, capital, and entrepreneurship are all required to produce products, and the prices of these resources affect supply. Suppose many firms are competing for computer programmers to design their software, and the salaries of these highly skilled workers increase. This increase in the price of labor adds to the cost of production. Along the original supply curve, extra costs must be added to each possible price. As a result, the supply of computer software shifts leftward (decreases) because sellers must charge more than before for any quantity supplied. Any reduction in production cost caused by a decline in the price of resources will have an opposite effect on the supply curve and it shifts rightward (increases). Along the original supply curve, cost declines, so the price can be reduced at each possible price.

3-6d TAXES AND SUBSIDIES

Certain taxes, such as sales taxes, have the same effect on supply as does an increase in the price of a resource. The impact of an increase in the sales tax is similar to a rise in the salaries of computer programmers. The higher sales tax imposes an additional production cost on, for example, Blu-rays, and the supply curve shifts leftward. Conversely, a payment from the government for each Blu-ray produced (an unlikely subsidy) would have the same effect as lower prices for resources or a technological advance. That is, the supply curve for Blu-rays shifts rightward.

3-6e EXPECTATIONS OF PRODUCERS

Expectations affect both current demand and current supply. Suppose a war in the Middle East causes oil producers to believe that oil prices will rise dramatically. Their initial response could be to hold back a portion of the oil in their storage tanks so that they can sell more and make greater profits later when oil prices rise. One approach used by the major oil companies might be to limit the amount of gasoline delivered to independent distributors. This response by the oil industry shifts the current supply curve to the left. Now suppose farmers anticipate that the price of wheat will soon fall sharply. The reaction is to sell their inventories stored in silos today before the price declines tomorrow. Such a response shifts the supply curve for wheat to the right.

3-6f PRICES OF OTHER GOODS THE FIRM COULD PRODUCE

Businesses are always considering shifting resources from producing one good to producing another good. A rise in the price of one product relative to the prices of other products signals to suppliers that switching production to the product with the higher relative price yields higher profit. Suppose the price of corn rises because of government incentives to grow corn for ethanol while the price of wheat remains the same; then many farmers will divert more of their land to corn and less to wheat. The result is an increase in the supply of corn and a decrease in the supply

PC Prices: How Low Can They Go?

Applicable Concept: nonprice determinants of demand and supply

Radio was in existence for 38 years before 50 million people tuned in. Television took 13 years to reach that benchmark. Sixteen years after the first PC kit was introduced, 50 million people were using one. Once available to the public, the Internet crossed that line in four years.[1] Before 1999, there were no blogs, and now there are millions. Today, over 80 percent of U.S. households have a computer. Following are quotes from articles that illustrate changes in supply and demand for computers over time.

An Associated Press article reported in 1998:

Personal computers, which tumbled below the $1,000-price barrier just 18 months ago, now are breaking through the $400 price mark—putting them within reach of the average U.S. family. The plunge in PC prices reflects declining wholesale prices for computer parts, such as microprocessors, memory chips, and hard drives. "We've seen a massive transformation in the PC business," said Andrew Peck, an analyst with Cowen & Co., based in Boston.[2]

In 1999, an article in *The Wall Street Journal* reported that PC makers and distributors smashed their industry's time-honored sales channels. PC makers such as Hewlett-Packard Company began using the Internet to sell directly to consumers.

In doing so, they are following the successful strategy of Dell, which for years bypassed storefront retailers and the PC distributors who traditionally keep them stocked, going instead straight to the consumer with catalogs, an 800 number, and Web sites.[3]

In 2001, an article in *The New York Times* described a computer price war:

We reached a situation where the market was saturated in 2000. People who needed computers had them. Vendors are living on sales of replacements, at least in the United States. But that doesn't give you the kind of growth these companies were used to. In the past, most price cuts came from falling prices for processors and other components. In addition, manufacturers have been narrowing profit margins for the last couple years. But when demand dried up last fall, the more aggressive manufacturers decided to try to gain market share by cutting prices to the bone. This is an all-out battle for market share.[4]

In 2012, an analyst in *USA Today* observed the following:

The TV market has been flat for the past two years, while PC sales—despite the enthusiasm for next generation products such as tablets and smartphones—are growing. The

Mircea BEZERGHEANU/Shutterstock.com

way consumers are actually using PCs "is expanding, not contracting," says Matt McRae, Vizio's chief technology officer. "They come home and use their PC for e-mail, but they're also using it for entertainments experiences."[5]

Finally, Wikipedia reports that over time, changes in supply and demand have continued to reduce PC prices. In 1982, for example, Dell offered a $3,000 PC. By 1998, the average selling price was below $1,000. Today, computers selling for less than $300 outperform computers from only a few years previously.

Analyze the Issue

Identify changes in quantity demanded, changes in demand, changes in quantity supplied, and changes in supply described in the article. For any change in demand or supply, also identify the nonprice determinant causing the change.

1. *The Emerging Digital Economy* (U.S. Department of Commerce, 1998), Chap. 1, p. 1.
2. David E. Kalish, "PC Prices Fall Below $400, Luring Bargain-Hunters," Associated Press/*Charlotte Observer*, Aug. 25, 1998, p. 3D.
3. George Anders, "Online Web Seller Asks: How Low Can PC Prices Go?" *The Wall Street Journal*, Jan. 19, 1999, p. B1.
4. Barnaby J. Feder, "Five Questions for Martin Reynolds: A Computer Price War Leaves Buyers Smiling," *The New York Times*, May 13, 2001.
5. Jefferson Graham, "Plans to Sell Budget, High-Performance PCs," *USA Today*, Jan. 9, 2012, p. 1B.

of wheat. This happens because the opportunity cost of growing wheat, measured in forgone corn profits, increases.

Exhibit 10 summarizes the relationship between changes in the nonprice determinants of supply and the supply curve, accompanied by examples for each type of nonprice factor change.

EXHIBIT 10	Summary of the Impact of Changes in Nonprice Determinants of Supply on the Supply Curve		
Nonprice Determinant of Supply	**Relationship to Changes in Supply Curve**	**Shift in the Supply Curve**	**Examples**
1. Number of sellers	Direct		• The United States lowers trade restrictions on foreign textiles, and the supply of textiles in the United States increases.
			• A severe drought destroys the orange crop, and the supply of oranges decreases.
2. Technology	Direct		• New methods of producing automobiles reduce production costs, and the supply of automobiles increases.
			• Technology is destroyed in war, and production costs increase; the result is a decrease in the supply of good X.
3. Resource prices	Inverse		• A decline in the price of computer chips increases the supply of computers.
			• An increase in the cost of farm equipment decreases the supply of soybeans.
4. Taxes and subsidies	Inverse		• An increase in the per-pack tax on cigarettes reduces the supply of cigarettes.
	Direct		• A government payment to dairy farmers based on the number of gallons produced increases the supply of milk.

Continued

Continued from previous page

Nonprice Determinant of Supply	Relationship to Changes in Supply Curve	Shift in the Supply Curve	Examples
5. Expectations	Inverse		• Oil companies anticipate a substantial rise in future oil prices, and this expectation causes these companies to decrease their current supply of oil.
			• Farmers expect the future price of wheat to decline, so they increase the present supply of wheat.
6. Prices of other goods and services	Inverse		• A rise in the price of brand-name drugs causes drug companies to decrease the supply of generic drugs.
			• A decline in the price of tomatoes causes farmers to increase the supply of cucumbers.

SOURCE: © Cengage Learning 2014

3-7 A Market Supply and Demand Analysis

"Teach a parrot to say 'supply and demand' and you've got an economist." Drumroll please! Buyer and seller actors are on center stage to perform a balancing act in a market. A market is any arrangement in which buyers and sellers interact to determine the price and quantity of goods and services exchanged. Let's consider the retail market for sneakers. Exhibit 11 displays hypothetical market demand and supply data for this product. Notice in column 1 of the exhibit that price serves as a common variable for both supply and demand relationships. Columns 2 and 3 list the quantity demanded and the quantity supplied for pairs of sneakers per year.

The important question for market supply and demand analysis is this: Which selling price and quantity will prevail in the market? Let's start by asking what will happen if retail stores supply 75,000 pairs of sneakers and charge $105 a pair. At this relatively high price for sneakers, consumers are willing and able to purchase only 25,000 pairs. As a result, 50,000 pairs of sneakers remain as unsold inventory on the shelves of sellers (column 4), and the market condition is a surplus (column 5). A surplus is a market condition existing at any price where the quantity supplied is greater than the quantity demanded.

How will retailers react to a surplus? Competition forces sellers to bid down their selling price to attract more sales (column 6). If they cut the selling price to $90, there will still be a surplus of 40,000 pairs of sneakers, and pressure on sellers

Market

Any arrangement in which buyers and sellers interact to determine the price and quantity of goods and services exchanged.

Surplus

A market condition existing at any price where the quantity supplied is greater than the quantity demanded.

(1) Price per pair	(2) Quantity demanded	(3) Quantity supplied	(4) Difference (3) – (2)	(5) Market condition	(6) Pressure on price
EXHIBIT 11	**Demand, Supply, and Equilibrium for Sneakers (pairs per year)**				
$105	25,000	75,000	+50,000	Surplus	Downward
90	30,000	70,000	+40,000	Surplus	Downward
75	40,000	60,000	+20,000	Surplus	Downward
60	50,000	50,000	0	Equilibrium	Stationary
45	60,000	35,000	−25,000	Shortage	Upward
30	80,000	20,000	−60,000	Shortage	Upward
15	100,000	5,000	−95,000	Shortage	Upward

SOURCE: © Cengage Learning 2014

to cut their selling price will continue. If the price falls to $75, there will still be an unwanted surplus of 20,000 pairs of sneakers remaining as inventory, and pressure to charge a lower price will persist.

Now let's assume sellers slash the price of sneakers to $15 per pair. This price is very attractive to consumers, and the quantity demanded is 100,000 pairs of sneakers each year. However, sellers are willing and able to provide only 5,000 pairs at this price. The good news is that some consumers buy these 5,000 pairs of sneakers at $15. The bad news is that potential buyers are willing to purchase 95,000 more pairs at that price, but cannot because the shoes are not on the shelves for sale. This out-of-stock condition signals the existence of a shortage. A shortage is a market condition existing at any price where the quantity supplied is less than the quantity demanded.

In the case of a shortage, unsatisfied consumers compete to obtain the product by bidding to pay a higher price. Because sellers are seeking the higher profits that higher prices make possible, they gladly respond by setting a higher price of, say, $30 and increasing the quantity supplied to 20,000 pairs annually. At the price of $30, the shortage persists because the quantity demanded still exceeds the quantity supplied. Thus, a price of $30 will also be temporary because the unfulfilled quantity demanded provides an incentive for sellers to raise their selling price further and offer more sneakers for sale. Suppose the price of sneakers rises to $45 a pair. At this price, the shortage falls to 25,000 pairs, and the market still gives sellers the message to move upward along their market supply curve and sell for a higher price.

Shortage
A market condition existing at any price at where the quantity supplied is less than the quantity demanded.

3-7a EQUILIBRIUM PRICE AND QUANTITY

Assuming sellers are free to sell their products at any price, trial and error will make all possible price-quantity combinations unstable except at equilibrium. Equilibrium occurs at any price and quantity where the quantity demanded and the quantity supplied are equal. Economists also refer to equilibrium as market clearing.

In Exhibit 11, $60 is the equilibrium price, and 50,000 pairs of sneakers is the equilibrium quantity per year. Equilibrium means that the forces of

Equilibrium
A market condition that occurs at any price and quantity at which the quantity demanded and the quantity supplied are equal.

supply and demand are "in balance" or "at rest" and there is no reason for price or quantity to change, ceteris paribus. In short, all prices and quantities except a unique equilibrium price and quantity are temporary. Once the price of sneakers is $60, this price will not change unless a nonprice factor changes demand or supply.

English economist Alfred Marshall (1842–1924) compared supply and demand to a pair of scissor blades. He wrote, "We might as reasonably dispute whether it is the upper or the under blade of a pair of scissors that cuts a piece of paper, as whether value is governed by utility [demand] or cost of production [supply]."[1] Joining market supply and market demand in Exhibit 12 allows us to clearly see the "two blades," that is, the demand curve, D, and the supply curve, S. We can measure the amount of any surplus or shortage by the horizontal distance between the demand and supply curves. At any price *above* equilibrium—say, $90—there is an *excess quantity supplied* (surplus) of 40,000 pairs of sneakers. For any price *below* equilibrium—$30, for example—the horizontal distance between the curves tells us there is an *excess quantity demanded* (shortage) of 60,000 pairs. When the price per pair is $60, the market supply curve and the market demand curve intersect at point E and the quantity demanded equals the quantity supplied at 50,000 pairs per year.

> **CONCLUSION:** *Graphically, the intersection of the supply curve and the demand curve is the market equilibrium price-quantity point. When all other nonprice factors are held constant, this is the only stable coordinate on the graph.*

3-8 Rationing Function of the Price System

Our analysis leads to an important conclusion. The predictable or stable outcome in the sneakers example is that the price will eventually come to rest at $60 per pair. All other factors held constant, the price may be above or below $60, but the forces of surplus or shortage guarantee that any price other than the equilibrium price is temporary. This is the theory of how the price system operates, and it is the cornerstone of microeconomic analysis. The price system is a mechanism that uses the forces of supply and demand to create an equilibrium through rising and falling prices. Stated simply, price plays a *rationing* role. The price system is important because it is a mechanism for distributing scarce goods and services. At the equilibrium price of $60, only those consumers willing to pay $60 per pair get sneakers, and there are no shoes for buyers unwilling to pay that price.

Why would you prefer a world with all markets in equilibrium? If all markets were in equilibrium, there would be no shortages or surpluses for any good or service. In this world, consumers are not frustrated because they want to buy something and it is not on the shelf. Sellers are not upset because unsold merchandise is piling up unsold in their storerooms. Everyone is happy!

Price system

A mechanism that uses the forces of supply and demand to create an equilibrium through rising and falling prices.

[1] Alfred Marshall, *Principles of Economics*, 8th ed. (New York: Macmillan, 1982), p. 348.

EXHIBIT 12 | The Supply and Demand for Sneakers

The supply and demand curves represent a market for sneakers. The intersection of the demand curve, *D*, and the supply curve, *S*, at point *E* indicates the equilibrium price of $60 and the equilibrium quantity of 50,000 pairs bought and sold per year. At any price above $60, a surplus prevails and pressure exists to push the price downward. At $90, for example, the excess quantity supplied of 40,000 pairs remains unsold. At any price below $60, a shortage provides pressure to push the price upward. At $30, for example, the excess quantity demanded of 60,000 pairs encourages consumers to bid up the price.

CAUSATION CHAINS

| Quantity supplied exceeds quantity demanded | → | Surplus | → | Price decreases to equilibrium price |

| Quantity demanded equals quantity supplied | → | Neither surplus nor shortage | → | Equilibrium price established |

| Quantity demanded exceeds quantity supplied | → | Shortage | → | Price increases to equilibrium price |

SOURCE: © Cengage Learning 2014

The Market Approach to Organ Shortages

Applicable concept: price system

There is a global market in human organs in spite of attempts to prevent these transactions. For example, China banned organ sales in 2006, and India did the same in 1994. The National Transplant Organ Act of 1984 made sale of organs illegal in the United States. Economist James R. Rinehart wrote the following on this subject:

> If you were in charge of a kidney transplant program with more potential recipients than donors, how would you allocate the organs under your control? Life and death decisions cannot be avoided. Some individuals are not going to get kidneys regardless of how the organs are distributed because there simply are not enough to go around. Persons who run such programs are influenced in a variety of ways. It would be difficult not to favor friends, relatives, influential people, and those who are championed by the press. Dr. John la Puma, at the Center for Clinical Medical Ethics, University of Chicago, suggested that we use a lottery system for selecting transplant patients. He feels that the present rationing system is unfair.
>
> The selection process frequently takes the form of having the patient wait at home until a suitable donor is found. What this means is that, at any given point in time, many potential recipients are just waiting for an organ to be made available. In essence, the organs are rationed to those who are able to survive the wait. In many situations, patients are simply screened out because they are not considered to be suitable candidates for a transplant. For instance, patients with heart disease and overt psychosis often are excluded. Others with end-stage liver disorders are denied new organs on the grounds that the habits that produced the disease may remain to jeopardize recovery....
>
> Under the present arrangements, owners receive no monetary compensation; therefore, suppliers are willing to supply fewer organs than potential recipients want. Compensating a supplier monetarily would encourage more people to offer their organs for sale. It also would be an excellent incentive for us to take better care of our organs. After all, who would want an enlarged liver or a weak heart ...?[1]

The following excerpt from a newspaper article illustrates the controversy:

> Mickey Mantle's temporary deliverance from death, thanks to a liver transplant, illustrated how the organ-donations system is heavily weighted against poor potential recipients who cannot pass what University of Pennsylvania medical ethicist Arthur Caplan calls the "wallet biopsy."... Thus, affluent patients like Mickey Mantle may get evaluated and listed simultaneously in different regions to increase their odds of finding a donor. The New Yorker found his organ donor in Texas' Region 4. Such a system is not only highly unfair, but it leads to other kinds of abuses.[2]

Based on altruism, the organ donor distribution system continues to result in shortages. In 2012, over 122,000 patients were on the waiting list for organs. To address the shortage of organ donation, some European countries such as Spain, Belgium, and Austria have implemented an "opt-out" organ donation system. In the "opt-out" system, people are automatically considered to be organ donors unless they officially declare that they do not wish to be donors. Also, Facebook encourages everyone to advertise their donor status on their pages.

Analyze the Issue

1. Draw supply and demand curves for the U.S. organ market and compare the U.S. market to the market in a country where selling organs is legal.
2. What are some arguments against using the price system to allocate organs?
3. Should foreigners have the right to buy U.S. organs and U.S. citizens have the right to buy foreign organs?

---

1. James R. Rinehart, "The Market Approach to Organ Shortages," *Journal of Health Care Marketing* 8, no. 1, March 1988, pp. 72–75.
2. Carl Senna, "The Wallet Biopsy," *Providence Journal*, June 13, 1995, p. B7.

✓ CHECKPOINT

Can the Price System Eliminate Scarcity?

You visit Cuba and observe that at "official" prices, there is a constant shortage of consumer goods in government stores. People explain that in Cuba, scarcity is caused by low prices combined with low production quotas set by the government. Many Cuban citizens say that the condition of scarcity would be eliminated if the government would allow markets to respond to supply and demand. Can the price system eliminate scarcity?

Key Concepts

Law of demand
Demand
Change in quantity demanded
Change in demand
Normal good
Inferior good

Substitute good
Complementary good
Law of supply
Supply
Change in quantity supplied
Change in supply

Market
Surplus
Shortage
Equilibrium
Price system

Summary

- The **law of demand** states there is an inverse relationship between the price and the quantity demanded, ceteris paribus. A market demand curve is the horizontal summation of individual demand curves.

- A **change in quantity demanded** is a movement along a stationary demand curve caused by a change in price. When any of the nonprice determinants of demand change, the demand curve responds by shifting. An *increase in demand* (rightward shift) or a *decrease in demand* (leftward shift) is caused by a change in one of the nonprice determinants.

Change in Quantity Demanded

(a) Increase in quantity demanded

SOURCE: © Cengage Learning 2014

Change in Demand

(b) Increase in demand

Price per Blu-ray (dollars)

Quantity of Blu-rays
(millions per year)

- **Nonprice determinants of demand** are as follows:
  a. Number of buyers
  b. Tastes and preferences
  c. Income (normal and inferior goods)
  d. Expectations of future price and income changes
  e. Prices of related goods (substitutes and complements)
- The **law of supply** states there is a direct relationship between the price and the quantity supplied, ceteris paribus. The market supply curve is the horizontal summation of individual supply curves.
- A **change in quantity supplied** is a movement along a stationary supply curve caused by a change in price. When any of the nonprice determinants of supply change, the supply curve responds by shifting. An *increase in supply* (rightward shift) or a *decrease in supply* (leftward shift) is caused by a change in one of the nonprice determinants.

Change in Quantity Supplied

(a) Increase in quantity supplied

Price per Blu-ray (dollars)

Quantity of Blu-rays
(millions per year)

Change in Supply

(b) Increase in supply

Price per Blu-ray (dollars)

Quantity of Blu-rays
(millions per year)

- **Nonprice determinants of supply** are as follows:
  a. Number of sellers
  b. Technology

c. Resource prices
d. Taxes and subsidies
e. Expectations of future price
   changes
f. Prices of other goods and services

- A **surplus** or **shortage** exists at any price where
  the quantity demanded and the quantity
  supplied are not equal. When the price of a
  good is higher than the equilibrium price,
  there is an excess quantity supplied, or *surplus*. When the price is less than the equilibrium price, there is an excess quantity
  demanded, or *shortage*.

- **Equilibrium** is the unique price and quantity
  established at the intersection of the supply
  and demand curves. Only at equilibrium
  does quantity demanded equal quantity
  supplied.

Equilibrium

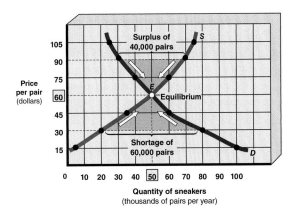

SOURCE: © Cengage Learning 2014

- The **price system** is the supply and demand
  mechanism that establishes equilibrium
  through the ability of prices to rise and fall.

Study Questions and Problems

1. Some people will pay a higher price for brand-
   name goods. For example, some people buy
   Rolls Royces and Rolex watches to impress
   others. Does knowingly paying higher prices
   for certain items just to be a "snob" violate the
   law of demand?

2. Draw graphs to illustrate the difference between a
   decrease in the quantity demanded and a decrease
   in demand for Mickey Mantle baseball cards.
   Give a possible reason for change in each graph.

3. Suppose oil prices rise sharply for years as a
   result of war in the Persian Gulf region. What
   happens and why to the demand for each of
   the following?
   a. Cars
   b. Home insulation
   c. Coal
   d. Tires

4. Draw graphs to illustrate the difference
   between a decrease in quantity supplied and a
   decrease in supply for condominiums. Give a
   possible reason for change in each graph.

5. Use supply and demand analysis to explain
   why the quantity of word processing software

exchanged increases from one year to
the next.

6. Predict the direction of change for either
   supply or demand in the following situations:
   a. Several new companies enter the cell phone
      industry.
   b. Consumers suddenly decide SUVs are
      unfashionable.
   c. The U.S. Surgeon General issues a report
      stating that tomatoes prevent colds.
   d. Frost threatens to damage the coffee crop,
      and consumers expect the price to rise
      sharply in the future.
   e. The price of tea falls. What is the effect on
      the coffee market?
   f. The price of sugar rises. What is the effect
      on the coffee market?
   g. Tobacco lobbyists convince Congress
      to remove the tax paid by sellers on each
      carton of cigarettes sold.
   h. A new type of robot is invented that will
      pick peaches.
   i. Nintendo anticipates that the future price
      of its games will fall much lower than the
      current price.

7. Explain the effect of the following situations:
   a. Population growth surges rapidly.
   b. The prices of resources used in the production of good X increase.
   c. The government is paying a $1-per-unit subsidy for each unit of a good produced.
   d. The incomes of consumers of normal good X increase.
   e. The incomes of consumers of inferior good Y decrease.
   f. Farmers are deciding what crop to plant and learn that the price of corn has fallen relative to the price of cotton.

8. Explain why the market price may not be the same as the equilibrium price.

9. If a new breakthrough in manufacturing technology reduces the cost of producing Blu-ray players by half, what will happen to the each of the following?
   a. Supply of Blu-ray players
   b. Demand for Blu-ray players
   c. Equilibrium price and quantity of Blu-ray players
   d. Demand for Blu-rays

10. The U.S. Postal Service is facing increased competition from firms providing overnight delivery of packages and letters. Additional competition has emerged because communications can be sent by emails, fax machine, and text messaging. What will be the effect of this competition on the market demand for mail delivered by the post office?

11. There is a shortage of college basketball and football tickets for some games, and a surplus occurs for other games. Why do shortages and surpluses exist for different games?

12. Explain the statement "People respond to incentives and disincentives" in relation to the demand curve and supply curve for good X.

For Online Exercises, go to the Tucker Web site at www.cengage.com/economics/tucker.

✔ CHECKPOINT ANSWERS

Can Gasoline Become an Exception to the Law of Demand?

As the price of gasoline began to rise, the expectation of still higher prices caused buyers to buy more now, and therefore, demand increased. As shown in Exhibit 13, suppose the price per gallon of gasoline was initially at P_1 and the quantity demanded was Q_1 on demand curve D_1 (point A). Then war in the Middle East caused the demand curve to shift rightward to D_2. Along the new demand curve, D_2, consumers increased their quantity demanded to Q_2 at the higher price of P_2 per gallon of gasoline (point B).

The expectation of rising gasoline prices in the future caused "an increase in demand," rather than "an increase in quantity demanded" in response to a higher price. If you said that there are no exceptions to the law of demand, **YOU ARE CORRECT.**

EXHIBIT 13

Price per gallon (dollars); Quantity of gasoline (millions of gallons per day)

SOURCE: © Cengage Learning 2014

Can the Law of Supply Be Repealed for the Oil Market?

There is not a single quantity of oil—say, 3 million barrels—for sale in the world on a given day. The supply curve for oil is not vertical. As the law of supply states, higher oil prices will cause greater quantities of oil to be offered for sale. At lower prices, oil producers have less incentive to drill deeper for oil that is more expensive to discover.

The government cannot repeal the law of supply. Price controls discourage producers from oil exploration and production, which causes a reduction in the quantity supplied. If you said U.S. oil production decreased in the 1970s when the government put a lid on oil prices, **YOU ARE CORRECT.**

Can the Price System Eliminate Scarcity?

Recall from Chapter 1 that scarcity is the condition in which human wants are forever greater than the resources available to satisfy those wants. Using markets free from government interference will not solve the scarcity problem. Scarcity exists at any price for a good or service. This means scarcity occurs at any disequilibrium price at

which a shortage or surplus exists, and scarcity remains at any equilibrium price at which no shortage or surplus exists.

Although the price system can eliminate shortages (or surpluses), if you said it cannot eliminate scarcity, **YOU ARE CORRECT.**

Sample Quiz

For an explanation of the correct answers, visit the Tucker website at www.cengage.com/economics/tucker.

1. Which of the following causes the demand for veggie burgers to increase?
   a. A decline in the price of veggie burgers
   b. An increase in the price of tofu burgers, perceived as a substitute by veggie burger consumers
   c. An increase in the price of burger buns
   d. A technological innovation that lowers the cost of producing veggie burgers

2. Which of the following would *not* cause market demand for a normal good to decline?
   a. An increase in the price of a substitute
   b. An increase in the price of a complement
   c. A decline in consumer income
   d. Consumer expectations that the good will go on sale in the near future
   e. An announcement by the Surgeon General that the product contributes to premature death

3. Low-income families consume proportionately more of which of the following kinds of goods?
   a. Luxury goods
   b. Substitute goods
   c. Normal goods
   d. Inferior goods

4. Suppose each of the seven dwarfs buys four mugs of ginger ale per week from Snow White's café when the price per mug is $2. If the seven dwarfs are the entire market demand for Snow White's ginger ale, which of the following is the correct value for market quantity demanded of ginger ale at a price of $2?
   a. 4
   b. 8
   c. 28
   d. 7

Sample Quiz *continued*

5. Which of the following increases the supply of corn?
   a. The farm worker's union successfully negotiates a pay increase for corn harvest workers.
   b. The Surgeon General announces that eating corn bread contributes to baldness in men.
   c. Congress and the President eliminate subsidies formerly paid to corn farmers.
   d. Farmers who grow soybeans can also grow corn, and the price of soybeans drops by 75 percent.

6. With an upward-sloping supply curve, which of the following is *true*?
   a. An increase in price results in a decrease in quantity supplied.
   b. An increase in price results in an increase in supply.
   c. A decrease in price results in a decrease in quantity supplied.
   d. A decrease in price results in an increase in supply.

7. A rightward shift in the demand curve is called a(an)
   a. decrease in output.
   b. decrease in demand.
   c. increase in demand.
   d. increase in income.

8. A surplus occurs when
   a. the quantity demanded exceeds the quantity supplied.
   b. price is below the equilibrium price.
   c. price is at the equilibrium.
   d. price is above the equilibrium.

9. A shortage occurs when
   a. the quantity supplied exceeds the quantity demanded.
   b. price is below the equilibrium price.
   c. price is at the equilibrium.
   d. price is above the equilibrium.

10. Which of the following decreases supply in the market for pizza?
    a. Pizza shop employees successfully organize a union and negotiate a pay increase.
    b. The Surgeon General announces that eating pizza reduces the incidence of stomach cancer.

   c. Cheese prices drop because price supports for dairy farmers are removed.
   d. Some hot sandwich shops can also make and sell pizzas, and consumer demand for hot sandwiches declines sharply, reducing the profitability of producing hot sandwiches.

11. Which of the following results from an increase in the price of a one-week vacation at beach resorts on the coast of Mexico?
    a. An increase in the supply of bicycle tires in Toledo, Ohio
    b. An increase in the demand for vacations at resorts on Caribbean islands
    c. An increase in the supply of vacation opportunities at resorts on the coast of Mexico
    d. A decrease in the demand for vacations at resorts on Caribbean islands

12. There is news that the price of Tucker's Root Beer will increase significantly next week. If the demand for Tucker's Root Beer reacts *only* to this factor and shifts to the right, the position of this demand curve has reacted to a change in
    a. tastes.
    b. income levels.
    c. the prices of related goods.
    d. the number of buyers.
    e. expectations.

13. Which of the following causes a shortage to become larger?
    a. An increase in market price
    b. An increase in supply
    c. A decrease in demand
    d. A decrease in price

14. Which of the following is *true* in ski towns such as Crested Butte, Colorado, and Whistler, British Columbia, during the peak winter ski season as compared to May and June?
    a. Demand for motel rooms is higher.
    b. Demand for motel rooms is lower.
    c. There is a surplus of motel rooms.
    d. The price of motel rooms will be lower.

15. In moving from a shortage toward the market equilibrium, which of the following is *true*?
    a. Price falls.
    b. Price rises.

Sample Quiz *continued*

c. Quantity demanded increases.
d. Quantity supplied decreases.

16. The law of demand is the principle that there is _____ relationship between the price of a good and the quantity buyers are willing to purchase in a defined time period, ceteris paribus.
    a. a direct
    b. no
    c. an inverse
    d. an independent

17. A curve that is derived by summing horizontally individual demand curves is called
    a. aggregate supply.
    b. market supply.
    c. aggregate demand.
    d. market demand.

18. A leftward shift in the demand curve is called a(an)
    a. decrease in demand.
    b. decrease in output.
    c. increase in demand.
    d. increase in income.

19. Under the law of demand, any increase in price will cause _____ in quantity demanded.
    a. a decrease
    b. an increase
    c. no change
    d. constant change

20. The law of supply is the principle that there is _____ relationship between the price of a good and the quantity sellers are willing to offer for sale in a defined time period, ceteris paribus.
    a. an inverse
    b. a direct
    c. no
    d. an independent

EXHIBIT 14	Demand and Supply Data for Video Games	
Price	Quantity demanded of video games	Quantity supplied of video games
$75	400	900
70	450	850
65	500	800
60	550	750
55	600	700
50	650	650
45	700	600
40	750	550

SOURCE: © Cengage Learning 2014

21. Exhibit 14 presents supply and demand data for the video game market. If the price of video games was currently $70, there would be an _____ of _____ video games in this market.
    a. excess demand; 450
    b. excess demand; 500
    c. excess supply; 400
    d. excess supply; 850
    e. excess demand; 400

22. In Exhibit 14, if the price of video games was currently $45, there would be an _____ of _____ video games in this market.
    a. excess demand; 700
    b. excess demand; 500
    c. excess supply; 100
    d. excess supply; 600
    e. excess demand; 100

Sample Quiz *continued*

23. In Exhibit 14, at any market price of video games above $50, a (an) _____ would result, causing price to _____.
    a. excess demand; rise
    b. excess supply; rise
    c. excess demand; fall
    d. excess supply; fall
    e. shortage; rise

24. In Exhibit 14, at any market price of video games below $50, a (an) _____ would result, causing price to _____.
    a. excess demand; rise
    b. excess supply; rise
    c. excess demand; fall
    d. excess supply; fall
    e. surplus; rise

25. In Exhibit 14, if there is a shortage of video games of 200 units, the current price of video games must be
    a. $60.
    b. $55.
    c. $50.
    d. $45.
    e. $40.

Consumer Surplus, Producer Surplus, and Market Efficiency

This chapter explained how the market forces of demand and supply establish the equilibrium price and output. Here it will be demonstrated that the equilibrium price and quantity determined in a competitive market are desirable because the result is *market efficiency*. To understand this concept, we use the area between the market price and the demand and supply curves to measure gains or losses from market transactions for consumers and producers.

3A-1a   CONSUMER SURPLUS

Consider the market demand curve shown in Exhibit A-1(a). The height of this demand curve shows the maximum willingness of consumers to purchase ground beef at various prices per pound. At a price of $4.00 (point X), no one will purchase ground beef. But if the price drops to $3.50 at point A, consumers will purchase 1 million pounds of ground beef per year. Moving downward along the demand curve to point B, consumers will purchase an additional million pounds of ground beef per year at a lower price of $3.00 per pound. If the price continues to drop to $2.50 per pound at point C and lower, consumers are willing to purchase more pounds of ground beef consistent with the law of demand.

Assuming the market equilibrium price for ground beef is $2.00 per pound, we can use the demand curve to measure the net benefit, or *consumer surplus*, in this market. Consumer surplus is the value of the difference between the price consumers are willing to pay for a product on the demand curve and the price actually paid for it. At point A, consumers are willing to pay $3.50 per pound, but they actually pay the equilibrium price of $2.00. Thus, consumers earn a surplus of $1.50 ($3.50 − $2.00) per pound multiplied by 1 million pounds purchased, which is a $15 million consumer surplus. This value is represented by the shaded vertical rectangle formed at point A on the demand curve. At point B, consumers who purchase an additional million pounds of ground beef at $3.00 per pound receive a lower extra consumer surplus than at point A, represented by a rectangle of lower height. At point C, the marginal consumer surplus continues to fall until at equilibrium point E, where there is no consumer surplus.

The total value of consumer surplus can be interpreted from the explanation given above. As shown in Exhibit A-1(b), begin at point X and instead of selected prices, now imagine offering ground beef to consumers at each possible price downward along the demand curve until the equilibrium price of $2.00 is reached at point E. The result is that the entire green triangular area between the demand curve and the horizontal line at the equilibrium price represents total consumer surplus. Note that a rise in the equilibrium price decreases total consumer surplus and a fall in the equilibrium price increases total consumer surplus.

Consumer surplus
The value of the difference between the price consumers are willing to pay for a product on the demand curve and the price actually paid for it.

| EXHIBIT A-1 | **Market Demand Curve and Consumer Surplus** |

As illustrated in part (a), consumers are willing at point *A* on the market demand curve to pay $3.50 per pound to purchase 1 million pounds of ground beef per year. Because the equilibrium price is $2.00, consumers receive a surplus of $1.50 for each pound of ground beef and the vertical shaded rectangular area is the consumer surplus earned only at point *A*. Others who pay less at points *B*, *C*, and *E* receive less consumer surplus and the height of the corresponding rectangles falls at each of these prices. In part (b), moving downward along all possible prices on the demand curve yields the green shaded triangle, which is equal to total consumer surplus (net benefit).

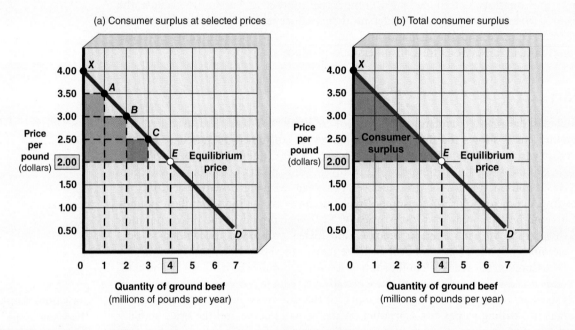

SOURCE: © Cengage Learning 2014

> **CONCLUSION:** *Total consumer surplus measured in dollars is represented by the total area under the market demand curve and above the equilibrium price.*

3A-1b PRODUCER SURPLUS

Similar to the concept of consumer surplus, the height of the market supply curve in Exhibit A-2(a) shows the producers' minimum willingness to accept payment for ground beef offered for sale at various prices per pound. At point *X*, firms offer no ground beef for sale at a price of zero and they divert their resources to an alternate use. At a price of $0.50 per pound (point *A*), the supply curve tells us that 1 million pounds will be offered for sale. Moving upward along the supply curve to point *B*, firms will offer an additional million pounds of ground beef for sale at the higher price of $1.00 per pound. If the price rises to $1.50 at point *C* and higher, firms allocate more resources to ground beef production and another million pounds will be supplied along the supply curve.

Again, we will assume the equilibrium price is $2.00 per pound, and the supply curve can be used to measure the net benefit, or *producer surplus.* Producer surplus is the value of the difference between the actual selling price of a product and the price producers are willing to sell it for on the supply curve. Now assume the first million pounds of ground beef is sold at point *A* on the supply curve. In this case, producer surplus is the difference between the equilibrium selling price of $2.00 and the $0.50 minimum price producers will accept to supply this quantity of ground beef. Thus, producer surplus is equal to $1.50 ($2.00 – $0.50) per pound multiplied by 1 million pounds sold, which is a $1.5 million producer surplus. This value is represented by the vertical shaded rectangle formed at point *A* on the supply curve. The second million pounds of ground beef offered for sale at point *B* also generates a producer surplus because the selling price of $2.00 exceeds the

Producer surplus

The value of the difference between the actual selling price of a product and the price producers are willing to sell it for on the supply curve.

EXHIBIT A-2	**Market Supply Curve and Producer Surplus**

In part (a), firms are willing at $0.50 (point *A*) to supply 1 million pounds of ground beef per year. Because $2.00 is the equilibrium price, the sellers earn a producer surplus of $1.50 per pound of ground beef sold. The first vertical shaded rectangle is the producer surplus earned only at point *A*. At points *B*, *C*, and *E*, sellers receive less producer surplus at each of these higher prices and the sizes of the rectangles fall. In part (b), moving upward along all possible selling prices on the supply curve yields the red-shaded triangle that is equal to total producer surplus (net benefit).

SOURCE: © Cengage Learning 2014

$1.00 price at which firms are willing to supply this additional quantity of ground beef. Note that producer surplus is lower at point *B* compared to point *A* and marginal producer surplus continues to fall at point *C* until it reaches zero at the equilibrium point *E*.

The total value of producer surplus is represented in Exhibit A-2(b). Start at point *X*, where none of the product will be supplied at the price of zero. Now consider the quantities of ground beef producers are willing to offer for sale at each possible price upward along the supply curve until the equilibrium price of $2.00 is reached at point *E*. The result is that the entire red triangular area between the horizontal line at the equilibrium price and the supply curve represents total producer surplus.

> **CONCLUSION:** *Total producer surplus measured in dollars is represented by the total area under the equilibrium price and above the supply curve.*

3A-1c MARKET EFFICIENCY

In this section, the equilibrium price and quantity will be shown to achieve market efficiency because at any other market price, the total net benefits to consumers and producers will be less. Stated differently, competitive markets are efficient when they maximize the sum of consumer and producer surplus. The analysis continues in Exhibit A-3(a), which combines part (b) from each of the two previous exhibits. The green triangle represents consumer surplus earned in excess of the $2.00 equilibrium price consumers pay for ground beef. The red triangle represents producer surplus producers receive by selling ground beef at $2.00 per pound in excess of the minimum price at which they are willing to supply it. The total net benefit (total surplus) is therefore the entire triangular area consisting of both the green consumer surplus and red producer surplus triangles.

Now consider in Exhibit A-3(b) the consequences to market efficiency of producers devoting fewer resources to ground beef production and only 2 million pounds being bought and sold per year compared with 4 million pounds at the equilibrium price of $2.00. The result is a deadweight loss. Deadweight loss is the net loss of consumer and producer surplus from underproduction or overproduction of a product. In Exhibit A-3(b), the deadweight loss is equal to the gray triangle *ABE*, which represents the total surplus of green and red triangles in part (a) that is not obtained because the market is operating below equilibrium point *E*.

Exhibit A-3(c) illustrates that a deadweight loss of consumer and producer surplus can also result from overproduction. Now suppose more resources are devoted to production and 6 million pounds of ground beef are bought and sold at the equilibrium price. However, from the producers' side of the market, the equilibrium selling price is only $2.00 and is below any possible selling price on the supply curve between points *E* and *C*. Therefore, firms have a net loss for each pound sold, represented by the area under the supply curve and bounded below by the horizontal equilibrium price line. Similarly, consumers pay the equilibrium price of $2.00, but this price exceeds any price consumers are willing to pay between points *E* and *D* on the demand curve. This means consumers

Deadweight loss

The net loss of consumer and producer surplus from underproduction or overproduction of a product.

EXHIBIT A-3 | Comparison of Market Efficiency and Deadweight Loss

In part (a), the green triangle represents consumer surplus and the red triangle represents producer surplus. The total net benefit, or total surplus, is the entire triangle consisting of the consumer and producer surplus triangles.

In part (b), too few resources are used to produce 2 million pounds of ground beef compared to 4 million pounds at equilibrium point E. The market is inefficient because the deadweight loss gray triangle ABE is no longer earned by either consumers or producers. As shown in part (c), overproduction at the equilibrium price of $2.00 can also be inefficient. If 6 million pounds of ground beef are offered for sale, too many resources are devoted to this product and a deadweight loss of area EDC occurs.

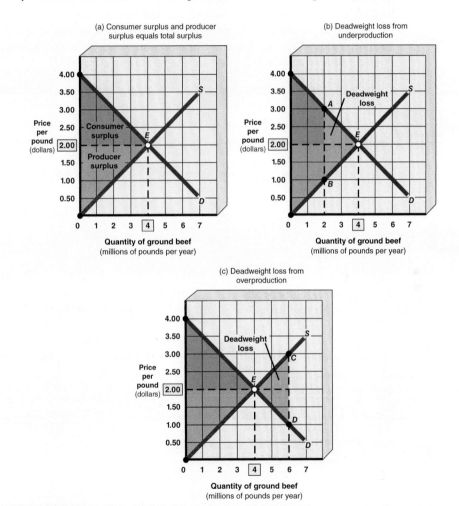

(a) Consumer surplus and producer surplus equals total surplus

(b) Deadweight loss from underproduction

(c) Deadweight loss from overproduction

SOURCE: © Cengage Learning 2014

experience a total net benefit loss for each pound purchased, represented by the rectangular area between the horizontal equilibrium price line above and the demand curve below. The total net loss of consumer and producer surplus (deadweight loss) is equal to the gray shaded area EDC.

> **CONCLUSION:** *The total dollar value of potential benefits not achieved is the deadweight loss resulting from too few or too many resources used in a given market.*

Looking ahead, the conclusion drawn from this appendix is that market equilibrium is efficient, but this conclusion is not always the case. In the next chapter, the topic of *market failure* will be discussed, in which market equilibrium under certain conditions can result in too few or too many resources being used to produce goods and services. For example, the absence of a competitive market, the existence of pollution, or vaccinations to prevent a disease can establish equilibrium conditions with misallocations of resources. In these cases, government intervention may be preferable in order to achieve optimal allocation of resources. In other cases, such as the government imposing price ceilings and price floors, the result of government intervention is a market that is no longer efficient.

Key Concepts

Consumer surplus   Producer surplus   Deadweight loss

Summary

- **Consumer surplus** measures the value between the price consumers are willing to pay for a product along the demand curve and the price they actually pay.
- **Producer surplus** measures the value between the actual selling price of a product and the price along the supply curve at which sellers are willing to sell the product. Total surplus is the sum of consumer surplus and producer surplus.
- **Deadweight loss** is the result of a market that operates in disequilibrium. It is the net loss of both consumer and producer surplus resulting from underproduction or overproduction of a product.

Summary of Conclusion Statements

- Total consumer surplus measured in dollars is represented by the total area under the market demand curve and above the equilibrium price.
- Total producer surplus measured in dollars is represented by the total area under the equilibrium price and above the supply curve.
- The total dollar value of potential benefits not achieved is the deadweight loss resulting from too few or too many resources used in a given market.

Study Questions and Problems

1. Consider the market for used textbooks. Use Exhibit A-4 to calculate the total consumer surplus.

EXHIBIT A-4	Used Textbook Market	
Potential buyer	Willingness to pay	Market price
Brad	$60	$30
Juan	45	30
Sue	35	30
Jamie	25	30
Frank	10	30
SOURCE: © Cengage Learning 2014		

2. Consider the market for used textbooks. Use Exhibit A-5 to calculate the total producer surplus.

EXHIBIT A-5	Used Textbook Market	
Potential seller	Willingness to sell	Market price
Forest	$60	$30
Betty	45	30
Alan	35	30
Paul	25	30
Alice	10	30
SOURCE: © Cengage Learning 2014		

3. Using Exhibits A-4 and A-5 above, calculate the total surplus. Then calculate the effect on consumer surplus, producer surplus, and total surplus of a fall in the equilibrium price of textbooks from $30 to $15 each. Explain the meaning of your calculations.

4. Using Exhibit A-6 and assuming the market is in equilibrium at Q_E, identify areas ACD, DCE, and ACE. Then explain the result of underproduction at Q in terms of areas BCG, GCF, and BCF.

EXHIBIT A-6	Used Textbook Market

SOURCE: © Cengage Learning 2014

Sample Quiz

For an explanation of the correct answers, visit the Tucker Web site at www.cengage.com/economics/tucker.

1. Consumer surplus measures the value between the price consumers are willing to pay and the:
   a. producer surplus price.
   b. deadweight gain price.
   c. actual price paid.
   d. preference price.

2. If Sam is willing to pay $50 for one good X, $30 for a second, $20 for a third, $8 for a fourth, and the market price is $10. What is Sam's consumer surplus?
   a. $10
   b. $40
   c. $70
   d. $100

3. Suppose Tucker Inc. is willing to sell one gizmo for $10, a second gizmo for $15, a third for $20 and the market price is $25. What is Tucker Inc.'s producer surplus?
   a. $10
   b. $15
   c. $30
   d. $50

4. In an efficient market, deadweight loss is
   a. maximum
   b. minimum
   c. constant
   d. zero

5. Deadweight loss results from
   a. equilibrium.
   b. underproduction.
   c. overproduction.
   d. none of the above.
   e. either b or c.

6. Deadweight loss is the net loss of
   a. consumer surplus.
   b. producer surplus.
   c. disequilibrium surplus.
   d. both a and b.

7. If the quantity supplied exceeds the quantity demanded in a market, what is the result?
   a. Deadweight loss
   b. Inefficiency

   c. Overproduction
   d. All of the above answers are correct

8. Suppose a consumer is willing to pay $20 for one good X, $10 for a second, and $5 for a third and the market price is $4. What is the consumer surplus?
   a. $16
   b. $6
   c. $1
   d. $23

9. Producer surplus measures the value between the actual selling price and the
   a. price at which sellers are willing to sell the product.
   b. deadweight loss price.
   c. lowest price at which sellers are willing to sell the product.
   d. profit-maximization price.

10. Suppose seller X is willing to sell one good X for $5, a second good X for $10, a third for $16, a fourth for $25 and the market price is $20. What is seller X's producer surplus?
    a. $15
    b. $20
    c. $22
    d. $29

11. Deadweight loss is the result of
    a. disequilibrium.
    b. underproduction.
    c. overproduction.
    d. all of the above.

12. Deadweight loss is computed as the net of
    a. consumer surplus minus producer surplus.
    b. disequilibrium surplus plus consumer surplus.
    c. producer surplus minus disequilibrium surplus.
    d. consumer surplus plus producer surplus.

13. Deadweight loss is *not* the result of
    a. an efficient market.
    b. an inefficient market.
    c. zero consumer surplus.
    d. zero producer surplus.

Sample Quiz *continued*

14. At the equilibrium price, deadweight loss is
    a. minimized.
    b. zero.
    c. maximized.
    d. equal to the equilibrium price multiplied by the quantity exchanged.

15. If the quantity supplied exceeds the quantity demanded in a market, what is the result?
    a. Deadweight loss
    b. Inefficiency
    c. Overproduction
    d. None of the above answers are correct

16. As shown in Exhibit A-7, if the market is in equilibrium, _____ represents consumer surplus.
    a. *ABEC*
    b. *AED*
    c. *EGH*
    d. *BEF*

17. As shown in Exhibit A-7, if the market is in equilibrium, _____ represents producer surplus.
    a. *ADFB*
    b. *CEFD*
    c. *EGH*
    d. *BEF*

18. As shown in Exhibit A-7, if the quantity supplied is 2 million pounds of ground beef per year, what is the result?
    a. Deadweight loss
    b. Inefficiency
    c. Underproduction
    d. All of the above
    e. None of the above

19. As shown in Exhibit A-7, if the quantity supplied is 6 million pounds of ground beef per year, what is the result?
    a. Deadweight loss
    b. Inefficiency
    c. Overproduction
    d. All of the above
    e. None of the above

20. As shown in Exhibit A-7, if the quantity supplied is 2 million pounds of ground beef per year, the result is a deadweight loss represented by area
    a. *ABEC*.
    b. *CEFD*.
    c. *EGH*.
    d. *BEF*.

EXHIBIT A-7	Comparison of Market Efficiency and Deadweight Loss

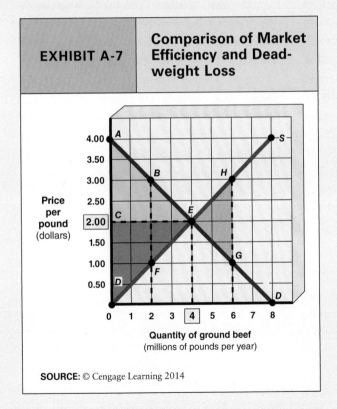

Quantity of ground beef
(millions of pounds per year)

SOURCE: © Cengage Learning 2014

chapter 4

Markets in Action

Once you understand how buyers and sellers respond to changes in equilibrium prices, you are progressing well in your quest to understand the economic way of thinking. This chapter begins by showing that changes in supply and demand influence the equilibrium price and quantity of goods and services exchanged around you every day. For example, you will study the impact of changes in supply and demand curves on the markets for Caribbean cruises, new homes, and AIDS vaccinations. Then you will see why the laws of supply and demand cannot be repealed. Using market supply and demand analysis, you will learn that government policies to control markets have predictable consequences. For example, you will understand what happens when the government limits the maximum rent landlords can charge and who benefits and who loses from the federal minimum wage law.

In this chapter, you will also study situations in which the market mechanism fails. Have you visited a city and lamented the smog that blankets the beautiful surroundings? Or have you ever wanted to swim or fish in a stream, but could not because of industrial waste? These are obvious cases in which market system magic failed and the government must consider cures to reach socially desirable results.

In this chapter, you will learn to solve these economics puzzles:

- How can a spotted owl affect the price of homes?
- How do demand and supply affect the price of ethanol fuel?
- Why might government warehouses overflow with cheese and milk?
- What do ticket scalping and rent controls have in common?
- Can vouchers fix our schools?

4-1 Changes in Market Equilibrium

Using market supply and demand analysis is like putting on glasses if you are near-sighted. Suddenly, the fuzzy world around you comes into clear focus. Many people believe that prices are set by sellers adding a certain percentage to their costs. If costs rise, sellers simply raise their prices by that percentage. In free markets, there is more to the story. In the following examples, you will open your eyes and see that economic theory has something important to say about so many things in the real world.

4-1a CHANGES IN DEMAND

The Caribbean cruise market shown in Exhibit 1(a) assumes market supply, S, is constant and market demand increases from D_1 to D_2. Why has the demand curve shifted rightward in the figure? We will assume the popularity of cruises to these vacation islands has suddenly risen sharply due to extensive advertising that influenced tastes and preferences. Given supply curve S and demand curve D_1, the initial equilibrium price is $600 per cruise, and the initial equilibrium quantity is 8,000 cruises per year, shown as point E_1. After the impact of advertising, the new equilibrium point, E_2, becomes 12,000 cruises per year at a price of $900 each. Thus, the increase in demand causes both the equilibrium price and the equilibrium quantity to increase.

It is important to understand the force that caused the equilibrium to shift from E_1 to E_2. When demand initially increased from D_1 to D_2, there was a temporary shortage of 8,000 cruises at $600 per cruise. Firms in the cruise business responded to the excess demand by hiring more workers, offering more cruises to the Caribbean, and raising the price. The cruise lines therefore move upward along the supply curve (increasing quantity supplied, but not changing supply). During some period of trial and error, Caribbean cruise sellers increase their price and quantity supplied until a shortage no longer exists at point E_2. Therefore, the increase in demand causes both the equilibrium price and the equilibrium quantity to increase.

What will happen to the demand for gas-guzzling automobiles (for example, SUVs) if the price of gasoline triples? Because gasoline and automobiles are complements, a rise in the price of gasoline decreases the demand for gas guzzlers from D_1 to D_2 in Exhibit 1(b). At the initial equilibrium price of $30,000 per gas guzzler ($E_1$), the quantity supplied now exceeds the quantity demanded by 20,000 automobiles per month. This unwanted inventory forces automakers to reduce the price and quantity supplied. As a result of this movement downward on the supply curve, market equilibrium changes from E_1 to E_2. The equilibrium price falls from $30,000 to $20,000, and the equilibrium quantity falls from 30,000 to 20,000 gas guzzlers per month.

4-1b CHANGES IN SUPPLY

Now reverse the analysis by assuming demand remains constant and allow some nonprice determinant to shift the supply curve. In Exhibit 2(a), begin at point E_1 in a market for babysitting services at an equilibrium price of $9 per hour and

EXHIBIT 1	The Effects of Shifts in Demand on Market Equilibrium

In part (a), demand for Caribbean cruises increases because of extensive advertising and the demand curve shifts rightward from D_1 to D_2. This shift in demand causes a temporary shortage of 8,000 cruises per year at the initial equilibrium of E_1. This disequilibrium condition encourages firms in the cruise business to move upward along the supply curve to a new equilibrium at E_2.

Part (b) illustrates a decrease in the demand for gas-guzzling automobiles (SUVs) caused by a sharp rise in the price of gasoline (a complement). This leftward shift in demand from D_1 to D_2 results in a temporary surplus of 20,000 gas guzzlers per month at the initial equilibrium of E_1. This disequilibrium condition forces sellers of these cars to move downward along the supply curve to a new equilibrium at E_2.

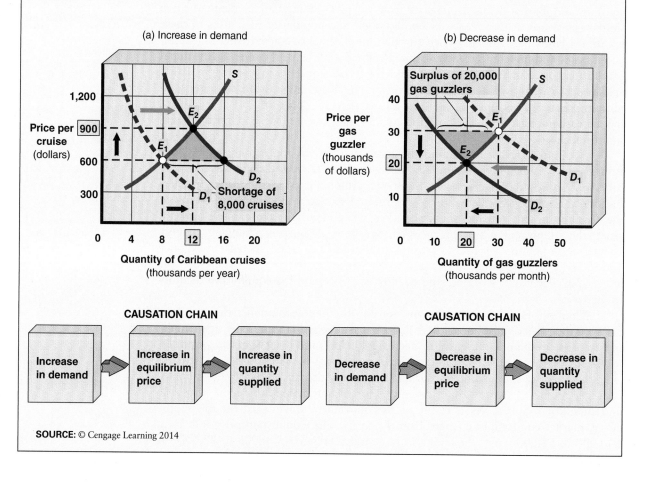

4,000 babysitters hired per month. Then assume there is a population shift and the number of people available to babysit rises. This increase in the number of sellers shifts the market supply curve rightward from S_1 to S_2 and creates a temporary surplus of 4,000 babysitters at point E_1 who offer their services but are not hired. The unemployed babysitters respond by reducing the price and the number of babysitters available for hire, which is a movement downward along S_2. As the price falls, buyers move down along their demand curve and hire more babysitters per month. When the price falls to $6 per hour, the market is in equilibrium again at point E_2, instead of E_1, and consumers hire 6,000 babysitters per month.

Exhibit 2(b) illustrates the market for lumber. Suppose this market is at equilibrium at point E_1, where the going price is $400 per thousand board

EXHIBIT 2	The Effects of Shifts in Supply on Market Equilibrium

In part (a), begin at equilibrium E_1 in the market for babysitters and assume an increase in the number of babysitters shifts the supply curve rightward from S_1 to S_2. This shift in supply causes a temporary surplus of 4,000 unemployed babysitters per month. This disequilibrium condition causes a movement downward along the demand curve to a new equilibrium at E_2. At E_2, the equilibrium price declines and the equilibrium quantity rises.

In part (b), steps to protect the environment cause the supply curve for lumber to shift leftward from S_1 to S_2. This shift in supply results in a temporary shortage of 4 billion board feet per year. Customer bidding for the available lumber raises the price. As a result, the market moves upward along the demand curve to a new equilibrium at E_2, and the quantity demanded falls.

EXHIBIT 3	Effect of Shifts in Demand or Supply on Market Equilibrium	
Change	**Effect on equilibrium price**	**Effect on equilibrium quantity**
Demand increases	Increases	Increases
Demand decreases	Decreases	Decreases
Supply increases	Decreases	Increases
Supply decreases	Increases	Decreases

SOURCE: © Cengage Learning 2014

feet, and 8 billion board feet are bought and sold per year. Now suppose a new Endangered Species Act is passed, and the federal government sets aside huge forest resources to protect the spotted owl and other wildlife. This means the market supply curve shifts leftward from S_1 to S_2, and a temporary shortage of 4 billion board feet of lumber exists at point E_1. Suppliers respond by hiking their price from $400 to $600 per thousand board feet, and a new equilibrium is established at E_2, where the quantity is 6 billion board feet per year. This higher cost of lumber, in turn, raises the price of a new home.

Exhibit 3 gives a concise summary of the impact of changes in demand or supply on market equilibrium.

✔ CHECKPOINT

Why the Higher Price for Ethanol Fuel?

Suppose more consumers purchased ethanol fuel for their cars, and at the same time, producers switched to ethanol fuel production. Within a year, the price of ethanol fuel shot up $2 per gallon. During this period, which increased more—demand, supply, or neither?

4-1c TREND OF EQUILIBRIUM PRICES OVER TIME

Basic demand and supply analysis allows us to explain a trend in prices over a number of years. Exhibit 4 shows the effect of changes in nonprice determinants that increase both the demand and supply curves for good X between 2000, 2005, and 2010. A line connects the equilibrium prices for each year in order to summarize the trend of equilibrium price and quantity changes over this time period. In this case, the observed prices trace an upward-sloping trend line.

EXHIBIT 4	Trend of Equilibrium Prices over Time

Nonprice determinants of demand and supply for good X have caused both the demand and supply curves to shift rightward between 2000 and 2010. As a result, the equilibrium price and quantity in this example rise along the upward-sloping trend line, connecting each observed equilibrium price.

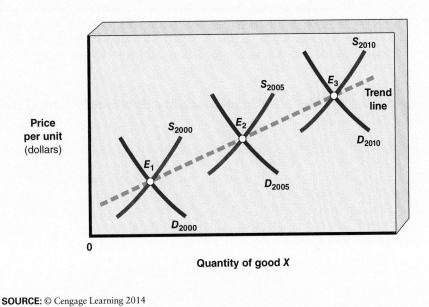

SOURCE: © Cengage Learning 2014

4-2 Can the Laws of Supply and Demand Be Repealed?

The government intervenes in some markets with the objective of preventing prices from rising to the equilibrium price. In other markets, the government's goal is to intervene and maintain a price higher than the equilibrium price. Market supply and demand analysis is a valuable tool for understanding what happens when the government fixes prices. There are two types of price controls: *price ceilings* and *price floors*.

4-2a PRICE CEILINGS

Case 1: Rent Controls   What happens if the government prevents the price system from setting a market price "too high" by mandating a price ceiling? A price ceiling is a legally established maximum price a seller can charge. Rent controls are an example of the imposition of a price ceiling in the market for rental units. New York City, Washington, D.C., Los Angeles, San Francisco, and other communities in the United States have some form of rent control. Since World War I, rent controls have been widely used in Europe. The rationale for rent controls is to provide an "essential service" that would otherwise be unaffordable by many people at the

Price ceiling

A legally established maximum price a seller can charge.

equilibrium rental price. Let's see why most economists believe that rent controls are counterproductive.

Exhibit 5 is a supply and demand diagram for the quantity of rental units demanded and supplied per month in a hypothetical city. We begin the analysis by assuming no rent controls exist and equilibrium is at point *E*, with a monthly rent of $1,200 per month and 6 million units occupied. Next, assume the city council imposes a rent control (ceiling price) that by law forbids any landlord from renting a unit for more than $800 per month. What does market supply and demand theory predict will happen? At the low rent ceiling of $800, the quantity demanded of rental units will be 8 million, but the quantity supplied will be only 4 million. Consequently, the price ceiling creates a persistent market shortage of 4 million rental units because suppliers cannot raise the rental price without being subjected to legal penalties.

EXHIBIT 5	Rent Control Results in a Shortage of Rental Units

If no rent controls exist, the equilibrium rent for a hypothetical apartment is $1,200 per month at point *E*. However, if the government imposes a rent ceiling of $800 per month, a shortage of 4 million rental units occurs. Because rent cannot rise by law, one outcome is that consumers must search for available units instead of paying a higher rent. Other outcomes include a black market, bribes, discrimination, and other illegal methods of dealing with a shortage of 4 million rental units per month.

CAUSATION CHAIN

Rent ceiling ⟹ Quantity demanded exceeds quantity supplied ⟹ Shortage

SOURCE: © Cengage Learning 2014

Note that a rent ceiling at or above $1,200 per month would have no effect. If the ceiling is set at the equilibrium rent of $1,200, the quantity of rental units demanded and the quantity of rental units supplied are equal regardless of the rent control. If the rent ceiling is set above the equilibrium rent, the quantity of rental units supplied exceeds the quantity of rental units demanded, and this surplus will cause the market to adjust to the equilibrium rent of $1,200.

What is the impact of rent controls on consumers? First, as a substitute for paying higher prices, consumers must spend more time on waiting lists and searching for housing. This means consumers incur an *opportunity cost* added to the $800 rent set by the government. Second, an illegal market, or *black market*, can arise because of the excess quantity demanded. Because the price of rental units is artificially low, the profit motive encourages tenants to risk breaking the law by subletting their unit to the highest bidder over $800 per month.

From the seller's perspective, rent control encourages two undesirable effects. First, faced with a mandated low rent, landlords may cut maintenance expenses, and housing deterioration will reduce the stock of rental units in the long run. Second, landlords may use discriminatory practices to replace the price system. Once owners realize there is an excess quantity demanded for rentals at the controlled price, they may resort to preferences based on pet ownership or family size to determine how to allocate scarce rental space.

Case 2: Gasoline Price Ceiling   The government placed ceilings on most nonfarm prices during World War II and, to a lesser extent, during the Korean War. In 1971, President Nixon "froze" virtually all wages, prices, and rents until 1973 in an attempt to control inflation. As a result of an oil embargo in late 1973, the government imposed a price ceiling of 55 cents per gallon of gasoline. To deal with the shortage, nonprice rationing schemes were introduced in 1974. Some states used a first-come, first-served system, while other states allowed consumers with even-numbered license plates to buy gas on even-numbered days and those with odd-numbered license plates to buy gas on odd-numbered days. Gas stations were required to close on Friday night and not open until Monday morning. Regardless of the scheme, long waiting lines for gasoline formed, just as the supply and demand model predicts. Finally, in the past, legally imposed price ceilings have been placed on such items as natural gas shipped in interstate commerce and on interest rates for loans. Internationally, as discussed later in the chapter on economies in transition, price ceilings on food and rent were common in the former Soviet Union. Soviet sociologists estimated that members of a typical urban household spent a combined total of 40 hours per week standing in lines to obtain various goods and services.

4-2b PRICE FLOORS

The other side of the price-control coin is a price floor set by government because it fears that the price system might establish a price viewed as "too low." A price floor is a legally established minimum price a seller can be paid. We now turn to two examples of price floors. The first is the minimum wage, and the second is agricultural price supports.

Case 1: The Minimum Wage Law   In Chapter 1, the second You're the Economist applied *normative* and *positive* reasoning to the issue of the minimum wage. Now you are prepared to apply market supply and demand analysis (positive reasoning) to this debate. Begin by noting that the demand for unskilled labor is the

Price floor

A legally established minimum price a seller can be paid.

EXHIBIT 6	A Minimum Wage Results in a Surplus of Labor

When the federal or state government sets a wage-rate floor above the equilibrium wage, a surplus of unskilled labor develops. The supply curve is the number of workers offering their labor services per year at possible wage rates. The demand curve is the number of workers employers are willing and able to hire at various wage rates. Equilibrium wage, W_e, will result if the price system is allowed to operate without government interference. At the minimum wage of W_m, there is a surplus of unemployed workers, $Q_s - Q_d$.

CAUSATION CHAIN

Minimum wage → Unemployment (surplus)

downward-sloping curve shown in Exhibit 6. The wage rate on the vertical axis is the price of unskilled labor, and the amount of unskilled labor employers are willing to hire varies inversely with the wage rate. At a higher wage rate, businesses will hire fewer workers. At a lower wage rate, they will employ a larger quantity of workers.

On the supply side, the wage rate determines the number of unskilled workers willing and able to work per year. At higher wages, workers will give up leisure or schooling to work, and at lower wages, fewer workers will be available for hire. The upward-sloping curve in Exhibit 6 is the supply of labor.

Assuming the freedom to bargain, the price system will establish an equilibrium wage rate of W_e and an equilibrium quantity of labor employed of Q_e. But suppose the government enacts a minimum wage, W_m, which is a price floor above the equilibrium wage, W_e. The intent of the legislation is to "wave a carrot" in front of people who will not work at W_e and to make lower-paid workers better off with a higher wage rate. But consider the undesirable consequences. One result of an artificially high minimum wage is that the number of workers willing to offer their labor increases upward along the supply curve to Q_s, but there are fewer jobs because the number of workers firms are willing to hire decreases to Q_d on the demand curve. The predicted outcome is a labor surplus of unskilled workers, $Q_s - Q_d$, who are unemployed. Moreover, employers are encouraged to substitute machines and skilled labor for the unskilled labor previously employed at equilibrium wage W_e. The minimum wage is therefore considered counterproductive because employers lay off the lowest-skilled workers, who ironically are the type of workers minimum wage legislation intends to help. Also, loss of minimum wage jobs represents a loss of entry-level jobs to those who seek to enter the workforce.

Supporters of the minimum wage are quick to point out that those employed (Q_d) are better off. Even though the minimum wage causes a reduction in employment, some economists argue that a more equal or fairer income distribution is worth the loss of some jobs. Moreover, the shape of the labor demand curve may be much more vertical than shown in Exhibit 6. If this is the case, the unemployment effect of a rise in the minimum wage would be small. In addition, they claim opponents ignore the possibility that unskilled workers lack bargaining power versus employers.

Finally, a minimum wage set at or below the equilibrium wage rate is ineffective. If the minimum wage is set at the equilibrium wage rate of W_e, the quantity of labor demanded and the quantity of labor supplied are equal regardless of the minimum wage. If the minimum wage is set below the equilibrium wage, the forces of supply of and demand for labor establish the equilibrium wage regardless of the minimum wage rate.

Case 2: Agricultural Price Supports   A farm price support is a well-known example of a price floor, which results in government purchases of surplus food and in higher food prices. Agricultural price support programs began in the 1930s as a means of raising the income of farmers, who were suffering from low market prices during the Great Depression. Under these programs, the government guarantees a minimum price above the equilibrium price and agrees to purchase any quantity the farmer is unable to sell at the legal price.

A few of the crops that have received price supports are corn, peanuts, soybeans, wheat, cotton, rice, tobacco, and dairy products. As predicted by market supply and demand analysis, a price support above the equilibrium price causes surpluses. Government warehouses therefore often overflow with such perishable products as butter, cheese, and dry milk purchased with taxpayers' money. The following You're the Economist on the dairy industry examines one of the best-known examples of U.S. government interference with agricultural market prices.

> **CONCLUSION:** *A price ceiling or price floor prevents market adjustment in which competition among buyers and sellers bids the price upward or downward to the equilibrium price.*

Rigging the Market for Milk

Applicable Concept: price supports

Each year the milk industry faces an important question: What does the federal government plan to do about its dairy price support program, which has helped boost farmers' income since 1949? Under the price support program, the federal government agrees to buy storable milk products, such as cheese, butter, and dry milk. If the farmers cannot sell all their products to consumers at a price exceeding the price support level, the federal government will purchase any unsold grade A milk production. Although state-run dairy commissions set their own minimum prices for milk, state price supports closely follow federal levels and are kept within 3 percent of levels in bordering states to reduce interstate milk price competition.

Members of Congress who advocate changes in the price support programs worry that milk surpluses are costing taxpayers too much. Each year the federal government pays billions of dollars to dairy farmers for milk products held in storage at a huge cost. Moreover, the problem is getting worse because the federal government encourages dairy farmers to use ultramodern farming techniques to increase the production per cow. Another concern is that the biggest government price support checks go to the largest farmers, while the number of dairy farmers continues to decline.

Congress is constantly seeking a solution to the milk price support problem. The following are some of the ideas that have been considered:

- Freeze the current price support level. This prospect dismays farmers, who are subject to increasing expenses

for feed, electricity, and other resources.
- Eliminate the price supports gradually in yearly increments over the next five years. This would subject the milk market to the price fluctuations of the free market, and farmers would suffer some bad years from low milk prices.
- Have the Department of Agriculture charge dairy farmers a tax of 50 cents for every 100 pounds of milk they produce. The

---

✔ CHECKPOINT

Is There Price Fixing at the Ticket Window?

At sold-out concerts, sports contests, and other events, some ticket holders try to resell their tickets for more than they paid—a practice known as scalping. For scalping to occur, must the original ticket price be legally set by a price floor, at the equilibrium price, or by a price ceiling?

4-2c MARKET FAILURE

In this chapter and the previous chapter, you have gained an understanding of how markets operate. Through the price system, society coordinates economic activity, but markets are not always "Prince Charmings" that achieve *market efficiency*

TOOS
USA

"I always wondered how the government set milk prices."

Finally, opponents of the dairy price support program argue that the market for milk is inherently a competitive industry and that consumers and taxpayers would be better served without government price supports for milk.

Analyze the Issue

1. Draw a supply and demand graph to illustrate the problem described in the case study and prescribe your own solution.
2. Which proposal do you think best serves the interests of small dairy farmers? Why?
3. Which proposal do you think best serves the interests of consumers? Why?
4. Which proposal do you think best serves the interest of a member of Congress? Why?

farmers oppose this approach because it would discourage production and run small farmers out of business.

- Have the federal government implement a "whole herd buyout" program. The problem is that using taxpayers' money to get farmers out of the dairy business pushes up the prices of milk products and rewards dairy farmers who own a lot of cows. Besides, what does the government do with the cows after it purchases them?

Source: © Cengage Learning 2014

without a misallocation of resources. It is now time to step back with a critical eye and consider markets that become "ugly frogs" by allocating resources inefficiently. Market failure occurs when market equilibrium results in too few or too many resources being used in the production of a good or service. In this section, you will study four important cases of market failure: lack of competition, externalities, public goods, and income inequality. Market failure is discussed in more detail in the chapter on environmental economics, except for the macroeconomics version of the text.

Market failure

A situation in which market equilibrium results in too few or too many resources being used in the production of a good or service. This inefficiency may justify government intervention.

4-2d LACK OF COMPETITION

There must be competition among both producers and consumers for markets to function properly. But what happens if the producers fail to compete? In *The Wealth of Nations*, Adam Smith stated, "People of the same trade seldom meet together, even for merriment and diversion, but the conversation ends in a

Adam Smith (1723–1790). The father of modern economics, who wrote *The Wealth of Nations* published in 1776.

conspiracy against the public, or in some diversion to raise prices."[1] This famous quotation clearly underscores the fact that in the real world, businesses seek ways to replace consumer sovereignty with "big business sovereignty." What happens when a few firms rig the market and they become the market's boss? By restricting supply through artificial limits on the output of a good, firms can enjoy higher prices and profits. As a result, firms may waste resources and retard technology and innovation.

Exhibit 7 illustrates how IBM, Apple, Gateway, Dell, and other suppliers of personal computers (PCs) could benefit from rigging the market. Without collusive action, the competitive price for PCs is $1,500, the quantity of 200,000 per month is sold, and efficient equilibrium prevails at point E_1. It is in the best interest of sellers, however, to take steps that would make PCs artificially scarce and raise the price. Graphically, the sellers wish to shift the competitive supply curve, S_1, leftward to the restricted supply curve, S_2. This could happen for a number of reasons, including an agreement among sellers to restrict supply (collusion) and government action. For example, the sellers could lobby the government to pass a law allowing an association of PC suppliers to set production quotas. The proponents might argue this action raises prices and, in turn, profits. Higher profits enable the industry to invest in new capital and become more competitive in world markets.

Opponents of artificially restricted supply argue that although the producers benefit, the lack of competition means the economy loses. The result of restricting supply is that the efficient equilibrium point, E_1, changes to the inefficient equilibrium point, E_2. At point E_2, the higher price of $2,000 is charged, and the lower equilibrium quantity means that firms devote too few resources to producing PCs and charge an artificially high price. Note that under U.S. antitrust laws, the Justice Department is responsible for prosecuting firms that collude to restrict supply to force higher prices.

4-2e EXTERNALITIES

Externality

A cost or benefit imposed on people other than the consumers and producers of a good or service.

Even when markets are competitive, some markets may still fail because they suffer from the presence of side effects economists call externalities. An externality is a cost or benefit imposed on people other than the consumers and producers of a good or service. Externalities are also called *spillover effects* or *neighborhood effects*. People other than consumers and producers who are affected by these side effects of market exchanges are called *third parties*. Externalities may be either negative or positive; that is, they may be detrimental or beneficial. Suppose you are trying to study and your roommate is listening to Steel Porcupines at full blast on the stereo. The action of your roommate is imposing an unwanted *external cost* or *negative externality* on you and other third parties who are trying to study or sleep. Externalities can also result in an *external benefit* or *positive externality* to nonparticipating parties. When a community proudly displays its neat lawns, gorgeous flowers, and freshly painted homes, visitors are third parties who did none of the work, but enjoy the benefit of the pleasant scenery.

A Graphical Analysis of Pollution   Exhibit 8 provides a graphical analysis of two markets that fail to include externalities in their market prices unless the government takes corrective action. Exhibit 8(a) shows a market for steel in which steel firms burn high-sulfur coal and pollute the environment. Demand curve D and supply curve S_1 establish the inefficient equilibrium, E_1, in the steel market. Not

---

[1]Adam Smith, *An Inquiry into the Nature and Causes of the Wealth of Nations* (1776; reprint, New York: Random House, The Modern Library, 1937), p. 128.

EXHIBIT 7	Rigging the PC Market

At efficient equilibrium point E_1, sellers compete. As a result, the price charged per PC is $1,500, and the quantity of PCs exchanged is 200,000. Suppose suppliers use collusion, government intervention, or other means to restrict the supply of this product. The decrease in supply from S_1 to S_2 establishes inefficient market equilibrium E_2. At E_2, firms charge the higher price of $2,000, and the equilibrium quantity of PCs falls to 150,000. Thus, the outcome of restricted supply is that the market fails because firms use too few resources to produce PCs at an artificially higher price.

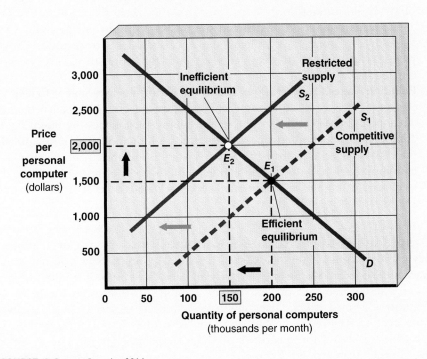

included in S_1 are the *external costs* to the public because the steel firms are not paying for the damage from smoke emissions. If steel firms discharge smoke and ash into the atmosphere, foul air reduces property values, raises health care costs, and generally erodes the quality of life. Because supply curve S_1 does not include these external costs, they are also not included in the price of steel, P_1. In short, the absence of the cost of pollution in the price of steel means the firms produce more steel and pollution than is socially desirable.

S$_2$ is the supply curve that would exist if the external costs of respiratory illnesses, dirty homes, and other undesirable side effects were included. Once S_2 includes the charges for environmental damage, the equilibrium price rises to P_2, and the equilibrium quantity becomes Q_2. At the efficient equilibrium point, E_2, the steel market achieves allocative efficiency. At E_2, steel firms are paying the full cost and using fewer resources to produce the lower quantity of steel at Q_2.

> **CONCLUSION:** *When the supply curve fails to include external costs, the equilibrium price is artificially low, and the equilibrium quantity is artificially high.*

Regulation and pollution taxes are two ways society can correct the market failure of pollution:

1. **Regulation.** Legislation can set standards that force firms to clean up their emissions as a condition of remaining in business. This means firms must buy, install, and maintain pollution-control equipment. When the extra cost of the pollution equipment is added to the production cost per ton of steel, the initial supply curve, S_1, shifts leftward to supply curve S_2. This means regulation has forced the market equilibrium to change from E_1 to E_2. At point E_2, the firms use fewer resources to produce Q_2 compared to Q_1 output of steel per year, and, therefore, the firms operate efficiently.

2. **Pollution Taxes.** Another approach would be for the government to levy a tax per ton of steel equal to the external cost imposed on society when the firm emits pollution into the air. This action inhibits production by imposing an additional production cost per ton of steel from the pollution taxes and shifts the supply curve leftward from S_1 to S_2. Again, the objective is to change the equilibrium from E_1 to E_2 and eliminate the overuse of resources devoted to steel production and its pollution. The tax revenue could be used to compensate those damaged by the pollution.

A Graphical Analysis of AIDS Vaccinations

As explained above, the supply curve can understate the *external costs* of a product. Now you will see that the demand curve can understate the *external benefits* of a product. Suppose a vaccination is discovered that prevents AIDS. Exhibit 8(b) illustrates the market for immunization against AIDS. Demand curve D_1 reflects the price consumers would pay for shots to receive the benefit of a reduced probability of infection by AIDS. Supply curve S shows the quantities of shots suppliers offer for sale at different prices. At equilibrium point E_1, the market fails to achieve an efficient allocation of resources. The reason is that when buyers are vaccinated, other people who do not purchase AIDS shots (called *free riders*) also benefit because this disease is less likely to spread. Once demand curve D_2 includes external benefits to nonconsumers of AIDS vaccinations (increase in the number of buyers), the efficient equilibrium of E_2 is established. At Q_2, sellers devote greater resources to AIDS vaccinations, and the underallocation of resources is eliminated.

How can society prevent the market failure of AIDS vaccinations? Two approaches follow.

1. **Regulation.** The government can boost consumption and shift the demand curve rightward by requiring all citizens to purchase AIDS shots each year. This approach to capturing external benefits in market demand explains why all school-age children must have polio and other shots before entering school.

2. **Special Subsidies.** Another possible solution would be for the government to increase consumer income by paying consumers for each AIDS vaccination.

EXHIBIT 8	Externalities in the Steel and AIDS Vaccination Markets

In part (a), resources are overallocated at inefficient market equilibrium E_1 because steel firms do not include the cost per ton of pollution in the cost per ton of steel. Supply curve S_2 includes the external costs of pollution. If firms are required to purchase equipment to remove the pollution or to pay a tax on pollution, the economy achieves the efficient equilibrium of E_2.

Part (b) demonstrates that external benefits cause an underallocation of resources. The efficient output at equilibrium point E_2 is obtained if people are required to purchase AIDS shots or if the government pays a subsidy equal to the external benefit per shot.

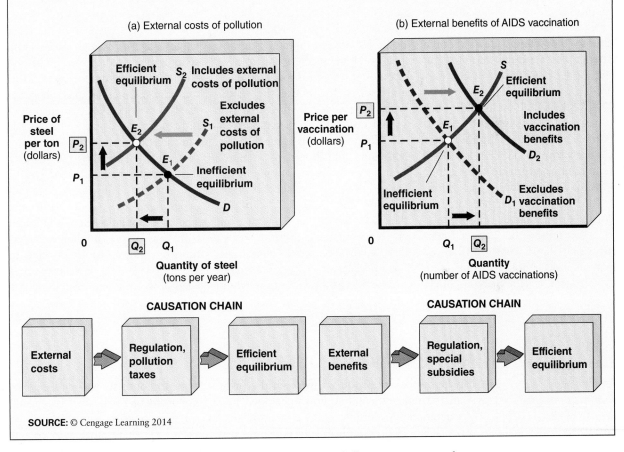

SOURCE: © Cengage Learning 2014

This would mean the government pays each citizen a dollar payment equal to the amount of external benefits per shot purchased. Because the subsidy amount is payable at any price along the demand curve, the demand curve shifts rightward until the efficient equilibrium price and quantity are reached.

CONCLUSION: *When externalities are present, market failure gives incorrect price and quantity signals, and as a result, resources are misallocated. External costs cause the market to overallocate resources, and external benefits cause the market to underallocate resources.*

Can Vouchers Fix Our Schools?

Applicable Concept: public goods versus private goods

In their book, *Free to Choose*, published in 1980, economists Milton Friedman and his wife Rose Friedman proposed a voucher plan for schools.[1] The objective of their proposal was to retain government financing, but give parents greater freedom to choose the schools their children attend. The Friedmans pointed out that under the current system, parents face a strong incentive not to remove their children from the public schools. The reason is because if parents decide to withdraw their children from a public school and send them to a private school, they must pay private tuition in addition to the taxes that finance children enrolled in the public schools.

To remove the financial penalty that limits the freedom of parents to choose schools, the government could give parents a voucher, which is a piece of paper redeemable for a sum of money payable to any approved school. For example, if the government spends $8,000 per year to educate a student, then the voucher could be for this amount. The voucher plan embodies the same principle as the GI Bill that provides educational benefits to military veterans. The veteran receives a voucher good only for educational expenses and is free to choose the school where it is used, provided the school satisfies certain standards.

The Friedmans argue that parents could, and should, be permitted to use the vouchers not only at private schools, but also at other public schools—and not only at schools in their own district, city, or state, but at any school that is willing to accept their child. That option would give every parent a greater opportunity to choose and at the same time would require public schools to charge tuition. The tuition would be competitive because public schools must compete for students both with other public schools and with private schools. It is important to note that this plan relieves no one of the burden of taxation to pay for schooling. It simply gives parents a wider choice as to which competing schools their children can attend, given the amount of funding per student that the community has obligated itself to provide. The plan also does not affect the present standards imposed on private schools to ensure that students attending them satisfy the compulsory attendance laws.

In 1990, Milwaukee began an experiment with school vouchers. The program gave selected children from low-income families taxpayer-funded vouchers to allow them to attend private schools. There has been a continuing heated debate

4-2f PUBLIC GOODS

Public good

A good or service with two properties: (1) users collectively consume benefits, and (2) there is no way to bar people who do not pay (free riders) from consuming the good or service.

Private goods are produced through the price system. In contrast, national defense is an example of a public good provided by the government because of its special characteristics. A public good is a good or service that, once produced, has two properties: (1) users collectively consume benefits, and (2) there is no way to bar people who do not pay (free riders) from consuming the good or service.

To see why the marketplace fails, imagine that Patriot Missiles Inc. offers to sell missile defense systems to people who want private protection against attacks from incoming missiles. First, once the system is operational, everyone in the defense area benefits from increased safety. Second, the *nonexclusive* nature of a public good means it is impossible or very costly for any owner of a Patriot missile defense system to prevent nonowners, the free riders, from reaping the benefits of its protection.

Given the two properties of a public good, why would any private individual purchase a Patriot missile defense system? Why not take a free ride and wait until someone else buys a missile system? Thus, each person wants a Patriot system, but does not want to bear the cost of the system when everyone shares in the benefits. As a result, the market fails to provide Patriot missile defense systems, and everyone among parents, politicians, and educators over the results. In 1998, Wisconsin's highest court ruled in a 4–2 decision that without violating the constitutional separation of church and state, Milwaukee could use public money for vouchers for students who attend religious schools.

A 2002 article in *USA Today* reported:

> Opponents of vouchers have repeatedly argued that they would damage the public schools, draining them of resources and better students. A recent study of the Milwaukee voucher program by Caroline Hoxby, a Harvard economist, suggests just the opposite. She wrote that "schools that faced the most potential competition from vouchers had the best productivity response." No

doubt, the nation's experience with vouchers is limited, yet the evidence cited in a recent Brookings Institution report shows that they do seem to benefit African-American youngsters.[2]

The controversy continues: For example, in a 2002 landmark case, the U.S. Supreme Court ruled that government vouchers for private or parochial schools are constitutional. In 2003, however, a Denver judge struck down Colorado's new school voucher law, ruling that it violated the state's constitution by stripping local school boards of their control over education. In 2006, the Florida Supreme Court ruled that Florida's voucher program for students in the lowest-rated public schools was unconstitutional. Then in 2010, Florida legislated a tax-credit voucher plan for low-income students.

And in 2011, Indiana began the nation's broadest school voucher program.

Analyze the Issue

1. In recent years, school choice has been a hotly debated issue. Explain whether education is a public good. If education is not a public good, why should the government provide it?

2. The Friedmans present a one-sided view of the benefits of a voucher system. Other economists disagree about the potential effectiveness of vouchers. Do you support a voucher system for education? Explain your reasoning.

1. Milton Friedman and Rose Friedman, *Free to Choose: A Personal Statement* (New York: Harcourt Brace Jovanovich, 1980), pp. 160–161.
2. Robert J. Bresler, "Vouchers and the Constitution," *USA Today*, May 2002, p. 15.

Source: © Cengage Learning 2014

hopes no missile attacks occur before someone finally decides to purchase one. Government can solve this public goods problem by producing Patriot missiles and taxing the public to pay. Unlike a private citizen, the government can use force to collect payments and prevent the free-rider problem. Other examples of public goods include global agreements to reduce emissions, the judicial system, the national emergency warning system, air traffic control, prisons, and traffic lights.

> **CONCLUSION:** *If public goods are available only in the marketplace, people wait for someone else to pay, and the result is an underproduction or zero production of public goods.*

4-2g INCOME INEQUALITY

In the cases of insufficient competition, externalities, and public goods, the marketplace allocates too few or too many resources to producing output. The market may also result in a very unequal distribution of income, thereby raising a very controversial issue. Under the impersonal price system, movie stars earn huge incomes for acting in movies, while homeless people roam the streets penniless. The controversy is therefore over how equal the distribution of income should be and how much government intervention is required to achieve this goal. Some people wish to remove most inequality of income. Others argue for the government to provide a "safety net" minimum income level for all citizens. Still others see high income as an incentive and a "fair" reward for productive resources.

To create a more equal distribution of income, the government uses various programs to transfer money from people with high incomes to those with low incomes. Unemployment compensation and food stamps are examples of such programs. The federal minimum wage is another example of a government attempt to raise the earnings of low-income workers.

✓ CHECKPOINT

Should There Be a War on Drugs?

The U.S. government fights the use of drugs, such as marijuana and cocaine, in a variety of ways, including spraying crops with poisonous chemicals; imposing jail sentences for dealers and users; and confiscating drug-transporting cars, boats, and planes. Which market failure motivates the government to interfere with the market for drugs: lack of competition, externalities, public goods, or income inequality?

Key Concepts

Price ceiling
Price floor

Market failure
Externality

Public good

Summary

- **Price ceilings** and **price floors** are maximum and minimum prices enacted by law, rather than allowing the forces of supply and demand to determine prices. A *price ceiling* is a maximum price mandated by government, and a *price floor*, or *support price* for agricultural products, is a minimum legal price. If a price ceiling is set below the equilibrium price, a shortage will persist. If a price floor is set above the equilibrium price, a surplus will persist.

Price Ceiling

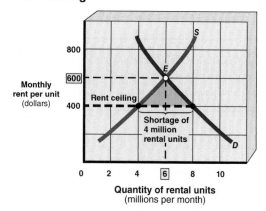

SOURCE: © Cengage Learning 2014

Price Floor

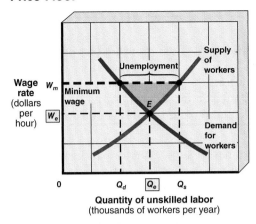

SOURCE: © Cengage Learning 2014

- **Market failure** occurs when the market mechanism does not achieve an efficient allocation of resources. Sources of market failure include lack of competition, externalities, public goods, and income inequality. Although controversial, government intervention is a possible way to correct market failure.

- An **externality** is a cost or benefit of a good imposed on people who are not buyers or sellers of that good. Pollution is an example of an *external cost*, which means too many resources are used to produce the product responsible for the pollution. Two basic approaches to solve this market failure are regulation and pollution taxes. Vaccinations provide *external benefits*, which means sellers devote too few resources to produce this product. Two basic solutions to this type of market failure are laws to require consumption of shots and special subsidies.

Externalities

(a) External costs of pollution

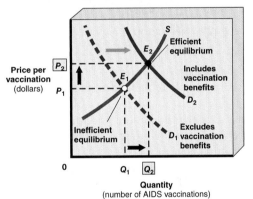

(b) External benefits of AIDS vaccination

SOURCE: © Cengage Learning 2014

- **Public goods** are goods that are consumed by all people in a society regardless of whether they pay or not. National defense, air traffic control, and other public goods can benefit many individuals simultaneously and are provided by the government.

Summary of Conclusion Statements

- A price ceiling or price floor prevents market adjustment in which competition among buyers and sellers bids the price upward or downward to the equilibrium price.
- When the supply curve fails to include external costs, the equilibrium price is artificially low, and the equilibrium quantity is artificially high.
- When externalities are present, market failure gives incorrect price and quantity signals, and

as a result, resources are misallocated. External costs cause the market to overallocate resources, and external benefits cause the market to underallocate resources.

- If public goods are available only in the marketplace, people wait for someone else to pay, and the result is an underproduction or zero production of public goods.

Study Questions and Problems

1. Market researchers have studied the market for milk, and their estimates for the supply of and the demand for milk per month are as follows:

Price per gallon	Quantity demanded (millions of gallons)	Quantity supplied (millions of gallons)
$10.00	100	500
8.00	200	400
6.00	300	300
4.00	400	200
2.00	500	100

a. Using the above data, graph the demand for and the supply of milk. Identify the equilibrium point as E, and use dotted lines to connect E to the equilibrium price on the price axis and the equilibrium quantity on the quantity axis.

b. Suppose the government enacts a milk price support of $8 per gallon. Indicate this action on your graph, and explain the effect on the milk market. Why would the government establish such a price support?

c. Now assume the government decides to set a price ceiling of $4 per gallon. Show and explain how this legal price affects your graph of the milk market. What objective could the government be trying to achieve by establishing such a price ceiling?

2. Use a graph to show the impact on the price of Japanese cars sold in the United States if the United States imposes import quotas on Japanese cars. Then draw another graph to show how the change in the price of Japanese cars affects the price of American-made cars in the United States. Explain the market outcome in each graph and the link between the two graphs.

3. Using market supply and demand analysis, explain why labor union leaders are strong advocates of raising the minimum wage above the equilibrium wage.

4. What are the advantages and disadvantages of the price system?

5. Suppose a market is in equilibrium and both demand and supply curves increase. What happens to the equilibrium price if demand increases more than supply?

6. Consider this statement: "Government involvement in markets is inherently inefficient." Do you agree or disagree? Explain.

7. Suppose coal-burning firms are emitting excessive pollution into the air. Suggest two ways the government can deal with this market failure.

8. Explain the impact of external costs and external benefits on resource allocation.

9. Why are public goods not produced in sufficient quantities by private markets?

10. Which of the following are public goods?
    a. Air bags
    b. Pencils
    c. Cycle helmets
    d. City streetlights
    e. Contact lenses

For Online Exercises, go to the Tucker Web site at www.cengage.com/economics/tucker.

✓ CHECKPOINT ANSWERS

Why the Higher Price for Ethanol Fuel?

As shown in Exhibit 9, an increase in demand leads to higher ethanol prices, while an increase in supply leads to lower prices. Because the overall direction of price in the ethanol market was up, the demand increase must have been larger than the supply increase. If you said demand increased by more than supply because consumers reacted more quickly than producers, **YOU ARE CORRECT.**

Is There Price Fixing at the Ticket Window?

Scalpers are evidence of a shortage whereby buyers are unable to find tickets at the official price. As shown in Exhibit 10, scalpers (often illegally) profit from the shortage by selling tickets above the official price. Shortages result when prices are restricted below equilibrium, as is the case when there is a price ceiling. If you said scalping occurs when there is a price ceiling because scalpers charge more than the official maximum price, **YOU ARE CORRECT.**

Should There Be a War on Drugs?

Drug use often affects not only the person using the drugs, but also other members of society. For example, higher crime rates are largely attributable to increased drug usage, and AIDS is often spread when users inject drugs using nonsterile needles. When one person's actions affect others not involved in the decision to buy or sell, the market fails to operate efficiently. If you said the market failure motivating government intervention in the drug market is externalities because drug users impose costs on nonusers, **YOU ARE CORRECT.**

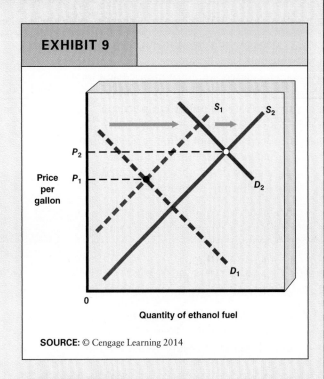

EXHIBIT 9

SOURCE: © Cengage Learning 2014

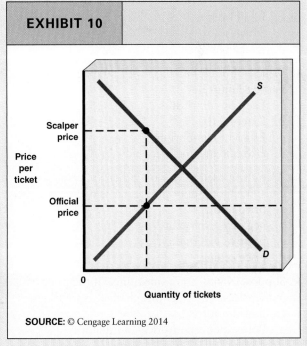

EXHIBIT 10

SOURCE: © Cengage Learning 2014

Sample Quiz

For an explanation of the correct answers, visit the Tucker Web site at www.cengage.com/economics/tucker.

1. A decrease in demand with the supply held constant leads to a(an)
   a. increased equilibrium price and an increased equilibrium quantity.
   b. decreased equilibrium price and a decreased equilibrium quantity.
   c. decreased equilibrium price and an increased equilibrium quantity.
   d. increased equilibrium price and a decreased equilibrium quantity.

2. An increased equilibrium price and a decreased equilibrium quantity results from a(an)
   a. decrease in demand.
   b. increase in supply.
   c. decrease in supply.
   d. increase in demand.

3. Assume no price ceiling exists in a market. Then a price ceiling is established below the market equilibrium. What would result?
   a. Shortage
   b. Equilibrium
   c. Surplus
   d. Exchange price

4. Which of the following is *not* an example of market failure?
   a. Lack of competition
   b. Externalities
   c. Efficient equilibrium
   d. Extreme income inequality

5. A cost imposed on people other than the consumers of a good or service is a
   a. price floor.
   b. negative externality.
   c. positive externality.
   d. price ceiling.

6. Suppose X and Y are substitutes. If the price of Y increases, how will this change the market equilibrium for X?
   a. Both equilibrium price and quantity decline.
   b. Both equilibrium price and quantity rise.

   c. Equilibrium price declines, and equilibrium quantity rises.
   d. Equilibrium price rises, and equilibrium quantity falls.

7. If the cost of producing a good rises for sellers, how will this affect the market equilibrium for that good?
   a. Price will rise, and quantity will fall.
   b. Price will fall, and quantity will rise.
   c. Both price and quantity will rise.
   d. Both price and quantity will fall.

8. If goods A and B are complements and the price of good B rises, how will this affect the market equilibrium for good A?
   a. Price will rise, and quantity will fall.
   b. Price will fall, and quantity will rise.
   c. Both price and quantity will rise.
   d. Both price and quantity will fall.

9. Suppose Big-Cat and Fat-Cat are rival cat food brands and the price of Fat-Cat is reduced. Following this price drop, is there a shortage or a surplus of Big-Cat at the old price of Big-Cat?
   a. Shortage
   b. Surplus
   c. Neither because equilibrium exists
   d. Neither because a price drop cannot cause a shortage or a surplus

10. Suppose the average equilibrium monthly rental price of apartments and rooms in a college town has been steady at $600, but then the college expands enrollment from 10,000 to 12,000. Suddenly, there is a shortage of rental housing at the prevailing price of $600. Which of the following is *most* likely true?
    a. The shortage occurred because demand increased, and a new market equilibrium will feature higher rental prices and more rental units available on the market.
    b. The shortage occurred because supply increased, and a new market equilibrium will feature lower rental prices and fewer rental units available on the market.
    c. The shortage occurred because demand decreased, and a new market equilibrium

Sample Quiz *continued*

will feature lower rental prices and fewer rental units available on the market.

d. The shortage occurred because demand increased, and a new market equilibrium will feature higher rental prices and fewer rental units available on the market.

11. If a price ceiling is set at $10 and the equilibrium market price is $8, which of the prices below will consumers actually pay?
   a. $10
   b. $8
   c. $18
   d. $2

12. Suppose the state of California imposes a minimum wage of $10 per hour. In the entry-level labor market in California fast-food restaurants, the quantity of labor demanded at $10 per hour is 800,000 and the quantity of labor supplied is 1.2 million. Which of the following is *true*?
   a. There is a shortage of 800,000 workers in the labor market.
   b. There is a surplus of 400,000 workers in the labor market.
   c. There is a shortage of 400,000 workers in the labor market.
   d. There is a surplus of 1.2 million workers in the labor market.

13. Suppose the federal government imposes a price floor (support price) in the milk market at a price of $6 per gallon. If market quantity demanded at $6 is 1 billion gallons, and market quantity supplied is 1.5 billion gallons, which of the following is true?
   a. There is a shortage of 500 million gallons of milk, and the federal government will buy 1 billion gallons to maintain the $6 price.
   b. There is a surplus of 500 million gallons of milk, and the federal government will buy these 500 million gallons to maintain the $6 price.
   c. There is a shortage of 500 million gallons of milk, and the federal government will buy an additional 500 million gallons to maintain the $6 price.

d. There is a surplus of 1 billion gallons of milk, and the federal government will buy 1.5 billion gallons to maintain the $6 price.

14. Suppose the city of Arcata, California, imposes rent control so that rents cannot exceed $1,000 per month on one-bedroom rental units. Suppose $500 had also been the equilibrium rental price in Arcata before a huge new apartment complex was built in the nearby town of McKinleyville, where rents are $800 per month. Which of the following is *most* likely true?
   a. There will be a shortage of rental housing in Arcata at the rent control price of $1,000.
   b. There will be a lasting surplus of rental housing in Arcata after the new apartment complex is built in McKinleyville.
   c. The equilibrium rental price in Arcata will fall below $1,000; thus, rent control will not affect the rental market in Arcata.
   d. The equilibrium price of $1,000 per month in Arcata will not change.

15. Suppose the federal government provides wheat farmers with a price floor above the market equilibrium price of wheat, creating a surplus. Which of the following causes a reduction in the surplus of wheat?
   a. Elimination of the price floor
   b. An increase in the price of wheat
   c. A decrease in the demand for wheat
   d. An increase in the supply of wheat

16. If society allows firms to freely pollute the environment, which of the following is *true*?
   a. Market equilibrium output will be too high relative to the efficient output level.
   b. Market equilibrium output will be too low relative to the efficient output level.
   c. Market equilibrium output will be equivalent to the efficient output level.
   d. The efficient output level can be achieved by giving firms a subsidy for the pollution they generate.

17. If there are external benefits for good X, which of the following is *true*?

Sample Quiz *continued*

a. The socially efficient amount of good X can be achieved if society taxes consumers of good X.
b. The socially efficient amount of good X can be achieved if society subsidizes consumers of good X.
c. The socially efficient amount of good X will be equivalent to the free market equilibrium quantity.
d. The socially efficient amount of good X does not exist.

18. Suppose the federal government imposes a new pollution tax of $0.01 per kilowatt-hour of electricity on coal-fired power producers. Which of the following describes how this tax will affect the market for electricity served by these power plants?
    a. Demand for electricity will decrease.
    b. Demand for electricity will increase.
    c. The supply of electricity will decrease.
    d. The supply of electricity will increase.

19. Why don't competitive markets do a good job providing public goods?
    a. Because people do not receive benefits from public goods
    b. Because firms cannot produce enough goods to satisfy market demand
    c. Because public goods generate negative externalities and pollution taxes reduce the incentive for firms to supply public goods
    d. Because it is difficult to exclude people from gaining benefits from public goods without paying for them; so market demand does not reflect the benefits to society from the public good

20. Which of the following is *not* an example of market failure?
    a. Lack of competition
    b. Externalities
    c. Efficient equilibrium
    d. Extreme income inequality

Applying Supply and Demand Analysis to Health Care

4

One out of every six dollars spent in the United States is spent for health care services. This is a greater percentage than in any other industrialized country.[1] And in 2010, historic health care legislation was enacted to dramatically reform the U.S. system. The topic of health care arouses deep emotions and generates intense media coverage. How can we understand many of the important health care issues? One approach is to listen to the normative statements made by politicians and other concerned citizens. Another approach is to use supply and demand theory to analyze the issue. Here again, the objective is to bring textbook theory to life and use it to provide you with a deeper understanding of third-party health service markets.

4A-1 The Impact of Health Insurance

There is a downward-sloping demand curve for health care services just as there is for other goods and services. Following the same law of demand that applies to cars, clothing, entertainment, and other goods and services, movements along the demand curve for health care occur because consumers respond to changes in the price of health care. As shown in Exhibit A-1, we assume that health care, including doctor visits, medicine, hospital bills, and other medical services, can be measured in units of health care. Without health insurance, consumers buy Q_1 units of health care services per year at a price of P_1 per unit. Assuming supply curve S represents the quantity supplied, the market is in equilibrium at point A. At this point, the total cost of health care can be computed by the price of health care (P_1) times the quantity demanded (Q_1) or represented geometrically by the rectangle $0P_1 A Q_1$.

Analysis of the demand curve for health care is complicated by the way health care is financed. About 80 percent of all health care is paid for by *third parties*, including private insurance companies and government programs, such as Medicare and Medicaid. The price of health care services therefore depends on the *copayment rate*, which is the percentage of the cost of services consumers pay out-of-pocket. To understand the impact, it is more realistic to assume consumers are insured and extend the analysis represented in Exhibit A-1. Because patients pay only 20 percent of the bill, the quantity of health care demanded in the figure increases to Q_2 at a lower price of P_2. At point B on the demand curve, insured consumers pay an amount equal to rectangle $0P_2BQ_2$, and insurers pay an amount represented by rectangle P_2P_3CB. Health care providers respond by increasing the quantity supplied from point A to point C on the supply curve S, where the quantity supplied equals the quantity demanded of Q_2. The reason there is no shortage in the health

---

[1]U.S. Census Bureau, *Statistical Abstract of the United States*, 2011, http://www.census.gov/compendia/statab, Table 1301.

EXHIBIT A-1	The Impact of Insurance on the Health Care Market

Without health insurance, the market is in equilibrium at point A, with a price of P_1 and a quantity demanded of Q_1. Total spending is $0P_1AQ_1$. With copayment health insurance, consumers pay the lower price of P_2, and the quantity demanded increases to Q_2. Total health care costs rise to $0P_3CQ_2$, with $0P_2BQ_2$ paid by consumers and P_2P_3CB paid by insurers. As a result, the quantity supplied increases from point A to point C, where it equals the quantity demanded of Q_2.

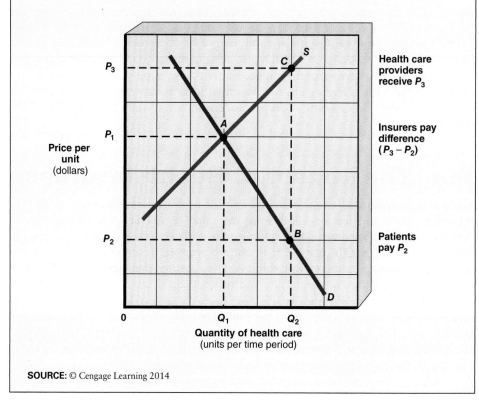

SOURCE: © Cengage Learning 2014

care market is that the combined payments from the insured consumers and insurers equal the total payment required for the movement upward along the supply curve. Stated in terms of rectangles, the total health care payment of $0P_3CQ_2$ equals $0P_2BQ_2$ paid by consumers plus P_2P_3CB paid by insurers.

CONCLUSION: *Compared to a health care market without insurance, the quantity demanded, the quantity supplied, and the total cost of health care are increased by copayment health care insurance.*

Finally, note that Exhibit A-1 represents an overall or general model of the health care market. Individual health care markets are subject to *market failure*. For example, there would be a lack of competition if hospitals, doctors, health maintenance organizations (HMOs), or drug companies conspired to fix prices. Externalities provide another source of market failure, as illustrated previously for vaccinations in Exhibit 8(b). We are also concerned that health care be distributed in a fair way. This concern explains why the government Medicare and Medicaid programs help the elderly and poor afford health care.

4A-2 Shifts in the Demand for Health Care

While changes in the price of health care cause movements along the demand curve, other factors can cause the demand curve to shift. The following are some of the nonprice determinants that can change the demand for health care.

4A-2a NUMBER OF BUYERS

As the population increases, the demand for health care increases. In addition to the total number of people, the distribution of older people in the population is important. As more people move into the 65-and-older age group, the demand for health care services becomes greater because older people have more frequent and prolonged spells of illness. An increase in substance abuse involving alcohol, tobacco, or drugs also increases the demand for health care. For example, if the percentage of babies born into drug-prone families increases, the demand for health care will shift rightward.

4A-2b TASTES AND PREFERENCES

Changes in consumer attitudes toward health care can also change demand. For example, television, movies, magazines, and advertising may be responsible for changes in people's preferences for cosmetic surgery. Moreover, medical science has improved so much that we believe there must be a cure for most ailments. As a result, consumers are willing to buy larger quantities of medical services at each possible price.

Doctors also influence consumer preferences by prescribing treatment. It is often argued that some doctors guard against malpractice suits or boost their incomes by ordering more tests or office visits than are really needed. Some estimates suggest that fraud and abuse account for about 10 percent of total health care spending. These studies reveal that as many as one-third of some procedures are inappropriate.

4A-2c INCOME

Health care is a normal good. Rising inflation-adjusted incomes of consumers in the United States cause the demand curve for health care services to shift to the right. On the other hand, if real median family income remains unchanged, there is no influence on the demand curve.

4A-2d PRICES OF SUBSTITUTES

The prices of medical goods and services that are substitutes can change and, in turn, influence the demand for other medical services. For example, treatment of a back problem by a chiropractor is an alternative for many of the treatments provided by orthopedic doctors. If the price of orthopedic therapy rises, then some people will switch to treatment by a chiropractor. As a result, the demand curve for chiropractic therapy shifts rightward.

4A-3 Shifts in the Supply of Health Care

Changes in the following nonprice factors change the supply of health care.

4A-3a NUMBER OF SELLERS

Sellers of health care include hospitals, nursing homes, physicians in private practice, HMOs, drug companies, chiropractors, psychologists, and a host of other suppliers. To ensure the quality and safety of health care, virtually every facet of the industry is regulated and licensed by the government or controlled by the American Medical Association (AMA). Primarily through medical school accreditation and licensing requirements, the AMA limits the number of people practicing medicine. The federal Food and Drug Administration (FDA) requires testing that delays the introduction of new drugs. Tighter restrictions on the number of sellers shift the health care supply curve leftward, and reduced restrictions shift the supply curve rightward.

4A-3b RESOURCE PRICES

An increase in the costs of resources underlying the supply of health care shifts the supply curve leftward. By far the single most important factor behind increasing health care spending has been technological change. New diagnostic, surgical, and therapeutic equipment is used extensively in the health care industry, and the result is higher costs. Wages, salaries, and other costs, such as the costs of malpractice suits, also influence the supply curve. If hospitals, for example, are paying higher prices for inputs used to produce health care, the supply curve shifts to the left because the same quantities may be supplied only at higher prices.

1

Agriculture

Rural America is home to a fifth of the Nation's people, keeper of natural amenities and national treasures, and safeguard of a unique part of American culture, tradition, and history.

—STATEMENT BY THE U.S. DEPARTMENT OF AGRICULTURE, *AN ENHANCED QUALITY OF LIFE FOR RURAL AMERICANS*, 2005

This introductory quotation paints an idyllic picture of rural America. Our nation takes pride in this environment that includes our natural resources, rural culture, and agricultural sector. Yet, we hear of problems in this sector—small farmers going bankrupt and farming towns losing residents. Indeed, annual Farm Aid concerts have raised $29 million since 1985. The September 2006 Farm Aid concert included singers Neil Young, Willie Nelson, John Mellencamp, Dave Matthews, and others; and their stated goals include support for family farms, a fight against corporate agriculture, advocacy for fair farm prices, and encouragement of consumers to buy locally grown food. Clearly, there is concern for the small and family farmer.

So, what's happening in agriculture? How does agricultural policy affect our farmers, and our small and family farmers in particular? How does it affect consumers? And how does it affect producers and consumers around the globe? In this chapter, we will discuss the unique characteristics of the American rural and agricultural sectors, the history and an evaluation of government policy toward agriculture, diversity and agriculture, the global context of agriculture, and the politics and outlook for agriculture in the future.

Characteristics of the Rural Sector

First, you probably know that the population of the U.S. rural sector is smaller than that of the urban sector. The rural sector is home to almost 50 million

The Economic Toolbox

- Inelastic demand
- Real price
- Immobile resources
- Agricultural subsidies
- Price supports (floors)
- Rationing function of price
- Dumping
- Concentration
- Biotechnology
- Target prices and deficiency payments (appendix)

inhabitants, while the urban sector comprises close to 250 million people. Rural incomes (an average per-person income of $25,000 per year) are lower than urban ones (an average of $35,000 per year). The rural poverty rate of 13.9 percent is higher than the urban poverty rate of 12.2 percent. Finally, the unemployment rate is 5.6 percent in the rural sector, whereas it is 5.0 percent in the urban sector.[1]

Clearly, in terms of these indicators, standards of living in our rural environments are poorer than those in our urban areas. Nevertheless, the rural sector is not synonymous with agriculture, so let's consider the characteristics of the agricultural sector specifically.

DIVERSITY

Characteristics of Agriculture

Before we even consider agriculture in detail, you should be aware that in the most recent farm census, about 1,890,000 men claimed farming as their primary occupation. In addition, about 240,000 women listed their primary occupation as farming. Many more women contribute to farming in important ways. We should be certain to think of the farmer as "she," as well as "he."

Certain characteristics of agriculture distinguish the farm sector from the remainder of the economy. Some of this discussion involves the short run (one year to the next) and some involves the long run (over several years). The characteristics are as follows:

1. An inelastic demand for farm products in the short run
2. Extensive technological change in the past half century
3. Immobile resources

Let's see how these characteristics affect farmers.

INELASTIC DEMAND FOR FARM PRODUCTS IN THE SHORT RUN

Inelastic demand

Demand in which buyers are relatively unresponsive to changes in price.

Recall our discussion of inelastic demand when we considered the market for addictive drugs in Chapter 2. When we say that a product has **inelastic demand**, we mean that its buyers are relatively unresponsive to changes in its price. This means that buyers show little variation in the quantity they buy when the price changes. This is the case for most farm commodities, as well as the many commodity exports from less-developed countries that we will discuss in Chapter 13. As discussed in previous chapters, we represent inelastic demand with a relatively steep demand curve. And, as we shall see, the inelasticity of demand has considerable significance for farm prices and farmers' incomes.

Price Instability

Let's begin by looking at the significance of the inelastic demand for farm products on the stability of farm prices in the short run. If demand is inelastic, the small fluctuations in supply that might result from either exceptionally good or exceptionally bad weather will have a resounding effect on the prices that farmers receive for their products. Figure 12-1 illustrates this effect. **The demand curve is shown to be relatively steep, reflecting the fact that any small percentage change on the horizontal axis (quantity) is associated with a large percentage change on the vertical axis (price).**

The graph in the figure shows a hypothetical demand curve for corn with an initial equilibrium price of $3 per bushel and an initial equilibrium quantity of 5 million bushels. Now consider an increase in supply from S to S' caused

FIGURE
12-1
THE EFFECT OF INELASTICITY ON PRICE AND FARM INCOMES IN THE CORN MARKET

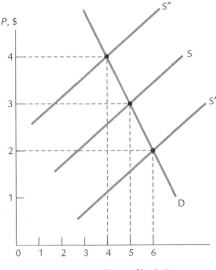

Quantity (millions of bushels)

Because the demand for farm products is inelastic, an increase in supply from S to S′ will cause a sharp decrease in price, as well as a decrease in farmers' incomes. Note that price falls from $3 to $2, while incomes decrease from $15 million to $12 million. Conversely, a decrease in supply to S″ will increase price to $4 and increase total farm incomes to $16 million.

by exceptionally good weather. The equilibrium quantity increases to 6 million bushels, which is a relatively small percentage increase (20 percent). Now consider the price change. Because of the inelastic demand, the effect of the supply shift on the market price is very large. The increase in supply causes the price to fall all the way to $2 per bushel (a relatively large decrease of 50 percent). Similarly, a relatively small decrease in supply caused by poor weather (from S to S″) would cause a relatively large increase in price up to $4 per bushel (a 50 percent increase). **The combination of short-run weather-related supply fluctuations and inelastic demand results in large fluctuations in agricultural prices in the short run.** To convince yourself of the outcomes of inelastic demand, try drawing the same graph but with a flatter demand curve. When demand is not inelastic, identical fluctuations in supply will cause much less price variation than when demand is inelastic.

Farm Income

Now let's consider how farmers' incomes are affected by this inelastic demand in the short run. If good weather causes an increase in supply (a **bumper crop**), which causes price to decrease, then overall farm income will also fall. This is because income from a corn crop is equal to the number of units sold times the price at which they are sold. Refer again to Figure 12-1. At the initial price of $3, farmers

Bumper crop

An unexpectedly large crop resulting from good growing conditions.

sold 5 million bushels, earning income of $15 million from their corn crop. (Five million bushels times $3 per bushel is $15 million.) After the increase in supply, farmers sold 6 million bushels at a price of $2 per bushel. They earned only $12 million for their corn crop. **Because consumers have an inelastic demand for agricultural products, a short-run decrease in price results in a short-run decrease in farm income.** Similarly, a short-run increase in price (from bad weather) results in a short-run increase in farm income. (For a more mathematical discussion of the effects of elasticity on prices and income, see Appendix 1 of this chapter.)

Note that these counterintuitive results are true for total farm income, not the income of an individual farmer. The farmer who has lost an entire crop will certainly not have higher income in the bad-weather year. Also note that these were short-run results. Demand is inelastic in the short run; and supply, price, and income fluctuate in the short run. These refer to year-to-year situations, as opposed to changes that occur over a long period of time. We now consider this long-run time period.

EXTENSIVE TECHNOLOGICAL CHANGE IN THE PAST HALF CENTURY

In the long run, technological change and slow growth in demand have caused the real prices of farm products to fall. (When we say **real price**, we mean the price as adjusted for inflation.) Commercial farmers have adopted new techniques and use new, efficient machinery. New high-yield crop varieties exist. Intensive use of fertilizers and pesticides increases yield per acre. Artificial insemination and other improved breeding techniques have resulted in more reliable growth in cattle herds. Center-pivot irrigation systems dot the Great Plains. And, as we discuss shortly, biotechnology is rapidly gaining supporters and opponents. In general, the results of these technological changes are a trend toward capital- and chemical-intensive agriculture, a move toward large-scale farming enterprises, and a pronounced increase in the supply of farm products. Although the number of farmers is much smaller than a half century ago, the supply of farm products has increased markedly.

As a result of this technological advance, American agriculture is highly productive, though it is not the most productive in the world. Table 12-1 reveals the productivity of many countries, where productivity is defined as agricultural value per worker.[2] The most productive countries, in order, are France, the Netherlands, Canada, and the United States. In general, the countries with the highest agricultural productivity are in the Western industrialized world. Eastern European and Latin American countries (with the exception of Haiti) tend to range in middle productivity, and the least productive countries tend to be in South Asia and Africa (with the exception of South Africa).

Compared with the large increase in supply, the increase in Americans' demand for food over time has been relatively small. That increase is attributable mainly to an increase in our population. We have grown more affluent over time, but we have spent our additional income on things other than food. As a people, we have been well fed for a great many years.

The combined effects of this large long-run increase in supply and the modest increase in demand have greatly decreased the real price of farm products. This change is not a year-to-year price fluctuation of the sort caused by agriculture's inelastic demand, but a long-run trend instead. This is shown in Figure 12-2,

Real price

Price as adjusted for the effects of inflation. We do this when we consider price changes over time.

TABLE 12-1	AGRICULTURAL PRODUCTIVITY; VALUE ADDED PER WORKER;[a] IN (CONSTANT 2000) DOLLARS; FOR THE HIGHEST, LOWEST,[b] AND SELECT COUNTRIES IN BETWEEN, 2002–2004

Country	Value ($)	Country	Value ($)
France	40,521	Iraq	2,271
Netherlands	39,358	El Salvador	1,607
Canada	38,509	Poland	1,408
United States	36,863	Haiti	427
Norway	32,779	Botswana	409
Sweden	31,716	China	373
Japan	26,557	Bangladesh	309
Argentina	9,311	Ukraine	231
Malaysia	4,690	Rwanda	229
Chile	3,222	Nepal	208
Mexico	2,727	Burkina Faso	166
South Africa	2,414	Ethiopia	118
Russia	2,297	Burundi	103

[a]This is the additional value contributed by each worker on average.
[b]Lowest among reporting countries.
Source: World Bank, *World Development Indicators 2006*, http://www.worldbank.org.

FIGURE 12-2	EFFECTS OF A LARGE INCREASE IN SUPPLY AND A SMALLER INCREASE IN DEMAND ON THE MARKET FOR FARM COMMODITIES IN THE LONG RUN

The larger increase in supply, coupled with the relatively small increase in demand, has caused the real prices of agricultural commodities to fall in the past 72 years.

where we see that the equilibrium quantity of agricultural products is larger but that the real price has decreased.

IMMOBILE FARM RESOURCES

The principal resource used in farming is, of course, land. With the exception of land near rapidly growing cities, which can be developed, most farmland has few alternative uses. So, although one farmer may leave farming and find a job in the city, land tends to remain in agriculture. Some other farmer buys the land and continues to farm it. If real prices fell as precipitously in other sectors as they have in farming, people and resources would rapidly flow out of these markets into other markets that are believed to be more profitable. But land is not removed from agriculture. Either farmland lies fallow or someone farms it. Agriculture's main resource is slow to respond to adverse industry conditions.

The U.S. Department of Agriculture (USDA) conducts a Census of Agriculture every five years. The most recent census as this book goes to print is for 2002. It is interesting to compare the percent of total land area in the United States classified as farmland for the last three censuses. In 1992 it was 41.8 percent; in 1997 it was 42.2 percent, and in 2002 it was 41.4 percent.[3] Clearly, the data support our thesis that farmland tends to be immobile.

Although the limited use to which farmland can be put undoubtedly contributes to this resource immobility, it can also be argued that the government's agricultural policies have kept agricultural resources *in* agriculture when they perhaps should have been transferred to other lines of production. Let's consider this policy.

Government Policy Toward Agriculture

The U.S. government has been extensively involved in agriculture since the Great Depression of the 1930s. The entire country (indeed, much of the world) was in distress during the 1930s, but agriculture suffered more than other sectors. Real farm prices fell, and farm income and profits plummeted. Furthermore, the prices that farmers received for their crops decreased more than the prices that they paid for their inputs.

Because the price of farm products was too low to cover farmers' costs, the government initiated a variety of policies to assist farmers. Congress passed the Agricultural Adjustment Act in 1933 to restore the standing of farm incomes relative to incomes in the rest of the economy. This was one of the first pieces of Franklin D. Roosevelt's New Deal legislation to be enacted. The government has been extensively involved in agriculture ever since.

The objectives of farm policy have been to stabilize conditions in farming and to increase real farm incomes. Accordingly, programs were devised to affect the supply of agricultural products, the demand for agricultural products, and the price received by farmers. Two policy instruments were used early on. These were price supports and programs to restrict supply. As time passed, price supports became less important policy instruments, and target prices and deficiency payments became more important. All forms of government payments to farmers are generally referred to as **agricultural subsidies**. Our government has also attempted to increase the demand for agricultural products in order to raise prices. We now discuss the price supports, programs to restrict supply, and policies to increase demand, and we leave the discussion of target prices and deficiency payments for Appendix 2 of this chapter.

Agricultural subsidies

Government payments to agricultural producers.

PRICE SUPPORTS

Price supports are examples of **price floors**, which are government-imposed minimum prices for a good or service. These minimum prices set a "floor" below which the market price is not permitted to fall. To be effective, which means to have an effect on the market, these price floors must be above the market equilibrium price. (A price floor set below the market equilibrium would not have an effect on the market, since the market-determined price would take over. There is no law that says the prices cannot go *above* a certain level.) Agricultural prices are thereby prevented from falling below the price floor. As we discussed in Chapter 1, markets tend to clear at an equilibrium price and quantity. In the process, shortages and surpluses are rationed away. This is the rationing function of price in a competitive market. When agricultural prices are kept artificially high, they cannot perform the rationing function. Let's look at this problem through a hypothetical example of the U.S. wheat market in Table 12-2.

The equilibrium price is $3.50, at which both quantity demanded and quantity supplied equal 2,500 million bushels of wheat. At this equilibrium price, 2,500 million bushels will be exchanged and the market will clear. If price is temporarily above equilibrium, at $4.00, a surplus will exist in the market. Figure 12-3, on page 278, shows the supply and demand data graphically, indicating the surplus at $4.00.

At the price of $4.00, farmers produce and offer 3,500 million bushels for sale, but consumers are willing to buy only 2,000 million, so only 2,000 million bushels are exchanged. The remaining 1,500 million bushels are an unsold surplus in the market. If the price is free to fall, the surplus will cause it to decrease. It will fall as long as there is a surplus to push it down. As price falls, a message is sent to buyers: increase the amount you demand, because price is falling. An opposite message is sent to sellers: decrease the amount you supply, because price is falling. Buyers and sellers each move down their respective demand or supply curve. When the equilibrium price ($3.50) is reached, quantity supplied equals quantity demanded, and there is no more surplus to drive the price down further. The falling price has rationed away the surplus. This process is what economists mean when they refer to the **rationing function of price**, which makes markets efficient means to allocate goods and services.

Now assume that the government had set the legal minimum price at $4.00, so that price could not fall in response to the surplus. The surplus would not be rationed away. Instead, the market would have a persistent surplus of wheat. And that is what happens when the government supports the prices of farm commodities. The price supports actually create surpluses.

The method by which some U.S. farm prices are supported is indirect, but the result is the same as the price floor. Prices are supported by granting farmers loans on their stored commodities through the Commodity Credit Corporation (CCC), which was established in 1933 for this purpose. Farmers can get loans on the

Price supports

Legally imposed minimum prices of goods or services. Price supports are specific examples of price floors.

Price floors

Legally imposed minimum prices of a good or service.

Rationing function of price

The ability of a flexible market price to clear the market of shortages and surpluses.

TABLE 12-2	DEMAND AND SUPPLY OF WHEAT (HYPOTHETICAL DATA)

Quantity Demanded (millions of bushels)	Price ($)	Quantity Supplied (millions of bushels)
1,500	4.50	4,500
2,000	4.00	3,500
2,500	3.50	2,500
3,000	3.00	1,500
3,500	2.50	500

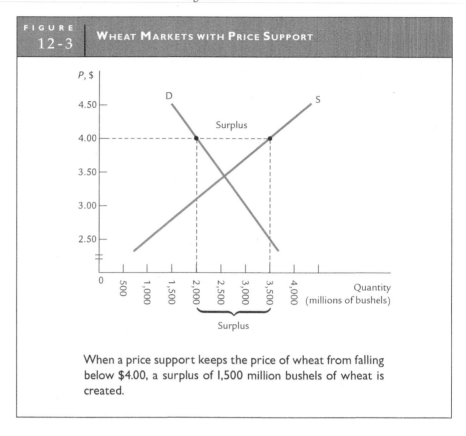

FIGURE 12-3 | **WHEAT MARKETS WITH PRICE SUPPORT**

When a price support keeps the price of wheat from falling below $4.00, a surplus of 1,500 million bushels of wheat is created.

value of their commodities at a rate established by the government (such as $4 per bushel). They put up their commodities as collateral. If the market price is above the loan rate, the farmer can withdraw the commodity from storage, sell the commodity, repay the loan, and keep the profits. On the other hand, if the market price is below the support price, the farmer simply surrenders the commodity to the government instead of repaying the loan. The loan rate is therefore the effective price support. The government is the buyer of the surplus, and it is the government (and taxpayers) that bear the losses.

We should note that the price floor set at $4.00 per bushel is more indicative of the price supports of the past than the present. In 2006, in line with falling support prices in recent times, the national average price support for wheat was only $2.75 per bushel.

By means of price supports, income is redistributed to the farm sector from taxpayers in general. Whenever income is redistributed, some groups gain and others lose. Let's look at the losers and the gainers. Taxpayers, who are also consumers, are obvious losers. Their taxes are used to buy and store the surplus at artificially high prices, and the higher prices lead to at least slightly higher food prices. (We say "slightly" because most of the price you pay for food results from the costs of processing and distributing the food, not from the cost of the farm products.)

Let's summarize the results of the agricultural price floors. Agricultural prices are held artificially high, which encourages excess production. Surplus crops result, which are costly for the government and taxpayers. At the same time that surplus crops are produced, consumers are discouraged from purchasing the crops because of the artificially high prices. Our agricultural system is inefficient, and it transfers benefits to our farm sector.

The farm sector is the gainer, but in a manner that many taxpayers do not understand. **The lion's share of the support goes to large farmers, because the subsidy is paid on a per-unit-of-output basis.** Large-scale farmers produce more bushels (units of output), so they receive bigger subsidy payments from the government. This reality undoubtedly conflicts with our vision of government farm programs as helping small, struggling American farmers. Most of us picture small-scale production on the "family farm" when we think of farmers. Agricultural economists Willard W. Cochrane and C. Ford Runge refer to the average citizen's false image of agriculture as the "Little House on the Prairie" image.[4] The average voter is far more likely to support farm programs that he or she believes guarantee a decent living to the hard-pressed, hardworking small farmer than to support programs that offer huge subsidies to large farms. We shall return to this topic shortly. Consider the following words of a farmer: "Nostalgically, many remember when farming was considered a comfortable, laid back, safe and healthy way of life. The farm was a 'good place to raise kids.' The hard work of farming was offset by a sense of independence, the joy of being your own boss."[5] This "nostalgic" view of farming does not apply to the bulk of agricultural production today.

PROGRAMS TO RESTRICT SUPPLY

Price supports have been combined with **programs to reduce supply**. Refer again to Figure 12-3 on page 278. Assume that government analysts believe that a "fair" price for farm commodities is $4. This price would cover the costs of production, including some level of wages for the average farmer. One way to ensure that farmers receive $4 per bushel is to support the price at $4 and create a surplus in the process, as we've just discussed. Another method would be to shift the supply curve back to the point at which supply intersects demand at $4. The effects of this method are shown in Figure 12-4.

Programs to reduce supply

Policies to decrease the amount produced and offered for sale.

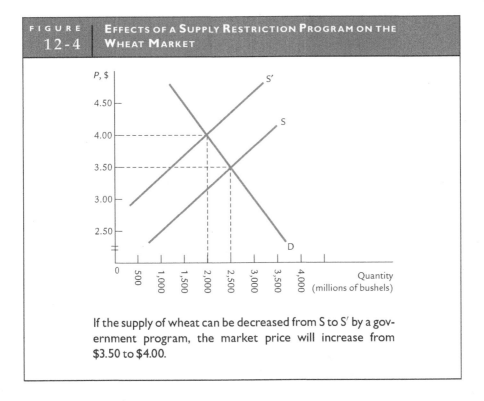

| FIGURE 12-4 | EFFECTS OF A SUPPLY RESTRICTION PROGRAM ON THE WHEAT MARKET |

If the supply of wheat can be decreased from S to S' by a government program, the market price will increase from $3.50 to $4.00.

After the decrease in supply, the equilibrium price is $4, and the market clears with 2,000 million bushels of wheat being exchanged. No surplus results for which the government is the buyer of last resort. No storage charges will be incurred. No loss of the stored grain due to damage from rodents or simple deterioration with age will occur. Programs to reduce the supply of farm products appeared preferable to rigid price supports in the 1930s, and these programs continue to receive support.

Accordingly, the history of U.S. farm policy is filled with efforts to reduce supply. Early efforts were voluntary and often involved land rent payments on acres taken out of the production of specific crops coupled with support prices on crops grown on the individual farmer's remaining land. Despite these attempts to control supply, the surpluses grew. Commercial warehouses were filled. Abandoned schoolhouses and (in some cases) churches were used for storage. Consequently, efforts to restrict supply became more formal and far-reaching.

In 1956, the Soil Bank was instituted. It encouraged the long-term withdrawal of farmland from production of any crops and stricter compliance with acreage controls on specific crops. Farmers were paid for not farming. In subsequent legislation, supply restriction programs were continued under other names: the Set-Aside program, the Payment-in-Kind (PIK) program, and the "10-year plan," which encouraged farmers to put highly erodible acres in a long-term supply restriction program. Under the Set-Aside program, farmers were paid for setting aside and not farming a proportion of their total acres. They were guaranteed support prices on crops grown on their remaining acreage. Under the PIK program, they were given surplus commodities from the government's storehouses instead of cash, but PIK resembled the Set-Aside program in other respects. The 10-year government plan required a longer commitment of farmers not to farm their entire acreage, and it restricted alternative uses of land by more than the two prior programs, but otherwise the programs were similar.

These supply restriction programs have not always worked. Acres were taken out of cultivation, but supply continued to increase, pushing down market prices. Why? Put yourself in the place of the American farmer. Would you put your best or your worst land in the Set-Aside program? Of course, you would put aside those swampy, poorly drained acres on which you get your tractor stuck every spring! You would be foolish to set aside well-drained, fertile acres in favor of your less-productive land. And that is what farmers have done: they have put their poorest land into supply restriction programs and then farmed the remaining acres more intensively. If rows of corn are planted closer together, and irrigation and fertilization of the crop is increased, the supply of corn increases despite acreage reduction programs. Simply by behaving in an economically rational way, the farmer dooms supply restriction programs to failure.

Like price supports, supply restriction programs favor large farms over small farms. The more acres put into the supply restriction program, the larger will be the payment to the farmer. And like price supports, supply restriction programs represent a redistribution of income from taxpayers at large to the agricultural sector.

The failures of price support and supply restriction policies are evident in the large stockpiles of agricultural products that have existed in the United States. These agricultural surpluses have pushed our government to experiment with demand-side programs in addition to supply restriction programs.

EFFORTS TO INCREASE DEMAND

Efforts to decrease supply have been accompanied by various efforts to increase domestic and international demand for U.S. agricultural products. You are undoubtedly familiar with some of the programs used in an attempt to increase domestic demand. Surplus commodities are distributed to the public school system for use in the school lunch program. (This practice explains some of the strange menus you encountered as an elementary school student.) Food stamps are distributed to poor families so that they can purchase more food. Surplus commodities such as cheese and milk powder have been distributed directly to the poor through various welfare agencies and food banks. The objectives of these programs are both humanitarian and pragmatic. Feeding the poor and seeing that schoolchildren receive a free or subsidized lunch are worthy humanitarian aims, and the pragmatic purposes of these programs are to increase the demand for agricultural products and to get rid of our surpluses.

Foreign demand for U.S. farm commodities has been affected by two types of programs: foreign food assistance programs (such as Food for Peace) and export subsidies. The foreign food assistance programs have been a means of disposing of surplus commodities abroad. When U.S. surpluses accumulate, we distribute more food abroad. When our surpluses are smaller, we send less humanitarian food aid to less-developed countries. After the first war in Iraq, surplus milk powder was made available to citizens of that country. During the 1980s, when Congress restricted foreign aid funds to Ecuador because of its brutal government, administration officials deliberately sent far more surplus milk powder to the country than its residents could possibly consume so that Ecuadorian sales of the milk to other countries could bring in desired revenue. In the world food crisis of the early 1970s, millions died of famine while the United States cut off food aid because our surpluses were relatively low. In many cases, our food aid programs have done more harm than good to Third World residents, as we will see shortly.

The U.S. government also pays export subsidies (government financial assistance) to U.S. agricultural exporters, as well as the assistance to U.S. farmers that we've discussed. These serve to make our agricultural exports "more competitive" (cheaper) to foreign consumers. This causes an increase in foreign consumption of U.S. agricultural products because U.S. prices will be lower than those of other countries. Indeed, we have lowered the world price of some commodities so much that we have been accused of **dumping**, or selling our farm products abroad at prices well below cost. These types of subsidies have also been used to a large extent in much of Western Europe and Japan. The decrease in the price of U.S., European, and Japanese commodities has greatly upset the other grain-producing and grain-exporting countries of the world, such as Canada, and has triggered retaliation. They also have negative effects on less-developed countries, as we shall see. We will return to this issue shortly.

Dumping
Exporting goods at low prices, even below the cost of production.

Efforts to increase the price of farm products by increasing demand have not been very effective. In most cases, we have merely disposed of accumulated surpluses. However, evidence indicates that some of the domestic programs meet their humanitarian objectives. For instance, the Food Stamp program increases poor families' access to food.

RECENT AGRICULTURAL POLICY

In recent years, the United States has attempted to coordinate and reevaluate these various farm programs. In 1990, for example, farmers were first required to put some of their acreage in a supply restriction program if they were to participate in the deficiency payments program. Attempts were made to decrease

EconNews

"Farmers Dump on Canada for Dumping"

Get more information on this news story by clicking Perfect Competition.

http://econapps.swlearning.com

farmers' incentives to continuously increase yields. Then, in 1996, Congress passed the so-called Freedom to Farm Bill, which eliminated the target prices and deficiency payments on some crops such as feed grains and wheat. It provided income support payments based on acreage. Restrictions on what farmers could plant and remain eligible for government farm programs were virtually eliminated, an action that was viewed as a major step toward "getting the government out of farming." The income support payments were scheduled to last for seven years until passage of the new farm bill.

The effects of the Freedom to Farm Act were what you probably would have predicted from reading the previous sections. At first, farmers were delighted to have less government interference with their decisions about what (and how much) to plant. But the supplies of grains and other crops affected by the act increased markedly, causing the market prices of corn and many other commodities to fall to historically low levels. Many farmers' incomes did not cover their costs. More farmers left agriculture. And in response to a number of natural disasters, such as floods and droughts, as well as the adverse market conditions just mentioned, Congress passed emergency farm aid measures in 1998, 1999, and 2000.

Most recently, President Bush signed the 2002 farm bill, entitled the Farm Security and Rural Investment Act. This bill covers the time period from 2002 to 2007, but specifies expenditures for a 10-year time period. Once again, the benefits of the farm bill are heavily targeted to large U.S. farms and agribusinesses. Little was done to alter the price distortions and commodity overproduction that have resulted from previous farm bills. The new farm bill also eliminated many provisions that would have targeted assistance to small- and medium-sized farms. While it does expand programs for farmland conservation and rural development, it failed to address concentration in the U.S. farm industry or strengthen competition in rural America. Instead, this bill (along with the crop insurance bill) was slated to provide $191 billion in direct subsidies to farmers over the 10-year time period (which was more than what was expected to be spent on K–12 education and environmental protection combined over the same 10-year time period). **Amazingly, almost 60 percent of all farm payments were projected to go to the largest 10 percent of farm producers.**[6]

As this book goes to press, the Bush administration has made proposals for the new 2007 farm bill. While the bill may be drastically altered in the legislative process, the current proposals mark a radical departure from the recent past. First, the bill would reduce payments to farmers by $10 billion over the next five years and cut off support for wealthy ones entirely. Specifically, it would cut off payments to farmers earning more than $200,000 per year, thereby affecting 75,000 of the 700,000 farmers who have been collecting government farm payments. In addition, it would reduce some of the trade distortions that have been harmful to less-developed countries, as we will discuss shortly. The proposal would also increase conservation financing and target almost $5 billion to fruit, vegetable, and other "specialty" growers who have received little federal assistance in the past. It would also provide money for research and development on cellulosic ethanol, which comes from agricultural waste and nonfood crops. Organizations concerned about the environment and poverty have praised the new proposals.

An Evaluation of U.S. Farm Policy

For 29 years, my family has made its living growing corn and soybeans in Mazon, Illinois—population 764. Most of my neighbors live on or near farms; they always *have. Many of the people I worship with every Sunday at Mazon Congregational Church still work on farms, though they're not sure how long they'll keep going. Still, the personal satisfaction—the sense of fulfilment—that we all used to experience from working hard and bringing in a harvest has dwindled, and for some, disappeared. My first year in farming was 1973, and that year we sold corn for $3.90 per bushel; I was able to buy a new tractor for $12,500. Last year I sold corn for $1.90, and a similar new tractor cost $100,000.[7]*

As is obvious to the farmer quoted here, government policies have not solved the core farm problem of declining real incomes to small- and medium-sized farmers, and they have had some unforeseen side effects. As we shall see, by treating a symptom rather than a cause, they have contributed to an increasingly concentrated agricultural sector and promoted productive techniques that have harmful environmental consequences. Additional issues involve farm workers and U.S. minority populations. The existence of biotechnology is just one more example of technical advance with questionable effects.

TREATING A SYMPTOM

The low price of farm products is a symptom of a resource allocation problem in the economy. We simply produce too many farm products in comparison with other goods. The solution to the problem is to decrease the resources devoted to farming. As long as prices are supported artificially, there will be an incentive to continue to overproduce. Indeed, government policies are a part of the farm problem because they encourage the retention in agriculture of resources that would otherwise leave farming and be used for other purposes.

INCREASING CONCENTRATION IN AGRICULTURE

A market is said to be concentrated if it contains a relatively few large firms. The current trend is toward greater **concentration** in agriculture. As we discussed previously, the "Little House on the Prairie" image of American agriculture is a false one today, but it was a more accurate image in the 1930s, when government involvement in agriculture began. The average farm was much smaller, and 25 percent of the population resided on farms.[8] Now, only about 1 percent of the population is engaged in farming, and the average size of farms has greatly increased. And while small family farms account for most of the farms in the nation, they produce a modest share of farm output.

The most recent Agricultural Census reveals that in 2002, the average farm size was 441 acres. This contrasts with 431 acres in the previous census in 1997. The average estimated market value of all machinery and equipment per farm was $66,570 in 2002, in contrast to $53,861 in 1997. Table 12-3, on page 284, reveals these and other differences between 2002 and 1997. We see that the very smallest farms have declined as a share of the total, and that the very largest farms have increased as a share of the total over just the five-year period shown in the table.

Growing concentration by the largest farms raises concern over potential market power among these farms. The effects of concentration were discussed in more detail in Chapter 11.

Concentration

The domination of a market by a few large firms.

HARMFUL ENVIRONMENTAL EFFECTS

Another false image of American agriculture noted by Cochrane and Runge is that farmers are "stewards of the land" or protectors of the land and

TABLE 12-3	FARM SIZE, 1997 AND 2002		
Farm Size		**1997**	**2002**
Average size (acres)		431	441
Average value of machinery and equipment per farm		$53,861	$66,570
Share of total farms by size:			
1–9 acres		9%	8%
10–49 acres		24	27
50–179 acres		31	30
180–499 acres		19	18
500–999 acres		8	8
1,000–1,999 acres		5	5
2,000 acres or more		3	5

Source: The U.S. Department of Agriculture, *Historical Highlights: 2002 and Earlier Census Years,* http://www.nass.usda.gov/census/census02, and *Farm Characteristics,* http://www.ers.usda.gov/StateFacts/US.

environment.[9] Farming is viewed as a healthy, wholesome way of life. In fact, modern farming has been reliant on chemical fertilizers to increase yield per acre to thereby obtain more government payments. It relies on pesticides to decrease insect damage and maximize yield. It creates nitrate pollution of water wells in farm states and other environmental problems. One year after the new farm bill, the Environmental Working Group criticized the bill for cutting farmland conservation and for funding controversial and environment-threatening operations.[10]

As people have left farming, they have been replaced by machines that are both expensive and dangerous. Farming is now one of the most dangerous sectors of the economy as measured by workplace accidents and deaths. Irrigation in the lower Midwest has damaged aquifers (underground water supplies serving large areas) but increased bushels per acre on which deficiency payments are earned. Commodity programs have encouraged the production of crops that are particularly likely to cause erosion, because these crops often have had high target prices. Farm life is neither particularly healthy nor environmentally benign. And our government programs have contributed to these adverse effects.

Some economists argue that the increasing concentration of agriculture worsens the environmental problems associated with large-scale production. Huge cattle feedlots, factory hog farms, and dairies with 1,200 cows on relatively few acres create significant problems of odor and waste disposal. Realistically, we will never return to the idealized notion of small family farms. We can, however, preserve the small- and medium-sized farms that remain if we adjust our national farm policy so that it no longer favors the largest producers. Policies that promote the greatest possible yield have proved self-defeating because they worsen the resource allocation problem and, in the process, increase concentration. Policies that promote a more diverse and less chemical-dependent agriculture appear to make more sense.

DIVERSITY AND AGRICULTURE

DIVERSITY

Ironically, the original farmers and inhabitants of the land in the United States; that is, Native Americans; experience high rates of poverty and hunger. Nearly one-third of Native Americans live in poverty, and nearly one-fourth of all Native households are considered food insecure.[11]

Another particularly at-risk population includes farm workers (often Hispanic migrants from within the United States or across national borders). Many of these farm workers harvest fruit and vegetable crops, which are not covered by government agricultural subsidies. Wages to farm workers are often very low and their housing and living conditions are often quite poor. Another issue involves pesticide poisoning. An estimated 10,000 to 20,000 hired farm workers are poisoned by pesticides on the job each year. For example, farm workers and their children have an increased risk of leukemia, non-Hodgkin's lymphoma, brain cancer, infertility, birth defects, and neurological disorders due to pesticide exposure. A recent study in Oregon found that migrant farm workers who had repeated exposures to neurotoxic pesticides scored far worse on tests of intellectual functioning, memory, and attention than did comparable immigrants who had no contact with pesticides. The problem is even more serious, given that poverty prevents many farm workers from receiving medical treatment when they are ill or injured. Despite the risks, the federal government has very few pesticide safety regulations that could protect harm workers.[12]

Finally, a 2006 investigation by the Environmental Working Group (EWG) and the Black Farmers' Association concluded that the USDA has failed in its responsibility to carry out compensation for African-American farmers who have filed for redress as a result of a historic civil rights case, known as *Pigford v. Veneman*. In this case, the USDA promised to pay billions of dollars to African-American farmers who claimed that the USDA had systematically discriminated against them for decades, denying them access to crop loans that were made to "similarly situated" white farmers in their communities. The EWG states that this lack of equal access to USDA loans is a partial cause of the dramatic decline in African-American farmers over the years since 1982. The EWG calls on the U.S. Congress to order full compensation and accountability by the USDA.[13]

BIOTECHNOLOGY

Production of genetically modified organisms (GMOs) has increased greatly over recent years. U.S. agricultural companies have taken the lead in developing biotechnology, in which seed varieties are genetically altered in order to increase yields. Farmers use the GMOs as a means of preventing crop disease and reducing pesticide use. Some people have characterized biotechnology as the means to solve the ever-present problem of world hunger, much as the Green Revolution was expected to relieve famine in earlier decades. Opponents maintain that the environmental and health risks of biotechnology are severe and that technology will do little to help with world hunger reduction. They argue that the development of GMOs will primarily benefit large multinational corporations. The debate over GMOs is expected to continue for some time and to create controversy between leaders of various governments. The effect of biotechnology, for better or worse, is probably most pronounced for less-developed countries, as we shall see.

Agriculture and Less-Developed Countries

FOOD PRODUCTION AND HUNGER

Some economists argue that our heavily subsidized agricultural sector produces commodities that compete unfairly with those of less-developed countries (LDCs). The LDCs often rely on their own agricultural exports for much-needed foreign currency. If, for example, the price of rice produced in Arkansas is artificially low because of U.S. government subsidies, Thailand's rice exports to the United States and to other trading partners will be diminished. This is an especially serious problem because the European countries and Japan, other potentially major markets for Third World agricultural exports, have policies similar to our own. Bread for the World, an organization concerned about world and domestic hunger, reports that the annual subsidy payments received by farmers in the rich countries (the United Sates, the European Union, and Japan) amount to about $280 billion, yet the total annual development assistance to the LDCs is about $60 billion, less than one-quarter of the subsidies.[14] Since U.S. and European farm subsidies, as well as the use of biotechnology, serve to increase food production, it is natural to assume that they will reduce world hunger and famine. Let's try to understand why this is probably not the case.

First, a lot of food is currently produced in the world. Except for the world food crisis years of the early 1970s, our world has been characterized as having abundant supplies and indeed surplus stocks of agricultural products that are never even consumed. The problem of world hunger has far less to do with global food production and a lot more to do with how this produce is distributed. Food, as well as other production, is distributed to people who have the incomes to buy it. Low-income people in poor countries cannot afford to buy enough food for themselves and their families. **Thus, hunger is a problem of poverty, not production.** In addition, civil war, political instability, bad weather, poor transportation, and lack of storage facilities can exacerbate problems of hunger.

Second, we must remember that most residents of less-developed countries live in the rural sector and earn their incomes through crop production. When U.S. and European subsidized agricultural products flood the world markets, causing very low agricultural prices, poor farmers in less-developed countries earn little income from their production of food and thus become poorer. They also have low incentive to produce food. They may seek employment in sectors that can more reliably provide for the needs of their families. Or they may swarm to cities in hopes of higher incomes, but in reality become unemployed and live in squalid conditions. **Although famine conditions require emergency food aid, prolonged food aid and dumping of agricultural products by developed countries actually exacerbate the problem of world hunger.**

A third reason that LDCs are disadvantaged in agriculture has to do with the trade restrictions imposed by the wealthy countries. The developed countries, including the United States, impose import tariffs on products that LDC country farmers can produce cheaper than rich country farmers, such as rice, sugar, and cotton. These trade restrictions prevent the agricultural commodities produced by LDCs from entering the United States and other prosperous countries. Rich-country governments receive large amounts of money from these trade barriers that cost the less-developed countries hundreds of billions of dollars in forgone sales. **Once again, this harm done to LDCs by developed country trade restrictions by far exceeds any amount of development assistance offered by rich countries to poor countries.**

EconNews

"Chiquita Going Bananas over Quotas"

Go to the International Trade category, and read more on the tariffs and trade restrictions.

http://econapps. swlearning.com

Finally, the patents owned by U.S. multinational corporations and agribusinesses prevent outsiders from producing genetically modified food and allow these large U.S. corporations to flood the world market with their agricultural products. Just as Green Revolution technology wasn't made available to many poor farmers in low-income countries in the past,[15] the new biotechnology is not available to poor farmers throughout the world today. In addition to health and environmental concerns about biotechnology, the most likely economic effects will be large increases in world food production, causing lower prices of agricultural products and preventing poor farmers from succeeding in agriculture. And it is the latter outcome that may serve to increase, rather than decrease, world hunger.

SUBSIDIES AND TRADE NEGOTIATIONS

The new round of international trade negotiations offers both optimism and frustration for the less-developed world. As discussed in more detail in Chapter 13 on international trade, the latest round of trade negotiations is called the Doha Round, named after the city of it location, Doha, Qatar. The Doha Round is also referred to as the "Development Round" and has the objective of assisting the economic development of less-developed countries. The optimistic side is that a "policy space" is now in place within which the world trading system can address the development needs of poor countries. The frustrating aspect is that little has been accomplished in this direction since the beginning of the round in 2001. The LDCs want a reduction in rich-country agricultural subsidies, from which the rich countries have so far refused to budge. We should closely watch international developments to discover the direction that the Doha Round will take. As this textbook goes to press, talks have continually broken down over the issue of developed country trade restrictions.

The Politics of U.S. Agricultural Policy

We've already noted that the benefits of government agricultural programs have mostly gone to large farms because subsidies have been designed to be paid on output or acres. In fact, by far, most of the benefits go to large farms and agribusinesses that earn more than $250,000 per year. According to the EWG, beneficiaries include 15 Fortune 500 companies and celebrities such as Sam Donaldson and Ted Turner. Payments to some of the Fortune 500 companies include $375,000 to International Paper Corporation, $269,000 to Westvaco Corporation, $260,000 to Chevron, and $189,000 to John Hancock Mutual Life Insurance. This compares with the average payment of $6,000 to the bottom 80 percent of farm subsidy recipients.[16] The Environmental Working Group has recently provided additional information on farm subsidies. A 2006 report assesses the "subsidy bonus" of 2005, which allocated 60 percent of the money to just the top 10 percent of recipients and 15 percent of the payments to just the top 1 percent of recipients. The latter received an average of over $21,000 per recipient. In contrast, the bottom 80 percent of recipients received about $370 each.[17]

No wonder some people ask why our taxpayers, many of whom have low or medium incomes themselves, should shift their earnings to higher-income farms. And why do farm payments dwarf expenditures for other programs that we've discussed in this text, including programs for education, environmental protection, poverty reduction, health care, and housing? And finally, why should high-income farmers and corporations receive government benefits when smaller farmers and other small business owners receive little, if any? What are the politics behind all this, and how could our policy be improved?

If most Americans are concerned about small- to medium-sized family farmers, then most farm payments should not go to the wealthiest farmers and agribusinesses. The fact that they do is the effect of politics and economics. How many consumer groups band together and advocate against farm policy that raises the price of food purchased in supermarkets? If you said none, you are probably right. *But*—how do you think the U.S. farm lobby compares with this diffuse and uninformed consumer group? Farm lobbying groups have organized in virtually every state in our nation. These groups are well financed by the large commercial farmers who use their vast financial resources to seek, not just beneficial agricultural policies, but policies that particularly benefit them as opposed to smaller farmers. Unfortunately, the smaller farmers that need the government benefits are neither informed about the effect of policies nor powerful as a lobbying group.

In addition, almost all members of the U.S. House of Representatives have at least one crop in their states whose producers vote pro-farmer. Senators are overrepresented by rural populations that vote pro-farmer as well. It is difficult to be re-elected when ignoring this group of farmers. Typically, lobbying and voting do not emphasize the need to target benefits to the poorest farmers. And, despite the publicity surrounding the Doha Round of trade talks, many legislators are still uninformed about or uninterested in the effect of our agricultural subsidies and trade policies on poor farmers in less-developed countries.

Can our agricultural policy be improved? Certainly! The 2007 Farm Bill presents the perfect opportunity for informed discussion and improved policy. First, politicians and the news media need to deflate the myths of the "Little House on the Prairie" farmer, as well as the myth that needy farmers benefit from our agricultural programs. Furthermore, our legislators should listen to our economists, who generally prefer programs that directly target needy groups, rather than policies that distort market prices and create poor incentives and disincentives (particularly the incentive to overproduce). One alternative is to untie the amount of food production from the amount of government benefit. Instead, the government might simply assure all farmers an adequate income, perhaps at twice the poverty line. If income for a full-time farmer falls below this, the government writes a check. If income for the farmer rises above this, the farmer receives no check. And, rather than distorting markets with artificial prices, the government can work on providing appropriate incentives (subsidies) to farmers who engage in environmental protection and appropriate disincentives (taxes) to farmers who do not engage in environmentally sound practices. This direct approach to incomes and the use of market incentives and disincentives for environmental protection would help to reduce the concentration in agricultural markets as well. Our policymakers should also pay attention to the special needs and issues of minority farmers, including farm workers. Finally, the problem of world hunger will not be solved until the problem of poverty is addressed. In this area, the world's wealthy countries have been called on to provide real development assistance rather than just food aid, and to reduce or eliminate their trade programs and agricultural subsidies that severely harm the well-being of less-developed country residents.

ViewPoint

CONSERVATIVE VERSUS LIBERAL

Conservative economists and politicians have argued for a long time that price supports, target prices, and supply restriction programs have contributed to our farm problem instead of solving it. Because of these programs, our country simply allocates too many resources to agriculture. Theoretically, conservatives would end virtually all farm programs and let market forces determine the outcomes for farmers. Also, by encouraging less government antitrust activity and fewer government environmental regulations (so that there is less government involvement in agricultural markets), the outcomes of conservative policy might be greater concentration in agricultural markets and unchecked environmental harm.

These conservative policies and outcomes might not actually take place, however, because politicians on both the left (liberal) and the right (conservative) face strong lobbying activity in favor of government programs that benefit farmers in their state. For example, conservative southern senators and representatives to Congress are under a great deal of pressure to support farm programs that benefit tobacco producers. There are other examples in almost every other state. And since large agribusinesses have more political power than do smaller farmers, the unequal distribution of the benefits of our farm programs has been accepted by many conservatives as a natural phenomenon.

Liberal economists and politicians, on the other hand, are more comfortable supporting agricultural programs both within and outside their states. Liberals do not wholeheartedly endorse the programs, however, and many believe that they should be gradually phased out. Their major objection to the programs is that the bulk of government payments go to large farms rather than small family farms. They would also like government efforts to reduce concentration in agricultural markets and to ensure environmental protection. Finally, globally minded economists and politicians are concerned about the effects of U.S. programs on the poor in less-developed countries.

Summary

Agriculture is characterized by inelastic demand in the short run, fluctuations in short-run supply, immobile resources, and such rapid technological change that supply has increased far more rapidly than demand. Thus, despite high productivity, agriculture has long been a troubled sector of the U.S. economy. Since the 1930s, government policies aimed at the farm problem have promoted the overallocation of resources to the agricultural sector. Furthermore, despite these policies, the proportion of our population engaged in farming has shrunk to about 1 percent. Supply restriction programs, price supports, and target prices have not saved the small American farm but instead have contributed to the farm problem.

Concentration has increased in agriculture, in part because of our farm policies. Policies that promote the greatest possible yield have proved self-defeating because they worsen the resource allocation problem and in the process increase concentration.

Finally, our farm policies affect the rest of the world. The policies of such a large and prosperous country can either help or hinder the development efforts of less-developed countries. Our agricultural subsidies and trade policies create harm. Food aid, development assistance, and biotechnology all become possible solutions or contributors to the problem of world hunger, depending on how they are managed.

Discussion and Action Questions

1. How does demand inelasticity affect farm prices and farmers' incomes? How does this issue compare between U.S. agricultural production and primary commodity production in less-developed countries (as discussed in Chapter 13 on international trade)?

2. What is the direction of the trend in concentration in farming? How have government programs contributed to this trend?

3. How do price floors interfere with the rationing function of price? Use price supports as an

example. Can you think of any other examples of price floors in our economy? (*Hint:* Remember that there are markets for *services* as well as for goods!)

4. Why don't supply restriction programs work well in increasing farm prices and incomes?

5. Do you believe that the government should be involved in agriculture? What kinds of policies would you suggest? Do you think that direct benefits to low-income farmers might be a possible solution?

6. Go to the Census Bureau Web site (http://www.census.gov). Look for information under *agriculture*. Can you find the number of farms in your state?

7. Visit the official Web site of the Department of Agriculture at http://www.usda.gov. What information can you find about current agricultural policy? What other type of material is available there?

8. Check out the statistical arm of the Department of Agriculture at http://www.nass.usda.gov. This site contains the latest of the agricultural censuses. Has the 2007 Farm Bill been enacted yet as you read this? If so, how does it differ from the 2002 bill?

9. Go to the Web site of the Farm Services Agency at http://www.fsa.usda.gov/pas/farmbill/fbfaqhome.asp. Read more about the latest Farm Bill, including the answers to frequently asked questions.

10. The Web site of the Food and Agriculture Organization of the United Nations (FAO) provides information about U.S. farm subsidies and how they affect the rest of the world. Go to the Web site at http://www.fao.org and investigate the effects of U.S. agricultural subsidies on the less-developed countries of the world. This site contains information about biotechnology, farm conservation, hazardous pesticides, and more.

11. Go to http://www.ewg.org to see the home page of the Environmental Working Group. This non-profit organization has assembled the records of farm benefits that have been paid to farmers as well as other types of information. Do you think this is a liberal or conservative Web site?

12. The USDA provides information that is not just beneficial to farmers. For example, go to the USDA Web site (http://www.usda.gov) and find information you may need about current food recalls!

13. Farmworker Justice is an organization dedicated to helping migrant and seasonal farm workers improve their working conditions and wages, labor and immigration policy, health and safety, and access to justice. Go to its Web site at http://www.fwjustice.org and find out more about these issues.

14. Have you ever thought about writing to your legislators about farm policy? Probably not! Have the issues raised in this chapter encouraged you to write such a letter? Do it!

15. For which nonfarm products is demand likely to be inelastic? Why is this the case? For which types of products is demand more likely to be elastic? (This topic is discussed in Appendix 1 of this chapter.)

16. How do target prices differ from price supports? Do different groups win or lose from these programs? (This topic is discussed in Appendix 2 of this chapter.)

Notes

1. The U.S. Department of Agriculture, Economic Research Service, *State Fact Sheets: United States*, http://www.ers.usda.gov/StateFacts/US. Estimated statistics for population are for 2005, income 2004, poverty rates 2003, and unemployment 2005. Unless otherwise indicated, other statistics in this chapter are from the same source.

2. Technically, the measure is "value added" and not simply "value." Value added refers to the additional value that the worker places on the product.

3. The U.S. Department of Agriculture, Economic Research Service, *State Facts: United States*, http://www.ers.usda.gov/StateFacts/US.

4. Willard W. Cochrane and C. Ford Runge, *Reforming Farm Policy* (Ames: Iowa State University Press, 1992), p. 21.

5. Jon Evert quoted in *Agriculture in the Global Economy: Hunger 2003* (Washington, DC: Bread for the World Institute, 2003), p. 44.

6. The Environmental Working Group (EWG), 2003 (http://www.ewg.org/farm).

7. Doug Harford quoted in *Agricultural in the Global Economy: Hunger 2003* (Washington, DC: Bread for the World Institute, 2003), p. 38.

8. Cochrane and Runge, *Reforming Farm Policy*, p. 22.

9. Ibid., p. 24.

10. The Environmental Working Group (EWG), 2003 (http://www.ewg.org/farm).

11. Bread for the World, *Agriculture in the Global Economy: Hunger 2003* (Washington, DC: Bread for the World Institute, 2003), p. 46.

12. Bread for the World, *Healthy Food, Farms & Families: Hunger 2007,* Washington, DC: Bread for the World Institute, 2007.

13. The Environmental Working Group, *USDA Stonewalls African American Farmers in Landmark Civil Rights Settlement,* http://www.ewg.org/reports/blackfarmers/execsumm, 2006.

14. Bread for the World Institute, Per Pinstrup-Anderson, "About Us," from the *2005 Annual Report on the State of World Hunger: Strengthening Rural Communities,* http://www.bread.org/about-us/institute/.

15. The Green Revolution consisted of new high-yielding seed varieties that were designed to withstand climate and other conditions in less-developed countries. If used with proper (and expensive) chemical fertilizers, irrigation, and other inputs, they resulted in greatly increased yields of wheat, rice, and corn. Larger and wealthier farmers were able to adapt the new seeds and corresponding inputs, causing large increases in food production, consequent reductions in food prices, and increases in their own incomes. The problem was that most poor people in LDCs are farmers who were unable to adapt the new seeds and corollary inputs, and who produced low yields sold at the prevailing low prices. Their incomes and standards of living suffered.

16. The Environmental Working Group (EWG), 2003 (http://www.ewg.org/farm).

17. The Environmental Working Group (EWG), *Bonus Subsidy 2006,* http://www.ewg.org/reports/agsupp2006/part5.

12 appendix 1

Inelastic Demand

The graph in Figure 12-5 shows the same hypothetical demand curve for corn that we discussed previously. The graph shows an initial equilibrium price of $3 per bushel and an initial equilibrium quantity of 5 million bushels. Now consider an increase in supply from S to S′ caused by exceptionally good weather. The equilibrium quantity increases to 6 million bushels, which is a relatively small increase of 20 percent. We calculate this increase in quantity by taking the 6 million bushels minus the 5 million bushels, giving us 1 million bushels. To express this in percentage terms, we take the 1 million bushels and divide by the original 5 million bushels, giving us a 20 percent reduction in quantity. This is shown in the following two steps:

1. 6 million bushels − 5 million bushels = 1 million bushels
2. 1 million bushels/5 million bushels = 1/5 = 0.20 = 20%

Recall that to transform a decimal (such as 0.20) into a percent (such as 20%), you would move the decimal two spaces to the right and add a percent sign.

Now consider the price change. Because of the inelastic demand, the effect of the supply shift on market price is great. The increase in supply causes the price to fall all the way to $2 per bushel, a decline of 50 percent. We calculate the 50 percent decline by taking $3 per bushel minus $2 per bushel, giving us a $1 per bushel price. To express this as a percent, we take the $1 and divide it by $2, giving us a 50 percent decrease in price. This is shown in the following two steps:

1. $3 per bushel − $2 per bushel = $1 per bushel
2. $1 per bushel/$2 per bushel = 1/2 = 0.50 = 50%

Alternatively, a relatively small decrease in supply caused by poor weather (from S to S″) would cause a large increase in price of 50 percent (up to $4 per bushel). **We summarize by stating that the combination of weather-related supply fluctuations and inelastic demand results in large fluctuations in agricultural prices in the short run.**

Now let's generalize the effects of an inelastic demand on farmers' *incomes* in the short run. We've already noted that if good weather causes an increase in supply, which causes price to decrease, then overall farm income will also fall. This is because income from a corn crop is equal to the number of units sold times the price at which they are sold. Refer again to Figure 12-5. At the initial price of $3, farmers sold 5 million bushels, earning income of $15 million from their corn crop. (Five million bushels times $3 per bushel is $15 million.) After the increase in supply, farmers sold 6 million bushels at a price of $2 per bushel. They earned only $12 million for their corn crop.

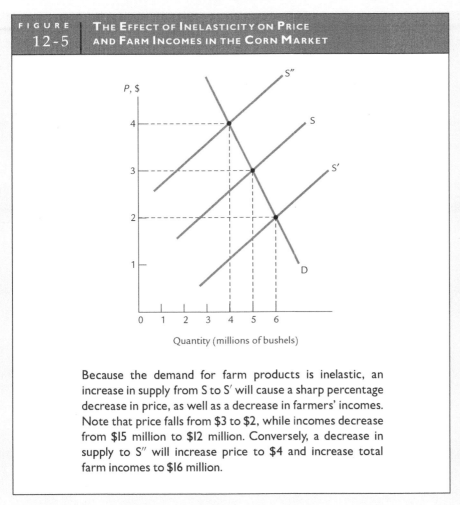

THE EFFECT OF INELASTICITY ON PRICE AND FARM INCOMES IN THE CORN MARKET

Because the demand for farm products is inelastic, an increase in supply from S to S′ will cause a sharp percentage decrease in price, as well as a decrease in farmers' incomes. Note that price falls from $3 to $2, while incomes decrease from $15 million to $12 million. Conversely, a decrease in supply to S″ will increase price to $4 and increase total farm incomes to $16 million.

Because the farmers face an inelastic demand, a short-run decrease in price results in a short-run decrease in farm income. Similarly, a short-run increase in price (from bad weather) results in a short-run increase in farm income. These outcomes, as well as the outcomes in situations in which demand is elastic (instead of inelastic), are shown in Table 12-4.

TABLE 12-4 **THE EFFECTS OF ELASTIC AND INELASTIC DEMAND ON TOTAL INCOME**

When demand is:	Then a decrease in price will cause:	And an increase in price will cause:
Inelastic	Farm income to fall	Farm income to rise
Elastic	Farm income to rise	Farm income to fall

12 appendix 2

Target Prices with Deficiency Payments

Target prices

A program in which farmers are paid the difference between the target price and the market price.

Deficiency payments

The target price minus the market price, multiplied by the number of units sold.

By the 1960s, the government had acquired huge surpluses under the price support program. Something had to be done. In many commodity markets, rigid price supports were replaced by flexible price supports based on past market prices. These price supports (loan rates) were markedly lower than those used previously. They became a less important instrument of farm policy for most commodities, whereas target prices became a more important instrument. Under target pricing, farmers received direct payments. These payments are called deficiency payments. They cover the gap between the target price and the actual market price.

Figure 12-6 illustrates how target pricing works. Suppose that policymakers determine that a $4.00 target price is justified by the costs of producing wheat, but

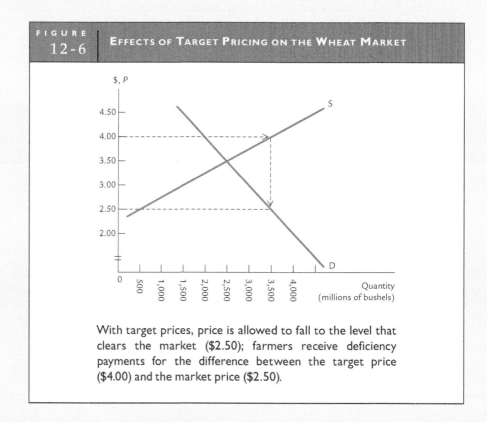

FIGURE 12-6 | EFFECTS OF TARGET PRICING ON THE WHEAT MARKET

With target prices, price is allowed to fall to the level that clears the market ($2.50); farmers receive deficiency payments for the difference between the target price ($4.00) and the market price ($2.50).

the market price is below $4.00. They establish $4.00 as the target price for wheat. At a target price of $4.00, farmers will offer 3,500 million bushels (quantity supplied) of wheat for sale.

Follow the arrow in the graph. The price at which buyers are willing to buy (quantity demanded) 3,500 million bushels is $2.50. So, the price will fall to $2.50, and the entire quantity supplied by farmers will be purchased. Farmers will receive $2.50 from the market for a bushel of wheat, but the government will send them a check for the difference between the target price ($4.00) and the market price ($2.50). So, for each bushel sold, the farmer will receive a government deficiency payment of $1.50. A farmer selling 10,000 bushels will receive a check for $15,000.

Target prices differ from the previously discussed price supports in a number of important ways. First, because the market price is much lower than the target price, the cost of farm commodities does not drive up the cost of food. Indeed, because target prices drive down the market price for farm products to below the free-market equilibrium, food is made cheaper for buyers. Second, because prices are lower for consumers whether they are in the U.S. or the export market, American farm products are more competitive on world markets at the lower prices. Of course, this causes the same problems for less-developed countries that we've already discussed. Third, the market is less distorted by target prices than by price supports, because no surplus is created. Finally, the costs to taxpayers of target prices and deficiency payments are easier to count because the costs associated with surpluses are not incurred.

Of course, some similarities occur between price supports, target prices, and supply restriction programs. They all result in a transfer of income from taxpayers to farmers. They all favor large-scale farmers over small farmers. And they all harm the exports of other nations, including the less-developed countries of the world.

index

Macroeconomics Fundamentals

part 3

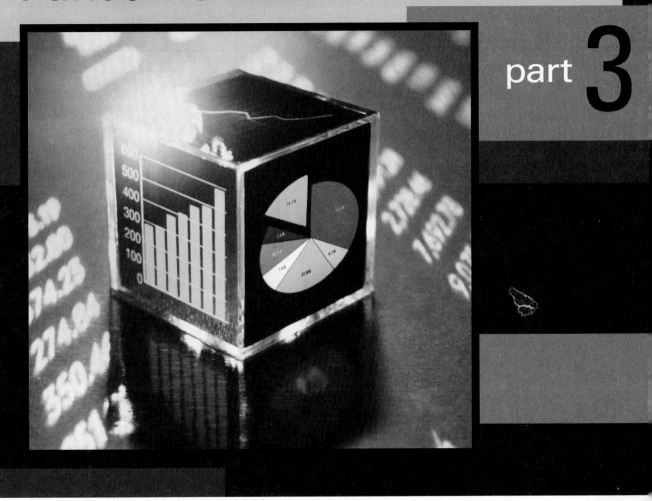

The three chapters in this part explain key measures of how well the macroeconomy is performing. Knowledge of this material is vital to the discussion of macro theory and policy in the next part. The first chapter in this part explains GDP computation. The next chapter begins by teaching how to measure business cycles and concludes with an examination of unemployment. The final chapter in this part explores the measurement and consequences of inflation.

chapter 5

Gross Domestic Product

Measuring the performance of the economy is an important part of life. Suppose one candidate for president of the United States proclaims that the economy's performance is the best in a generation, and the opposing presidential candidate argues that the economy could perform better. Which statistics would you seek to determine how well the economy is doing? The answer requires understanding some of the nuts and bolts of *national income accounting*. National income accounting is the system used to measure the aggregate income and expenditures for a nation. Despite certain limitations, the national income accounting system provides a valuable indicator of an economy's performance. For example, you can visit the Internet and check the annual *Economic Report of the President* to compare the size or growth of the U.S. economy between years.

Prior to the Great Depression, there were no national accounting procedures for estimating the data required to assess the economy's performance. To provide accounting methodologies for macro data, the late economist Simon Kuznets published a small report in 1934 titled *National Income, 1929–32*. For his pioneering work, Kuznets, the "father of GDP," earned the 1971 Nobel Prize in Economics. Today, thanks in large part to Kuznets, most countries use common national accounting methods. National income accounting serves a nation similar to the manner in which accounting serves a business or household. In each case, accounting methodology is vital for identifying economic problems and formulating plans for achieving goals.

In this chapter, you will learn to solve these economics puzzles:

- Why doesn't economic growth include increases in spending for welfare, Social Security, and unemployment programs?

- Can one newscaster report that the economy grew while another reports that for the same year the economy declined, and both reports be correct?

- How is the calculation of national output affected by environmental damage?

5-1 Gross Domestic Product

The most widely reported measure throughout the world of a nation's economic performance is gross domestic product (GDP), which is the market value of all final goods and services produced in a nation during a period of time, usually a year. GDP therefore excludes production abroad by U.S. businesses. For example, GDP excludes Microsoft's earnings on its foreign operations. On the other hand, GDP includes Toyota's profits from its car plants in the United States. Why is GDP important? It tells a country how well its economy is doing. One advantage of GDP is that it avoids the "apples and oranges" measurement problem. If an economy produces 10 apples one year and 10 oranges the next, can we say that the value of output has changed in any way? To answer this question, we must attach price tags in order to evaluate the relative monetary value of apples and oranges to society. This is the reason GDP measures value using dollars, rather than listing the number of cars, heart transplants, legal cases, toothbrushes, and tanks produced. Instead, the market-determined dollar value establishes the monetary importance of production. In GDP calculations, "money talks." That is, GDP relies on markets to establish the relative value of goods and services.

GDP is compiled by the Bureau of Economic Analysis (BEA), which is an agency of the Department of Commerce. GDP requires that the following two points receive special attention: (1) GDP counts only new domestic production, and (2) it counts only final goods.

5-1a GDP COUNTS ONLY NEW DOMESTIC PRODUCTION

National income accountants calculating GDP carefully exclude transactions in two major areas: secondhand transactions and nonproductive financial transactions.

Secondhand Transactions GDP includes only current transactions. It does not include the sale of a used car or the sale of a home constructed some years ago. Such transactions are merely exchanges of previously produced goods and not *current* production of new goods that add to the existing stock of cars and homes. Used items were counted previously in GDP for the year when they were newly produced. However, the sales commission on a used car or a home produced in another GDP period counts in current GDP because the salesperson performed a service during the present period of time.

Nonproductive Financial Transactions GDP does not count purely private or public financial transactions, such as giving private gifts, buying and selling stocks and bonds, and making transfer payments. A transfer payment is a government payment to individuals not in exchange for goods or services currently produced. Welfare, Social Security, veterans' benefits, and unemployment benefits are transfer payments. These transactions are considered nonproductive because they do not represent production of any new or *current* output. Transfer payments are made to people who are entitled to them. The reason could be because of being poor or reaching a certain age. Similarly, stock market transactions represent only the exchange of certificates of ownership (stocks) or indebtedness (bonds) and not actual new production.

Gross domestic product (GDP)

The market value of all final goods and services produced in a nation during a period of time, usually a year.

Transfer payment

A government payment to individuals not in exchange for goods or services currently produced.

5-1b GDP COUNTS ONLY FINAL GOODS

Final goods

Finished goods and services produced for the ultimate user.

The popular press usually defines GDP as simply "the value of all goods and services produced." This is technically incorrect because GDP counts only final goods, which are finished goods and services produced for the ultimate user. Including all goods and services produced would inflate GDP by *double counting* (counting many items more than once). In order to count only final goods and avoid overstating GDP, national income accountants must take care not to include intermediate goods. Intermediate goods are goods and services used as inputs for the production of final goods. Stated differently, intermediate goods are not produced for consumption by the ultimate user.

Intermediate goods

Goods and services used as inputs for the production of final goods.

Suppose a wholesale distributor sells glass to an automaker. This transaction is not included in GDP. The glass is an intermediate good used in the production of cars. When a customer buys a new car from the car dealer, the value of the glass is included in the car's selling price, which is the value of a final good counted in GDP. Let's consider another example. A wholesale distributor sells glass to a hardware store. GDP does not include this transaction because the hardware store is not the final user. When a customer buys the glass from the hardware store to repair a broken window, the final purchase price of the glass is added to GDP as a consumer expenditure.

5-2 Measuring GDP

GDP is like an enormous puzzle with many pieces to fit together, including markets for products, markets for resources, consumers spending and earning money, and businesses spending and earning money. How can one fit all these puzzle pieces together? One way to understand how all these concepts fit together is to use a simple macroeconomic model called the circular flow model. The circular flow model shows the exchange of money, products, and resources between households and businesses. In exchange for these resources, money payments flow between businesses and households. Exhibit 1 shows the circular flow in a hypothetical economy with no government, no financial markets, and no foreign trade. In this ultra-simple pure market economy, only the households and the businesses make decisions.

Circular flow model

A diagram showing the exchange of money, products, and resources between households and businesses.

5-2a THE CIRCULAR FLOW MODEL

The upper half of the diagram in Exhibit 1 represents *product markets*, in which households exchange money for goods and services produced by firms. The red *supply* arrow in the top loop represents all finished products and the value of services produced, sold, and delivered to consumers. The blue *demand* arrow in the top loop shows why the businesses make this effort to satisfy the consuming households. When consumers decide to buy products, they are actually voting with their dollars. This flow of consumption expenditures from households is sales revenues to businesses and expenses from the viewpoint of households. Notice that the box labeled *product markets* contains a supply and demand graph. This means the forces of supply and demand in individual markets determine the price and quantity of each product exchanged without government interference.

The bottom half of the circular flow diagram consists of the *factor markets*, in which firms *demand* the natural resources, labor, capital, and entrepreneurship needed to produce the goods and services sold in the product markets. Our hypothetical economy is capitalistic, and the model assumes for simplicity that households own the factors of production. Businesses therefore must purchase all their resources from the households. The red *supply* arrow in the bottom loop represents this flow of resources from households to firms, and the blue *demand* arrow is the flow of money payments to households for these resources. These

EXHIBIT 1	The Basic Circular Flow Model

In this simple economy, households spend all their income in the upper loop and demand consumer goods and services from businesses. Businesses seek profits by supplying goods and services to households through the product markets. Prices and quantities in individual markets are determined by the market supply and demand model. In the factor markets in the lower loop, resources (land, labor, and capital) are owned by households and supplied to businesses that demand these factors in return for money payments. The forces of supply and demand determine the returns to the factors, for example, wages and the quantity of labor supplied. Overall, goods and services flow clockwise, and the corresponding payments flow counterclockwise.

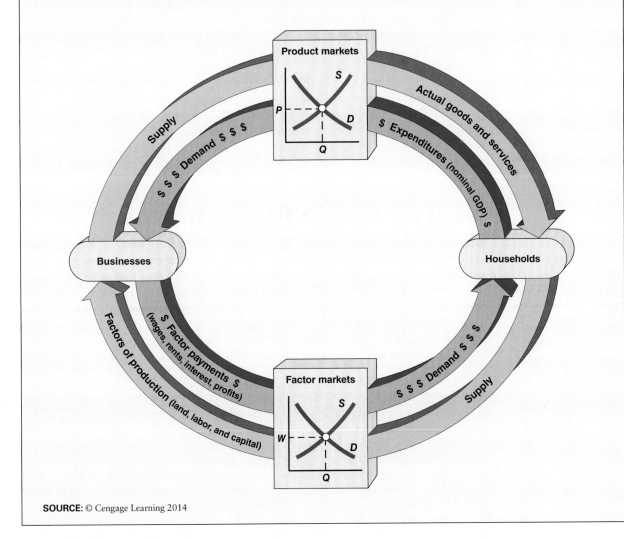

payments are also income earned by households in the form of wages, rents, interest, and profits. As in the product markets, market supply and demand determine the price and quantity of factor payments.

This simple model also assumes all households live from hand to mouth. That is, households spend all the income they earn in the factor markets on products. Households therefore do not save. Likewise, all firms spend all their income earned in the product markets on resources from the factor markets. The simple circular flow model therefore fails to mirror the real world. But it does aid your understanding of the relationships between product markets, factor markets, the flow of money, and the theory behind GDP measurement.

5-2b FLOW VERSUS STOCK

Flow

A rate of change in a quantity during a given time period, such as dollars per year. For example, income and consumption are flows that occur per week, per month, or per year.

Stock

A quantity measured at one point in time. For example, an inventory of goods or the amount of money in a checking account.

The arrows in Exhibit 1 are *flows*, rather than *stocks*. A flow is a rate of change in a quantity during a given time period. Changes in the amount of steel produced per month, the number of computer games purchased per day, the amount of income earned per year, and the number of gallons of water pouring into a bathtub per minute are examples of flows. Flows are always measured in units per time period, such as tons per month, billions of dollars per year, or gallons per hour. A stock is a quantity measured at one point in time. An inventory of goods, the amount of money in a checking account, and the amount of water in a bathtub are examples of stocks. Stocks are measured in tons, dollars, gallons, and so on, at a given point in time.

The important point is this: *All measurements in the circular flow model are rates of change (flows) and tell us nothing about the total amounts (stocks) of goods, services, money, or anything else in the economy.* Consumption expenditures, business production, wages, rents, interest payments, and profits are *flows* of money for newly produced products or resources that affect the level of *stocks* not shown in the model.

5-3 The Expenditure Approach

Expenditure approach

The national income accounting method that measures GDP by adding all the spending for final goods during a period of time.

How does the government actually calculate GDP? One way national income accountants calculate GDP is to use the expenditure approach to measure total spending flowing through product markets in the circular flow diagram. The expenditure approach measures GDP by adding all the spending for final goods during a period of time. Exhibit 2 shows 2011 GDP using the expenditure approach, which breaks down expenditures into four components. The data in this exhibit show that all production in the U.S. economy is ultimately purchased by spending from households, businesses, government, or foreigners. Let's discuss each of these expenditure categories.

5-3a PERSONAL CONSUMPTION EXPENDITURES (*C*)

The largest component of GDP in 2011 was $10.7 trillion for the category national income accountants call *personal consumption expenditures*, represented by the letter C. Personal consumption expenditures comprise total spending by households for durable goods, nondurable goods, and services. Durable goods include items such as automobiles, appliances, and furniture because they last longer than three

EXHIBIT 2	Gross Domestic Product Using the Expenditure Approach, 2011		
National income account		**Amount (trillions of dollars)**	**Percentage of GDP**
Personal consumption expenditures (*C*)		$10.7	71%
Durable goods	$1.2		
Nondurable goods	2.4		
Services	7.1		
Gross private domestic investment (*I*)		1.9	12
Fixed investment	1.9		
Change in business inventories	0.04		
Government consumption expenditures and gross investment (*G*)		3.0	20
Federal	1.2		
State and local	1.8		
Net exports of goods and services (*X − M*)		−0.5	−3
Exports (X)	2.1		
Imports (M)	2.6		
Gross domestic product (**GDP**)		$15.1	100%

SOURCE: Bureau of Economic Analysis, *National Economic Accounts*, http://www.bea.gov/national/nipaweb/SelectTable.asp?Selected=Y, Table 1.1.5.

years. Food, clothing, soap, and gasoline are examples of nondurables, because they are considered used up or consumed in less than these years. Services, which is the largest category, include recreation, legal advice, medical treatment, education, and any transaction not in the form of a tangible object. This is why the U.S. economy is often referred to as a service economy.

5-3b GROSS PRIVATE DOMESTIC INVESTMENT (*I*)

In 2011, $1.9 trillion was spent for what is officially called *gross private domestic investment* (*I*). This national income account includes "gross" (all) "private" (not government) "domestic" (not foreign) spending by businesses for investment in capital assets that are expected to earn profits in the future. Gross private domestic investment is the sum of two components: (1) *fixed investment* expenditures for newly produced capital goods, such as commercial and residential structures, machinery, equipment, tools, and computers, and (2) change in *business inventories*, which is the net change in spending for unsold finished goods. Note that gross private domestic investment is simply the national income accounting category for "investment," defined in Chapter 2. The only difference is that investment in Exhibit 5 in Chapter 2 was in physical capital, such as manufacturing plants, oil wells, or fast-food restaurants, rather than the dollar value of capital used here.

Now we will take a closer look at gross private domestic investment. Note that national income accountants include the rental value of newly constructed residential housing in the $1.9 trillion spent for fixed investment. A new factory, warehouse, or robot is surely a form of investment, but why include residential housing as business investment rather than consumption by households? The debatable answer is that a new home is considered investment because it provides services in the future that the owner can rent for financial return. For this reason, all newly produced housing is considered investment whether the owner rents or occupies the property.

Finally, the –$121 billion change in business inventories means this amount of net dollar value of unsold finished goods and raw materials was subtracted from the stock of inventories during 2011. A decline in inventories would reduce GDP because households consumed more output than firms produced during this year. When businesses have more on their shelves this year than last, more new production has taken place than has been consumed during this year.

5-3c GOVERNMENT CONSUMPTION EXPENDITURES AND GROSS INVESTMENT (*G*)

This official category simply called *government spending* includes the value of goods and services government at all levels purchased measured by their costs. For example, spending for police and state university professors enters the GDP accounts at the prices the government pays for them. In addition, the government spends for investment additions to its stock of capital, such as tanks, schools, highways, bridges, and government buildings. In 2011, federal, state, and local government spending (*G*) totaled $3.0 trillion. As the figures in Exhibit 2 reveal, government purchases by state and local governments far exceeded those of the federal government. It is important to understand that the government spending category of GDP excludes *transfer payments* because, as explained at the beginning of the chapter, they do not represent newly produced goods and services. Instead, transfer payments are paid to those entitled to Social Security benefits, veterans' benefits, welfare, unemployment compensation, and benefits from other programs.

5-3d NET EXPORTS (X – M)

The last GDP account is net exports, expressed in the formula (*X* − *M*). Exports (*X*) are spending by foreigners for U.S. domestically produced goods. Imports (*M*) are the dollar amount of U.S. purchases of Japanese automobiles, French wine, clothes from China, and other goods produced abroad. The positive sign (+*X*) means that money flows into the United States from foreigners to pay for our exports. The negative sign (−*M*) indicates dollars are flowing out of the United States to pay for imports. In 2011, export spending was $2.1 trillion and import spending was −$2.6 trillion. Net exports were therefore −$0.5 trillion. What is the effect of a negative sign for net exports? It means the United States is spending more dollars to purchase foreign products than it is receiving from abroad for U.S. goods. The effect of a negative net exports figure is to reduce U.S. GDP. Stated another way, higher exports (*X*) relative to imports (*M*) increases GDP. Prior to the early 1980s, the United States was a consistent net exporter, selling more goods and services to the rest of the world than we purchased from abroad. Since 1983, the United States has been a net importer. International trade is discussed in more detail in the last section of the text.

5-3e A FORMULA FOR GDP

Using the expenditure approach, GDP is expressed mathematically in trillions of dollars as

$$GDP = C + I + G + (X - M)$$

For 2011 (see Exhibit 2),

$$\$15.1 = \$10.7 + \$1.9 + \$3.0 + (\$2.1 - \$2.6)$$

This simple equation plays a central role in macroeconomics. It is the basis for analyzing macro problems and formulating macro policy. When economists study the macro economy, they can apply this equation to predict the behavior of the major sectors of the economy: consumption (C) is spending by households, investment (I) is spending by firms, government spending (G) is spending by the government, and net exports (X – M) is net spending by foreigners.

5-4 The Income Approach

The second, somewhat more complex approach to measuring GDP is the income approach. The income approach measures GDP by adding all the incomes earned by households in exchange for the factors of production during a period of time. Both the expenditure approach and the income approach yield identical GDP calculations. As shown in the basic circular flow model, each dollar of expenditure paid by households to businesses in the product markets means a dollar of income flows to households through the factor markets as a payment for the land, labor, and capital required to produce the product. Using the income approach, GDP is expressed as follows:

Income approach

The national income accounting method that measures GDP by adding all incomes, including compensation of employees, rents, net interest, and profits.

GDP = compensation of employees + rents + profits + net interest
+ indirect taxes + depreciation

In practice, it is necessary to add depreciation (capital consumption allowance) to factor payments so that national income equals GDP. Exhibit 3 presents actual 2011 GDP calculated following the income approach, and then each component is discussed in turn.

5-5 Compensation of Employees

Employees' compensation is the largest of the national income accounts. About 55 percent of GDP in 2011 ($8.3 trillion) was income earned from wages, salaries, and certain supplements paid by firms and government to suppliers of labor. Since labor services play such an important role in production, it is not surprising that employee compensation represents the largest share of the GDP income pie. The supplements consist of employer taxes for Social Security and unemployment

EXHIBIT 3	Gross Domestic Product Using the Income Approach, 2011	
National income account	Amount (trillions of dollars)	Percentage of GDP
Compensation of employees	$8.3	55%
Rental income	0.4	3
Profits	3.0	20
Proprietors' income	1.1	
Corporate profits	1.9	
Net interest	0.5	3
Indirect business taxes	1.2	8
Depreciation	1.7	11
Gross domestic product (GDP)	$15.1	100%

SOURCE: Bureau of Economic Analysis, *National Income Accounts*, http://www.bea.doc/bea.gov/national/nipaweb/SelectTable.asp?Selected=Y, Table 1.7.5.

insurance. Also included are fringe benefits from a variety of private health insurance and pension plans.

5-5a RENTAL INCOME

The smallest source of income is from rent and royalties received by property owners who permit others to use their assets during a time period. For example, this category includes house and apartment rents received by landlords. In 2011, $0.4 trillion was earned in rental income.

5-5b PROFITS

Proprietors' Income   All forms of income earned by unincorporated businesses totaled $1.1 trillion in 2011. Self-employed proprietorships and partnerships simultaneously own their businesses and pay themselves for labor services to their firms.

Corporate Profits   This income category includes all income earned by the stockholders of corporations regardless of whether stockholders receive it. The $1.9 trillion of corporate profits in 2011 was the sum of three sources: (1) dividends, (2) undistributed corporate profits (retained earnings for expanding plant and equipment), and (3) corporate income taxes. Thus, corporate profits using the income approach are "before taxes."

5-5c NET INTEREST

Households both receive and pay interest. Persons who make loans to businesses earn interest income. Suppose you purchase a bond issued by Apple. When Apple pays interest on its bonds, the interest payments are included in the national income accounts. Households also received interest from savings accounts and certificates of deposits (CDs). On the other hand, households borrow money and pay interest on, for example, credit cards, installment loans, and mortgage loans. The net interest of $0.5 trillion in 2011 is the difference between interest income earned and interest payments.

5-5d INDIRECT BUSINESS TAXES

As reported in Exhibit 3, $1.2 trillion was collected by government in the form of indirect business taxes. Why do national income accountants include business taxes in the income approach to GDP competition? Indirect business taxes are levied as a percentage of the prices of goods sold and therefore become part of the revenue received by firms. These taxes include sales taxes, federal excise taxes, license fees, business property taxes, and customs duties. Indirect taxes are not income payments to suppliers of resources. Instead, firms collect indirect taxes and send these funds to the government. Suppose you purchased a new automobile for $20,000, including a $1,000 federal excise tax and state sales tax. These taxes are included in the price, but are income for the government, which represents the public interest of households.

Indirect business taxes

Taxes levied as a percentage of the prices of goods sold and therefore collected as part of the firm's revenue. Firms treat such taxes as production costs. Examples include general sales taxes, excise taxes, and customs duties.

5-5e DEPRECIATION

To reconcile the above income accounts with GDP requires adding the category labeled *consumption of fixed capital*. Consumption of fixed capital is an estimate of the depreciation of capital. This somewhat imposing term is simply an allowance for the portion of capital worn out producing GDP. Over time, capital goods, such as buildings, machines, and equipment, wear out and become less valuable. Depreciation (capital consumption allowance) is therefore a portion of GDP that is not available for income payments. Because it is impossible to measure depreciation accurately, an estimate is entered. In 2011, $1.7 trillion was the estimated amount of GDP attributable to depreciation during the year.

Exhibit 4 presents the conceptual frameworks of the expenditure and income approaches to computing GDP.

✔ CHECKPOINT

How Much Does Mario Add to GDP?

Mario works part-time at Pizza Hut and earns an annual wage plus tips of $15,000. He sold 4,000 pizzas at $15 per pizza during the year. He was unemployed part of the year, so he received unemployment compensation of $3,000. During the past year, Mario bought a used car for $5,000. Using the expenditure approach, how much has Mario contributed to GDP?

EXHIBIT 4 | **Expenditure and Income Approaches to GDP**

Expenditure approach

Consumption (*C*)
  expenditures by households
    plus
Investment (*I*) expenditures
  by businesses
    plus
Government consumption
  expenditures and
  gross investment (*G*)
    plus
Net exports (*X – M*)
  expenditures by
  foreign economies

= GDP =

Income approach

Compensation of
  employees
    plus
Rents
    plus
Profits
    plus
Net Interest
    plus
Indirect business taxes
    plus
Depreciation

SOURCE: © Cengage Learning 2014

5-6 GDP in Other Countries

Exhibit 5 compares GDP for selected countries in 2011. The United States had the world's highest GDP, and China had the second largest GDP. U.S. GDP, for example, was about twice China's GDP.

5-7 GDP Shortcomings

For various reasons, GDP omits certain measures of overall economic well-being. Because GDP is the basis of government economic policies, there is concern that GDP may be giving us a false impression of the nation's material well-being. GDP is a less-than-perfect measure of the nation's economic pulse because it excludes the following factors.

5-7a NONMARKET TRANSACTIONS

Because GDP counts only market transactions, it excludes certain unpaid activities, such as homemaker production, child rearing, and do-it-yourself home repairs and services. For example, if you take your dirty clothes to the laundry, GDP increases by the amount of the cleaning bill paid. But GDP ignores the value of laundering these same clothes if you wash them yourself at home.

There are two reasons for excluding nonmarket activities from GDP. First, it would be extremely imprecise to attempt to collect data and assign a dollar value to services people provide for themselves or others without compensation. Second, it is difficult to decide which nonmarket activities to exclude and which ones to include. Perhaps repairing your own roof, painting your own house, and repairing your

| EXHIBIT 5 | An International Comparison of GDPs, 2011 |

This exhibit shows GDPs in 2011 for selected countries. The United States had the world's highest GDP, and China has the second largest GDP. U.S. GDP, for example, is about twice the size of China's GDP.

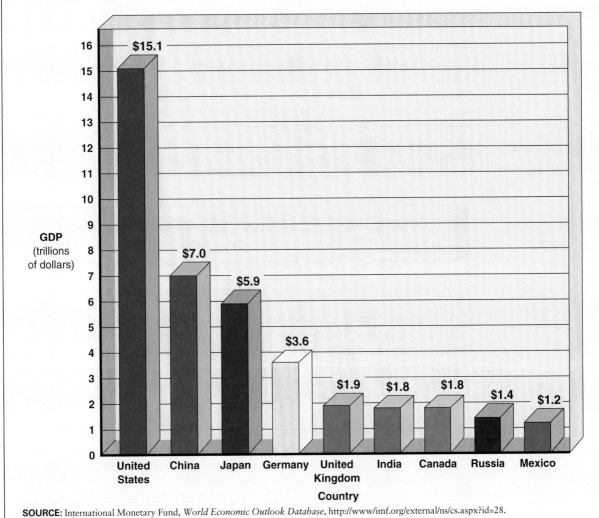

SOURCE: International Monetary Fund, *World Economic Outlook Database*, http://www.imf.org/external/ns/cs.aspx?id=28.

own car should be included. Now consider the value of washing your car. GDP does include the price of cleaning your car if you purchase that service at a car wash, so it could be argued that GDP should include the value of you washing your car at home.

The issue of unpaid do-it-yourself activities affects comparisons of the GDPs of different nations. One reason some less-developed nations have lower GDPs than major industrialized nations is that a greater proportion of people in less-developed nations farm, clean, make repairs, and perform other tasks for their families rather than hire someone else to do the work.

5-7b DISTRIBUTION, KIND, AND QUALITY OF PRODUCTS

GDP is blind to whether a small fraction of the population consumes most of a country's GDP or consumption is evenly divided. GDP also wears a blindfold with respect to the quality and kinds of goods and services that make up a nation's GDP. Consider the fictional economies of Zuba and Econa. Zuba has a GDP of $2,000 billion, and Econa has a GDP of $1,000 billion. At first glance, Zuba appears to possess superior economic well-being. However, Zuba's GDP consists of only military goods, and Econa's products include computers, cell phones, tractors, wheat, milk, houses, and other consumer items. Moreover, assume the majority of the people of Zuba could care less about the output of military goods and would be happier if the country produced more consumer goods. Now consider, for example, the difference in quality between a cell phone purchased today and a cell phone with only few capabilities purchased years ago. Such qualitative improvements are not reflected in GDP.

> **CONCLUSION:** *GDP is a quantitative, rather than a qualitative, measure of the output of goods and services.*

5-7c NEGLECT OF LEISURE TIME

GDP does not directly measure quality-of-life or "happiness" variables such as leisure time. In general, the wealthier a nation becomes, the more leisure time its citizens can afford. Rather than working longer hours, workers often choose to increase their time for recreation and travel. Since 1900, the length of the typical workweek in the United States declined steadily from about 50 hours to about 33 hours in 2011.[1] The last chapter discusses quality-of-life variables in more detail.

> **CONCLUSION:** *It can be argued that GDP understates national well-being because no allowance is made for people working fewer hours than they once did.*

5-7d THE UNDERGROUND ECONOMY

Illegal gambling, prostitution, loan-sharking, illegal guns, and illegal drugs are goods and services that meet all the requirements for GDP. They are final goods with a value determined in "black" markets, but GDP does not include unreported criminal activities because no record is made of these transactions. The "underground" economy also includes tax evasion. One way to avoid paying taxes on a legal activity is to trade or barter goods and services rather than selling them. One person fixes a neighbor's car in return for babysitting services, and the value of the

---

[1] *Economic Report of the President, 2012,* http://www.gpoaccess.gov/eop/, Table B-47.

exchange is unreported. Other individuals and businesses make legal sales for cash and do not report the income earned to the Internal Revenue Service.

Estimates of the size of this subterranean economy vary. Some studies by economists estimate the size of the underground sector is about 9 percent of GDP. This range of estimates is slightly less than the estimated size of the underground economy in most European countries.

> **CONCLUSION:** *If the underground economy is sizable, GDP will understate an economy's performance.*

5-7e ECONOMIC BADS

More production means a larger GDP, regardless of the level of pollution created in the process. Recall from Chapter 4 the discussion of *negative externalities*, such as pollution caused by steel mills, chemical plants, and cigarettes. Air, water, and noise pollution are *economic bads* that impose costs on society not reflected in private market prices and quantities bought and sold. When a polluting company sells its product, this transaction increases GDP. However, critics of GDP argue that it fails to account for the diminished quality of life from the "bads" not reported in GDP.

Stated another way, if production results in pollution and environmental damage, GDP overstates the nation's well-being.

> **CONCLUSION:** *Since the costs of negative by-products are not deducted, GDP overstates the national well-being.*

5-8 Other National Income Accounts

In addition to GDP, the media often report several other national income accounts because they are necessary for studying the macro economy. We now take a brief look at each.

5-8a NATIONAL INCOME (NI)

It can be argued that depreciation should be subtracted from GDP. Recall that GDP is not entirely a measure of newly produced output because it includes an estimated value of capital goods required to replace those worn out in the production process. The measurement designed to correct this deficiency is national income (NI), which is the gross domestic product minus depreciation of the capital worn out in producing output. Stated as a formula

NI = GDP − depreciation (consumption of fixed capital)

In 2011, $1.7 trillion was the estimated amount of GDP attributable to depreciation during the year. Exhibit 6 shows the actual calculation of NI from GDP in

National income (NI)

The total income earned by resource owners, including wages, rents, interest, and profits. NI is calculated as gross domestic product minus depreciation of the capital worn out in producing output.

Is GDP a False Beacon Steering Us into the Rocks?

Applicable Concept: national income accounting "goods" and "bads"

Suppose a factory in your community has been dumping hazardous wastes into the local water supply and people develop cancer and other illnesses from drinking polluted water. The Environmental Protection Agency (EPA) discovers this pollution and, under the federal "Superfund" law, orders a cleanup and imposes a fine for the damages. The company defends itself against the EPA by hiring lawyers and experts to take the case to court. After years of trial, the company loses the case and has to pay for the cleanup and damages.

In terms of GDP, an amazing "good" result occurs. The primary measure of national economic output, GDP, increases. GDP counts the millions of dollars spent to clean up the water supply. GDP even includes the health care expenses of anyone who develops cancer or other illnesses caused by drinking polluted water. GDP also includes the money spent by the company on lawyers and experts to defend itself against the EPA. And GDP includes the money spent by the EPA to regulate the polluting company.

Now consider what happens when trees are cut down and oil and minerals are used to produce houses, cars, and other goods. The value of the wood, oil, and minerals is an intermediate good implicitly computed in GDP because the value of the final goods is explicitly computed in GDP. Using scarce resources to produce goods and services therefore raises GDP and is considered a "good" result. On the other hand, don't we lose the value of trees, oil, and minerals in the production process, so isn't this a "bad" result?

The Bureau of Economic Analysis (BEA) is an agency of the U.S. Department of Commerce. The BEA is the nation's economic accountant, and it is the source of GDP data cited throughout this text. Critics have called for a new measure designed to estimate the kinds of damage described above. These new accounts would adjust for changes in air and water quality and depletion of oil and minerals. These accounts would also adjust for changes in the stock of renewable natural resources, such as forests and fish stocks. In addition, accounts should be created to measure global warming and destruction of the ozone layer.

As explained in this chapter, a dollar estimate of capital depreciation is subtracted from GDP to compute national income (NI). The argument here is that a dollar estimate of the damage to the environment should also be subtracted. To ignore measuring such environmental problems, critics argue, threatens future generations. In short, conventional GDP perpetuates a false dichotomy between economic growth and environmental protection.

Critics of this approach argue that assigning a dollar value to environmental damage and resource depletion requires a methodology that is extremely subjective and complex. Nevertheless, national income accountants have not ignored these criticisms, and the National Academy of Sciences has reviewed BEA proposals for ways to account for interactions between the environment and the economy.

Analyze the Issue

Suppose a nuclear power plant disaster occurs. How could GDP be a "false beacon" in this case?

Source: © Cengage Learning 2014

2011. NI measures how much income is *earned* by households that own and supply resources. It includes the total flow of payments to the owners of the factors of production, including wages, rents, interest, and profits. Another way to compute national income is to add compensation of employees, rents, profits, net interest, and indirect business taxes using the income approach demonstrated in Exhibit 3.

EXHIBIT 6	National Income Calculated from Gross Domestic Product, 2011
	Amount (trillions of dollars)
Gross domestic product (GDP)	$15.1
Depreciation	−1.7
National income (NI)	$13.4

SOURCE: Bureau of Economic Analysis, *National Economic Accounts*, http://www.bea.gov/national/nipaweb/SelectTable.asp?Selected=Y, Table 1.7.5.

Exhibit 7 illustrates the transition from GDP to NI and two other measures of the macro economy.[2]

5-8b PERSONAL INCOME (PI)

National income measures the total amount of money *earned*, but determining the amount of income actually *received* by households (not businesses) requires a measurement of personal income (PI). Personal income is the total income received by households that is available for consumption, saving, and payment of personal taxes. Suppose we want to measure the total amount of money individuals receive that they can use to consume products, save, and pay taxes. National income is not the appropriate measure for two reasons. First, NI excludes transfer payments, which constitute unearned income that can be spent, saved, or used to pay taxes. Second, NI includes corporate profits, but stockholders do not receive all these profits. A portion of corporate profits is paid in corporate taxes. Also, retained earnings are not distributed to stockholders, but are channeled back into business operations.

Exhibit 7 illustrates the relationship between personal income and national income, and Exhibit 8 gives the figures for 2011. National income accountants adjust national income by subtracting corporate profits and payroll taxes for Social Security (FICA deductions). Next, *transfer payments* and other income individuals receive from net interest and dividends are added. The net result is the personal income received by households, which in 2011 amounted to $13.0 trillion.

Personal income (PI)

The total income received by households that is available for consumption, saving, and payment of personal taxes.

5-8c DISPOSABLE PERSONAL INCOME (DI)

One final measure of national income is shown at the far right of Exhibit 7. Disposable personal income (DI) is the amount of income that households actually have to spend or save after payment of personal taxes. Disposable, or *after-tax*,

Disposable personal income (DI)

The amount of income that households actually have to spend or save after payment of personal taxes.

[2]As a result of a revision in national income accounting, the only difference between net domestic product (NDP) and national income (NI) is a statistical discrepancy. Because NI is more widely reported in the media, and to simplify, NDP is not calculated here.

EXHIBIT 7	Four Measures of the Macro Economy

The four bars show major measurements of the U.S. macro economy in 2011 in trillions of dollars. Beginning with gross domestic product, depreciation is subtracted to obtain national income. Next, personal income equals national income minus corporate profits and contributions for Social Security insurance (FICA payments) plus transfer payments and other income. Subtracting personal taxes from personal income yields disposable personal income.

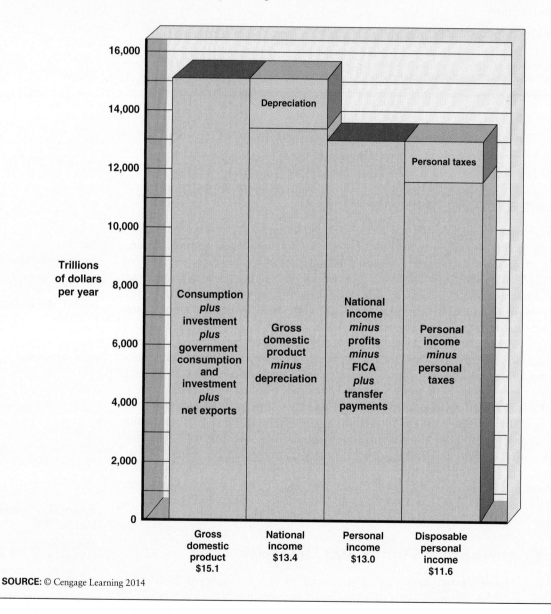

SOURCE: © Cengage Learning 2014

income is equal to personal income minus personal taxes paid to federal, state, and local governments. Personal taxes consist of personal income taxes, personal property taxes, and inheritance taxes. As tabulated in Exhibit 9, disposable personal income in 2011 was $11.6 trillion.

EXHIBIT 8	Personal Income Calculated from National Income, 2011	
		Amount (trillions of dollars)
National income (NI)		$13.4
Corporate profits		−1.9
Contributions for Social Security (FICA)		−0.9
Transfer payments and other income		2.4
Personal income (PI)		$13.0

SOURCE: Bureau of Economic Analysis, *National Economic Accounts*, http://www.bea.gov/national/nipaweb/SelectTable.asp?Selected=Y, Table 1.7.5.

5-9 Changing Nominal GDP to Real GDP

So far, GDP has been expressed as nominal GDP. Nominal GDP is the value of all final goods based on the prices existing during the time period of production. Nominal GDP is also referred to as *current-dollar* or *money GDP*. Nominal GDP grows in three ways. First, output rises and prices remain unchanged. Second, prices rise and output is constant. Third, in the typical case, both output and prices rise. The problem, then, is how to adjust GDP so it reflects only changes in output and not changes in prices. This adjusted GDP allows meaningful comparisons over time when prices are changing.

Changing prices can have a huge impact on how we compare dollar figures. Suppose a newspaper headline reports that a film entitled *The History of Economic Thought* is the biggest box-office sales movie of all time. You ask, How can this be? What about *Gone with the Wind*? Reading the article reveals that this claim is based on the nominal measure of gross box-office receipts. This gives a recent movie with higher ticket prices an advantage over a movie released in 1939 when the average ticket price was about $1. A better measure of popularity would be to compare "real" box-office receipts by multiplying actual attendance figures for each movie by a base year movie price.

Measuring the difference between changes in output and changes in the price level involves making an important distinction between nominal GDP and real GDP. Real GDP is the value of all final goods produced during a given time period based on the prices existing in a selected base year. The U.S. Department of Commerce currently uses 2005 prices as the base year. Real GDP is also referred to as *constant dollar GDP*.

5-9a THE GDP CHAIN PRICE INDEX

The most broadly based measure used to take the changes-in-the-price-level "air" out of the nominal GDP "balloon" and compute real GDP is officially called the GDP chain price index. The GDP chain price index is a measure that compares

Nominal GDP

The value of all final goods based on the prices existing during the time period of production.

Real GDP

The value of all final goods produced during a given time period based on the prices existing in a selected base year.

GDP chain price index

A measure that compares changes in the prices of all final goods during a given year to the prices of those goods in a base year.

EXHIBIT 9	Disposable Personal Income Calculated from Personal Income, 2011
	Amount (trillions of dollars)
Personal income (PI)	$13.0
Personal taxes	−1.4
Disposable personal income (DI)	$11.6

SOURCE: Bureau of Economic Analysis, *National Economic Accounts*, http://www.bea.gov/national/nipaweb/SelectTable.asp?Selected=Y, Table 2.1.

changes in the prices of all final goods produced during a given time period relative to the prices of those goods in a base year. The GDP chain price index is a broad "deflator" index calculated by a complex chain-weighted geometric series (you are spared the details). It is highly inclusive because it measures not only price changes of consumer goods, but also price changes of business investment, government purchases, exports, and imports. Do not confuse the GDP chain price index with the *consumer price index* (CPI), which is widely reported in the news media. The CPI is a different index, measuring only consumer prices, which we will discuss in the chapter on inflation.

Now it's time to see how the GDP chain price index works. We begin with the following conversion equation:

$$\text{Real GDP} = \frac{\text{nominal GDP}}{\text{GDP chain price index}} \times 100$$

Using 2005 as the base year, suppose you are given the 2011 nominal GDP of $15.1 trillion and the 2011 GDP chain price index of 113.5. To calculate 2011 real GDP, use the above formula as follows:

$$\$13.3 \text{ trillion} = \frac{\$15.1 \text{ trillion}}{113.5} \times 100$$

Exhibit 10 shows actual U.S. nominal GDP, real GDP, and the GDP chain price index for selected years. Column (1) reports nominal GDP, column (2) gives real GDP figures for these years, and column (3) lists corresponding GDP chain price indexes. Notice that the GDP chain price index exceeds 100 in years beyond 2005. This means that prices, on average, have risen since 2005, causing the real purchasing power of the dollar to fall. In years before 2005, the GDP chain price index is less than 100, which means the real purchasing power of the dollar was higher relative to the 2005 base year. At the base year of 2005, nominal and real GDP are identical, and the GDP price index equals 100.

The graph in Exhibit 10 traces real GDP and nominal GDP for the U.S. economy since 1960. Note that nominal GDP usually grows faster than real GDP because inflation is included in the nominal figures. For example, if we calculate the economy's average rate in nominal GDP between 1990 and 2000, we find it was 7.2 percent. If instead we calculate average real GDP growth between the

EXHIBIT 10 | Nominal GDP, Real GDP, and the GDP Chain Price Index for Selected Years

Real GDP reflects output valued at 2005 base-year prices, but nominal GDP is annual output valued at prices prevailing during the current year. The intersection of real and nominal GDP occurs in 2005 because in the base year, both nominal GDP and real GDP measure the same output at 2005 prices. Note that the nominal GDP curve has risen more sharply than the real GDP curve as a result of inflation included in the nominal figures.

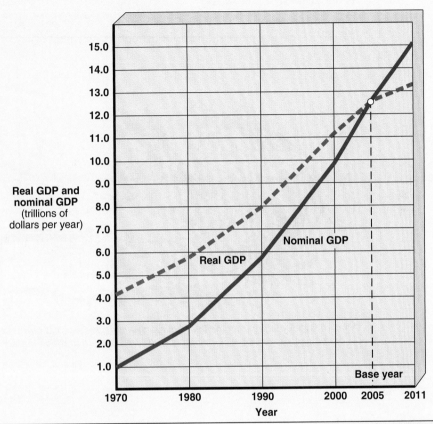

Year	(1) Nominal GDP (trillions of dollars)	(2) Real GDP (trillions of 2005 dollars)	(3) GDP chain price index (2005 = 100)
1970	1.0	4.3	23.3
1980	2.8	5.8	48.3
1990	5.8	8.0	72.5
2000	9.9	11.2	88.4
2005	12.6	12.6	100.0
2011	15.1	13.3	113.5

SOURCE: Bureau of Economic Analysis, *National Economic Accounts*, http://www.bea.gov/national/nipaweb/ SelectTable.aspSelected=Y, Tables 1.1.5, 1.1.6, and *Economic Report of the President*, http://www.gpoaccess.gov/ eop/, Tables B-1, B-2, and B-7.

same years, we find the growth rate was 4.0 percent. You must therefore pay attention to which GDP is being used in an analysis.

✓ CHECKPOINT

Is the Economy Up or Down?

One person reports, "GDP rose this year by 8.5 percent." Another says, "GDP fell by 0.5 percent." Can both reports be right?

"And so, extrapolating from the best figures available, we see that current trends, unless dramatically reversed, will inevitably lead to a situation in which the sky will fall."

Key Concepts

Gross domestic product (GDP)
Transfer payment
Final goods
Intermediate goods
Circular flow model
Flow

Stock
Expenditure approach
Income approach
Indirect business taxes
National income (NI)
Personal income (PI)

Disposable personal income (DI)
Nominal GDP
Real GDP
GDP chain price index

Summary

- **Gross domestic product (GDP)** is the most widely used measure of a nation's economic performance. GDP is the market value of all

final goods produced in the United States during a period of time, regardless of who owns the factors of production. Secondhand and financial transactions are not counted in GDP. To avoid double counting, GDP also does not include **intermediate goods**. GDP is calculated by either the expenditure approach or the income approach.

- The **circular flow model** is a diagram representing the flow of products and resources between businesses and households in exchange for money payments. **Flows** must be distinguished from **stocks**. Flows are measured in units per time period—for example, dollars per year. Stocks are quantities that exist at a given point in time measured in dollars.

- The **expenditure approach** sums the four major spending components of GDP consumption, investment, government spending, and net exports. Algebraically, GDP = $C + I + G + (X - M)$, where X equals foreign spending for domestic exports and M equals domestic spending for foreign products.

- The **income approach** sums the major income components of GDP, consisting of compensation of employees, rents, profits, net interest, **indirect business taxes**, and depreciation. Indirect business taxes are levied as a percentage of product prices and include sales taxes, excise taxes, and customs duties.

- **National income (NI)** is total income *earned* by households that own and supply resources. It is calculated as GDP minus depreciation.

- **Personal income (PI)** is the total income *received* by households and is calculated as NI minus corporate taxes and Social Security taxes plus transfer payments and other income.

- **Disposable personal income (DI)** is personal income minus personal taxes. DI is the amount of income a household has available to consume or save.

Circular Flow Model

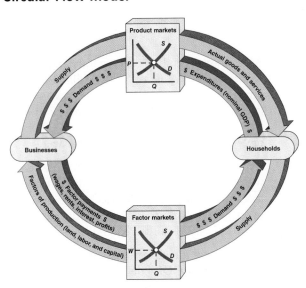

SOURCE: © Cengage Learning 2014

Measures of the Macro Economy

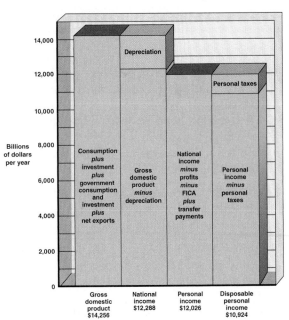

SOURCE: © Cengage Learning 2014

- **Nominal GDP** measures all final goods and services produced in a given time period valued at the prices existing during the time period of production.
- **Real GDP** measures all final goods and services produced in a given time period valued at the prices existing in a base year.
- The **GDP chain price index** is a broad price index used to convert nominal GDP to real

GDP. The GDP chain price index measures changes in the prices of consumer goods, business investment, government spending, exports, and imports. Real GDP is computed by dividing nominal GDP for year X by year X's GDP chain price index and then multiplying the result by 100.

Summary of Conclusion Statements

- GDP is a quantitative, rather than a qualitative, measure of the output of goods and services.
- It can be argued that GDP understates national well-being because no allowance is made for people working fewer hours than they once did.

- If the underground economy is sizable, GDP will understate an economy's performance.
- Because the costs of negative by-products are not deducted, GDP overstates our national well-being.

Study Questions and Problems

1. Which of the following are final goods or services, and which are intermediate goods or services?
   a. A haircut purchased from a hair salon
   b. A new automobile
   c. An oil filter purchased in a new automobile
   d. Crude oil

2. Using the basic circular flow model, explain why the value of businesses' output of goods and services equals the income of households.

3. A small economy produced the following final goods and services during a given month: 3 million pounds of food, 50,000 shirts, 20 houses, 50,000 hours of medical services, 1 automobile plant, and 2 tanks. Calculate the value of this output at the following market prices:

   - $1 per pound of food
   - $20 per shirt
   - $50,000 per house
   - $20 per hour of medical services
   - $1 million per automobile plant
   - $500,000 per tank

4. An economy produces final goods and services with a market value of $5,000 billion in a given year, but only $4,500 billion worth of goods and services is sold to domestic or foreign buyers. Is this nation's GDP $5,000 billion or $4,500 billion? Explain your answer.

5. Explain why a new forklift sold for use in a warehouse is a final good even though it is fixed investment (capital) used to produce other goods. Is there a double-counting problem if this sale is added to GDP?

6. Explain why the government spending (G) component of GDP falls short of actual government expenditures.

7. Explain how net exports affect the U.S. economy. Describe both positive and negative impacts on GDP. Why do national income accountants use net exports to compute GDP, rather than simply adding exports to the other expenditure components of GDP?

8. Suppose the data in Exhibit 11 are for a given year from the annual *Economic Report of the President*. Calculate GDP using the expenditure and income approaches.

EXHIBIT 11	National Income Data
	Amount (billions of dollars)
Corporate profits	$ 305
Depreciation	479
Gross private domestic investment	716
Personal taxes	565
Personal saving	120
Government spending	924
Imports	547
Net interest	337
Compensation of employees	2,648
Rental income	19
Exports	427
Personal consumption expenditures	2,966
Indirect business taxes	370
Contributions for Social Security (FICA)	394
Transfer payments and other income	967
Proprietors' income	328

SOURCE: © Cengage Learning 2014

9. Using the data in Exhibit 11, compute national income (NI) by making the required subtraction from GDP. Explain why NI might be a better measure of economic performance than GDP.

10. Again using the data from Exhibit 11, derive personal income (PI) from national income (NI). Then make the required adjustments to PI to obtain disposable personal income (DI).

11. Suppose U.S. nominal GDP increases from one year to the next year. Can you conclude that these figures present a misleading measure of economic growth? What alternative method would provide a more accurate measure of the rate of growth?

12. Which of the following are counted in this year's GDP? Explain your answer in each case.
    a. Flashy Car Company sold a used car.
    b. Juanita Jones cooked meals for her family.
    c. IBM paid interest on its bonds.
    d. José Suarez purchased 100 shares of Microsoft stock.
    e. Bob Smith received a welfare payment.
    f. Carriage Realty earned a brokerage commission for selling a previously owned house.
    g. The government makes interest payments to persons holding government bonds.
    h. Air and water pollution increase.
    i. Gambling is legalized in all states.
    j. A retired worker receives a Social Security payment.

13. Explain why comparing the GDPs of various nations might not tell you which nations are better off.

For Online Exercises, go to the Tucker Web site at www.cengage.com/economics/tucker.

✓ CHECKPOINT ANSWERS

How Much Does Mario Add to GDP?

Measuring GDP by the expenditure approach, Mario's output production is worth $60,000 because consumers purchased 4,000 pizzas at $15 each. Transfer payments and purchases of goods produced in other years are excluded from GDP. The $3,000 in unemployment compensation received and the $5,000 spent for a used car are therefore not counted in GDP. Mario's income of $15,000 is also not counted using the expenditure approach. If you said using the expenditure approach to measure GDP, Mario contributed $60,000 to GDP, **YOU ARE CORRECT.**

Is the Economy Up or Down?

Between 1973 and 1974, for example, nominal GDP rose from $1,382 to $1,500 billion—an 8.5 percent increase. During the same period, real GDP fell from $4,917 to $4,890 billion—a 0.5 percent decrease. If you said both reports can be correct because of the difference between nominal and real GDP, **YOU ARE CORRECT.**

Sample Quiz

For an explanation of the correct answers, visit the Tucker Web site at www.cengage.com/economics/tucker.

1. Gross domestic product is officially measured by adding together the
   a. quantity of each good and service produced by U.S. residents.
   b. market value of all final goods and services produced within the borders of a nation.
   c. quantity of goods and services produced by companies owned by U.S. citizens.
   d. None of the answers above are correct.

2. Which of the following items is included in the calculation of GDP?
   a. purchase of 100 shares of Microsoft stock
   b. purchase of a used car
   c. the value of a homemaker's services
   d. sale of Gulf War military surplus
   e. None of the above would be included.

3. Which of the following expenditures would *not* be included in GDP?
   a. purchase of a new lawnmower
   b. purchase of a silver cup previously sold new in 1950

   c. purchase of a ticket to the latest movie
   d. All of the above would be counted in GDP.

4. Gross domestic product (GDP) includes
   a. intermediate as well as final goods.
   b. foreign goods as well as domestically produced goods.
   c. used goods sold in the current time period.
   d. only final goods and services.

5. GDP includes
   a. the negative attributes in our quest for more goods and services, such as soil erosion and deforested landscape.
   b. all quality improvements resulting from higher-quality goods replacing inferior goods.
   c. the cleanup expenses associated with pollution.
   d. the value of leisure time.

Sample Quiz *continued*

6. The largest component of GDP is
   a. personal consumption expenditures.
   b. government spending.
   c. durable goods.
   d. net exports.

7. The circular flow of economic activity is a model of the
   a. flow of goods, resources, payments, and expenditures between the sectors of the economy.
   b. influence of government on business behavior.
   c. influence of business on consumers.
   d. role of unions and government in the economy.

8. All final goods and services that make up GDP can be expressed as
   a. $GDP = C + I - G + (X + M)$.
   b. $GDP = C + I + G + (X + M)$.
   c. $GDP = C + I + G + (X - M)$.
   d. $GDP = C + I + (X - M)$.
   e. $GDP = C + I + G$.

9. The expenditure approach for the calculation of GDP includes spending on
   a. consumption, investment, durable goods, and exports.
   b. consumption, gross private domestic investment, government spending for goods and services, and exports.
   c. consumption, gross private domestic investment, government spending for goods and services, and net exports.
   d. consumption, net private domestic investment, government spending for goods and services, and net exports.
   e. consumption, gross private domestic investment, all government spending including transfer payments, and net exports.

10. Which of the following is a shortcoming of GDP?
    a. GDP excludes changes in inventories.
    b. GDP includes an estimate of illegal transactions.

c. GDP excludes nonmarket transactions.
d. GDP excludes business investment spending.

11. National income (NI) is calculated by adjusting GDP for
    a. depreciation.
    b. investment and net exports.
    c. Social Security insurance contributions and transfer payments.
    d. corporate and personal income taxes.

12. Which of the following is included in personal income but *not* in national income?
    a. compensation for workers
    b. proprietors' income
    c. corporate profits
    d. Social Security payments

13. Which national income account should be examined to discover trends in the after-tax income that people have to save and spend?
    a. gross domestic product (GDP)
    b. gross national product (GNP)
    c. national income (NI)
    d. disposable personal income (DI)

14. The equation for determining real GDP for year X is
    a. $\dfrac{\text{nominal GDP for year } X}{\text{average nominal GDP}}$.
    b. $\dfrac{\text{nominal GDP for year } X}{\text{GDP for year } X} - 100$.
    c. $\dfrac{\text{nominal GDP for year } X}{\text{GDP chain price index for year } X} \times 100$.
    d. $\dfrac{\text{nominal GDP for year } X}{\text{average family income}} \times 100$.

15. The most broadly based price index is the
    a. real GDP price index.
    b. consumer price index.
    c. producer price index.
    d. GDP chain price index.

16. Which of the following would be counted as a final good for inclusion in GDP?
    a. a piece of glass bought this year by a consumer to fix a broken window
    b. a sheet of glass produced this year by Ford to use for windows in a new car

Sample Quiz *continued*

c. a tire produced this year and sold to a car maker for a new car sold this year

d. None of the answers are correct.

17. Based on the circular flow model, money flows from households to businesses in
   a. factor markets.
   b. product markets.
   c. neither factor nor product markets.
   d. both factor and product markets.

18. If the underground economy is sizable, GDP will
   a. understate the economy's performance.
   b. overstate the economy's performance.
   c. fluctuate unpredictably.
   d. accurately reflect this subterranean activity.

19. The income that people earn in resource or factor markets is called
   a. national income.
   b. personal income.
   c. disposable personal income.
   d. transfer payments.
   e. net national product.

20. Increased production, but *not* increased inflation, will result in higher
   a. nominal GDP.
   b. money GDP.
   c. real GDP.
   d. current dollar GDP.

A Four-Sector Circular Flow Model

5

Sound the trumpets! This exhibit is going to put all the puzzle pieces together. Exhibit A-1 presents a more complex circular flow model by adding three sectors: financial markets, government, and foreign markets. In addition to the spending of households for the output of firms shown in the simplified model in Exhibit A-1, these additions add three *leakages* from the amount of income paid to households. First, part of households' income is saved. Second, part of it is taxed. Third, part of the income is spent on imports. On the other hand, this model includes three sources of spending *injections* for firms' output other than from households. First, firms purchase new plants, equipment, and inventories (investment) from other firms. Second, government consumption purchases are for goods and services from firms. Third, foreigners purchase exports from the firms.

This exhibit presents a circular flow model for an economy, such as the United States, that engages in international trade. The theoretical model includes links between the product and factor markets in the domestic economy and the financial markets, government, and foreign economies. To simplify the model, only dollar payments are shown for the foreign sector.

EXHIBIT A-1	The Circular Flow Model of an Open Economy

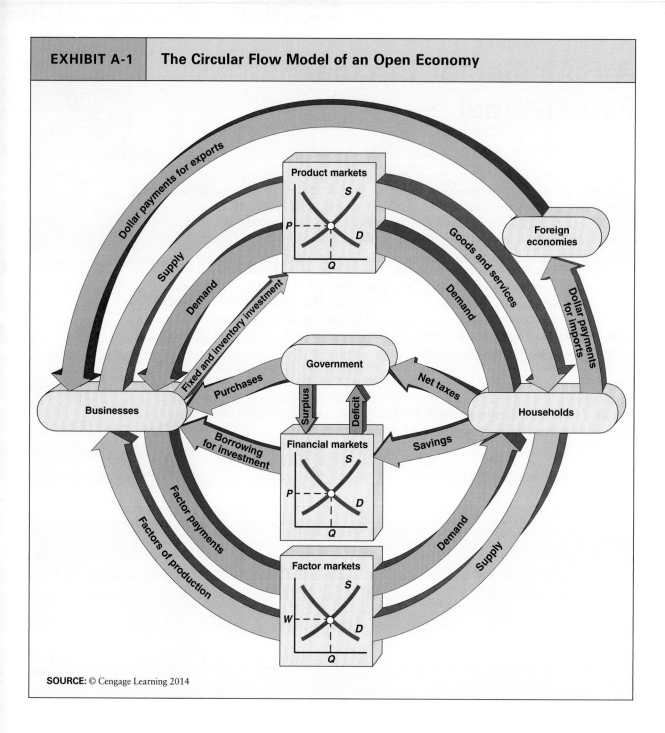

chapter 6

Business Cycles and Unemployment

The headline in the morning newspaper reads, "The Economy is in Deep Recession." Later in the day, a radio announcer begins the news by saying, "The unemployment rate rose for the tenth consecutive month." On television, the evening news broadcasts an interview with several economists who predict that the slump will last for another year. Next, a presidential candidate appears on the screen and says, "It's time for change," and the media are abuzz with speculation on the political implications. The growth rate of the economy and the unemployment rate are headline-catching news. Indeed, these measures of macroeconomic instability are important because they affect your future. When real GDP rises and the economy "booms," jobs are more plentiful. A fall in real GDP means a "bust" because the economy forces some firms into bankruptcy and workers lose their jobs. Not being able to find a job when you want one is a painful experience not easily forgotten.

This chapter looks behind the macro economy at a story that touches each of us. It begins by discussing the business cycle. How are the expansions and contractions of business cycles measured? And what causes the business-cycle roller coaster? Finally, you will learn what the types of unemployment are, what "full employment" is, and what the monetary, nonmonetary, and demographic costs of unemployment are.

In this chapter, you will learn to solve these economics puzzles:

- What is the difference between a recession and a depression?
- Is a worker who has given up searching for work counted as unemployed?
- Can an economy produce more output than its potential?

6-1 The Business-Cycle Roller Coaster

A central concern of macroeconomics is the upswings and downswings in the level of real output called the business cycle. The business cycle consists of alternating periods of economic growth and contraction. Business cycles are inherent in market economies. Market-based economies are driven by ever-changing forces of supply and demand. A key measure of cycles is the rise and fall in real GDP, which mirrors changes in employment and other key measures of the macro economy. Recall from the previous chapter that changes in real GDP measure changes in the value of national output, while ignoring changes in the price level.

6-1a THE FOUR PHASES OF THE BUSINESS CYCLE

Exhibit 1(a) illustrates a theoretical business cycle. Although business cycles vary in duration and intensity, each cycle is divided into four phases: *peak, recession, trough,* and *recovery*. The business cycle looks like a roller coaster. It begins at a peak, drops to a bottom, climbs steeply, and then reaches another peak. Once the trough is reached, the upswing starts again. Although forecasters cannot precisely predict the phases of a cycle, the economy is always operating along one of these phases. Over time, there has been a long-term upward trend with shorter-term cyclical fluctuations around the long-run trend.

Two peaks are illustrated in Exhibit 1(a). At each of these peaks, the economy is close to or at full employment. At a peak, real GDP reaches its maximum. That is, as explained in Chapter 2, the economy is operating near its production possibilities curve, and real GDP is at its highest level relative to recent years. However, a peak is a temporary high point. A macro setback called a recession (or *contraction*) follows each peak. A recession is a downturn in the business cycle during which real GDP declines, business profits fall, the percentage of the workforce without jobs rises, and production capacity is underutilized. A general rule is that a recession consists of at least two consecutive quarters (six months) in which there is a decline in real GDP. Stated differently, during a recession, the economy is functioning inside and farther away from its production possibilities curve.

What is the difference between a *recession* and a *depression*? According to the old saying, "A recession is when your neighbor loses his or her job, and a depression is when you also lose your job!" This one-liner is close to the true distinction between these two concepts. The answer is because no subsequent recession has approached the prolonged severity of the Great Depression from 1929 to 1933, the term *depression* is primarily a historical reference to this extremely deep and long recession. The Great Depression is discussed at the end of this chapter, the chapter on aggregate demand and supply, and the chapter on monetary policy.

The trough is where the level of real GDP "bottoms out." The length of time between the peak and the trough is the duration of the recession. Since the end of World War II, recessions in the United States have averaged 11 months. As shown in Exhibit 2, the last recession, called the Great Recession, lasted 18 months, from December 2007 to June 2009. The percentage decline in real GDP was 4.1 percent, and the national unemployment rate hit a high of 9.7 percent. The Great Recession is the longest recession since the Great Depression, which lasted 43 months.

Business cycle
Alternating periods of economic growth and contraction, which can be measured by changes in real GDP.

Peak
The phase of the business cycle in which real GDP reaches its maximum after rising during a recovery.

Recession
A downturn in the business cycle during which real GDP declines, and the unemployment rate rises. Also called a *contraction*.

Trough
The phase of the business cycle in which real GDP reaches its minimum after falling during a recession.

EXHIBIT 1	Hypothetical and Actual Business Cycles

Part (a) illustrates a hypothetical business cycle consisting of four phases: peak, recession, trough, and recovery. These fluctuations of real GDP can be measured by a growth trend line, which shows that over time, real GDP has trended upward. In reality, the fluctuations are not so clearly defined as those in this graph.

Part (b) illustrates actual ups and downs of the business cycle. After a recession in 2001, an upswing continued until the Great Recession began in 2007.

(a) Hypothetical business cycle

(b) Actual business cycle

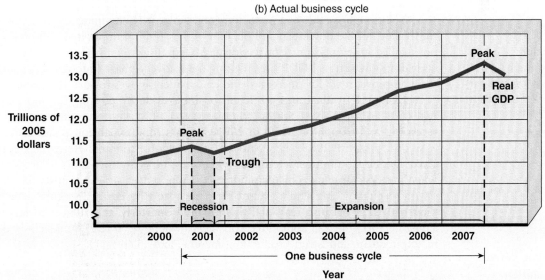

SOURCE: Bureau of Economic Analysis, *National Income Accounts*, http://www.bea.gov/national/nipaweb/SelectTable.asp?Selected=Y, Table 1.1.6.

EXHIBIT 2	Severity of Post-World War II Recessions		
Recession dates	Duration (months)	Percentage decline in real GDP	Peak unemployment rate
Nov. 1948–Oct. 1949	11	−1.7%	7.9%
July 1953–May 1954	10	−2.7	5.9
Aug. 1957–Apr. 1958	8	−1.2	7.4
Apr. 1960–Feb. 1961	10	−1.6	6.9
Dec. 1969–Nov. 1970	11	−0.6	5.9
Nov. 1973–Mar. 1975	16	−3.1	8.6
Jan. 1980–July 1980	6	−2.2	7.8
July 1981–Nov. 1982	16	−2.9	10.8
July 1990–Mar. 1991	8	−1.3	6.8
Mar. 2001–Nov. 2001	8	−0.5	5.6
Dec. 2007–June 2009	18	−4.1	9.7
Average	**11**	**−2.8**	**7.6**

SOURCE: National Bureau of Economic Research, *Business Cycle Expansion and Contractions,* http://www.nber.org/cycles/cyclesmain.html. Real GDP and unemployment rate data added by author.

Expansion

An upturn in the business cycle during which real GDP rises. Also called a *recovery*.

The trough is both bad news and good news. It is simultaneously the bottom of the "valley" of the downturn and the foot of the "hill" of improving economic conditions called an expansion or a recovery. An expansion is an upturn in the business cycle during which real GDP rises. During the recovery phase of the cycle, profits generally improve, real GDP increases, and employment moves toward full employment.

Exhibit 1(b) illustrates an actual business cycle by plotting the movement of real GDP in the United States from 2000 to 2007. The economy's initial peak, recession, and trough occurred in 2001, and a strong expansion phase lasted until a second peak in 2007. The National Bureau of Economic Research's Business Cycle Dating Committee determines when the U.S. economy enters a recession and when a recession ends. This committee is composed of six economists who decide on the beginning and ending dates for a recession based on monthly data rather than real GDP because real GDP is measured quarterly and subject to large revisions. Factors that the committee considers in defining a recession include decline in employment, industrial production, income, and sales.

Economic growth

An expansion in national output measured by the annual percentage increase in a nation's real GDP.

6-1b ECONOMIC GROWTH

We will now expand the definition of economic growth given in Chapter 2. In this chapter, recall that an outward shift of the production possibilities curve illustrated economic growth. Also recall that factors such as increases in resources and technological advances were key reasons for economic growth. Here the discussion of economic growth is explained. Economic growth is defined by economists as an expansion in national output measured by the annual percentage increase in a nation's real GDP. The growth trend line in the hypothetical model in Exhibit 1(a) illustrates that over time, our real GDP tends to rise. This general, long-term upward trend in real GDP persists in spite of the peaks, recessions, troughs, and recoveries. As shown by the dashed line in Exhibit 3, since 1930, real GDP in the United States has grown at an average annual rate of 3.5 percent. This annual change may seem small, but about 3 percent annual growth will lead to a doubling of real GDP in only 24 years. The largest expansion in U.S. history occurred over ten years from 1991 to 2001.

CONCLUSION: *We value economic growth as one of our nation's economic goals because it increases our standard of living—it creates a bigger "economic pie."*

EXHIBIT 3	**A Historical Record of Business Cycles in the United States, 1929–2011**

Real GDP has increased at an average annual growth rate of 3.5 percent since 1930. Above-average annual growth rates have alternated with below-average annual growth rates. Following the Great Depression of 2007, the annual growth rate was a negative 3.5 percent in 2009 and therefore below the zero growth line. In 2011, the growth rate was a below- average 1.7 percent.

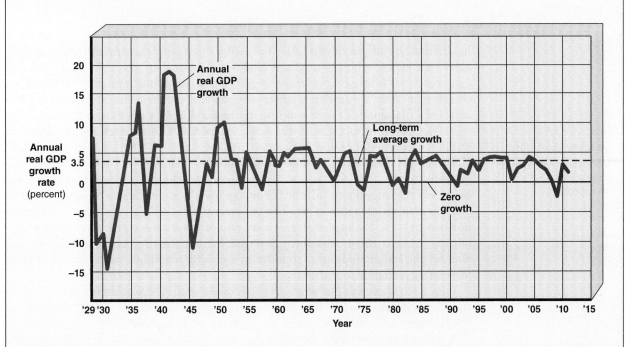

SOURCE: Bureau of Economic Analysis, *National Economic Accounts*, http://www.bea.gov/national/nipaweb/SelectTable.asp?Selected=Y, Table 1.1.6.

Closer examination of Exhibit 3 reveals that the growth path of the U.S. economy over time is not a smooth, rising trend, but instead is a series of year-to-year variations in real GDP. Following the Great Recession beginning in 2007, the growth rate was again a negative 3.5 percent in 2009 before rising to a below-average 1.7 percent in 2011.

✓ CHECKPOINT

Where Are We on the Business-Cycle Roller Coaster?

Suppose the economy is in a recession and everyone is asking when the economy will recover. To find an answer to the state of the economy's health, a television reporter interviews Terrence Carter, a local car dealer. Carter says, "I do not see any recovery. The third quarter of this year we sold more cars than in the second quarter, but sales in these two quarters were far below the first quarter." Is Mr. Carter correct? Are his observations consistent with the peak, recession, trough, or expansion phase of the business cycle?

6-1c REAL GDP GROWTH RATES IN OTHER COUNTRIES

Exhibit 4 presents real GDP growth rates for selected countries in 2011. China and India had the largest rates of growth at 9.5 and 7.8 percent, respectively. The United States and other countries throughout the world had lower growth rates, with Greece having a negative 5 percent rate.

6-1d BUSINESS-CYCLE INDICATORS

In addition to changes in real GDP, the media often report several other macro variables that measure business activity and are published by the U.S. Department of Commerce in *Business Conditions Digest*. These economic *indicator* variables are classified in three categories: leading indicators, coincident indicators, and lagging indicators. Exhibit 5 lists the variables corresponding to each indicator series.

Leading indicators

Variables that change before real GDP changes.

The government's chief forecasting gauge for business cycles is the index of leading indicators. Leading indicators are key variables that change before real GDP changes. This index captures the headlines when there is concern over swings in the economy. The first set of 10 variables in Exhibit 5 is used to forecast the business cycle months in advance. For example, a slump ahead is signaled when declines exceed advances in the components of the leading indicators data series. But beware! The leading indicators may rise for two consecutive months and then fall for the next three consecutive months. Economists are therefore cautious and wait for the leading indicators to move in a new direction for several months before forecasting a change in the cycle.

Is a recession near, or when will a recession end? The Conference Board's Consumer Confidence Index is often reported in the news as a key measure of the economy's health. It is based on a survey of households who are asked their expectations of how well the economy will perform over the next six months. Prolonged consumer pessimism can result in less consumer spending and contribute to

EXHIBIT 4	Global Comparison of Real GDP Growth Rates, 2011

The exhibit shows that China and India had the largest rates of growth at 9.5 and 7.5 percent, respectively. In contrast, the United States and other countries had lower growth rates for the year, with Greece the lowest at –5.0 percent.

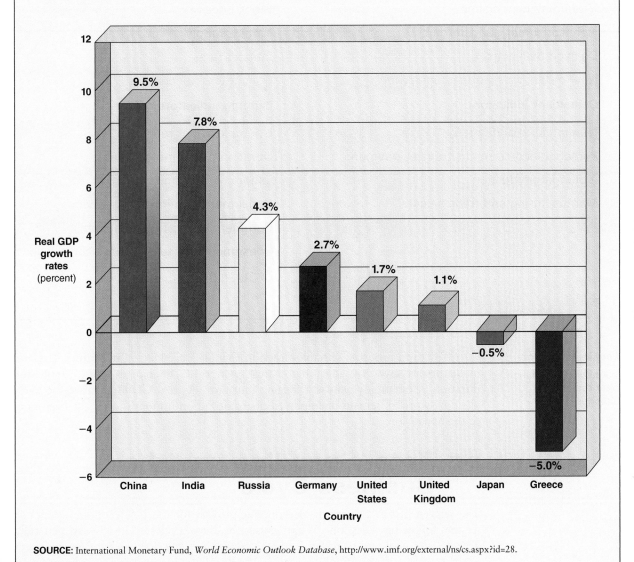

SOURCE: International Monetary Fund, *World Economic Outlook Database*, http://www.imf.org/external/ns/cs.aspx?id=28.

slowing economic growth. Stated differently, persistent consumer pessimism can result in lower personal consumption expenditures (C) and business investment (I) because businesses reduce investment when consumers' purchases of their products fall.

The second data series of key variables listed in Exhibit 5 are four coincident indicators. Coincident indicators are variables that change at the same time that real GDP changes. For example, as real GDP rises, economists expect employment, personal income, industrial production, and sales to rise.

Coincident indicators

Variables that change at the same time real GDP changes.

EXHIBIT 5	Business-Cycle Indicators
Leading indicators	
Average workweek	New building permits
Unemployment claims	Stock prices
New consumer goods orders	Money supply
Delayed deliveries	Interest rates
New orders for plant and equipment	Consumer expectations
Coincident indicators	**Lagging indicators**
Nonagricultural payrolls	Unemployment rate
Personal income minus transfer payments	Duration of unemployment
Industrial production	Labor cost per unit of output
Manufacturing and trade sales	Consumer price index for services
	Commercial and industrial loans
	Consumer credit to personal income ratio
	Prime rate

SOURCE: © Cengage Learning 2014

Lagging indicators

Variables that change after real GDP changes.

The third group of variables listed in Exhibit 5 are lagging indicators. Lagging indicators are seven variables that change after real GDP changes. For example, the duration of unemployment is a lagging indicator. As real GDP increases, the average time workers remain unemployed does not fall until months after the beginning of the expansion.

6-2 Total Spending and the Business Cycle

The uneven historical pattern of economic growth for the U.S. economy gives rise to the following question: What causes business cycles? The theory generally accepted by economists today is that changes in total or aggregate expenditures are the cause of variations in real GDP. Recall from the previous chapter that aggregate expenditures refer to total spending for *final goods* by households, businesses, government, and foreign buyers. Expressed as a formula:

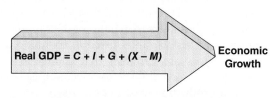

Real GDP = C + I + G + (X − M)   Economic Growth

SOURCE: © Cengage Learning 2014

Why do changes in total spending cause the level of GDP to rise during an expansion? Suppose consumers are optimistic about the economic future. If consumer spending (C) increases, then businesses find it profitable to increase investment (I) in plants and equipment. When firms become more productive, they use more land, labor, and capital. Such increased spending leads to economic growth in output, employment, and incomes. Economic growth occurs when government spending (G) increases. Growth also comes from increases in spending for exports (X) versus imports spending (M). A recession is the result of declines in sectors of real GDP. Now assume consumers become pessimistic about their economic future. If consumer spending (C) decreases, then business profits fall, and businesses decrease investment (I) in plants and equipment. Business becomes less productive and uses fewer resources. Economic growth can also fall if government spending (G) decreases or export spending (X) falls relative to import spending (M).

6-3 Unemployment

Since the abyss of the Great Depression, a major economic goal of the United States has been to achieve a high level of employment. The *Employment Act of 1946* declared it the responsibility of the federal government to use all practical means consistent with free competitive enterprise to create conditions under which all able individuals who are willing to work and seeking work will be afforded useful employment opportunities. Later, Congress amended this act with the *Full Employment and Balanced Growth Act of 1978*, which established specific goals for unemployment and the level of prices.

Each month the Bureau of Labor Statistics (BLS) of the U.S. Department of Labor, in conjunction with the Bureau of the Census, conducts a survey of a random sample of about 60,000 households in the United States. Each member of the household who is 16 years of age or older is asked whether he or she is employed or unemployed. If a person works at least 1 hour per week for pay or at least 15 hours per week as an unpaid worker in a family business, he or she is counted as employed. If the person is not employed, the question then is whether he or she has looked for work in the last month. If so, the person is said to be unemployed. Based on its survey data, the BLS publishes the unemployment rate and other employment-related statistics monthly.

The unemployment rate is the percentage of people in the civilian labor force who are without jobs and are actively seeking jobs. But who is actually counted as an unemployed worker, and which people belong to the labor force? Certainly, all people without jobs are not classified as unemployed. Babies, full-time students, and retired persons are not counted as unemployed. Likewise, individuals who are ill or severely disabled are not included as unemployed. And there are other groups not counted.

Turn to Exhibit 6. The *civilian labor force* is the number of people 16 years of age and over who are either employed or unemployed, excluding members of the armed forces and other groups listed in the "persons not in labor force" category. Based on survey data, the BLS computes the *civilian unemployment rate* using the following formula:

$$\text{Unemployment rate} = \frac{\text{unemployed}}{\text{civilian labor force}} \times 100$$

In 2011, the unemployment rate was

$$8.9\% = \frac{13.7 \text{ million persons}}{153.6 \text{ million persons}} \times 100$$

Unemployment rate

The percentage of people in the civilian labor force who are without jobs and are actively seeking jobs.

Civilian labor force

The number of people 16 years of age and older who are employed or who are actively seeking a job, excluding armed forces, homemakers, discouraged workers, and other persons not in the labor force.

EXHIBIT 6	Population, Employment, and Unemployment, 2011

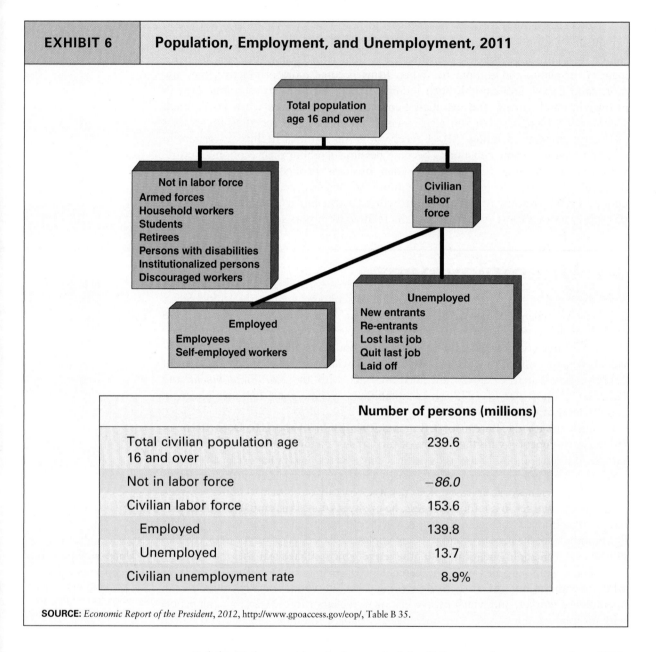

	Number of persons (millions)
Total civilian population age 16 and over	239.6
Not in labor force	*−86.0*
Civilian labor force	153.6
Employed	139.8
Unemployed	13.7
Civilian unemployment rate	8.9%

SOURCE: *Economic Report of the President, 2012*, http://www.gpoaccess.gov/eop/, Table B 35.

Exhibit 7 charts a historical record of the U.S. unemployment rate since 1929. Note that the highest unemployment rate was 25 percent in 1933 during the Great Depression. At the other extreme, the lowest unemployment rate we have attained was 1.2 percent in 1944. Following the Great Recession, the unemployment rate surged to 9.6 percent in 2010, which was the highest annual rate since 1983. In 2011, the unemployment rate was 8.9 percent.

6-3a UNEMPLOYMENT IN OTHER COUNTRIES

Exhibit 8 shows unemployment rates for selected countries in 2011. South Africa and Greece had unemployment rates higher than the United States. Other industrialized

EXHIBIT 7	The U.S. Unemployment Rate, 1929–2011

This exhibit shows fluctuations in the civilian unemployment rate since 1929. The unemployment rate reached a high point of 25 percent in 1933 during the Great Depression. The lowest unemployment rate of 1.2 percent was achieved during World War II in 1944. In 2010, the unemployment rate was 9.6 percent, which was the highest annual rate since 1983. In 2011, the unemployment rate was 8.9 percent.

SOURCE: *Economic Report of the President, 2010,* http://www.gpoaccess.gov/eop/, Table B 35.

countries such as Japan and China had unemployment rates much lower than the United States.

6-3b UNEMPLOYMENT RATE CRITICISMS

The unemployment rate is criticized for both understating and overstating the "true" unemployment rate. An example of *overstating* the unemployment rate occurs when respondents to the BLS survey falsely report they are seeking employment. The motivation may be that their eligibility for unemployment compensation or welfare benefits depends on actively pursuing a job. Or possibly an individual is "employed" in illegal activities.

The other side of the coin is that the official definition of unemployment *understates* the unemployment rate by not counting so-called discouraged workers. A discouraged worker is a person who wants to work, but has given up searching

Discouraged worker

A person who wants to work, but who has given up searching for work because he or she believes there will be no job offers.

EXHIBIT 8	Unemployment Rates for Selected Nations, 2011

In 2011, other nations shown had a higher unemployment rate than that of the United States. For example, the unemployment rate of Greece was 7.6 percent higher than the U.S. rate. The United States had an unemployment rate of 8.9 percent, while Canada and Japan had lower rates.

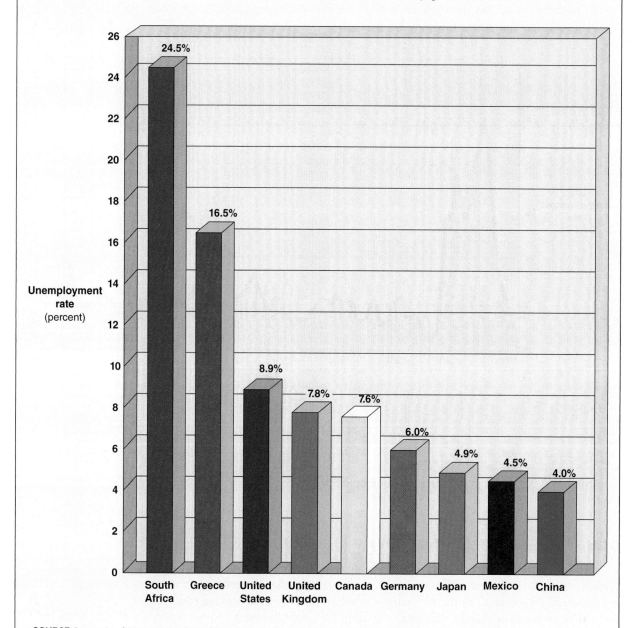

SOURCE: International Monetary Fund, *World Economic Outlook Database*, http://www.imf.org/external/ns/cs.aspx?id=28.

for work because he or she believes there will be no job offers. After repeated rejections, discouraged workers often turn to their families, friends, and public welfare for support. The BLS counts a discouraged worker as anyone who has looked for work within the last 12 months, but is no longer actively looking. The BLS simply includes discouraged workers in the "not in labor force" category listed in Exhibit 6. Because the number of discouraged workers rises during a recession, the underestimation of the official unemployment rate increases during a downturn.

Another example of *understating* the unemployment rate occurs because the official BLS data include all part-time workers as fully employed. These workers are actually partially employed, and many would work full-time if they could find full-time employment. The unemployment rate does not measure *underemployment*. If jobs are scarce and a college graduate takes a job not requiring his or her level of skills, a human resource is underutilized. Or suppose an employer cuts an employee's hours of work from 40 to 20 per week. Such losses of work potential are greater during a recession, but are not reflected in the unemployment rate.

6-4 Types of Unemployment

The unemployment rate is determined by three different types of unemployment: *frictional*, *structural*, and *cyclical*. Understanding these conceptual categories of unemployment aids in understanding and formulating policies to ease the burden of unemployment. In fact, each type of unemployment requires a different policy prescription to reduce it.

6-4a FRICTIONAL UNEMPLOYMENT

For some unemployed workers, the absence of a job is only temporary. At any given time, some people with marketable skills are fired, and others voluntarily quit jobs to accept or look for new ones. And there are always young people who leave school and search for their first job. Workers in some industries such as construction experience short periods of unemployment between projects, and temporary layoffs are common. Other workers are "seasonally unemployed." For example, ski resort workers will be employed in the winter, but not in the summer, and certain crops are harvested "in season." Because jobs requiring the skills of these unemployed workers are available, the unemployed workers and the job vacancies are matched and such workers are therefore considered "between jobs." This type of unemployment is called frictional unemployment, and it is not of great concern. Frictional unemployment is temporary unemployment caused by the time required of workers to move from one job to another. Frictional unemployment is unemployment caused by the normal search time required by workers with marketable skills who are changing jobs, initially entering the labor force, or reentering the labor force. The cause of frictional unemployment is either the transition time to a new job or the lack of information required to match a job applicant immediately with a job vacancy. For this reason, frictional unemployment is sometimes called *transitional unemployment* or *search unemployment*.

The fact that job market information is imperfect and operates with "friction" causes frictional unemployment in the economy. Because it takes time to search

Frictional unemployment

Temporary unemployment caused by the time required of workers to move from one job to another.

for the information required to match employer and employees, some workers will always be frictionally unemployed. Frictional unemployment is therefore a normal condition in an economic system permitting freedom of job choice. Improved methods of distributing job information through job listings on the Internet help unemployed workers find jobs more quickly and reduce frictional unemployment.

6-4b STRUCTURAL UNEMPLOYMENT

Structural unemployment

Unemployment caused by a mismatch of the skills of workers out of work and the skills required for existing job opportunities.

Unlike frictional unemployment, structural unemployment is not a short-term situation. Instead, it is long-term, or possibly permanent, unemployment. Structural unemployment is unemployment caused by a mismatch of the skills of workers who are out of work and the skills required for existing job opportunities. Note that changing jobs and lack of job information are *not* problems for structurally unemployed workers. Unlike frictionally unemployed workers who have marketable skills, structurally unemployed workers require additional education or retraining. The following are four causes of structural unemployment.

Lack of Education   Workers may face joblessness because they lack the education or the job-related skills to perform available jobs. This type of structural unemployment particularly affects teenagers and minority groups, but other groups of workers can be affected as well. For example, environmental concerns, such as protecting the spotted owl by restricting trees from being cut, cost some loggers their jobs. Reducing such structural unemployment requires retraining loggers for new jobs as, say, forest rangers.

Changes in Consumer Demand   The consuming public may decide to increase the demand for computer products and decrease the demand for Chevrolet Corvettes. This shift in demand would cause U.S. autoworkers who lose their jobs in Bowling Green, Kentucky, to become structurally unemployed. To regain employment, these unemployed autoworkers must retrain and find job openings in other industries, for example, manufacturing computer printers in North Carolina. Another example involves the reduction in defense spending after a war. This situation creates structural unemployment for discharged military personnel who require retraining after a war for, say, teaching, nursing, or police jobs.

Technological Advances   Implementation of the latest technology may also increase the pool of structural unemployment in a particular industry and region. For example, the U.S. textile industry, located primarily in the South, can fight less expensive foreign textile imports by installing modern machinery. This new capital may replace textile workers. But suppose these unemployed textile workers do not wish to move to a new location where new types of jobs are available. The costs of moving, fear of the unknown, and family ties are understandable reasons for being reluctant to move, and instead, the workers become structurally unemployed until they are retrained for other jobs.

To summarize, there are many causes of structural unemployment, including poor schools, new products, new technology, foreign competition, geographic differences, restricted entry into jobs, and shifts in government priorities. Because of the numerous sources of mismatching between skills and jobs, economists consider a certain level of structural unemployment inevitable. Public and private programs that train employees to fill existing job openings decrease structural unemployment. Conversely, one of the concerns about the minimum wage is that it may contribute to structural unemployment. In Exhibit 6 of Chapter 4, we demonstrated that a minimum wage set by legislation above the equilibrium wage causes unemployment. One approach intended to offset such undesirable effects of the minimum wage is a subminimum wage paid during a training period to give employers an incentive to hire unskilled workers.

Globalization   Certain jobs can be globally resourced, which means they can be performed anywhere in the world. U.S. companies sometimes use outsourcing of U.S. jobs to India, China, and other countries. Outsourcing is the practice of a company having its work done by another company in another country. As a result, U.S. workers can lose their jobs and require retraining for other jobs. It can be argued that outsourcing allows U.S. companies to reduce their costs, lower the prices of U.S. goods, and therefore be more competitive in global markets. In short, jobs are saved from being lost to more efficient competitors, and consumers benefit from lower prices.

Outsourcing
The practice of a company having its work done by another company in another country.

A company also has the choice of having a job performed by its own employees in the United States, where the product is sold, or in another country. Offshoring occurs when a U.S. company hires employees from another country to perform jobs once done by the company's American employees. Suppose, for example, a U.S. company hires engineers in India to do jobs once done for this company in the United States. Assume the result is that the average salary paid by the company to these engineers drops $100,000 per year. A benefit is that the company reduces it costs, although some Americans may lose their jobs and must find new jobs.

Offshoring
The practice of work for a company performed by the company's employees located in another country.

In conclusion, there will always be mismatching between skills and jobs. Economists therefore consider a level of structural unemployment inevitable.

6-4c CYCLICAL UNEMPLOYMENT

Cyclical unemployment is directly attributable to the lack of jobs caused by the business cycle. Cyclical unemployment is unemployment caused by the lack of jobs during a recession. When real GDP falls, companies close, jobs disappear, and workers scramble for fewer available jobs. Similar to the game of musical chairs, there are not enough chairs (jobs) for the number of players (workers) in the game.

Cyclical unemployment
Unemployment caused by the lack of jobs during a recession.

The Great Depression is a dramatic example of cyclical unemployment. There was a sudden decline in consumption, investment, government spending, and net exports. As a result of this striking fall in real GDP, the unemployment rate rose to about 25 percent (see Exhibit 7). Now notice what happened to the unemployment rate when real GDP rose sharply during World War II. The Great Recession beginning in 2007 is another example of cyclical unemployment. Falling home prices and a plunge in stock prices caused households to cut back on consumption spending and, in combination with a fall in business investment spending, caused a negative growth rate and a sharp rise in the unemployment rate to a high of 9.7 percent at the end of the recession in 2009. To smooth out these swings in unemployment, a focus of macroeconomic policy is to moderate cyclical unemployment.

✓ CHECKPOINT

What Kind of Unemployment Did the Invention of the Wheel Cause?

But Egor, what about the effect on labor?

Did the invention of the wheel cause frictional, structural, or cyclical unemployment?

Courtesy of Irwin Tucker

6-5 The Goal of Full Employment

Full employment

The situation in which an economy operates at an unemployment rate equal to the sum of the frictional and structural unemployment rates. Also called the *natural rate of unemployment*.

In this section, we take a closer look at the meaning of full employment, also called the *natural rate of unemployment*. Because both frictional and structural unemployment are present in good and bad times, *full employment* does not mean "zero" percent unemployment. Full employment is the situation in which an economy operates at an unemployment rate equal to the sum of the frictional and structural unemployment rates. Full employment therefore is the rate of unemployment that exists without cyclical unemployment.

Unfortunately, economists cannot state with certainty what percentages of the labor force are frictionally and structurally unemployed at any particular point in time. In practice, therefore, full employment is difficult to define. Moreover, the full-employment rate of unemployment, or natural rate of unemployment, changes over time. In the 1960s, 4 percent unemployment was generally considered to represent full employment. In the 1980s, the accepted rate was 6 percent. Currently, the consensus among economists is that the natural rate is close to 5 percent. However, some economists argue that the rate is closer to 7 percent.

What Kind of Unemployment Do Robot Musicians Cause?

Applicable Concept: types of unemployment

 The following is a classic article from the late 1980s that illustrates the types of unemployment and describes a recurring labor market situation:

People looking for job security have rarely chosen the music industry. But these days, musicians say, competition from machines has removed what little stability there was. Modern machines can effectively duplicate string sections, drummers, and even horn sections, so with the exception of concerts, the jobs available to live musicians are growing fewer by the day....

It is not the first time that technology has thrown a wrench into musical careers. When talking pictures helped usher in the death of vaudeville, and again, when recorded music replaced live music in radio station studios, the market for musicians took a beating from which it never fully recovered.... The musicians' plight is not getting universal sympathy. Some industry insiders say that the current job problems are an inevitable price of progress, and that musicians should update their skills to deal with the new instruments....

But others insist that more than musicians' livelihood is at stake. Mr. Glasel, [Musicians' Union] Local 802's president, warns that unbridled computerization of music could eventually threaten the quality of music. Jobs for trumpet players, for instance, have dropped precipitously since the synthesizer managed a fair approximation of the trumpet. And without trumpet players, he asked, "where is the next generation going to get its Dizzy Gillespie?"[1]

The threat to musicians' jobs continues: The Toyota Motor Corp. unveiled its instrument-playing humanoid robots at the 2005 World Exposition. The robots played drums and horn instruments, such as trumpets and tubas. And in 2008, a humanoid robot walked on the stage, said, "Hello, everyone," lifted the baton, and conducted the Detroit Symphony Orchestra. Its timing was judged to be impeccable, but the robot conductor lacked any spur-of-the-moment emotions. In 2011 Honda's humanoid robot named ASIMO was displayed at international events. ASIMO is the world's most advanced humanoid robot that can perform complicated tasks, such as playing soccer, dancing, and opening a sealed bottle and pouring a drink in a paper cup.

There is a Robot Hall of Fame at Carnegie Mellon University. The robots fall into two categories—robots from science and robots from science fiction. A panel of experts, each serving a two-year term, chooses robots in each category to be inducted into the Hall of Fame.

Rick Lord/Shutterstock.com

Envelope please! The first winners were the Unimate, the first industrial robot; the Sojourner robot from NASA's Mars Pathfinder mission; R2D2, the "droid" from the Stars Wars films; and HAL-9000, the rogue computer from the film *2001: A Space Odyssey*. And in 2012, robots played a soccer match at the RoboCup in Mexico City.

Analyze the Issue

1. Are the musicians experiencing frictional, structural, or cyclical unemployment? Explain.
2. What solution would you propose for the trumpet players mentioned above?

---

1. James S. Newton, "A Death Knell Sounds for Musical Jobs," *The New York Times*, March 1, 1987, sec. 3, p. 9.

Several reasons are given for why full employment is not fixed. One reason is that between the early 1960s and the early 1980s, the participation of women and teenagers in the labor force increased. This change in the labor force composition increased the full-employment rate of unemployment because both women and young workers (under age 25) typically experience higher unemployment rates than men do. Another frequently cited and controversial reason for the rise in the full-employment rate of unemployment is that larger unemployment compensation payments, food stamps, welfare, and Social Security benefits from the government make unemployment less painful. In the 1990s, the natural rate of unemployment declined somewhat because the entry of females and teenagers into the labor force slowed. Also, the baby boom generation has aged, and middle-aged workers have lower unemployment rates.

6-6 The GDP Gap

GDP gap

The difference between actual real GDP and potential or full-employment real GDP.

When people in an economy are unemployed, society forfeits the production of goods and services. To determine the dollar value of how much society loses if the economy fails to reach the natural rate of unemployment, economists estimate the GDP gap. The GDP gap is the difference between actual real GDP and full-employment real GDP. The level of GDP that could be produced at full employment is also called *potential real GDP*. Expressed as a formula:

$$\text{GDP gap} = \text{actual real GDP} - \text{potential real GDP}$$

The GDP gap can be either positive if actual real GDP exceeds potential real GDP or negative if actual real GDP is less than potential real GDP. Because the GDP gap is calculated on the basis of the difference between GDP at the actual unemployment rate and estimated GDP at the full-employment rate of unemployment, the GDP gap measures the cost of cyclical unemployment. A positive GDP gap measures a boom in the economy when workers are employed overtime, and a negative GDP gap increases during a recession. Exhibit 9 shows the size of the GDP gap (in 2005 prices) from 1997 to 2011, based on potential real GDP and actual real GDP for each of these years. Prior to the 2001 recession, the economy operated above its potential (positive GDP gap). After the 2001 recession, the economy operated below its potential (negative gap) until 2005, when the gap was positive through 2007. Since the Great Recession's beginning in 2007, the U.S. economy has experienced large negative GDP gaps.

> **CONCLUSION:** *The gap between actual and potential real GDP measures the monetary losses of real goods and services to the nation from operating at less than full employment.*

6-6a NONMONETARY AND DEMOGRAPHIC CONSEQUENCES OF UNEMPLOYMENT

The burden of unemployment is more than the loss of potential output measured by the GDP gap. Unemployment also has nonmonetary costs. Some people endure unemployment pretty well because they have substantial savings to draw on, but others sink into despair. Without work, many people lose their feeling of

EXHIBIT 9	Actual and Potential GDP, 1997–2011

The GDP gap is the difference between actual real GDP and potential real GDP, which is based on the assumption that the economy operates at full employment. A positive GDP gap measures a boom in the economy when workers are employed overtime. Between 1997 and 2000, the U.S. economy experienced a positive GDP gap. The recession in 2001 reversed the GDP gap, and the economy has operated with a negative GDP gap below its potential until 2004, when the gap was positive through 2007. Since the Great Recession beginning in 2007, the U.S. economy has experienced large negative GDP gaps.

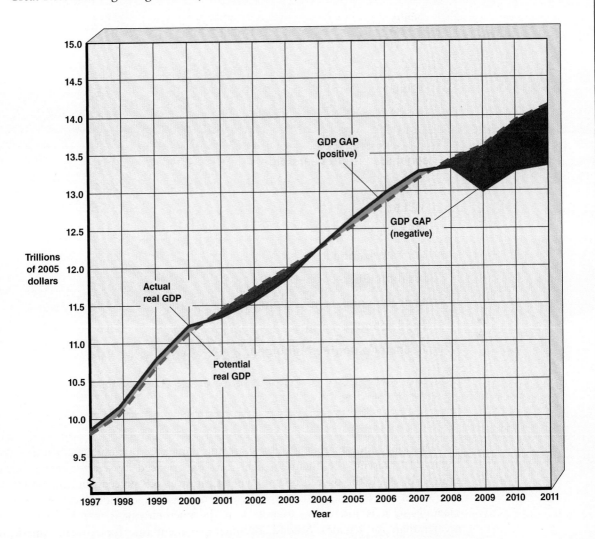

SOURCE: International Monetary Fund, *World Economic Outlook Database*, http://www.imf.org/external/ns/cs.aspx?id=28.

worth. A person's self-image suffers when he or she cannot support a family and be a valuable member of society. Research has associated high unemployment with suicides, crime, mental illness, heart attacks, and other maladies. Moreover, severe unemployment causes despair, family breakups, and political unrest.

EXHIBIT 10	Civilian Unemployment Rates by Selected Demographic Groups, 2011

Demographic Group	Unemployment Rate (percent)
Overall	8.9%
Gender	
Male	9.4
Female	8.5
Race	
White	7.9
Hispanic	11.5
African American	15.8
Teenagers (16–19 years old)	
All	24.4
White	21.7
Hispanics	31.1
African American	41.3
Education (25 years and over)	
Less than high school diploma	14.1
High school graduates	9.4
Bachelor's degree and higher	4.3

SOURCE: Bureau of Labor Statistics, *Current Population Survey*, http://stats.bls.gov/cps/cpsatabs.htm, Table 1-4.

Various labor market groups share the impact of unemployment unequally. Exhibit 10 presents the unemployment rates experienced by selected demographic groups. In 2011, the overall unemployment rate was 8.9 percent, but the figures in the exhibit reveal the unequal burden by gender, race, age, and educational attainment. First, it is interesting to note that the unemployment rate for males was greater than for females. Second, the unemployment rate for African Americans was higher than for whites and Hispanics. Third, teenagers experienced a high unemployment rate because they are new entrants to the workforce who have little employment experience, high quit rates, and little job mobility. Again, race is a strong factor, and the unemployment rate for African-American teenagers was greater than for white teenagers. Among the explanations are discrimination; the concentration of African-Americans in the inner city, where job opportunities for less skilled (blue-collar) workers are inadequate; and the minimum wage law.

Brother Can You Spare a Dime?

Applicable Concept: human costs of *unemployment*

The unemployment rate does not measure the full impact of unemployment on individuals. Prolonged unemployment not only means lost wages, but it also impairs health and social relationships. The United States fought its most monstrous battle against unemployment during the Great Depression of the 1930s. Return to Exhibit 7 and note that the unemployment rate stayed at 20 percent or more from 1932 through 1935. In 1933, it reached almost 25 percent of the civilian labor force; that is, about one out of every four people who wanted to work could not. This meant 16 million Americans were out of work when our country's population was less than half its present size.[1] For comparison, at the low point of the 1990–1991 recession, about 10 million Americans were officially unemployed.

But these statistics tell only part of the horror story. Millions of workers were "discouraged workers" who had simply given up looking for work because there was no work available, and these people were not counted. People were standing in line for soup kitchens, selling apples on the street, and living in cardboard shacks. "Brother can you spare a dime?" was a common greeting. Some people jumped out of windows, and others roamed the country trying valiantly to survive.

John Steinbeck's great novel *The Grapes of Wrath* described millions of midwesterners who drove in caravans to California after being wiped out by drought in what became known as the Dust Bowl.

A 1992 study estimated the frightening impact of sustained unemployment that is not reflected in official unemployment data. Mary Merva, a University of Utah economist, co-authored a study of unemployment in 30 selected big cities from 1976 to 1990. This research found that a 1 percentage point increase in the national unemployment rate resulted in the following:

- 6.7 percent more murders
- 3.1 percent more deaths from stroke
- 5.6 percent more deaths from heart disease
- 3.9 percent increase in suicides[2]

Hard times during the recession of 2007 caused people to cut back on their medical care. According to a survey by the American Heart Association (AHA), 42 percent of the respondents said they trimmed health-related expenses, 32 percent skipped some preventive care, such as a mammogram or an annual physical, and 10 percent stopped or diminished the use of medicine for chronic conditions. And a 2011 article in *The New York Times* reported the finding in a Harvard School of Public Health survey that workers who lost a job through no fault of their own were twice as likely to report developing a new ailment such as high blood pressure, diabetes, or heart disease over the next year and a half, compared with people who were continuously employed.[3]

Although these estimates are subject to statistical qualifications, they underscore the notion that prolonged unemployment poses a real danger to many individuals. As people change their behavior in the face of layoffs, cutbacks, or a sudden drop in net worth, more and more Americans find themselves clinically depressed.

1. U.S. Bureau of the Census, *Historical Statistics of the United States, Colonial Times to 1957* (Washington, D.C.: U.S. Government Printing Office, 1960), Series D46–47, p. 73.
2. Robert Davis, "Recession's Cost: Lives," *USA Today*, Oct. 16, 1992, p. 1A.
3. Roni Caryn Rabin, "Losing Job May Be Hazardous to Health," *The New York Times*, May 9, 2011.

Source: © Cengage Learning 2014

Finally, comparison of the unemployment rates in 2011 by educational attainment reveals the importance of education as an insurance policy against unemployment. Firms are much less likely to lay off a higher-skilled worker with a college education, in whom they have a greater investment in terms of training and salaries, than a worker with only a high school diploma.

Key Concepts

Business cycle
Peak
Recession
Trough
Expansion
Economic growth
Leading indicators

Coincident indicators
Lagging indicators
Unemployment rate
Civilian labor force
Discouraged worker
Frictional unemployment
Structural unemployment

Outsourcing
Offshoring
Cyclical unemployment
Full employment
GDP gap

Summary

- **Business cycles** are recurrent rises and falls in real GDP over a period of years. Business cycles vary greatly in duration and intensity. A cycle consists of four phases: peak, recession, trough, and recovery. The generally accepted theory today is that changes in the forces of demand and supply cause business cycles. A **recession** is generally defined as at least two consecutive quarters of real GDP decline. A **trough** is the turning point in national output between recession and recovery. During an **expansion**, there is an upturn in the business cycle, during which real GDP rises. A **peak** occurs when real GDP reaches its maximum level during a recovery.

Hypothetical Business Cycle

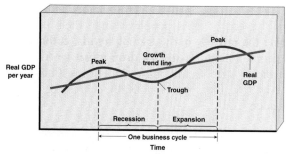

SOURCE: Bureau of Economic Analysis, *National Income Accounts*, http://www.bea.gov/national/nipaweb/SelectTable.asp?Selected=Y, Table 1.1.6.

- **Economic growth** is measured by the annual percentage change in real GDP in a nation. The long-term average annual growth rate since 1930 in the United States has been 3.5 percent.
- **Leading, coincident,** and **lagging indicators** are economic variables that change before, at the same time as, and after changes in real GDP, respectively.
- The **unemployment rate** is the ratio of the number of unemployed to the number in the civilian labor force multiplied by 100. The nation's **civilian labor force** consists of people who are employed plus those who are out of work, but seeking employment.
- **Discouraged workers** are a reason critics say the unemployment rate is *understated*. Discouraged workers are persons who want to work, but have given up searching for work. Another criticism of the unemployment rate is that it *overstates* unemployment because respondents can falsely report they are seeking a job.
- **Frictional, structural,** and **cyclical unemployment** are different types of unemployment. **Frictional unemployment,** including seasonal unemployment, results when workers are

seeking new jobs that exist. The problem is that imperfect information prevents matching the applicants with the available jobs. **Structural unemployment** is long-term unemployment caused by factors in the economy, including lack of education, changes in consumer demand, technological change, and globalization. **Cyclical unemployment** is unemployment resulting from insufficient aggregate demand.

- **Full employment** occurs when the unemployment rate is equal to the total of the frictional and structural unemployment rates. Currently, the full-employment rate of unemployment (natural rate of unemployment) in the United States is considered to be close to 5 percent. At this rate of unemployment, the economy is producing at its maximum potential.

- The **GDP gap** is the difference between actual real GDP and full employment, or potential real GDP. Therefore, the GDP gap measures the loss of output due to cyclical unemployment.

Summary of Conclusion Statements

- We value economic growth as one of our nation's economic goals because it increases our standard of living—it creates a bigger "economic pie."

- The gap between actual and potential real GDP measures the monetary losses of real goods and services to the nation from operating at less than full employment.

Study Questions and Problems

1. What is the basic cause of the business cycle?

2. Following are real GDP figures for 10 quarters:

Quarter	Real GDP (billions of dollars)
1	$ 400
2	500
4	200
5	300
6	500
7	800
8	900
9	1,000
10	500

Plot these data points, and identify the four phases of the business cycle. Give a theory that may explain the cause of the observed business cycle. What are some of the consequences of a prolonged decline in real GDP? Is the decline in real GDP from $1,000 billion to $500 billion a recession?

3. In a given year, there are 10 million unemployed workers and 120 million employed workers in an economy. Excluding members of the armed forces and persons in institutions and assuming these figures include only civilian workers, calculate the civilian unemployment rate.

4. Describe the relevant criteria that government statisticians use to determine whether a person is "unemployed."

5. How has the official unemployment rate been criticized for overestimating and underestimating unemployment?

6. Why is frictional unemployment inevitable in an economy characterized by imperfect job information?

7. How does structural unemployment differ from cyclical unemployment?

8. Is it reasonable to expect the unemployment rate to fall to zero for an economy? What is the relationship of frictional, structural, and cyclical unemployment to the full-employment rate of unemployment, or natural rate of unemployment?

9. In the 1960s, economists used 4 percent as their approximation for the natural rate of unemployment. Currently, full employment is on the order of 5 percent unemployment. What is the major factor accounting for this rise?

10. Speculate on why teenage unemployment rates exceed those for the overall labor force.

11. Explain the GDP gap.

For Online Exercises, go to the Tucker Web site at www.cengage.com/economics/tucker.

✓ CHECKPOINT ANSWERS

Where Are We on the Business-Cycle Roller Coaster?

The car dealer's sales in the first quarter conformed to the recession phase of the business cycle, and those in the second quarter, to the trough. Then car sales in the third quarter were below those in the first quarter, but the increase over the second quarter indicated a recovery. If you said real GDP during an expansion can be lower than real GDP during a recession, **YOU ARE CORRECT.**

What Kind of Unemployment Did the Invention of the Wheel Cause?

The invention of the wheel represented a new technology for primitive people. Even in the primitive era, many workers who transported goods lost their jobs to the more efficient cart with wheels. If you said the invention of the wheel caused structural unemployment, **YOU ARE CORRECT.**

Sample Quiz

For an explanation of the correct answers, visit the Tucker website at www.cengage.com/economics/tucker.

1. A business cycle is the
   a. period of time in which expansion and contraction of economic activity are equal
   b. period of time in which there are three phases: peak, depression, and expansion
   c. recurring growth and decline in real GDP
   d. period of time in which a business is established and ceases operations

2. A business cycle is the period of time in which
   a. a business is established and ceases operations.
   b. there are four phases: peak, recession, trough, and expansion.
   c. the price level changes.
   d. expansion and contraction of economic activity are equal.

3. The phase of the business cycle follows a recession.
   a. expansion
   b. recession
   c. peak
   d. trough

Sample Quiz *continued*

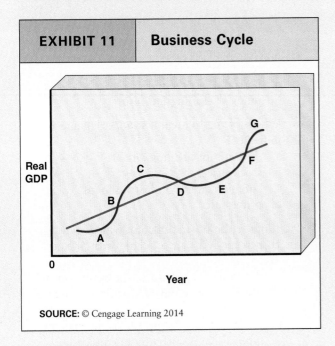

EXHIBIT 11 | **Business Cycle**

Real GDP

Year

0

G

F

C

B

A

D

E

SOURCE: © Cengage Learning 2014

4. In Exhibit 11, the expansion phase of the business cycle is represented by points
   a. *A* and *C*
   b. *B* and *F*
   c. *B* and *D*
   d. *C* and *G*

5. A general rule is that economy is experiencing a recession when
   a. real GDP declines for at least three months.
   b. real GDP declines for at least nine months.
   c. nominal GDP declines for at least nine months.
   d. real GDP declines for at least six months.

6. A person who has given up searching for work is called
   a. frictionally unemployed.
   b. structurally unemployed.
   c. a discouraged worker.
   d. unemployed.

7. John Steinbeck's *Cannery Row* describes a character who takes his own life because of poor job prospects. If he was an unemployed person who gave up looking for work, he would be considered
   a. chronically unemployed.
   b. a discouraged worker.
   c. a member of the labor force.
   d. frictionally unemployed.

8. Unemployment that is of a short duration to allow a person time to find a new job is
   a. structural unemployment.
   b. cyclical unemployment.
   c. frictional unemployment.
   d. durational unemployment.

9. A person who voluntarily quits their job in New York and expects to get a similar job in Los Angeles is an example of
   a. structural unemployment.
   b. cyclical unemployment.
   c. durational unemployment.
   d. frictional unemployment.

10. Frictional unemployment refers to
    a. people who are out of work and have no job skills.
    b. short periods of unemployment needed to match jobs and job seekers.
    c. people who spend relatively long periods out of work.
    d. unemployment related to the ups and downs of the business cycle.

11. Sam is a musician who is out of work because electronic equipment replaced live musicians. This is an example of
    a. frictional unemployment.
    b. cyclical unemployment.
    c. structural unemployment.
    d. involuntary unemployment.

12. Louise is unemployed due to a decrease in the demand for workers with knowledge of a certain word processing language. This is an example of
    a. cyclical unemployment.
    b. frictional unemployment.
    c. involuntary unemployment.
    d. structural unemployment.

Sample Quiz *continued*

13. Consider a broom factory that permanently closes because of foreign competition. If the broom factory's workers cannot find new jobs because their skills are no longer marketable, they are classified as
    a. seasonally unemployed.
    b. frictionally unemployed.
    c. structurally unemployed.
    d. cyclically unemployed.

14. The increase in unemployment associated with a recession is called
    a. structural unemployment.
    b. frictional unemployment.
    c. discouraged unemployment.
    d. cyclical unemployment.

15. Which of the following is *true*?
    a. The GDP gap is the difference between full-employment real GDP and actual real GDP.
    b. We desire economic growth because it increases the nation's standard of living.
    c. Economic growth is measured by the annual percentage increase in a nation's real GDP.
    d. Discouraged workers are a reason critics say the unemployment rate is understated.
    e. All of the above answers are correct.

16. What stage of the business cycle immediately follows the trough?
    a. peak
    b. expansion
    c. recession
    d. depression

17. The government's chief forecasting gauge for business cycles is the
    a. unemployment rate.
    b. real GDP.
    c. personal income index.
    d. index of leading indicators.

18. Which of the following is *not* a lagging indicator?
    a. duration of unemployment
    b. stock prices
    c. commercial and industrial loans
    d. prime rate

19. Suppose the official unemployment rate is 10 percent. We can conclude without question that
    a. the same 10 percent of the people in the economy were out of work for the entire year.
    b. 1 out of every 10 people in the civilian labor force is currently unemployed.
    c. the same 10 percent of the people in the civilian labor force was out of work for the entire year.
    d. every person in the civilian labor force was out of work for 10 percent of the year.

20. Sally lost her job when her company went out of business because of a recession. This is an example of
    a. frictional unemployment.
    b. structural unemployment.
    c. cyclical unemployment.
    d. technological unemployment.

chapter 7

Inflation

In addition to the goals of full employment and economic growth discussed in the previous chapter, keeping prices stable is one of the most important economic goals facing a nation. In the United States, the Great Depression of the 1930s and the Great Recession of 2007 produced profound changes in people's lives from the consequences of unemployment. Similarly, the "Great Inflation" of the 1970s and early 1980s left memories of the miseries of inflation. In fact, every American president since Franklin Roosevelt has resolved to keep the price level stable. Politicians are aware that, as with high unemployment, voters are quick to blame any administration that fails to keep inflation rates under control.

This chapter explains what inflation is: What does it mean when a 50 percent hike in the price of gasoline causes pain at the pump, eggs jump by 35 percent, a gallon of milk is up 23 percent, a loaf of bread climbs 16 percent, and around the world others feel the pinch of higher prices? Here you will study how the government actually measures changes in the price level and computes the rate of inflation. The chapter concludes with a discussion of the consequences and root causes of inflation. It explains who the winners are and who the losers are. For example, you will see what happened in Zimbabwe when the inflation rate reached 231,000,000 percent. After studying this chapter, you will have a much clearer understanding of why inflation is so feared.

In this chapter, you will learn to solve these economics puzzles:

- What is the inflation rate of your college education?
- Can a person's income fall even though he or she received a raise?
- What would Babe Ruth's salary be worth today?
- What is the real price of gasoline?
- Can an interest rate be negative?
- Does inflation harm everyone equally?

7-1 Meaning and Measurement of Inflation

Inflation

An increase in the general (average) price level of goods and services in the economy.

Deflation

A decrease in the general (average) price level of goods and services in the economy.

After World War II, a 12-ounce bottle of Pepsi sold for 5 cents. Today, a 12-ounce can of Pepsi sells for more than 20 times that much. This is not inflation. Inflation is an increase in the *general* (average) price level of goods and services in the economy. Inflation's opposite is deflation. Deflation is a decrease in the *general* (average) price level of goods and services in the economy. Note that inflation does not mean that *all* prices of *all* products in the economy rise during a given period of time. For example, the annual percentage change in the average overall price level during the 1970s reached double digits, but the prices of pocket calculators and digital watches actually declined. The reason that the average price level rose in the 1970s was that the rising prices of Pepsi, houses, and other goods outweighed the falling prices of pocket calculators, digital watches, and other goods.

> **CONCLUSION:** *Inflation is an increase in the overall average level of prices and not an increase in the price of any specific product.*

7-1a THE CONSUMER PRICE INDEX

Consumer price index (CPI)

An index that measures changes in the average prices of consumer goods and services.

The most widely reported measure of inflation is the consumer price index (CPI), which measures changes in the average prices of consumer goods and services. The CPI is sometimes called the *cost-of-living index*. It includes only consumer goods and services in order to determine how rising prices affect the income of consumers. Unlike the *GDP chain price index* explained in the previous chapter on GDP, the CPI does not consider items purchased by businesses and government.

The Bureau of Labor Statistics (BLS) of the Department of Labor prepares the CPI. Each month the bureau's "price collectors" contact retail stores, homeowners, and tenants in selected cities throughout the United States. Based on these monthly inquiries, the BLS records average prices for a "market basket" of different items purchased by the typical *urban* family. These items are included under the following categories: food, housing, apparel, transportation, medical care, entertainment, and other expenditures. Exhibit 1 presents a more detailed breakdown of these categories and shows the relative importance of each as a percentage of total expenditures. The survey reveals, for example, that 33 cents out of each consumer dollar is spent

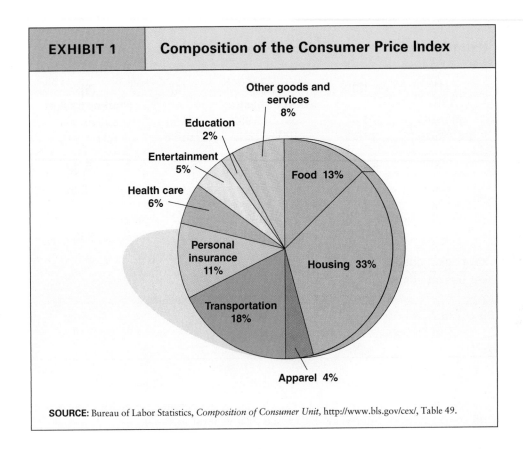

| EXHIBIT 1 | Composition of the Consumer Price Index |

Other goods and services 8%

Education 2%

Entertainment 5%

Health care 6%

Personal insurance 11%

Transportation 18%

Food 13%

Housing 33%

Apparel 4%

SOURCE: Bureau of Labor Statistics, *Composition of Consumer Unit*, http://www.bls.gov/cex/, Table 49.

for housing and 18 cents for transportation. The composition of the market basket generally remains unchanged from one period to the next, so the CPI is called a *fixed-weight price index*. If 33 percent of consumer spending was on housing during a given base year, the assumption is that 33 percent of spending is still spent on housing in, say, 2011. Over time, particular items in the CPI change. For example, personal computers, digital cameras, and cell phones have been added. The base period is changed periodically.

7-1b HOW THE CPI IS COMPUTED

Exhibit 2 illustrates the basic idea behind the CPI using hypothetical data to show how this price index measures inflation. Suppose, in 1982, a typical family in the United States lived a very meager existence and purchased a market basket of only hamburgers, gasoline, and jeans. Column (1) shows the quantity purchased for each of these items, and column (2) lists the corresponding average selling price. Multiplying the price times the quantity gives the market basket cost in column (3) of each consumer product purchased in 1982. The total cost paid by our typical family for the market basket, based on 1982 prices and quantities purchased, is $245.

Years later it is 2011, and we wish to know the impact of rising prices on consumer purchases. To calculate the CPI, we determine the cost of the *same* market basket, valued at 2011 *current-year prices*, and compare this to the cost at 1982

EXHIBIT 2	A Hypothetical Consumer Price Index for a Simple Economy				
Products in consumers' market basket	**(1) 1982 quantity purchased**	**(2) 1982 price**	**(3) Market basket cost in 1982 [(1) × (2)]**	**(4) 2011 price**	**(5) Market basket cost in 2011 [(1) × (4)]**
Hamburgers	50	$ 0.80	$ 40	$ 1.00	$ 50
Gallons of gasoline	250	0.70	175	0.90	225
Jeans	2	15.00	30	30.00	60
			Total 1982 cost = $245		Total 2011 cost = $335

$$2011 \text{ CPI} = \frac{2011 \text{ market basket cost}}{1982 \text{ market basket cost}} \times 100$$

$$2011 \text{ CPI} = \frac{\$335}{\$245} \times 100 = 136.7$$

SOURCE: © Cengage Learning 2014

Base year

A year chosen as a reference point for comparison with some earlier or later year.

base-year prices. A base year is a year chosen as a reference point for comparison with some earlier or later year. Expressed as a general formula:

$$\text{CPI} = \frac{\text{cost of market basket of products at current-year (2011) prices}}{\text{cost of same market basket of products at base-year (1982) prices}} \times 100$$

As shown in Exhibit 2, the 2011 cost for our market basket example is calculated by multiplying the 2011 price for each item in column (4) times the 1982 quantity purchased in column (1). Column (5) lists the result for each item in the market basket, and the total market basket cost in 2011 is $335. The CPI value of 136.7 is computed in Exhibit 2 as the ratio of the current 2011 cost of the market basket ($335) to the cost of the same market basket in the 1982 base year ($245) multiplied by 100.

The value of the CPI in the base year is always 100 because the numerator and the denominator of the CPI formula are the same in the base year. Currently, the CPI uses 1982–1984 spending patterns as its base year. Once the BLS selects the base year and uses the market basket technique to generate the CPI numbers, the annual *inflation rate* is computed as the percentage change in the official CPI from one year to the next. Mathematically,

$$\text{Anual rate of inflation} = \frac{\text{CPI in given year} - \text{CPI in previous year}}{\text{CPI in previous year}} \times 100$$

Exhibit 3 lists actual CPI for selected years. You can use the above formula and calculate the inflation rate for any given year using the base year of 1982–84 = 100. In 2011, for example, the CPI was 225.0, while in 2010, it was 218.1. The rate of inflation for 2011 is computed as follows:

$$3.2\% = \frac{225.0 - 218.1}{218.1} \times 100$$

EXHIBIT 3	Consumer Price Indexes and Inflation Rates, Selected Years	
Year	CPI	Inflation rate
1931	15.2	—
1932	13.7	−9.9%
1979	72.6	—
1980	82.4	13.5
2000	172.2	—
2001	177.1	2.8
2002	179.9	1.6
2008	215.3	—
2009	214.5	−0.4

SOURCE: Bureau of Labor Statistics, *Consumer Price Index*, http://data.bls.gov/cgi-bin/surveymost?cu.

The negative inflation rate of 9.9 percent for 1932 was deflation, and the 13.5 percent inflation rate for 1980 illustrates a relatively high rate in recent U.S. history. The fall in the inflation rate from 2.8 percent to 1.6 percent between 2001 and 2002 was disinflation. Disinflation is a reduction in the rate of inflation. Disinflation does not mean that prices are falling; rather, it means that the rate of increases in prices is falling. The negative inflation rate of −0.4 percent in 2009 was the first U.S. deflation since 1955.

Disinflation
A reduction in the rate of inflation.

✓ CHECKPOINT

The College Education Price Index
Suppose your *market basket* for a college education consisted of only the four items listed in the following table:

Item	2010	2011
Tuition and fees[1]	$4,500	$5,000
Room and board[2]	6,000	6,200
Books[3]	1,000	1,200
Soft drinks[4]	150	200

[1]Tuition for two semesters.
[2]Payment for nine months.
[3]Ten textbooks.
[4]Two hundred 12-ounce Coca-Colas.

Using 2010 as your base year, what is the percentage change in the college education price index in 2011?

How Much More Does It Cost to Laugh?

Applicable Concept: consumer price index

Are we paying bigger bucks for smaller yuks? Or is it a lower fee for more glee? Is there a bone to pick with the price of rubber chickens? Is the price of Groucho glasses raising eyebrows? The cost of *Mad* magazine driving you mad? Well, you get the idea. Malcolm Kushner, an attorney-turned-humor consultant based in Santa Cruz, California, developed an index based on a compilation of leading humor indicators to measure price changes in things that make us laugh. Kushner created the cost-of-laughing index to track how trends in laughter affect the bottom line. He is a humor consultant who advises corporate leaders on making humor work for business professionals. For example, humor can make executives better public speakers, and laughter reduces stress and can even cure illnesses. Kushner believes humor is America's greatest asset, and his consulting business

gets a lot of publicity from publication of the index. To combat rising humor costs, Kushner has established a Web site at http://www.kushner group.com. It organizes links to databases of funny quotes, anecdotes, one-liners, and other material for business speakers and writers.

The exhibit with the Groucho face traces annual percentage changes in the cost of laughing that Kushner has reported to the media. On an annual basis, the inflation rate for laughing remained almost flat as a pancake at about 3 percent from 2000 through 2005. Then in 2006, the humor index took a slippery slide on a banana peel to a disinflation rate of only one-tenth of 1 percent. In 2007, the index rode a roller coaster ride up to 4.7 percent, which was the largest increase since 1999, and then down to −1.4 percent in 2009. This deflation was the first negative percent change in the index history that began in 1987.

Closer examination of the cost-of-laughing index over the years and some other items gives both smiley and sad faces. The good news in 2011 is that the price of a whoopee cushion decreased, but the bad news is that the price of Groucho glasses rose. The major reason for more expensive humor is the price of writing a half-hour television situation comedy. Just like the CPI, Kushner's index has been criticized. Note that the fee for writing a TV sitcom dominates the index. Kushner responds to this issue by saying, "Well, I wanted the index to be truly national. The fact that this price dominates the index reflects that TV comedy shows dominate our national culture. If you can laugh for free at a sitcom, you don't need to buy a rubber chicken or go to a comedy club."

Analyze the Issue
No question here. This one is just for fun.

Cost of Laughing Index				
Item	2008	2009	2010	2011
Rubber chicken[1]	$51.00	$51.00	$ 72.00	$ 78.00
Groucho glasses[1]	15.00	15.00	21.00	24.00
Whoopee cushion[1]	5.40	5.40	3.00	1.20
Mad magazine[2]	4.99	4.99	5.99	5.99
Singing telegrams[3]				
Pink gorilla	250.00	150.00	185.00	185.00
Dancing chicken	250.00	150.00	185.00	185.00
Fee for writing a TV sitcom[4]	15,482.00	15,482.00	15,946.00	16,437.00
Comedy clubs[5]				
Atlanta: The Punch Line	23.00	20.00	20.00	20.00
Chicago: Second City	25.00	25.00	27.00	27.00
Houston: Laff Stop	25.00	20.00	15.00	15.00
Denver: Comedy Works	25.00	28.00	25.00	25.00
Indianapolis: Crackers Comedy	13.00	15.00	13.00	13.00
Los Angeles: Laugh Factory	20.00	20.00	20.00	20.00
New York: Comic Strip	22.00	25.00	25.00	25.00
Pittsburgh: The Funny Bone	15.00	15.00	15.00	15.00
San Francisco: Punch Line	25.00	21.00	21.00	21.00
Seattle: Comedy Underground	15.00	15.00	15.00	15.00
Total cost of humor basket	$16,266.39	$16,062.39	$16,613.99	$17,112.19
Annual inflation rate	**4.3%**	**−1.4%**	**3.4%**	**3%**

1. One dozen wholesale from Franco-American Novelty Company, Long Island City, New York.
2. April issue.
3. Available from Bellygrams, Manhattan, New York.
4. Minimum fee under Writers Guild of America basic agreement.
5. Admission on Saturday night.

Source: Data provided by Malcolm Kushner.

7-1c HISTORY OF U.S. INFLATION RATES

Exhibit 4 shows how prices have changed in the United States since 1929, as measured by annual changes in the CPI. During the early years of the Great Depression, the nation experienced *deflation*, and the CPI declined at almost a double-digit rate. In contrast, the CPI reached a double-digit inflation rate during and immediately following World War II. After 1950, the inflation rate generally remained below 3 percent until the inflationary pressures from the Vietnam War in the late 1960s. In fact, the average inflation rate between 1950 and 1968 was only 2 percent. Then the inflation rate climbed to more than 10 percent in 1974, 1979, 1980, and 1981, reaching a high of 13.5 percent in 1980. During the 1973–1982 period, the average annual inflation rate was 8.8 percent. Following the 1990–1991 recession, the annual inflation rate moderated, and it averaged 2.5 percent between 1992 and 2010. In 2009 during the Great Recession, the deflation rate was −0.4 percent. In 2011, the inflation rate was 3.2 percent.

EXHIBIT 4	The U.S. Inflation Rate, 1929–2011

During the Great Depression, the economy experienced deflation as prices plunged. During and immediately after World War II, the annual rate of inflation reached the double-digit level. After 1950, the inflation rate was generally below 3 percent until the inflationary pressures from the Vietnam War in the late 1960s. During the 1950–1968 period, the average inflation rate was only 2 percent. In contrast, the inflation rate climbed sharply to an average of 7.6 percent between 1969 and 1982. Between 1992 and 2009, inflation moderated and averaged 2.6 percent annually. In 2009 during the Great Recession, the deflation rate was −0.4 percent. In 2011, the inflation rate was 3.2 percent.

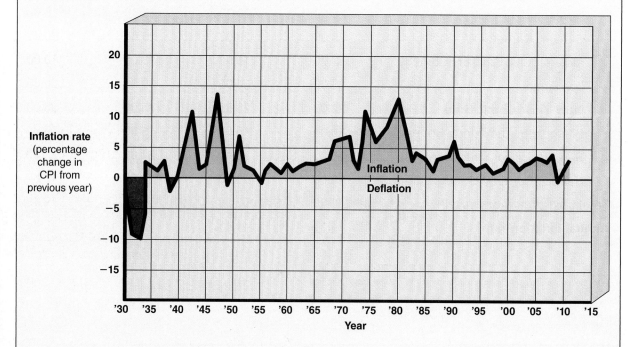

SOURCE: *Economic Report of the President*, 2012, http://www.gpoaccess.gov/eop/, Table B-64.

7-1d CONSUMER PRICE INDEX CRITICISMS

Just as there is criticism of the unemployment rate, the CPI is not a perfect measure of inflation, and it has been the subject of much public debate. There are reasons for this criticism:

1. Changes in the CPI are based on a typical market basket of products that does not match the actual market basket purchased by many consumers. Suppose you spend your nominal annual income entirely on lemonade, hot dogs, and jeans. During this year, the inflation rate is 5 percent, but assume the prices of lemonade, hot dogs, and jeans actually fall. In this case, your real income will rise, and the official inflation rate based on the CPI will *overstate* the impact of inflation on your standard of living. Retired persons, for example, buy a bundle of products that differs from that of the "typical" family. Because retired persons purchase proportionally more medical services than the typical family, the inflation rate may understate the impact of inflation on older persons.

2. The BLS has difficulty adjusting the CPI for changes in *quality*. Compare a TV made in the past with a new TV. The new TV may cost more, but it is much better than the old TV. A portion of the price increase therefore reflects better quality instead of simply a higher price for the same item. If the quality of items improves, increases in the CPI *overstate* inflation. Similarly, deteriorating quality *understates* inflation. The BLS attempts to make adjustments for quality changes in automobiles, electronic equipment, and other products in the market basket, but these adjustments are difficult to determine accurately.

3. The use of a single base-year market basket ignores the law of demand. If the price of a product rises, consumers purchase substitutes, and a smaller quantity is demanded. Suppose orange growers suffer from severe frosts and the supply of oranges decreases. Consequently, the price of oranges increases sharply. According to the *law of demand*, consumers will decrease the quantity demanded of oranges and substitute consumption of, say, apples for oranges. Because the market basket does not automatically change by reducing the percentage or weight of oranges and increasing the percentage of apples, the CPI will *overstate* the impact of higher prices for oranges on the price level. To deal with this *substitution* bias problem, the BLS takes annual surveys to keep up with changing consumption patterns and correct for the fixed market basket limitations of the CPI.

7-2 Consequences of Inflation

We will now turn from measuring inflation to examining its effects on people's income and wealth. Why should inflation cause concern? You will learn in this section that inflation is feared because it can significantly alter one's standard of living. You will see that inflation can create winners, who enjoy a larger slice of the national income pie, and losers, who receive a smaller slice as a result of inflation.

7-2a INFLATION SHRINKS INCOME

Economist Arthur Okun once stated, "This society is built on implicit and explicit contracts.... They are linked to the idea that the dollar means something. If you cannot depend on the value of the dollar, this system is undermined. People will constantly feel they've been fooled and cheated." When prices rise, people worry whether the rise in their income will keep pace with inflation. And the more quickly prices rise, the more people suffer from the stresses of inflation and its uncertainties.

Inflation tends to reduce your standard of living through declines in the purchasing power of money. The greater the rate of inflation, the greater the decline in the quantity of goods we can purchase with a given nominal income, or *money income*. Nominal income is the actual number of dollars received over a period of time. The source of income can be wages, salary, rent, dividends, interest, or pensions.

Nominal income does not measure your real purchasing power. Finding out if you are better or worse off over time requires converting nominal income to real income. Real income is the actual number of dollars received (nominal income) adjusted for changes in the CPI. Real income measures the amount of goods and services that can be purchased with one's nominal income. If the CPI increases and your nominal income remains the same, your real income (purchasing power) falls. In short, if your nominal income fails to keep pace with inflation, your standard of living falls. Suppose your nominal income in Year *1* was $50,000 and the Year *2* CPI value is 207.3. Your real income relative to a base year is

Nominal income

The actual number of dollars received over a period of time.

Real income

The actual number of dollars received (nominal income) adjusted for changes in the CPI.

$$\text{Real income} = \frac{\text{nominal income}}{\text{CPI (as decimal, or CPI}/100)}$$

$$\text{Year } 1 \text{ real income} = \frac{\$50,000}{2.07} = \$24,155$$

Now assume your nominal income rose in the next year (Year *2*) by 10 percent, from $50,000 to $55,000, and the CPI increases by 3.8 percent, from 207.3 to 215.3. Thus, you earn more money, but how much better off are you? To answer this question, you must compute your Year *2* real income as follows:

$$\text{Year } 2 \text{ real income} = \frac{\$55,000}{2.15} = \$25,581$$

Using the preceding two computed real-income figures, the percentage change in your real income between Year *1* and Year *2* was 5.9 percent ($1,426/$24,155 × 100). This means that your standard of living has risen because you have an extra $1,426 to spend on entertainment, clothes, or travel. Even though the general price level has risen, your purchasing power has increased because the percentage rise in nominal income more than offsets the rate of inflation. Instead of precisely calculating this relationship, a good approximation can be obtained through the following simple formula:

SOURCE: © Cengage Learning 2014

It should be noted that workers with union contracts are largely unaffected by inflation because their wages automatically increase with increases in the CPI, which is called a *cost-of-living adjustment (COLA)*. For example, under union contracts, an inflation rate of 3 percent in a given year would automatically increase wages by 3 percent.

> **CONCLUSION:** *People whose nominal incomes rise faster than the rate of inflation gain purchasing power, while people whose nominal incomes do not keep pace with inflation lose purchasing power.*

Now suppose someone asks you the following question: In 1932, Babe Ruth, the New York Yankees home run slugger, earned $80,000. How much did he earn in 2011 dollars? Economists convert a past salary into a salary today by using this formula:

$$\text{Salary in given year} = \text{salary in previous year} \times \frac{\text{CPI in given year}}{\text{CPI in previous year}}$$

$$\text{Salary in 2011 dollars} = \$80,000 \times \frac{225.0}{13.7} = \$1,313,868$$

In other words, a salary of $80,000 in 1932 was equivalent to a salary of about $1.3 million today.

✓ CHECKPOINT

What Is the Real Price of Gasoline?

In 1981, consumers were shocked when the average price for gasoline reached $1.35 per gallon because only a few years previously, gasoline was selling for one-half this price. If the CPI is 1981 was 90.9 and the CPI in 2011 was 225.0, what is the average inflation adjusted price in 2011 dollars?

"I've called the family together to announce that, because of inflation, I'm going to have to let two of you go."

7-2b INFLATION AND WEALTH

Wealth

The value of the stock of assets owned at some point in time.

Income is one measure of economic well-being, and wealth is another. Income is a flow of money earned by selling factors of production. Wealth is the value of the stock of assets owned at some point in time. Wealth includes real estate, stocks, bonds, bank accounts, life insurance policies, cash, and automobiles. A person can have a high income and little wealth or great wealth and little income.

Inflation can benefit holders of wealth because the value of assets tends to increase as prices rise. Consider a home purchased for $200,000 that sells ten years later for $300,000. This 50 percent increase can be largely the result of inflation. People who own forms of wealth that increase in value faster than the inflation rate, such as real estate and stocks, are winners. On the other hand, the impact of inflation on wealth penalizes people without it. Consider younger couples wishing to purchase a home. As prices rise, it becomes more difficult for them to buy a home or acquire other assets.

7-2c INFLATION AND THE REAL INTEREST RATE

Nominal interest rate

The actual rate of interest without adjustment for the inflation rate.

Real interest rate

The nominal rate of interest minus the inflation rate.

Borrowers and savers may be winners or losers, depending on the rate of inflation. Understanding how this might happen requires making a distinction between the nominal interest rate and the real interest rate. The nominal interest rate is the actual rate of interest earned over a period of time. The nominal interest rate, for example, is the interest rate specified on a loan or savings account. If you borrow $10,000 from a bank at a 5 percent annual interest rate for five years, this is more accurately called a 5 percent annual nominal interest rate. Similarly, a $10,000 certificate of deposit that yields 5 percent annual interest is said to have a 5 percent annual nominal interest rate.

The real interest rate is the nominal interest rate minus the inflation rate. The occurrence of inflation means that the real rate of interest will be less than the nominal rate. Suppose the inflation rate during the year is 5 percent. This means that a 5 percent annual nominal interest rate paid on a $10,000 loan amounts to a 2 percent *real interest rate* and a certificate of deposit that yields 5 percent annual nominal interest also earns 2 percent *real interest*.

To understand how inflation can make those who borrow winners, suppose you receive a one-year loan from your parents to start a business. Earning a profit is not your parents' motive, and they know you will repay the loan. Their only concern is that you replace the decline in purchasing power of the money they loaned you. Both you and your parents anticipate the inflation rate will be 2 percent during the year; so the loan is made, and you agree to repay the principal plus the 2 percent to offset inflation. In short, both parties assume payment of a zero real interest rate (the 2 percent nominal interest rate minus the 2 percent rate of inflation). Now consider what happens if the inflation rate is actually 5 percent during the year of the loan. The clear unintentional winner is you, the debtor, because your creditor parents are paid the principal plus 2 percent interest, but their purchasing power still falls by 3 percent because the actual inflation rate is 5 percent. Stated differently, instead of zero, the real interest rate paid on the loan was −3 percent (the 2 percent nominal interest rate minus the 5 percent rate of inflation). In real terms, your parents paid you to borrow from them.

During the late 1970s, the rate of inflation rose frequently. This forced mortgage lenders to protect themselves against declining real interest rates on their loans by offering adjustable-rate mortgages (ARMs) in addition to conventional fixed-rate mortgages. ARMs are home loans that adjust the nominal interest rate to changes in an index, such as rates on Treasury securities. The *subprime loan crisis* resulted from homeowners who were unable to make payments as the interest rate rose on their ARMs. This subject is discussed in more depth in the chapter on monetary policy.

A nest egg in the form of a savings account set aside for a rainy day is also affected by inflation. For example, if the interest rate on a one-year $10,000 certificate of deposit is 5 percent and the inflation rate is zero (5 percent real interest rate), the certificate holder will earn a 5 percent return on his or her savings. If the inflation rate exceeds the nominal rate of interest, the real interest rate is negative, and the saver is hurt because the interest earned does not keep pace with the inflation rate. This is the reason: Suppose, after one year, the saver withdraws the original $10,000 plus the $500 interest earned and the inflation rate during the year has been 10 percent. The real value of $10,500 adjusted for loss of purchasing power is only $9,500 [$10,000 + ($10,000 × −0.05)].

Finally, it is important to note that the nominal interest rate is never negative, but the real interest rate can be either positive or negative.

> **CONCLUSION:** *When the real rate of interest is negative, lenders and savers lose because interest earned does not keep up with the inflation rate.*

7-3 Demand-Pull and Cost-Push Inflation

Economists distinguish between two basic types of inflation, depending on whether it originates from the buyers' or the sellers' side of the market. The analysis presented in this section returns to the cause-and-effect relationship between total spending and the business cycle discussed in the previous chapter.

7-3a DEMAND-PULL INFLATION

Perhaps the most familiar type of inflation is demand-pull inflation, which is a rise in the general price level resulting from an excess of total spending (demand). Demand-pull inflation is often expressed as "too much money chasing too few goods." When sellers are unable to supply all the goods and services buyers demand, sellers respond by raising prices. In short, the general price level in the economy is "pulled up" by the pressure from buyers' total expenditures.

Demand-pull inflation occurs at or close to full employment, when the economy is operating at or near full capacity. Recall that at full employment, all but the frictionally and structurally unemployed are working and earning income. Therefore, total, or aggregate, demand for goods and services is high. Businesses find it profitable to expand their plants and production to meet the buyers' demand, but cannot in the short run. As a result, national output remains fixed, and prices rise as buyers try to outbid one another for the available supply of goods and services. If total spending subsides, so will the pressure on the available supply of products, and prices will not rise as rapidly or may even fall.

Adjustable-rate mortgage (ARM)

A home loan that adjusts the nominal interest rate to changes in an index rate, such as rates on Treasury securities.

Demand-pull inflation

A rise in the general price level resulting from an excess of total spending (demand).

A word of caution: Consumers may not be the only villain in the demand-pull story. Recall that total aggregate spending includes consumer spending (C), business investment (I), government spending (G), and net exports (X − M). Even foreigners may contribute to inflation by bidding up the price of U.S. exports.

7-3b COST-PUSH INFLATION

Cost-push inflation
An increase in the general price level resulting from an increase in the cost of production.

An excess of total spending is not the only possible explanation for rising prices. For example, suppose the Organization of Petroleum Exporting Countries (OPEC) sharply increases the price of oil. This action means a significant increase in the cost of producing goods and services. The result could be cost-push inflation. Cost-push inflation is a rise in the general price level resulting from an increase in the cost of production.

The source of cost-push inflation is not always such a dramatic event as an OPEC price hike. Any sharp increase in costs to businesses can be a potential source of cost-push inflation. This means that upward pressure on prices can be caused by cost increases for labor, raw materials, construction, equipment, borrowing, and so on. Businesses can also contribute to cost-push inflation by raising prices to increase profits.

The influence of *expectations* on both demand-pull and cost-push inflation is an important consideration. Suppose buyers see prices rise and believe they should purchase that new house or car today before these items cost much more tomorrow. At or near full employment, this demand-pull results in a rise in prices. On the suppliers' side, firms might expect their production costs to rise in the future, so they raise prices in anticipation of the higher costs. The result is cost-push inflation.

Here you should take note of coming attractions. The chapter on aggregate demand and supply develops a modern macro model that you can use to analyze with more precision the factors that determine national output, employment, and the price level. In particular, the last section of this chapter applies the aggregate demand and supply model to the concepts of demand-pull and cost-push inflation. Also, the chapter on monetary policy will discuss the theory that inflation is the result of increases in the money supply in excess of increases in the production of goods and services.

7-4 Inflation in Other Countries

GLOBAL ECONOMICS

Exhibit 5 reveals that inflation rates vary widely among nations. In 2011, Venezuela, Congo, and other countries experienced very high rates of inflation. In contrast, the United States had an inflation rate of 3.2 percent, while Italy and France had lower rates. Ireland and other countries had negative inflation rates.

7-4a INFLATION ON A RAMPAGE

Hyperinflation
An extremely rapid rise in the general price level.

Some people must carry a large stack of money to pay for a chocolate bar because of the disastrous consequences of hyperinflation. Hyperinflation is an extremely rapid rise in the general price level. There is no consensus on when a particular rate of inflation becomes "hyper." However, most economists would agree that an inflation rate of about 100 percent per year or more is hyperinflation. Runaway

EXHIBIT 5	Annual Inflation Rates in Selected Countries, 2011

As shown by the bars, inflation was a serious problem in 2011 for Venezuela, Congo, and other countries. The United States experienced an inflation rate of 3.2 percent, while Italy and France had lower rates.

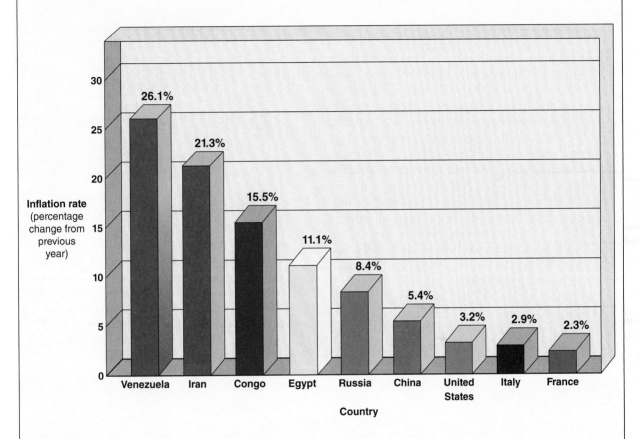

SOURCE: International Monetary Fund, *World Economic Outlook Database*, http://www.imf.org/external/ns/cs.aspx?id=28.

inflation is conducive to rapid and violent social and political change stemming from four causes.

First, individuals and businesses develop an *inflation psychosis*, causing them to buy quickly today in order to avoid paying even more tomorrow. Everyone feels pressure to spend their earnings before their purchasing power deteriorates. Regardless of whether you are paid once, twice, or any number of times per day, you will be eager to spend it immediately.

Second, huge unanticipated inflation jeopardizes debtor-lender contracts, such as credit cards, home mortgages, life insurance policies, pensions, bonds, and other forms of savings. For example, if nominal interest rates rise unexpectedly in response to higher inflation, borrowers find it more difficult to make their monthly payments.

Who Wants to Be a Trillionaire?

Applicable Concept: hyperinflation

The following articles are two historical examples of hyperinflation:

A 1985 *Wall Street Journal* article described hyperinflation in La Paz, Bolivia:

> A courier stumbles into Banco Boliviano Americano, struggling under the weight of a huge bag of money he is carrying on his back. He announces that the sack contains 32 million pesos, and a teller slaps on a notation to that effect. The courier pitches the bag into a corner. "We don't bother counting the money any-more," explains Max Lowes Stah, a loan officer standing nearby. "We take the client's word for what's in the bag." Pointing to the courier's load, he says, "That's a small deposit." At that moment the 32 million pesos—enough bills to stuff a mail sack—were worth only $500. Today, less than two weeks later, they are worth at least $180 less. Life's like that with quadruple-digit inflation....
>
> Prices go up by the day, the hour or the customer. If the pace continues all year it would mean an annual rate of 116,000 percent. The 1,000-peso bill, the most commonly used,

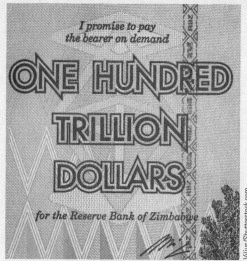

> costs more to print than it purchases. To purchase an average-size television set with 1,000-peso bills, customers have to haul money weighing more than 68 pounds into the showroom. Inflation makes use of credit cards impossible here, and merchants generally can't take checks, either. Restaurant owners often covered their menus with cellophane and chan-ged prices several times daily using a dry-erase marker.[1]

Wage-price spiral

A situation that occurs when increases in nominal wage rates are passed on in higher prices, which, in turn, result in even higher nominal wage rates and prices.

Third, hyperinflation sets a wage-price spiral in motion. A wage-price spiral occurs in a series of steps when increases in nominal wage rates are passed on in higher prices, which, in turn, result in even higher nominal wage rates and prices. A wage-price spiral continues when management believes it can boost prices faster than the rise in labor costs. As the cost of living moves higher, however, labor must again demand even higher wage increases. Each round yields higher and higher prices as wages and prices chase each other in an upward spiral.

Fourth, because the future rate of inflation is difficult or impossible to antici-pate, people turn to more speculative investments that might yield higher financial returns. To hedge against the high losses of purchasing power from hyperinflation, funds flow into gold, silver, stamps, jewels, art, antiques, and other currencies, rather than into new factories, machinery, and technological research that expand an economy's production possibilities curve.

A *San Francisco Chronicle* article reported on hyperinflation in Zimbabwe:

> What is happening is no laughing matter. (In 2008, the annual inflation rate was 231 million percent.) For untold numbers of Zimbabweans, bread, margarine, meat and even the morning cup of tea have become unimaginable luxuries. The city suffers rolling electrical blackouts because the state cannot afford parts or technicians to fix broken down power turbines. Mounds of uncollected garbage pile up on the streets of slums. Public-school fees and other ever-rising government surcharges have begun to exceed the monthly incomes of many urban families lucky enough to work. Those with spare cash put it not in banks, but in gilt-edged investments like bags of cornmeal and sugar, guaranteed not to lose their value.[2]

In 2010, Zimbabwe's central bank announced the introduction of new 100 trillion, 50 trillion, 20 trillion, and 10 trillion notes. Want to be a multi-trillionaire?

A *Newsweek* article made the following thoughtful observation:

> Hyperinflation is the worst economic malady that can befall a nation, wiping out the value of money, savings, assets, and thus work. It is worse even than a deep recession. Hyperinflation robs you of what you have now (savings), whereas a recession robs you of what you might have had (higher standards of living if the economy had grown). That's why it so often toppled governments and produced revolution. Recall that it was not the Great Depression that brought the Nazis to power in Germany but rather hyperinflation, which destroyed the middle class of that country by making its savings worthless.[3]

Analyze the Issue

1. Can you relate inflation psychosis to these excerpts? Give an example of a debtor-lender relationship that is jeopardized by hyperinflation.
2. Explain why the workers in Bolivia were striking even though wages rose at an annual rate of 1,500 percent. Do you see any connection between hyperinflation and the political system?

---

1. Sonia L. Nazario, "When Inflation Rate Is 116,000 Percent, Prices Change by the Hour," *The Wall Street Journal*, Feb. 7, 1985, p. 1.
2. Michale Wines, "Zimbabwe: Inflation Capitol," *San Francisco Chronicle*, May 2, 2006, p. A-2.
3. Fareed Zakaria, "Is This the End of Inflation? Turkey's Currency Crisis May Be the Last Battle in the Global War Against Hyperinflation," *Newsweek*, Mar. 19, 2001, p. 38.

History reveals numerous hyperinflation examples. One of the most famous occurred during the 1920s in the German Weimar Republic. Faced with huge World War I reparations payments, the Weimar government simply printed money to pay its bills. By late 1923, the annual inflation rate in Germany had reached 35,000 percent per month. Prices rose frequently, sometimes increasing in minutes, and German currency became so worthless that it was used as kindling for stoves. No one was willing to make new loans, and credit markets collapsed. Wealth was redistributed because those who were heavily in debt easily paid their debts, and people's savings were wiped out.

Finally, hyperinflation is invariably the result of a government's ill-advised decision to increase a country's money supply. Moreover, hyperinflation is not a historical relic, as illustrated in the above Global Economics article.

Key Concepts

Inflation
Deflation
Consumer price index (CPI)
Base year
Disinflation

Nominal income
Real income
Wealth
Nominal interest rate
Real interest rate

Adjustable-rate mortgage (ARM)
Demand-pull inflation
Cost-push inflation
Hyperinflation
Wage-price spiral

Summary

- **Inflation** is an increase in the general (average) price level of goods and services in the economy.
- **Deflation** is a decrease in the general level of prices. During the early years of the Great Depression, there was deflation, and the CPI declined at about a double-digit rate.
- The **consumer price index (CPI)** is the most widely known price-level index. It measures the cost of purchasing a market basket of goods and services by a typical household during a time period relative to the cost of the same bundle during a base year. The annual rate of inflation is computed using the following formula:

  annual rate of inflation =
  $$\frac{\text{CPI in given year} - \text{CPI in previous year}}{\text{CPI in previous year}} \times 100$$

- **Disinflation** is a reduction in the inflation rate. This does not mean that prices were falling, only that the inflation rate fell.
- The **inflation rate** determined by the CPI is criticized because (1) it is not representative, (2) it has difficulty adjusting for quality changes, and (3) it ignores the relationship between price changes and the importance of items in the market basket.

- **Nominal income** is income measured in actual money amounts. Measuring your purchasing power requires converting nominal income into **real income**, which is nominal income adjusted for inflation.

SOURCE: © Cengage Learning 2014

- The **real interest rate** is the *nominal interest rate* adjusted for inflation. If real interest rates are negative, lenders incur losses.
- An **adjustable-rate mortgage** is a home loan that adjusts the nominal interest rate to changes in an index rate, such as rates on Treasury securities.
- **Demand-pull inflation** is caused by pressure on prices originating from the buyers' side of the market. In contrast, **cost-push inflation** is caused by pressure on prices originating from the sellers' side of the market.
- **Hyperinflation** can seriously disrupt an economy by causing inflation psychosis, credit market collapses, a wage-price spiral, and speculation. A **wage-price spiral** occurs when increases in nominal wages cause higher prices, which, in turn, cause higher wages and prices.

Summary of Conclusion Statements

- Inflation is an increase in the overall average level of prices and not an increase in the price of any specific product.

- People whose nominal incomes rise faster than the rate of inflation gain purchasing power, while people whose nominal incomes do

not keep pace with inflation lose purchasing power.
- When the real rate of interest is negative, lenders and savers lose because interest

earned does not keep up with the inflation rate.

Study Questions and Problems

1. Consider this statement: "When the price of a good or service rises, the inflation rate rises." Do you agree or disagree? Explain.

2. Suppose, in the base year, a typical market basket purchased by an urban family cost $250. In Year 1, the same market basket cost $950. What is the consumer price index (CPI) for Year 1? If the same market basket cost $1,000 in Year 2, what is the CPI for Year 2? What was the Year 2 rate of inflation?

3. What are three criticisms of the CPI?

4. Suppose you earned $100,000 in a given year. Calculate your real income, assuming the CPI is 200 for this year.

5. Explain how a person's purchasing power can decline in a given year even though he or she received a salary increase.

6. Who loses from inflation? Who wins from inflation?

7. Suppose you borrow $100 from a bank at 5 percent interest for one year and the inflation rate that year is 10 percent. Was this loan advantageous to you or to the bank?

8. Suppose the annual nominal rate of interest on a bank certificate of deposit is 12 percent. What would be the effect of an inflation rate of 13 percent?

9. When the economy approaches full employment, why does demand-pull inflation become a problem?

10. How does demand-pull inflation differ from cost-push inflation?

11. Explain this statement: "If everyone expects inflation to occur, it will."

For Online Exercises, go to the Tucker Web site at http://www.cengage.com/economics/tucker.

✔ CHECKPOINT ANSWERS

The College Education Price Index

$$2010 \text{ college education price index} = \frac{\text{market basket cost at 2010 prices}}{\text{market basket cost at base-year (2010) prices}} \times 100$$

$$= \frac{\$11,650}{\$11,650} \times 100 = 100$$

$$2011 \text{ college education price index} = \frac{\text{market basket cost at 2011 prices}}{\text{market basket cost at base-year (2010) prices}} \times 100$$

$$= \frac{\$12,600}{\$11,650} \times 100 = 108.1$$

$$\text{Percentage change in price level of college education} = \frac{108.1 - 100}{100} \times 100 = 8.1\%$$

If you said the price of a college education increased 8.1 percent in 2011, **YOU ARE CORRECT.**

What s the Real Price of Gasoline?

$$\text{Average gasoline price in 2011 dollars} = \$1.35 \times \frac{225.0}{90.9} = \$3.34$$

If you said the price of $1.35 per gallon for gasoline in 1981 was $3.34 per gallon in 2011 after adjusting for inflation over these years, **YOU ARE CORRECT.**

To update this calculation, click on the CPI Inflation Calculator at http://data.bls.gov/cgi-bin/cpicalc.pl.

Sample Quiz

For an explanation of the correct answers, visit the Tucker Web site at www.cengage.com/economics/tucker.

1. Inflation is defined as an increase in
   a. real wages of workers.
   b. real GDP.
   c. the average price level.
   d. all consumer products.

2. Inflation is measured by an increase in
   a. homes, autos, and basic resources.
   b. prices of all products in the economy.
   c. the consumer price index (CPI).
   d. None of the answsers above is correct.

3. Which one of the following groups benefits from inflation?
   a. borrowers
   b. savers
   c. landlords
   d. lenders

4. Price indexes such as the CPI are calculated using a base year. The term *base year* refers to
   a. the first year that price data are available.
   b. any year in which inflation is higher than 5 percent.
   c. the most recent year in which the business cycle hit the trough.
   d. an arbitrarily chosen reference year.

5. If the consumer price index (CPI) in Year 1 was 200 and the CPI in Year 2 was 215, the rate of inflation is
   a. 215 percent.
   b. 15 percent.
   c. 5 percent.
   d. 7.5 percent.
   e. 8 percent.

6. Which of the following statements is *true*?
   a. Deflation is an increase in the general level of prices.
   b. The consumer price index (CPI) measures changes in the average prices of consumer goods and services.
   c. Disinflation is an increase in the rate of inflation.
   d. Real income is the actual number of dollars received over a period of time.

7. Suppose the price of banana rises over time and consumers respond by buying fewer bananas. This situation contributes to which bias in the consumer price index?
   a. substitution bias
   b. transportation bias
   c. quality bias
   d. indexing bias

Sample Quiz *continued*

8. Deflation means a decrease in
   a. the rate of inflation.
   b. the prices of all products in the economy.
   c. homes, autos, and basic resources.
   d. the general level of prices in the economy.

9. Real income in Year X is equal to
   a. $\dfrac{\text{Year } X \text{ nominal income}}{\text{Year } X \text{ real GDP}} \times 100.$

   b. $\dfrac{\text{Year } X \text{ nominal income}}{\text{Year } X \text{ real output}} \times 100.$

   c. $\dfrac{\text{Year } X \text{ nominal income}}{\text{CPI}/100}.$

   d. Year X nominal income $\times$ CPI.

10. The real interest rate is defined as the
    a. actual interest rate.
    b. fixed rate on consumer loans.
    c. nominal interest rate minus the inflation rate.
    d. expected interest rate minus the inflation rate.

11. If the inflation rate exceeds the nominal rate of interest,
    a. the real interest rate is negative.
    b. lenders lose.
    c. savers lose.
    d. All of the above answers are correct.

12. Suppose you place $10,000 in a retirement fund that earns a nominal interest rate of 8 percent. If you expect inflation to be 5 percent or lower, then you are expecting to earn a real interest rate of at least
    a. 1.6 percent.
    b. 3 percent.
    c. 4 percent.
    d. 5 percent.

13. Which of the following can create demand-pull inflation?
    a. excessive aggregate spending
    b. sharply rising oil prices
    c. higher labor costs
    d. recessions and depressions

14. Which of the following statements is *true*?
    a. Demand-pull inflation is caused by excess total spending.
    b. Cost-push inflation is caused by an increase in resource costs.
    c. If nominal interest rates remain the same and the inflation rate falls, real interest rates increase.
    d. If real interest rates are negative, lenders incur losses.
    e. All of the above answers are correct.

15. Cost-push inflation is due to
    a. labor cost increases.
    b. energy cost increases.
    c. raw material cost increases.
    d. All of the above answers are correct.

16. During periods of hyperinflation, which of the following is the *most* likely response of consumers?
    a. Save as much as possible
    b. Spend money as fast as possible
    c. Invest as much as possible
    d. Lend money

17. The base year in the consumer price index (CPI) is
    a. given a value of zero.
    b. a year chosen as a reference for prices in all other years.
    c. always the first year in the current decade.
    d. established by law.

18. Deflation
    a. was prevalent during the oil shocks of the 1970s.
    b. will cause consumers' purchasing power to shrink under current trends.
    c. has been persistent in the U.S. economy since the Great Depression.
    d. refers to none of the answers above.

19. As the price of gasoline rose during the 1970s, consumers cut back on their use of gasoline relative to other consumer goods. This situation contributed to which bias in the consumer price index?

Sample Quiz *continued*

a. substitution bias
b. transportation bias
c. quality bias
d. indexing bias

20. If the rate of inflation in a given time period turns out to be lower than lenders and borrowers anticipated, then the effect will be a

a. redistribution of wealth from borrowers to lenders.
b. redistribution of wealth from lenders to borrowers.
c. net loss in purchasing power for lenders relative to borrowers.
d. net gain in purchasing power for borrowers relative to lenders.

Road Map
Macroeconomic Fundamentals

part **3**

This road map feature helps you tie together material in the part as you travel the Economic Way of Thinking highway. The following are review questions listed by chapter from the previous part.

CHAPTER 5. GROSS DOMESTIC PRODUCT

1. **Key Concept: Gross Domestic Product**
   Which of the following items is included in the calculation of GDP?
   a. Purchase of 100 shares of General Motors stock
   b. Purchase of a used car
   c. The value of a homemaker's services
   d. Sale of Gulf War military surplus
   e. None of the above

2. **Key Concept: Expenditure Approach**
   Using the expenditure approach, GDP equals:
   a. $C + I + G + (X - M)$.
   b. $C + I + G + (X + M)$.
   c. $C + I - G + (X - M)$.
   d. $C + I + G - (X - M)$.

3. **Key Concept: GDP Shortcomings**
   If the underground economy is sizable, then GDP will:
   a. understate the economy's performance.
   b. overstate the economy's performance.
   c. fluctuate unpredictably.
   d. accurately reflect this subterranean activity.

4. **Key Concept: Real GDP**
   What is the equation for determining real GDP for year X?
   a. $\dfrac{\text{nominal GDP for year } X}{\text{average nominal GDP}}$
   b. $\dfrac{\text{nominal GDP for year } X}{\text{GDP for year } X} - 100$
   c. $\dfrac{\text{nominal GDP for year } X}{\text{GDP chain price index for year } X} \times 100$
   d. $\dfrac{\text{nominal GDP for year } X}{\text{average family income}} \times 100$

CHAPTER 6. BUSINESS CYCLES AND UNEMPLOYMENT

5. Key Concept: Business Cycle
A business cycle is:
a. the period of time in which expansion and contraction of economic activity are equal.
b. the period of time in which there are three phases: peak, depression, and recovery.
c. recurring growth and decline in real GDP.
d. the period of time in which a business is established and ceases operations.

6. Key Concept: Business Cycle
A business cycle is the period of time in which:
a. a business is established and ceases operations.
b. there are four phases: peak, recession, trough, and recovery.
c. the price level varies with real GDP.
d. expansion and contraction of economic activity are equal.
e. none of the above occur.

7. Key Concept: Unemployment
John Steinbeck's *Cannery Row* describes a character who takes his own life because of poor job prospects. If he was an unemployed person who gave up looking for work, he would be considered:
a. chronically unemployed.
b. a discouraged worker.
c. a member of the labor force.
d. frictionally unemployed.

8. Key Concept: Unemployment
Consider a broom factory that permanently closes because of foreign competition. If the broom factory's workers cannot find new jobs because their skills are no longer marketable, then they are classified as:
a. seasonally unemployed.
b. frictionally unemployed.
c. structurally unemployed.
d. cyclically unemployed.

CHAPTER 7. INFLATION

9. Key Concept: Inflation
Inflation is measured by an increase in:
a. homes, autos, and basic resources.
b. prices of all products in the economy.
c. the consumer price index (CPI).
d. none of the above.

10. **Key Concept: Consumer Price Index Bias**

As the price of gasoline rose during the 1970s, consumers cut back on their use of gasoline relative to other consumer goods. This situation contributed to which bias in the consumer price index?

   a. Substitution bias
   b. Transportation bias
   c. Quality bias
   d. Indexing bias

11. **Key Concept: Real Income**

Real income in Year X is equal to:

   a. $\dfrac{\text{Year } X \text{ nominal income}}{\text{Year } X \text{ real GDP}} \times 100.$

   b. $\dfrac{\text{Year } X \text{ nominal income}}{\text{Year } X \text{ real output}} \times 100.$

   c. $\dfrac{\text{Year } X \text{ nominal income}}{\text{CPI}/100}.$

   d. Year X nominal income $\times$ CPI.

12. **Key Concept: Cost-Push Inflation**

Cost-push inflation is due to:

   a. labor cost increases.
   b. energy cost increases.
   c. raw material cost increases.
   d. all of the above.

Macroeconomic Theory and Policy

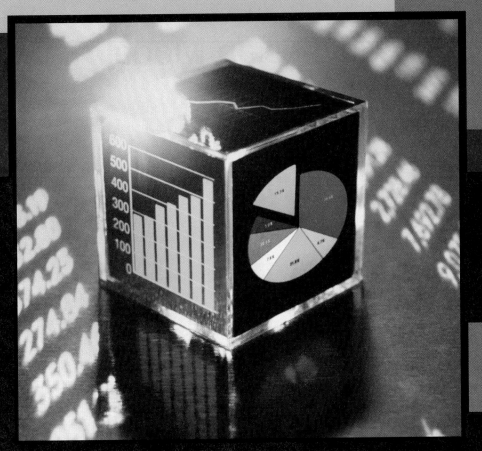

This part begins with two chapters that present a theoretical model originating in a book published in 1936 by British economist John Maynard Keynes. The purpose of the Keynesian model is to understand the causes and cures of the Great Depression. The next chapter explains another theoretical macro model based on aggregate demand and aggregate supply. The following chapter discusses the federal government's taxing and spending policies, and the next chapter explains actual data measures of government spending and taxation patterns. The part concludes with a chapter on hotly debated topics: federal deficits, surpluses, and the national debt.

chapter 8

The Keynesian Model

In U.S. history, the 1920s are known as the "Roaring 20s." It was a time of optimism and prosperity. The spirit of the times was captivated in the lyrics of a popular song of the day: "Nothing but blue skies do I see." Between 1920 and 1929, real GDP rose by 42 percent. Stock prices soared year after year and made many investors rich. As business boomed, companies invested in new factories, and the U.S. economy was a job-creating machine. People bought fine clothes, had parties, and danced the popular Charleston. Then the business cycle took an abrupt downturn on October 29, 1929, Black Tuesday. The most severe recession in recent U.S. history had begun. During the Great Depression, stock prices fell. Wages fell. Real output fell. Banks failed. Businesses closed their doors, and the unemployment rate soared to 25 percent. Unemployed workers would fight over a job, sell apples on the corner to survive, and walk the streets in bewilderment.

The misery of the Great Depression created a revolution in economic thought. Prior to the Great Depression, economists recognized that over the years, business downturns would interrupt the nation's prosperity, but they believed these episodes were temporary. They argued that in a short time, the price system would automatically restore an economy to full employment without government intervention.

Why didn't the economy self-correct to its 1929 level of real GDP? What went wrong? The stage was set for a new idea offered by British economist **John Maynard Keynes** (pronounced "canes"). Keynes argued that the economy was not self-correcting and therefore could indeed remain below full employment indefinitely because of inadequate aggregate spending. Keynes's work not only explained the crash, but also offered cures requiring the government to play an active rather than a passive role in the economy.

Whether or not economists agree with Keynes's ideas, this famous economist still influences macroeconomics today. This chapter begins with a discussion of classical economic theory before Keynes. Then you will learn what determines the level of consumption and investment expenditures, which are the first two components of Keynes's aggregate expenditures model. In the next chapter, these two components are added to government spending and net exports to form the complete Keynesian aggregate expenditures model.

In this chapter, you will learn to solve these economics puzzles:

- Why did economists believe the Great Depression was impossible?

- According to Keynes, what determines a family's spending for consumption?

- Why did Keynes believe that "animal spirits" and government policy were important to maintain full employment?

8-1 Introducing Classical Theory and the Keynesian Revolution

Prior to the Great Depression of the 1930s, a group of economists known as the classical economists dominated economic thinking.[1] The founder of the classical school of economics was Adam Smith (discussed in the chapter on economies in transition). Macroeconomics had not developed as a separate economic theory, and classical economics was therefore based primarily on microeconomic market equilibrium theory. The classical school of economics was mainstream economics from the 1770s to the Great Depression era. The classical economists believed in the *laissez-faire* "leave it alone" theory that our economy was self-regulating and would correct itself without government interference. The classical economists believed, as you studied in Chapter 4, that the forces of supply and demand naturally achieve full employment in the economy because flexible prices (including wages and interest rates) in competitive markets bring all markets to full-employment equilibrium. After a temporary adjustment period, markets always clear because firms sell all goods and services offered for sale. In short, recessions would naturally cure themselves because the capitalistic price system would automatically restore full employment. The classical model is explained in more detail in the chapter on aggregate demand and supply.

> **CONCLUSION:** *The classical economists believed that a continuing depression is impossible because markets eliminate persistent shortages or surpluses.*

The simple idea known as Say's Law, developed in the early 1800s by *Jean-Baptiste Say*, convinced classical economists that a prolonged depression was impossible. Say's Law is the theory that supply creates its own demand. Say's Law was the cornerstone of classical economics. Simply put, this theory states that long-term underspending is impossible because the production of goods and services (supply) generates an equal amount of total spending (demand) for these goods and services. Recall the circular flow model explained in the chapter on GDP. Suppose a firm produces $1 worth of bread in the product market. This supply decision creates $1 of income to the household sector through the factor markets. In other words, Say's Law is a theory that a glut of unsold products causing workers to lose

John Maynard Keynes

British economist (1883–1946) whose influential work offered an explanation of the Great Depression and suggested, as a cure, that the government should play an active role in the economy.

Classical economists

A group of economists whose theory dominated economic thinking from the 1770s to the Great Depression. They believed recessions would naturally cure themselves because the price system would automatically restore full employment.

Say's Law

The theory that supply creates its own demand.

---

[1]The classical economists included Adam Smith, J. B. Say, David Ricardo, John Stuart Mill, Thomas Malthus, Alfred Marshall, and others.

their jobs is a temporary problem because there is just the right amount of income in the economy to purchase all products produced without layoffs.

> **CONCLUSION:** *In the classical view, unemployment is the result of a short-lived adjustment period in which wages and prices decline or people voluntarily choose not to work. Thus, there is a natural tendency for the economy to restore full employment over time.*

In 1936, seven years after the beginning of the Great Depression and three years before the beginning of World War II, John Maynard Keynes published *The General Theory of Employment, Interest, and Money*.[2] Keynes, a Cambridge University economist, wrote in a time of great uncertainty and instability. His book established macroeconomics as a separate field of economics and challenged the baffled classical economists by turning Say's Law upside down. Keynesian theory argues that "demand creates its own supply." Keynes explained that *aggregate expenditures (demand)* can be forever inadequate for an economy to achieve full employment. Aggregate expenditures are the sum of consumption (C), investment (I), government spending (G), and net exports (X − M). Aggregate expenditures are also known as *aggregate spending* or *aggregate demand*. Recall from the chapter on GDP that C, I, G, and (X − M) are national accounting categories used to calculate GDP following the expenditures approach.

8-1a THE CONSUMPTION FUNCTION

Consumption function

The graph or table that shows the amount households spend for goods and services at different levels of real disposable income.

What determines your family's spending for food, clothing, automobiles, education, and other consumer goods and services? According to Keynes, the most important factor is disposable income (personal income to spend after taxes; see Exhibit 9 in the chapter on GDP). Keynes argued it is a fundamental psychological law that if take-home pay increases, consumers will increase their spending and saving. Keynes's focus on the relationship between consumption and real disposable income is represented by the consumption function. The consumption function shows the amount households spend for goods and services at different levels of real disposable income. Recall from Exhibit 2 in the chapter on GDP that consumption is the largest single component of aggregate expenditures.

Exhibit 1 provides data on real disposable income (Y_d) in column (1), consumption (C) in column (2), and saving (S) in column (3) for a hypothetical economy. Since households spend each dollar of real disposable income either for consumption or for saving, the formula for saving is

$$S = Y_d - C$$

From the above equation, it follows that

$$Y_d = C + S$$

Autonomous consumption

Consumption that is independent of the level of real disposable income.

Note that if real disposable income is zero, consumption expenditures will be $1 trillion of autonomous consumption. Autonomous consumption is consumption that is independent of the level of real disposable income. It is the amount of

---

[2]John Maynard Keynes, *The General Theory of Employment, Interest, and Money* (New York: Harcourt, Brace, and World, 1936).

EXHIBIT 1	The Consumption Function

This exhibit shows the consumption function for a hypothetical economy. The break-even income is $4 trillion real disposable income, where households spend each dollar of real disposable income, $C = Y_d$, and savings are zero. Below $4 trillion, households spend more than their real disposable income by borrowing or withdrawing from past savings. Above the break-even income, households spend less than their real disposable income, and saving occurs. The marginal propensity to consume (MPC) is 0.75 because the slope of the consumption schedule shows that for each dollar increase in income (ΔY_d), consumption increases (ΔC) by 75 cents, and the remaining 25 cents is saved.

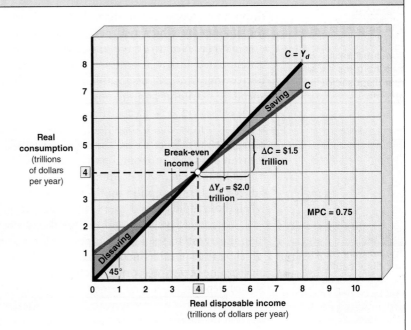

Consumption, Dissaving, Saving, MPC, and MPS Data

(1) Real disposable income (Y_d)	(2) Consumption (C)	(3) Dissaving (−) or Saving (+)	(4) Marginal propensity to consume (MPC) [$\Delta C/\Delta Y_d$ or $\Delta 2/\Delta 1$]	(5) Marginal propensity to save (MPS) [$\Delta S/\Delta Y_d$ or $\Delta 3/\Delta 1$]
$0	$1.00	−$1.00	—	—
1.00	1.75	−0.75	0.75	0.25
2.00	2.50	−0.50	0.75	0.25
3.00	3.25	−0.25	0.75	0.25
4.00	4.00	0	0.75	0.25
5.00	4.75	0.25	0.75	0.25
6.00	5.50	0.50	0.75	0.25
7.00	6.25	0.75	0.75	0.25
8.00	7.00	1.00	0.75	0.25

NOTE: All amounts are in trillions of dollars per year.

consumption expenditures that occur even when real disposable income is zero. At other low levels of real disposable income, households also spend more on consumer goods and services than they earn in income during the year. If annual real disposable income is any level below $4 trillion, households dissave. Dissaving is the amount by which real personal consumption expenditures exceed real disposable income. Negative saving, or dissaving, is financed by drawing down previously accumulated financial assets, such as savings accounts, stocks, and bonds, or by borrowing. At a real disposable income of $2 trillion per year, for example, families spend $2.5 trillion and thereby dissave $0.5 trillion.

Dissaving

The amount by which real personal consumption expenditures exceed real disposable income.

Dissaving is shown in the graph as the vertical distance below the consumption function to the *45-degree line*. The 45-degree line is a geometric construct that represents all points where the value measured on the vertical axis equals the value measured on the horizontal axis. This makes it easier to identify the *break-even, or no-saving income*, which equates real disposable income measured on the horizontal axis and consumption on the vertical axis. In our example, $C = Y_d$ at $4 trillion, where households spend every dollar earned and saving is therefore zero.

At higher levels beyond the break-even income, households earn more income than they wish to spend, and a portion of income is saving. Saving is the amount by which real disposable income exceeds real personal consumption expenditures. Savings can be in various forms, such as funds in a passbook savings account, a certificate of deposit, stocks, or bonds. In Exhibit 1, positive saving is the vertical distance above the consumption function to the 45-degree line. For example, at a real disposable income of $8 trillion, households save $1 trillion.

Saving

The amount by which real disposable income exceeds real personal consumption expenditures.

> **CONCLUSION:** *The 45-degree line is a geometric construct. It indicates all points where real disposable income (measured on the horizontal axis) and real consumption (measured on the vertical axis) are equal. Consequently, the 45-degree line makes it easier to identify the break-even, or no-saving income level.*

8-1b MARGINAL PROPENSITIES TO CONSUME AND SAVE

Keynes argued that as income grows, so does consumption, but by less than income. This crucial concept is called the marginal propensity to consume (MPC). The marginal propensity to consume is "the change" or "extra" in consumption resulting from a given change in real disposable income. Stated differently, the MPC is the ratio of the change in real consumption (ΔC) to the change in real disposable income (ΔY_d). The Greek letter Δ (delta) means "a change in." Mathematically,

Marginal propensity to consume (MPC)

The change in consumption resulting from a given change in real disposable income.

$$\text{MPC} = \frac{\text{change in consumption}}{\text{change in real disposable income}} = \frac{\Delta C}{\Delta Y_d}$$

As shown in column (4) of Exhibit 1, the MPC is 0.75. This means for every dollar increase (decrease) in disposable income (ΔY_d), consumption (ΔC) increases (decreases) 75 cents. In each model developed throughout this text, we assume the MPC is constant for all income levels. In our numerical example, real disposable income rises by $1 trillion between each level of income listed in column (1) of Exhibit 1, and consumption rises by $0.75 trillion. Mathematically,

$$MPC = \frac{\Delta C}{\Delta Y_d} = \frac{\$0.75 \text{ trillion}}{\$1 \text{ trillion}} = 0.75$$

What do households do with an extra dollar of real disposable income if they do not spend it? There is only one other choice—they save it. The marginal propensity to save (MPS) is the change in saving resulting from a given change in real disposable income. That is, the MPS is the ratio of the change in saving (ΔS) to the change in real disposable income (ΔY_d). Mathematically,

$$MPS = \frac{\text{change in saving}}{\text{change in real disposable income}} = \frac{\Delta S}{\Delta Y_d}$$

The MPS given in column (5) of Exhibit 1 is 0.25. Each dollar increase (decrease) in disposable income (ΔY_d) yields a rise (fall) of 25 cents in the amount of savings (ΔS). Mathematically,

$$MPS = \frac{\Delta S}{\Delta Y_d} = \frac{\$0.25 \text{ trillion}}{\$1 \text{ trillion}} = 0.25$$

As derived previously, $Y_d = C + S$, so it follows that $\Delta C + \Delta S = \Delta Y_d$. Dividing both sides of this equation by ΔY_d yields

$$\frac{\Delta C}{\Delta Y_d} + \frac{\Delta S}{\Delta Y_d} = \frac{\Delta Y_d}{\Delta Y_d}$$

or

$$MPC + MPS = 1$$

In our example, $0.75 + 0.25 = 1$, which means any change in real disposable income is divided between changes in consumption and changes in saving. Hence, if you know the MPC, you can calculate the MPS and vice versa.

8-1c GRAPHICAL ANALYSIS OF MPC

Exhibit 1 shows a graphic representation of the MPC. The consumption function has a positive slope because consumption spending increases with real disposable income. The MPC (slope) of the consumption function, C, for example, between the break-even income of $4 trillion and $6 trillion is measured by dividing $\Delta C = \$1.5$ trillion (the rise) by $\Delta Y_d = \$2.0$ trillion (the run). Since the MPC is constant, the ratio $\Delta C/\Delta Y_d$ between any two levels of real disposable income is 0.75. As a formula:

$$\text{Slope of consumption function} = \frac{\text{rise}}{\text{run}} = \frac{\Delta C}{\Delta Y_d} = \frac{\$1.5 \text{ trillion}}{\$2.0 \text{ trillion}} = 0.75$$

The points along the consumption function, C, in Exhibit 1 can be expressed by the following equation:

$$C = a + bY_d$$

where a is autonomous consumption and b is the MPC, which falls between 0 and 1. Keynes used this basic equation to derive consumption (C), and it is called the Keynesian consumption function.

Marginal propensity to save (MPS)

The change in saving resulting from a given change in real disposable income.

Using this equation,

$$C = \$1 \text{ trillion} + 0.75\ Y_d$$

For example, at $Y_d = \$4$ trillion,

$$C = \$1 \text{ trillion} + 0.75\ (\$4 \text{ trillion})$$
$$C = \$4 \text{ trillion}$$

To demonstrate how changes in MPC affect the consumption function, Exhibit 2 shows two consumption functions with the same autonomous

EXHIBIT 2	Consumption Functions for Two Marginal Propensities to Consume

The MPC is the slope of the consumption function. Here two consumption functions are shown for MPCs of 0.50 and 0.75. The autonomous consumption of $1 trillion is the same for both consumption functions. The higher the MPC, the steeper the consumption function.

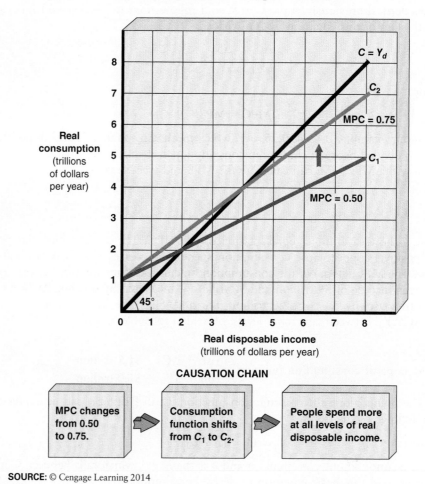

Real consumption (trillions of dollars per year)

Real disposable income (trillions of dollars per year)

CAUSATION CHAIN

| MPC changes from 0.50 to 0.75. | Consumption function shifts from C_1 to C_2. | People spend more at all levels of real disposable income. |

SOURCE: © Cengage Learning 2014

consumption of \$1 trillion, but each has a different slope. C_1 has an MPC of 0.50, and C_2 has a larger MPC of 0.75. Thus, the higher the marginal propensity to consume, the steeper the consumption function.

How do changes in taxes cause movements along the consumption function? Suppose there is an income-tax cut. As a result, real disposable income (Y_d) increases and, in turn, induces higher consumption represented by an upward movement along the consumption function. An income-tax hike, on the other hand, reduces real disposable income and causes less consumption shown by a downward movement along the consumption function.

Exhibit 3 provides recent empirical evidence that supports Keynes's theoretical consumption function. Each point in the exhibit represents a pair of values for real personal consumption spending and real disposable income in the United States for years since 2000. Note that the relationship is close to an upward-sloping linear line. As real disposable income rises, real consumption spending also rises.

| EXHIBIT 3 | U.S. Personal Consumption and Disposable Income, 2000–2011 |

Keynes argued that a fundamental psychological law exists whereby real disposable income strongly influences real consumption. Actual data on real personal consumption expenditures and real disposable income are consistent with Keynes's theory.

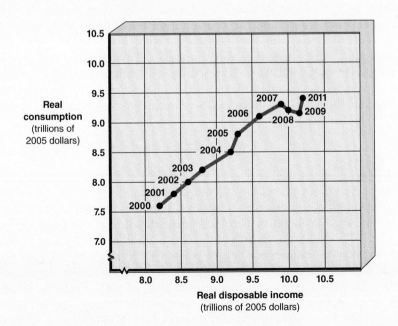

SOURCE: Bureau of Economic Research, *National Economic Accounts*, http://www.bea.gov/national/nipaweb/ SelectTable.asp?Selected=Y, Tables 1.1.6 and 2.1.

CONCLUSION: *There is a direct relationship between changes in real disposable income and changes in consumption.*

✓ CHECKPOINT

What's Your MPC?

As your income increases over time, your marginal propensity to consume (MPC) can remain constant, or it can change. Would you expect your MPC to increase, decrease, or remain constant as your income increases throughout your career?

8-2 Reasons the Consumption Function Shifts

Just as nonprice factors in the market supply and demand model, such as consumer tastes and income, shift the demand curve, changes in certain *nonincome* factors cause the consumption function to shift. Exhibit 4 uses hypothetical data to illustrate this difference in terminology. The sole cause of the change in consumption spending from $3 trillion (point *A*) to $4 trillion (point *B*) movement along the stable consumption schedule, C_1, is a $2 trillion change in the level of real disposable income. A change in a nonincome determinant, on the other hand, can cause the consumption schedule to shift upward from $C_1 = a_1 + bY_d$ to $C_2 = a_2 + bY_d$. As a result, households spend an extra $1 trillion $(a_2 - a_1)$ at each point along C_2. This means that the level of autonomous consumption has increased by $1 trillion from $1.5 trillion to $2.5 trillion because of some influence other than current Y_d. Nonincome variables that can shift the consumption function include expectations, wealth, the price level, and the interest rate.

8-2a EXPECTATIONS

Consumer expectations are optimistic or pessimistic views of the future that can change consumption spending in the present. Expectations may involve the future inflation rate, the likelihood of becoming unemployed, the likelihood of receiving higher income, or the future shortage of products resulting from a war or other circumstances. Suppose households believe prices will be much higher next year and buy now, rather than paying more in the future. The effect of such expectations would be to trigger current spending at each level of real disposable income and shift the consumption function parallel upward. The anticipation of a recession and fears about losing jobs would make families more tightfisted in their current spending. This means an autonomous decrease in consumption, and the consumption function shifts downward.

EXHIBIT 4	Movement along and Shifts in the Consumption Function

The movement from real consumption spending of $3 trillion (point A) to $4 trillion (point B) along the stable consumption schedule, C_1, is a change in real consumption caused by a $2 trillion change in the level of real disposable income (Y_d). A change in a nonincome determinant causes the consumption function to shift. For example, some nonincome factors may increase autonomous consumption by $1 trillion from a_1 to a_2. As a result, the entire consumption function shifts upward from C_1 to C_2. Nonincome factors include changes in expectations, wealth, the price level, and the interest rate.

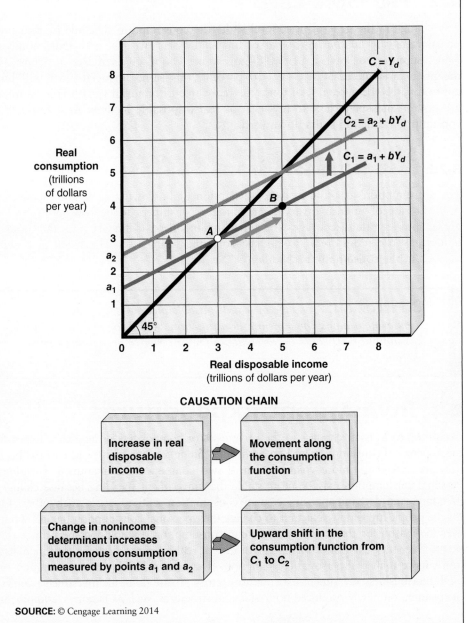

CAUSATION CHAIN

Increase in real disposable income → Movement along the consumption function

Change in nonincome determinant increases autonomous consumption measured by points a_1 and a_2 → Upward shift in the consumption function from C_1 to C_2

8-2b WEALTH

Holding all other factors constant, the more wealth households accumulate, the more they spend at any level of real disposable income, causing the consumption function to shift upward. Wealth owned by households includes both *real* assets, such as homes, automobiles, and land, and *financial* assets, including cash, savings accounts, stocks, bonds, insurance policies, and pensions. Changes in prices of stocks, real estate, and other assets affect the value of wealth and, in turn, can shift the nation's consumption function. A so-called wealth effect occurred in the 1990s when stock values rose and households increased their spending. And during the financial turmoil in 2008, the fall in stock prices and housing prices was a significant factor in depressing consumption.

Wealth effect

A shift in the consumption function caused by a change in the value of real and financial assets.

8-2c THE PRICE LEVEL

Any change in the general price level shifts the consumption schedule by reducing or enlarging the *purchasing power* of financial assets (wealth) with fixed nominal value. Suppose you own a $100,000 government bond or certificate of deposit. If the price level increases by, say, 10 percent, this same financial asset will buy approximately 10 percent less. Once the real value of financial wealth falls, families are poorer and spend less at any level of real disposable income. As a result, the consumption function shifts downward.

8-2d THE INTEREST RATE

The consumption schedule includes the option of borrowing to finance spending. A lower rate of interest on loans encourages consumers to borrow more, and a higher interest rate discourages consumer indebtedness. If interest rates fall, households may use more credit to finance consumer purchases. The result is a shift upward in the consumption schedule.

CONCLUSION: *A change in real disposable income is the sole cause of a movement along the consumption function. A shift or relocation in the consumption schedule occurs when a factor other than real disposable income changes.*

8-3 Investment Expenditures

According to Keynes, changes in the private-sector components of aggregate expenditures (personal consumption and investment spending) are the major cause of the business cycle. And the more volatile of these two components is investment spending. Personal consumption may be more stable than investment spending because changes in nonincome determinants of personal consumption tend to offset each other. Or maybe people are simply reluctant to change their personal consumption habits. Whatever the reason for the stability of personal consumption, Exhibit 5 demonstrates this point. Over the years, the annual growth rate of real investment has indeed fluctuated much more than real personal consumption. Recall from Exhibit 2 in the chapter on GDP that business investment expenditures (gross private domestic investment) consist of spending on newly produced nonresidential structures, such as factories, equipment,

EXHIBIT 5	A Comparison of the Volatility of Real Investment and Real Consumption, 1965–2011

Real investment spending is highly volatile compared to real personal consumption. The data since 1965 confirm that the annual growth rate of real investment (gross private domestic investment) fluctuates much more than the annual growth rate of real personal consumption.

SOURCE: Bureau of Economic Analysis, *National Economic Accounts*, http://www.bea.gov/national/nipaweb/SelectTable.asp?Selected=Y, Table 1.1.1.

changes in inventories, and residential structures. Note that during the Great Recession (2007–2009), both the consumption and investment growth rates were negative with investment spending dropping sharply to −24 percent.

8-3a THE INVESTMENT DEMAND CURVE

The classical economists believed that the interest rate alone determines the level of investment spending. Keynes disputed this idea. Instead, Keynes argued that expectations of future profits are the primary factor in determining investment, and the interest rate is the financing cost of any investment proposal.

Using a micro example to illustrate the investment decision-making process, suppose a consulting firm plans to purchase a new computer program for $1,000 that will be obsolete in a year. It anticipates that the new software will increase the firm's revenue by $1,100. Thus, assuming no taxes or expenses exist, the expected rate of return or profit is 10 percent. Now consider the impact of the cost of borrowing funds to finance the software investment. If the interest rate is less than 10 percent, the business will earn a profit, so it will make the investment expenditure to buy the computer program. On the other hand, a rate of interest higher than 10 percent means the software investment will be a loss, so this project will not be undertaken.

Investment demand curve

The curve that shows the amount businesses spend for investment goods at different possible rates of interest.

Understanding a single firm's investment decision from a micro perspective allows us to develop the investment demand curve from the macro vantage point. The investment demand curve shows the amount businesses spend for investment goods at different possible rates of interest. Exhibit 6 expresses the interest rate as annual percentages on the vertical axis. As shown in part (a), changes in the interest rate generate movements along the firm's investment demand curve. If the interest rate falls from, say, 6 percent at point *A* to 4 percent at point *B*, an additional $5 million of real investment spending occurs because *marginal* planned projects become profitable. Stated another way, as a result of this fall in the rate of interest, the firm's real investment increases from $5 million to $10 million.

The relationship among the expected rate of profit, the interest rate, and investment follows this investment rule: *Businesses will undertake all planned investment projects for which the expected rate of profit equals or exceeds the interest rate.*

8-4 Why Investment Demand Is Unstable

Why did Keynes view investment spending as so susceptible to ups and downs? The reason is there are several volatile determinants that cause the investment demand curve to be quite unstable. In short, any factor that changes the expected rate of profit shifts the investment demand curve and thereby changes the investment component of real GDP. As shown in Exhibit 6(b), the initial investment demand curve, I_1, has shifted rightward to I_2, and at an interest rate of 4 percent, $5 million of additional investment spending occurs between points *B* and *C*. The next sections discuss major factors that can shift the investment demand curve.

8-4a EXPECTATIONS

Keynes argued that swings in "animal spirits" cause volatile investment expenditures. Translated this means businesspersons are quite susceptible to moods of optimism and pessimism about future economic conditions. Their expectations about the future translate into estimates of future sales, future costs, and future profitability of investment projects. These forecasts involve a clouded crystal ball, requiring a degree of intuition or normative analysis. There are always many ever-changing factors, such as government spending and tax policies, world events, population growth, and stock market conditions, that make forecasting difficult.

When a wave of pessimism becomes pervasive, businesspeople reduce their expectations for profitability at each rate of interest. Such a pessimistic attitude can become contagious and shift the investment demand curve leftward. This was the case during the Great Depression, when the outlook was dismal. At other times, such as during the 1990s, businesspersons become very optimistic and revise upward their expected rate of profit for investment at each interest rate. If so, the investment demand curve shifts rightward. Thus, Keynes viewed changes in business confidence (expectations) as a major cause of investment spending volatility.

EXHIBIT 6	Movement along and a Shift in a Firm's Investment Demand

Part (a) shows that investment spending by a hypothetical business firm depends on the interest rate. Ceteris paribus, lowering the interest rate from 6 percent at point A to 4 percent at point B increases the quantity of real investment purchases from $5 million to $10 million during the year.

Keynes argued that investment spending is unstable because a change in volatile factors, such as expectations, technological change, capacity utilization, and business taxes, can shift the location of the investment demand curve. As shown in part (b), the initial investment demand curve, I_1, has shifted rightward to I_2, and at an interest rate of 4 percent, $5 million in additional investment spending occurs between points B and C.

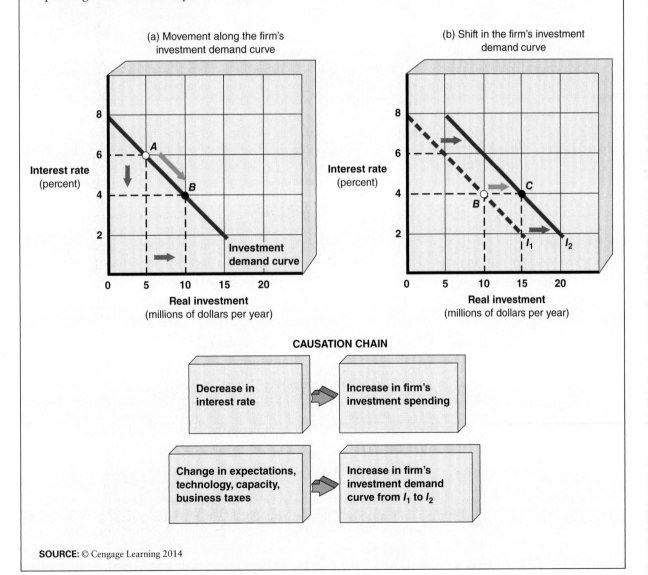

(a) Movement along the firm's investment demand curve

(b) Shift in the firm's investment demand curve

CAUSATION CHAIN

SOURCE: © Cengage Learning 2014

YOU'RE THE ECONOMIST

Does a Stock Market Crash Cause Recession?

Applicable Concept: consumption and investment

The stock market soared during the "Roaring 20s." Lavish spending was in style as people enjoyed their new wealth. Then, on October 29, 1929, Black Tuesday, the stock market crashed. During the Great Depression, banks failed, businesses closed their doors, real GDP plummeted, and unemployment soared. Over the years, much debate has occurred over whether the 1929 stock market crash was merely a symptom or a major cause of the downturn. Evidence exists that the 1929 stock market crash only reflected an economic decline already in progress. For example, months before Black Tuesday, national production had already fallen.

The argument over the impact of a stock market crash on the economy was renewed in 2001. The National Association for Business Economics (NABE) was holding its annual meeting in the World Trade Center when disaster struck the building on September 11, 2001. "The chandeliers shook, we heard a concussive sound, and as we were herding out, we could see that one tower was burning," said Carl Tannenbaum, the chief economist of LaSalle Bank in Chicago, who was attending the meeting.[1] Just the day before, a panel of NABE economists predicted slow growth for the economy, but no recession. That forecast became obsolete the moment the first plane hit. Analysts predicted a recession, and one reason was that they expected the stock market would dive as profit expectations fell. Indeed, as a result of the September terrorist attacks, the stock market suffered its worst one-week loss since the Great Depression. In the immediate aftermath, equities losses were estimated to be an extraordinary $1.2 trillion in value.[2]

Prior to the September attacks, the Dow Jones Industrial Average had reached a high of about 11,500 in May, but it had already fallen almost 2,000 points to a low of 9,431 on September 10, 2001. During this period of time, the economy was plagued by the implosion of the dot-com companies and sharp declines in high-tech stocks. After the attacks, the

8-4b TECHNOLOGICAL CHANGE

Technological progress includes the introduction of new products and new ways of doing things. Robots, personal computers, iPhones, the Internet, and similar new inventions provide less costly ways of production. New technologies create a flurry of investment spending as firms buy the latest innovations in order to improve their production capabilities, thereby causing the investment demand curve to shift rightward.

8-4c CAPACITY UTILIZATION

During the Great Depression and the Great Recession, many businesses operated at far less than full capacity. Capacity is defined as the maximum possible output of a firm or an industry. When much of the nation's capital stock stands idle, firms have little incentive to buy more. As a result, the investment demand curve shifts far to the left. Conversely, firms may be operating their plants at a high rate of capacity utilization, and the outlook for sales growth is optimistic. In this case, there is pressure on firms to invest in new investment projects, and the investment demand curve shifts to the right.

stock market closed for the remainder of the week and reopened the following Monday, September 17, 2001, with the famous statue of the Wall Street Bull decorated with American flags and the National Guard patrolling the streets. The result of trading was a huge sell-off and another loss of 1,371 points during the week. Throughout the remainder of the year, the Dow Jones Industrial Average gradually rose toward its pre-September 11 levels, closing at 10,022 on December 31, 2001. Real GDP contracted at a 1.3 percent annual rate in the third quarter of 2001 and then rose in the final three months of 2001 by 1.7 percent, which was a surprisingly strong performance under the circumstances. The six-member panel at the National Bureau of Economic Research (NBER), which is considered the nation's arbiter of U.S. business cycles,

declared in November 2001 that a recession had begun in March and ended eight months later in November of that year.

Stock market plunges are widely reported headline news. One result of these plunges is that many Americans feel poorer because of the threat to their life's savings. In only a few hours, spectacular paper losses reduce the wealth that people are counting on to pay for homes, automobiles, college tuition, or retirement. Although not all U.S. households own stock, everyone fears a steep downhill ride on the Wall Street roller coaster. If a stock market crash leads to a recession, it will cause layoffs and cuts in profit sharing and pension funds. Businesses fear that many families will postpone buying major consumer items in case they need their cash to tide them over the difficult economic times ahead. Reluctance of

consumers to spend lowers aggregate demand, and, in turn, prices and profits fall. Falling sales and anxiety about a recession may lead many business executives to postpone modernization plans. Rather than buying new factories and equipment, businesses continue with used plants and machinery, which means lower private investment spending, employment, output, and income for the overall economy.

Analyze the Issue

Immediately following the attack on the United States on September 11, 2001, the stock market plunged and many observers predicted a recession. Using the consumption and investment functions, explain their predictions.

---

1. "Worldwide, Hope for Recovery Dims," *Business Week*, Sept. 24, 2001, p. 42.
2. "Economy under Siege," *Fortune*, October 15, 2001, p. 86.

Source: © Cengage Learning 2014

8-4d BUSINESS TAXES

As explained earlier, changes in income taxes on individuals affect disposable income and the level of consumption. Similarly, taxes on business firms can shift the investment demand curve. Business decisions, in reality, depend on the expected *after-tax* rate of profit. An increase in business taxes therefore would lower profitability and shift the investment demand curve to the left. On the other hand, the U.S. government may wish to encourage investment by allowing, say, a *tax credit* for new investment. A 10 percent *investment tax credit* means that if ExxonMobil decides to invest $10 million in a new plant, the corporation's tax bill to the IRS will be cut by $1 million. The effect of this tax policy is that the government increases the profitability of new investment projects by 10 percent and the investment demand curve shifts to the right.

8-4e INVESTMENT AS AN AUTONOMOUS EXPENDITURE

Assuming none of the above factors changes in the short run, Keynes argued that investment spending is an autonomous expenditure. An autonomous expenditure

Autonomous expenditure

Spending that does not vary with the level of real disposable income.

is spending that does not vary with the level of real disposable income. Stated simply, autonomous expenditures in the Keynesian model remain a fixed amount, regardless of the level of disposable income. Exhibit 7 shows how the rate of interest determines the aggregate level of autonomous investment for all firms in an economy, regardless of or external to the level of real disposable income. In part (a), at an interest rate of 8 percent, *all* businesses spend $1 trillion for capital goods and inventory. Part (b) shows this $1 trillion is the amount of real investment spending, no matter what the level of real disposable income. If the rate of interest is lower, investment increases, and the horizontal investment demand curve shifts vertically upward. A higher rate of interest discourages investment and shifts the horizontal investment demand curve vertically downward.

EXHIBIT 7	The Aggregate Investment Demand and Autonomous Investment Demand Curves

In part (a), the level of real investment for all firms in an economy is determined by the investment rule that all investment projects for which the expected rate of profit equals or exceeds the interest rate will be undertaken. If the interest rate is 8 percent, real autonomous investment will be $1 trillion, shown as point A on the investment demand curve, I.

In part (b), autonomous real investment expenditures are shown to be independent of the level of real disposable income per year. This means firms will spend $1 trillion regardless of the level of real disposable income per year.

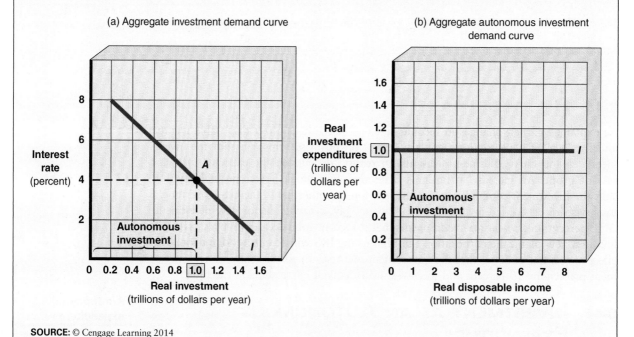

Key Concepts

John Maynard Keynes
Classical economists
Say's Law
Consumption function
autonomous consumption

Dissaving
Saving
Marginal propensity to
  consume (MPC)
Marginal propensity to save (MPS)

Wealth effect
Investment demand curve
Autonomous expenditure

Summary

- **Say's Law** is the classical theory that "supply creates its own demand," and therefore, the Great Depression was impossible. Say's Law is the theory that the value of production generates an equal amount of income and, in turn, total spending. The classical economists rejected the argument that underconsumption is possible because they believed flexible prices, wages, and interest rates would soon establish a balance between supply and demand.

- **John Maynard Keynes** rejected the classical theory that the economy self-corrects in the long run to full employment. The key in Keynesian theory is aggregate demand, rather than the classical economists focus on aggregate supply. Unless aggregate spending is adequate, the economy can experience prolonged and severe unemployment.

- The **consumption function (C)** is determined by changes in the level of real disposable income. **Autonomous consumption** is consumption that occurs even if real disposable income equals zero. Changes in such nonincome determinants as expectations, wealth, the price level, and interest rates can cause shifts in the consumption function.

- The **marginal propensity to consume (MPC)** is the change in consumption associated with a given change in real disposable income. The MPC tells how much of an additional dollar of disposable income households will spend for consumption.

- The **marginal propensity to save (MPS)** is the change in saving associated with a given change

in real disposable income. The MPS measures how much of an additional dollar of disposable income households will save.

Consumption Function

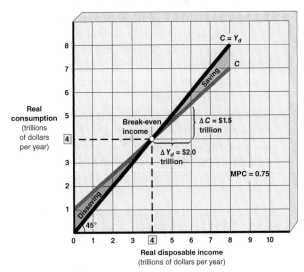

SOURCE: © Cengage Learning 2014

- The **investment demand curve (I)** shows the amount businesses spend for investment goods at different possible rates of interest. The determinants of this schedule are the expected rate of profit and rate of interest. Shifts in the investment demand curve result from changes in expectations, technology, capacity utilization, and business taxes.

Causation Chains

SOURCE: © Cengage Learning 2014

- An **autonomous expenditure** is spending that does not vary with the current level of disposable income. The Keynesian model applies this simplifying assumption to investment. As a result, the investment demand curve is a fixed amount determined by the rate of profit and the interest rate.

Summary of Conclusion Statements

- The classical economists believed that a continuing depression is impossible because markets eliminate persistent shortages or surpluses.
- In the classical view, unemployment is the result of a short-lived adjustment period in which wages and prices decline or people voluntarily choose not to work. Thus, there is a natural tendency for the economy to restore full employment over time.
- The 45-degree line is a geometric construct. It indicates all points where real disposable income (measured on the horizontal axis) and real consumption (measured on the vertical axis) are equal. Consequently, the 45-degree line makes it easier to identify the break-even or no-saving income level.
- There is a direct relationship between changes in real disposable income and changes in consumption.
- A change in real disposable income is the sole cause of a movement along the consumption function. A shift or relocation in the consumption schedule occurs when a factor other than real disposable income changes.
- Businesses will undertake all planned investment projects for which the expected rate of profits equals or exceeds the interest rate.

Study Questions and Problems

1. Explain how the classical economists concluded that Say's Law is valid and long-term unemployment impossible.

2. Use the following consumption function data to answer the questions below.
   a. Calculate the saving schedule.
   b. Determine the marginal propensities to consume (MPC) and save (MPS).
   c. Determine the break-even income.
   d. What is the relationship between the MPC and the MPS?

3. Explain why the MPC and the MPS must always add up to one.

Keynesian Consumption Function (billions of dollars per year)

Real disposable income	Consumption	Saving	MPC	MPS
$100	$150	$__	__	__
200	200	__	__	__
300	250	__	__	__
400	300	__	__	__
500	350	__	__	__

4. How do households "dissave"?

5. Explain how each of the following affects the consumption function:
   a. The expectation is that a prolonged recession will occur in the next year.
   b. Stock prices rise sharply.
   c. The price level rises by 10 percent.
   d. The interest rate on consumer loans rises sharply.
   e. Income taxes increase.

6. Your college is considering investing $6 million to add 10,000 seats to its football stadium. The athletic department forecasts it can sell all these extra seats at each game for a ticket price of $20 per seat, and the team plays six home games per year. If the school can borrow at an interest rate of 14 percent, should the school undertake this project? What would happen if the school expected a losing season and could sell tickets for only half of the 10,000 seats?

7. Why is the investment demand curve less stable than the consumption and saving schedules? What are the basic determinants that can shift the investment demand curve?

8. Suppose most business executives expect a slowdown in the economy. How might this situation affect the economy?

9. The levels of real disposable income and aggregate expenditures for a two-sector economy (consumption and investment) are given in the following table:

Real disposable income (trillions of dollars per year)	Consumption (C) (trillions of dollars per year)
$0	$3.00
1	3.25
2	3.50
3	3.75
4	4.00
5	4.25
6	4.50
7	4.75
8	5.00

a. Construct a graph of the consumption function (C).
b. Determine the autonomous consumption, MPC, and MPS for this hypothetical economy.
c. What is the break-even income consumption of real disposable income?
d. What is the amount of dissavings at $2 trillion real disposable income and the savings at $7 trillion.

For Online Exercises, go to the Tucker Web site at www.cengage.com/economics/tucker.

✓ CHECKPOINT ANSWER

What's Your MPC?

Early in your career when your income is relatively low, you are likely to spend your entire income, and perhaps even dissave, just to afford necessities. During this stage of your life, your MPC will be close to 1. As your income increases and you have purchased the necessities, additional income can go to luxuries. If you become wealthier, you have a higher marginal propensity to save and consequently a lower marginal propensity to consume. If you said your MPC will probably decrease as your income increases, **YOU ARE CORRECT.**

Sample Quiz

For an explanation of the correct answers, visit the Tucker Web site at www.cengage.com/economics/tucker.

1. The popular theory prior to the Great Depression that the economy will automatically adjust to achieve full employment in the long run is
   a. supply-side economics.
   b. Keynesian economics.
   c. classical economics.
   d. mercantilism.

2. The French economist Jean-Baptiste Say transformed the equality of total output and total spending into a law that can be expressed as
   a. unemployment is not possible in the short run.
   b. demand and supply are never equal.
   c. supply creates its own demand.
   d. demand creates its own supply.

3. If the economy is experiencing less than full equilibrium, the Keynesian school recommends that the government
   a. do nothing to stimulate the economy.
   b. undertake fiscal policy to stimulate aggregate demand.
   c. undertake fiscal policy to stimulate aggregate supply.
   d. balance the budget to stimulate aggregate demand.

4. The school of thought that emphasizes the natural tendency for an economy to move toward equilibrium full employment is known as the
   a. Keynesian school.
   b. supply-side school.
   c. noninterventionist school.
   d. classical school.

5. What is the title of the John Maynard Keynes's book published in 1936 that challenged the classical self-correction economic theory?
   a. *In the Long Run, We Are Dead.*
   b. *Classical Economics Revised.*
   c. *General Theory of Employment, Interest, and Money.*
   d. *A Keynesian Approach to Economic Policy.*

6. What is the vertical intercept of the consumption function that represents the portion of consumption expenditure *not* associated with a level of disposable income?
   a. consumption intercept
   b. disposable income intercept
   c. autonomous consumption
   d. automatic consumption line

7. John Maynard Keynes's central proposition that a dollar increase in disposable income would increase consumption, but by less than the increase in disposable income, implies a marginal propensity to consume (MPC) that is
   a. greater than or equal to one.
   b. equal to one.
   c. less than one but greater than zero.
   d. negative.

8. The marginal propensity to consume (MPC) is the slope of the
   a. GDP curve.
   b. disposable income curve.
   c. consumption function.
   d. autonomous consumption curve.

9. The sum of the marginal propensity to consume (MPC) and the marginal propensity to save (MPS) always equals
   a. 1.
   b. 0.
   c. the interest rate.
   d. the marginal propensity to invest (MPI).

10. The relationship between MPC and MPS is
    a. $1 + \text{MPC} = \text{MPS}$.
    b. $1 - \text{MPC} = \text{MPS}$.
    c. $1 + \text{MPS} = \text{MPC}$.
    d. $\text{MPC} - \text{MPS} = 1$.

11. If the marginal propensity to consume $= 0.75$, then
    a. the marginal propensity to save $= 0.75$.
    b. the marginal propensity to save $= 1.33$.
    c. the marginal propensity to save $= 0.20$.
    d. the marginal propensity to save $= 0.25$.

Sample Quiz *continued*

EXHIBIT 8 | **Consumption Function**

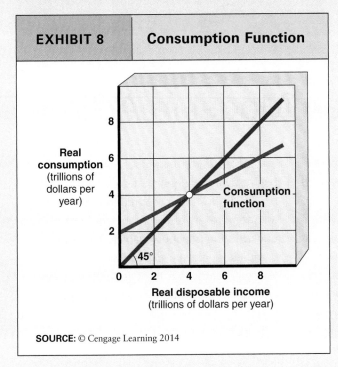

Real consumption (trillions of dollars per year)

Real disposable income (trillions of dollars per year)

Consumption function

45°

SOURCE: © Cengage Learning 2014

12. As shown in Exhibit 8, autonomous consumption is
   a. 0.
   b. $2 trillion.
   c. $4 trillion.
   d. $6 trillion.
   e. $8 trillion.

13. As shown in Exhibit 8, savings occurs
   a. at 0.
   b. between 0 and $4 trillion.
   c. where disposable income is greater than $4 trillion.
   d. at $2 trillion.

14. As shown in Exhibit 8, dissaving occurs
   a. at $5 trillion.
   b. between 0 and $4 trillion.
   c. where disposable income is greater than $4 trillion.
   d. at $8 trillion.

15. As shown in Exhibit 8, the marginal propensity to consume (MPC) is
   a. 0.33.
   b. 0.50.

c. 0.67.
d. 0.75.

16. As shown in Exhibit 8, the break-even income is
   a. $2 trillion.
   b. $4 trillion.
   c. $6 trillion.
   d. $8 trillion.

17. As shown in Exhibit 8, the 45° line represents
   a. autonomous consumption.
   b. real consumption spending.
   c. real disposable income.
   d. all points where real consumption equals real disposable income.

18. The consumption function is drawn on a graph with disposable income on the horizontal axis. Assume autonomous consumption increases. The effect is
   a. an upward adjustment in the vertical intercept.
   b. no change in the adjustment in the vertical intercept.
   c. an increase in the slope of the consumption function.
   d. a decrease in the slope of the consumption function.

19. The investment demand curve shows the amount businesses spend for investment goods at different possible
   a. price levels.
   b. levels of GDP.
   c. rates of interest.
   d. levels of taxation.

20. A rightward shift of the investment demand curve would be caused by a(an)
   a. increase in the expected rate of return on investment caused by an increase in business confidence.
   b. decrease in the expected rate of return on investment caused by a decrease in business confidence.
   c. increase in the rate of interest.
   d. decrease in the rate of interest.

chapter 9

The Keynesian Model in Action

In 1935, George Bernard Shaw received a letter from John Maynard Keynes, which stated, "I believe myself to be writing a book [*The General Theory*] on economic theory which will largely revolutionize—not, I suppose, at once but in the course of the next ten years—the way the world thinks about economic problems." Indeed, Keynes's macroeconomic theory offered powerful ideas whose time had come during the Great Depression. Building on the foundation of the previous chapter, this chapter describes how Keynes conceived the economy as driven by aggregate demand that can be separated and analyzed under the individual components of consumption (C), investment (I), government spending (G), and net exports (X − M).

You must keep in mind that during the Great Depression era, plants had idle capacity and unemployment was massive. Under these conditions, inflation was not the problem. The Keynesian model therefore generally ignores price level changes and focuses instead on how full-employment output can be achieved by changes in aggregate expenditures.

Like adding icing to a cake, this chapter begins by adding government spending and global trade to the consumption function and autonomous investment demand curve introduced in the previous chapter. The result is the complete aggregate expenditures model. Next, you will learn how the economy gravitates to an equilibrium where aggregate expenditures equal aggregate output (real GDP). And you will look at the link between the equilibrium real GDP and the level of employment in an economy. The analysis will make clear why Keynes argued that there is no self-correction mechanism that eventually moves the nation to the full-employment equilibrium output.

Finally, you will understand one of Keynes's most powerful ideas—the spending multiplier. At the very heart of Keynesian theory is the concept that an initial increase in aggregate spending of $1 in an economy can increase equilibrium output by more than $1. Thus, Keynesian economics offers a cure for an economy in deep recession: government policies that expand aggregate demand, raise national output, create jobs, and restore full employment.

In this chapter, you will learn to solve these economics puzzles:

- Why did Keynes reject the classical theory that "supply creates its own demand"?

- Why did Keynes argue that the government should adopt active policies, rather than allowing the price system to prevail?

- Can the Keynesian model explain an ice cream war?

9-1 Adding Government and Global Trade to the Keynesian Model

In this chapter, we continue our study of the Keynesian model begun in the previous chapter. Consumption and investment are not the only forms of spending. As shown earlier in the chapter on GDP (Exhibit 2), consumption and investment represent 83 percent of total spending, while government spending and net exports account for the remaining 17 percent of GDP.

9-1a GOVERNMENT SPENDING

Government spending is the second largest component of aggregate expenditures in the United States. Like investment, government spending can be considered an autonomous expenditure. The reasoning is that government spending is primarily the result of political decisions made independent of the level of national output.

Exhibit 1(a) shows hypothetical government spending as a horizontal line labeled G at $1 trillion. If government officials increase government spending, the G line shifts vertically upward at each possible level of real GDP to G_1, and reduced government spending shifts the G line vertically downward at each possible level of real GDP to G_2. The amount of the shift is equal to the amount of change in government spending.

Here we must pause to take special note of the change from real disposable income to real GDP on the horizontal axis of the graph. Does it make a difference? No, it makes little difference. In the previous chapter, real disposable income was used following the theory Keynes himself developed. However, it is important to connect aggregate output and income measures. Recall from Exhibit 7 in the chapter on GDP the adjustments required to convert GDP into disposable income (Y_d). As it turns out, real disposable income is a sizable portion of real GDP. Over the last decade, real disposable income, on average, has consistently been about 70 percent of real GDP. If we assume that real disposable income remains the same high proportion of real GDP each year, then we can substitute real GDP for real disposable income in the Keynesian model. Changes in real GDP therefore reflect changes in both real national output and income (real disposable income).

9-1b NET EXPORTS

Like investment and government spending, exports and imports can be treated as autonomous expenditures unaffected by a nation's domestic level of real GDP. Economic conditions in the countries that buy U.S. products affect the level of our exports. On the other hand, the level of imports purchased by U.S. citizens is

GLOBAL ECONOMICS

EXHIBIT 1	Autonomous Government Spending and Net Exports Curves

In part (a), government spending (G) is assumed to be determined by the political decision-making process. The autonomous government spending line, G, is therefore a horizontal line indicating that government spending is independent of the level of real GDP. An increase in government spending shifts G upward to G_1. A decrease shifts G downward to G_2.

Part (b) also shows that net exports are assumed to be independent of the level of GDP. Horizontal line $(X - M)_1$ is negative because imports exceed exports. If exports equal imports, then the net export line shifts upward to $(X - M)$. If exports exceed imports, the net exports line is represented by a positive net exports line, $(X - M)_2$.

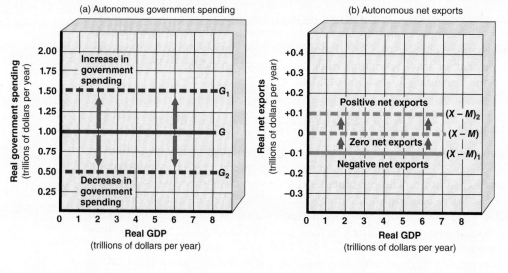

SOURCE: © Cengage Learning 2014

influenced by economic conditions in the United States. As shown in Exhibit 1(b), net exports, $(X - M)$, can be positive, zero, or negative. The level of net exports, or the $(X - M)$ line, is horizontal because net exports are assumed to be independent of the level of real GDP. Since for many years the value of imports we have purchased from foreigners has exceeded the value of exports we have been selling them, the model assumes net exports are negative at line $(X - M)_1$. If exports and imports are equal, the net exports line shifts upward to zero at line $(X - M)$. If exports exceed imports, the positive $(X - M)$ line shifts farther upward to line $(X - M)_2$.

9-2 The Aggregate Expenditures Model

Keynes countered classical theory by developing an alternative theory that explained how a depressed economy can be stuck forever in a below-full-employment equilibrium without adequate aggregate expenditures. In this section, a basic Keynesian model is developed to explain what Keynes meant by his famous saying, "In the long run, we are all dead."

9-2a THE AGGREGATE EXPENDITURES FUNCTION (AE)

A little drum roll please! Now we are ready to tie together concepts and point the spotlight on an important concept called the aggregate expenditures function (AE) necessary to understand Keynes's cure for the Great Depression. The aggregate expenditures function (AE) is the total spending in an economy at different levels of real GDP. The AE function or line is conceptually derived graphically in Exhibit 2 by vertically summing $C + I + G + (X - M)$ at each level of GDP on the horizontal axis. The consumption function (C) explained in the previous chapter begins the AE function with a given level of autonomous consumption spending (a). Next, recall that the consumption function is determined by its slope, which equals the MPC. As

Aggregate expenditures function (AE)

The total spending in an economy at different levels of real GDP.

EXHIBIT 2	Aggregate Expenditures and Keynesian Equilibrium

The aggregate expenditures function (AE) begins with the consumption function (C). Then we add investment (I), government spending (G), and net exports (X − M). Note that I, G, and (X − M) are assumed to be autonomous expenditures and are therefore lines parallel to the C line. The slope of the AE line is determined by the slope of the consumption function, which equals the MPC ($\Delta C/\Delta Y$). At Y^* real GDP, aggregate expenditures equals aggregate income/output (real GDP) along the 45-degree line (AE = Y), and the economy is in equilibrium.

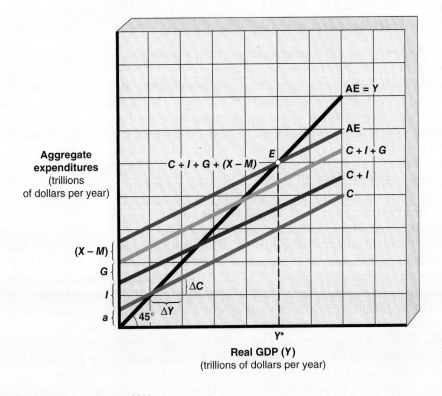

SOURCE: © Cengage Learning 2014

shown in Exhibit 2, MPC is represented by the ratio of the change in consumption to the change in real GDP ($\Delta C/\Delta Y$). Since consumption spending rises by less than real GDP, the MPC is less than 1. Note that it is the slope of the consumption function that gives the entire AE function its upward slope.

The next step in graphing a conceptual AE line is to add expenditures for I, G, and $(X - M)$. To do this, we assume businesses plan to spend a constant amount of investment at all levels of GDP. Therefore, autonomous investment (I) is added parallel to consumption (C) at each level of real GDP. As a result, the AE line shifts vertically upward and consists of $C + I$. Like consumption and investment, government spending and net exports are also assumed to be autonomous spending that remains unchanged regardless of the level of real GDP. Adding government spending (G) results in a parallel upward shift in the AE line to $C + I + G$. The aggregate expenditures function is completed by adding net exports to the $C + I + G$ line, and the AE line shifts parallel upward to $C + I + G$ $(X - M)$. Finally, macro equilibrium is established at point E where aggregate expenditures equal real GDP at Y^* along the 45-degree line.

> **CONCLUSION:** *At the equilibrium level of real GDP, the total value of goods and services produced (real GDP, Y) is precisely equal to the total spending for these goods and services (aggregate expenditures, AE).*

9-2b TABULAR ANALYSIS OF KEYNESIAN EQUILIBRIUM

In this section, we will further explain macro equilibrium using hypothetical data. Exhibit 3 illustrates the relationship between employment, aggregate output and income (real GDP), and aggregate expenditures for our hypothetical economy. Real GDP (Y) is listed in column (1), consumption (C) is listed in column (2), and investment (I) in column (3) is an autonomous expenditure of $1 trillion from Exhibit 7(b) in the previous chapter. Government spending (G) in column (4) is also an autonomous expenditure of $1 trillion from Exhibit 1(a), and net exports ($X - M$) in column (5) are taken from Exhibit 1(b). The aggregate expenditures function (AE) in column (6) is the sum of the $C + I + G + (X - M)$ components of aggregate expenditures in columns (2) through (5).

Examination of the levels of real GDP in column (1) and the levels of aggregate expenditures in column (6) indicate that an equality exists only at the $5 trillion level of real GDP. All output levels other than $5 trillion are unsustainable macro disequilibrium levels. Consider what happens if businesses employ only enough workers to produce an output of $1 trillion real GDP. Business managers expect total spending to equal aggregate output at this level of production, but this does not happen. At the level of $1 trillion, aggregate expenditures of $3 trillion exceed aggregate output by an *unplanned inventory investment depletion* of $2 trillion, listed in column (7). Firms respond to this happy state of affairs by hiring more workers, expanding output, and generating additional aggregate income. As a result of this process, the economy moves toward the equilibrium of $5 trillion real GDP. Thus, the pressure of empty shelves and warehouses drives our hypothetical economy to create jobs and reduce the unemployment rate (not explicitly shown in the model).

EXHIBIT 3	Equilibrium and Disequilibrium Levels of Employment, Output, and Income						
(1)	(2)	(3)	(4)	(5)	(6)	(7)	(8)
Aggregate Output and Income (real GDP) (Y)	Consumption (C)	Investment (I)	Government (G)	Net Exports (X − M)	Aggregate Expenditures (AE)	Unplanned Inventory Investment Depletion (−) or Accumulation (+)	Direction of Real GDP and Employment
$ 0	$0.6	$1	$1	$−0.1	$2.5	$−2.S	Increase
1.0	1.1	1	1	−0.1	3.0	−2.0	Increase
2.0	1.6	1	1	−0.1	3.5	−1.5	Increase
3.0	2.1	1	1	−0.1	4.0	−1.0	Increase
4.0	2.6	1	1	−0.1	4.5	−0.5	Increase
5.0	3.1	1	1	−0.1	5.0	0	Equilibrium
6.0	3.6	1	1	−0.1	5.5	+0.5	Decrease
7.0	4.1	1	1	−0.1	6.0	+1.0	Decrease
8.0	4.6	1	1	−0.1	6.5	+1.5	Decrease

NOTE: All amounts are in trillions of dollars per year.
SOURCE: © Cengage Learning 2014

The reverse is true for all levels of real GDP above the $5 trillion equilibrium level. Now suppose firms hire more workers and aggregate output is $7 trillion real GDP. At the real GDP disequilibrium level of $7 trillion, *unplanned inventory investment accumulation* occurs because aggregate expenditures of $6 trillion are insufficient to purchase $7 trillion of output. The result is that unwanted inventories worth $1 trillion remain unsold on the shelves and in the warehouses of business firms. Producers react to this undesirable condition by cutting the rate of output and employment. In this case, real GDP declines toward the equilibrium level of $5 trillion, jobs are lost, and unemployment rises.

> **CONCLUSION:** *Aggregate expenditures in Keynesian economics pull aggregate output either higher or lower toward equilibrium in the economy, as opposed to the classical view that aggregate output generates an equal amount of aggregate spending.*

9-2c   GRAPHICAL ANALYSIS OF KEYNESIAN EQUILIBRIUM

Using the data from Exhibit 3, Exhibit 4 presents a graph measuring real aggregate expenditures on the *y*-axis and real GDP on the *x*-axis. Exhibit 4 illustrates the complete aggregate expenditures model. The aggregate expenditures model determines the equilibrium level of real GDP by the intersection of the aggregate

Aggregate expenditures model

The model that determines the equilibrium level of real GDP by the intersection of the aggregate expenditures and aggregate output and income (real GDP) curves.

EXHIBIT 4	The Keynesian Aggregate Expenditures Model

Aggregate expenditures (AE) equal aggregate output (Y) at the equilibrium level of $5 trillion real GDP. Below the equilibrium level of real GDP, an undesired inventory depletion causes businesses to expand production, which pushes the economy toward equilibrium output. Above the equilibrium level of real GDP, an unintended inventory accumulation causes businesses to reduce production, which pushes the economy toward equilibrium output. In Keynesian theory, the full-employment output of $6 trillion real GDP can be reached only by shifting the AE curve upward until the full-capacity output of $6 trillion real GDP is reached.

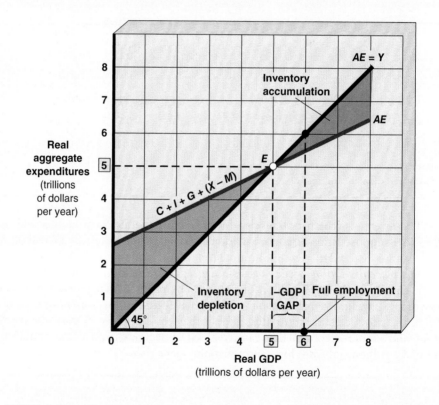

SOURCE: © Cengage Learning 2014

expenditures and aggregate output and income (real GDP) curves. The aggregate expenditure model is sometimes called the *Keynesian Cross*. The 45-degree line now takes on a special significance. Each point along this line is equidistant from the horizontal and vertical axes. Therefore, each point reflects a *possible* equilibrium between real GDP aggregate output (Y) and aggregate expenditures (AE). Note that the AE line indicates aggregate expenditures along a line less steep than the 45-degree line. This is because the slope of the AE line is determined by the marginal propensity to consume (MPC), which is less than 1. Aggregate expenditures equal aggregate output at the $5 trillion real GDP level, and any other level of output is unstable. If businesses produce at some output level that is higher than equilibrium GDP, such as $7 trillion real GDP, the vertical distance between the 45-degree equilibrium line and the AE line measures an undesired inventory accumulation of $1 trillion. This leads businesses to reduce employment, and production drops downward until the economy reaches equilibrium at $5 trillion. You may have already recognized that the difference of $1 trillion between the equilibrium output (actual real GDP) at point E and the full-employment output (potential real GDP) is a negative *GDP gap*, discussed in the chapter on business cycles and unemployment (see Exhibit 9).

Now consider the case in which businesses hire only enough workers to produce aggregate output where the AE line is above the 45-degree equilibrium line. Because aggregate expenditures exceed aggregate output, businesses sell more than they currently produce, which depletes their inventories. Business managers react to this excess aggregate demand condition by hiring more workers and expanding production, causing movement upward along the AE function toward the equilibrium level of $5 trillion real GDP.

Now it's time to pause, take a breath, and appreciate what you have been studying so diligently. It's a powerful idea! Exhibit 4 illustrates the basic explanation offered by Keynes for the Great Depression: *Contrary to classical theory, once an equilibrium is established between aggregate expenditures and aggregate output, there is no tendency for the economy to change, even when equilibrium is well below full employment.* The solution Keynes offered Western economies facing the Great Depression is to shift the AE line upward until the full-employment equilibrium is reached. Otherwise, prolonged unemployment persists indefinitely, and the economy never self-corrects. We now turn to the key idea behind changes in aggregate spending to stabilize the macro economy.

9-3 The Spending Multiplier Effect

Changes in aggregate expenditures in the Keynesian model make things happen. The crux of Keynesian macroeconomic policy depends on a change in aggregate expenditures, which is multiplied or amplified by rounds of spending and respending throughout the economy. Exhibit 5 is an enlarged version of Exhibit 4. Our analysis begins at the initial equilibrium of $5 trillion real GDP (point E), which is below the full-employment output level of $6 trillion real GDP. Now let's assume the government decides to increase government spending by $0.5 trillion. An increase in autonomous government spending of $0.5 trillion per year shifts the aggregate expenditures curve *vertically* upward by this amount from point E on AE_1 to point a on AE_2. This means at the initial output of $5 trillion real GDP, aggregate demand expands by $0.5 trillion to $5.5 trillion. The initial expansion of spending causes inventories (not shown in the graph) to decline by $0.5 trillion because aggregate spending of $5.5 trillion exceeds aggregate output of $5.0 trillion real GDP. Firms respond by stepping up output by $0.5 trillion real GDP per year to replace inventories. The exhibit shows this by the move from point a to point b. Now the marginal propensity to consume enters the picture. Assuming the MPC is 0.50, the expansion of output from $5 trillion to $5.5 trillion puts an extra $500 billion of income into the pockets of workers. Given the MPC of 0.50, these workers increase spending on goods and services by $250 billion (movement from point b to point c). This expansion of consumer spending again causes inventories to decline and output, in turn, to expand by $250 billion,

EXHIBIT 5 — The Spending Multiplier Effect of a Change in Government Spending

This graph is an enlargement of the spending multiplier process beginning at the point where the economy is in equilibrium at $5 trillion. Then an initial increase of $500 billion in government spending shifts the aggregate expenditures line up vertically from AE_1 to AE_2. After all spending-output-spending rounds are complete, a new equilibrium is restored at point E_1 with a full-employment output of $6 trillion. Thus, the $500 billion initial increase in government spending has caused a $1 trillion increase in real GDP, and the value of the multiplier is 2.

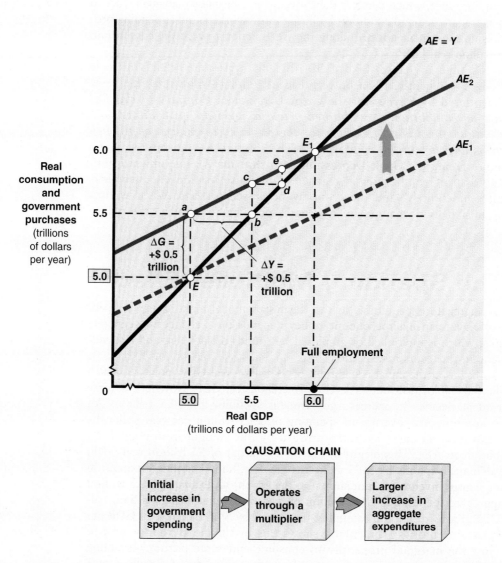

represented by the distance between point *c* and point *d*. This again puts extra income into workers' pockets, of which $125 billion (the distance between points *d* and *e*) is spent (MPC $\times \Delta Y = 0.50 \times$ $250 billion = $125 billion).

This process of spending-output-spending continues through an infinite number of rounds until output reaches the new equilibrium level of $6 trillion per year at point E_1. Thus, an initial expansion of government spending of $0.5 trillion expands equilibrium output by $1 trillion, which is twice the magnitude of the increase in government spending. Hence, the spending multiplier (SM) is 2. The spending multiplier is the ratio of the change in real GDP to the initial change in any component of aggregate expenditures, including consumption, investment, government spending, and net exports. The formula to compute the amount of change in government spending or other aggregate expenditures required to shift equilibrium aggregate output measured by real GDP is

$$\text{Spending multiplier} = \frac{\text{change in equilibrium real GDP}}{\textit{initial} \text{ change in aggregate expenditures}}$$

In the example presented in Exhibit 5, the spending multiplier is computed as

$$\text{Spending multiplier} = \frac{\Delta Y}{\Delta G} = \frac{\$1,000 \text{ billion}}{\$500 \text{ billion}} = 2$$

Spending multiplier (SM)

The ratio of the change in real GDP to an initial change in any component of aggregate expenditures, including consumption, investment, government spending, and net exports. As a formula, the spending multiplier equals 1/(1 − MPC) or 1/MPS.

9-3a SPENDING MULTIPLIER ARITHMETIC

The graphical presentation of the spending multiplier process should make the basic mechanics clear to you, but we need to be more specific and derive a formula. Therefore, let's pause to tackle the task of explaining in more detail the spending multiplier of 2 used in the above example. Exhibit 6 illustrates numerically the cumulative increase in aggregate expenditures resulting from a $500 billion increase in government spending. In the initial round, the government spends this amount for bridges, national defense, and so forth. Households receive this amount of income. In the second round, these households spend $250 billion (0.50 × $500 billion) on houses, cars, groceries, and other products. In the third round, the incomes of realtors, auto workers, grocers, and others are boosted by $250 billion, and they spend $125 billion (0.50 × $250 billion). These rounds of spending create income for respending in a downward spiral throughout the economy in smaller and smaller amounts until the total level of aggregate expenditures rises by an extra $1,000 billion.

CONCLUSION: *Any initial change in spending by the government, households, or firms creates a chain reaction of further spending, which causes a greater cumulative change in aggregate expenditures.*

You might recognize from algebra that the spending multiplier effect is a process based on an infinite geometric series. The formula for the sum of such a series of numbers is the initial number times 1/(1 − *r*), where *r* is the ratio that relates the numbers. Using this formula, the sum (total spending) is calculated as $500 billion (ΔG) × [1/(1 − 0.50)] = $1,000 billion. By simply defining *r* in the

EXHIBIT 6	Spending Multiplier Effect	
Round	Component of total spending	New consumption spending
1	Government spending	$500
2	Consumption	250
3	Consumption	125
4	Consumption	63
.	.	.
.	.	.
.	.	.
All other rounds	Consumption	62
Total spending		$1,000

NOTE: All amounts are rounded to the nearest billion dollars per year.
SOURCE: © Cengage Learning 2014

infinite series formula as MPC, the spending multiplier for aggregate demand is expressed as

$$\text{Spending multiplier} = \frac{1}{1 - \text{MPC}}$$

Applying this formula to our example:

$$\text{Spending multiplier} = \frac{1}{1 - 0.50} = \frac{1}{0.50} = 2$$

Recall from the previous chapter that MPC + MPS = 1; therefore, MPS = 1 − MPC. Hence, the above multiplier formula can be rewritten as

$$\text{Spending multiplier} = \frac{1}{\text{MPS}}$$

Applying the multiplier formula to our example:

$$\text{Spending multiplier} = \frac{1}{\text{MPS}} = \frac{1}{1 - 0.50} = 2$$

Because MPS and MPC are related, the size of the multiplier depends on the size of the MPC. What will the result be if people spend 80 percent or 33 percent of each dollar of income instead of 50 percent? If the MPC increases (decreases), consumers spend a larger (smaller) share of each additional dollar of output/income in each round, and the size of the multiplier increases (decreases). Exhibit 7 lists the multiplier for different values of MPC and MPS. Economists use real-world macroeconomic data to estimate a more complex multiplier than the simple multiplier formula developed in this chapter. Their estimates of the long-run real-world MPC range from 0.80 to 0.90. An MPC of 0.50 is used in the above examples for simplicity.

EXHIBIT 7	Relationship between MPC, MPS, and the Spending Multiplier	
(1) Marginal propensity to consume (MPC)	**(2)** Marginal propensity to save (MPS)	**(3)** Spending multiplier
0.90	0.10	10
0.80	0.20	5
0.75	0.25	4
0.67	0.33	3
0.50	0.50	2
0.33	0.67	1.5

SOURCE: © Cengage Learning 2014

9-4 Recessionary and Inflationary Gaps

The multiplier is important in the Keynesian model because it means that the initial change in aggregate expenditures results in an amplified change in the equilibrium level of real GDP. Such inherent instability can mean bad or good news for an economy. The bad news occurs, for example, when the multiplier amplifies small declines in total spending from, say, consumer and business manager pessimism into downturns in national output, income, and employment. The good news is that, in theory, macroeconomic policy can manage, or manipulate, the economy's performance by a relatively small initial change in aggregate expenditures.

9-4a RECESSIONARY GAP

Using Government Spending to Close a Recessionary Gap
Consider the aggregate expenditures function AE_1 in Exhibit 8. Beginning at point E_1, this hypothetical economy's initial equilibrium level is $4 trillion real GDP. The MPC is 0.50, and the spending multiplier is therefore 2. The full-employment output is $6 trillion real GDP, which means the economy faces a negative GDP gap of $2 trillion. Along the vertical line at the full-employment output level, look at the segment between point a on the initial AE_1 line and point E_2 on the AE_2 line, which is labeled a recessionary gap. A recessionary gap is the amount by which aggregate expenditures fall short of the amount required to achieve full-employment equilibrium. In our example, the recessionary gap is $1 trillion. What is the importance of the recessionary gap? The recessionary gap is the initial increase in autonomous spending required to trigger the multiplier, shift the

Recessionary gap

The amount by which the aggregate expenditures curve must be increased to achieve full-employment equilibrium.

aggregate expenditures function upward from AE_1 to AE_2, and eliminate the positive GDP gap. Stated as an expression,

Initial increase in autonomous expenditures × spending multiplier

= increase in equilibrium output

Using the data in our example,

$1 trillion × 2 = $2 trillion

We now turn to the important question of how to inject an additional $1 trillion spending into the economy, cause AE_1 to shift upward to AE_2, and thereby increase the equilibrium output from $4 trillion to $6 trillion real GDP. Under

EXHIBIT 8	A Recessionary Gap

The hypothetical economy begins in equilibrium at point E_1, with an equilibrium output of $4 trillion real GDP. With aggregate expenditures of AE_1, real GDP will not automatically increase to the $6 trillion full-employment output. The $1 trillion deficiency in total spending required to achieve full employment is the recessionary gap measured by the vertical distance between points a and E_2. Given a multiplier of 2, an initial increase in autonomous expenditures equal to the recessionary gap works through the spending multiplier and causes the economy to move from E_1 to E_2 and achieve full employment.

Keynesian theory, when market forces do not automatically do the job, then the central government should take aggressive action and adopt policies that boost autonomous spending [C, I, G, or (X − M)] by an amount equal to the recessionary gap.

Using a Tax Cut to Close a Recessionary Gap   Instead of increasing government spending, let's assume the government decides to cut taxes to close the negative recessionary GDP gap in Exhibit 8. This is an option we have not yet discussed in the context of the aggregate expenditures model, and it requires special consideration. The government may consider changes in two types of taxes: autonomous taxes and income taxes. For simplicity, here the analysis is confined to the simpler concept of autonomous taxes, such as property taxes, which are independent of the levels of real output and income.

Suppose in Exhibit 8 the government reduces autonomous taxes by $800 billion. Would this tax cut be enough to restore full employment? Since real disposable income rises at every level of GDP, so does consumption at all levels of real GDP. As a result, the consumption function and, in turn, the aggregate expenditures function shifts upward, but not by the full amount of the tax cut. Since the MPC is 0.50, this means households spend only $400 billion of the additional $800 billion of disposable income from the tax cut. The remaining $400 billion of the tax cut is added to savings. Hence, after multiplying the tax cut by the MPC, the result of the tax cut is computed as above. That is, in this case, the increase in equilibrium real GDP is $400 billion × 2 = $800 billion. Since GDP would increase only from $4 trillion to $4.8 trillion, the economy would operate below the full-employment real GDP of $6 trillion.

An approach similar to a cut in taxes would be for the government to raise *transfer payments* (welfare, unemployment, and Social Security payments) by $800 billion. This increase in transfer payments, holding taxes constant, increases disposable income dollar for dollar at each level of real GDP. Hence, the consumption and aggregate expenditures lines shift upward by $400 billion. This initial boost in total spending is computed by multiplying the MPC of 0.50 times the increase of $800 billion in transfer payments. The increase in transfer payments has the same effect as an identical cut in taxes, and the equilibrium real GDP increases by $800 billion. Hence, a transfer payment is simply a cut in net taxes.

Another simpler method of calculating the impact of a change in taxes is to use a tax multiplier. The tax multiplier is the change in aggregate expenditures (total spending) resulting from an initial change in taxes. Expressed as a formula:

Tax multiplier = 1 − spending multiplier

After you calculate the tax multiplier, multiply your answer by the amount of the tax increase or decrease in order to determine the change in aggregate expenditures. Expressed as a formula:

Change in taxes (ΔT) × tax multiplier = change in aggregate expenditures

Returning to the example shown in Exhibit 8, suppose we wish to calculate the tax cut required to increase real GDP by $2 trillion from $4 trillion to $6 trillion and achieve full employment. Using the tax multiplier formula:

$$\text{Tax multiplier} = 1 - 2 = -1$$
$$\Delta T \times (-1) = \$2 \text{ trillion}$$
$$\Delta T = -\$2 \text{ trillion}$$

Tax multiplier

The change in aggregate expenditures (total spending) resulting from an initial change in taxes. As a formula, the tax multiplier equals 1 − spending multiplier.

Therefore, in this hypothetical economy, a $2 trillion tax cut will increase GDP by the $2 trillion required to achieve full employment.

> ✔ **CHECKPOINT**
>
> **Full-Employment Output, Where Are You?**
>
> Suppose the U.S. economy is in equilibrium at $15 trillion real GDP with a recessionary gap. Given an MPC of 0.50, the government estimates that a tax cut of $500 billion is just enough to restore full employment. What is the full-employment real GDP target?

9-4b INFLATIONARY GAP

Inflationary gap

The amount by which the aggregate expenditures curve must be decreased to achieve full-employment equilibrium.

Under other circumstances, an inflationary gap may burden an economy. An inflationary gap is the amount by which aggregate expenditures exceed the amount required to achieve full-employment equilibrium. In Exhibit 9, the inflationary gap of $1 trillion is the vertical distance between point a on the initial AE_1 line and point E_2 on the AE_2 line. Since the economy can produce only $4 trillion in real output, this excess aggregate demand puts upward pressure on prices as buyers compete for this limited real output. If aggregate spending declines from AE_1 to AE_2, the economy moves from an equilibrium of $6 trillion at point E_1 to the full-employment equilibrium of $4 trillion at point E_2, and the inflationary pressure cools.

Again, the Keynesian prescription is for the central government to take aggressive action and adopt policies that reduce autonomous spending [C, I, G, or $(X - M)$] by an amount equal to the inflationary gap. Note from the analysis in the previous section that the government could cut government spending or use a tax hike or a cut in transfer payments to reduce consumption. Stated as an expression,

Initial decrease in autonomous expenditures × spending multiplier
= decrease in equilibrium output

In our example, the MPC is 0.50, so the multiplier is 2. The actual real GDP of $6 trillion is greater than the potential real GDP of $4 trillion, so the negative real GDP gap is –$2 trillion. Hence,

$$-\$1 \text{ trillion} \times 2 = -\$2 \text{ trillion}$$

> ✔ **CHECKPOINT**
>
> **How Much Spending Must Uncle Sam Cut?**
>
> Suppose the U.S. economy is troubled by inflation. The economy is in equilibrium at a real GDP of $15.5 trillion, the MPC is 0.90, and the full-employment output is $15 trillion. If the government decides to eliminate the inflationary gap by cutting government spending, what will be the size of the cut?

EXHIBIT 9 | An Inflationary Gap

The hypothetical economy begins in equilibrium at point E_1 with an equilibrium output of $6 trillion real GDP. Given an initial aggregate expenditures function of AE_1, real GDP will not self-correct to the full-employment output of $4 trillion. The $1 trillion excess of total spending over the amount required at full employment is the inflationary gap measured by the vertical distance between points a and E_2. Given a multiplier of 2, an initial decrease in autonomous expenditures of $1 trillion causes the economy to move from point E_1 to E_2, achieve full employment, and cool the upward pressure on prices.

SOURCE: © Cengage Learning 2014

The Great Ice Cream War

Applicable concept: aggregate expenditures model

The following article from *The Wall Street Journal* provides a rare insight into the politics of global trade, and the Analyze the Issue connects trade policy to the macro model developed in this chapter:

> While many people relish American-made ice cream with deliberately foreign-sounding names, few people realize that the U.S. government declared war on ice cream imports by restricting them to less than one-tenth of one percent of U.S. consumption. With quotas so low and transportation costs high, few countries bothered to ship any ice cream at all to the United States. For example, in 1988 the United States exported hundreds of thousands of gallons of ice cream to Canada, yet Canadian ice cream was banned from the United States. Only 576 gallons was imported from New Zealand and 12 gallons from Denmark. This was not enough ice cream to stock a large grocery store on a summer Saturday.
>
> The U.S. ice cream quotas dated back to December 31, 1970, when President Nixon decreed that future ice cream imports could not exceed 431,330 gallons a year. Why? That year, according to Deputy Secretary of Agriculture Ann Veneman, testifying before the ITC [U.S. International Trade Commission], the United States was hit with a "flood of imports." This so-called "flood" amounted to barely 1 percent of U.S. ice cream consumption.
>
> How did Mr. Nixon decide to limit imports to exactly 431,330 gallons a year? Section 22 of the Agriculture Adjustment Act allowed the U.S. government to protect domestic price-support programs by restricting imports to 50 percent of the annual average imports for a representative period. Ice cream imports did not begin until 1969, so the U.S. government chose 1969 and the two previous years with no ice cream imports in order to calculate a low annual average import quota for this product.

> Finally, the article concluded that the U.S. government probably spent more than $1,000 in administrative expenses for each gallon of ice cream imported into the United States. The article's author concluded, "Global trade disputes are rapidly degenerating into a full employment program for government bureaucrats."

Analyze the Issue

Assume the U.S. economy is in an inflationary gap condition. Use the Keynesian aggregate expenditures model to explain why increasing U.S. exports and restricting imports is or is not a desirable policy.

Source: Reprinted from The Wall Street Journal © 1989 Dow Jones & Company. All rights reserved.

Key Concepts

Aggregate expenditures function (AE)	Spending multiplier (SM)	Tax multiplier
Aggregate expenditures model	Recessionary gap	Inflationary gap

Summary

- The **Keynesian theory** argues that the economy is inherently unstable and may require government intervention to control aggregate expenditures and restore full employment. If we assume that real disposable income remains the same high proportion of real GDP, then we can substitute real GDP for real disposable income in the Keynesian model. **Investment, government spending** and **net exports** can be treated as autonomous expenditures. Adding consumption (C), investment (I), government spending (G), and net exports ($X - M$) equals the aggregate expenditures function (AE).

Keynesian Equilibrium

SOURCE: © Cengage Learning 2014

- The **Keynesian aggregate expenditures model** determines the equilibrium level of real GDP by the intersection of the aggregate expenditures and the aggregate output and income curves. Each equilibrium level in the economy is associated with a level of employment and corresponding unemployment rate. Aggregate expenditures and real GDP are equal, graphically, where the AE = $C + I + G + (X - M)$ line intersects the 45-degree line. At any output greater or less than the equilibrium real GDP, unintended inventory investment pressures businesses to alter aggregate output and income until equilibrium at full-employment real GDP is restored.

Keynesian Aggregate Expenditures Model

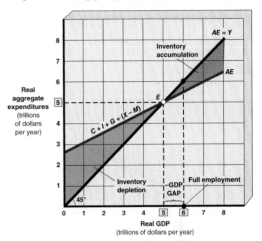

SOURCE: © Cengage Learning 2014

- The **spending multiplier** is the ratio of the change in equilibrium output to the initial change in any of the components of aggregate expenditures. Algebraically, the multiplier is the reciprocal of the marginal propensity to save. The multiplier effect causes the equilibrium level of real GDP to change by several times the initial change in spending.

Spending Multiplier

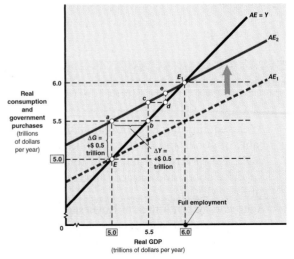

SOURCE: © Cengage Learning 2014

- A **recessionary gap** is the amount by which aggregate expenditures fall short of the amount necessary for the economy to operate at full-employment real GDP. To eliminate a negative GDP gap, the Keynesian solution is to increase autonomous spending by an amount equal to the recessionary gap and operate through the multiplier to increase equilibrium output and income.

Recessionary Gap

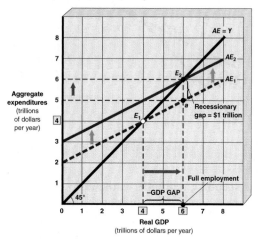

- The **tax multiplier** is the multiplier by which an initial change in taxes changes aggregate demand (total spending) after an infinite number of spending cycles. Expressed as a formula, the tax multiplier = 1 − spending multiplier.

- An **inflationary gap** is the amount by which aggregate expenditures exceed the amount necessary to establish full-employment equilibrium and indicates upward pressure on prices. To eliminate a positive GDP gap, the Keynesian solution is to decrease autonomous spending by an amount equal to the inflationary gap and operate through the multiplier to decrease equilibrium output and income.

Inflationary Gap

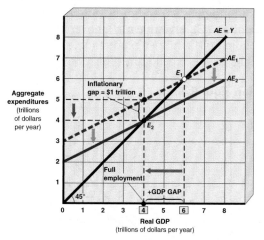

Summary of Conclusion Statements

- At the equilibrium level of real GDP, the total value of goods and services produced (real GDP, Y) is precisely equal to the total spending for these goods and services (aggregate expenditures, AE).
- Aggregate expenditures in Keynesian economics pull aggregate output either higher or lower toward equilibrium in the economy, as opposed to the classical view that aggregate output generates an equal amount of aggregate spending.
- Any initial change in spending by the government, households, or firms creates a chain reaction of further spending, which causes a greater cumulative change in aggregate expenditures.

Study Questions and Problems

1. Assume the level of autonomous investment is $100 billion and aggregate expenditures equal consumption and investment. Based on the following table, answer the questions below.

Employment, Output, Consumption, and Unplanned Inventory

Possible levels of employment (millions of workers)	Real GDP (output) equals disposable income (billions of dollars)	Consumption (billions of dollars)	Unplanned inventory (billions of dollars)
40	$325	$300	$_____
45	375	325	_____
50	425	350	_____
55	475	375	_____
60	525	400	_____
65	575	425	_____
70	625	450	_____

a. Fill in the unplanned inventory column.
b. Determine the MPC and MPS.
c. If this economy employs a labor force of 40 million, what will happen to this level of employment? Explain and identify the equilibrium level of output.

2. Using the data given in question 1, what is the impact of adding net exports? Let imports equal $75 billion, and assume exports equal $50 billion. What is the equilibrium level of employment and output?

3. Explain the determination of equilibrium real GDP by drawing an abstract graph of the aggregate expenditures model. Label the aggregate expenditures line AE and the aggregate output line AO. Explain why the interaction of AE and AO determines the Keynesian equilibrium level of real GDP.

4. Use the aggregate expenditures model to demonstrate the multiplier effect.

5. How are changes in the MPC, changes in the MPS, and the size of the multiplier related? Answer the following questions:
a. What is the multiplier if the MPC is 0? 0.33? 0.90?
b. Suppose the equilibrium real GDP is $100 billion and the MPC is 4/5. How much will the equilibrium output change if businesses increase their level of investment by $10 billion?
c. Using the data given in question 5(b), what will be the change in equilibrium real GDP if the MPC equals 2/3?

6. Assume the MPC is 0.90 and autonomous investment increases by $500 billion. What will be the impact on real GDP?

7. Suppose autonomous investment increases by $100 billion and the MPC is 0.75.
a. Use the following table to compute four rounds of the spending multiplier effect:

Round	Components of total spending	New consumption spending (billions of dollars)
1	Investment	$_____
2	Consumption	_____
3	Consumption	_____
4	Consumption	_____
	Total spending	_____

b. Use the spending multiplier formula to compute the final cumulative impact on aggregate spending.

8. First, use the data given in question 1, and assume the level of autonomous investment is $50 billion. If the full-employment level of output is $525 billion, what is the equilibrium level of output and employment? Does a recessionary gap or an inflationary gap exist? Second, assume the level of autonomous

investment is $150 billion. What is the equilibrium level of output and employment? Does a recessionary gap or an inflationary gap exist? Explain the consequences of an inflationary gap using the aggregate expenditures model.

9. Assume an economy is in recession with a MPC of 0.75 and there is a GDP gap of $100 billion. How much must government spending increase to eliminate the gap? Instead of increasing government spending by the amount

you calculate, what would be the effect of the government cutting taxes by this amount?

10. Suppose the government wishes to eliminate an inflationary gap of $100 billion and the MPC is 0.50. How much must the government cut its spending? Instead of decreasing government spending by the amount you calculate, what would be the effect of the government increasing taxes by this amount?

For Online Exercises, go to Tucker Web site at www.cengage.com/economics/tucker.

✓ CHECKPOINT ANSWERS

Full-Employment Output, Where Are You?

A tax cut of $500 billion boosts consumer income by this amount. Because the MPC is 0.50, consumers will spend $250 billion of the tax cut and save the remaining $250 billion. To compute the impact of the rise in consumption (ΔC) on real GDP (ΔY), use this formula:

$$\Delta C \times \text{multiplier} = \Delta Y$$

where

$$\text{Multiplier} = \frac{1}{\text{MPS}} = \frac{1}{1 - \text{MPC}} = \frac{1}{1 - 0.50} = 2$$

Thus, $250 billion × 2 = $500 billion. The increase in real GDP from the tax cut equals $500 billion, which is added to the initial equilibrium real GDP of $15 trillion to achieve full-employment output. If you said the full-employment real GDP is $15.5 trillion, **YOU ARE CORRECT.**

How Much Spending Must Uncle Sam Cut?

The GDP gap is $500 billion real GDP. To calculate the size of the government spending cut (ΔG) required to decrease real GDP (ΔY) by $500 billion, use this formula:

$$\Delta G \times \text{multiplier} = -\Delta Y$$

where

$$\text{Multiplier} = \frac{1}{\text{MPS}} = \frac{1}{1 - \text{MPC}} = \frac{1}{1 - 0.90} = 10$$

Thus,

$$\Delta G = \frac{-\Delta Y}{\text{multiplier}} = \frac{-\$500 \text{ billion}}{10} = -\$50 \text{ billion}$$

If you said the size of the cut in government spending is $50 billion, **YOU ARE CORRECT.**

Sample Quiz

For an explanation of the correct answers, visit the Tucker Web site at www.cengage.com/economics/tucker.

1. Using C to represent consumption, I to represent investment, G to represent government spending, S to represent saving, X to represent exports, and M to represent imports, aggregate expenditures (AE) can be represented by
   a. $C + I + G + (X + M)$.
   b. $(C - S) + G + (X - M)$.
   c. $C + I + G + (X - M)$.
   d. $C + I + G + (X - M) - S$.

2. In the aggregate expenditures model, if aggregate expenditures (AE) are less than GDP, then
   a. inventory is depleted.
   b. inventory is unchanged.
   c. employment decreases.
   d. employment increases.

3. Which of the following are the components of aggregate expenditures?
   a. household consumption, business investment, government spending for goods and services, and net exports
   b. household consumption, business investment, government transfer payments, and net exports
   c. household consumption, business investment, government spending for goods and services, and exports
   d. household consumption, business investment, government spending for goods and services, and saving

4. In the Keynesian model, investment, government spending, and net exports are treated as autonomous expenditures, which means they are independent of
   a. expectations.
   b. the price level.
   c. political processes.
   d. real GDP.

5. As shown in Exhibit 10, equilibrium GDP is
   a. $2 trillion.
   b. $6 trillion.
   c. $10 trillion.
   d. $12 trillion.

EXHIBIT 10 | Keynesian Aggregate Expenditures Model

SOURCE: © Cengage Learning 2014

6. As shown in Exhibit 10, if GDP is $6 trillion, the economy experiences unplanned inventory
   a. depletion of $2 trillion.
   b. depletion of $6 trillion.
   c. accumulation of $2 trillion.
   d. accumulation of $6 trillion.

7. As shown in Exhibit 10, if GDP is $14 trillion, the economy experiences unplanned inventory
   a. accumulation of $12 trillion.
   b. depletion of $14 trillion.
   c. accumulation of $2 trillion.
   d. depletion of $4 trillion.

8. The ratio of the change in GDP to an initial change in aggregate expenditures (AE) is the
   a. spending multiplier.
   b. permanent income rate.
   c. marginal expenditure rate.
   d. marginal propensity to consume.

9. The formula to compute the spending multiplier is
   a. $1/(MPC + MPS)$.
   b. $1/(1 - MPC)$.
   c. $1/(1 - MPS)$.
   d. $1/(C + I)$.

Sample Quiz *continued*

10. If the marginal propensity to consume (MPC) is 0.80, the value of the spending multiplier is
    a. 2.
    b. 5.
    c. 8.
    d. 10.

11. When households' marginal propensity to consume (MPC) increases, the size of the spending multiplier
    a. also increases.
    b. decreases.
    c. remains unchanged.
    d. reacts unpredictably.

12. Mathematically, the value of the spending multiplier is given by the formula
    a. MPC − 1.
    b. (MPC − 1)/MPC.
    c. 1/MPC.
    d. 1/MPS.

13. Assume the economy is in recession, the MPC is 0.80, and an increase of $200 billion in spending is needed to reach full employment. The target can be reached if government spending is increased by
    a. $20 billion.
    b. $200 billion.
    c. $80 billion.
    d. $40 billion.

14. Using the aggregate expenditures model, assume the aggregate expenditures (AE) line is above the 45-degree line at full-employment GDP. This vertical distance is called a(an)
    a. inflationary gap.
    b. recessionary gap.
    c. negative GDP gap.
    d. marginal propensity to consume gap.

15. Assume that full-employment real GDP is $Y =$ $1,200 billion, the current equilibrium real GDP is $Y =$ $1,600 billion, and the MPC = 0.8. To bring the economy to a full-employment real GDP,
    a. a recessionary gap must be bridged by increasing aggregate expenditures by $80 billion.

    b. an inflationary gap must be bridged by cutting aggregate expenditures by $80 billion.
    c. nothing is needed to bring the economy into full-employment equilibrium.
    d. a recessionary gap must be bridged by increasing aggregate expenditures by $400 billion.
    e. an inflationary gap must be bridged by cutting aggregate expenditures by $400 billion.

16. If the MPC is 0.70, then the spending multiplier is equal to
    a. 0.70.
    b. 0.30.
    c. 0.14.
    d. 3.33.
    e. 5.

17. The equilibrium level of real GDP is $1,000, the target full-employment level of real GDP is $1,500, and the marginal propensity to consume is 0.75. The target can be reached if government spending is
    a. increased by $100 billion.
    b. increased by $125 billion.
    c. increased by $500 billion.
    d. held constant.

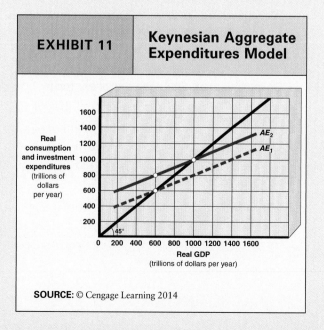

EXHIBIT 11 | **Keynesian Aggregate Expenditures Model**

Real consumption and investment expenditures (trillions of dollars per year)

Real GDP (trillions of dollars per year)

SOURCE: © Cengage Learning 2014

Sample Quiz *continued*

18. In Exhibit 11, an increase in aggregate expenditures causes
    a. a movement down the aggregate expenditures curve from equilibrium real GDP of $600 to equilibrium real GDP $1,000.
    b. a movement up the aggregate expenditures curve from equilibrium real GDP of $1,200 to equilibrium real GDP $1,000.
    c. a shift of the aggregate expenditures curve to the right, causing equilibrium real GDP to increase from $600 to $1,000.
    d. a shift of the aggregate expenditures curve to the left, causing equilibrium real GDP to decrease from $1,200 to $1,000.
    e. no change in equilibrium real GDP.

19. In Exhibit 11, the value of the spending multiplier is
    a. 3.
    b. 4.
    c. 5.
    d. 2.
    e. 6.

20. In Exhibit 11, assume the AE_2 line is aggregate expenditures and $1,000 is full-employment real GDP. If the economy operates at a real disposable income of $600, there will be
    a. inventory accumulation of $100.
    b. inventory accumulation of $200.
    c. zero inventory.
    d. inventory depletion of $200.

chapter **10**

Aggregate Demand and Supply

Classical economic theory held that the economy would bounce back to full employment as long as prices and wages were flexible. As the unemployment rate soared and remained high during the Great Depression, British economist John Maynard Keynes formulated a new theory with new policy implications. Instead of taking a wait-and-see policy until markets self-correct the economy, Keynes argued that policymakers must take action to influence aggregate spending through changes in government spending. The prescription for the Great Depression was simple: Increase government spending and jobs will be created. Faced with the current financial crisis, Keynesian management of the economy is currently being used to stabilize the U.S. and global economy. Keynes himself would be amazed at the scale and scope of what is happening. The opposition view today is based on the classical model that rejects the federal government

stimulus package concept because the economy will self-correct to full employment.

In this chapter, you will use aggregate demand and supply analysis to study the business cycle. The chapter opens with a presentation of the aggregate demand curve and then the aggregate supply curve. Once these concepts are developed, the analysis shows why modern macroeconomics teaches that shifts in aggregate supply or aggregate demand can influence the price level, the equilibrium level of real GDP, and employment. For example, although Keynes was not concerned with the problem of inflation, his theory has implications for fighting demand-pull inflation. In this case, the government must cut spending or increase taxes to reduce aggregate demand. You will probably return to this chapter often because it provides the basic tools with which to organize your thinking about the macro economy.

In this chapter, you will learn to solve these economics puzzles:

- Why does the aggregate supply curve have three different segments?
- Would the greenhouse effect cause inflation, unemployment, or both?
- Was John Maynard Keynes's prescription for the Great Depression right?

10-1 The Aggregate Demand Curve

Here we view the collective demand for *all* goods and services, rather than the *market* demand for a particular good or service. Exhibit 1 shows the aggregate demand curve (AD), which slopes downward and to the right for a given year. The aggregate demand curve shows the level of real GDP purchased by households, businesses, government, and foreigners (net exports) at different possible price levels during a time period, ceteris paribus. Stated differently, the aggregate demand curve shows us the total dollar amount of goods and services that will be demanded in the economy at various price levels. As for the demand curve for an individual market, the lower the economy-wide price level, the greater the aggregate quantity demanded for real goods and services, ceteris paribus.

The downward slope of the aggregate demand curve shows that at a given level of aggregate income, people buy more goods and services at a lower average price level. While the horizontal axis in the market supply and demand model measures

Aggregate demand curve (AD)

The curve that shows the level of real GDP purchased by households, businesses, government, and foreigners (net exports) at different possible price levels during a time period, ceteris paribus.

EXHIBIT 1	The Aggregate Demand Curve

The aggregate demand curve (AD) shows the relationship between the price level and the level of real GDP, other things being equal. The lower the price level, the larger the GDP demanded by households, businesses, government, and foreigners. If the price level is 300 at point *A*, a real GDP of $8 trillion is demanded. If the price level is 200 at point *B*, the real GDP demanded increases to $12 trillion.

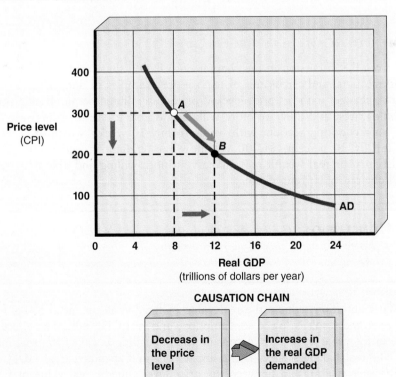

SOURCE: © Cengage Learning 2014

physical units, such as bushels of wheat, the horizontal axis in the aggregate demand and supply model measures the value of *final* goods and services included in real GDP. Note that the horizontal axis represents the quantity of aggregate production demanded, measured in base-year dollars. The vertical axis is an *index* of the overall price level measured by the consumer price index (CPI), rather than the price per bushel of wheat. As shown in Exhibit 1, if the price level measured by the CPI is 300 at point *A*, a real GDP of $8 trillion is demanded in a given year. If the price level is 200 at point *B*, a real GDP of $12 trillion is demanded. Note that hypothetical data is used throughout this chapter and the next unless otherwise stated.

Although the aggregate demand curve looks like a market demand curve, these concepts are different. As we move along a market demand curve, the price of related goods is assumed to be constant. But when we deal with changes in the general or average price level in an economy, this assumption is meaningless because we are using a market basket measure for *all* goods and services.

> **CONCLUSION:** *The aggregate demand curve and the demand curve are not the same concept.*

10-2 Reasons for the Aggregate Demand Curve's Shape

The reasons for the downward slope of an aggregate demand curve include the *real balances effect*, the *interest-rate effect*, and the *net exports effect*.

10-2a REAL BALANCES EFFECT

Recall from the discussion in the chapter on inflation that cash, checking deposits, savings accounts, and certificates of deposit are examples of financial assets whose real value changes with the price level. If prices are falling, the purchasing power of households rises, and they are more willing and able to spend. Suppose you have $1,000 in a checking account with which to buy 10 weeks' worth of groceries. If prices fall by 20 percent, $1,000 will now buy enough groceries for 12 weeks. This rise in your real wealth may make you more willing and able to purchase a new iPhone out of current income.

> **CONCLUSION:** *Consumers spend more on goods and services when lower prices make their dollars more valuable. Therefore, the real value of money is measured by the quantity of goods and services each dollar buys.*

Real balances effect

The impact on total spending (real GDP) caused by the inverse relationship between the price level and the real value of financial assets with fixed nominal value.

When inflation reduces the real value of fixed-value financial assets held by households, the result is lower consumption, and real GDP falls. The effect of the change in the price level on real consumption spending is called the real balances effect. The real balances effect is the impact on total spending (real GDP) caused by the inverse relationship between the price level and the real value of financial assets with fixed nominal value.

10-2b INTEREST-RATE EFFECT

A second reason why the aggregate demand curve is downward sloping involves the interest-rate effect. The interest-rate effect is the impact on total spending (real GDP) caused by the direct relationship between the price level and the interest rate. A key assumption of the aggregate demand curve is that the supply of money available for borrowing remains fixed. A high price level means people must take more dollars from their wallets and checking accounts in order to purchase goods and services. At a higher price level, the demand for borrowed money to buy products also increases and results in a higher cost of borrowing, that is, higher interest rates. Rising interest rates discourage households from borrowing to purchase homes, cars, and other consumer products. Similarly, at higher interest rates, businesses cut investment projects because the higher cost of borrowing diminishes the profitability of these investments. Thus, assuming fixed credit, an increase in the price level translates through higher interest rates into a lower real GDP.

Interest-rate effect

The impact on total spending (real GDP) caused by the direct relationship between the price level and the interest rate.

10-2c NET EXPORTS EFFECT

Whether American-made goods have lower prices than foreign goods is another important factor in determining the aggregate demand curve. A higher domestic price level tends to make U.S. goods more expensive than foreign goods, and imports rise because consumers substitute imported goods for domestic goods. An increase in the price of U.S. goods in foreign markets also causes U.S. exports to decline. Consequently, a rise in the domestic price level of an economy tends to increase imports, decrease exports, and thereby reduce the net exports component of real GDP. This condition is the net exports effect. The net exports effect is the impact on total spending (real GDP) caused by the inverse relationship between the price level and the net exports of an economy.

Exhibit 2 summarizes the three effects that explain why the aggregate demand curve in Exhibit 1 is downward sloping.

GLOBAL ECONOMICS

Net exports effect

The impact on total spending (real GDP) caused by the inverse relationship between the price level and the net exports of an economy.

10-3 Nonprice-level Determinants of Aggregate Demand

As was the case with individual demand curves, we must distinguish between *changes in real GDP demanded*, caused by changes in the price level, and *changes in aggregate demand*, caused by changes in one or more of the *nonprice-level determinants*. Once the ceteris paribus assumption is relaxed, changes in variables other than the price level cause a change in the location of the aggregate demand curve. Nonprice-level determinants include the consumption (C), investment (I), government spending (G), and net exports ($X - M$) components of aggregate expenditures explained in the chapter on GDP.

> **CONCLUSION:** *Any change in the individual components of aggregate expenditures shifts the aggregate demand curve.*

EXHIBIT 2	Why the Aggregate Demand Curve Is Downward Sloping
Effect	**Causation chain**
Real balances effect	Price level decreases → Purchasing power rises → Wealth rises → Consumers buy more goods → Real GDP demanded increases
Interest-rate effect	Price level decreases → Purchasing power rises → Demand for fixed supply of credit falls → Interest rates fall → Businesses and households borrow and buy more goods → Real GDP demanded increases
Net exports effect	Price level decreases → U.S. goods become less expensive than foreign goods → Americans and foreigners buy more U.S. goods → Exports rise and imports fall → Real GDP demanded increases

SOURCE: © Cengage Learning 2014

Exhibit 3 illustrates the link between an increase in expenditures and an increase in aggregate demand. Begin at point A on aggregate demand curve AD_1, with a price level of 200 and a real GDP of $12 trillion. Assume the price level remains constant at 200 and the aggregate demand curve increases from AD_1 to AD_2. Consequently, the level of real GDP rises from $12 trillion (point A) to $16 trillion (point B) at the price level of 200. The cause might be that consumers have become more optimistic about the future and their consumption expenditures (C) have risen. Another cause might be that a tax cut increased take-home (disposable income) and consumer purchases increased at each possible price level. Or possibly an increase in business optimism has increased profit expectations, and the level of investment (I) has risen because businesses are spending more for plants and equipment. The same increase in aggregate demand could also have been caused by a boost in government spending (G) or a rise in net exports ($X - M$). A swing to pessimistic expectations by consumers or firms will cause the aggregate demand curve to shift leftward. A leftward shift in the aggregate demand curve may also be caused by a tax increase or a decrease in government spending or net exports.

10-4 The Aggregate Supply Curve

Aggregate supply curve (AS)

The curve that shows the level of real GDP produced at different possible price levels during a time period, ceteris paribus.

Just as we must distinguish between the aggregate demand and market demand curves, the theory for a market supply curve does not apply directly to the aggregate supply curve. Keeping this condition in mind, we can define the aggregate supply curve (AS) as the curve that shows the level of real GDP produced at different possible price levels during a time period, ceteris paribus. Stated simply, the aggregate supply curve shows us the total dollar amount of goods and services produced in an economy at various price levels. Given this general definition, we must pause to discuss two opposing views—the Keynesian horizontal aggregate supply curve and the classical vertical aggregate supply curve.

EXHIBIT 3	A Shift in the Aggregate Demand Curve

At the price level of 200, the real GDP level is $12 trillion at point A on AD_1. An increase in one of the nonprice-level determinants of consumption (C), investment (I), government spending (G), or net exports ($X - M$) causes the level of real GDP to rise to $16 trillion at point B on AD_2. Because this effect occurs at any price level, an increase in aggregate expenditures shifts the AD curve rightward. Conversely, a decrease in aggregate expenditures shifts the AD curve leftward.

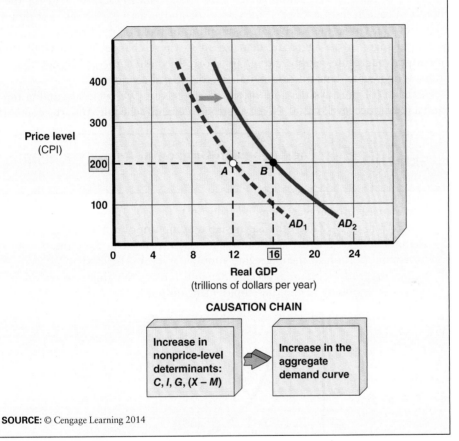

CAUSATION CHAIN

Increase in nonprice-level determinants: C, I, G, (X − M) ⇒ Increase in the aggregate demand curve

10-4a KEYNESIAN VIEW OF AGGREGATE SUPPLY

Keynes wrote in a time of great uncertainty and instability. In 1936, seven years after the beginning of the Great Depression and three years before the beginning of World War II, John Maynard Keynes published *The General Theory of Employment, Interest, and Money*. In this book, Keynes, a Cambridge University economist, argued that price and wage inflexibility during a recession means that unemployment can be a prolonged affair. Unless an economy trapped in a depression or severe recession is rescued by an increase in aggregate demand, full employment will not be achieved. This Keynesian prediction calls for government to intervene and actively manage aggregate demand to avoid a depression or recession.

Why do Keynesians assume that product prices and wages are fixed? Reasons for upward inflexibility include the following: First, during a deep recession, there are many idle resources in the economy. Consequently, producers are willing to sell at current prices because there are no shortages to put upward pressure on prices. Second, the supply of unemployed workers willing to work for the prevailing wage rate diminishes the power of workers to increase their wages. Reasons for downward inflexibility include: First, union contracts prevent businesses from lowering wage rates. Second, minimum wage laws prevent lower wages. Third, employers believe that cutting wages lowers worker morale and productivity. Therefore, during a recession, employers prefer to freeze wages and lay off or reduce hours for some of their workers until the economy recovers. In fact, the CPI for the last month of each recession since 1948 was at or above the CPI for the first month of the recession. Given the Keynesian assumption of fixed or rigid product prices and wages, changes in the aggregate demand curve cause changes in real GDP along a horizontal aggregate supply curve. In short, Keynesian theory argues that only shifts in aggregate demand can revitalize a depressed economy.

Exhibit 4 portrays the core of Keynesian theory. We begin at equilibrium E_1, with a fixed price level of 200. Given aggregate demand schedule AD_1, the equilibrium

EXHIBIT 4	The Keynesian Horizontal Aggregate Supply Curve

The increase in aggregate demand from AD_1 to AD_2 causes a new equilibrium at E_2. Given the Keynesian assumption of a fixed price level, changes in aggregate demand cause changes in real GDP along the horizontal portion of the aggregate supply curve, AS. Keynesian theory argues that only shifts in aggregate demand possess the ability to restore a depressed economy to the full-employment output.

CAUSATION CHAIN

Government spending (G) increases ⇒ Aggregate demand increases and the economy moves from E_1 to E_2 ⇒ Price level remains constant, while real GDP and employment rise

SOURCE: © Cengage Learning 2014

level of real GDP is $8 trillion. Now government spending (G) increases, causing aggregate demand to rise from AD_1 to AD_2 and equilibrium to shift from E_1 to E_2 along the horizontal aggregate supply curve (AS). At E_2, the economy moves to $12 trillion, which is closer to the full-employment GDP of $16 trillion.

> **CONCLUSION:** *When the aggregate supply curve is horizontal and an economy is in recession below full employment, the only effects of an increase in aggregate demand are increases in real GDP and employment, while the price level does not change. Stated simply, the Keynesian view is that "demand creates its own supply."*

10-4b CLASSICAL VIEW OF AGGREGATE SUPPLY

Prior to the Great Depression of the 1930s, a group of economists known as the *classical economists* dominated economic thinking.[1] The founder of the classical school of economics was Adam Smith (discussed in the chapter on economies in transition). Macroeconomics had not developed as a separate economic theory, and classical economics was therefore based primarily on microeconomic market equilibrium theory. The classical school of economics was mainstream economics from the 1770s to the Great Depression era. The classical economists believed in the *laissez-faire* "leave it alone" theory that the economy was self-regulating and would correct itself over time without government intervention. The classical economists believed, as you studied in Chapter 4, that the forces of supply and demand naturally achieve full employment in the economy because flexible prices (including wages and interest rates) in competitive markets bring all markets to equilibrium. After a temporary adjustment period, markets always clear because firms sell all goods and services offered for sale. In short, recessions naturally cure themselves because the capitalistic price system automatically restores full employment.

Exhibit 5 uses the aggregate demand and supply model to illustrate the classical view that the aggregate supply curve, AS, is a vertical line at the full-employment output of $16 trillion. The vertical shape of the classical aggregate supply curve is based on two assumptions. First, the economy normally operates at its full-employment output level. Second, the price level of products and production costs change by the same percentage, that is, proportionally, in order to maintain a full-employment level of output. This classical theory of flexible prices and wages is at odds with the Keynesian concept of sticky (inflexible) prices and wages.

Exhibit 5 also illustrates why classical economists believe a market economy over time automatically self-corrects without government intervention to full employment. Following the classical scenario, the economy is initially in equilibrium at E_1, the price level is 300, real output is at its full-employment level of $16 trillion, and the aggregate demand curve AD_1 traces total spending. Now suppose private spending falls because households and businesses are pessimistic about economic conditions. This condition causes AD_1 to shift leftward to AD_2. At a price level of 300, the immediate effect is that aggregate output exceeds aggregate spending by $4 trillion ($E_1$ to E'), and unexpected inventory accumulation occurs. To eliminate unsold inventories resulting from the decrease in aggregate demand, business firms temporarily cut back on production and reduce the price level from 300 to 200.

---

[1]The classical economists included Adam Smith, J. B. Say, David Ricardo, John Stuart Mill, Thomas Malthus, Alfred Marshall, and others.

EXHIBIT 5 | The Classical Vertical Aggregate Supply Curve

Classical theory teaches that prices and wages adjust to keep the economy operating at its full-employment output of $16 trillion. A decline in aggregate demand from AD_1 to AD_2 will temporarily cause a surplus of $4 trillion, the distance from E' to E_1. Businesses respond by cutting the price level from 300 to 200. As a result, consumers increase their purchases because of the real balances effect, and wages adjust downward. Thus, classical economists predict the economy is self-correcting and will restore full employment at point E_2. E_1 and E_2 therefore represent points along a classical vertical aggregate supply curve, AS.

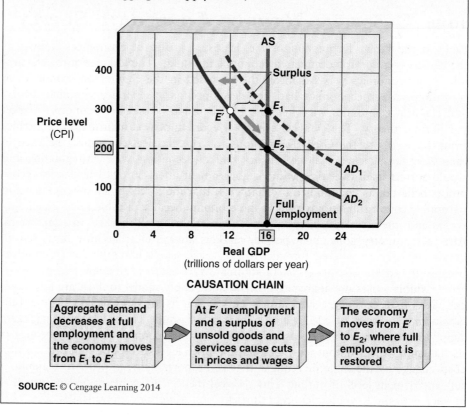

CAUSATION CHAIN

Aggregate demand decreases at full employment and the economy moves from E_1 to E' → At E' unemployment and a surplus of unsold goods and services cause cuts in prices and wages → The economy moves from E' to E_2, where full employment is restored

SOURCE: © Cengage Learning 2014

At E', the decline in aggregate output in response to the surplus also affects prices in the factor markets. As a result of the economy moving from point E_1 to E', there is a decrease in the demand for labor, natural resources, and other inputs used to produce products. This surplus condition in the factor markets means that some workers who are willing to work are laid off and compete with those who still have jobs by reducing their wage demands. Owners of natural resources and capital likewise cut their prices.

How can the classical economists believe that prices and wages are completely flexible? The answer is contained in the *real balances effect*, explained earlier. When businesses reduce the price level from 300 to 200, the cost of living falls by the same proportion. Once the price level falls by 33 percent, a nominal or money wage rate of, say, $21 per hour will purchase 33 percent more groceries after the fall in product prices than it would have before the fall. Workers will therefore accept a pay cut of 33 percent, or $7 per hour. Any worker who refuses the lower wage rate of $14 per hour will be replaced by an unemployed worker willing to accept the going rate.

Exhibit 5 shows an economy-wide proportional fall in prices and wages by the movement downward along AD_2 from E' to a new equilibrium at E_2. At E_2, the economy has self-corrected through downwardly flexible prices and wages to its full-employment level of $16 trillion worth of real GDP at the lower price level of 200. E_1 and E_2 therefore represent points along a classical vertical aggregate supply curve, AS. (The classical model is explained in more detail in the appendix to this chapter.)

CONCLUSION: *When the aggregate supply curve is vertical at the full-employment GDP, the only effect over time of a change in aggregate demand is a change in the price level. Stated simply, the classical view is that "supply creates its own demand."*[2]

Although Keynes himself did not use the AD-AS model, we can use Exhibit 5 to distinguish between Keynes's view and the classical theory of flexible prices and wages. Keynes believed that once the demand curve has shifted from AD_1 to AD_2, the surplus (the distance from E' to E_1) will persist because he rejected price-wage downward flexibility. The economy therefore will remain at the less-than-full-employment output of $12 trillion until the aggregate demand curve shifts rightward and returns to its initial position at AD_1.

CONCLUSION: *Keynesian theory rejects classical theory for an economy in recession because Keynesians argue that during a recession, prices and wages do not adjust downward to restore an economy to full-employment real GDP.*

10-5 Three Ranges of the Aggregate Supply Curve

Having studied the differing theories of the classical economists and Keynes, we will now discuss an eclectic or general view of how the shape of the aggregate supply curve varies as real GDP expands or contracts. The aggregate supply curve, AS, in Exhibit 6 has three distinct ranges or segments, labeled (1) *Keynesian range*, (2) *intermediate range*, and (3) *classical range*.

The Keynesian range is the horizontal segment of the aggregate supply curve, which represents an economy in a severe recession. In Exhibit 6, below real GDP Y_K, the price level remains constant as the level of real GDP rises. Between Y_K and the full-employment output of Y_F, the price level rises as the real GDP level rises. The intermediate range is the rising segment of the aggregate supply curve, which

Keynesian range

The horizontal segment of the aggregate supply curve, which represents an economy in a severe recession.

Intermediate range

The rising segment of the aggregate supply curve, which represents an economy as it approaches full-employment output.

---

[2]This quotation is known as Say's Law, named after the French classical economist Jean-Baptiste Say (1767–1832).

EXHIBIT 6	The Three Ranges of the Aggregate Supply Curve

The aggregate supply curve shows the relationship between the price level and the level of real GDP supplied. It consists of three distinct ranges: (1) a Keynesian range between 0 and Y_K, wherein the price level is constant for an economy in severe recession; (2) an intermediate range between Y_K and Y_F, where both the price level and the level of real GDP vary as an economy approaches full employment; and (3) a classical range, where the price level can vary while the level of real GDP remains constant at the full-employment level of output, Y_F.

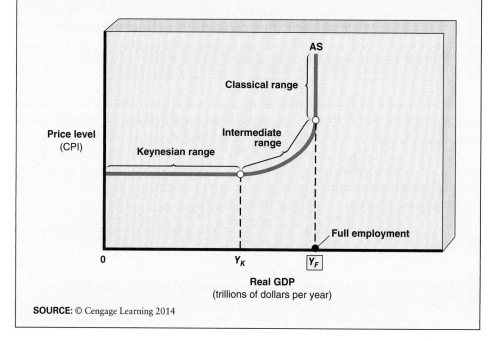

SOURCE: © Cengage Learning 2014

Classical range

The vertical segment of the aggregate supply curve, which represents an economy at full-employment output.

represents an economy approaching full-employment output. Finally, at Y_F, the level of real GDP remains constant, and only the price level rises. The classical range is the vertical segment of the aggregate supply curve, which represents an economy at full-employment output. We will now examine the rationale for each of these three distinct ranges.

10-5a AGGREGATE DEMAND AND AGGREGATE SUPPLY MACROECONOMIC EQUILIBRIUM

In Exhibit 7, the macroeconomic equilibrium level of real GDP corresponding to the point of equality, E, is $8 trillion, and the equilibrium price level is 200. This is the unique combination of price level and output level that equates how much people want to buy with the amount businesses want to produce and sell. Because the entire real GDP value of final products is bought and sold at the price level of 200, there is no upward or downward pressure for the macroeconomic equilibrium

EXHIBIT 7	The Aggregate Demand and Aggregate Supply Model

Macroeconomic equilibrium occurs where the aggregate demand curve, AD, and the aggregate supply curve, AS, intersect. In this case, equilibrium, *E*, is located at the far end of the Keynesian range, where the price level is 200 and the equilibrium output is $8 trillion. In macroeconomic equilibrium, businesses neither overestimate nor underestimate the real GDP demanded at the prevailing price level.

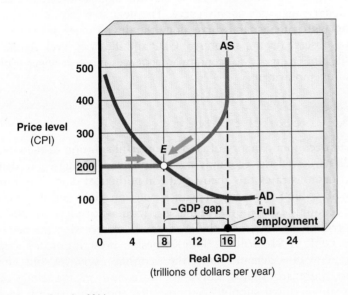

SOURCE: © Cengage Learning 2014

to change. Note that the economy shown in Exhibit 7 is operating on the edge of the Keynesian range, with a negative GDP gap of $8 trillion.

Suppose that in Exhibit 7, the level of output on the AS curve is below $8 trillion and the AD curve remains fixed. At a price level of 200, the real GDP demanded exceeds the real GDP supplied. Under such circumstances, businesses cannot fill orders quickly enough, and inventories are drawn down unexpectedly. Business managers react by hiring more workers and producing more output. Because the economy is operating in the Keynesian range, the price level remains constant at 200. The opposite scenario occurs if the level of real GDP supplied on the AS curve exceeds the real GDP in the intermediate range between $8 trillion and $16 trillion. In this output segment, the price level is between 200 and 400, and businesses face sales that are less than expected. In this case, unintended inventories of unsold goods pile up on the shelves, and management will lay off workers, cut back on production, and reduce prices.

This adjustment process continues until the equilibrium price level and output level are reached at point *E* and there is no upward or downward pressure for the price level to change. Here the production decisions of sellers in the economy equal the total spending decisions of buyers during the given period of time.

> **CONCLUSION:** *At macroeconomic equilibrium, sellers neither overestimate nor underestimate the real GDP demanded at the prevailing price level.*

10-6 Changes in the AD-AS Macroeconomic Equilibrium

One explanation of the business cycle is that the aggregate demand curve moves along a stationary aggregate supply curve. The next step in our analysis therefore is to *shift* the aggregate demand curve along the three ranges of the aggregate supply curve and observe the impact on real GDP and the price level. As the macroeconomic equilibrium changes, the economy experiences more or fewer problems with inflation and unemployment.

10-6a KEYNESIAN RANGE

Keynes's macroeconomic theory offered a powerful solution to the Great Depression. Keynes perceived the economy as being driven by aggregate demand, and Exhibit 8(a) demonstrates this theory with hypothetical data. The range of real GDP below $8 trillion is consistent with Keynesian price and wage inflexibility. Assume the economy is in equilibrium at E_1, with a price level of 200 and a real GDP of $4 trillion. In this case, the economy is in recession far below the full-employment GDP of $16 trillion. The Keynesian prescription for a recession is to increase aggregate demand until the economy achieves full employment. Because the aggregate supply curve is horizontal in the Keynesian range, "demand creates its own supply." Suppose demand shifts rightward from AD_1 to AD_2 and a new equilibrium is established at E_2. Even at the higher real GDP level of $8 trillion, the price level remains at 200. Stated differently, aggregate output can expand throughout this range without raising prices. This is because in the Keynesian range, substantial idle production capacity (including property and unemployed workers competing for available jobs) can be put to work at existing prices.

> **CONCLUSION:** *As aggregate demand increases in the Keynesian range, the price level remains constant as real GDP expands.*

10-6b INTERMEDIATE RANGE

The intermediate range in Exhibit 8(b) is between $8 trillion and $16 trillion worth of real GDP. As output increases in the range of the aggregate supply curve near the full-employment level of output, the considerable slack in the economy disappears. Assume an economy is initially in equilibrium at E_3 and aggregate demand increases from AD_3 to AD_4. As a result, the level of real GDP rises from $8 trillion to $12 trillion, and the price level rises from 200 to 250. In this output range,

EXHIBIT 8   Effects of Increases in Aggregate Demand

The effect of a rightward shift in the aggregate demand curve on the price and output levels depends on the range of the aggregate supply curve in which the shift occurs. In part (a), an increase in aggregate demand causing the equilibrium to change from E_1 to E_2 in the Keynesian range will increase real GDP from $4 trillion to $8 trillion, but the price level will remain unchanged at 200.

In part (b), an increase in aggregate demand causing the equilibrium to change from E_3 to E_4 in the intermediate range will increase real GDP from $8 trillion to $12 trillion, and the price level will rise from 200 to 250.

In part (c), an increase in aggregate demand causing the equilibrium to change from E_5 to E_6 in the classical range will increase the price level from 300 to 400, but real GDP will not increase beyond the full-employment level of $16 trillion.

(a) Increasing demand in the Keynesian range

(b) Increasing demand in the intermediate range

(c) Increasing demand in the classical range

several factors contribute to inflation. First, *bottlenecks* (obstacles to output flow) develop when some firms have no unused capacity and other firms operate below full capacity. Suppose the steel industry is operating at full capacity and cannot fill all its orders for steel. An inadequate supply of one resource, such as steel, can hold up auto production even though the auto industry is operating well below capacity. Consequently, the bottleneck causes firms to raise the price of steel and, in turn, autos. Second, a shortage of certain labor skills while firms are earning higher profits causes businesses to expect that labor will exert its power to obtain sizable wage increases, so businesses raise prices. Wage demands are more difficult to reject when the economy is prospering because businesses fear workers will change jobs or strike. Besides, businesses believe higher prices can be passed on to consumers quite easily because consumers expect higher prices as output expands to near full capacity. Third, as the economy approaches full employment, firms must use less productive workers and less efficient machinery. This inefficiency creates higher production costs, which are passed on to consumers in the form of higher prices.

> **CONCLUSION:** *In the intermediate range, increases in aggregate demand increase both the price level and the real GDP.*

10-6c   CLASSICAL RANGE

While inflation resulting from an outward shift in aggregate demand was no problem in the Keynesian range and only a minor problem in the intermediate range, it becomes a serious problem in the classical, or vertical, range.

> **CONCLUSION:** *Once the economy reaches full-employment output in the classical range, additional increases in aggregate demand merely cause inflation, rather than more real GDP.*

Assume the economy shown in Exhibit 8(c) is in equilibrium at E_5, which intersects AS at the full-capacity output. Now suppose aggregate demand shifts rightward from AD_5 to AD_6. Because the aggregate supply curve AS is vertical at $16 trillion, this increase in the aggregate demand curve boosts the price level from 300 to 400, but it fails to expand real GDP. The explanation is that once the economy operates at capacity, businesses raise their prices in order to ration fully employed resources to those willing to pay the highest prices.

In summary, the AD-AS model presented in this chapter is a combination of the conflicting assumptions of the Keynesian and classical theories separated by an intermediate range, which fits neither extreme precisely. Be forewarned that in later chapters, you will encounter a continuing great controversy over the shape of the aggregate supply curve. Modern-day classical economists believe the entire aggregate supply curve is steep, or vertical. In contrast, Keynesian economists contend that the aggregate supply curve is much flatter, or horizontal.

10-6d THE AD-AS MODEL FOR 2008–2009 DURING THE GREAT RECESSION

Exhibit 9 uses actual data to illustrate the AD-AS model. At E_1, the economy in the third quarter of 2008 was operating at a CPI of 219 and a real GDP of $13.3 trillion, which was below the full-employment real GDP of $13.4 trillion. In 2008, the combination of home prices falling sharply and a plunge in stock prices destroyed household wealth. At the same time, new home construction fell rapidly, which decreased investment spending. Recall from the chapter on gross domestic product that new residential housing is included in investment spending (I). This recessionary condition is illustrated by a movement between E_1 and E_2 caused by the aggregate demand curve decreasing from AD_1 to AD_2 along the intermediate range of the aggregate supply curve AS. At E_2 in the fourth quarter of 2008, the CPI dropped to 212, and real GDP decreased from $13.3 trillion to $13.1 trillion. Next, the aggregate demand curve decreased again from AD_2 to AD_3 in the second

EXHIBIT 9	Effect of Decreases in Aggregate Demand During 2008–2009 of the Great Recession

Beginning in the third quarter of 2008 at E_1, the aggregate demand curve shifted leftward from E_1 to E_2 in the fourth quarter of 2008 along the intermediate range of the aggregate supply curve, AS. The CPI fell from 219 to 212, and real GDP fell from $13.3 trillion to $13.1 trillion. Next, the aggregate demand curve decreased from AD_2 at E_2 to AD_3 at E_3 in the second quarter of 2009 along the Keynesian range of the aggregate supply curve. Here the price level remained constant, and real GDP fell from $13.1 trillion to $12.9 trillion.

SOURCES: Bureau of Economic Analysis, *National Income Accounts*, http://www.bea.gov/national/nipaweb/SelectTable.asp?Selected=Y, Table 1.1.6 and Bureau of Labor Statistics, *Consumer Price Index*, http://data.bls.gov/cgi-bin/surveymost?cu.

quarter of 2009 along the flat Keynesian range between E_2 and E_3. Here the price level remained approximately constant at 212, while real GDP declined from $13.1 trillion to $12.9 trillion. Although not shown explicitly in the exhibit, the unemployment rate rose during this period from 4.7 percent to 9.5 percent.

10-7 Nonprice-Level Determinants of Aggregate Supply

Our discussion so far has explained changes in real GDP supplied resulting from changes in the aggregate demand curve, given a stationary aggregate supply curve. Now we consider the situation when the aggregate demand curve is stationary and the aggregate supply curve shifts as a result of changes in one or more of the *nonprice-level determinants*. The nonprice-level factors affecting aggregate supply include resource prices (domestic and imported), technological change, taxes, subsidies, and regulations. Note that each of these factors affects production costs. At a given price level, the profit businesses make at any level of real GDP depends on production costs. If costs change, firms respond by changing their output. Lower production costs shift the aggregate supply curve rightward, indicating greater real GDP is supplied at any price level. Conversely, higher production costs shift the aggregate supply curve leftward, meaning less real GDP is supplied at any price level.

Exhibit 10 represents a supply-side explanation of the business cycle, in contrast to the demand-side case presented in Exhibit 8. (Note that for simplicity, the aggregate supply curve can be drawn using only the intermediate segment.) The economy begins in equilibrium at point E_1, with real GDP at $10 trillion and the price level at 175. Then suppose labor unions become less powerful, and their weaker bargaining position causes the wage rate to fall. With lower labor costs per unit of output, businesses seek to increase profits by expanding production at any price level. Hence, the aggregate supply curve shifts rightward from AS_1 to AS_2, and equilibrium changes from E_1 to E_2. As a result, real GDP increases $2 trillion, and the price level decreases from 175 to 150. Changes in other nonprice-level factors also cause an increase in aggregate supply. Lower oil prices, greater entrepreneurship, lower taxes, and reduced government regulation are other examples of conditions that lower production costs and therefore cause a rightward shift of the aggregate supply curve.

What kinds of events might raise production costs and shift the aggregate supply curve leftward? Perhaps there is war in the Persian Gulf or the Organization of Petroleum Exporting Countries (OPEC) disrupts supplies of oil, and higher energy prices spread throughout the economy. Under such a "supply shock," businesses decrease their output at any price level in response to higher production costs per unit. Similarly, larger-than-expected wage increases, higher taxes to protect the environment (see Exhibit 8(a) in Chapter 4), greater government regulation, or firms having to pay higher health insurance premiums would increase production costs and therefore shift the aggregate supply curve leftward. A leftward shift in the aggregate supply curve is discussed further in the next section.

Exhibit 11 summarizes the nonprice-level determinants of aggregate demand and supply for further study and review. In the chapter on monetary policy, you will learn how changes in the supply of money in the economy can also shift the aggregate demand curve and influence macroeconomic performance.

EXHIBIT 10	A Rightward Shift in the Aggregate Supply Curve

Holding the aggregate demand curve constant, the impact on the price level and real GDP depends on whether the aggregate supply curve shifts to the right or the left. A rightward shift of the aggregate supply curve from AS_1 to AS_2 will increase real GDP from $10 trillion to $12 trillion and reduce the price level from 175 to 150.

CAUSATION CHAIN

Change in one or more nonprice-level determinants: resource prices, technological change, taxes, subsidies, and regulations	→	Increase in the aggregate supply curve

SOURCE: © Cengage Learning 2014

10-8 Cost-Push and Demand-Pull Inflation Revisited

We now apply the aggregate demand and aggregate supply model to the two types of inflation introduced in the chapter on inflation. This section begins with a historical example of *cost-push inflation* caused by a decrease in the aggregate supply curve. Next, another historical example illustrates *demand-pull inflation*, caused by an increase in the aggregate demand curve.

During the late 1970s and early 1980s, the U.S. economy experienced stagflation. Stagflation is the condition that occurs when an economy experiences the twin maladies of high unemployment and rapid inflation simultaneously.

Stagflation

The condition that occurs when an economy experiences the twin maladies of high unemployment and rapid inflation simultaneously.

EXHIBIT 11	Summary of the Nonprice-Level Determinants of Aggregate Demand and Aggregate Supply
Nonprice-level determinants of aggregate demand (total spending)	Nonprice-level determinants of aggregate supply
1. Consumption (C)	1. Resource prices (domestic and imported)
2. Investment (I)	2. Taxes
3. Government spending (G)	3. Technological change
4. Net exports ($X - M$)	4. Subsidies
	5. Regulation

SOURCE: © Cengage Learning 2014

Cost-push inflation

An increase in the general price level resulting from an increase in the cost of production that causes the aggregate supply curve to shift leftward.

Demand-pull inflation

A rise in the general price level resulting from an excess of total spending (demand) caused by a rightward shift in the aggregate demand curve.

How could this happen? The dramatic increase in the price of imported oil in 1973–1974 was a villain explained by a *cost-push inflation* scenario. Cost-push inflation, defined in terms of our macro model, is a rise in the price level resulting from a decrease in the aggregate supply curve while the aggregate demand curve remains fixed. As a result of cost-push inflation, real output and employment decrease.

Exhibit 12(a) uses actual data to show how a leftward shift in the supply curve can cause stagflation. In this exhibit, aggregate demand curve AD and aggregate supply curve AS_{73} represent the U.S. economy in 1973. Equilibrium was at point E_1, with the price level (CPI) at 44.4 and real GDP at \$4,341 billion. Then, in 1974, the impact of a major supply shock shifted the aggregate supply curve leftward from AS_{73} to AS_{74}. The explanation for this shock was the oil embargo instituted by OPEC in retaliation for U.S. support of Israel in its war with the Arabs. Assuming a stable aggregate demand curve between 1973 and 1974, the punch from the energy shock resulted in a new equilibrium at point E_2, with the 1974 CPI at 49.3. The inflation rate for 1973 was 6.2 percent and for 1974 was 11 percent [(49.3 − 44.4]/44.4] × 100. Real GDP fell from \$4,341 billion in 1973 to \$4,319 billion in 1974, and the unemployment rate (not shown directly in the exhibit) climbed from 4.9 percent to 5.6 percent between these two years.[3]

In contrast, an outward shift in the aggregate demand curve can result in *demand-pull inflation*. Demand-pull inflation, in terms of our macro model, is a rise in the price level resulting from an increase in the aggregate demand curve while the aggregate supply curve remains fixed. Again, we can use aggregate demand and supply analysis and actual data to explain demand-pull inflation. In 1965, when the unemployment rate of 4.5 percent was close to the 4 percent natural rate of unemployment, real government spending increased sharply to fight the Vietnam War without a tax increase (an income tax surcharge was enacted in 1968). The inflation rate jumped sharply from 1.6 percent in 1965 to 2.9 percent in 1966.

---

[3] *Economic Report of the President, 2012*, http://www.gpo.gov/fdsys/pkg/ERP-2012/content-detail.html, Tables B-2, B-42, B-62, and B-64.

| EXHIBIT 12 | Cost-Push and Demand-Pull Inflation |

Parts (a) and (b) illustrate the distinction between cost-push inflation and demand-pull inflation. Cost-push inflation is inflation that results from a decrease in the aggregate supply curve. In part (a), higher oil prices in 1973 caused the aggregate supply curve to shift leftward from AS_{73} to AS_{74}. As a result, real GDP fell from $4,341 billion to $4,319 billion, and the price level (CPI) rose from 44.4 to 49.3. This combination of higher price level and lower real output is called stagflation.

As shown in part (b), demand-pull inflation is inflation that results from an increase in aggregate demand beyond the Keynesian range of output. Government spending increased to fight the Vietnam War without a tax increase, causing the aggregate demand curve to shift rightward from AD_{65} to AD_{66}. Consequently, real GDP rose from $3,191 billion to $3,399 billion, and the price level (CPI) rose from 31.5 to 32.4.

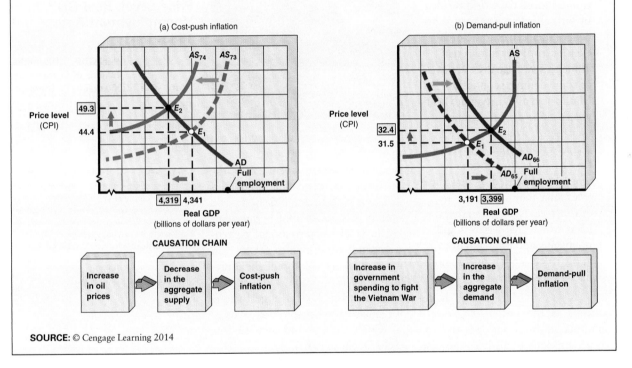

SOURCE: © Cengage Learning 2014

Exhibit 12(b) illustrates what happened to the economy between 1965 and 1966. Suppose the economy was operating in 1965 at E_1, which is in the intermediate output range. The impact of the increase in military spending shifted the aggregate demand curve from AD_{65} to AD_{66}, and the economy moved upward along the aggregate supply curve until it reached E_2. Holding the aggregate supply curve constant, the AD-AS model predicts that increasing aggregate demand at near full employment causes demand-pull inflation. As shown in Exhibit 12(b), real GDP increased from $3,191 billion in 1963 to $3,399 billion in 1966, and the CPI rose from 31.5 to 32.4. Thus, the inflation rate for 1966 was 2.9 percent $[(32.4 − 31.5)/31.5] \times 100$. Corresponding to the rise in real output, the unemployment rate of 4.5 percent in 1965 fell to 3.8 percent in 1966.[4]

[4]Ibid.

Was John Maynard Keynes Right?

Applicable Concept: aggregate demand and aggregate supply analysis

In *The General Theory of Employment, Interest, and Money,* Keynes wrote:

The ideas of economists and political philosophers, both when they are right and when they are wrong, are more powerful than is commonly understood. Indeed the world is ruled by little else. Practical men, who believe themselves to be quite exempt from any intellectual influences, are usually the slaves of some defunct economist. Madmen in authority, who hear voices in the air, are distilling their frenzy from some academic scribbler of a few years back.... There are not many who are influenced by new theories after they are twenty-five or thirty years of age, so that the ideas which civil servants and politicians and even agitators apply to current events are not likely to be the newest.[1]

Keynes (1883–1946) is regarded as the father of modern macroeconomics. He was the son of an eminent English economist, John Neville Keynes, who was a lecturer in economics and logic at Cambridge University. Keynes was educated at Eton and Cambridge in mathematics and probability theory, but ultimately he selected the field of economics and accepted a lectureship in economics at Cambridge.

Keynes was a many-faceted man who was an honored and supremely successful member of the British academic, financial, and political upper class. He amassed a $2 million personal fortune by speculating in stocks, international currencies, and commodities. (Use CPI index numbers to compute the equivalent amount in today's dollars.) In addition to making a huge fortune for himself, Keynes served as a trustee of King's College and increased its endowment over tenfold.

Keynes was a prolific scholar who is best remembered for *The General Theory*, published in 1936. This work made a convincing attack on the classical theory that capitalism would self-correct from a severe recession. Keynes based his model on the belief that increasing aggregate demand will achieve full employment, while prices and wages remain inflexible. Moreover, his bold policy prescription was for the government to raise its spending and/or reduce taxes in order to increase the economy's aggregate demand curve and put the unemployed back to work.

Price Level, Real GDP, and Unemployment Rate, 1933–1941

Year	CPI	Real GDP (billions of 2000 dollars)	Unemployment rate (percent)
1933	13.0	$ 635	24.9%
1939	13.9	951	17.2
1940	14.0	1,034	14.6
1941	14.7	1,211	9.9

SOURCES: Bureau of Labor Statistics, ftp://ftp.bls.gov/pub/special.requests/cpi/cpiai.txt, Bureau of Economic Analysis, *National Economic Accounts*, http://www.bea.gov/iTable/iTable.cfm?ReqID=9&step=1, Table 1.1.6 and *Economic Report of the President, 2012,* http://www.gpo.gov/fdsys/pkg/ERP-2012/content-detail.html, Table B-35.

Analyze the Issue

Was Keynes correct? Based on the above data, use the aggregate demand and aggregate supply model to explain Keynes's theory that increases in aggregate demand propel an economy toward full employment.

---

1. J. M. Keynes, *The General Theory of Employment, Interest, and Money* (London: Macmillan, 1936), p. 383.

Sources: © Cengage Learning 2014z

In summary, the aggregate supply and aggregate demand curves shift in different directions for various reasons in a given time period. These shifts in the aggregate supply and aggregate demand curves cause upswings and downswings in real GDP—the business cycle. A leftward shift in the aggregate demand curve, for example, can cause a recession. Whereas, a rightward shift of the aggregate demand curve can cause real GDP and employment to rise, and the economy recovers. A leftward shift in the aggregate supply curve can cause a downswing, and a rightward shift might cause an upswing.

> **CONCLUSION:** *The business cycle is a result of shifts in the aggregate demand and aggregate supply curves.*

10-9 Increase in Both Aggregate Demand and Aggregate Supply Curves

Let the trumpets blow! Aggregate demand and supply curves will now edify you by explaining the U.S. economy from the mid-1990s through 2000. Begin in Exhibit 13 at E_1 with real GDP at \$8,031 billion and the CPI at 152. As shown in the AD-AS model for 1995, the economy operated below full employment (5.6 percent unemployment rate, not explicitly shown). Over the next five years, the U.S. economy moved to E_2 in 2000 and experienced strong growth in real GDP (from \$8,031 billion to \$9,817 billion) and mild inflation (the CPI increased from 152 to 172, which is 13.1 percent, or 2.6 percent per year).

The movement from E_1 (below full employment) to E_2 (full employment) was caused by an increase in AD_{95} to AD_{00} and an increase in AS_{95} to AS_{00}. The rightward shift in the AS curve was the result of technological advances, such as the Internet and electronic commerce, which produced larger-than-usual increases in productivity at each possible price level. And as shown earlier in Exhibit 9 of the chapter on business cycles and unemployment, the economy has returned to operating below its full-employment potential real GDP since the recession of 2001, and this negative GDP rose sharply during the recession beginning in 2007.

✓ CHECKPOINT

Would the Greenhouse Effect Cause Inflation, Unemployment, or Both?

You are the chair of the president's Council of Economic Advisers. There has been an extremely hot and dry summer due to a climatic change known as the greenhouse effect. As a result, crop production has fallen drastically. The president calls you to the White House to discuss the impact on the economy. Would you explain to the president that a sharp drop in U.S. crop production would cause inflation, unemployment, or both?

EXHIBIT 13	A Rightward Shift in the Aggregate Demand and Supply Curves

From late 1995 through 2000, the aggregate demand curve increased from AD_{95} to AD_{00}. Significant increases in productivity from technology advances shifted the aggregate supply curve from AS_{95} to AS_{00}. As a result, the U.S economy experienced strong real GDP growth to full employment with mild inflation (the CPI increased from 152 to 172).

SOURCE: © Cengage Learning 2014

Key Concepts

Aggregate demand curve (AD)	Aggregate supply curve (AS)	Stagflation
Real balances effect	Keynesian range	Cost-push inflation
Interest-rate effect	Intermediate range	Demand-pull inflation
Net exports effect	Classical range	

Summary

- The **aggregate demand curve** shows the level of real GDP purchased in the economy at different price levels during a period of time.
- **Reasons why the aggregate demand curve is downward sloping** include the following three effects: (1) The **real balances effect** is the impact on real GDP caused by the inverse relationship between the purchasing power of fixed-value financial assets and inflation, which causes a shift in the consumption schedule. (2) The **interest-rate effect** assumes a fixed money supply; therefore, inflation increases the demand for money. As the demand for money increases, the interest rate rises, causing consumption and investment spending to fall. (3) The **net exports effect** is the impact on real GDP caused by the inverse relationship between net exports and inflation. An increase in the U.S. price level tends to reduce U.S. exports and increase imports, and vice versa.

Shift in the Aggregate Demand Curve

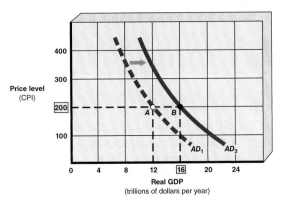

SOURCE: © Cengage Learning 2014

- The **aggregate supply curve** shows the level of real GDP that an economy will produce at different possible price levels. The shape of the aggregate supply curve depends on the flexibility of prices and wages as real GDP expands and contracts. The aggregate supply

curve has three ranges: (1) The **Keynesian range** of the curve is horizontal because neither the price level nor production costs will increase or decrease when there is substantial unemployment in the economy. (2) In the **intermediate range**, both prices and costs rise as real GDP rises toward full employment. Prices and production costs rise because of bottlenecks, the stronger bargaining power of labor, and the utilization of less productive workers and capital. (3) The **classical range** is the vertical segment of the aggregate supply curve. It coincides with the full-employment output. Because output is at its maximum, increases in aggregate demand will only cause a rise in the price level.

Aggregate Supply Curve

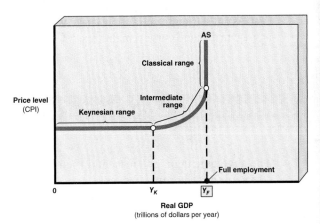

SOURCE: © Cengage Learning 2014

- **Aggregate demand and aggregate supply analysis** determines the equilibrium price level and the equilibrium real GDP by the intersection of the aggregate demand and aggregate supply curves. In macroeconomic equilibrium, businesses neither overestimate nor underestimate the real GDP demanded at the prevailing price level.

Cost-Push Inflation

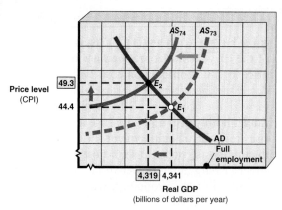

Price level (CPI): 49.3, 44.4

Real GDP (billions of dollars per year): 4,319 4,341

SOURCE: © Cengage Learning 2014

- **Stagflation** exists when an economy experiences inflation and unemployment simultaneously. Holding aggregate demand constant, a decrease in aggregate supply results in the unhealthy condition of a rise in the price level and a fall in real GDP and employment.
- **Cost-push inflation** is inflation that results from a decrease in the aggregate supply curve while the aggregate demand curve remains fixed. Cost-push

inflation is undesirable because it is accompanied by declines in both real GDP and employment.

- **Demand-pull inflation** is inflation that results from an increase in the aggregate demand curve in both the classical and the intermediate ranges of the aggregate supply curve, while the aggregate supply curve is fixed.

Demand-Pull Inflation

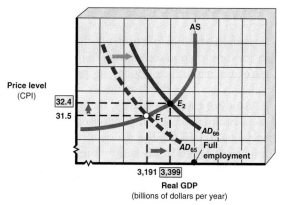

Price level (CPI): 32.4, 31.5

Real GDP (billions of dollars per year): 3,191 3,399

SOURCE: © Cengage Learning 2014

Summary of Conclusion Statements

- The aggregate demand curve and the demand curve are not the same concept.
- Consumers spend more on goods and services when lower prices make their dollars more valuable. Therefore, the real value of money is measured by the quantity of goods and services each dollar buys.
- Any change in the individual components of aggregate expenditures shifts the aggregate demand curve.
- When the aggregate supply curve is horizontal and an economy is in recession below full employment, the only effects of an increase in aggregate demand are increases in real GDP and employment, while the price level does not change. Stated simply, the Keynesian view is that "demand creates its own supply."

- When the aggregate supply curve is vertical at the full-employment GDP, the only effect over time of a change in aggregate demand is a change in the price level. Stated simply, the classical view is that "supply creates its own demand."
- Keynesian theory rejects classical theory for an economy in recession because Keynesians argue that during a recession, prices and wages do not adjust downward to restore an economy to full-employment real GDP.
- At macroeconomic equilibrium, sellers neither overestimate nor underestimate the real GDP demanded at the prevailing price level.
- As aggregate demand increases in the Keynesian range, the price level remains constant as real GDP expands.

- In the intermediate range, increases in aggregate demand increase both the price level and the real GDP.
- Once the economy reaches full-employment output in the classical range, additional increases in aggregate demand merely cause inflation, rather than more real GDP.
- The business cycle is a result of shifts in the aggregate demand and aggregate supply curves.

Study Questions and Problems

1. Explain why the aggregate demand curve is downward sloping. How does your explanation differ from the reasons behind the downward-sloping demand curve for an individual product?

2. Explain the theory of the classical economists that flexible prices and wages ensure that the economy operates at full employment.

3. In which direction would each of the following changes in conditions cause the aggregate demand curve to shift? Explain your answers.
   a. Consumers expect an economic downturn.
   b. A new U.S. president is elected, and the profit expectations of business executives rise.
   c. The federal government increases spending for highways, bridges, and other infrastructure.
   d. The United States increases exports of wheat and other crops to Russia, Ukraine, and other former Soviet republics.

4. Identify the three ranges of the aggregate supply curve. Explain the impact of an increase in the aggregate demand curve in each segment.

5. Consider this statement: "Equilibrium GDP is the same as full employment." Do you agree or disagree? Explain.

6. Assume the aggregate demand and aggregate supply curves intersect at a price level of 100. Explain the effect of a shift in the price level to 120 and to 50.

7. In which direction would each of the following changes in conditions cause the aggregate supply curve to shift? Explain your answers.
   a. The price of gasoline increases because of a catastrophic oil spill.
   b. Labor unions and all other workers agree to a cut in wages to stimulate the economy.
   c. Power companies switch to solar power, and the price of electricity falls.
   d. The federal government increases the excise tax on gasoline in order to finance a deficit.

8. Assume an economy operates in the intermediate range of its aggregate supply curve. State the direction of shift for the aggregate demand or aggregate supply curve for each of the following changes in conditions. What is the effect on the price level? On real GDP? On employment?
   a. The price of crude oil rises significantly.
   b. Spending on national defense doubles.
   c. The costs of imported goods increase.
   d. An improvement in technology raises labor productivity.

9. What shifts in aggregate supply or aggregate demand would cause each of the following conditions for an economy?
   a. The price level rises, and real GDP rises.
   b. The price level falls, and real GDP rises.
   c. The price level falls, and real GDP falls.
   d. The price level rises, and real GDP falls.
   e. The price level falls, and real GDP remains the same.
   f. The price level remains the same, and real GDP rises.

10. Explain cost-push inflation verbally and graphically, using aggregate demand and aggregate supply analysis. Assess the impact on the price level, real GDP, and employment.

11. Explain demand-pull inflation graphically using aggregate demand and supply analysis. Assess the impact on the price level, real GDP, and employment.

For Online Exercises, go to the Tucker Web site at www.cengage.com/economics/tucker.

✓ CHECKPOINT ANSWER

Would the Greenhouse Effect Cause Inflation, Unemployment, or Both?

A drop in food production reduces aggregate supply. The decrease in aggregate supply causes the economy to contract, while prices rise. In addition to the OPEC oil embargo between 1972 and 1974, worldwide weather conditions destroyed crops and contributed to the supply shock that caused stagflation in the U.S. economy. If you said that a severe greenhouse effect would cause both higher unemployment and inflation, **YOU ARE CORRECT.**

Sample Quiz

For an explanation of the correct answers, visit the Tucker Web site at www.cengage.com/economics/tucker.

1. The aggregate demand curve shows how real GDP purchased varies with changes in
   a. unemployment.
   b. output.
   c. the price level.
   d. the interest rate.

2. Which of the following is *not* a component of the aggregate demand curve?
   a. government spending (G)
   b. investment (I)
   c. consumption (C)
   d. net exports (X – M)
   e. saving

3. The real balances effect occurs because a higher price level will reduce the real value of people's
   a. financial assets.
   b. wages.
   c. unpaid debt.
   d. physical investments.

4. The real balance effect is the impact on real GDP caused by the _____ relationship between the price level and the real value of financial assets.
   a. direct
   b. inverse
   c. independent
   d. linear

5. The interest-rate effect is the impact on real GDP caused by the _____ relationship between the price level and the interest rate.
   a. direct
   b. independent
   c. linear
   d. inverse

6. The net exports effect is the _____ relationship between net exports and the price level of an economy.
   a. inverse
   b. independent
   c. direct
   d. linear

7. Which of the following would shift the aggregate demand curve to the left?
   a. an increase in exports
   b. an increase in investment
   c. an increase in government spending
   d. a decrease in government spending

8. Suppose workers become pessimistic about their future employment, which causes them to save more and spend less. If the economy is on the intermediate range of the aggregate supply curve, then
   a. both real GDP and the price level will fall.
   b. real GDP will fall, and the price level will rise.

Sample Quiz *continued*

c. real GDP will rise, and the price level will fall.

d. both real GDP and the price level will rise.

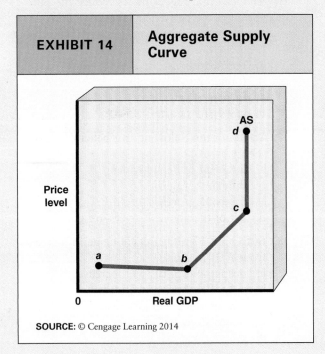

EXHIBIT 14 — Aggregate Supply Curve

Price level / Real GDP (points a, b, c, d; AS)

SOURCE: © Cengage Learning 2014

9. In Exhibit 14, resources are fully employed, and competition among producers for resources will lead to a higher price level in
a. the segment labeled *ab*.
b. the segment labeled *bc*.
c. the segment labeled *cd*.
d. segments *bc* and *cd*.

10. In Exhibit 14, as production increases, firms resort to offering higher wage rates to attract the dwindling supply of unemployed resources in
a. the segment labeled *ab*.
b. the segment labeled *bc*.
c. the segment labeled *cd*.
d. segments *bc* and *cd*.

11. An increase in oil prices will shift the aggregate
a. demand curve leftward.
b. demand curve rightward.
c. supply curve leftward.
d. supply curve rightward.

12. Stagflation is a period of time when the economy is experiencing
a. inflation and low unemployment.
b. high unemployment and low levels of inflation at the same time.
c. high inflation and high unemployment at the same time.
d. low inflation and low unemployment at the same time.

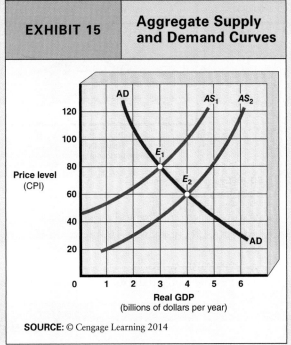

EXHIBIT 15 — Aggregate Supply and Demand Curves

Price level (CPI) / Real GDP (billions of dollars per year); AD, AS_1, AS_2, E_1, E_2

SOURCE: © Cengage Learning 2014

13. The shift from AS_1 to AS_2 in Exhibit 15 could be caused by a (an)
a. sudden increase in the price of oil.
b. increase in input prices for most firms.
c. increase in workers' wages.
d. All of the answers above are correct.

14. As the economy moves to the right in Exhibit 16 along the upward-sloping aggregate supply curve, the
a. unemployment rate rises.
b. unemployment rate falls.
c. inflation rate falls.
d. None of the above occur.

Sample Quiz *continued*

EXHIBIT 16	Aggregate Supply and Demand Curves

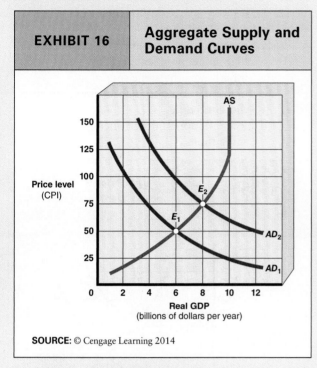

SOURCE: © Cengage Learning 2014

15. As the aggregate demand curve shifts from AD_1 to AD_2 in Exhibit 16, the economy experiences
a. cost-push inflation.
b. demand-pull inflation.

c. wage-push inflation.
d. hyperinflation.

16. The idea that higher prices reduce the purchasing power of financial assets and lead to less consumption and more saving is known as the
a. real wealth effect.
b. foreign purchases effect.
c. income effect.
d. aggregate demand effect.

17. Which of the following is a belief of classical theory?
a. long-run full employment
b. inflexible wages
c. inflexible prices
d. All of the above answers are correct

18. In Exhibit 17, if aggregate demand increases from AD_1 to AD_2,
a. output and prices will increase.
b. output and prices will decrease.
c. output alone will increase.
d. prices alone will decrease.
e. prices alone will increase.

EXHIBIT 17	Aggregate Supply and Demand Curves

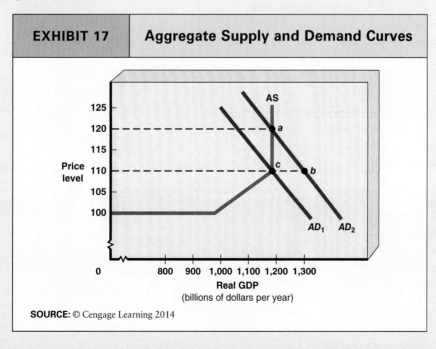

SOURCE: © Cengage Learning 2014

Sample Quiz *continued*

19. In Exhibit 17, the aggregate demand and supply curves reflect an economy in which
    a. full employment is at $1,000 billion GDP.
    b. excess aggregate supply is created when there is a shift from AD_1 to AD_2.
    c. excess aggregate demand forces prices up to P = 120.
    d. excess aggregate demand causes prices to stabilize at P = 110.
    e. a new equilibrium is found at point *b*.

20. In Exhibit 17, choosing to operate the economy at GDP = $1,200 billion and P = 110 would be opting for an economy of
    a. no unemployment with inflation.
    b. full employment without inflation.
    c. full employment with inflation.
    d. moderate cyclical unemployment without inflation.

10
The Self-Correcting Aggregate Demand and Supply Model

It can be argued that the economy is self-regulating. This means that over time, the economy will move itself to full-employment equilibrium. Stated differently, this classical theory is based on the assumption that the economy might ebb and flow around it, but full employment is the normal condition for the economy regardless of gyrations in the price level. To understand this adjustment process, the AD-AS model presented in the chapter must be extended into a more complex model called the self-correcting AD-AS model. First, a distinction will be made between the short-run and long-run aggregate supply curves. Indeed, one of the most controversial areas of macroeconomics is the shape of the aggregate supply curve and the reasons for that shape. Second, we will explain long-run equilibrium using the self-correcting AD-AS model. Third, this appendix concludes by using the self-correcting AD-AS model to explain short-run and long-run adjustments to changes in aggregate demand.

10A-1 Why the Short-Run Aggregate Supply Curve Is Upward Sloping

Short-run aggregate supply curve (SRAS)

The curve that shows the level of real GDP produced at different possible price levels during a time period in which nominal incomes do not change in response to changes in the price level.

Exhibit A-1(a) shows the short-run aggregate supply curve (SRAS), which does not have either the perfectly flat Keynesian segment or the perfectly vertical classical segment developed in Exhibit 6 of this chapter. The short-run supply curve shows the level of real GDP produced at different possible price levels during a time period in which nominal wages and salaries (incomes) do not change in response to changes in the price level. Recall from the chapter on inflation that

$$\text{Real income} = \frac{\text{nominal income}}{\text{CPI (as decimal)}}$$

As explained by this formula, a rise in the price level measured by the CPI decreases real income, and a fall in the price level increases real income. Given the definition of the short-run aggregate supply curve, there are two reasons why one can assume nominal wages and salaries remain fixed in spite of changes in the price level:

1. **Incomplete knowledge.** In a short period of time, workers may be unaware that a change in the price level has changed their real incomes. Consequently, they do not adjust their wage and salary demands according to changes in their real incomes.
2. **Fixed-wage contracts.** Unionized employees, for example, have nominal or money wages stated in their contracts. Also, many professionals receive set

EXHIBIT A-1   Aggregate Supply Curves

The short-run aggregate supply curve (SRAS) in part (a) is based on the assumption that nominal wages and salaries are fixed based on an expected price level of 100 and full-employment real GDP of $8 trillion. An increase in the price level from 100 to 150 increases profits, real GDP, and employment, moving the economy from point *A* to point *B*. A decrease in the price level from 100 to 50 decreases profits, real GDP, and employment, moving the economy from point *A* to point *C*.

The long-run aggregate supply curve (LRAS) in part (b) is vertical at full-employment real GDP. For example, if the price level rises from 100 at point *A* to 150 at point *B*, workers now have enough time to renegotiate higher nominal incomes by a percentage equal to the percentage increase in the price level. This flexible adjustment means that real incomes and profits remain unchanged, and the economy continues to operate at full-employment real GDP.

(a) Short-run aggregate supply curve

(b) Long-run aggregate supply curve

SOURCE: © Cengage Learning 2014

salaries for a year. In these cases, nominal incomes remain constant, or "sticky," for a given time period regardless of changes in the price level.

Given the assumption that changes in the prices of goods and services measured by the CPI do not in a short period of time cause changes in nominal wages, let's examine Exhibit A-1(a) and explain the SRAS curve's upward-sloping shape. Begin at point *A* with a CPI of 100 and observe that the economy is operating at the full-employment real GDP of $8 trillion. Also assume that labor contracts are based on this expected price level. Now suppose the price level unexpectedly increases from 100 to 150 at point *B*. At higher prices for products, firms' revenues increase, and with nominal wages and salaries fixed, profits rise. In response, firms increase output from $8 trillion to $12 trillion, and the economy operates beyond its full-employment output. This occurs because firms increase work hours and train and hire homemakers, retirees, and unemployed workers who were not profitable at or below full-employment real GDP.

Now return to point *A* and assume the CPI falls to 50 at point *C*. In this case, the prices firms receive for their products drop while nominal wages and salaries remain fixed. As a result, firms' revenues and profits fall, and they reduce output from $8 trillion to $4 trillion real GDP. Correspondingly, employment (not shown explicitly in the model) falls below full employment.

> **CONCLUSION:** *The upward-sloping shape of the short-run aggregate supply curve (SRAS) is the result of fixed nominal wages and salaries as the price level changes.*

10A-2 Why the Long-Run Aggregate Supply Curve Is Vertical

Long-run aggregate supply curve (LRAS)

The curve that shows the level of real GDP produced at different possible price levels during a time period in which nominal incomes change by the same percentage as the price level changes.

The long-run aggregate supply curve (LRAS) is presented in Exhibit A-1(b). The long-run aggregate supply curve shows the level of real GDP produced at different possible price levels during a time period in which nominal incomes change by the same percentage as the price level changes. Like the classical vertical segment of the aggregate supply curve developed in Exhibit 6 of the chapter, the long-run aggregate supply curve is vertical at full-employment real GDP.

To understand why the long-run aggregate supply curve is vertical requires the assumption that sufficient time has elapsed for labor contracts to expire, so that nominal wages and salaries can be renegotiated. Stated another way, over a long enough time, workers will calculate changes in their real incomes and obtain increases in their nominal incomes to adjust proportionately to changes in purchasing power. Suppose the CPI is 100 (or as a decimal, 1.0) at point *A* in Exhibit A-1(b) and the average nominal wage is $10 per hour. This means the average real wage is also $10 ($10 nominal wage divided by 1.0). But if the CPI rises to 150 at point *B*, the $10 average real wage falls to $6.67 ($10/1.5). In the long run, workers will demand and receive a new nominal wage of $15, returning their real wage to $10 ($15/1.5). Thus, both the CPI (rise from 100 to 150) and the nominal wage (rise from $10 to $15) changed by the same rate of 50 percent, and the economy moved from point *A* to point *B*, upward along the long-run aggregate supply curve. Note that because both the prices of products measured by the CPI and the nominal wage rise by the same percentage, profit margins remain unchanged in real terms, and firms have no incentive to produce either more or less than the full-employment real GDP of $8 trillion. And because this same adjustment process occurs between any two price levels along LRAS, the curve is vertical, and potential real GDP is independent of the price level. Regardless of rises or falls in the CPI, potential real GDP remains the same.

> **CONCLUSION:** *The vertical shape of the long-run aggregate supply curve (LRAS) is the result of nominal wages and salaries eventually changing by the same percentage as the price level changes.*

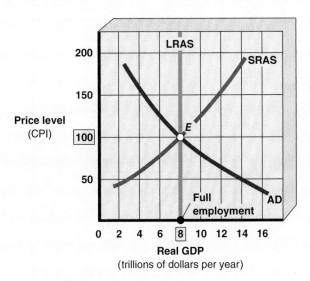

EXHIBIT A-2 Self-Correcting AD-AS Model

The short-run aggregate supply curve (SRAS) is based on an expected price level of 100. Point E shows that this equilibrium price level occurs at the intersection of the aggregate demand curve AD, SRAS, and the long-run aggregate supply curve (LRAS).

SOURCE: © Cengage Learning 2014

10A-3 Equilibrium in the Self-Correcting AD-AS Model

Exhibit A-2 combines aggregate demand with the short-run and long-run aggregate supply curves from the previous exhibit to form the self-correcting AD-AS model. Equilibrium in the model occurs at point E, where the economy's aggregate demand curve (AD) intersects the vertical long-run aggregate supply curve (LRAS) and the short-run aggregate supply curve (SRAS). In long-run equilibrium, the economy's price level is 100, and full-employment real GDP is $8 trillion.

10A-4 The Impact of an Increase in Aggregate Demand

Now you're ready for some actions and reactions using the model. Suppose that beginning at point E_1 in Exhibit A-3, a change in a nonprice determinant (summarized in Exhibit 11 at the end of the chapter) causes an increase in aggregate demand from AD_1 to AD_2. For example, the shift could be the result of an increase in consumption spending (C), government spending (G), or business investment (I), or greater demand for U.S. exports. Regardless of the cause, the short-run effect is for the economy to move upward along $SRAS_{100}$ to the intersection with AD_2 at the temporary or short-run equilibrium point E_2 with a price level of 150. Recall

EXHIBIT A-3	Adjustments to an Increase in Aggregate Demand Supply Curves

Beginning at long-run equilibrium E_1, the aggregate demand curve increases from AD_1 to AD_2. Because nominal incomes are fixed in the short run, firms raise product prices, earn higher profits, and expand output to short-run equilibrium point E_2. After enough time passes, workers increase their nominal incomes to restore their purchasing power, and the short-run supply curve shifts leftward along AD_2 to a transitional point such as E_3. As the economy moves from E_2 to E_4, profits fall, and firms cut output and employment. Eventually, long-run equilibrium is reached at E_4, with full employment restored by the self-correction process.

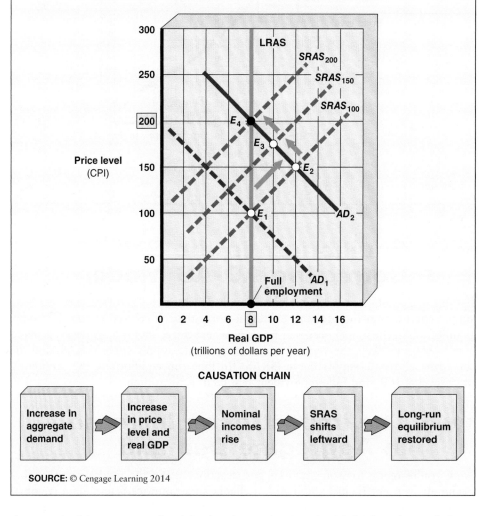

CAUSATION CHAIN

Increase in aggregate demand → Increase in price level and real GDP → Nominal incomes rise → SRAS shifts leftward → Long-run equilibrium restored

SOURCE: © Cengage Learning 2014

that nominal incomes are fixed in the short run. Faced with higher demand, firms raise prices for products, and because the price of labor remains unchanged, firms earn higher profits and increase employment by hiring workers who were not profitable at full employment. As a result, for a short period of time, real GDP increases above the full-employment real GDP of $8 trillion to $12 trillion. However, the economy cannot produce in excess of full employment forever. What forces are at work to bring real GDP back to full-employment real GDP?

Assume time passes and labor contracts expire. The next step in the transition process at E_2 is that workers begin demanding nominal income increases that will eventually bring their real incomes back to the same real incomes established initially at E_1. Since firms are anxious to maintain their output levels and they are competing for workers, firms meet the wage increase demands of labor. These increases in nominal incomes shift the short-run aggregate supply curve leftward, which causes an upward movement along AD_2. One of the successions of possible intermediate adjustment short-run supply curves along AD_2 is $SRAS_{150}$. This short-run intermediate adjustment is based on an expected price level of 150 determined by the intersection of $SRAS_{150}$ and LRAS. Although the short-run aggregate supply curve $SRAS_{150}$ intersects AD_2 at E_3, the adjustment to the increase in aggregate demand is not yet complete. Workers negotiated increases in nominal incomes based on an expected price level of 150, but the leftward shift of the short-run aggregate supply curve raised the price level to about 175 at E_3. Workers must therefore negotiate another round of higher nominal incomes to restore purchasing power. This process continues until long-run equilibrium is restored at E_4, where the adjustment process ends.

The long-run forecast for the price level at full employment is now 200 at point E_4. $SRAS_{100}$ has shifted leftward to $SRAS_{200}$, which intersects LRAS at point E_4. As a result of the shift in the short-run aggregate supply curve from E_2 to E_4 and the corresponding increase in nominal incomes, firms' profits are cut, and they react by raising product prices, reducing employment, and reducing output. At E_4, the economy has self-adjusted to both short-run and long-run equilibrium at a price level of 200 and full-employment real GDP of $8 trillion. If there are no further shifts in aggregate demand, the economy will remain at E_4 indefinitely. Note that nominal income is higher at point E_4 than it was originally at point E_1, but real wages and salaries remain unchanged, as explained in Exhibit A-1(b).

> **CONCLUSION:** *An increase in aggregate demand in the long run causes the short-run aggregate supply curve to shift leftward because nominal incomes rise and the economy self-corrects to a higher price level at full-employment real GDP.*

10A-5 The Impact of a Decrease in Aggregate Demand

Point E_1 in Exhibit A-4 begins where the sequence of events described in the previous section ends. Now let's see what happens when the aggregate demand curve decreases from AD_1 to AD_2. The reason might be that a wave of pessimism from a stock market crash causes consumers to cut back on their spending and firms postpone buying new factories and equipment. As a result, firms find their sales and profits have declined, and they react by cutting product prices, output, and employment. Workers' nominal incomes remain fixed in the short run with contracts negotiated based on an expected price level of 200. The result of this situation is that the economy moves downward along $SRAS_{200}$ from point E_1 to short-run equilibrium point E_2. Here the price level falls from 200 to 150, and real GDP has fallen from $8 trillion to $4 trillion.

EXHIBIT A-4	Adjustments to a Decrease in Aggregate Demand

Assume the economy is initially at long-run equilibrium point E_1 and aggregate demand decreases from AD_1 to AD_2. Nominal incomes in the short run are fixed based on an expected price level of 200. In response to the fall in aggregate demand, firms' profits decline, and they cut output and employment. As a result, the economy moves downward along $SRAS_{200}$ to temporary equilibrium at E_2. When workers lower their nominal incomes because of competition from unemployed workers, the short-run aggregate supply curve shifts downward to an intermediate point, such as E_3. As workers decrease their nominal incomes based on the new long-run expected price level of 150 at point E_3, profits rise, and firms increase output and employment. In the long run, the short-run aggregate supply curve continues to automatically adjust downward along AD_2 until it again returns to long-run equilibrium at E_4.

CAUSATION CHAIN

Decrease in aggregate demand ⇒ Decrease in price level and real GDP ⇒ Nominal incomes fall ⇒ SRAS shifts rightward ⇒ Long-run equilibrium restored

At E_2, the economy is in a serious recession, and after, say, a year, workers will accept lower nominal wages and salaries when their contracts are renewed in order to keep their jobs in a time of poor profits and competition from unemployed workers. This willingness to accept lower nominal incomes is made easier by the realization that lower prices for goods means it costs less to maintain the workers' standard of living. As workers make a series of downward adjustments in nominal incomes, the short-run aggregate supply curve moves downward along AD_2 toward E_4. $SRAS_{150}$ illustrates one possible intermediate position corresponding to the long-run expected price level of 150 determined by the intersection of $SRAS_{150}$ and LRAS. However, like E_2, E_3 is not the point of long-run equilibrium. Workers negotiated decreases in nominal increases based on an expected price level of 150, but the rightward shift of the short-run aggregate supply curve has lowered the price level to about 125 at E_3. Under pressure from unemployed workers who will work for still lower real wages and salaries, workers will continue this process of adjusting their nominal incomes lower until $SRAS_{150}$ shifts rightward to point E_4.

Eventually, the long-run expected full-employment price level returns to 100 at point E_4, where the economy has self-corrected to long-run full-employment equilibrium. The result of this adjustment downward along AD_2 between E_2 and E_4 is that lower nominal incomes raise profits and firms respond by lowering prices of products, increasing employment, and increasing output so that real GDP increases from \$4 trillion to \$8 trillion. Unless aggregate demand changes, the economy will be stable at E_4 indefinitely. Finally, observe that average nominal income has decreased by the same percentage between points E_1 and E_4 as the percentage decline in the price level. Therefore, real incomes are unaffected as explained in Exhibit A-1(b).

> **CONCLUSION:** *A decrease in aggregate demand in the long run causes the short-run aggregate supply curve to shift rightward because nominal incomes fall and the economy self-corrects to a lower price level at full-employment real GDP.*

10A-6 Changes in Potential Real GDP

Like the aggregate demand and short-run aggregate supply curves, the long-run aggregate supply curve also changes. As explained in Chapter 2, changes in resources and technology shift the production possibilities curve outward. We now extend this concept of economic growth to the long-run aggregate supply curve as follows:

1. *Changes in resources.* For example, the quantity of land can be increased by reclaiming land from the sea or revitalizing soil. Over time, potential real GDP increases if the full-employment number of workers increases, holding capital and technology constant. Such growth in the labor force can result from population growth. Greater quantities of plants, production lines, computers, and other forms of capital also produce increases in potential real GDP. Capital includes *human capital*, which is the accumulation of education, training, experience, and health of workers.
2. *An advance in technology.* Technological change enables firms to produce more goods from any given amount of inputs. Even with fixed quantities of labor and capital, the latest computer-age machinery increases potential GDP.

EXHIBIT A-5	Trend of Macro Equilibrium Price Level over Time

Each hypothetical long-run equilibrium point shows the CPI and real GDP for a given year determined by the intersection of the aggregate demand curve, short-run aggregate supply curve, and long-run aggregate supply curve. Over time, these curves shift, and both the price level and real GDP increase.

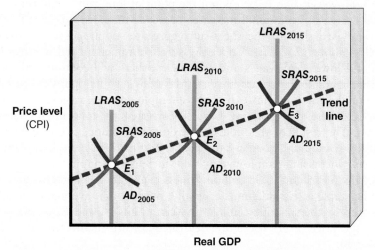

Real GDP
(trillions of dollars per year)

SOURCE: © Cengage Learning 2014

CONCLUSION: *A rightward shift of the long-run aggregate supply curve represents economic growth in potential full-employment real GDP.*

Over time, the U.S. economy typically adds resources and improves technology, and growth occurs in full-employment output. Exhibit A-5 uses basic aggregate demand and supply analysis to explain a hypothetical trend in the price level measured by the CPI between 2005, 2010, and 2015. The trend line connects the macro equilibrium points for each year. The following section uses real-world data to illustrate changes in the long-run aggregate supply curve over time.

10A-7 Increase in the Aggregate Demand and Long-Run Aggregate Supply Curves

The self-correcting AD-AS model shown in Exhibit A-5 revisits Exhibit 13 in the chapter, which illustrated economic growth that occurred between 1995 and 2000 in the U.S. economy. Exhibit A-6, however, uses short-run and long-run aggregate supply curves to expand the analysis. (For simplicity, the real GDP amounts have

EXHIBIT A-6	A Rightward Shift in the Aggregate Demand and Long-Run Aggregate Supply Curves

In 1995, the U.S. economy was operating at $8.0 trillion below full-employment real GDP of $8.3 trillion at $LRAS_{95}$. Between 1995 and 2000, the aggregate demand curve increased from AD_{95} to AD_{00}, and the U.S economy moved upward along the short-run aggregate supply curve $SRAS_{95}$ from point E_1 to point E_2. Nominal or money incomes of workers increased, and $SRAS_{95}$ shifted leftward to $SRAS_{00}$, establishing long-run full-employment equilibrium at E_3 on long-run aggregate supply curve $LRAS_{00}$. Technological changes and capital accumulation over these years caused the rightward shift from $LRAS_{95}$ to $LRAS_{00}$, and potential real GDP grew from $8.3 trillion to $9.8 trillion.

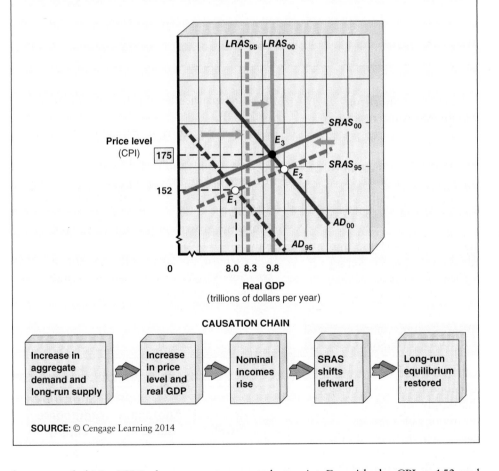

CAUSATION CHAIN

| Increase in aggregate demand and long-run supply | ⇨ | Increase in price level and real GDP | ⇨ | Nominal incomes rise | ⇨ | SRAS shifts leftward | ⇨ | Long-run equilibrium restored |

SOURCE: © Cengage Learning 2014

been rounded.) In 1995, the economy operated at point E_1, with the CPI at 152 and a real GDP of $8.0 trillion. Since $LRAS_{95}$ at E_1 was estimated to be $8.3 trillion real GDP, the economy was operating below its full-employment potential with an unemployment rate of 5.6 percent (not explicitly shown in the model). Over the next five years, the U.S. economy moved to full employment at point E_3 in 2000 and experienced growth in real GDP from $8.0 trillion to $9.8 trillion. The CPI increased from 152 to 175 (mild inflation), and the unemployment rate fell to 4.0 percent.

During this time period, extraordinary technological change and capital accumulation, particularly in high-tech industries, caused economic growth in potential real GDP, represented by the rightward shift in the vertical long-run supply curve from $LRAS_{95}$ to $LRAS_{00}$. The movement from E_1 below full-employment real GDP was caused by an increase in AD_{95} to AD_{00} and a movement upward along short-run aggregate supply curve $SRAS_{95}$ to point E_2. Over time, the nominal or money wage rate increased, and $SRAS_{95}$ shifted leftward to $SRAS_{00}$. At point E_3, the price level was 175 and equal to potential real GDP of $9.8 trillion.

Key Concepts

Short-run aggregate supply curve (SRAS)   Long-run aggregate supply curve (LRAS)

Summary

- The **upward-sloping shape of the short-run aggregate supply curve (SRAS)** is the result of fixed nominal wages and salaries as the price level changes.
- The **vertical shape of the long-run aggregate supply curve (LRAS)** is the result of nominal wages and salaries eventually changing by the same percentage as the price level changes.
- An **increase in aggregate demand (AD) in the long run** causes the short-run aggregate supply curve (SRAS) to shift leftward because nominal incomes rise and the economy self-corrects to a higher price level at full-employment real GDP.
- A **decrease in aggregate demand in the long run** causes the short-run aggregate supply curve (SRAS) to shift rightward because nominal incomes fall and the economy self-corrects to a lower price level at full-employment real GDP.
- **Economic growth in potential real GDP** is represented by a rightward shift in the long-run aggregate supply curve (LRAS). Shifts in LRAS are caused by changes in resources and advances in technology.

Study Questions and Problems

1. The economy of Tuckerland has the following aggregate demand and supply schedules, reflecting real GDP in trillions of dollars:
   a. Graph the aggregate demand curve and the short-run aggregate supply curve.
   b. What are short-run equilibrium real GDP and the price level?
   c. If Tuckerland's potential real GDP is $12 trillion, plot the long-run aggregate supply curve (LRAS) in the graph.

Price level (CPI)	Aggregate demand	Short-run aggregate supply
250	$ 4	$16
200	8	12
150	12	8
100	16	4

2. Using the graph from question 1 and assuming long-run equilibrium at $12 trillion, explain the impact of a 10 percent increase in workers' income.

3. Use the graph drawn in question 1 and assume the initial equilibrium is E_1. Next, assume aggregate demand increases by $4 trillion. Draw the effect on short-run equilibrium.

4. Based on the assumptions of question 3, explain verbally the impact of an increase of $4 trillion in aggregate demand on short-run equilibrium.

5. The economy shown in Exhibit A-7 is initially in equilibrium at point E_1, and the aggregate demand curve decreases from AD_1 to AD_2. Explain the long-run adjustment process.

6. In the first quarter of 2001, real GDP was $9.88 trillion, and the price level measured by the GDP chain price index was 101. Real GDP was approximately equal to potential GDP. In the third quarter, aggregate demand decreased to $9.83 trillion, and the price level rose to 103. Draw a graph of this recession.

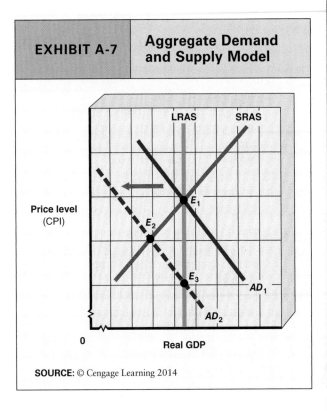

EXHIBIT A-7	Aggregate Demand and Supply Model

SOURCE: © Cengage Learning 2014

For Online Exercises, go to the Tucker Web site at www.cengage.com/economics/tucker.

Sample Quiz

For an explanation of the correct answers, visit the Tucker Web site at www.cengage.com/economics/tucker.

1. One reason for the short-run aggregate supply curve (SRAS) is
   a. a fixed CPI market basket.
   b. perfect knowledge of workers.
   c. fixed-wage contracts.
   d. the upward-sloping production function.

2. The full-employment level of real GDP is the level that can be produced with
   a. given technology and productive resources.
   b. frictional and structural unemployment equal to zero.
   c. cyclical unemployment equal to zero.
   d. both a and b.
   e. both a and c.

3. Which of the following would cause a decrease in the short-run aggregate supply curve (SRAS)?
   a. an increase in oil prices
   b. an advance in technology
   c. an increase in the CPI
   d. an increase in the long-run aggregate supply curve (LRAS)

4. If nominal wages and salaries are fixed as firms change product prices, the short-run aggregate supply curve (SRAS) is
   a. vertical.
   b. horizontal.
   c. negatively sloped.
   d. positively sloped.

Sample Quiz *continued*

5. Which of the following explains why the short-run aggregate supply curve is upward sloping?
   a. The quantity of real output supplied is inversely related to the aggregate supply curve.
   b. Nominal incomes are fixed.
   c. The capital-output ratio.
   d. An increase in price will increase the supply of money.

6. In an economy where nominal incomes adjust equally to changes in the price level, we would expect the long-run aggregate supply curve to be
   a. vertical.
   b. horizontal.
   c. negatively sloped.
   d. positively sloped.

7. In the AD-AS model, a point where the economy's long-run AS curve, short-run AS curve, and AD curve all intersect at a single point represents a point where
   a. real GDP is equal to its full-employment level.
   b. the conditions of short-run equilibrium are fulfilled.
   c. the conditions of long-run equilibrium are fulfilled.
   d. All of the above answers are correct.
   e. Answers a and c are correct.

8. The intersection between the long-run aggregate supply and aggregate demand curves determines the
   a. level of full-employment real GDP.
   b. average level of prices (CPI).
   c. marginal product.
   d. both a and b.

9. The adjustment of nominal incomes to changes in the price level (CPI) is fixed because of the
   a. volatility of investment spending.
   b. existence of long-term contracts.
   c. complete information possessed by workers.
   d. All of the above answers are correct.

10. In the self-correcting AD-AS model, the economy's short-run equilibrium position is indicated by the intersection of which two curves?
    a. short-run aggregate supply and long-run aggregate supply
    b. short-run aggregate supply and aggregate demand
    c. long-run aggregate supply and aggregate demand
    d. long-run aggregate demand and short-run personal consumption expenditures

11. Which of the following causes a leftward shift in the short-run aggregate supply curve?
    a. an increase of goods prices while nominal incomes are unchanged
    b. an increase in nominal incomes
    c. an increase of full-employment real GDP
    d. an increase of personal consumption expenditures while the price level is unchanged

12. In parts (a) and (b) of Exhibit A-8, the intersection of AD with SRAS indicates
    a. a short-run equilibrium.
    b. a long-run equilibrium.
    c. that the economy needs policies to reduce unemployment.
    d. that the economy is at full employment.

13. In part (a) of Exhibit A-8, suppose the initial equilibrium is at real GDP level Y_1 and price level P_2. At real GDP level Y_1, there is
    a. an inflationary gap.
    b. a recessionary gap.
    c. full employment.
    d. long-run equilibrium.

14. In part (b) of Exhibit A-8, the intersection of SRAS with AD indicates
    a. an economy experiencing a recessionary gap.
    b. an economy experiencing an inflationary gap.
    c. that the economy is in long-run equilibrium.
    d. that the economy has an unemployment rate currently less than the natural rate of unemployment.

Sample Quiz *continued*

15. In part (b) of Exhibit A-8, the intersection of SRAS with LRAS indicates
    a. an economy experiencing a recessionary gap.
    b. long-run equilibrium if the aggregate demand curve (AD) shifts leftward to this point.

c. that the economy is in long-run equilibrium.
d. that the economy has an unemployment rate currently greater than the natural rate of unemployment.

16. As shown in Exhibit A-9 and assuming the aggregate demand curve shifts from AD_1 to AD_2, the full-employment level of real GDP is
    a. $10 billion.
    b. $4 billion.
    c. $100 billion.
    d. unable to be determined.

17. Beginning from a point of short-run equilibrium at point E_2 in Exhibit A-9, the economy's movement to a new position of long-run equilibrium from that point would *best* be described as
    a. a movement downward along the AD_2 curve with a shift in the $SRAS_1$ curve to $SRAS_2$.
    b. a movement along the $SRAS_2$ curve with a shift in the AD_2 curve.
    c. a shift in the LRAS curve to an intersection at E_3.
    d. no shift of any kind.

18. Based on Exhibit A-10, when the aggregate demand curve shifts to the position AD_2 and the economy is operating at point E_2, the economy's position of long-run equilibrium corresponds to point
    a. E_1.
    b. E_2.
    c. E_3.
    d. E_1 or E_3.

19. Beginning in Exhibit A-10, from long-run equilibrium at point E_1, the aggregate demand curve shifts to AD_2. The economy's path to a new long-run equilibrium is represented by a movement from
    a. E_3 to E_1 to E_2.
    b. E_1 to E_3 to E_2.
    c. E_2 to E_1 to E_2.
    d. E_1 to E_2 to E_3.

EXHIBIT A-8	Macro AD-AS Models

(a)

(b)

SOURCE: © Cengage Learning 2014

Sample Quiz *continued*

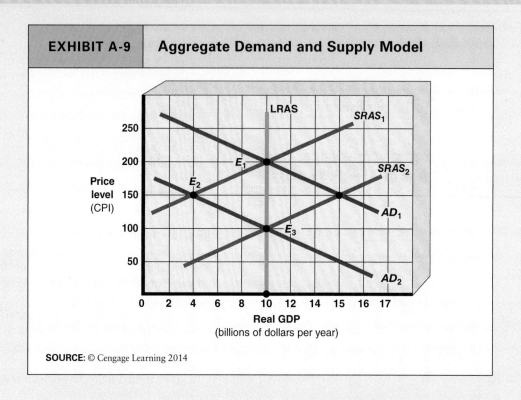

EXHIBIT A-9 | Aggregate Demand and Supply Model

SOURCE: © Cengage Learning 2014

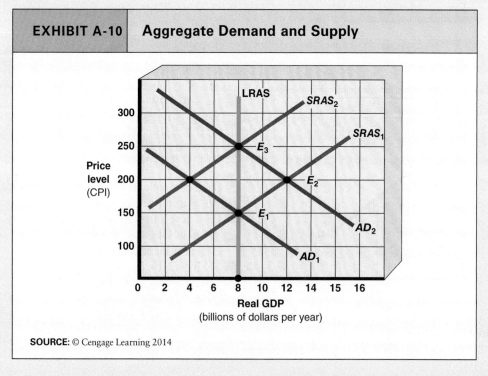

EXHIBIT A-10 | Aggregate Demand and Supply

SOURCE: © Cengage Learning 2014

Sample Quiz *continued*

20. Economic growth would be represented in Exhibit A-10 by a(an)
    a. leftward shift in the long-run aggregate supply curve (LRAS).
    b. inward shift of the production possibilities curve.
    c. rightward shift in the long-run aggregate supply curve (LRAS).
    d. movement along the long-run aggregate supply curve (LRAS).

TKKNOK - An Allegory by Sam Stenard

Far across the blue ocean whose bottom is sand,
Where the sigglethrush hunt for fine places to land,
By the Mishler still fishing for figs in the deep,
And cacophonous caves where the Caterwall sleeps...

Far beyond all these places there exists a fine spot,
Where the sun's always shining quite bright and quite hot,
It's the land of the Neetches! The fine land of Knox!
All surrounded by mountains with glass on their tops.

Now these Knobbly-Kneed Neetches (as most know them best)
Are famous for the feathers on their wings and their breasts,
Very useful for catching a mid-morning breeze,
And the envy of those without knobs on their knees.

Also existing in this country of Knox,
Stands the Cliffs of Much Tallness, a pile of rocks
That reach their way upward, past the day's glow,
And casts a long shadow on things far below.

On the face of that cliff grows a plant that's quite rare:
The fresh Ju-Ju Fruit that is found only there.

The juice of this fruit turns Neetch feathers bright,
Makes them grow large and allows them their flight.
On these fine feathers they soar to great heights,
Eating the Ju-Jus with great beaky bites.

Searching the sky on one sunny day,
The Neetches in Charge were rather dismayed
To see their fellows in flight for so long;
They decided right there it mustn't go on.

So they came up with a plan,
A method, a way,
To keep Neetches on land
All through the day.

"We'll make a device, a great big machine!
That will fly up the rocks and pick the cliffs clean!"

"No need for Neetches flying about,
Exhausting themselves day in and day out;
All we need is a feather or two,
From each of the Neetches
To see our plan through."

The Neetches freely obeyed without fuss.
But faced a dilemma really quite rough:
That despite all their giving...
                                    There wasn't enough!

When the Neetches in Charge again begged their fellows,
They found that their feathers had withered and yellowed.
For fewer feathers on the wings of the Neetches
Meant trouble ascending to the Cliff's highest reaches.

Yet it was here that the finest fruit could be found,
And without they must settle for the fruit on the ground.
But the juice of this fruit didn't make feathers so bright,
It actually did nothing but inhibit their flight.

So with feathers smaller than ever they'd seen,
It'd take two times the number to complete the machine!
Yet again they gave as the leaders implored,
Only to find that they still needed more.

But they had picked all the feathers, every last one.
And still the machine wasn't done.

chapter 11

Fiscal Policy

In the early 1980s, under President Ronald Reagan, the federal government reduced personal income tax rates. The goal was to expand aggregate demand and boost real GDP output and employment in order to end the recession of 1980–1981. In the 1990s, a key part of President Bill Clinton's programs was to stimulate economic growth by boosting government spending on long-term investment, including highways, bridges, and education. In 2001, the United States experienced a recession, and during the next two years, President George W. Bush proposed and signed into law tax cuts to stimulate the economy. And in 2008, Americans received a $170 billion tax-rebate stimulus package, followed by another $787 billion federal stimulus package under the Obama administration in 2009 intended to jump-start the economy into recovery from the recession.

Fiscal policy is one of the major issues that touches everyone's life. Fiscal policy is the use of government spending and taxes to influence the nation's output, employment, and price level. Federal government spending policies affect Social Security benefits, price supports for dairy farmers, and employment in the defense industry. Tax policies can change the amount of your paycheck and therefore influence whether you purchase a car or attend college.

Using fiscal policy to influence the performance of the economy has been an important idea since the Keynesian revolution of the 1930s. This chapter removes the political veil and looks at fiscal policy from the viewpoint of two opposing economic theories. First, you will study Keynesian demand-side fiscal policies that "fine-tune" aggregate demand so that the economy grows and achieves full employment with a higher price level. Second, you will study supply-side fiscal policy, which gained prominence during the Reagan administration. Supply-siders view aggregate supply as far more important than aggregate demand. Their fiscal policy prescription is to increase aggregate supply so that the economy grows and achieves full employment with a lower price level.

In this chapter, you will learn to solve these economics puzzles:

- Does an increase in government spending or a tax cut of equal amount provide the greater stimulus to economic growth?

- Can Congress fight a recession without taking any action?

- How could one argue that the federal government can increase tax revenues by cutting taxes?

11-1 Discretionary Fiscal Policy

Here we begin where the previous chapter left off, that is, discussing the use of discretionary fiscal policy, as Keynes advocated, to influence the economy's performance. Discretionary fiscal policy is the deliberate use of changes in government spending or taxes to alter aggregate demand and stabilize the economy. Exhibit 1 lists three basic types of discretionary fiscal policies and the corresponding ways in which the government can pursue each of these options. The first column of the table shows that the government can choose to increase aggregate demand by following an *expansionary* fiscal policy. The second column lists *contractionary* fiscal policy options the government can use to restrain aggregate demand.

11-1a INCREASING GOVERNMENT SPENDING TO COMBAT A RECESSION

Suppose the U.S. economy represented in Exhibit 2 has fallen into recession at equilibrium point E_1, where aggregate demand curve AD_1 intersects the aggregate supply curve, AS, in the near-full-employment range. The price level measured by the CPI is 210, and a real GDP gap of $1 trillion exists below the full-employment output of $14 trillion real GDP. As explained in the previous chapter (Exhibit 5), one approach the president and Congress can follow is provided by classical theory. The classical economists' prescription is to wait because the economy will self-correct to full employment in the long run by adjusting downward along AD_1. But election time is approaching, so there is political pressure to do something about the

Fiscal policy

The use of government spending and taxes to influence the nation's spending, employment, and price level.

Discretionary fiscal policy

The deliberate use of changes in government spending or taxes to alter aggregate demand and stabilize the economy.

EXHIBIT 1	Discretionary Fiscal Policies
Expansionary fiscal policy	**Contractionary fiscal policy**
Increase government spending	Decrease government spending
Decrease taxes	Increase taxes
Increase government spending and taxes equally	Decrease government spending and taxes equally

SOURCE: © Cengage Learning 2014

EXHIBIT 2 | **Using Government Spending to Combat a Recession**

The economy in this exhibit is in recession at equilibrium point E_1 on the intermediate range of the aggregate supply curve, AS. The price level is 210, with an output level of $13 trillion real GDP. To reach the full-employment output of $14 trillion in real GDP, the aggregate demand curve must be shifted to the right by $2 trillion real GDP, measured by the horizontal distance between point E_1 on curve AD_1 and point X on curve AD_2. The necessary increase in aggregate demand from AD_1 to AD_2 can be accomplished by increased government spending. Given a spending multiplier of 2, a $1 trillion increase in government spending brings about the required $2 trillion rightward shift in the aggregate demand curve, and equilibrium in the economy changes from E_1 to E_2. Note that the equilibrium real GDP changes by $1 trillion and not by the full amount by which the aggregate demand curve shifts horizontally.

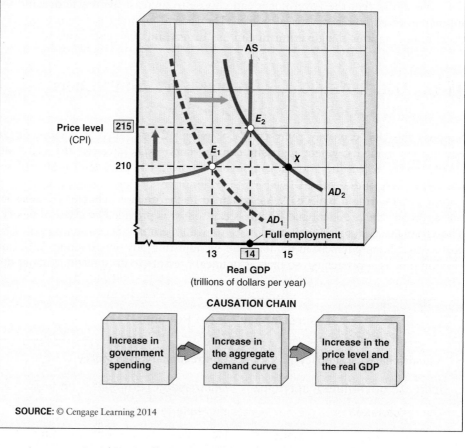

CAUSATION CHAIN

Increase in government spending ⇒ Increase in the aggregate demand curve ⇒ Increase in the price level and the real GDP

SOURCE: © Cengage Learning 2014

recession now. Besides, recall Keynes's famous statement, "In the long run, we are all dead." Hence, policymakers follow Keynesian economics and decide to shift the aggregate demand curve rightward from AD_1 to AD_2 and thereby cure the recession.

How can the federal government do this? In theory, any increase in consumption (C), investment (I), or net exports (X − M) can spur aggregate demand. But these spending boosts are not directly under the government's control as is government spending (G). After all, there is always a long wish list of spending proposals for federal highways, health care, education, environmental programs, and so forth. Rather than crossing their fingers and waiting for things to happen in the long run, suppose members of Congress gladly increase government spending to boost employment now.

But just how much new government spending is required? Note that the economy is operating $1 trillion below its full-employment output, but the horizontal distance between AD_1 and AD_2 is $2 trillion. This gap between AD_1 and AD_2 is indicated by the dotted line between points E_1 and X ($15 trillion − $13 trillion). This means that the aggregate demand curve must be shifted to the right by $2 trillion. But it is not necessary to increase government spending by this amount. The following formula can be used to compute the amount of additional government spending required to shift the aggregate demand curve rightward and establish a new full-employment real GDP equilibrium:

Initial change in government spending (ΔG) × spending multiplier

= change in aggregate demand (total spending)

The spending multiplier (SM) in the formula amplifies the amount of new government spending. The spending multiplier is the change in aggregate demand (total spending) resulting from an initial change in any component of aggregate demand, including consumption, investment, government spending, and net exports. Assume the value for the spending multiplier in our example is 2. The next section explains the algebra behind the spending multiplier so that the example can be solved:

$$\Delta G \times 2 = \$2 \text{ trillion}$$

$$\Delta G = \$1 \text{ trillion}$$

Note that the Greek letter Δ (delta) means "a change in." Thus, it takes $1 trillion worth of new government spending to shift the aggregate demand curve to the right by $2 trillion. As described in the previous chapter (Exhibit 6), bottlenecks occur throughout the upward-sloping range of the AS curve. This means prices rise as production increases in response to greater aggregate demand. Returning to Exhibit 2, you can see that $1 trillion worth of new government spending shifts aggregate demand from AD_1 to AD_2. As a result, firms increase output upward along the aggregate supply curve, AS, and total spending moves upward along aggregate demand curve AD_2. This adjustment mechanism moves the economy to a new equilibrium at E_2, with full employment, a higher price level of 215, and a real GDP of $14 trillion per year. At point E_2, the economy experiences *demand-pull inflation*. And here is the important point: Although the aggregate demand curve has increased by $2 trillion, the equilibrium real GDP has increased by only $1 trillion, from $13 to $14 trillion.

Spending multiplier (SM)

The change in aggregate demand (total spending) resulting from initial change in any component of aggregate expenditures, including consumption, investment, government spending, and net exports. As a formula, spending multiplier equals 1/(1 − MPC) or 1/MPS.

> **CONCLUSION:** *In the intermediate segment of the aggregate supply curve, the equilibrium real GDP changes by less than the change in government spending times the spending multiplier.*

11-1b SPENDING MULTIPLIER ARITHMETIC REVISITED[1]

Marginal propensity to consume (MPC)

The change in consumption spending resulting from a given change in income.

Now let's pause to tackle the task of explaining in more detail the spending multiplier of 2 used in the above example. The spending multiplier begins with a concept called the marginal propensity to consume (MPC). The marginal propensity to consume is the change in consumption spending resulting from a given change in income. Algebraically,

$$\text{MPC} = \frac{\text{change in consumption spending}}{\text{change in income}}$$

Exhibit 3 illustrates numerically the cumulative increase in aggregate demand resulting from a $1 trillion increase in government spending. In the initial round, the government spends this amount for bridges, national defense, and so forth. Households receive this amount of income. In the second round, these households spend $500 billion (0.50 × $1 trillion, or $1,000 billion) on houses, cars, groceries, and other products. In the third round, the incomes of realtors, autoworkers, grocers, and others are boosted by $500 billion, and they spend $250 billion (0.50 × $500 billion). Each round of spending creates income for consumption respending in a downward spiral throughout the economy in smaller and smaller amounts until the total level of aggregate demand rises by an extra $2,000 billion ($2 trillion).

EXHIBIT 3	The Spending Multiplier Effect	
Round	**Component of total spending**	**New consumption spending (billions of dollars)**
1	Government spending	$1,000
2	Consumption	500
3	Consumption	250
4	Consumption	125
.	.	.
.	.	.
.	.	.
All other rounds	Consumption	125
	Total spending	$2,000

NOTE: All amounts are rounded to the nearest billion dollars per year.
SOURCE: © Cengage Learning 2014

---

[1]This section duplicates material presented earlier in the chapters titled "The Keynesian Model" and "The Keynesian Model in Action." The reason for repeating this material is that an instructor may choose to skip the Keynesian model presented in these two chapters.

> **CONCLUSION:** *Any initial change in spending by the government, households, or firms creates a chain reaction of further spending, which causes a greater cumulative change in aggregate demand.*

You might recognize from algebra that the spending multiplier effect is a process based on an *infinite geometric series*. The formula for the sum of such a series of numbers is the initial number times $1/(1 - r)$, where r is the ratio that relates the numbers. Using this formula, the sum (total spending) is calculated as $1 trillion ($\Delta G$) $\times$ [1/(1 - 0.50)] = $2 trillion. By simply defining r in the infinite series formula as MPC, the spending multiplier for aggregate demand is expressed as follows:

$$\text{Spending multiplier} = \frac{1}{1 - \text{MPC}}$$

Applying this formula to our example:

$$\text{Spending multiplier} = \frac{1}{1 - 0.50} = \frac{1}{0.50} = 2$$

If households spend a portion of each extra dollar of income, then the remaining portion of each dollar is saved. The marginal propensity to save (MPS) is the change in saving resulting from a given change in income. Therefore,

$$\text{MPC} + \text{MPS} = 1$$

rewritten as

$$\text{MPS} = 1 - \text{MPC}$$

Hence, the above spending multiplier formula can be rewritten as

$$\text{Spending multiplier} = \frac{1}{\text{MPS}}$$

Because MPS and MPC are related, the size of the multiplier depends on the size of the MPC. What will the result be if people spend 80 percent or 33 percent of each dollar of income instead of 50 percent? If the MPC increases (decreases), consumers spend a larger (smaller) share of each additional dollar of output/income in each round, and the size of the multiplier increases (decreases). Exhibit 4 lists the multiplier for different values of MPC and MPS.

Marginal propensity to save (MPS)

The change in saving resulting from a given change in income.

✔ CHECKPOINT

What is the MPC for Uncle Sam's Stimulus Package?

Assume the economy is in a recession, and a stimulus package of $800 billion is passed by the federal government. The administration predicts that this measure will provide a $2,400 billion boost to GDP this year because consumers will spend their extra cash on HD televisions and other items. For this amount of stimulus, what is the established value of MPC used in this forecast?

EXHIBIT 4	Relationship between MPC, MPS, and the Spending Multiplier	
(1) Marginal propensity to consume (MPC)	(2) Marginal propensity to save (MPS)	(3) Spending multiplier
0.90	0.10	10
0.80	0.20	5
0.75	0.25	4
0.67	0.33	3
0.50	0.50	2
0.33	0.67	1.5

SOURCE: © Cengage Learning 2014

11-1c CUTTING TAXES TO COMBAT A RECESSION

Another expansionary fiscal policy intended to increase aggregate demand and restore full employment calls for the government to cut taxes. Let's return to point E_1 in Exhibit 2. As before, the problem is to shift the aggregate demand curve to the right by $2 trillion. But this time, instead of a $1 trillion increase in government spending, assume Congress votes for a $1 trillion tax cut. How does this cut in taxes affect aggregate demand? First, *disposable personal income* (take-home pay) increases by $1 trillion—the amount of the tax reduction. Second, once again assuming the MPC is 0.50, the increase in disposable personal income induces new consumption spending of $500 billion (0.50 × $1 trillion). Thus, a cut in taxes triggers a multiplier process similar to, but smaller than, the spending multiplier.

Exhibit 5 demonstrates that a tax reduction adds less to aggregate demand than does an equal increase in government spending. Column (1) reproduces the effect of increasing government spending by $1 trillion, and column (2) gives for comparison the effect of lowering taxes by $1 trillion. Note that the only difference between increasing government spending and cutting taxes by the same amount is the impact in the initial round. The reason is that a tax cut injects zero new spending into the economy because the government has purchased no new goods and services. The effect of a tax reduction in round 2 is that people spend a portion of the $1 trillion boost in after-tax income from the tax cut introduced in round 1. Subsequent rounds in the tax multiplier chain generate a cumulative increase in consumption expenditures that totals $1 trillion. Comparing the total changes in aggregate demand in columns (1) and (2) of Exhibit 4 leads to the following:

CONCLUSION: *A tax cut has a smaller multiplier effect on aggregate demand than an equal increase in government spending.*

EXHIBIT 5	Comparison of the Spending and Tax Multipliers		
		Increase in aggregate demand from a	
Round	Component of total spending	(1) $1 trillion increase in government spending ($+\Delta G$)	(2) $1 trillion cut in taxes ($-\Delta T$)
1	Government spending	$1,000	$ 0
2	Consumption	500	500
3	Consumption	250	250
4	Consumption	125	125
.	.	.	.
.	.	.	.
.	.	.	.
All other rounds	Consumption	125	125
	Total spending	$2,000	$1,000

NOTE: All amounts are rounded to the nearest billion dollars per year.
SOURCE: © Cengage Learning 2014

The tax multiplier (TM) can be computed by using a formula and the information from column 2 of Exhibit 5. The tax multiplier is the change in aggregate demand (total spending) resulting from an initial change in taxes. Mathematically, the tax multiplier is given by this formula:

Tax multiplier = 1 − spending multiplier

Returning to Exhibit 2, the tax multiplier formula can be used to calculate the cumulative increase in the aggregate demand from a $1 trillion tax cut. Applying the formula given above and a spending multiplier of 2 yields a tax multiplier of −1. Note that the sign of the tax multiplier is always negative. Thus, a $1 trillion tax cut shifts the aggregate demand curve rightward by only $1 trillion and fails to restore full-employment equilibrium at point E_2. Mathematically,

Change in taxes (ΔT) × tax multiplier (TM) = change in aggregate demand (AD)

−$1 trillion × −1 = $1 trillion

The key to the amount of real GDP growth achieved from a stimulus package depends on the size of the MPC. What proportion of the government spending increase or tax cut is spent for consumption? The answer means the difference between a deeper or milder recession as well as the speed of recovery. What are estimates of real-world multipliers? In Congressional testimony given in July 2008,

Tax multiplier

The change in aggregate demand (total spending) resulting from an initial change in taxes. As a formula, tax multiplier equals 1 − spending multiplier.

Mark Zandi, chief economist for Moody's Economy.com, provided estimates for the one-year multiplier effect for several fiscal policy options. The spending multiplier varied from 1.36 to 1.73 for different federal government spending programs, such as food stamps, extended unemployment insurance benefits, aid to state governments, or bridges and highways. The tax multiplier also varied from 0.27 to 1.29 for different temporary tax cut plans.

11-1d USING FISCAL POLICY TO COMBAT INFLATION

So far, Keynesian expansionary fiscal policy, born of the Great Depression, has been presented as the cure for an economic downturn. Contractionary fiscal policy, on the other hand, can serve in the fight against inflation. Exhibit 6 shows an economy operating at point E_1 on the classical range of the aggregate supply curve, AS. Hence, this economy is producing the full-employment output of $14 trillion real GDP, and the price level is 220. In this situation, any increase in aggregate demand only causes inflation, while real GDP remains unchanged.

Suppose Congress and the president decide to use fiscal policy to reduce the CPI from 220 to 215 because they fear the wrath of voters suffering from the consequences of inflation. Although a fall in consumption, investment, or net exports might do the job, Congress and the president may be unwilling to wait, and they prefer taking direct action by cutting government spending. Given a marginal propensity to consume of 0.50, the spending multiplier is 2. As shown by the horizontal distance between point E_1 on AD_1 and point E' on AD_2 in Exhibit 6, aggregate demand must be decreased by $1 trillion in order to shift the aggregate demand curve from AD_1 to AD_2 and establish equilibrium at E_2, with a price level of 215. Mathematically,

$$\Delta G \times 2 = -\$1 \text{ trillion}$$

$$\Delta G = -\$500 \text{ billion}$$

Using the above formula, a $500 billion cut in real government spending would cause a $1 trillion decrease in the aggregate demand curve from AD_1 to AD_2. The result is a temporary excess aggregate supply of $1 trillion, measured by the distance from E' to E_1. As explained in Exhibit 5 of the previous chapter, the economy follows classical theory and moves downward along AD_2 to a new equilibrium at E_2. Consequently, inflation cools with no change in the full-employment real GDP.

Another approach to the inflation problem would be for Congress and the president to raise taxes. Although tax increases are often considered political suicide, let's suppose Congress calculates just the correct amount of a tax hike required to reduce aggregate demand by $1 trillion.

Assuming a spending multiplier of 2, the tax multiplier is -1. Therefore, a $1 trillion tax hike provides the necessary $1 trillion leftward shift in the aggregate demand curve from AD_1 to AD_2. As a result, the desired equilibrium change from E_1 to E_2 is achieved, and the price level drops from 220 to 215 at the full-employment output of $14 trillion. Mathematically,

$$\Delta T \times -1 = -\$1 \text{ trillion}$$

$$\Delta T = \$1 \text{ trillion}$$

EXHIBIT 6 — Using Fiscal Policy to Combat Inflation

The economy in this exhibit is in equilibrium at point E_1 on the classical range of the aggregate supply curve, AS. The price level is 220, and the economy is operating at the full-employment output of $14 trillion real GDP. To reduce the price level to 215, the aggregate demand curve must be shifted to the left by $1 trillion, measured by the horizontal distance between point E_1 on curve AD_1 and point E' on curve AD_2. One way this can be done is by decreasing government spending. With MPC equal to 0.50, and therefore a spending multiplier of 2, a $500 billion decrease in government spending results in the needed $100 billion leftward shift in the aggregate demand curve. As a result, the economy reaches equilibrium at point E_2, and the price level falls from 220 to 215, while real output remains unchanged at full capacity.

An identical decrease in the aggregate demand curve can be obtained by a hike in taxes. A $1 trillion tax increase works through a tax multiplier of -1 and provides the needed $1 trillion decrease in the aggregate demand curve from AD_1 to AD_2.

CAUSATION CHAIN

Decrease in government spending or increase in taxes → Decrease in the aggregate demand curve → Decrease in the price level

11-1e THE BALANCED BUDGET MULTIPLIER

The analysis of Keynesian discretionary fiscal policy presented in the previous section supposes the federal government selects a change in *either* government spending or taxes as a remedy for recession or inflation. However, a controversial fiscal policy requires the government to match, or "balance," any new spending with new taxes. Understanding the impact on the economy of this fiscal policy requires derivation of the balanced budget multiplier. The balanced budget multiplier is an equal change in government spending and taxes, which, as shown below, changes aggregate demand by the amount of the change in government spending. Expressed as a formula,

Balanced budget multiplier

An equal change in government spending and taxes, which changes aggregate demand by the amount of the change in government spending.

$$\text{Cumulative change in aggregate demand } (\Delta AD)$$
$$= \text{government spending multiplier effect}$$
$$+ \text{ tax multiplier effect}$$

rewritten as

$$\text{Cumulative change in aggregate demand } (\Delta AD)$$
$$= (\text{initial change in government spending} \times \text{spending multiplier})$$
$$+ (\text{initial change in taxes} \times \text{tax multiplier})$$

To see how the balanced budget multiplier works, suppose Congress enacts a $1 billion increase in government spending for highways and it finances these purchases with a $1 billion increase in gasoline taxes. Mathematically,

$$\Delta AD = \left(\$1 \text{ billion} \times \frac{1}{1 - \text{MPC}} \right) + \left(\$1 \text{ billion} \times 1 - \frac{1}{1 - \text{MPC}} \right)$$

$$= \left(\$1 \text{ billion} \times \frac{1}{1 - 0.50} \right) + \left(\$1 \text{ billion} \times 1 - \frac{1}{1 - 0.50} \right)$$

$$= (\$1 \text{ billion} \times 2) + (\$1 \text{ billion} \times -1)$$

$$= \$2 \text{ billion} - \$1 \text{ billion}$$

$$= \$1 \text{ billion}$$

Hence, the balanced budget multiplier is always equal to 1, and the cumulative change in aggregate demand is $1 billion—*the amount of the initial change in government spending.*

CONCLUSION: *Regardless of the MPC, the net effect on the economy of an equal initial increase (decrease) in government spending and taxes is an increase (decrease) in aggregate demand equal to the initial increase (decrease) in government spending.*

✓ CHECKPOINT

Walking the Balanced Budget Tightrope

Suppose the president proposes an $800 billion economic stimulus package intended to create jobs. A major criticism of this new spending proposal is that it is not matched by a tax increase. Assume the U.S. economy is below full employment and Congress has passed a law requiring that any increase in spending be matched or balanced by an equal increase in taxes. The MPC is 0.75, and aggregate demand must be increased by $1,000 billion to reach full employment. Will the economy reach full employment if Congress increases spending by $800 billion and increases taxes by the same amount?

11-2 Automatic Stabilizers

Unlike discretionary fiscal policy, automatic stabilizers are policy tools built into the federal budget that help fight unemployment and inflation, while spending and tax laws remain unchanged. Automatic stabilizers are federal expenditures and tax revenues that automatically change levels in order to stabilize an economic expansion or contraction. Automatic stabilizers are sometimes referred to as *nondiscretionary fiscal policy*. Exhibit 7 illustrates the influence of automatic stabilizers on the economy. The downward-sloping line, *G*, represents federal government expenditures, including such *transfer payments* as unemployment compensation, Medicaid, and welfare. This line falls as real GDP rises. When the economy expands, unemployment falls, and government spending for unemployment compensation, welfare, and other transfer payments decreases. During a downturn, people lose their jobs, and government spending automatically increases because unemployed individuals become eligible for unemployment compensation and other transfer payments.

The direct relationship between tax revenues and real GDP is shown by the upward-sloping line, *T*. During an expansion, jobs are created, unemployment falls, and workers earn more income and therefore pay more taxes. Thus, income tax collections automatically vary directly with the growth in real GDP.

We begin the analysis of automatic stabilizers with a balanced federal budget. Federal spending, *G*, is equal to tax collections, *T*, and the economy is in equilibrium at $14 trillion real GDP. Now assume consumer optimism soars and a spending spree increases the consumption component (*C*) of total spending. As a result, the economy moves to a new equilibrium at $16 trillion real GDP. The rise in real GDP creates more jobs and higher tax collections. Consequently, taxes rise to $2 trillion on line *T*. Also, government expenditures fall to $1 trillion because fewer people are collecting transfer payments, such as unemployment compensation and welfare. As a result, the vertical distance between lines *T* and *G* represents a federal budget surplus of $1 trillion. A budget surplus occurs when government revenues exceed government expenditures in a given time period.

Automatic stabilizers

Federal expenditures and tax revenues that automatically change levels in order to stabilize an economic expansion or contraction; sometimes referred to as *nondiscretionary fiscal policy*.

Budget surplus

A budget in which government revenues exceed government expenditures in a given time period.

EXHIBIT 7	Automatic Stabilizers

Federal government spending varies inversely with real GDP and is represented by the downward-sloping line, *G*. Taxes, in contrast, vary directly with real GDP and are represented by the upward-sloping line, *T*. This means government spending for welfare and other transfer payments declines and tax collections rise as real GDP rises. Thus, if real GDP falls below $14 trillion, the budget deficit rises automatically. The size of the budget deficit is shown by the vertical distance between lines *G* and *T*. This budget deficit assists in offsetting a recession because it stimulates aggregate demand. Conversely, when real GDP rises above $14 trillion, a federal budget surplus increases automatically and assists in offsetting inflation.

CAUSATION CHAIN

Now begin again with the economy at $14 trillion in Exhibit 7, and let's change the scenario. Assume that business managers lower their profit expectations. Their revised outlook causes business executives to become pessimistic, so they cut investment spending (*I*), causing aggregate demand to decline. The corresponding decline in real GDP from $14 trillion to $12 trillion causes tax revenues to fall from $1.5 trillion to $1 trillion on line *T*. The combined effect of the rise in government spending and the fall in taxes creates a budget deficit. A budget deficit occurs when government expenditures exceed government revenues in a given time period. The vertical distance between lines *G* and *T* at $12 trillion real GDP illustrates a federal budget deficit of $1 trillion.

The key feature of automatic stabilization is that it "leans against the prevailing wind." In short, changes in federal spending and taxes moderate changes in aggregate demand. Stated differently, built-in stabilizers diminish or reduce swings in real GDP. When the economy expands, the fall in government spending for transfer payments and the rise in the level of taxes result in a budget surplus. As the budget surplus grows, people send more money to Washington, which applies braking power against further increases in real GDP. When the economy contracts, the rise in government spending for transfer payments and the fall in the level of taxes yield a budget deficit. As the budget deficit grows, people receive more money from Washington to spend, which slows further decreases in real GDP.

> **CONCLUSION:** *Automatic stabilizers assist in offsetting a recession when real GDP falls and in offsetting inflation when real GDP expands.*

11-3 Supply-Side Fiscal Policy

The focus so far has been on fiscal policy that affects the macro economy solely through the impact of government spending and taxation on aggregate demand. Supply-side economists, whose intellectual roots are in classical economics, argue that *stagflation* in the 1970s was the result of the federal government's failure to follow the theories of supply-side fiscal policy. Supply-side fiscal policy emphasizes government policies that increase aggregate supply in order to achieve long-run growth in real output, full employment, and a lower price level. Supply-side policies became an active economic idea with the election of Ronald Reagan as president in 1980. As discussed in the previous chapter, the U.S. economy in the 1970s experienced high rates of both inflation and unemployment. Stagflation aroused concern about the ability of the U.S. economy to generate long-term advances in the standard of living. This set the stage for a new macroeconomic policy.

Suppose the economy is initially at E_1 in Exhibit 8(a), with a CPI of 150 and an output of $8 trillion real GDP. The economy is experiencing high unemployment, so the goal is to achieve full employment by increasing real GDP to $12 trillion. As described earlier in this chapter, the federal government might follow Keynesian expansionary fiscal policy and shift the aggregate demand curve

Budget deficit

A budget in which government expenditures exceed government revenues in a given time period.

Supply-side fiscal policy

A fiscal policy that emphasizes government policies that increase aggregate supply in order to achieve long-run growth in real output, full employment, and a lower price level.

EXHIBIT 8	Keynesian Demand-Side versus Supply-Side Effects

In part (a), assume an economy begins in equilibrium at point E_1, with a price level of 150 and a real GDP of $8 trillion. To boost real output and employment, Keynesian economists prescribe that the federal government raise government spending or cut taxes. By following such demand-side policies, the policymakers work through the multiplier effect and shift the aggregate demand curve from AD_1 to AD_2. As a result, the equilibrium changes to E_2, where real GDP rises to $12 trillion, but the price level also rises to 200. Hence, full employment has been achieved at the expense of higher inflation.

The initial situation for the economy at point E_1 in part (b) is identical to that shown in part (a). However, supply-siders offer a different fiscal policy prescription than the Keynesians. Using some combination of cuts in resource prices, technological advances, tax cuts, subsidies, and regulation reduction, supply-side fiscal policy shifts the aggregate supply curve from AS_1 to AS_2. As a result, the equilibrium in the economy changes to E_2, and real GDP increases to $12 trillion, just as in part (a). The advantage of the supply-side stimulus over the demand-side stimulus is that the price level falls to 100, rather than rising to 200.

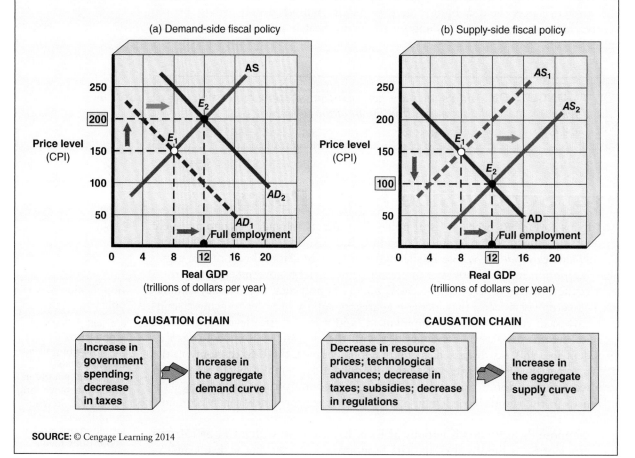

rightward from AD_1 to AD_2. Higher government spending or lower taxes operate through the multiplier effect and cause this increase in aggregate demand. The good news from such a demand-side fiscal policy prescription is that the economy moves toward full employment, but the bad news is that the price level rises. In this case, *demand-pull inflation* would cause the price level to rise from 150 to 200.

Exhibit 8(b) represents the supply-siders' alternative to Keynesian fiscal policy. Again, suppose the economy is initially in equilibrium at E_1. Supply-side economists argue that the federal government should adopt policies that shift the aggregate supply curve rightward from AS_1 to AS_2. An increase in aggregate supply would move the economy to E_2 and achieve the full-employment level of real GDP. Under supply-side theory, there is an additional bonus to full employment. Instead of rising as in Exhibit 8(a), the price level in Exhibit 8(b) falls from 150 to 100. Comparing the two graphs in Exhibit 8, you can see that the supply-siders have a better theoretical case than proponents of demand-side fiscal policy when both inflation and unemployment are concerns.

Note the causation chain under each graph in Exhibit 8. The demand-side fiscal policy options are from column 1 of Exhibit 1 in this chapter, and the supply-side policy alternatives are similar to Exhibit 10 in the previous chapter. For supply-side economics to be effective, the government must implement policies that increase the total output that firms produce at each possible price level. An increase in aggregate supply can be accomplished by some combination of cuts in resource prices, technological advances, subsidies, and reductions in government taxes and government regulations.

Although a laundry list of supply-side policies was advocated during the Reagan administration, the most familiar policy action taken was the tax cuts implemented in 1981. By reducing tax rates on wages and profits, the Reagan administration sought to increase the aggregate supply of goods and services at any price level. However, tax cuts are a Keynesian policy intended to increase aggregate demand, so supply-siders must have a different view of the impact of tax cuts on the economy. To explain these different views of tax cuts, let's begin by stating that both Keynesians and supply-siders agree that tax cuts increase disposable personal income. In Keynesian economics, this boost in disposable personal income works through the *tax multiplier* to increase aggregate demand, as shown earlier in Exhibit 5. Supply-side economists argue instead that changes in disposable income affect the incentive to supply work, save, and invest.

Consider how a supply-side tax cut influences the labor market. Suppose supply and demand in the labor market are initially in equilibrium at point E_1 in Exhibit 9. Before a cut in personal income tax rates, the equilibrium hourly wage rate is W_1, and workers supply L_1 hours of labor per year at this wage rate. When the tax rates are cut, supply-side theory predicts the labor supply curve will shift rightward and establish a new equilibrium at E_2. The rationale is that an increase in the after-tax wage rate gives workers the incentive to work more hours per year. Those in the labor force will want to work longer hours and take fewer vacations. And because Uncle Sam takes a smaller bite out of workers' paychecks, many of those not already in the labor force will now supply their labor. As a result of the increase in the labor supply curve,

EXHIBIT 9	How Supply-Side Fiscal Policies Affect Labor Markets

Begin with equilibrium in the labor market at point E_1. Here the intersection of the labor supply and demand curves determines a wage rate of W_1 and L_1 hours of labor per year. By lowering tax rates, supply-side fiscal policies increase net after-tax earnings. This extra incentive causes workers to provide additional hours of labor per year. As a result, the labor supply curve increases and establishes a new equilibrium at point E_2. The new wage rate paid by employers falls to W_2, and they use more labor hours per year, L_2.

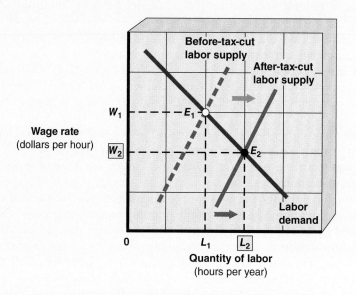

SOURCE: © Cengage Learning 2014

the price of labor falls to W_2 per hour, and the equilibrium number of labor hours increases to L_2.

Supply-side tax cuts of the early 1980s also provided tax breaks that subsidized business investment. Tax credits were available for new equipment and plants and for research and development to encourage technological advances. The idea here was to increase the nation's productive capacity by increasing the quantity and quality of capital. Consequently, the aggregate supply curve would shift rightward because businesses have an extra after-tax profit incentive to invest and produce more at each price level.

The idea of using tax cuts to shift the aggregate supply curve outward is controversial. Despite its logic, the Keynesians argue that the magnitude of any rightward shift in aggregate supply is likely to be small and occur only in the long run. They point out that it takes many years before tax cuts for business generate any change in actual plants and equipment or technological advances. Moreover, individuals can accept tax cuts with a "thank you, Uncle Sam" and not work longer or harder. Meanwhile, unless a reduction in government spending offsets the tax cuts, the effect will be a Keynesian increase in the aggregate demand curve and a higher price level. Exhibit 10 summarizes the important distinction between the supply-side and Keynesian theories on tax cut policy.

Laffer curve

A graph depicting the relationship between tax rates and total tax revenues.

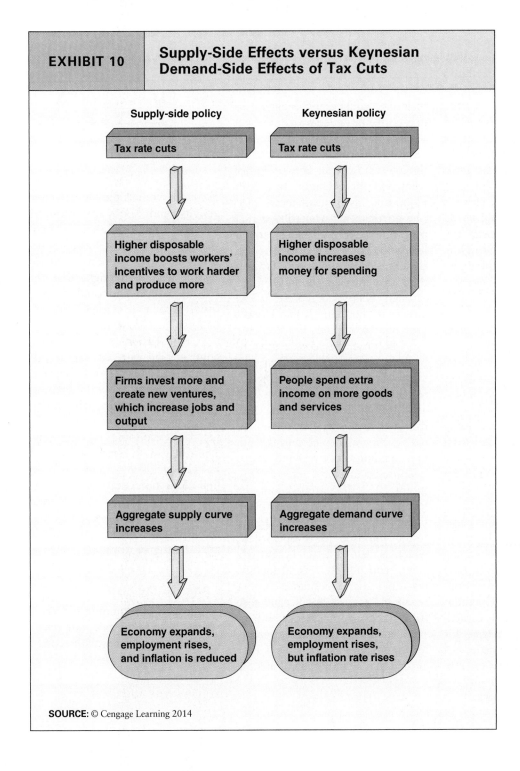

EXHIBIT 10	Supply-Side Effects versus Keynesian Demand-Side Effects of Tax Cuts

Supply-side policy

Tax rate cuts

↓

Higher disposable income boosts workers' incentives to work harder and produce more

↓

Firms invest more and create new ventures, which increase jobs and output

↓

Aggregate supply curve increases

↓

Economy expands, employment rises, and inflation is reduced

Keynesian policy

Tax rate cuts

↓

Higher disposable income increases money for spending

↓

People spend extra income on more goods and services

↓

Aggregate demand curve increases

↓

Economy expands, employment rises, but inflation rate rises

SOURCE: © Cengage Learning 2014

The Laffer Curve

Applicable Concept: supply-side fiscal policy

Supply-side economics became popular during the presidential campaign of 1980. This fiscal policy prescription gained prominence after supply-side economist Arthur Laffer, using his pen to draw on a paper napkin, explained what has come to be known as the Laffer curve to an editor of *The Wall Street Journal* at a restaurant in Washington, D.C., in 1974. The Laffer curve is a graph depicting the relationship between tax rates and total tax revenues. As shown in the figure, the hypothetical Laffer curve can be drawn with the federal tax rate on the horizontal axis and tax revenue on the vertical axis. The idea behind this curve is that the federal tax rate affects the incentive for people to work, save, invest, and produce, which in turn influences tax revenue. As the tax rate climbs, Laffer and other supply-siders argue that the erosion of incentives shrinks national income and total tax collections. The editor kept the napkin and published the curve in an editorial in *The Wall Street Journal*. And a theory was born.

Here is how the Laffer curve works. Suppose the federal government sets the federal income tax rate at zero (point *A*). At a zero income tax rate, people have the maximum incentive to produce, and optimum national income would be earned, but there is zero tax revenue for Uncle Sam. Now assume the federal government sets the income tax rate

at the opposite extreme of 100 percent (point *D*). At a 100 percent confiscating income tax rate, people have no reason to work, take business risks, produce, and earn income. People seek ways to reduce their tax liabilities by engaging in unreported or underground transactions or by not working at all. As a result, no tax revenue is collected by the Internal Revenue Service. Laffer compared this situation to Robin Hood and his band of merry men (the government) who robbed rich people (taxpayers) traveling through Sherwood Forest to give to the poor. Laffer posed this question, "Do you think that travelers continued to go through Sherwood Forest?" The answer is "no," and Robin Hood's "revenue" would fall.

Because the federal government does not want to collect zero tax revenue, Congress sets the federal income tax rate between zero and 100 percent. Assuming that the income tax rate is related to tax revenue as depicted in the figure, maximum tax revenue, R_{max}, is collected at a tax rate of T_{max} (point *B*). Laffer argued that the federal income tax rate of *T* (point *C*) in 1981 exceeded T_{max} and the result would be tax revenue of *R*, which is below R_{max}. In Laffer's view, reducing the federal income tax rate leads to an increase in tax revenue because people increase their work effort, saving, and investment and reduce their attempts to avoid paying taxes. Thus, Laffer argued that a cut in federal income

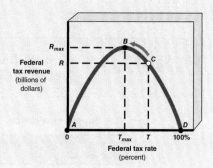

SOURCE: © Cengage Learning 2014

tax rates would unleash economic activity and boost tax revenues needed to reduce the federal budget deficit. President Reagan's belief in the Laffer curve was a major reason why he thought that the federal government could cut personal income tax rates and still balance the federal budget.

The Laffer curve remains a controversial part of supply-side economics. There is still considerable uncertainty about the shape of the Laffer curve and at what point, *B*, *C*, or otherwise, along the curve the U.S. economy is operating. There is also no certainty for what tax rate yields maximum tax revenue. And note that below T_{max}, tax rate increases do increase total revenue. Thus, the existence and the usefulness of the Laffer curve are a matter of dispute.

Analyze the Issue

Compare the common perception of how a tax rate cut affects tax revenues with economist Laffer's theory.

Source: © Cengage Learning 2014

Key Concepts

Fiscal policy
Discretionary fiscal policy
Spending multiplier (SM)
Marginal propensity to consume
  (MPC)

Marginal propensity to save (MPS)
Tax multiplier (TM)
Balanced budget multiplier
Automatic stabilizers
Budget surplus

Budget deficit
Supply-side fiscal policy
Laffer curve

Summary

- **Fiscal policy** is the use of government spending and taxes to stabilize the economy.
- **Discretionary fiscal policy** follows the Keynesian argument that the federal government should manipulate aggregate demand in order to influence the output, employment, and price levels in the economy. Discretionary fiscal policy requires new legislation to change either government spending or taxes in order to stabilize the economy.

Discretionary Fiscal Policies

Expansionary fiscal policy	Contractionary fiscal policy
Increase government spending	Decrease government spending
Decrease taxes	Increase taxes
Increase government spending and taxes equally	Decrease government spending and taxes equally

- The **spending multiplier (SM)** is the multiplier by which an initial change in one component of aggregate demand, for example, government spending, alters aggregate demand (total spending) after an infinite number of spending cycles. Expressed as a formula, the spending multiplier = $1/(1 - MPC)$.
- **Expansionary fiscal policy** is a deliberate increase in government spending, a deliberate decrease in taxes, or some combination of these two options.
- **Contractionary fiscal policy** is a deliberate decrease in government spending, a deliberate

increase in taxes, or some combination of these two options. Using either expansionary or contractionary fiscal policy, the government can shift the aggregate demand curve in order to combat recession, cool inflation, or achieve other macroeconomic goals.
- The **marginal propensity to consume (MPC)** is the change in consumption spending divided by the change in income.
- The **marginal propensity to save (MPS)** is the change in savings divided by the change in income.
- The **tax multiplier** is the change in aggregate demand (total spending) that results from an initial change in taxes after an infinite number of spending cycles. Expressed as a formula, the tax multiplier (TM) = 1 − spending multiplier.
- **Combating recession and inflation** can be accomplished by changing government spending or taxes. The total change in aggregate demand from a change in government spending is equal to the change in government spending times the spending multiplier.
- The total change in aggregate demand from a change in taxes is equal to the change in taxes times the tax multiplier.

Combating Recession

SOURCE: © Cengage Learning 2014

Combating Inflation

- The **balanced budget multiplier** is not neutral. A dollar of government spending increases real GDP more than a dollar cut in taxes. Thus, even though the government does not spend more than it collects in taxes, it is still stimulating the economy.
- A **budget surplus** occurs when government revenues exceed government expenditures. A **budget deficit** occurs when government expenditures exceed government revenues.
- **Automatic stabilizers** are changes in taxes and government spending that occur automatically in response to changes in the level of real GDP. The business cycle therefore creates braking power: A *budget surplus* slows an expanding

economy; a *budget deficit* reverses a downturn in the economy.

Automatic Stabilizers

- According to **supply-side fiscal policy**, lower taxes encourage work, saving, and investment, which shift the aggregate supply curve rightward. As a result, output and employment increase without inflation.
- The **Laffer curve** represents the relationship between the income tax rate and the amount of income tax revenue collected by the government.

Summary of Conclusion Statements

- In the intermediate segment of the aggregate supply curve, the equilibrium real GDP changes by less than the change in government spending times the spending multiplier.
- Any initial change in spending by the government, households, or firms creates a chain reaction of further spending, which causes a greater cumulative change in aggregate demand.
- A tax cut has a smaller multiplier effect on aggregate demand than an equal increase in government spending.

- Regardless of the MPC, the net effect on the economy of an equal initial increase (decrease) in government spending and taxes is an increase (decrease) in aggregate demand equal to the initial increase (decrease) in government spending.
- Automatic stabilizers assist in offsetting a recession when real GDP falls and in offsetting inflation when real GDP expands.

Study Questions and Problems

1. Explain how discretionary fiscal policy fights recession and inflation.

2. How does each of the following affect the aggregate demand curve?
   a. Government spending increases.
   b. The amount of taxes collected decreases.

3. In each of the following cases, explain whether the fiscal policy is expansionary, contractionary, or neutral.
   a. The government decreases government spending.
   b. The government increases taxes.
   c. The government increases spending and taxes by an equal amount.

4. Why does a reduction in taxes have a smaller multiplier effect than an increase in government spending of an equal amount?

5. Suppose you are an economic adviser to the president and the economy needs a real GDP increase of $500 billion to reach full-employment equilibrium. If the marginal propensity to consume (MPC) is 0.75 and you are a Keynesian, by how much do you believe Congress must increase government spending to restore the economy to full employment?

6. Consider an economy that is operating at the full-employment level of real GDP. Assuming the MPC is 0.90, predict the effect on the economy of a $50 billion increase in government spending balanced by a $50 billion increase in taxes.

7. Why is a $100 billion increase in government spending for goods and services more expansionary than a $100 billion decrease in taxes?

8. What is the difference between discretionary fiscal policy and automatic stabilizers? How are federal budget surpluses and deficits affected by the business cycle?

9. Assume you are a supply-side economist who is an adviser to the president. If the economy is in recession, what would your fiscal policy prescription be?

10. Suppose Congress enacts a tax reform law and the average federal tax rate drops from 30 percent to 20 percent. Researchers investigate the impact of the tax cut and find that the income subject to the tax increases from $600 billion to $800 billion. The theoretical explanation is that workers have increased their work effort in response to the incentive of lower taxes. Is this a movement along the downward-sloping or the upward-sloping portion of the Laffer curve?

11. Indicate how each of the following would change either the aggregate demand curve or the aggregate supply curve.
    a. Expansionary fiscal policy
    b. Contractionary fiscal policy
    c. Supply-side economics
    d. Demand-pull inflation
    e. Cost-push inflation

For Online Exercises, go to the Tucker Web site at www.cengage.com/economics/tucker.

✔ CHECKPOINT ANSWERS

What is the MPC for Uncle Sam's Stimulus Package?

To calculate the value of the MPC required to increase real GDP (ΔY) by $2,400 billion from an increase in government spending (ΔG) of $800 billion, use this formula:

$$\Delta G \times \text{multiplier} = \Delta Y$$

where

$$\$800 \text{ billion} \times \text{multiplier} = \$2,400 \text{ billion}$$

Thus,

$$\text{Multiplier} = \frac{\$2,400 \text{ billion}}{\$800 \text{ billion}} = 3$$

Using Exhibit 4, if you said that the MPC is 0.67, **YOU ARE CORRECT.**

Walking the Balanced Budget Tightrope

An $800 billion increase in government spending increases aggregate demand by $3,200 billion [government spending increase × spending multiplier, where the spending multiplier = 1/(1 − MPC) = 1/0.25 = 4]. On the other hand, an $800 billion increase in taxes reduces aggregate demand by $2,400 billion (tax cut × tax multiplier, where the tax multiplier = 1 − spending multiplier = 1 − 4 = −3). Thus, the net effect of the spending multiplier and the tax multiplier is an increase in aggregate demand of $800 billion. If you said

Congress has missed its goal of a $1,000 billion boost in aggregate demand by $200 billion and has not restored full employment, **YOU ARE CORRECT.**

Sample Quiz

For an explanation of the correct answers, visit the Tucker Website at academic.cengage.com/economics/tucker.

1. Which of the following is an example of expansionary fiscal policy?
   a. an increase in taxes
   b. a decrease in government spending
   c. an increase in government spending
   d. an increase in taxes and a decrease in government spending equally

2. In the _____ range of the aggregate supply curve, expansionary fiscal policy causes aggregate _____ to increase, which results in a higher price level and a higher equilibrium level of real GDP.
   a. Keynesian, supply
   b. classical, demand
   c. intermediate, demand
   d. intermediate, supply

3. An expansionary fiscal policy may include
   a. increases in government spending.
   b. discretionary increases in transfer payments.
   c. reductions in taxes.
   d. All of the answers above are correct.

4. Suppose the economy in Exhibit 11 is in equilibrium at point E_1 and the marginal propensity to consume (MPC) is 0.80. Following Keynesian economics, to restore full employment, the government should increase its spending by
   a. $200 billion.
   b. $250 billion.

   c. $500 billion.
   d. $1 trillion.

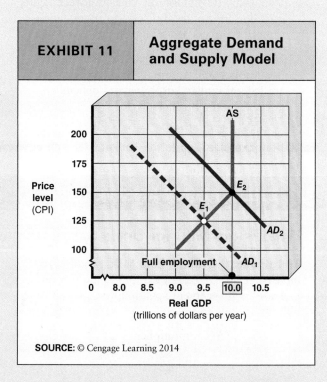

EXHIBIT 11   **Aggregate Demand and Supply Model**

SOURCE: © Cengage Learning 2014

5. Beginning at equilibrium E_1 in Exhibit 11, when the government increases spending or cuts taxes, the economy will experience
   a. an inflationary recession.
   b. stagflation.

Sample Quiz *continued*

c. cost-push inflation.

d. demand-pull inflation.

| EXHIBIT 12 | **Aggregate Demand and Supply Model** |

SOURCE: © Cengage Learning 2014

6. Suppose the economy in Exhibit 12 is in equilibrium at point E_1 and the marginal propensity to consume (MPC) is 0.75. Following Keynesian economics, the federal government can move the economy to point E_2 and reduce inflation by

   a. decreasing government spending by $750 billion.

   b. decreasing government spending by $100 billion.

   c. increasing government spending by $25 billion.

   d. decreasing government spending by $25 billion.

7. Mathematically, the value of the tax multiplier in terms of the marginal propensity to consume (MPC) is given by the formula

   a. $MPC - 1$.

   b. $(MPC - 1)/MPC$.

   c. $1/MPC$.

   d. $1 - [1/(1 - MPC)]$.

8. A tax multiplier equal to -4.30 would imply that a $100 tax increase would lead to a

   a. $430 decline in real GDP.

   b. $430 increase in real GDP.

   c. 4.3 percent increase in real GDP.

   d. 4.3 percent decrease in real GDP.

   e. 43 percent decrease in real GDP.

9. Equal increases in government spending and taxes will

   a. cancel each other out so that the equilibrium level of real GDP remains unchanged.

   b. lead to an equal decrease in the equilibrium level of real GDP.

   c. lead to an equal increase in the equilibrium level of real GDP.

   d. lead to an increase in the equilibrium level of real GDP output that is larger than the initial change in government spending and taxes.

10. When the economy enters a recession, automatic stabilizers create

    a. higher taxes.

    b. more discretionary spending.

    c. budget deficits.

    d. budget surpluses.

11. Automatic stabilizers "lean against the prevailing wind" of the business cycle because

    a. wages are controlled by the minimum wage law.

    b. federal expenditures and tax revenues change as the level of real GDP changes.

    c. the spending and tax multipliers are constant.

    d. they include the power of special interests.

12. Unemployment compensation payments

    a. rise during a recession and thus reduce the severity of the recession.

    b. rise during a recession and thus increase the severity of the recession.

Sample Quiz *continued*

c. rise during inflationary episodes and thus reduce the severity of the inflation.

d. fall during a recession and thus increase the severity of the recession.

13. According to supply-side fiscal policy, reducing tax rates on wages and profits will
   a. create demand-pull inflation.
   b. lower the price level but may trigger a recession.
   c. result in stagflation.
   d. reduce both unemployment and inflation.

14. Supply-side economics calls for
   a. lower taxes on businesses and individuals.
   b. regulatory reforms to increase productivity.
   c. government subsidies to promote technological advance.
   d. All of the above answers are correct.

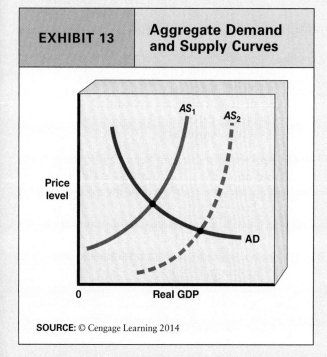

EXHIBIT 13   **Aggregate Demand and Supply Curves**

SOURCE: © Cengage Learning 2014

15. In Exhibit 13, supply-siders claimed that the shift from AS_1 to AS_2 would occur if the government

a. increased tax rates and increased the amount of government regulation.

b. increased tax rates and decreased the amount of government regulation.

c. decreased tax rates and increased the amount of government regulation.

d. decreased tax rates and decreased the amount of government regulation.

16. The Laffer curve belongs to which of the following schools of economic thought?
   a. Keynesian
   b. supply-side
   c. demand management
   d. classical

17. According to the Laffer curve, when the tax rate is 100 percent, tax revenue will be
   a. 0.
   b. at the maximum value.
   c. the same as it would be at a 50 percent tax rate.
   d. greater than it would be at a 50 percent tax rate.
   e. the same as it would be at a 20 percent tax rate.

18. Assume the marginal propensity to consume (MPC) is 0.75 and the government increases taxes by $250 billion. The aggregate demand curve will shift to the
   a. left by $1,000 billion.
   b. right by $1,000 billion.
   c. left by $750 billion.
   d. right by $750 billion.

19. When the government levies a $100 million tax on people's income and puts the $100 million back into the economy in the form of a spending program, such as new interstate highway construction, the
   a. tax then generates a $100 million decline in real GDP.
   b. level of real GDP expands by $100 million.
   c. effect on real GDP is uncertain.
   d. tax multiplier overpowers the income multiplier, triggering a rollback in real GDP.

Sample Quiz *continued*

20. Assume the economy is in recession and real GDP is below full employment. The marginal propensity to consume (MPC) is 0.75, and the government follows Keynesian economics by using expansionary fiscal policy to increase aggregate demand (total spending). If an increase of $1,000 billion aggregate demand can restore full employment, the government should
    a. increase spending by $250 billion.
    b. decrease spending by $750 billion.
    c. increase spending by $1,000 billion.
    d. increase spending by $750 billion.

chapter 12

The Public Sector

In the early 1980s, President Ronald Reagan adopted the Laffer curve theory that the federal government could cut tax rates and increase tax revenues. Critics said the result would be lower tax revenues. During the 2000 campaign for the Republican presidential nomination, Steve Forbes continued his attempt to win support for a flat tax, and George W. Bush advocated cutting individual marginal tax rates. However, President Bill Clinton said cutting taxes was not a good idea because ensuring the integrity of Social Security should come first. Between 2001 and 2004, President George W. Bush signed laws that provided for phased-in cuts in the marginal tax rates and increased spending for the war in Iraq and homeland defense. Critics argued that changing the tax structure while increasing spending would worsen the long-term federal budget outlook. And in 2011, grassroots "Tea Parties" were conducted across the nation to protest a too-large federal government that is spending large amounts on economic stimulus packages to deal with the recession.

These events illustrate the persistent real-world controversy surrounding fiscal policy. The previous chapter presented the theory behind fiscal policy. In this chapter, you will examine the practice of fiscal policy. Here the facts of taxation and government expenditures are clearly presented and placed in perspective. You can check, for example, the trend in federal taxes and expenditures during the Obama administration and compare these figures to those of other countries. And you will discover why the government uses different types of taxes and tax rates.

The final section of the chapter challenges the economic role of the public sector. Here you will learn a theory called *public choice*, which examines public sector decisions of politicians, government bureaucrats, voters, and special-interest groups.

In this chapter, you will learn to solve these economics puzzles:

- How does the tax burden in the United States compare to other countries?
- How does the Social Security tax favor the upper-income worker?
- Is a flat tax fair?
- Should we replace the income tax with a national sales tax or a flat tax?

12-1 Government Size and Growth

How big is the public sector in the United States? If we look at Exhibit 1, we see total government expenditures or outlays—including those of federal, state, and local governments—as a percentage of GDP for the 1929–2011 period. When we refer to *government expenditures*, we refer to more than the *government consumption expenditures and investment* (G) account used by national income accountants to calculate GDP (see Exhibit 3 in the chapter on GDP). Government expenditures, or outlays, equal government purchases plus *transfer payments*. Recall from the chapter on GDP that the government national income account (G) includes federal government spending for defense, highways, and education. Transfer payments, not

Government expenditures

Federal, state, and local government outlays for goods and services, including transfer payments.

EXHIBIT 1	The Growth of Government Expenditures as a Percentage of GDP in the United States, 1929–2011

The graph shows the growth of the federal, state, and local governments as measured by government expenditures as a percentage of GDP since 1929. Expenditures rose dramatically during World War II and fell dramatically after the war, but not to previous peacetime levels. Taking account of all government outlays, including transfer payments, the government sector has grown from about one-quarter of GDP in 1950 to about one-third of GDP beginning in 1975 and remained at this level until total government expenditures increased sharply following the Great Recession to 40 percent of GDP in 2009. In 2011, total government expenditures fell slightly to 38 percent.

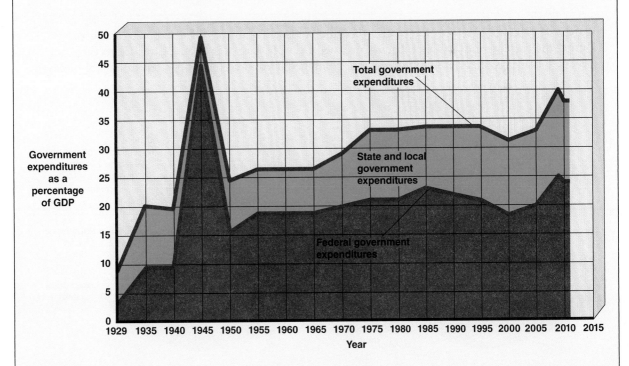

SOURCES: *Economic Report of the President*, 2012, http://www.gpo.gov/fdsys/pkg/ERP-2012/content-detail.htm1, Table B-79; and Bureau of Economic Analysis, *National Income Accounts*, http://www.bea.gov/national/nipaweb/SelectTable.asp?Selected=Y, Tables 1.1.5 and 3.3.

in (G), include payments to persons entitled to welfare, Social Security, and unemployment benefits.

As shown in Exhibit 1, total government expenditures skyrocketed as a percentage of GDP during World War II and then took a sharp plunge, but not to previous peacetime levels. Since 1950, total government expenditures grew from about one-quarter of GDP to about one-third beginning in 1975 and remained at this level until total expenditures increased sharply following the Great Recession to a 40 percent of GDP in 2009. In 2011, total government expenditures fell slightly to 38 percent of GDP. The other side of the coin is that today the private sector's share of national output is 62 percent of GDP. Issues concerning federal government spending and financing its debt are discussed in the next chapter.

12-1a   GOVERNMENT EXPENDITURES PATTERNS

Exhibit 2 shows program categories for federal government expenditures for 1970 and 2011. The largest category by far in the federal budget for 2011 was a category called *income security*. "Security" means these payments provide income to the elderly or disadvantaged, including Social Security, Medicare, unemployment compensation, public assistance (welfare), federal retirement, and disability benefits. These entitlements are transfer payments in the form of either direct cash payments or in-kind transfers that redistribute income among persons. In 2011, 40 percent of

EXHIBIT 2	Federal Government Expenditures, 1970 and 2011

Between 1970 and 2011, income security became the largest category of federal expenditures. During the same period, national defense declined from the largest spending category to the second largest. Income security and national defense combined accounted for 70 percent of federal outlays in 2011.

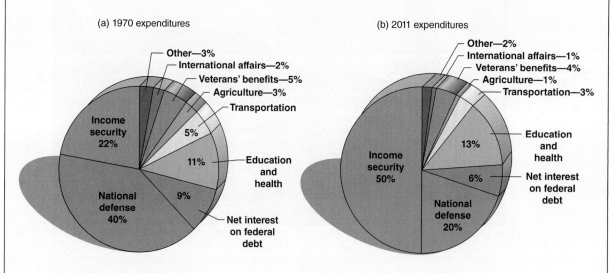

SOURCES: *Economic Report of the President,* 1975, Table C-65, p. 325; and *Economic Report of the President,* 2012, http://www.gpo.gov/fdsys/pkg/ERP-2012/content-detail.htm1, Table B-81.

income security expenditures was spent for Social Security and 28 percent for Medicare.

The second largest category of federal government expenditures in 2011 was national defense. Note that the percentage of the federal budget spent for defense declined from 40 percent in 1970 to 20 percent in 2011, while income security ("safety net") expenditures grew from 22 percent in 1970 to 50 percent in 2011. Hence, the dominant trend in federal government spending between 1970 and 2011 was an increase in the redistribution-of-income role of the federal government and a decrease in the portion of the budget spent for defense.

Federal expenditures for education and health were in third place in 2011, and net interest on the federal debt was in fourth place. Net interest paid is the interest on federal government borrowings minus the interest earned on federal government loans, and in 2011, this category of the budget was 6 percent. Thus, the federal government spent about the same proportion of the budget on financing its debt as on international affairs, veterans' benefits, and agriculture combined.

Finally, you need to be aware that the size and growth of government are measured several ways. We could study *absolute* government spending rather than percentages or compare the growth of spending after adjusting for inflation. Still another technique is to measure the proportion of the population that the public sector employs. Using any of these measurements confirms the following conclusion reached from Exhibits 1 and 2:

CONCLUSION: *The government's share of total economic activity has generally increased since World War II ended in 1945. Most of the growth in combined government expenditures as a percentage of GDP reflects rapidly growing federal government transfer programs.*

12-1b GOVERNMENT EXPENDITURES IN OTHER COUNTRIES

In 2011, U.S. government spending for all levels as a percentage of GDP was lower than that of other advanced industrial countries. As shown in Exhibit 3, the governments of France, Sweden, Germany, and other countries spent a higher percentage of their GDPs than did the federal, state, and local governments of the United States.

GLOBAL ECONOMICS

12-2 Financing Government Budgets

Where does the federal government obtain the funds to finance its outlays? Exhibit 4 tells the story. We find that the largest revenue source in 2011 was individual income taxes (47 percent), followed closely by social insurance taxes (36 percent), which include payroll taxes paid by employers and employees for Social Security, workers' compensation, and unemployment insurance. The third best revenue collector was corporate income taxes (8 percent). An excise tax is a sales tax on the purchase of a particular good or service. Excise taxes contributed

EXHIBIT 3	Government Expenditures in Other Countries, 2011

In 2011, the U.S. government was less of a spender than other advanced industrial countries. As shown in this exhibit, the governments of France, Sweden, Germany, and other countries spent a higher percentage of their GDPs than did the federal, state, and local governments of the United States.

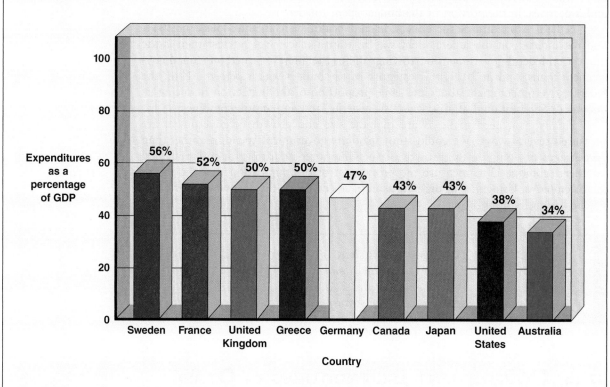

SOURCE: OECD (2011), "*OECD Economic Outlook* No. 90", OECD Economic Outlook: Statistics and Projections (database). http://dx.doi.org/10.1787/data-00588-en

3 percent of total tax receipts. The "Other" category includes receipts from such taxes as customs duties, estate taxes, and gift taxes.

12-2a THE TAX BURDEN IN OTHER COUNTRIES

Before turning our attention in the next section to the criteria for selecting which tax to impose, we must ask how burdensome overall taxation in the United States is. It may surprise you to learn that by international standards, U.S. citizens are among the most lightly taxed people in the industrialized world. Exhibit 5 reveals that in 2011, the tax collector was clearly much more heavy-handed in most other advanced industrial countries based on the fraction of GDP paid in taxes. The French, Swedes, Germans, Greeks, and British, for example, pay far higher taxes as a percentage of GDP than do Americans. It should be noted that countries that tax more heavily also are expected to provide more public services compared to those of the United States.

EXHIBIT 4	Federal Government Receipts, 2011

In 2011, the largest source of revenue for the federal government was individual income taxes, and the second largest source was social insurance taxes.

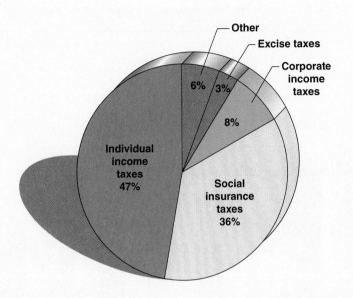

SOURCE: *Economic Report of the President*, 2012, http://www.gpo.gov/fdsys/pkg/ERP-2012/content-detail.html, Table B-81.

Another way to study the burden of taxation in the United States is to observe how it has changed over time. Exhibit 6 charts the growth of taxes as a percentage of GDP in the United States since 1929. Total government taxes, including federal, state, and local taxes, climbed from 11 percent of GDP in 1929 to their highest level of 34 percent in 2000 and then fell to 29 percent in 2011. The exhibit also shows that in 2000, federal taxes as a percentage of GDP rose to a post-World War II high of 21 percent before falling to about 15 percent in 2010 and 2011, which is the lowest percentage since 1950.

12-3 The Art of Taxation

Jean-Baptiste Colbert, finance minister to King Louis XIV of France, once said, "The art of taxation consists of so plucking the goose as to obtain the largest amount of feathers while promoting the smallest amount of hissing." Each year with great zeal, members of Congress and other policymakers debate various ways of raising revenue without causing too much "hissing." As you will learn, the task is difficult because each kind of tax has a different characteristic. Government must decide which tax is "appropriate" based on two basic philosophies of fairness—benefits received and ability-to-pay.

EXHIBIT 5	The Tax Burden in Selected Countries, 2011

Americans were more lightly taxed in 2011 than the citizens of other advanced industrial countries. For example, the Swedes, French, Germans, Greeks, and British pay higher taxes as a percentage of GDP.

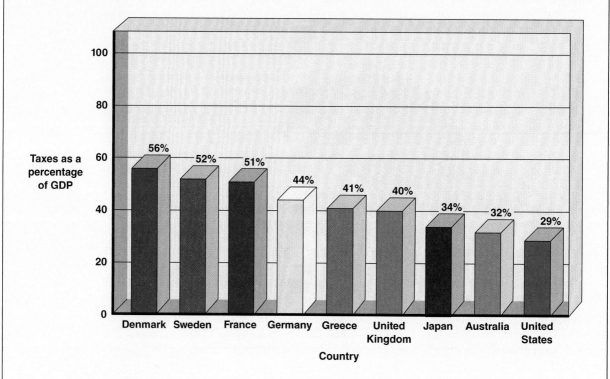

SOURCE: OECD (2011), "*OECD Economic Outlook* No. 90", OECD Economic Outlook: Statistics and Projections (database). http://dx.doi.org/10.1787/data-00588-en

12-3a THE BENEFITS-RECEIVED PRINCIPLE

Benefits-received principle

The concept that those who benefit from government expenditures should pay the taxes that finance their benefits.

What standard or guideline can we use to be sure everyone pays his or her "fair" share of taxes? One possibility is the benefits-received principle of taxation, which is the concept that those who benefit from government expenditures should pay the taxes that finance their benefits. The gasoline tax is an example of a tax that follows the *benefits-received principle*. The number of gallons of gasoline bought is a measure of the amount of highway services used, and the more gallons purchased, the greater the tax paid. Applying benefit-cost analysis, voters will approve additional highways only if the benefits they receive exceed the costs in gasoline taxes they must pay for highway construction and repairs.

Although the benefits-received principle of taxation is applicable to a private good such as gasoline, the nature of *public goods* often makes it impossible to apply this principle. Recall from Chapter 4 that national defense is a public good, which users collectively consume. So how can we separate those who benefit from national defense and make them pay? We cannot, and there are other goods and services for which the benefits-received principle is inconsistent with societal goals.

EXHIBIT 6	The Growth of Taxes as a Percentage of GDP in the United States, 1929–2011

The graph shows the growth in federal, state, and local government taxes as a percentage of GDP since 1929. Total government taxes climbed from about 11 percent of GDP in 1929 to their highest level of 34 percent in 2000 before falling to 29 percent in 2010 and 2011. In 2000, federal taxes as a percentage of GDP reached a post-World War II high of 21 percent before falling to 15 percent in 2010 and 2011, which is the lowest percentage since 1950.

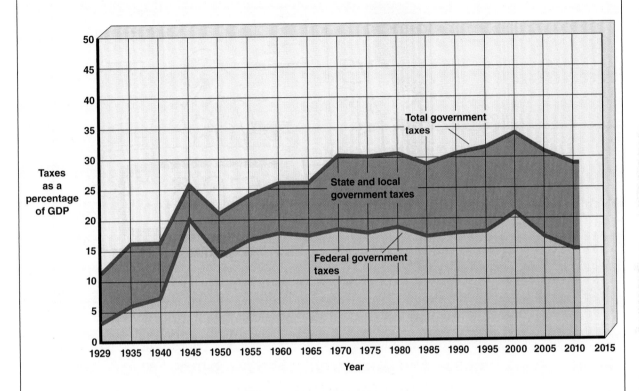

SOURCES: *Economic Report of the President*, 2012, http://www.gpo.gov/fdsys/pkg/ERP-2012/content-detail.htm1, Table B-79; and Bureau of Economic Analysis, *National Income Accounts*, http://www.bea.gov/national/nipaweb/SelectTable.asp?Selected=Y, Tables 1.1.5 and 3.3.

It would be foolish, for example, to ask families receiving food stamps to pay all the taxes required to finance their welfare benefits.

12-3b THE ABILITY-TO-PAY PRINCIPLE

A second popular principle of fairness in taxation sharply contrasts with the benefits-received principle. The ability-to-pay principle of taxation is the concept that those who have higher incomes can afford to pay a greater proportion of their income in taxes, regardless of benefits received. Under this tax philosophy, the rich may send their children to private schools or use private hospitals, but they should bear a heavier tax burden because they are better able to pay. How could there possibly be a problem with such an approach? An individual who earns

Ability-to-pay principle

The concept that those who have higher incomes can afford to pay a greater proportion of their income in taxes, regardless of benefits received.

$200,000 per year should pay X more taxes than an individual who earns only $10,000 per year. The difficulty lies in determining exactly how much more the higher-income individual should pay in taxes to ensure he or she is paying a "fair" amount. Unfortunately, no scientific method can measure precisely what one's "ability" to pay taxes means in dollars or percentage of income. Nevertheless, in the U.S. economy, the ability-to-pay principle dominates the benefits-received principle.

Where is the money I gave you last year?

12-3c PROGRESSIVE, REGRESSIVE, AND PROPORTIONAL TAXES

As we have seen, governments raise revenues from various taxes, such as income taxes, sales taxes, excise taxes, and property taxes. For purposes of analysis, economists classify each of these taxes into three types of taxation—*progressive*, *regressive*, and *proportional*. The focus of these three classifications is the relationship between changes in the tax rates and increases or decreases in income. Income is the tax base because people pay taxes out of income, even though a tax is levied on property, such as land, buildings, automobiles, and furniture.

Progressive tax

A tax that charges a higher percentage of income as income rises.

Progressive Taxes   Following the ability-to-pay principle, individual and corporate income taxes are progressive taxes. A progressive tax charges a higher percentage of income as income rises. For example, if a person earning $10,000 a year pays $1,500 in taxes, the *average* tax rate is 15 percent. If another person earns $100,000 a year and pays $28,000 in taxes, the average tax rate is 28 percent. This tax rate progressivity is the principle behind the federal and state income tax systems. Exhibit 8 illustrates the progressive nature of the federal income tax for a single person filing a 2011 tax return.

EXHIBIT 7	Federal Individual Income Tax Rate Schedule for a Single Taxpayer, 2011					
(1) Taxable income		**(2)**	**(3)** Average tax rate [(2)/(1)]	**(4)** Change in taxable income	**(5)** Change in tax	**(6)** Marginal tax rate [(5)/(4)]
Over	**But not over**	**Tax***				
$ 0	$ 8,500	$ 850	10%	$ 8,500	$ 850	10%
8,500	34,500	4,750	14	26,000	3,900	15
34,500	83,600	17,025	20	49,100	12,275	25
83,600	174,400	42,449	24	90,800	25,424	28
174,400	379,150	110,016	29	204,750	67,567	33
379,150	...	...	...	...	...	35

*Tax calculated at the top of the taxable income brackets.

SOURCE: Internal Revenue Service, Publication 17, *Your Federal Income Tax*, 2012, http://www.irs.gov/publications/index.html, Tax Rate Schedules, p. 274.

Column (1) of Exhibit 7 lists the *taxable income* tax brackets. Taxable income is gross income minus the personal exemption and the standard deduction. The personal exemption and the standard deduction are adjusted each year so inflation does not push taxpayers into higher tax brackets. Column (2) shows the tax bill that a taxpayer at the upper income of each of the five lowest taxable income brackets must pay, and the figures in column (3) are the corresponding average tax rates. The average tax rate is the tax divided by the income:

Average tax rate

The tax divided by the income.

$$\text{Average tax rate} = \frac{\text{total tax due}}{\text{total taxable income}}$$

Thus, at a taxable income of $34,500, the average tax rate is 14 percent ($4,750 divided by $34,500), and at $83,600, it is 20 percent ($17,025 divided by $83,600). A taxable income of over $379,150 is included to represent the upper-income bracket. As these figures indicate, our federal individual income tax is a progressive tax because the average tax rate rises as income increases.

Another key tax rate measure is the marginal tax rate, which is the fraction of additional income paid in taxes. The marginal tax rate formula is expressed as

Marginal tax rate

The fraction of additional income paid in taxes.

$$\text{Marginal tax rate} = \frac{\text{change in taxes due}}{\text{change in taxable income}}$$

Column (6) in Exhibit 7 computes the marginal tax rate for each federal tax bracket in the table. You can comprehend the marginal tax rate by observing in column (1) that when taxable income rises from $8,500 to $34,500 in the second lowest tax bracket, the tax rises from $850 to $4,750 in column (2). Column (4) reports this change in taxable income, and column (5) shows the change in the tax. The marginal tax rate in column (6) is therefore 15 percent ($3,900 divided by $26,000). Apply the same analysis when taxable income increases by $49,100 from $34,500 to $83,600 in the next bracket. An additional $12,275 is added to the $4,750 tax bill, so the marginal tax rate on this extra income is 25 percent ($12,275 divided by $49,100). Similar computations provide the marginal tax rates for the remaining taxable income brackets. The marginal tax rate is important because it determines how much a taxpayer's tax bill changes as his or her income rises or falls within each tax bracket.

Regressive tax

A tax that charges a lower percentage of income as income rises.

Regressive Taxes   A tax can also be a regressive tax. A regressive tax charges a lower percentage of income as income rises. Suppose Mutt, who is earning $10,000 a year, pays a tax of $5,000, and Jeff, who earns $100,000 a year, pays $10,000 in taxes. Although Jeff pays twice the absolute amount, this would be regressive taxation because richer Jeff pays an average tax rate of 10 percent and poorer Mutt suffers a 50 percent tax bite. Such a tax runs afoul of the ability-to-pay principle of taxation.

We will now demonstrate that sales and excise taxes are regressive taxes. Assume that there is a 5 percent sales tax on all purchases and that the Jones family earned $80,000 during the last year, while the Jefferson family earned $20,000. A sales tax is regressive because the richer Jones family will spend a smaller portion of their income to buy food, clothing, and other consumption items. The Joneses, with an $80,000 income, can afford to spend $40,000 on groceries and clothes and save the rest, while the Jeffersons, with a $20,000 income, spend their entire income to feed and clothe their family. Because each family pays a 5 percent sales tax, the lower-income Jeffersons pay sales taxes of $1,000 (0.05 × $20,000). This $1,000 sales tax is 5 percent of their income ($1,000/$20,000). The higher-income Joneses, on the other hand, pay sales taxes of $2,000 (0.05 × $40,000). This $2,000 sales tax is only 2.5 percent of their income ($2,000/$80,000). Although the richer Jones family pays twice the amount of sales tax to the tax collector, the sales tax is regressive because their average tax rate is lower than the Jefferson family's tax rate.

In practice, an example of a regressive tax is the Social Security payroll tax, FICA. The payroll tax is a fixed percentage levied on each worker's earnings and deducted from the worker's paycheck by the employer.

Payroll taxes are regressive for two reasons. First, only wages and salaries are subject to this tax, while other sources of income, such as interest and dividends, are not. Because wealthy individuals typically receive a larger portion of their income from sources other than wages and salaries than do lower-income individuals, the wealthy pay a smaller fraction of their total income in payroll taxes. Second, earnings above a certain level are exempt from the Social Security tax. Thus, the *marginal tax rate* above a given threshold level is zero. In 2011, this level was $110,000 for wage and salary income subject to Social Security tax. Hence, any additional dollars earned above this figure add no additional taxes, and the average tax rate falls. On the other hand, there is no wage base limit for the Medicare tax. It is noteworthy that one idea for reforming Social Security is to adjust or remove the limit on income subject to Social Security tax.

Finally, property taxes are also considered regressive for two reasons. First, property owners add this tax to the rent paid by tenants who generally are lower-income persons. Second, property taxes are a higher percentage of income for poor families than rich families because the poor spend a much greater proportion of their incomes for housing.

| EXHIBIT 8 | The Progressive Income Tax versus a Flat Tax |

The taxable income tax brackets for 2011 are drawn from Exhibit 7. In contrast to the "stair step" tax rates, a flat tax would charge a single rate of, say, 17 percent. This reform proposal is controversial and is discussed in the You're the Economist, "Is It Time to Trash the 1040s?"

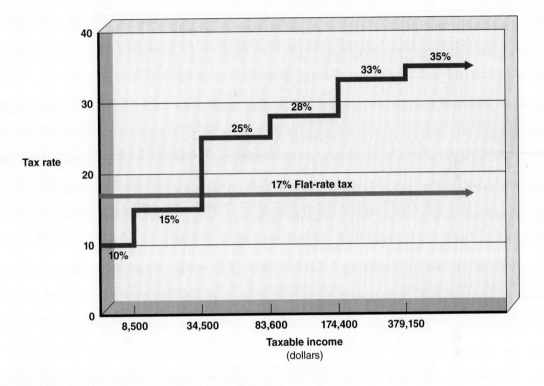

Proportional Taxes There continues to be considerable interest in simplifying the federal progressive income tax by substituting a proportional tax, also called a *flat tax*. A proportional tax charges the same percentage of income, regardless of the size of income. For example, one way to reform the federal progressive tax rate system would be to eliminate all deductions, exemptions, and loopholes and simply apply the same tax rate, say, 17 percent of income to everyone. Such a reform is illustrated in Exhibit 8. This would avoid the "hissing" from taxpayers who would no longer require legions of accountants and lawyers to file their tax returns. Actually, most flat-tax proposals are not truly proportional because they exempt income below some level and are therefore somewhat progressive. Also, it is debatable that a 17 percent flat tax would raise enough revenue.

Let's look at whether the flat tax satisfies the benefits-received principle and the ability-to-pay principle. First, the flat tax does not necessarily relate to

Proportional tax

A tax that charges the same percentage of income, regardless of the size of income. Also called a *flat-tax rate* or simply a *flat tax*.

Is It Time to Trash the 1040s?

Applicable Concepts: flat tax, national sales tax, and Value Added Tax (VAT)

Two controversial fundamental tax reform ideas are often hot news topics. One proposal is the flat tax discussed earlier in this chapter, and the other is a national sales tax. The flat tax is favored by former presidential candidate and publisher Steve Forbes. It would grant a personal exemption of about $36,000 for a typical family and then tax income above this amount at 17 percent with no deductions. As stated by recent presidential candidate John McCain, the argument for a flat tax is that it would allow people to file their tax returns on a postcard and reduce the number of tax cheats. McCain proposed that the flat tax would be optional to the current tax system.

The flat-tax plan described above creates serious political problems by eliminating taxes on income from dividends, interest, capital gains, and inheritances. Also, eliminating deductions and credits would face strong opposition from the public. For example, eliminating the mortgage interest deduction and exemptions for health care and charity would be a difficult political battle. And there is the fairness question. People at the lower end of the current system of six progressive rates could face a tax increase while upper-income people would get the biggest tax break. The counterargument is that under the current tax system, many millionaires pay nothing because they shelter their income. Under a flat-tax scheme, they would lose deductions and credits.

A national retail sales tax is another tax reform proposal. In 2008, Mike Huckabee, Republican candidate for president, made this

the benefits received from any particular government goods or services. Second, consider a 17 percent tax that collects $17,000 from Ms. "Rich," who is earning $100,000 a year, and $1,700 from Mr. "Poor," who is earning $10,000 a year. Both taxpayers pay the same proportional 17 percent of their incomes, but the $1,700 tax is thought to represent a much greater sacrifice to Mr. Poor than does the $17,000 tax paid by Ms. Rich. After paying her taxes, Ms. Rich can still live comfortably, but Mr. Poor complains that he desperately needed the $1,700 to buy groceries for his family. To be fair, one can argue that the $17,000 paid by Ms. Rich is not enough based on the ability-to-pay principle.

12-3d REFORMING THE TAX SYSTEM

The Supreme Court declared the personal income tax unconstitutional in 1895. This changed in 1913 when the states ratified the Sixteenth Amendment to the Constitution, granting Congress the power to levy taxes on income. The federal income tax was an inconsequential source of revenue until World War II, but since then, it has remained a major source. Currently, 41 states have income taxes, idea, called the Fair Tax, central to his campaign. A consumption tax could eliminate all federal income taxes entirely (personal, corporate, and Social Security) and tax only consumer purchases at a given percentage. Like the flat tax, loopholes would be eliminated, and tax collection would become so simple that the federal government could save billions of dollars by cutting or eliminating the IRS. Taxpayers could save because they would no longer need to hire tax preparers and lawyers to prepare their complicated 1040 tax returns. Also, the tax base would broaden because, while not everyone earns income, almost everyone makes purchases.

Critics of a national sales tax argue that retail businesses would have the added burden of being tax collectors for the federal government, and the IRS would still be required to ensure that taxes are collected on billions of sales transactions. Moreover, huge price increases from the national sales tax would lead to "black market" transactions. The counterargument is that this problem would be no worse than current income tax evasion, and a sales tax indirectly taxes participants in illegal markets when they spend their income in legal markets. Also, a sales tax is regressive because the poor spend a greater share of their income on food, housing, and other necessities. To offset this problem, sales tax advocates propose subsidy checks paid up to some level of income. Critics also point out that retired people who pay little or no federal income tax will not welcome paying a national sales tax.

There are also debates on using a value-added tax (VAT) that is popular in Europe and many other countries. VAT is a consumption tax levied at each stage of production. Suppose a vendor buys apples from a farmer to sell at a market. The vendor's VAT is based on a percentage of the difference (value added) between the cost the vendor paid and the sales price customers pay. Customers who buy the apples bear the VAT cost built in the price of the apples they purchase.

> ### Analyze the Issue
> Assume the federal government replaces the federal income tax with a national sales tax on all consumption expenditures. Analyze the impact of this tax change on taxation efficiency and equity. Note that the federal government already collects a nationwide consumption tax through excise taxes on gasoline, liquor, and tobacco.

Source: © Cengage Learning 2014

and personal income taxes may become an increasingly important source of state and local revenues in years to come.

Over the years, Congress has enacted various reforms of the federal tax system. The Tax Reform Act of 1986, for example, marked the first time Congress has completely rewritten the Federal Tax Code since 1954. This law removed millions of households from the tax rolls by roughly doubling the personal exemption allowed for each taxpayer and his or her dependents. Before the tax law changed, there were 15 marginal tax brackets for individuals, ranging from 11 to 50 percent. The Tax Reform Act of 1986 reduced the number of tax brackets to only four. Most taxpayers are in the lower brackets, so the loss in tax revenue that resulted from lowering the individual tax rates was offset by raising taxes on corporations and closing numerous tax loopholes. Consistent with the two key taxation objectives, the intention of this major revision of the federal income tax law was to improve efficiency and make the system fairer by shifting more of the tax burden to corporations. As shown in Exhibits 7 and 8, there are currently six tax brackets, and critics argue that another tax reform act is long overdue. The You're the Economist titled "Is It Time to Trash the 1040s?" discusses ideas to reform the current federal tax system.

12-4 Public Choice Theory

Public choice theory

The analysis of the government's decision-making process for allocating resources.

James Buchanan, who won the 1986 Nobel Prize in economics, is the founder of a body of economic literature called public choice theory. Public choice theory is the analysis of the government's decision-making process for allocating resources. Recall from Chapter 4 that private-market failure is the reason for government intervention in markets. The theory of public choice considers how well the government performs when it replaces or regulates a private market. Rather than operating as the market mechanism to allocate resources, the government is a non-market, political decision-making force. Instead of behaving as private-interest buyers or sellers in the marketplace, actors in the political system have complex incentives in their roles as elected officials, bureaucrats, special-interest lobbyists, and voters.

Buchanan and other public choice theorists raise the fundamental issue of how well a democratic society can make efficient economic decisions. The basic principle of public choice theory is that politicians follow their own self-interest and seek to maximize their reelection chances, rather than promote the best interests of society. Thus, a major contribution of Buchanan has been to link self-interest motivation to government officials just as Adam Smith earlier identified the pursuit of self-interest as the motivation for consumers and producers. In short, individuals within any government agency or institution will act analogously to their private-sector counterparts; they will give first priority to improving their own earnings, working conditions, and status, rather than to being altruistic.

Given this introduction to the subject, let's consider a few public choice theories that explain why the public sector, like the private sector, may also "fail."

12-4a MAJORITY-RULE PROBLEM

Benefit-cost analysis

The comparison of the additional rewards and costs of an economic alternative.

To evaluate choices, economists often use a technique called benefit-cost analysis. Benefit-cost analysis is the comparison of the additional rewards and costs of an economic alternative. If a firm is considering producing a new product, its benefit ("carrots") will be the extra revenue earned from selling the product. The firm's cost ("sticks") is the opportunity cost of using resources to make the product. How many units of the product should the firm manufacture?

> **CONCLUSION:** *Rationally, a profit-maximizing firm follows the marginal rule and produces additional units so long as the marginal benefit exceeds the marginal cost.*

The basic rule of benefit-cost analysis is that undertaking a program whose cost exceeds its benefit is an inefficient waste of resources. In the competitive market system, undertaking projects that yield benefits greater than costs is a sure bet. In the long run, any firm that does not follow the benefit-cost rule will either go out of business or switch to producing products that yield benefits equal to or greater than their costs. Majority-rule voting, however,

EXHIBIT 9	Majority-Rule Benefit-Cost Analysis of Two Park Projects					
	Park Project A			Park Project B		
(1) Voter	(2) Marginal cost (taxes)	(3) Marginal benefit	(4) Vote	(5) Marginal cost (taxes)	(6) Marginal benefit	(7) Vote
Bob	$100	$ 0	No	$100	$ 90	No
Juan	100	101	Yes	100	90	No
Theresa	100	101	Yes	100	301	Yes
Total	$300	$202	Passes	$300	$481	Fails

SOURCE: © Cengage Learning 2014

can result in the approval of projects whose costs outweigh their benefits. Exhibit 9 illustrates how an inefficient economic decision can result from the ballot box.

As shown in Exhibit 9, suppose Bob, Juan, and Theresa are the only voters in a mini-society that is considering whether to add two publicly financed park projects, A and B. The total cost to taxpayers of either park project is $300, and the marginal cost of park A or park B to each taxpayer is an additional tax of $100 [columns (2) and (5)]. Next, assume each taxpayer determines his or her additional dollar value derived from the benefits of park projects A and B [columns (3) and (6)]. Assuming each person applies marginal analysis, each will follow the *marginal rule* and vote for a project only if his or her benefit exceeds the cost of the $100 tax. Consider park project A. This project is worth $0 to Bob, $101 to Juan, and $101 to Theresa, and this means two Yes votes and one No vote: the majority votes for park A [column (4)]. This decision would not happen in the business world. The Walt Disney Company, for example, would rationally reject such a project because the total of all consumers' marginal benefits is only $202, which is less than its $300 marginal cost.

The important point here is that majority-rule voting can make the correct benefit-cost marginal analysis, but it can also lead to a rejection of projects with marginal total benefits that exceed marginal costs. Suppose park project B costs $300 as well, and Bob's benefits are $90, Juan's $90, and Theresa's $301 [column (6)]. The total of all marginal benefits from constructing park B is $481, and this project would be undertaken in a private-sector market. But because only Theresa's benefits exceed the marginal $100 tax, park project B in the political arena receives only one Yes vote against two No votes and fails.

Why is there a distinction between political majority voting and benefit-cost analysis? The reason is that dollars can measure the intensity of voter preferences and "one-person, one-vote" does not. A count of ballots can determine whether a proposal passes or fails, but this count may not be proportional to the dollar strength of benefits among the individual voters.

12-4b SPECIAL-INTEREST GROUP EFFECT

In addition to benefit-cost errors from majority voting, special-interest groups can create government support for programs with costs outweighing their benefits. The *special-interest effect* occurs when the government approves programs that benefit only a small group within society, but society as a whole pays the costs. The influence of special-interest groups is indeed a constant problem for effective government because the benefits of government programs to certain small groups are great and the costs are relatively insignificant to each taxpayer. For example, let's assume the benefits of support prices for dairy farmers are $100 million. Because of the size of these benefits to dairy farmers, this special-interest group can well afford to hire professional lobbyists and donate a million dollars or so to the reelection campaigns of politicians voting for dairy price supports.

In addition to the incentive of financial support from special interests, politicians can also engage in *logrolling*. Logrolling is the political practice of trading votes of support for legislated programs. Politician A says to politician B, "You vote for my dairy price support bill, and I will vote for your tobacco price support bill."

But who pays for these large benefits to special-interest groups? Taxpayers do, of course, but the extra tax burden per taxpayer is very low. Although Congress may enact a $200 million program to favor, say, a few defense contractors, this expenditure costs 100 million taxpayers only $2 per taxpayer. Because in a free society it is relatively easy to organize special-interest constituencies and lobby politicians to spread the cost, it is little wonder that spending programs are popular. Moreover, the small cost of each pet program per taxpayer means there is little reward for a single voter to learn the details of the many special-interest legislation proposals.

12-4c RATIONAL VOTER IGNORANCE

Rational ignorance

The voter's choice to remain uninformed because the marginal cost of obtaining information is higher than the marginal benefit from knowing it.

Politicians, appointed officials, and bureaucrats constitute the supply side of the political marketplace. The demand side of the political market consists of special-interest groups and voters who are subject to what economists call rational ignorance. Rational ignorance is a voter's decision that the benefit of becoming informed about an issue is not worth the cost. A frequent charge in elections is that the candidates are not talking about the issues. One explanation is that the candidates realize that a sizable portion of the voters will make a calculated decision not to judge the candidates based on in-depth knowledge of their positions on a wide range of issues. Instead of going to the trouble of reading position papers and doing research, many voters choose their candidates based simply on party affiliation or on how the candidate appears on television. This approach is rational if the perceived extra effort required to be better informed exceeds the marginal benefit of knowing more about the candidate.

The principle of rational ignorance also explains why eligible voters fail to vote on election day. A popular explanation is that low voter participation results from apathy among potential voters, but the decision can be an exercise in practical benefit-cost analysis. Nonvoters presumably perceive that the opportunity cost of going to the polls outweighs the benefit gained from any of the candidates or issues on the ballot. Moreover, nonvoters perceive that one extra vote is unlikely to change the outcome.

Public choice theorists argue that one reason benefits are difficult to measure is that the voter confronts an *indivisible* public service. In a grocery store, the consumer can decide to spend so much on apples, oranges, and other *divisible* items, but voting involves candidates who take stands on many issues. The point is that voting does not allow the voter to pick and choose among the candidate's good and bad positions. Most voters, in short, must "buy" a confusing mixture of "wants" and "unwants" that are difficult to interpret as a benefit.

12-4d BUREAUCRATIC INEFFICIENCY

The bureaucracy is the body of nonelected officials and administrators who operate government agencies. As government grows, one of the concerns is that the bureaucracy may become more powerful than the executive, legislative, and judicial branches. Public choice theory also considers how bureaucratic behavior affects economic decision making. One principle is that the government bureaucracy tends to be inefficient because of the absence of the profit motive.

What happens when a government agency performs poorly? First, there is no competition from other producers to take away market share. There are no shareholders demanding reform when profits are falling because taxpayers are a poor substitute for stockholder pressure. Second, the typical government response each year is to request a larger budget. Without profits as a measure of performance, the tendency is to use the size of an agency's budget and staff as an indicator of success. In brief, the basic incentive structure of government agencies encourages inefficient management because, unlike the market system, there is a lack of incentive to be cost-conscious or creative. Instead, the hallmark of the bureaucrat is to be extremely cautious and make all decisions "by the book." Such behavior may maximize prestige and security, but it usually fails to minimize costs.

12-4e SHORTSIGHTEDNESS EFFECT

Finally, it can be argued that democracy has a bias toward programs offering clear benefits and hidden costs. The reason is that political officeholders must run for reelection after a relatively short period of two to six years. Given this reality, politicians tend to favor proposals providing immediate benefits, with future generations paying most of the costs. Conversely, they reject programs that have easily identifiable short-run high costs, but offer benefits only after a decade. Hence, the essence of the hidden costs bias, or *shortsightedness effect*, is that both voters and politicians suffer from a short time horizon. Such a myopic view of either future costs or future benefits can cause an irrational acceptance of a program, even though long-run costs exceed short-run benefits, or an irrational rejection of a program with long-run benefits that outweigh short-run costs.

✓ CHECKPOINT

What Does Public Choice Say about a Budget Deficit?

In 2002, the situation switched from a few years in which the federal government spent less than it collected in taxes to spending more than tax revenues (discussed in the next chapter). James Buchanan predicted over 30 years ago that growing government deficits would be inevitable. He maintained that government officials would increase spending for their constituents in order to gain votes. Furthermore, politicians would shy away from tax increases for fear of alienating voters. The net effect would be deficits. Was Buchanan's prediction based on the rational ignorance effect, government inefficiency, or the shortsightedness effect?

Key Concepts

Government expenditures	Average tax rate	Public choice theory
Benefits-received principle	Marginal tax rate	Benefit-cost analysis
Ability-to-pay principle	Regressive tax	Rational ignorance
Progressive tax	Proportional tax or flat tax	

Summary

- **Government expenditures**, including transfer payments, have grown from about one-quarter of GDP in 1950 to about 40 percent of GDP today.

- **Federal tax revenues** are collected primarily from individual income taxes and social insurance taxes.

Federal Tax Revenues

Government Expenditures

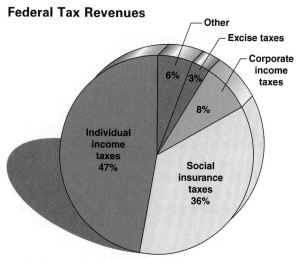

SOURCES: *Economic Report of the President*, 2012, http://www.gpo.gov/fdsys/pkg/ERP-2012/content-detail.htm1, Table B-79; and Bureau of Economic Analysis, *National Income Accounts*, http://www.bea.gov/national/nipaweb/SelectTable.asp?Selected=Y, Tables 1.1.5 and 3.3.

SOURCE: *Economic Report of the President*, 2012, http://www.gpo.gov/fdsys/pkg/ERP-2012/content-detail.htm1, Table B-81.

- The **taxation burden,** measured by taxes as a percentage of GDP, is lighter in the United States than in many other advanced industrial countries.

Taxation Burden

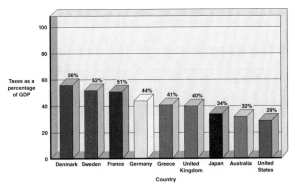

SOURCE: OECD (2011), "*OECD Economic Outlook* No. 90", OECD Economic Outlook: Statistics and Projections (database). http://dx.doi .org/10.1787/data-00588-en

- **Total tax revenues** amounted to about 11 percent of GDP in 1929 and reached the highest level of close to 34 percent in 2000 before falling to 29 percent in 2011. Federal taxes take a larger share of GDP than state and local governments.

Total tax Revenues

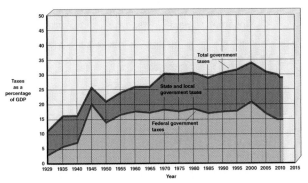

SOURCES: *Economic Report of the President,* 2012, http://www.gpo .gov/fdsys/pkg/ERP-2012/content-detail.htm1, Table B-79; and Bureau of Economic Analysis, *National Income Accounts,* http://www.bea.gov/ national/nipaweb/SelectTable.asp?Selected=Y, Tables 1.1.5 and 3.3.

- The **benefits-received principle** and the **ability-to-pay principle** are two basic philosophies of taxation fairness. The gasoline tax is a classic example of the benefits-received principle because users of the highways pay the gasoline tax. Progressive income taxes follow the ability-to-pay principle because there is a direct relationship between the average tax rate and income size. Sales, excise, property, and flat-rate taxes violate this principle because each results in a greater burden on the poor than on the rich.

- **Public choice theory** reveals the government's decision-making process. For example, government failure can occur for any of the following reasons: (1) majority voting may not follow benefit-cost analysis; (2) special-interest groups can obtain large benefits and spread their costs over many taxpayers; (3) rational voter ignorance means a sizable portion of the voters will decide not to make informed judgments; (4) bureaucratic behavior may not lead to cost-effective decisions; and (5) politicians suffer from a short time horizon, leading to a bias toward hiding the costs of programs.

Summary of Conclusion Statements

- The government's share of total economic activity has generally increased since World War II ended in 1945. Most of the growth in combined government expenditures as a percentage of GDP reflects rapidly growing federal government transfer programs.

- Rationally, a profit-maximizing firm follows the marginal rule and produces additional units so long as the marginal benefit exceeds the marginal cost.

Study Questions and Problems

1. Explain why federal, state, and local expenditures account for about 40 percent of GDP, but total government spending (G in GDP) is only about 20 percent of GDP.

2. Identify the major differences between federal government outlays and spending by state and local governments.

3. What are the primary tax revenue sources at the federal, state, and local levels of government?

4. Which of the following taxes satisfy the benefits-received principle, and which satisfy the ability-to-pay principle?
   a. Gasoline tax
   b. Federal income tax
   c. Tax on Social Security benefits

5. What is the difference between the marginal tax rate and the average tax rate?

6. Explain why a 5 percent sales tax on gasoline is regressive.

7. Ms. Jones has a taxable income of $30,000, and she must pay $3,000 in taxes. Mr. Smith has a taxable income of $60,000. How much tax must Mr. Smith pay for the tax system to be
   a. progressive?
   b. regressive?
   c. proportional?

8. Explain why each of the following taxes is progressive or regressive.
   a. A $1 per pack federal excise tax on cigarettes
   b. The federal individual income tax
   c. The federal payroll tax

9. Complete the following table, which describes the sales tax paid by individuals at various income levels. Indicate whether the tax is progressive, proportional, or regressive.

Income	Total spending	Sales tax paid	Sales tax paid as a percentage of income
$ 1,000	$ 1,000	$ 100	_____%
5,000	3,500	350	_____
10,000	6,000	600	_____
100,000	40,000	4,000	_____

10. Calculate the average and marginal tax rates in the following table, and indicate whether the tax is progressive, proportional, or regressive. What observation can you make concerning the relationship between marginal and average tax rates?

Income	Tax paid	Average tax rate	Marginal tax rate
$ 0	$ 0	0%	0%
100	10	_____	_____
200	30	_____	_____
300	60	_____	_____
400	100	_____	_____
500	150	_____	_____

11. Compare "dollar voting" in private markets with "majority voting" in the political decision-making system.

For Online Exercises, go to the Tucker Web site at www.cengage.com/economics/tucker.

✓ CHECKPOINT ANSWER

What Does Public Choice Say about a Budget Deficit?

The government uses the deficit to finance clear short-term benefits, paying little attention to long-term consequences. If you said public choice predicts that government officials will emphasize near-term benefits to gain votes (the shortsightedness effect), **YOU ARE CORRECT.**

Sample Quiz

For an explanation of the correct answers, visit the Tucker Web site at www.cengage.com/economics/tucker.

1. Currently, total government expenditures in the United States is approximately
   a. 40 percent of GDP.
   b. 50 percent of GDP.
   c. 75 percent of GDP.
   d. 80 percent of GDP.

2. Which of the following categories accounted for the largest percentage of total federal government expenditures in recent years?
   a. income security
   b. national defense
   c. education and health
   d. interest on the national debt

3. Which of the following taxes contributed the greatest percentage of total federal government tax revenues in recent years?
   a. individual income taxes
   b. corporate income taxes
   c. Social Security taxes
   d. excise taxes

4. How do total taxes as a percentage of GDP in the United States compare to those of Western European countries, such as the United Kingdom, Germany, and Sweden?
   a. U.S. taxation is smaller.
   b. U.S. taxation is about the same.
   c. U.S. taxation is slightly larger.
   d. U.S. taxation is substantially larger.

5. The benefits-received principle of taxation is *most* evident in
   a. progressive tax rates.
   b. excise taxes on gasoline.
   c. the personal income tax.
   d. the corporate income tax.

6. A tax is regressive if it collects a
   a. larger amount as income rises.
   b. constant amount as income rises.
   c. smaller fraction of income as income falls.
   d. smaller fraction of income as income rises.

7. Which of the following is an example of a progressive tax?
   a. the excise tax on cigarettes
   b. the federal tax on gasoline
   c. the federal personal income tax
   d. All of the above answers are correct

8. A tax structured so that people with the same income pay the same percentage of their income in taxes is called a(an)
   a. flat tax.
   b. regressive tax.
   c. progressive tax.
   d. excise tax.

Sample Quiz *continued*

EXHIBIT 10 | **Marginal Tax Rate Lines**

Marginal tax rate (percent)

Income

S

C

A

SOURCE: © Cengage Learning 2014

9. In Exhibit 10, line *A* represents a(an)
   a. regressive tax.
   b. progressive tax.
   c. proportional tax.
   d. ability-to-pay tax.

10. In Exhibit 10, line *B* represents a
    a. regressive tax.
    b. progressive tax.
    c. proportional tax.
    d. flat tax.

11. In Exhibit 10, line *C* represents a
    a. regressive tax.
    b. progressive tax.
    c. proportional tax.
    d. ability-to-pay tax.

12. In Exhibit 10, if *A* represents state and local taxes and *B* represents federal income taxes, what is the result of imposing both types of taxes?
    a. a regressive tax
    b. a progressive tax
    c. a proportional tax
    d. an ability-to-pay tax

13. The study of the decision-making process of government is the study of
    a. Keynesian economics.
    b. public choice theory.
    c. rational expectations theory.
    d. social economics.

14. People who often create benefits for the minority and impose the cost on the majority are called
    a. fair-interest groups.
    b. encounter groups.
    c. laissez-faire groups.
    d. special-interest groups.

15. Voters may choose to remain uninformed about an issue because of
    a. the special-interest effect.
    b. rational ignorance.
    c. bureaucratic inefficiency.
    d. the shortsightedness effect.

16. Which of the following categories accounted for the lowest percentage of total federal government expenditures in recent years?
    a. income security
    b. national defense
    c. education and health
    d. interest on the national debt

17. Since 1929, total government taxes as a percentage of GDP
    a. climbed from 10 percent to about 30 percent.
    b. remained close to 30 percent.
    c. climbed from 30 percent to about 50 percent.
    d. climbed from 15 percent to about 50 percent.

18. "It would be an undue hardship to require people whose income is below $15,000 per year to pay income taxes." This statement reflects which of the following principles for a tax?
    a. benefits-received
    b. inexpensive-to-collect

Sample Quiz *continued*

c. ability-to-pay
d. fairness of contribution

19. If a person is taxed $100 on an income of $1,000, taxed $180 on an income of $2,000, and taxed $220 on an income of $3,000, this person is paying a
a. progressive tax.
b. poll tax.

c. proportional tax.
d. regressive tax.

20. According to the shortsightedness effect, politicians tend to favor projects with
a. short-run benefits and short-run costs.
b. short-run benefits and long-run costs.
c. long-run benefits and short-run costs.
d. long-run benefits and long-run costs.

Economics

OF

Natural Disasters

SUPPLEMENTAL MODULE

by

Bill Boyes
Arizona State University

Mike Melvin
Arizona State University

CENGAGE
Learning

Australia • Brazil • Japan • Korea • Mexico • Singapore • Spain • United Kingdom • United States

Economics of Natural Disasters

On August 29, 2005, Hurricane Katrina, a Category 5 storm, came ashore a few miles east of New Orleans, Louisiana. Katrina caused waters to rise and pressure to build until the levees protecting the city of New Orleans from the waters of Lake Pontchartrain and the Mississippi River collapsed. Flooding occurred throughout most of the city, leaving more than 1,000 people dead. In addition, the hurricane seriously damaged the oil industry, putting about 25 percent of the U.S. domestic production out of commission. On September 29, 2005, just when the area was beginning to recover, Hurricane Rita, a Category 3 storm, landed near Galveston, Texas—close enough to Katrina's path to add to its misery.

While these two hurricanes may be the worst natural disaster to strike the United States, they are far from the most devastating natural disasters in the world. The most devastating earthquake of the 20th century (magnitude 7.8) hit the city of Tangshan in northeast China in 1976. The death toll was somewhere between 300,000 and 655,000. The greatest volcanic eruption occurred July 1991 at Mt. Pinatubo on Luzon Island in the Philippines, blanketing 430 square miles with volcanic ash and killing more than 800 people. The July 1991 cyclone in Bangladesh and the flooding that resulted killed 138,000. Hurricane Mitch in October 1998 was the deadliest hurricane to hit the Americas, killing 11,000 in Honduras and Nicaragua. The tsunami of 2004 caused an estimated death toll of 250,000 and extended from Indonesia in the east to the coast of Africa, some 4,000 miles away.

In this chapter, we discuss some of the economic issues of natural disasters. We begin with microeconomic considerations: looking at why natural disasters are made worse by development in disaster-prone areas, examining Katrina's effect on the U.S. oil industry, and considering the impact government policies had on the disaster. We then turn to the macroeconomic issues involved and analyze the effects of natural disasters on real GDP and prices, and investigate the Federal Reserve and Government's policy responses. We will see how natural disasters in one part of the country and world affect other parts of the country and world, and how, conversely, global markets help to ameliorate the economic effects of a natural disaster in one part of the world.

1. Hurricanes, Floods, and Earthquakes in the United States

Hurricanes, floods, and earthquakes are the natural disasters that cause the greatest damage in the United States. The deadliest hurricane in U.S. history occurred in September 1900 in Galveston, Texas, where 12,000 people lost their lives. The costliest hurricanes have been Katrina (estimated at $100 billion), Andrew in 1992 ($27 billion), and Camille in 1969 ($1.5 billion). The severity of hurricanes is rated on a scale of Category 1 to Category 5, with Category 5 being the most powerful. Four Category 5 storms have struck the U.S. since 1935. Most U.S. hurricanes hit the Gulf Coast—Florida, Mississippi, and Louisiana—although many come ashore on the Atlantic seaboard from the Florida Keys to North Carolina.

Earthquakes, measured on the Richter scale, are not uncommon in California. Quakes of magnitude 7 or larger—considered serious—struck that state in 1999 at Hector Mine, in 1989 at San Francisco, and in 1992 at Northridge. But smaller quakes strike daily throughout California. Figure 1 shows the pattern of earthquake activity in the United States. Clearly, the earthquake corridor is throughout coastal California and inland Southern California.

FIGURE 1

Earthquakes in the United States

Shades represent probabilities of damage in 100 years. Black indicates greatest probability, and dark gray the lowest.

Source: Faults and Earthquakes, Steven Dutch, Natural and Applied Sciences, University of Wisconsin—Green Bay.

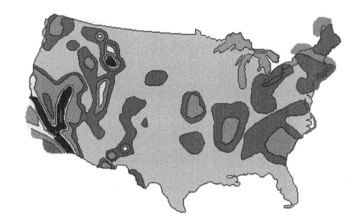

Floods are the costliest and most chronic natural hazard in the United States, causing an average of 140 fatalities and $5 billion damage each year. Damage from floods results from a combination of the great power of flowing water and the concentration of people and property along rivers. In the United States, about 3,800 towns and cities of more than 2,500 inhabitants are on floodplains. The greatest concentration of flood plains lies along the Appalachian Mountains and the Mississippi River, in the coastal areas of southern and northern California, in the Willamette Valley of Oregon, and in northern Washington State. Figure 2 shows where floods occur in the United States.

RECAP

1. Hurricanes, earthquakes and floods are the most damaging natural disasters in the United States.
2. Hurricanes land primarily along the Gulf Coast and secondly along the eastern seaboard from the Florida Keys to North Carolina.
3. Earthquakes occur primarily in California.
4. Flooding occurs most often along the Mississippi River Valley, in the Appalachian Mountains, and in Oregon.

2. A Recipe for Disaster

While hurricanes, earthquakes, and floods are considered "natural disasters," some would argue that human activities have contributed to their effects. How land is developed can adversely affect the ecology of an area, making it more susceptible to damage from storms. When people choose to live in "disaster-prone" areas, they can contribute to this effect—in addition to putting themselves in harm's way. A natural disaster would be far less disastrous if no one inhabited the place where it occurred. Why do people choose to live and work where they do? Climate, type of job, pay, family, and other factors enter into this decision. People choose to maximize utility. They want to be as happy as possible, and when faced with a choice—

FIGURE 2

Flooding in the United States

The dots show flood occurrences since the 1930s.

Source: Jim E. O'Connor and John E. Costa, "Large Floods in the United States: Where They Happen and Why," *U.S. Geological Survey Circular 1245.*

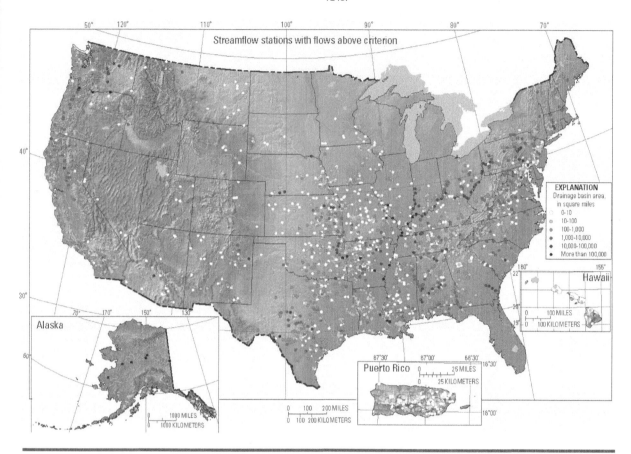

such as where to live—they compare what they perceive to be the costs to what they perceive to be the benefits of the options they have. We know that consumer equilibrium occurs when the last dollar spent on something yields the same enjoyment as would occur if that dollar had been spent on something else. In equation form, the consumer equilibrium is:[1]

$$MU_x/P_x = MU_y/P_y = MU_z/P_z$$

Marginal utility of x divided by the price of x equals the marginal utility of y divided by the price of y, which equals the marginal utility of z divided by the price of z. Items x, y, and z are being purchased, and P_x, P_y, and P_z are the prices of the items; MU_x, MU_y, and MU_z are the marginal utilities of the items—the additional utility another unit of the item gives you.

The equation illustrates that quantities of the items selected depend on their relative prices. As the price of item z rises while prices of x and y do not change, people

---

[1] See Chapter 7 in Micro Split, or Chapter 21 in Economics.

purchase less z and may purchase more of y and z. They will change what they buy (i.e., they will reallocate their income among goods and services), until the marginal utility per dollar of expenditure is the same on all the items. This applies to all goods and services, including housing and where to live.

2.a. Living in Disaster-Prone Locations

Each of us has a preference for where we want to live. Some prefer to live near the ocean, others in the mountains; some people prefer cold climates, while others prefer warm climates. Those who prefer to live in a warm climate can be induced to live in a colder climate if the reward for living in the colder climate is high enough. This means that the relative cost of living in the warm climate must be sufficiently high that the colder climate seems to be a good deal. Once having selected a climate and general location, we choose where to establish our housing.

Let's say we have two choices, on a hill or next to the river. The river represents a location prone to experiencing natural disasters; the hill represents a location that is much less likely to experience natural disasters. Locating next to the river means that floods could destroy your house, whereas living on the hill means no floods. Suppose you prefer the river location. If you choose to locate next to the river, you know that you could experience a flood, yet you are willing to risk it because you prefer river living.

Suppose that P_H is the price of hill living and P_R is the price of river living. Consumer equilibrium occurs when $MU_R / P_R = MU_H / P_H$, which tells us that the consumer will choose between river and hill living so as to equate the marginal utility per dollar of expenditure on river and hill living. As the price of river living rises relative to hill living, the consumer will then shift purchases away from river living. If someone prefers the river living twice as much as they do hill living, then living on the hill will occur only if the price of river living is more than twice hill living. We can illustrate this in equation form as: $MU_R = 2MU_H$.[2] The person will choose to live on the hill only if $P_R > 2P_H$. If another person prefers living near the river about 1.2 times as much as living on the hill, then that person will be induced to live on the hill only if $P_R > 1.2P_H$. As the price of river living rises relative to hill living, fewer people will choose to live near the river.

People's choice of living location depends on their tastes and preferences (the MUs) and the total cost of each living location. Most people are risk averse, which means that when offered \$1,000 for sure or a 50% chance of earning \$2,000 and a 50% chance of earning \$0, most people choose the for-sure \$1,000 option. Why would risk-averse people gamble with their most valuable assets—themselves and their family's well being—by locating in a flood plain, hurricane alley, earthquake fault, or other location that has a high probability of experiencing a natural disaster? Are people uninformed about the risks they are exposing their families to when they choose to live in an area prone to natural disasters? Some are for sure, but those who are not quickly learn about the risks once a hurricane or an earthquake occurs in the area, even if it doesn't cause them personal losses.

In the case of Katrina and Rita, there were few in New Orleans and Houston who did not know about the potential of a hurricane hitting their area. Information of the potential devastation that would be caused by a Category 3 or higher hurricane hit-

---

[2] Since we do not divide housing into small units—one brick, one board, etc.—when making living decisions, when we talk about the marginal utility of another unit of river living, we should think of it more like the total enjoyment one gets from living on the river or on the hill rather than the additional utility one gets from the last brick placed on the river house. Then, using the formula $MU_R = 2MU_H$ to represent the idea that river living is preferred twice as much as hill living makes a little more sense. We are not saying that the last brick put on the river house provided twice the enjoyment as the last brick put on the hill house.

ting New Orleans was widespread. The inability of the levees to keep the waters of Lake Pontchartrain and the Mississippi River from flooding New Orleans was well known by local officials and the Army Corps of Engineers; they had been discussing potential repairs and fortifications to the levees for years. Why then did development continue to take place in what was clearly a disaster-prone area?

2.b. Government-Induced Changes in Relative Prices

If the price of river living relative to hill living declines, more people will choose river living. Insurance can cause the relative price to change. Suppose the full cost to an individual of a natural disaster is his personal loss multiplied by his expectation that the disaster will strike him. For instance, if a flood to Ben's property would cause $10,000 in estimated damages and Ben thinks there is a 10 percent chance that flooding will occur this year, his full cost of the disaster is $1,000. Let's represent that full cost as F. If the price of river living is represented by P_R, then $P_R + F$ is the full cost of river living.

Insurance reduces the value of F. If, for example, insurance would pay for 80 percent of Ben's loss from the flood, then instead of $1,000, his loss would be $200. Since F is lower with the insurance, the full cost of river living, $P_R + F$, is lower. If private insurance can be purchased, then the cost of river living is reduced relative to no insurance, and more people would choose river living. Risk-averse people tend to buy insurance instead of taking the chance of experiencing the full loss that would result from a natural disaster.

The companies offering the private insurance have to be able to earn a profit by offering the insurance. They do this by having many policyholders, most of whom do not experience losses, and by setting fees appropriate to the risk—the greater the chance of losses, the higher the annual fee. However, if the risk is so high that the company cannot make a profit on the insurance, it simply won't offer it. Without the insurance, fewer people would choose river living.

For decades, when floods and other natural disasters caused serious damage, the government would provide assistance, dishing out disaster relief dollars so people could rebuild homes and businesses. What does the government program do to the calculation of costs and benefits for individuals? It lowers F and thus decreases the cost of river living. People know that if they experience damages from a natural disaster, the government provides funds to reduce these damages. For instance, rather than costing someone $30,000 to repair his house following flooding, the cost to the individual might be just $10,000 because the government would provide low-cost loans or money to rebuild.

Federal government disaster relief aid began in 1936 when Congress passed the Flood Control Act. From then until the 1980s, expenditures by the government on disaster relief rose continually. In 1980, Congress decided to try a different approach—providing insurance rather than just shipping dollars after a disaster occurred. The program it created is called the National Federal Insurance Program (NFIP) and is run by the Federal Emergency Management Assistance Agency (FEMA). The program offers flood insurance to any locale that has agreed to work with FEMA. Participation in the NFIP is based on an agreement between local communities and FEMA that states if a community will adopt and enforce a floodplain management ordinance to reduce future flood risks to new construction in Special Flood Hazard Areas, the Federal Government will make flood insurance available within the community. Government programs, whether they are in the form of disaster relief or subsidized insurance, alter the relative prices of river and hill living, reducing the price of living in the more risky (river) areas. As a result, more people live in those risky areas than would be the case if the government was not providing assistance. And in contrast to private insurance, it does not matter how risky one's location is, as one can get insurance through the NFIP.

In general, more people live in the hurricane-prone areas than would be the case if government-subsidized insurance and disaster relief funds were not available.

RECAP

1. Consumer equilibrium occurs when the consumer has allocated her budget among goods and services such that the marginal utility of the last dollar spent on any item is the same as that spent on any other item.
2. If people would rather live near a river, they will do so unless it is just too expensive relative to a less preferred location.
3. When something changes the relative prices of different locations, then some people will change where they locate. Government disaster assistance makes the relative cost of living in a disaster-prone area less than it would be without the government assistance.

3. The Oil Industry[3]

When a natural disaster strikes some part of oil-producing machinery, it has a global impact. Approximately 4,000 oil-producing structures are located in the Gulf of Mexico. These structures range from single-well to large multi-well installations. The oil and natural gas extracted from the wells is fed into 33,000 miles of underwater pipelines that lead to refineries along the coast. Approximately 35 percent of the entire United States' oil and 20 percent of its natural gas are extracted and transported to refineries via pipeline in the Gulf of Mexico. In addition, 10 percent of U.S. oil *imports* come into the United States via the Gulf. Katrina and Rita ripped through this complex. Approximately 25 percent of the platforms were damaged by hurricane-force winds, and 30 of the platforms were lost. The combination of damage to platforms and to the underwater pipelines caused a loss of as much as 1.4 million barrels of oil per day and 8 billion cubic feet of natural gas per day—nearly 80 percent of the production from the Gulf region, or 20 percent of the total U.S. production.

3.a. Crude Oil

Crude oil is extracted from the ground, placed into containers, transported to refineries, and then refined into various petroleum products, including gasoline. Crude oil is measured in barrels that hold 42 gallons. In 2003, one barrel of crude oil, when refined, yielded 19.7 gallons of finished motor gasoline, as well as smaller quantities of many other petroleum products, as noted in Table 1.

3.b. Crude Oil Prices

The pattern of crude prices since 1970 is shown in Figure 3. Until the late 1970s, the price of crude was pretty stable, at around $15 per barrel in constant 2004 dollars.

---

[3] While the natural gas industry was also damaged by the hurricanes, the issues involved are not much different from those of crude oil and gasoline. Thus, the natural gas market is not discussed here.

TABLE 1

Output from Crude Oil

Petroleum Products Yielded from One Barrel of Crude	
Product	**Gallons**
Finished Motor Gasoline	19.69
Distillate Fuel Oil	9.70
Kero-Type Jet Fuel	3.99
Residual Fuel Oil	1.76
Still Gas	1.89
Petroleum Coke	2.14
Liquefied Refinery Gas	1.76
Asphalt and Road Oil	1.34
Naptha for Feedstocks	0.63
Other Oils for Feedstocks	0.50
Lubricants	0.46
Special Naphthas	0.13
Kerosene	0.17
Miscellaneous Products	0.17
Finished Aviation Gasoline	0.04
Waxes	0.04
Total	**44.41**

FIGURE 3

Crude Oil Prices, 1970–2006

The price of crude oil rose from June 2005 to about $60 a gallon prior to Katrina. With Katrina, prices hit $70 a barrel and then fell to about $62, only to be driven to $68 with Rita. *SOURCE:* WTRG Economics. www.wtrg.com. Accessed October 2005.

NYMEX Crude Oil Futures Close (Front Month)

Oct 1, 2004 - Oct 7, 2005

WTRG Economics ©2005
www.wtrg.com
(479) 293-4081

—— Close

Events in the Middle East brought about oil shortages and large price increases in the late 1970s and through the mid-1980s. Then the price of crude oil re-stabilized and remained reasonably stable until 1999; it has risen since then. In late June 2005, the price of crude oil had reached a high of $60.95 per barrel. The devastation of Hurricane Katrina drove the price up to over $70; within a week, the price had declined to the mid-$60 range. When Rita hit two weeks later, crude prices again jumped up, but when it was found that little damage had been sustained by the refineries and oil platforms, prices returned to the pre-Rita level.

3.b.1. Demand   *"Step right up, Ladies and Gentleman. In this bottle is a remedy of wonderful efficacy. Its curative powers are calculated to remove pain and alleviate much human suffering and disease."* Just what was that elixir, commonly referred to as "snake oil," proffered by traveling hucksters of the 19th century? It was petroleum. Petroleum's use as a medicine has a long history. Ancient Persians, 10th century Sumatrans, and pre-Columbian Indians all believed that crude oil had medicinal benefits. Marco Polo found it used in the Caspian Sea region to treat camels for mange, and the first oil exported from Venezuela (in 1539) was intended as a gout treatment for the Holy Roman Emperor Charles V.

Although the belief that petroleum had restorative powers was widespread, the demand for it was on a relatively small scale. In fact, until the late 19th century, an oil discovery was viewed as frustrating: When pioneers in the American West dug wells to find water or brine, they were disappointed when they struck oil. But the invention of the kerosene lamp changed all that. Invented in 1854, the kerosene lamp created the first large-scale demand for petroleum. (Kerosene was made first from coal, but by the late 1880s, most was derived from crude oil.) Demand grew dramatically as the gasoline engine was developed and used in automobiles. Gasoline is now the number one use of petroleum. Approximately 55 percent of crude oil pulled from the ground is used for gasoline.

The demand for crude oil is essentially the demand for gasoline. That demand is very price-inelastic in the short term because there are no good substitutes—you might share rides with others, use mass transit, or rely on your bicycle or feet for transportation, but these are not reliable alternatives for many people. The price elasticity of demand for gasoline in the short run is about 0.2. This means that as the price of gas increases by 10 percent, the quantity demanded declines by 0.2 (10 percent), or 2 percent. The price at the pump immediately following Katrina was about $3 a gallon, $1 higher than in September 2004. This is a 33 percent increase. Given the price elasticity of demand, what would a 33 percent increase in prices at the pump mean for gas purchases? The quantity of gasoline demanded would decline by just 6.6 percent. Although expenditures are slightly lower, the prices are so much higher that total expenditures on gasoline rose by about 24 percent.

The greater household expenditures on gasoline mean that expenditures on other items would decline now or in the future (as debt created today to buy things was paid off). It would also mean that people would begin seeking alternatives—if prices are expected to remain high for years to come, then substitutes to gasoline-powered automobiles as well as other transportation modes would be sought after by consumers.

The long-run price elasticity of demand is much less inelastic than the short run. But how long is the long run? Most believe it is decades rather than years. Yet, rising prices do have immediate effects—in the month following Katrina and Rita and their impact on gasoline prices, the demand for automobiles changed dramatically. Fewer people wanted SUVs, and more people wanted fuel-efficient cars.

3.b.2. Supply   The world's top six crude oil-producing countries (in order) are Saudi Arabia, Russia, United States, Iran, and China and Mexico both tied for fifth place. The United States accounts for about 8 percent, Russia 12 percent, and the Organization of Petroleum Exporting Countries (OPEC) 40 percent of the total crude oil produced in the world. OPEC was formed in 1960 with five founding members: Iran, Iraq, Kuwait, Saudi Arabia, and Venezuela. By the end of 1971, six other nations had joined the group: Qatar, Indonesia, Libya, United Arab Emirates, Algeria, and Nigeria.

Over one-fourth of the crude oil produced in the United States is produced offshore in the Gulf of Mexico. The five largest oil-producing companies in the United States— ExxonMobil, BP-Amoco, ChevronTexaco, Phillips-Tosco, and Marathon—account for about 65 percent of the U.S. gasoline sales. Globally, the market is dominated by state-owned (i.e., government-owned) companies. Half of the biggest oil producers are state-controlled, and over 77 percent of the world's 1.1 trillion barrels in proven oil reserves is controlled by governments that significantly restrict access to international companies. Much of those reserves are in the hands of countries belonging to OPEC. The country with the world's largest reserves is Saudi Arabia, which has its own national oil company, Saudi Aramco, and does not allow foreign companies to pump oil.

The price elasticity of *supply* is inelastic in the short run but much less so in the long run. Surging prices induce consumers to attempt to reduce their future demand for oil by better insulating new homes, increasing insulation in older homes, using more energy efficient industrial processes, and purchasing automobiles that get better gas mileage. The higher prices also result in increased exploration and production outside of OPEC. From 1980 to 1986, non-OPEC production increased 10 million barrels per day, and the second largest recoverable oil field in the world, second to Saudi Arabia, which exists in Alberta, Canada, is being brought on line. The oil there is in a semi-solid form known as bitumen and is mixed with sand. The deposits are either mined in open pits or in mines that have to be injected with steam to turn the bitumen into a liquid form that can be brought to the surface. At $30 or even $40 per barrel, it has been too costly in the past to extract oil from the Alberta fields. But with the price of crude expected to remain above $45, the oil from this area can be profitably extracted.

While Hurricanes Katrina and Rita affected oil supplies extracted and refined in the Gulf Coast of the United States, it is necessary to recognize that crude oil is a global market. Oil pumped in Nigeria or Saudi Arabia may be transported to refineries in the United States, Malaysia, China, or elsewhere. This means that the price of crude is determined in the world market; it is not a distinct U.S. market. So when the United States lost about 25 percent of its Gulf Coast oil production, the world oil price was forced up. The U.S. oil companies had to acquire oil from non-U.S. sources to make up for the amount lost from Gulf Coast production.

3.b.3. Gasoline   The price of a gallon of gasoline at the pump depends on the price of crude oil, taxes, cost of refining, and the profits that the oil companies take out. The price of crude is the largest part—when the price of gasoline was about $1.50, the cost of crude was $0.65—about 43 percent of the price of gasoline. Taxes can add as much as 15 percent to the price per gallon (cpg). According to the American Petroleum Institute (API), Alaska had the lowest gasoline taxes in the country, at 26.4 cpg (total federal and state), while New York and Hawaii had the highest, at 58.0 cpg and 57.2 cpg, respectively. California is third highest at 56.6 cpg. According to Figure 4, taxes constituted about 15 percent of the price of a gallon of gasoline in 2003; at a 2005 price of $3, taxes would account for a smaller percentage of the price. The Federal tax is 18.4 cents per gallon in all states. State taxes are levied in different ways. Some states levy a flat cents-per-gallon, while others

FIGURE 4

What Goes Into the Price of Gas

The price of a gallon of gasoline depends primarily on the price of crude oil. In addition, refining costs, distribution and marketing costs, and federal and state taxes are passed along to consumers. *Source:* Energy Information Administration. http://www.eia.doe.gov/ Accessed October 26, 2005.

What We Pay For In a Gallon of Regular Gasoline
(September 2005)
Retail Price: $2.90/gallon

Taxes — 15%
Distribution & Marketing — 8%
Refining — 27%
Crude Oil — 50%

apply a percent of pump price. So as the price of crude oil rises and the price of a gallon of gasoline rises, taxes will rise in some states yet remain the same in others.

Although crude oil accounts for nearly one-half of gas prices, gasoline is not the global market that crude oil is. Government regulations impact gasoline prices. For example, environmental regulations adopted by various state and local agencies require refiners to manufacture a wide variety of gasoline types to meet federal and state emissions regulations. Gasoline sold in California is not the same as gasoline sold in Arizona. This inhibits the ability of refiners and marketers to move supplies from one region to another. As a result, the price of supply is much less elastic than it otherwise would be, i.e., price changes do not bring on additional quantities supplied in the short term. If there is a demand surge or a supply shock, the price will shoot up more than if supply was price elastic.

3.c. The Impact of the Hurricanes

Gasoline prices rose to a national average exceeding $3 per gallon immediately after Katrina landed, as shown in Figures 5a and 5b. Katrina decreased the supply of gasoline because it damaged the refineries and pipelines. Rita had a much smaller impact on the supply of gasoline. The price of gasoline declined but at a much slower rate than it had risen. Legislators and attorney generals around the country were holding inquiries into price gouging and calling for price controls and penalties on oil/gas companies.

Gasoline prices rise very fast when an emergency or international event reduces oil supplies, but they do not decline as quickly once the supply of crude oil recovers. You can see in Figures 5a and 5b how the price rose between 8/29 and 9/2 (Katrina's impact) from about $2.58 per gallon to $3.08 and then took from 9/2 to 9/9 to decline just to $2.98 per gallon. The reason that price increases occur more rapidly than price decreases is due primarily to the structure of the gasoline industry and the price elasticities of demand and supply. When crude prices rise, the costs of supplying gasoline rise. If a gas station is to maintain its profits, it has to raise

Effect of Hurricanes Katrina and Rita on U.S. Gas Prices

Source: http://www.newjerseygasprices.com/retail_price_chart.aspx; http://tonto.eia.doe.gov/dnav/pet/hist/mg_rt_usw.htm

Daily price of gasoline from 10/24/04 through 10/07/05 in Alaska and Washington, D.C., compared with the U.S. average

Gas prices were rising before the hurricanes but jumped considerably as a result of the damage to oil-producing structures. *Source:* http://www.newjerseygasprices.com/retail_price_chart.aspx; http://tonto.eia.doe.gov/dnav/pet/hist/mg_rt_usw.htm

prices as well. If consumers could simply switch from gasoline to some other way to get around, the stations would not be able to pass the increased costs along to consumers. But because demand is so price inelastic, the gas stations are able to increase prices without losing many sales. So whenever their costs rise, the gas stations pass along their increased costs immediately to the customer. The price inelasticity also means that gasoline prices decrease slowly following a drop in crude prices. Competition does eventually force prices back down. As the cost of supplying gasoline declines, a few stations lower prices a few cents just to pull in more traffic. Competitors follow, not wanting to lose customers. This competition occurs until prices gradually work their way back down to the earlier prices (assuming crude returns to its prior price). While the retailers may make a greater profit for a few days, competition eventually forces them back to their original profit margins.

The price of gasoline actually declines more rapidly than we might expect given the price inelasticity of demand. The reason is that gasoline is not the most profitable aspect of a gas station; in fact, gasoline may serve as a loss leader for the stations. A loss leader is an item that is sold near or even below cost in order to attract customers who purchase more profitable items. Gas stations make the bulk of their profits on the convenience store associated with the station, not on fuel. Thus, stations have an incentive to match or beat the gas prices of nearby stations in order to draw you in as a customer. The demand for gasoline at a single station is quite a bit more elastic than the demand for gasoline in general.

4. Policy Response to Gasoline Price Increases

The average U.S. gasoline price increase of 20 percent after Katrina struck was primarily the result of the expectation of reduced supplies and higher crude oil prices. Some stations charged several dollars more than that, and some ran out of gas. Officials called for price controls as well as penalties for those stations raising prices above the "fair" level. Some suggested that taxes on gasoline at the pump should be rescinded. Officials also asked the public to conserve and not to "top off the tank." What do these policies mean, and do they work?

4.a. Price Gouging

Consider Figure 6, which illustrates the demand for and supply of gasoline in a specific location in the United States. The price on August 27, 2005, was $2.54 per gallon. This is the price determined by demand and supply. You could see the listed price on the signs outside the station—$2.54 (and 0.99 cents)—and know that when purchasing regular, unleaded, that is the price you would pay. You would also know that the station would not run out of gas—you could buy as much as you were willing and able to.

FIGURE 6

Equilibrium, Effects of Hurricane Katrina, and Price Controls

The natural disaster damaged oil-producing structures, thereby causing the supply of oil to decrease and the equilibrium price to increase to $3. A price fixed by government to $2.54 causes a shortage. Demand is increased as drivers change their behavior and "top off" their tanks.

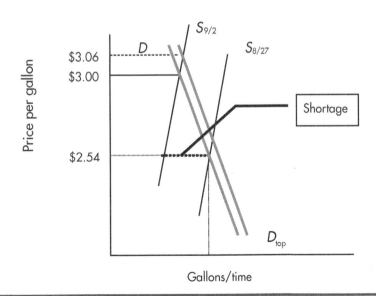

When Katrina struck, the expected supply of gasoline declined, shifting the supply curve inward to $S_{8/27}$. The market price rose to $3.00 per gallon. This is the market price, determined by demand and supply. The price rose primarily because of the actual or expected reduced supply of gasoline. People began "topping off the tank" because they were afraid gas would cost a lot more the next day and that stations might run out of gas. By topping off their tanks, they were demanding gasoline during a time period in which they otherwise would not be demanding. If the demand before topping off was D in Figure 6, then topping off would mean the demand curve shifts out, as shown by D_{top}. This drove the price up even more, to $3.06, as shown in Figure 6.

Although the price increase was substantial, it was what demand and supply were dictating. The higher price means a lower quantity demanded—people would drive less and do what they could to consume less gasoline. They would "conserve" to avoid having to pay the high price. But the public and government officials called this price gouging. Typical language in price-gouging legislation is similar to Florida's law that states:

> In the wake of natural disaster, essentials—such as food, ice, generators, lanterns, lumber, etc.—may be in short supply. Charging **exorbitant** or **excessive** prices for these and other necessities following a disaster is not only unethical, it's illegal. It is illegal to charge **unconscionable** prices for goods or services following a declared state of emergency. Individuals or businesses found guilty of price-gouging could face fines up to $1,000 per violation.

Notice that the words to define *gouging* are "exorbitant," "excessive," and "unconscionable." What do these words mean? Who defines them?

Following Katrina, there were reports that at a station or two, people would drive up to the pump and see a notice that the price was double the listed price—the gas was selling for $6 per gallon. Is this price gouging? If you drove up to the pump and saw this sign, what would you do? Most people would drive off and find another station. But, if there were no other stations available so that the customer either had to pay the very high price or not get gasoline, would that be price gouging? A grocery store that raises the price of bottled water from $1 to $20 a bottle because, due to an emergency, drinking water is unavailable and there are no other sources of bottled water would surely be considered to be engaging in price gouging. Yet, even in this case, notice that demand and supply have determined the $20 price; some consumers are willing and able to pay the price and are grateful to have the water. An equilibrium price is called price gouging if the equilibrium price is the result of a temporary situation of increased demand and/or reduced supply resulting from an emergency and if that price is generally considered "unfair" by customers.

There is an old saying in the business world: "If you gouge them at Christmas time, they won't be back in Spring." This means that if you charge what customers think is an unfair price because of the increased demand during the Christmas season, the customers will remember that unfavorably and will refuse to do business with you again. Similarly, if customers are treated in a way they believe to be unfair by a gas station during an emergency, they are unlikely to do business with that station once the emergency situation has been resolved. Price gouging, therefore, would seem to be a temporary strategy undertaken by someone who does not expect to do business with the same customers in the future. Anyone who relies on repeat business would be extremely shortsighted to gouge the customers.

Should price gouging be illegal? Twenty-three states have laws against price gouging, with others considering similar laws. The laws read as noted above, using words like "unconscionable," "excessive," and so on. Who defines what these words are? What is an unconscionable price? The legal approach is to look at the cost of inputs and then determine what a reasonable return on those inputs would be. Suppose that the crude oil, taxes, and other costs of gasoline add up to $2.20 a gallon. If the profit rate that is typically earned by stations is 10 percent, then a reasonable price would be $2.42 per gallon. If the station is charging $3.50 per gallon, that might be considered unconscionable.

There is no doubt that gasoline supplies were constrained by Hurricanes Katrina and Rita. About 12 percent of the nation's refining capacity was damaged, and the pipelines that deliver fuel from the Gulf Coast were offline for several days. So, how should the limited pool of gasoline be rationed? In a free market, scarce goods are typically rationed by price. People who value gasoline most are willing to pay higher prices than those who value it less. Those who value it more highly and are able to purchase it get the gasoline; others go without. Some find this terribly unfair. The poor motorist may value the gasoline as much as the rich motorist, but his willingness to pay is constrained by his inability to pay. And even when he does pay, the economic pain caused by those high prices is far beyond anything inflicted on the rich. Accordingly, price controls are offered as a means to cushion the blow on the poor and to ensure a more equitable distribution of fuel.

Price controls come at a cost, however. Lower prices result in more quantity demanded than do higher prices. That's why the first thing we notice about price controls is that they lead to shortages, as illustrated in Figure 6. If the price of $2.54 becomes the fixed price (i.e., the highest price allowed to be charged) and if the equilibrium price is $3, a shortage exists. A shortage in the case of gasoline means that customers will be unable to find stations that have gasoline or that long lines will exist at stations that have not sold out of their supplies. In addition, less will be supplied to the stations, because the gas is being sold at a loss.

Price controls are policy responses to rising prices that cause more problems. The price set below the intersection of the supply-and-demand curves causes the supply of whatever you are attempting to keep inexpensive to disappear. In 1973, for example, when President Nixon imposed price controls on oil, the result was very long gasoline lines or stations without gasoline. And when California Governor Gray Davis refused in 2000–2001 to lift retail price controls on electricity, blackouts followed.

Price controls are also inefficient when it comes to allocating fuel among competing users. Rather than price being the allocation mechanism, it becomes first-come, first-served. Those who don't really need gasoline have as much chance of getting fuel as those who desperately need it. Whoever gets in line first gets the gas.

Allowing prices to rise to the equilibrium level sets off an economic chain reaction that remedies the shortage quicker than any conceivable government plan to do likewise. That is because $2 gasoline and exhortations of moral duty from government officials to conserve fuel will not produce the same degree of conservation that $6 gasoline would deliver. Likewise, pleas to the oil industry to "help thy fellow man" will not do as much for getting gasoline to the market as the promise of a profit to suppliers. As Figure 6 illustrates, allowing the price to rise to the equilibrium level reduces the quantity demanded and increases quantity supplied. Fixing prices below equilibrium reduces quantity supplied while stimulating quantity demanded.

4.b. Reducing Taxes

Many state legislators and governors reacted to the rising gasoline prices by suggesting that state and federal governments repeal taxes on gasoline. Others rejected these pleas by noting that the demand for gasoline is very price inelastic in the short term, making a tax cut ineffectual on the price of gasoline. Who is correct?

If a $0.20 per gallon tax is repealed, the gas station manager must decide whether to keep the $0.20 per gallon or to give it to customers. Knowing that if he doesn't pass the tax cut on to consumers, his profits will rise while sales don't really change, the station manager has little incentive to lower his prices. But if one station lowers its price by a few cents and attracts more customers, what will other stations do? Can we argue that demand is very price inelastic?

When the Governor of Georgia suspended Georgia's gasoline tax effective midnight September 2, 2005, the retail price in Georgia immediately fell relative to the prices in the neighboring states of Florida and South Carolina. This does not sound like a price inelastic demand. In fact, while the demand for gasoline is very price inelastic, the demand for gasoline at any particular gas station is not so inelastic. One station might find that it attracts business from other stations when it lowers its price by a few cents; that is, when the price is reduced and demand is price elastic, the quantity demanded will increase and total revenue will rise. If costs haven't changed, the station's profit will increase. A higher profit by one station will attract competition by other stations, who in turn will cut prices.

4.c. Why Wasn't the City Prepared?

In the wake of Hurricane Katrina, President Bush declared that a "Great City will Rise Again." Lawmakers proposed to spend about $200 billion on disaster relief. In addition, Senator Kennedy proposed a $150 billion government agency specifically dedicated to Gulf area infrastructure. Economics says that questions need to be asked about these spending proposals. Do they make sense? Do they cause more harm than good?

The incentives that individuals, companies, and local governments have to locate plants, oil-drilling rigs, refineries, factories, homes, roads, levees, and bridges is affected by government insurance and subsidies. Location decisions would make more economic sense if those making these decisions had to bear the full social cost of any damages to their property and person from a disaster. Without government programs, greater insurance premiums in areas that are prone to hurricanes, earthquakes, tsunamis, and other disasters would reflect the greater risk to life and property in these areas. The expected loss for those not insuring would rise in proportion to the greater risk. People, companies, and governments would then build homes, roads, businesses, etc., in disaster-prone regions only if the benefits exceeded the full cost of damages. But when the government fully repairs any damages and spends about $75,000 per person residing in the Gulf Coast region to rebuild, the incentives are changed.

Why wasn't New Orleans better prepared for the disaster? Why hadn't the levees been rebuilt and other protective measures constructed? For years, the Army Corps of Engineers had stated that the chance in any given year that a storm would inundate New Orleans was between one in 200 and one in 300. If the cost of a flooded New Orleans is $200 billion, and the annual chance of that flood is one in 200, then the expected cost each year is $1 billion ($200 billion/200). Thus, it would pay the residents and businesses to spend some amount less than $1 billion a year to keep such a flood from happening. But $1 billion is a hefty price tag, averaging $1,000 per person per year. Would a family of four rather spend $4,000 a year on flood levees or on food and recreation? Would an elected official rather spend money on a new hotel or gambling casino, new roads, new bridges, and other infrastructure or on levees to protect the city in the event of a hurricane with a 1 in 200 chance of striking?

1. The market for crude oil is a global market. The United States supplies only about 8 percent of total crude oil, and of that, about 25 percent was damaged in the Gulf Coast area by the hurricanes.

2. The market for gasoline is dependent on the market for crude oil, since the price of gasoline is about 45 percent of crude oil. Yet, gasoline supplies and prices depend on local conditions. Government rules and regulations impact the price and supply of gasoline.

3. When the crude-producing area of the Gulf Coast was damaged by Hurricanes Katrina and Rita, world crude oil prices rose from about $60 per barrel to nearly $70 per barrel for a short while. A week or so after Rita, the price had returned to a little over $60 per barrel. The price of gasoline rose to $3 per gallon, rising immediately when Katrina struck and falling to only about $2.95 several weeks after Rita hit.

4. The demand for gasoline is price inelastic, about 0.2. Thus, when costs of supplying gasoline temporarily rise, the cost is passed on to customers. Competition slowly drives the price back down.

5. The demand for gasoline at a single gas station is substantially more price elastic than the demand for gasoline in general.

6. Price gouging is a normative term referring to prices that rise during emergencies to levels that are considered unfair or unconscionable.

7. Price controls lead to shortages.

8. Decreasing the tax on gasoline means a lower cost of supplying gasoline and higher profits to gas stations. But, competition among stations eventually lowers the price to customers. When the tax on gasoline is reduced at some stations but not others, some of the reduced costs will be passed on to customers as the lower-tax stations attempt to attract customers from the higher-taxed stations.

9. Rebuilding and preparing for future disasters makes little economic sense to individuals if they have to pay the price. But if government assistance and subsidies provide the funding, rebuilding in the disaster-prone areas will occur.

5. Macroeconomic Implications of Disasters

Disasters such as hurricanes, earthquakes, and terrorist attacks have implications for macroeconomic concerns such as incomes and employment. The effects are not all negative, as the harmful initial effects of disasters may later be followed by stimulative effects associated with rebuilding and restoring housing, commercial activity, and infrastructure such as highways, bridges, and communication systems. The Center for Research on the Epidemiology of Disasters defines a natural disaster as an event where 10 or more people are killed; 100 or more people are affected, injured, or left homeless; significant damage is incurred; and a declaration of a state of emergency and/or an appeal for international assistance is made. Table 2 lists the disasters with the greatest number of deaths since 1980. The death toll from recent disasters has, at times, been well beyond what anyone could have expected: 250,000 killed by a tsunami in the Indian Ocean in 2004; 30,000 killed in an earthquake in Pakistan in 2005; 14,802 killed due to extreme heat in France in 1998; 30,000 dead in Venezuelan floods in 1999; and 138,866 dead from a windstorm in Bangladesh in

Disasters with the Greatest Loss of Life Since 1980

Type of Disaster	Year	Death Count	Country
Earthquake	1990	40,000	Iran
	2005	30,000	Pakistan
	2001	20,005	India
	1999	17,980	Turkey
Extreme Temperature	2003	14,802	France
	1998	2,541	India
	2003	2,099	Portugal
	2003	2,045	U.K.
	2002	1,030	India
	1987	1,000	Greece
Flooding	1999	30,000	Venezuela
	1980	6,200	China
	1998	3,656	China
Landslide	1987	640	Colombia
	2002	472	Nepal
	1995	400	India
Windstorm	1991	138,866	Bangladesh
	1998	14,600	Honduras
	1985	10,000	Bangladesh
Industrial	1984	2,500	India
	1998	1,082	Nigeria
	1984	508	Brazil
Tsunami	2004	275,000	Indonesia, Sri Lanka, India, Thailand, and South Africa

Sources: Matthew E. Kahn, "The Death Toll from Natural Disasters: The Role of Income, Geography, and Institutions," *Review of Economics and Statistics,* May 2005; World Health Organization, "Climate Change and Adaption Strategies for Human Health," www.euro.who.int; and Wikipedia, the free encyclopedia, "2004 Indian Ocean Earthquake," http://en.wikipedia.org/wiki/Main_Page.

1991. Besides the human life lost, the damage resulting from disasters imposes huge costs in terms of lower living standards and suffering.

5.a. Disasters as a Supply Shock

Hurricane Katrina serves as a case study of the adverse effects of disasters on aggregate supply. In addition to the direct effects on the supply of energy, interrupted flows of imports coming through the port of New Orleans meant reduced supplies of steel, coal, chemicals, fertilizers, and concrete, as well as other key material. The effect of reduced supplies of material needed to produce other goods and services meant that the ability of the U.S. economy to produce new output was temporarily lowered.

FIGURE 7

The Aggregate Supply Effect of Disasters

The figure shows a decrease in aggregate supply as productive capacity is decreased due to the disaster. This raises the equilibrium price level and lowers the equilibrium level of real GDP.

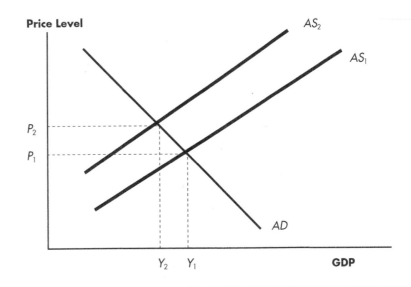

Figure 7 illustrates the effect of natural disasters on aggregate supply. This reduction in aggregate supply has adverse effects on the level of employment and income and temporarily reduces economic growth. We see that the equilibrium level of real GDP falls from Y_1 to Y_2. In addition, a reduction in aggregate supply puts upward pressure on prices as the equilibrium price level rises from P_1 to P_2, leading to a temporarily higher inflation rate. Of course, the equilibrium level of real GDP and price depends upon both aggregate demand and aggregate supply. So, we must also consider any potential effects on aggregate demand of disasters.

5.b. Disasters as a Demand Shock

Disasters destroy businesses along with opportunities for employment and income they represent. Individuals who lose their jobs as a result of a disaster have lower incomes and must reduce their expenditures. Owners and employees of New Orleans restaurants and hotels suffered in the aftermath of Hurricane Katrina; even establishments not seriously damaged experienced diminished business from lack of customers due to the prolonged loss of residents and visitors to the city. Employees and owners of business firms that suffer serious loss associated with disasters must rely on government subsidies and private charity to maintain a minimal standard of living. In turn, the firms and workers who would have been selling goods and services to these displaced workers lose business and *their* incomes and living standards suffer. In this sense, disasters have effects that can extend beyond the area that directly takes the hit. Reduced spending from residents of a disaster region has a ripple effect that spreads throughout the economy—lowering incomes, employment, and living standards.

Figure 8 illustrates the effects of disasters on aggregate demand. Initially, *AD* falls from AD_1 to AD_2 following the disaster, but over time, as rebuilding creates new jobs, incomes start rising and *AD* increases. The net effect may be positive, negative, or neutral on the equilibrium level of real GDP and price. In Figure 8 there is a neutral effect once the short-run decreases in *AD* due to destruction of jobs and incomes are

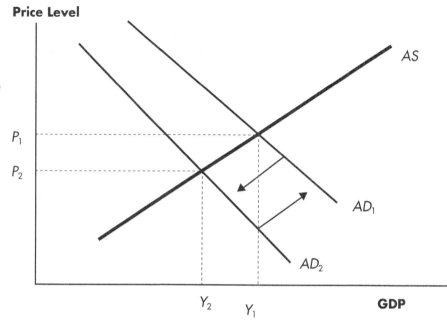

FIGURE 8

The Aggregate Demand Effects of Disasters

Initially, disasters are associated with a decrease in *AD,* as in the decrease from AD_1 to AD_2, due to the destruction of jobs and incomes. This lowers the equilibrium level of real GDP and income. Over time, the rebuilding effort creates new jobs and incomes, and aggregate demand rises to a higher level. In this example, *AD* rises back to where it started, AD_1, so that real GDP and price return to their initial level. In reality, *AD* could shift to where the new price level and real GDP are higher or lower than initially.

offset by the longer-run effects of new jobs and incomes associated with the rebuilding efforts. *AD* rises from AD_2 back to the initial aggregate demand curve AD_1 so that the original equilibrium levels of price and real GDP are restored. In reality, the increase in *AD* may be less than the initial decrease so that even with the rebuilding effect on aggregate demand, real GDP is still lower than before the disaster.

What sort of real world numbers may be associated with aggregate demand reductions due to disasters? The economic costs of Hurricanes Charley, Frances, Ivan, and Jeanne that struck the United States (largely Florida) in 2004 are estimated to include −$5.5 billion to proprietor's income, −$14.6 billion to rental income, and −$93 billion to corporate profits. These are substantial losses to aggregate demand that impacted lives and incomes of many workers both in and beyond the directly affected region.

5.c. Economic Growth Effects of Disasters

Economic growth results from combining labor and capital with technology to produce goods and services. While we normally do not think of technology (ways of producing) as being affected by disasters, growth can be reduced due to a reduction in the quantity of labor or the quantity of capital. A disaster may destroy significant productive capacity of a region and country. For instance, if factories are left inoperable by the disaster and workers are killed or displaced, then both capital and labor shrink and output falls both in the current period and in the near future.

The U.S. Congressional Budget Office estimated that Hurricane Katrina will reduce U.S. economic growth by 0.5%–1.0% for the second half of 2005. This means that if the economy would have grown at a rate of, say, 3.3% (annual rate of growth), the hurricane will reduce that growth rate to around 2.3%–2.8%. While such a small impact may seem trivial, for an economy the size of the United States, this would translate into a potential loss of $123 billion in output of goods and services. This is output lost forever due to the impact of the hurricane. The reduction in the growth of the economy is likely to be slowed beyond the immediate period until the effects of rebuilding are well underway.

RECAP

1. Disasters reduce aggregate supply, which raises the equilibrium price level and lowers the equilibrium level of real GDP.
2. The initial effect of a disaster is to lower aggregate demand as the loss of jobs and incomes reduces spending. Disasters can also lead to later increases in aggregate demand associated with the rebuilding effort. This will tend to raise the equilibrium level of real GDP and price.
3. The net effect of a disaster on aggregate demand will depend upon the relative magnitudes of the shifts in initial fall and later rise in *AD*.
4. In the short run, economic growth is lowered due to a disaster. This may have long-lasting impacts on living standards.

6. Economic Policy Effects of Disasters

Macroeconomic policy is comprised of monetary and fiscal policy.[4] Fiscal policy refers to government spending and taxes, whereas monetary policy refers to control of money, credit, and financial conditions. In the United States, fiscal policy is the responsibility of the President and Congress, and monetary policy is managed by the Federal Reserve. We explore the impact of disasters on macroeconomic policy next.

6.a. Fiscal Policy

Disasters affect government budgets since costs for emergency and humanitarian aid to the affected region are components of government spending that are usually not anticipated and, therefore, not included in planned spending. While a disaster is clearly devastating to the area in which it occurred, its effects on the entire U.S. economy may not be so obvious. For instance, the three states most affected by Hurricane Katrina account for the following shares of U.S. GDP: Louisiana, 1.2%; Mississippi, 0.7%; and Alabama, 1.2%. One might conclude that the costs of the hurricane borne by U.S. taxpayers might be quite small. However, the initial costs to the federal government, and thus to U.S. taxpayers, were $62 billion. Such costs include the obvious costs of rebuilding the Port of New Orleans, a critically important port for the United States, the cost of rebuilding infrastructure such as transportation systems, and the costs associated with providing support in the form of income subsidies and housing for people displaced by the disaster. For example, in the period immediately following Hurricane Katrina, the number of people filing claims for unemployment benefits related to the hurricane was estimated to be 68,000.

---

[4] See Chapters 12 and 14 in Macroeconomics and Economics.

One possible implication of an increase in spending for disaster relief could be that other worthy programs face reduced funding or receive no funding. Cutbacks in social programs, defense, education, or any of the multitudes of government-financed items may suffer if the unexpected rise in spending associated with a disaster forces reductions elsewhere.

Fiscal policy refers to government spending and taxing. Taxes tend to fall following a disaster because working people and business firms pay taxes. Unemployed workers and closed businesses result in lower tax revenue, as income taxes fall with declines in income. In addition, when people are forced out of jobs and businesses are forced to close, sales taxes fall. Such taxes are a critical component of local government spending that pays for local services such as schools, fire, and police protection.

If government spending increases and tax revenues fall, the difference between spending and revenue, the government budget deficit will rise. Governments must fund deficits by borrowing. When the deficit is unexpectedly large due to a disaster, then governmental borrowing will be unexpectedly large. The cost of borrowed funds is the interest rate that the borrower must pay. So other things being equal, if government borrows more, the cost of borrowing (i.e., the interest rate) rises in order to induce people to lend more money to the government. Interest rate increases fueled by governmental borrowing can have adverse effects on the rest of the economy, as higher costs of borrowing may lead business firms and households to cut back on their spending plans. For instance, a business firm that was planning to borrow to finance the construction of a new factory may decide to postpone such plans if the cost of borrowing rises. Similarly, a household that was planning to buy a new house or car may decide to postpone the purchase if the cost of borrowing the money to finance the purchase rises. In this way, higher interest rates resulting from governmental borrowing may "crowd out" private spending and lower the level of economic activity that would have otherwise existed.

6.b. Monetary Policy

Monetary policy is the control of money and credit. In the United States, this is the job of the Federal Reserve. In times of disaster, central banks have the job of ensuring the economy has sufficient money and credit available to support continued spending. For instance, immediately after the terrorist attacks of September 11, 2001, some banks and other financial institutions were temporarily closed due to damage and disruption. This meant that the money that would typically have flowed from these institutions to other financial institutions, other business firms, and households was interrupted. For instance, suppose large Bank A owes Bank B a payment of $1 billion and Bank A is temporarily closed due to a disaster. This means that Bank B will not receive the payment as originally scheduled. The problem is that Bank B must make payments to others, and if it does not receive the expected payment from Bank A, then it cannot pay those to whom it owes money. This so-called "systemic risk"—that one bank may not make good on its debts, causing a ripple effect of payment defaults throughout the banking system—could lead to a global financial meltdown. In order to prevent this from happening after 9/11, the Federal Reserve injected very large sums of money into the banking system to ensure that all banks would be able to meet their obligations.

When a central bank is concerned about a disaster leading to a recession, or contraction in real GDP, it can increase the money supply and/or lower interest rates to stimulate spending. This leads to an increase in aggregate demand and, other things being equal, a higher equilibrium real GDP. In Figure 8, we saw that a decrease in aggregate demand associated with a disaster causes real GDP to fall as well as the price level. In this case, the appropriate monetary policy would be fairly clear: increase the money supply, lower interest rates, and stimulate spending so that aggregate demand increases. However, in Figure 7, the appropriate monetary policy is not as clear. If aggregate supply falls, real GDP falls, which would seem to call for a stimulative monetary policy. But the equilibrium price level rises, which might lead to greater inflation, so that by stimulating the economy the central bank could contribute to higher inflation.

After Hurricanes Katrina and Rita, the Federal Reserve decided to raise interest rates rather than cut them, due to concerns over building inflationary pressures. The president of the Federal Reserve Bank of Philadelphia was quoted as saying, "The U.S. economy has proved to be surprisingly capable of absorbing such shocks, and after a short period, the effects of Katrina are likely to slow but not stall the forward progress of the national economy." At this time, the U.S. economy was experiencing robust growth, and the general expectation was only a relatively modest slowdown. As stated earlier in the chapter, the forecasters were calling for only about a 0.5 percent reduction in real GDP growth. It was this outlook for continued solid economic growth that led to the Federal Reserve's concern with inflation, rather than recession after Hurricanes Katrina and Rita.

<table>
<tr><td>RECAP</td><td>
1. Disasters lead to greater government spending and lower tax revenues. This means that the government budget deficit will widen following a disaster, which may mean cutbacks in other worthy programs supported by government spending.

2. Monetary policy following a disaster typically includes increasing the money supply to ensure that there is adequate level of money flowing through the banking system to support normal business operations. Monetary policy may also aim at lowering interest rates to encourage economic growth. After Hurricanes Katrina and Rita, the Federal Reserve raised interest rates due to a fear of rising inflation.
</td></tr>
</table>

7. The Effect of Natural Disasters on Developing Countries

Both rich and poor nations experience natural disasters, but rich nations suffer less damage, due to their ability to prepare and respond to such shocks. Recent analysis indicates that a 10 percent increase in per capita GDP is associated with a decrease in national earthquake deaths by 5.3 percent.[5] This is due in part because in wealthy nations, building codes are stricter and more likely to be enforced. Better building codes mean that homes and other structures are built more soundly and therefore better able to survive a disaster with minimal damage.

Also, the transformation from largely rural to urban populations in developing countries has increased the exposure of such countries to disasters. Poor infrastructure, lax regulation of low-income neighborhoods, overcrowding, and the tendency

---

[5] See Matthew E. Kahn, "The Death Toll from Natural Disasters: The Role of Income, Geography, and Institutions," *Review of Economics and Statistics,* May 2005.

for the poor to occupy land that is more prone to disasters contribute to the greater susceptibility of poor countries to damage and loss of life from disasters.

For the individual living in a poor country that experiences a disaster, the harmful effects tend to be longer lasting than for those in rich countries. For instance, in Sri Lanka's coastal areas, an estimated 66 percent of the fishing fleet was destroyed by the tsunami of 2004. Fishing provided employment for about 250,000 people and is a major economic activity. The loss of fishing boats and consequent loss of jobs imposes hardships to the local coastal economies as well as the national economy. In addition, the countries hit by the tsunami have suffered contamination of drinking water and farm fields by the seawater that spread throughout the coastal regions. It will take several years for the soil to return to the fertile conditions that previously existed.

The loss of jobs is particularly devastating in a poor country, as it cannot afford to provide income support payments to those who lose their jobs due to a disaster. As a result, the degree of human suffering is greater. After the U.S. Gulf Coast hurricanes of 2005, those who lost jobs and incomes were provided temporary housing and income support payments to allow them to maintain a modest living standard. In a poor country, any government-provided support is likely to be funded by donations from citizens of a wealthier country and will be lower and of shorter duration than in a developed country.

Finally, the rapid rebuilding effort that follows a disaster in a wealthy country is likely to be much slower and of longer duration than in a poor country. The lack of funds to finance rebuilding and restoration of transportation and communication systems and reestablish private business activity will result in a more prolonged recovery period and more persistent human suffering as a result of a disaster.

RECAP

1. Disasters cause a greater loss of life and property damage in poor countries than in wealthy countries due to those countries' weaker building codes and lax enforcement of good construction practices.

2. Human suffering associated with a disaster tends to be more prolonged and more extreme in poor countries, since governments in these countries do not have the resources to provide income to those who lose jobs or housing to those who need shelter.

3. Rebuilding efforts following disasters last longer in poor countries and may never restore damaged areas to their prior state, due to a lack of funds for reconstruction.

Summary

❓ Why do people live where natural disasters are likely to occur?

1. In the United States, the most damaging natural disasters are hurricanes, earthquakes, and floods. U.S. hurricanes land primarily along the Gulf Coast and secondly along the Eastern seaboard from the Florida Keys to North Carolina. Earthquakes occur most frequently in California. Flooding occurs along the Mississippi River, the Appalachians, and Oregon.

2. People choose where to live in the same way they choose anything else: they allocate their income so as to maximize utility. This occurs when the last dollar spent on one good generates the same marginal utility as that dollar would generate spent on anything else.

3. Part of the cost of living in a certain location is the risk of a natural disaster. The higher the risk, the fewer the number of people that will choose to live in the risky area.

4. Insurance is a way to reduce the potential damage from a natural disaster. Risk-averse individuals will purchase insurance from private insurance companies. The insurance lowers the cost of living in a disaster-prone area for risk-averse individuals.

5. Government disaster assistance lowers the cost of living in risky areas and induces more people to live in the risky areas.

? What did Hurricanes Katrina and Rita do to the oil and gas industry?

6. The hurricanes knocked about 25 percent of U.S. oil production out of commission.

7. The reduced oil production affected the world oil market, causing the price of crude oil to rise.

8. The higher price of crude oil caused gasoline prices to rise.

? Why do gasoline prices rise rapidly but decline slowly?

9. The demand for gasoline is price inelastic. Thus, price increases do not reduce sales much and total revenue rises. Gas companies have an incentive to increase prices anytime their costs rise.

10. The demand for gasoline at individual gas stations is much more elastic than the demand for gasoline in general. As a result, gasoline stations will compete with each other. Prices will be reduced when crude oil prices decline as stations slowly reduce price, a few cents at a time.

? What is price gouging?

11. Price gouging is referred to as exorbitant, unfair, unconscionably high prices during a disaster or emergency.

12. If the supply of a good is reduced whether it is due to an emergency or to a regular event, the equilibrium price will increase. If the price did not rise, then shortages would exist. Price controls would create shortages.

13. If a firm sets a very high price on its product during an emergency, customers may pay the price but are likely to remember the high price once the emergency is over. If the firm does a repeat business, its high price may lose customers in the future.

14. A reduction in the tax on gasoline will drive the price of gasoline down because the demand for gasoline at a specific gas station is price elastic or at least significantly less inelastic than the demand for gasoline in general.

? What are the aggregate supply effects of disasters?

15. Disasters reduce aggregate supply (shift the AS curve to the left).

16. A lower AS causes equilibrium real GDP to fall and the equilibrium price level to rise.

? What are the aggregate demand effects of disasters?

17. Disasters lower AD (shift the AD curve to the left), initially due to loss of jobs and incomes.

18. Some time after the disaster, rebuilding begins and this increases AD (shifts the AD curve to the right).

19. The net effect of a disaster on AD will depend upon the relative magnitudes of the immediate fall versus the later rise.

? What effects do disasters have on economic growth?

20. Disasters lower the rate of economic growth in the short run as resources and labor inputs are lost.

21. In the long run following a disaster, economic growth may recover to the pre-disaster growth rates but the economy will have lost forever the output that would have been produced but was not following the disaster.

? What should the Central Bank do when a natural disaster strikes?

22. Central banks must provide adequate money to the banking system to support normal levels of business activity.

23. Since disasters may have inflationary consequences, central banks must be careful not to support higher inflation by continued high rates of money supply growth.

24. Human suffering tends to be greater and longer-lasting in poor countries, as governments lack resources to provide income to those who have lost jobs or shelter to those who have lost housing.

25. Poor nations often have weaker building codes and lax enforcement of good construction practices.

Key Terms

natural disaster
risk averse
systemic risk

Exercises

1. Explain why people choose to live on the hillsides of Malibu, California, where the likelihood of a flood and damages to residential structures is very high.

2. Would your behavior be the same in the following two circumstances?
   a. When you receive a low grade in a class, you can retake the class but have to pay full tuition.
   b. When you receive a low grade in a class, you may retake the class without paying any additional tuition.

3. Why does government disaster relief cause potentially greater disasters in the future?

4. What is price gouging? What would occur if it was against the law to increase prices during an emergency that causes supply to decline?

5. Why is the demand for gasoline price inelastic? Why is the demand for gasoline at a particular gas station not price inelastic?

6. Draw an *AD/AS* diagram and use this diagram to illustrate and explain the effects of a disaster on an economies equilibrium level of real GDP and price level.

7. Following up on Exercise 6, draw two *AD/AS* diagrams, one for poor countries and one for wealthy countries. Use these diagrams to explain likely differences between the two types of countries in terms of the macroeconomic effects of a disaster.

8. If disasters cause lower output and income, why might a central bank adhere to a more restrictive monetary policy following a disaster than it had prior to the disaster?

9. How can disasters "crowd out" government spending on worthy social programs that existed prior to the disaster?

chapter 13

Federal Deficits, Surpluses, and the National Debt

The U.S. government has been in the red almost continuously since the Revolutionary War forced the Continental Congress to borrow money. The only exception was a brief interlude more than a century and a half ago when our government was debt-free. In December 1834, President Andrew Jackson proudly reported to Congress what he considered to be a major accomplishment of his administration. By New Year's Day 1835, the federal government would succeed in paying off the national debt. It was Jackson's second term as president. Since the close of the War of 1812, the country had experienced tremendous growth, and revenues flowed into the U.S. Treasury from import tariffs and the sale of public land. By early 1836, the nation had been out of debt for two years, and there was a budget surplus of $37 million. The dilemma in those days was how to use the surplus. In 1836, Congress simply decided to divide all but $5 million of the surplus among the states. Then the financial panic of 1837 caused the government to plunge into debt again, where it remains today and for the foreseeable future.

Unlike Andrew Jackson, Abraham Lincoln, in his 1864 Annual Message to Congress, expressed no concern for paying off the national debt. Lincoln stated:

> The great advantage of citizens being creditors as well as debtors, with relation to the public debt, is obvious. Men can readily perceive that they cannot be much oppressed by a debt which they owe to themselves.

As this text is written in 2012, federal government borrowing to cover its budget deficits had accumulated a national debt of about $16 trillion. To the average citizen, this is an incomprehensible amount of money for even the government to owe. Perhaps the best way to picture this sea of red ink is that your individual share is over $50,000 and rising.

In this chapter, you will learn to solve these economics puzzles:

- Can Uncle Sam go bankrupt?

- How does the national debt of the United States compare to the debt of other countries?

- Are we passing the debt burden to our children?

- Who owns the national debt?

13-1 The Federal Budget Balancing Act

What will happen next? Like a high-wire performer swinging one way and then another while the crowd below gazes transfixed, the public in the late 1990s and early 2000s watched the federal budget sway back and forth between deficits and surpluses. As you learned in the preceding chapter on fiscal policy, a federal budget deficit occurs whenever the government spends more than it collects in taxes. The accumulation of these budget deficits over the years is the origin of the national debt. When the federal government has a surplus in its budget, some or all of the surplus can be used to retire the national debt, and it decreases. Here you will take a closer look at the actual budgetary process that creates and finances our national debt.

13-1a THE FEDERAL BUDGETARY PROCESS

In theory, Keynesian discretionary fiscal policy requires that legislation be enacted to change government spending or taxes in order to shift the aggregate demand curve represented in the AD-AS model. In practice, the federal budgetary process, which determines the level of spending and taxation, is not so orderly. The annual "battle of the budget" on Capitol Hill involves political decisions on how much the government plans to spend and where the money will come from to finance these outlays. Wrangling takes place between all sorts of camps: the president versus Congress, Republicans versus Democrats, national security versus economic equality, price stability versus full employment, health care versus tax cuts, and so on. Given the complexities of world events, special-interest groups, volatile public opinion, and political ambitions that complicate the budget process, it is no wonder actual fiscal policy often ignores textbook macroeconomics.

The following brief look at the federal budgetary process shows how Congress and the president make federal spending and tax decisions each year:

Stage 1: Presidential Budget Submission   The president must submit the budget to Congress on or before the first Monday in February of each year. The official title is *The Budget of the United States*. This unveiling of the administration's budget is always big news. Does the president recommend that less money be spent for defense and more for education? Is there an increase in the Social Security payroll tax or the income tax? And how large is the national debt? Is there a budget deficit or a budget surplus?

Stage 2: Budget Resolution   After the president submits the budget in January, Congress takes the lead in the budgetary process. The president's budget now becomes the starting point for congressional consideration. The Congressional Budget Office (CBO) employs a professional staff that advises Congress on the budget. The CBO analyzes the budget by February and reports its evaluation at budget committee hearings in both the House of Representatives and the Senate. After debate, in May, Congress approves an overall budget outline called the *budget resolution*, which sets target levels for spending, tax revenues, and the budget deficit or surplus.

Stage 3: Budget Passed   Throughout the summer and supposedly ending by October 1, Congress and the president debate while congressional committees and subcommittees prepare specific spending and tax law bills. The budget resolution is supposed to guide the spending and revenue decisions of these committees. After Congress passes and the president signs the spending and revenue bills, the federal government has its actual budget for spending and tax collection.

As summarized in Exhibit 1, the budgetary process seems orderly enough, but in practice, it does not work so smoothly. The process can, and often does, go astray. One problem is that Congress does not necessarily follow its own rules. The budget bills are not always passed on time, and when that happens, the fiscal year starts without a budget. Then federal agencies must operate on the basis of *continuing resolutions*, which means each agency operates as it did the previous year until spending bills are approved. In some years, Congress even fails to pass a continuing resolution, and the federal government must shut down and workers stay home until Congress approves the necessary funds.

EXHIBIT 1	**Major Steps in the Federal Budgetary Process**

The first step is the president's transmittal of the administration's budget to Congress. In the second step, Congress passes a budget resolution that sets targets for spending, taxes, and the deficit or surplus. In the third step, Congress passes the budget consisting of specific spending and tax bills. When the president signs the spending and revenue bills, the federal government has its actual budget.

SOURCE: © Cengage Learning 2014

13-1b FINANCING THE NATIONAL DEBT

Over the years, the federal government budget experiences imbalances. A budget deficit occurs when federal expenditures, including spending for final goods plus transfer payments, exceed tax revenues collected. A surplus occurs when the government collects more in taxes than it spends. For example, for four years between 1998 and 2001, budget surpluses existed, as discussed in the next You're the Economist feature. As shown in Exhibit 2, deficits returned after the 2001 recession, and following the Great Recession of 2007–2009, deficits reached record highs. In 2009, a record-breaking federal deficit was $1.4 trillion. In 2011, the deficit was $1.3 trillion.

What happens when the government overspends, and the U.S. Treasury must borrow to finance the difference between expenditures and revenues? The answer to that question is the U.S. Treasury borrows by selling Treasury bills (T-bills), notes, and bonds promising to make specified interest payments and to repay the loaned funds on a given date. These government securities are IOUs of the federal government. They are considered a safe haven for idle funds and are purchased by Federal Reserve banks, government agencies, private banks, corporations, individual U.S. citizens, and foreigners. If you own a U.S. government savings bond, for example, you have loaned your funds to the federal government. The stock of these federal government IOUs accumulated over the years is called the *gross public debt*, *federal debt*, or national debt. The national debt is the total amount owed by the federal government to owners of government securities. There are national debt clocks on the Internet and in several cities around the United States that display the amount of money owed by the federal government.

National debt

The total amount owed by the federal government to owners of government securities.

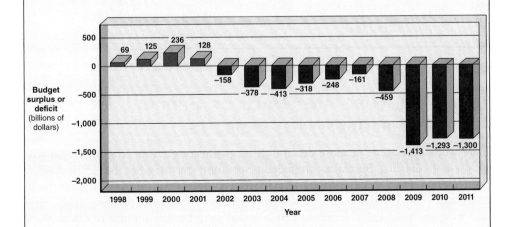

EXHIBIT 2	U.S. Federal Budget Surpluses and Deficits, 1998–2011

During 1998 through 2001, the annual federal government budget was in surplus each year. After the recession of 2001, these surpluses disappeared and deficits appeared, exploding to $1.4 trillion in 2009. In 2011, the deficit was $1.3 trillion.

SOURCE: *Economic Report of the President*, 2012, http://www.gpo.gov/fdsys/pkg/ERP-2012/content-detail.html1, Table B-78.

Note that the national debt does not include state and local governments' debt. Also, as mentioned above, the national debt does include U.S. Treasury securities purchased by various federal agencies, such as the Social Security trust fund. When the Social Security trust fund collects more in taxes than it pays out in retirement benefits, it lends the extra money to the federal government for spending. This means federal budget deficits would be significantly higher, or budget surpluses would be significantly lower, without federal government borrowing from this trust fund. If we subtract the portion of the national debt held by all government agencies (what the federal government owes to itself), we can compute the net public debt. Beware! Confusion sometimes occurs when the media use the term *public debt* without specifying whether the reference is to "gross" or "net" public debt.

Net public debt

National debt minus all government interagency borrowing.

Before proceeding, let's pause and explain the Social Security trust fund in a little more detail. A misconception is that the Social Security Administration (SSA) collects the annual Social Security surpluses and stacks the cash with reserve cash from previous surpluses in a vault, or special checking account. When the trust fund is in deficit as the baby boomers retire and the ratio of workers paying into the system to people drawing benefits shrinks, the SSA will open the vault and/or write a check to draw on trust fund reserves to pay its obligations.

Here is what really happens to Social Security tax dollars. When excess Social Security taxes are collected by the SSA, these surplus funds must, by law, be immediately withdrawn and given to the Treasury, which, in turn, issues "nonmarketable" interest-bearing Treasury bonds to the SSA. The Treasury then spends this money on welfare, roads, tax cuts, defense, or whatever the federal government decides. On the other hand, if the trust fund cannot pay for retirees' needs, then the SSA will ask the Treasury to redeem its bonds for cash to pay benefits. In this situation, where will the Treasury get the money to repay the SSA? It will either print it, borrow it, levy additional taxes, or cut benefits. In short, the full faith and credit of the U.S. federal government promises to pay itself enough money when needed to pay for Social Security.

CONCLUSION: *The national debt includes the Social Security trust fund, and as a result, federal budget deficits are reduced or budget surpluses are raised.*

13-1c THE RISE AND FALL OF FEDERAL BUDGET SURPLUSES AND DEFICITS

Here we will examine in more detail influences affecting recent federal budget surpluses and deficits. Restraint on federal spending began with the 1990 Budget Enforcement Act (BEA), which set spending caps on broad areas of discretionary spending. The BEA also required that any proposal to increase spending or decrease tax revenues over agreed limits had to be offset by an equal amount of tax revenue increases or new spending cuts. This pay-as-you-go legislation is called a "PayGo" rule. In 1993, Congress passed the Deficit Reduction Act, which increased tax revenues. This act took into account the ability-to-pay principle by increasing the highest marginal tax rate for individuals and raising the corporate income tax rate. It also increased the federal tax on gasoline. A gasoline tax offers the extra benefit of reducing the quantity of energy demanded and conforms to the benefits-received principle. However, a gasoline tax suffers from the problem of being regressive.

The spending caps combined with tax increases and a growing high-employment economy driven by technological advances, for example, the Internet, transformed federal budget deficits into surpluses during the late 1990s. Exhibit 3(a) shows federal expenditures and tax revenues expressed as a percentage of GDP. The difference between these two curves represents the federal deficit or surplus, also expressed as a percentage of GDP. Between 1991 and 2000, federal government expenditures as a percentage of GDP declined from 22 percent to 18 percent of GDP, and federal government tax revenues as a percentage of GDP crept steadily upward from 18 percent to 21 percent of GDP. The result of these changes in tax and spending percentages of GDP was four years of federal surpluses from 1998 to 2001. However, in 2002, the PayGo budget rule expired, and from 2002 through today, the federal budget has returned to red ink deficits.

After the Great Recession beginning in 2007, the deficit surged to historic highs when in 2009, federal expenditures climbed sharply to 25 percent of GDP, while tax revenues plummeted to a record low of only 15 percent of GDP. Recall from the automatic stabilizers explained in the previous chapter that during a recession, government expenditures rise for transfer payments when people lose jobs and tax revenues decline from individuals and companies making less money. Moreover, these unprecedented deficit figures flowed from the Wall Street bailout and economic stimulus bill, which sharply increased federal government spending relative to tax collections. In 2011, expenditures were 25 percent of GDP.

Exhibit 3(b) provides an alternate graph of the federal budget deficit or surplus as a percentage of GDP. During President Reagan's first term in the early 1980s, the combined effect of recession, a military spending buildup, and a cut in income taxes caused a rise in the deficit to 5 percent of GDP. During the 1990–1991 recession, the deficit as a percentage of GDP again reached close to 5 percent. However, during the Great Recession in 2009, the federal deficit soared to a record high since World War II of 10 percent of GDP. In 2011, the deficit fell slightly to 9 percent of GDP.

It is interesting to note that during the Great Depression, federal deficits were unimpressive by today's standards. As a share of GDP, Roosevelt's New Deal deficits (stimulus package) peaked at 6 percent of GDP in 1934. It is also noteworthy that in 2010, President Obama requested and the Senate passed a new PayGo law. But there are 50 programs whose spending is exempt from this law, including Social Security, veterans, trust funds, and emergency spending, such as a jobs bill or unemployment benefits.

13-1d DEBT CEILING

The debt ceiling is a method for curbing the national debt. A debt ceiling is a legislated legal limit on the national debt. This means that the federal government cannot legally allow a budget deficit to raise the national debt beyond the ceiling.

Debt ceiling

A legislated legal limit on the national debt.

EXHIBIT 3	Federal Expenditures, Revenues, and Deficits as a Percentage of GDP, 1990–2011

Part (a) shows that after the 1990–1991 recession, federal government expenditures as a percentage of GDP declined until 2000, while federal government tax revenues rose steadily. The results were federal surpluses between 1998 and 2001. After the Great Recession beginning in 2007, the deficit reached a record high when expenditures rose to 25 percent of GDP in 2009, and tax revenues plummeted to only 15 percent of GDP. In 2011, expenditures were 24 percent of GDP and taxes were 15 percent.

Part (b) focuses on the federal deficit or surplus as a percentage of GDP. In 1992, the federal deficit as a percentage of GDP was about 5 percent. After reaching a budget surplus peak of 2.4 percent in 2000, the federal budget deficit soared to a historic high of 10 percent of GDP in 2009. In 2011, the deficit was 9 percent of GDP.

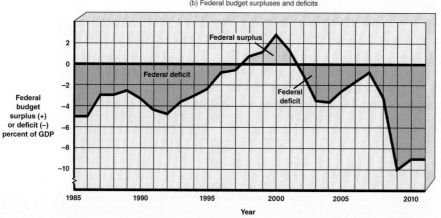

SOURCE: *Economic Report of the President*, 2012, http://www.gpo.gov/fdsys/pkg/ERP-2012/content-detail.htm1, Table B-79.

The Great Federal Budget Surplus Debate

Applicable Concept: federal budget surplus

As unprecedented deficit figures flowed during the Great Recession, it is hard to believe that for four years the federal budget was in surplus. After a one-year small budget surplus in 1969, it took 29 contentious years to eliminate federal budget deficits. And then surpluses occurred between 1998 and 2001, as shown in Exhibits 2 and 3, before becoming today what seems to be a historic relic. These federal budget surpluses aroused as much controversy in their time as deficits do in their years. In short, the hotly contested debate involved whether the surplus should be saved, spent, or devoted to tax cuts. The case for tax cuts and smaller government is based on the view that a surplus is the result of excess tax collections. Proponents of tax cuts pointed out that in 2000, federal tax revenues as a percentage of GDP were the highest since revenues during World War II. Moreover, tax rate cuts would spur the economy and result in higher future tax revenues. The argument for spending a surplus is based on "unmet needs." Instead of tax cuts, the surplus could be used to finance spending for defense, public infrastructure, research and development, and social programs such as education or health care. Also, a large proportion of American households pay no income taxes. Tax cuts therefore do not benefit people who are not prosperous enough to pay taxes.

An alternative to tax cuts and spending increases is paying down

Federal budget deficit projections
(billions of dollars)

Source: Office of Management and Budget, http://www.whitehouse.gov/OMB/budget/overview, Summary Table 5.1.

the national debt. Former Federal Reserve Chairman Alan Greenspan supported this approach. He said Congress faced the quandary of trying to establish fiscal policy based on long-range forecasts that may prove inaccurate. He stated that if Congress cuts taxes, it also has to be prepared to cut spending significantly in the event that the forecasts on which the cuts were based are proved wrong. On the other hand, using the budget surplus to fund "irrevocable spending programs" would be "the worst of all outcomes." Testifying before the Senate Budget Committee in 2001, Greenspan suggested that the proposed tax cut bill include provisions that would limit the tax cuts if specified future targets for the budget surpluses or debt reduction were not met. These provisions were not included in the 2001 tax bill.

The outcome of the "Great Federal Budget Surplus Debate" was that President George W. Bush signed a $1.35 trillion tax cut bill in 2001 spread over ten years. It was the largest and most widespread tax cut since the 1980s, during Ronald Reagan's presidency. And in spite of the tax cuts, the outlook for surpluses in the future was optimistic. In August 2001, the Office of Management and Budget (OMB) projected continuously growing budget surpluses that would peak at about $400 billion in 2007. The actual federal budget in 2007 was a $161 billion deficit, and the OMB dramatically changed its projections to deficits that exploded to $1.4 trillion in 2009 at the conclusion of the Great Recession. As actual deficit figures become available, check the accuracy of OMB estimates reported here.

Analyze the Issue

1. Refer to Exhibit 8 in the chapter on fiscal policy. Using demand-side and supply-side fiscal policy theories, explain how a tax cut could either increase or decrease the price level.

2. Using the Laffer curve discussed in the You're the Economist box in the chapter on fiscal policy, explain how proponents could claim that the tax cut would increase tax revenues.

Source: © Cengage Learning 2014

It works like the credit limit on your charge card. When you reach the limit, you cannot charge any more and you must pay cash. When the federal government hits the debt limit, it cannot borrow any more to supplement its cash from taxes and other sources. What usually happens when the budget pushes against the debt ceiling is that the federal government raises its own ceiling to accommodate the budget deficit. Raising the debt ceiling often provokes a fiery political debate over government spending. Failure to raise the debt ceiling means no money for the government to pay its bills, meet its payroll, or pay interest due on the national debt. In 1990, Congress rejected President George H. W. Bush's spending plan, and the government shut down throughout the three-day Columbus Day weekend. Most workers were off for the holiday, and few government agencies were affected. In 2009, a provision of the stimulus bill raised the U.S. debt ceiling in order to allow the record budget deficit described in the previous section.

In 2011 after many months of debate, a bill to raise the debt ceiling was passed just hours before the deadline. The bill raised the debt limit in stages until 2013 while providing dollar-for-dollar spending cuts. Exempt from spending cuts are Social Security, Medicaid, veteran's benefits, military pay, and programs for women, infants, and children. A 12-member bipartisan congressional committee was established to identify future deficit reductions and tax reforms.

13-1e BUDGET SURPLUSES AND DEFICITS IN OTHER COUNTRIES

Exhibit 4 shows numerous countries with government budget deficits as a percentage of GDP in 2011. While Norway had a budget surplus of 13 percent of GDP, Canada, France, and Greece, for example, had deficit percentages lower than the U.S. deficit percentage of 9 percent of GDP. Ireland had a deficit greater than the United States.

13-2 Why Worry over the National Debt?

In 2011, Greece was in financial crisis with a national debt-to-GDP ratio of 165 percent. Fearing default on Greece's debt, creditors have demanded solutions. In response, Greece cut civil service salaries, froze pensions, and enacted new taxes on a long list of items, including fuel, cigarettes, alcohol, jewelry, leather goods, yachts, private jets, and high-end automobiles. Also, Greece accepted international bailout packages, but as this text is written in 2012, there are fears that this crisis could spread.

As shown in Exhibit 5(a), the result of the accumulation of federal deficits in the United States is that the national debt is rising at a rapid rate. The national debt crossed $1 trillion in 1982. And it took 14 years before another $4 trillion was added, reaching the $5 trillion mark in 1996. Fourteen years later in 2010, the national debt accelerated by $9 trillion to $14 trillion. In 2011, the national debt reached $15 trillion.

EXHIBIT 4	A Global Comparison of Government Surpluses and Deficits as a Percentage of GDP, 2011

In 2011, Norway had a budget surplus of 13 percent of GDP. Other nations, such as Canada, France, and Greece, had budget deficits lower than the U.S. deficit of 9 percent of GDP. Ireland had a deficit greater than that of the United States.

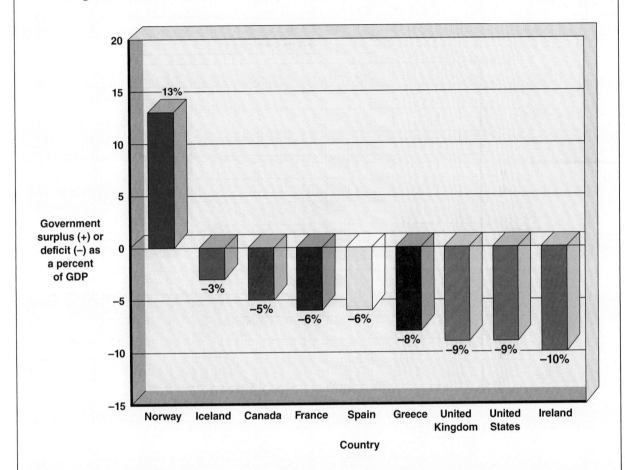

SOURCE: OECD (2011), "OECD Economic Outlook No. 90", OECD Economic Outlook: Statistics and Projections (database). http://dx.doi.org/10.1787/data-00588-en

What are some major causes of the rising national debt? Observe in Exhibit 5(a) the increase in the debt during World War II. In wartime, the government must increase military expenditures sharply and escalate the national debt. Recession also causes the national debt to rise dramatically. Cyclical downturns such as the 1930s, 1974–1975, 1981–1982, 1990–1991, 2001, and 2007–2009 also cause the debt to rise rapidly because a decline in real GDP automatically increases the budget deficit due to lower tax collections and

EXHIBIT 5	The National Debt, 1930–2011

In part (a), we see that the federal debt has skyrocketed since 1980. A concern is that sooner or later the U.S. government will be bankrupt. The counterargument is shown in part (b). The national debt as a percentage of GDP has declined since the end of World War II, when it reached a peak of about 122 percent. After 1980, the federal debt as a percentage of GDP increased and has risen sharply to a historic high since World War II of 99 percent in 2011.

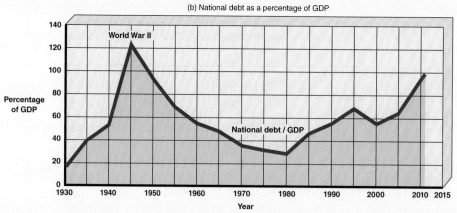

SOURCES: *Economic Report of the President*, 2012, http://www.gpo.gov/fdsys/pkg/ERP-2012/content-detail.htm1, Table B-79; Tables B-78 and B-79.

greater spending for unemployment compensation and welfare. Currently, as a result of the bailout plans and stimulus spending to boost troubled credit markets, the federal government is financing these plans with government borrowing that has caused a rise in the federal deficit, debt ceiling, and national debt.

Politicians and nonpoliticians alike often speak of the gloom and doom of the national debt. Should we lose sleep over it? To find out, we'll consider three controversial questions:

13-2a   1. CAN UNCLE SAM GO BANKRUPT?

Reasons to Worry   If households and firms persistently operate in the red, as the federal government does, they will go bankrupt sooner or later. How long can a national debt continue to rise before the U.S. government is broke?

Reasons Not to Worry   Whether private or public debt is the issue, debt must be judged relative to the debtor's ability to repay the principal and interest on the debt. Exhibit 5(b) shows that the national debt as a percentage of GDP is lower today than at the end of World War II. In 1945, public debt was about 122 percent of GDP, and by 1980, the ratio of debt to GDP had fallen to 33 percent. This means the debt grew considerably slower than GDP between 1945 and 1980. Since 1980, however, the trend reversed, and the debt has grown faster than GDP. Between 1980 and 2011, the national debt grew from 33 percent to 99 percent of GDP. Still, the United States was not bankrupt in 1945 or 2011. In the future, it can be argued that the debt will again grow slower than the GDP and the ratio will fall again.

There is an even more important point: Uncle Sam never has to pay off the national debt. At the maturity date on a government security, the U.S. Treasury has the constitutional authority to collect taxes levied by Congress, print money, or refinance its obligations. Suppose the government decides not to raise taxes or cause inflation by simply printing money, so it refinances the debt. When a $1 million government bond comes due, as described earlier in this chapter, the U.S. Treasury can simply "roll over" the debt. This financial trade expression means a borrower (here the federal government) pays off its $1 million bond that reaches maturity by issuing a new $1 million bond. In short, the federal government refinances its debt by replacing old bonds with new bonds. This means the federal government never has to pay off the national debt. These debts can be rolled over forever, provided bond buyers have faith in Uncle Sam.

Global Perspective on National Debt   Exhibit 6 provides a global perspective on the national debt. This figure shows the ratio of national debt to GDP for several industrialized nations. Japan, Greece, Italy, and Portugal have a higher debt in relation to GDP than does the United States. The United States, on the other hand, has a national debt-to-GDP ratio about four times as large as Australia's ratio.

EXHIBIT 6	A Global Comparison of National Debt Ratios, 2011

This exhibit shows estimated ratios of national debt to GDP in 2011 for selected industrialized countries. Compared to the United States, Japan, Greece, Italy, and Portugal have higher national debt-to-GDP ratios. On the other hand, the United States has a debt ratio about four times as large as Australia's.

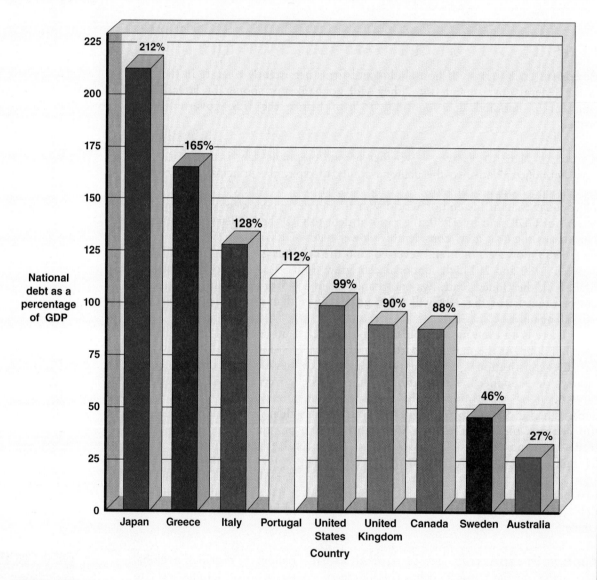

SOURCE: OECD (2011), "OECD Economic Outlook No. 90", OECD Economic Outlook: Statistics and Projections (database). http://dx.doi.org/10.1787/data-00588-en

✔ **CHECKPOINT**

What's Behind the National Debt?

Suppose the federal government has balanced budgets each year and the entire national debt comes due. How could the federal government pay off the national debt without refinancing, raising taxes, or printing money?

13-2b   2. ARE WE PASSING THE DEBT BURDEN TO OUR CHILDREN?

Reasons to Worry   The fear is that interest payments to finance the national debt will swallow an enormous helping of the federal government's budget pie. This means future generations will pay more of their tax dollars to the government's creditors and have less to spend for highways, health care, defense, and other public sector programs. Exhibit 7 shows net interest payments as a percentage of GDP. The net interest payment was only 1.7 percent of GDP right after World War II in 1950, but it increased dramatically after the mid-1970s to more than 3 percent in 1995. Since 1995, the interest payment burden declined to 1.8 percent of GDP in 2011.

Reasons Not to Worry   The burden of the national debt on present and future generations depends on who owns the accumulated national debt. Stated more precisely, the burden of the debt depends on whether it is held internally or externally. The bulk of the public debt is internal national debt. Internal national debt is the portion of the national debt owed to a nation's own citizens. Internal debt financing is viewed as "we owe it to ourselves." One U.S. citizen buys a government security and lends Uncle Sam the money to pay the interest and principal on a maturing government security held by another U.S. citizen. Although this redistribution of income and wealth does indeed favor bondholders, who are typically upper-income individuals, transferring dollars between U.S. citizens does not alter the overall purchasing power in the U.S. economy.

Those on the "not to worry" side of this issue also concede that an external national debt is a concern. External national debt is the portion of the national debt owed to foreign citizens. Financing the external national debt means interest and principal payments are transfers of money from U.S. citizens to other nations. If foreign governments, banks, corporations, and individual investors hold part of the national debt, the "we owe it to ourselves" argument is weakened. Exhibit 8 shows who owns the securities the U.S. Treasury has issued. In 2011, foreigners owned 31 percent of the total national debt. The largest foreign holder of the debt was China with 8 percent of the total national debt, and next was Japan with 6 percent. Forty-two percent was held by the federal, state, and local governments, primarily by federal agencies such as the U.S. Treasury, the Social Security Administration, and Federal Reserve banks. The Federal Reserve is an independent government agency, as explained in the next chapter. The private sector, consisting

Internal national debt

The portion of the national debt owed to a nation's own citizens.

External national debt

The portion of the national debt owed to foreign citizens.

EXHIBIT 7	Federal Net Interest as a Percentage of GDP, 1940–2011

Some fear that interest payments on the national debt will swallow an enormous portion of the federal budget. The exhibit shows that the net interest payment as a proportion of GDP was only about 1.7 percent right after World War II. In the 1980s and early 1990s, however, the interest rate burden increased dramatically to more than 3 percent in 1995. Since 1995, it declined to 1.8 percent in 2011.

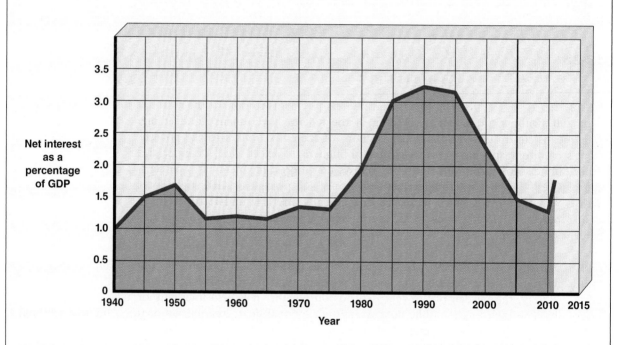

SOURCES: *Economic Report of the President*, 2012, http://www.gpo.gov/fdsys/pkg/ERP-2012/content-detail.html, Tables B 1 and B 80 and Bureau of Economic Analysis, *National Economic Accounts*, http://www.bea.gov/national/nipaweb/SelectTable.asp?Selected=Y, Table 1.1.

of individuals, banks, corporations, and insurance companies, held 27 percent of the national debt. The debt held by the private sector and government entities constitutes the internal national debt.

Although 69 percent of the national debt was internal, the 31 percent of total U.S. debt that is external debt is not necessarily undesirable. Foreign investment in the United States supplements domestic saving. Borrowing from abroad can prevent the higher interest rates that would exist if the U.S. Treasury relied only on domestic savers to purchase federal government securities. A lower interest rate increases U.S. investment and consumer spending, causing the aggregate demand curve to shift rightward.

If we do not need to worry about shifting the burden to future generations, can the current generation escape the debt burden? The answer is *No*. During World War II, for example, the United States operated at full employment along its *production possibilities curve*. As illustrated earlier in Exhibit 2 of

Chapter 2, the people at that time in history were forced to trade off consumer goods production for military goods production. Because massive amounts of resources were diverted to fight World War II, people at that time were forced to give up private consumption of houses, cars, refrigerators, and so on. After the war was over, resources were again devoted to producing more consumer goods and fewer military goods. The same analysis can be used today. At full employment, the burden of the national debt on the current generation is the opportunity cost of private-sector goods and services forgone because land, labor, and capital are used to produce public-sector goods and services.

In other words, the burden of the national debt is incurred when production takes place; it is not postponed until the debt is paid by future generations. When the debt comes due in the future, the government can simply refinance the debt and redistribute money from one group of citizens to another. This redistribution of income does not cause a reallocation of resources away from consumer goods and services in favor of government programs.

EXHIBIT 8	Ownership of the National Debt, 2011

In 2011, 42 percent of the national debt was held by the public sector, including federal, state, and local governments and Federal Reserve banks. The private sector, including individuals, banks, corporations, and insurance companies, held 27 percent, and foreigners owned the remaining 31 percent.

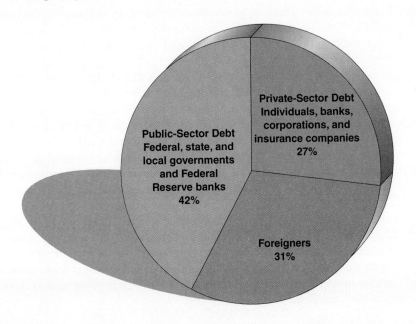

SOURCE: *Economic Report of the President*, 2012, http://www.gpo.gov/fdsys/pkg/ERP-2012/content-detail. htm1, Table B-89.

13-2c 3. DOES GOVERNMENT BORROWING CROWD OUT PRIVATE-SECTOR SPENDING?

Crowding-out effect

A reduction in private-sector spending as a result of federal budget deficits financed by U.S. Treasury borrowing. When federal government borrowing increases interest rates, the result is lower consumption by households and lower investment spending by businesses.

Reasons to Worry   Critics of Keynesian fiscal policy believe that government spending financed by borrowing designed to boost aggregate demand has little, if any, effect on growth of real GDP. The reason is that the crowding-out effect dampens the stimulus to aggregate demand from increased federal government spending. The crowding-out effect is a reduction in private-sector spending as a result of higher interest rates caused by U.S. Treasury borrowing (selling securities) to finance government spending. For example, suppose the federal government spends and borrows, rather than collecting taxes, to finance new health care programs. In this case, the size of the national debt rises, and interest rates are pushed up in loan markets. Interest rates rise because the federal government competes with private borrowers for available savings, and less credit is available to consumers and business borrowers. The result of this crowding-out effect is lower consumption $(-\Delta C)$ and business investment $(-\Delta I)$, which offset the boost in aggregate demand $(+\Delta AD)$ from increased government spending $(+\Delta G)$ operating through the spending multiplier.

The crowding-out effect contradicts the theory, explained in the previous Reasons Not to Worry section, that future generations do not bear some of today's debt burden. Recall from Chapter 2 that current investment spending increases living standards in the future by shifting the production possibilities curve outward (Exhibit 5 in Chapter 2). If federal borrowing crowds out private investment in plants and equipment, future generations will have a smaller possible productive capacity.

The AD-AS model will help you understand the crowding-out concept. Exhibit 9 reproduces the situation in which government spending is used to combat a recession, depicted earlier in Exhibit 2 of the chapter on fiscal policy. Begin at E_1, with an equilibrium GDP of $13 trillion, and assume the government increases its spending and uses the spending multiplier to shift the aggregate demand curve rightward from AD_1 to AD_2. Following Keynesian theory, there is zero crowding out, and the economy achieves full employment at equilibrium point E_2, corresponding to real GDP of $14 trillion. Critics of Keynesian theory, however, argue that crowding out occurs. The result of expansionary fiscal policy is not E_2, but some equilibrium point along the AS line between E_1 and E_2. For example, a fall in private expenditures might partially offset the government spending stimulus. With incomplete crowding out, the aggregate demand curve increases only to AD'_2 because of the decline in consumption and investment. The economy therefore moves to E'_2 at a real GDP of $13.5 trillion and does not achieve full employment at E_2. Or crowding out can completely offset the multiplier effect of increased government spending. The fall in private expenditures by consumers and businesses can result in no change in aggregate demand curve AD_1. In this case, the economy remains at E_1, with unemployment unaffected by expansionary policy. Meanwhile, the deficit required to finance extra government spending increases the national debt.

Crowding-in effect

An increase in private-sector spending as a result of federal budget deficits financed by U.S. Treasury borrowing. At less than full employment, consumers hold more Treasury securities and this additional wealth causes them to spend more. Business investment spending increases because of optimistic profit expectations.

Reasons Not to Worry   The crowding-out effect is controversial. Keynesian economists counter critics by saying that any crowding-out effect is small or nonexistent. Instead, at below full-employment real GDP, their counterargument is the crowding-in effect. For example, government capital spending for highways, dams, universities, and infrastructure financed by borrowing might offset any decline in private investment. Another Keynesian argument is that consumers and businesspersons may believe that federal spending is "just what the doctor ordered" for an ailing economy. Federal borrowing incurred to finance the new spending would boost consumption and therefore increase aggregate demand.

EXHIBIT 9	Zero, Partial, and Complete Crowding Out

Beginning at equilibrium E_1, the federal government borrows to finance a deficit created by expansionary fiscal policy. Keynesian theory predicts zero crowding out, which means that an increase in government spending operates through the spending multiplier to shift aggregate demand from AD_1 to AD_2. If crowding out is zero, consumption and investment spending are unaffected by the increase in government spending financed by borrowing. Partial crowding out occurs when a decrease in private spending partially offsets the multiplier effect from an increase in deficit-financed government spending. Partial crowding out results in a shift only from AD_1 to AD'_2 and an equilibrium at E'_2, rather than E_2. If crowding out is complete, a decrease in private spending completely offsets the increase in government spending financed by debt. In this case, the aggregate demand curve remains at AD_1, and the economy remains at E_1.

CAUSATION CHAIN

SOURCE: © Cengage Learning 2014

How Real Is Uncle Sam's Debt?

Applicable Concepts: national debt and federal deficit

Perhaps the national debt and federal budget deficits are really not so large and threatening. For example, it can be argued that we should use real rather than nominal values to report the national debt—similar to using real GDP to report economic growth. Suppose the national debt rises from $10 trillion to $10.3 trillion and the price level increases by 3 percent in a given year. The nominal value of the national debt therefore has risen by $300 billion because the government must issue $300 billion in newly issued government securities due to higher prices, and real growth in the national debt is therefore zero.

Critics also warn that federal accounting rules are an economic policy disaster. Private businesses, as well as state and local governments, use two budgets. One is the *operating budget*, which includes salaries, interest payments, and other current expenses. The second type of budget, called a *capital budget*, includes spending for investment items, such as machines, buildings, and roads. Expenditures on the capital budget yield benefits over time and may be paid for by long-term borrowing. The federal government does not use a capital

iStockphoto.com/james steidl

The reason is because holders of Treasury bills, notes, and bonds feel richer. As a result of their greater wealth, consumers spend more now and plan to spend more in the future. Such a blush of optimism may also raise the profit expectations of business managers, and they may increase investment spending. The effect of increased private-sector spending could nullify some or all of the crowding-out effect, which would otherwise offset the boost in aggregate demand from increased government spending. Hence, as explained in the graphical analysis in Exhibit 9, the spending multiplier shifts the aggregate demand curve from AD_1 to AD_2, with zero crowding out.

Finally, both sides of the debate agree that complete crowding out occurs in one situation. Suppose the economy is operating at full employment (point E_2). This is comparable to being on the economy's production possibilities curve. If the government shifts the aggregate demand curve rightward by increasing spending or cutting taxes, the result will be higher prices and a replacement of private sector output with public sector output.

> **CONCLUSION:** *Crowding out is complete if the economy is at full employment, but it is debatable at less than full employment.*

budget. Capital budgeting allows spreading the cost of long-lasting assets over future years. For example, the federal budget makes no distinction between the rental cost of a federal office building and the cost of constructing a new federal office building to replace rented office space. However, payments on borrowing for a new building provide the benefit of a long-lasting asset that offsets rent payments. If a capital budgeting system were used, the public would see that most federal borrowing really finances assets yielding long-term benefits. In short, proponents of a capital budget believe the public's focus should be on the operating budget, which gives a truer measure of the federal deficit. Opponents of changing the accounting rules argue that controversial expenditures would be placed in the capital budget in order to manipulate the size of the deficit or surplus in the operating budget for political reasons.

Finally, some economists argue for other numerical adjustments that show the federal deficit or surplus is really not as it seems. They say it is not the federal deficit or surplus that really matters, but the combined deficits or surpluses of federal, state, and local governments. When state and local governments run budget surpluses, these surpluses are a source of savings in financial markets that adds to federal surpluses or offsets federal borrowing to finance its deficit.

Analyze the Issue

1. Do households make a distinction between spending for current expenses and spending for capital expenses? Compare borrowing $5,000 to take a vacation in Hawaii to borrowing $125,000 to buy a condominium and move out of your rented apartment.

2. Critics of "new accounting" for federal borrowing argue that it does not matter what the government spends the money for. What matters is the total amount that the government spends minus taxes collected. Explain this viewpoint.

Source: © Cengage Learning 2014

Key Concepts

National debt
Net public debt
Debt ceiling

Internal national debt
External national debt
Crowding-out effect

Crowding-in effect

Summary

- The **national debt** is the dollar amount that the federal government owes holders of government securities. It is the cumulative sum of past deficits. The U.S. Treasury issues government securities to finance the deficits. The debt has increased sharply since 1980.

National Debt

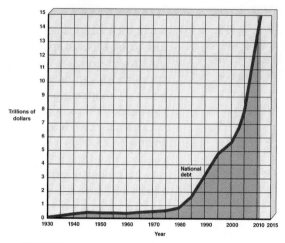

SOURCES: *Economic Report of the President*, 2012, http://www.gpo.gov/fdsys/pkg/ERP-2012/content-detail.htm1, Table B-79; Tables B-78 and B-79.

- The **net public debt** is the national debt minus all government interagency borrowing (the debt that the federal government owes to itself).
- A **debt ceiling** is a method used to restrict the growth of the national debt.
- **Internal national debt** is the percentage of the national debt a nation owes to its own citizens, including individuals, banks, corporations, insurance companies, and government entities. The "we owe it to ourselves" argument over the debt is that U.S. citizens own the bulk of the U.S. national debt. **External national debt** is a burden because it is the portion of the national debt a nation owes to foreigners. The interest paid on external debt transfers purchasing power to other nations.

Internal and External National Debt

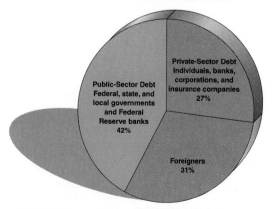

SOURCE: *Economic Report of the President*, 2012, http://www.gpo.gov/fdsys/pkg/ERP-2012/content-detail.htm1, Table B-89.

- The **burden of the debt debate** involves controversial questions:
  1. **Can Uncle Sam Go Bankrupt?** The U.S. government will not go bankrupt because it never has to pay off its debt. When government securities mature, the U.S. Treasury can refinance, or roll over, the debt by issuing new securities.
  2. **Are We Passing the Debt Burden to Our Children?** One side of this argument is that the burden of the debt falls only on the current generation when the trade-off between public-sector goods and private-sector goods along the production possibilities curve occurs. In short, when resources are used to make missiles today, citizens are forced to give up, say, airplane production in the current period and not later. The counterargument is that there is a sizable external national debt that transfers purchasing power to foreigners.
  3. **Does Government Borrowing Crowd Out Private-Sector Spending?** The **crowding-out effect** is a burden of the national debt that occurs when the government borrows to finance its deficit, causing the interest rate to rise. As the interest rate rises, consumption and business investment fall. If crowding out occurs, reduced private spending completely or partially offsets the multiplier effect of increased government spending. As a result, the expected magnitude of the rightward shift in the aggregate demand curve is partially or completely offset.

  Opponents believe in the **crowding-in effect**. In this view, government capital spending for highways, dams, universities, and infrastructure offsets any decline in business investment from crowding out.

Zero, Partial, and Complete Crowding Out

SOURCE: © Cengage Learning 2014

Summary of Conclusion Statements

- The national debt includes the Social Security trust fund and as a result, federal budget deficits are reduced or budget surpluses are raised.

- Crowding out is complete if the economy is at full employment, but it is debatable at less than full employment.

Study Questions and Problems

1. Explain the relationship between budget deficits and the national debt.

2. Discuss various ways of measuring the size of the national debt.

3. Explain this statement: "The national debt is like taking money out of your left pocket and putting it into your right pocket."

4. Explain this statement: "The most unlikely problem of the national debt is that the government will go bankrupt."

5. Suppose the percentage of the federal debt owned by foreigners increases sharply. Would this trend concern you? Why or why not?

6. Explain the theory that crowding out can weaken or nullify the effect of expansionary fiscal policy financed by federal government borrowing.

7. Suppose the federal government has no national debt and spends $100 billion, while raising only $50 billion in taxes.
   a. What amount of government bonds will the U.S. Treasury issue to finance the deficit?
   b. Next year, assume tax revenues remain at $50 billion. If the government pays a 10 percent rate of interest, add the debt-servicing interest payment to the government's $100 billion expenditure for goods and services the second year.
   c. For the second year, compute the deficit, the amount of new debt issued, and the new national debt.

8. Suppose the media report that the federal deficit this year is $200 billion. The national debt was $5,000 billion last year, and it is $5,200 billion this year. The price level this year is 3 percent higher than it was last year. What is the real deficit?

9. During the presidential campaign of 1932 in the depth of the Great Depression, candidates Herbert Hoover and Franklin D. Roosevelt both advocated reducing the budget deficit using tax hikes and/or expenditure reductions. Evaluate this fiscal policy.

10. Consider this statement: "Our grandchildren may not suffer the entire burden of a federal deficit." Do you agree or disagree? Explain.

11. Suppose you are the economic policy adviser to the president and are asked what should be done to eliminate a federal deficit. What would you recommend?

For Online Exercises, go to the Tucker Web site at www.cengage.com/economics/tucker.

✓ CHECKPOINT ANSWER

What's behind the National Debt?

Every item owned by the federal government, including the White House, office buildings, tanks, and computers, is an asset standing behind the national debt. If you said the assets of the federal government could be sold to pay off the national debt, **YOU ARE CORRECT**.

Sample Quiz

For an explanation of the correct answers, visit the Tucker Web site at www.cengage.com/economics/tucker.

1. Each year, the president must submit a budget proposal to Congress by
   a. February.
   b. April.
   c. July.
   d. October.

2. If the fiscal year begins without a budget and Congress fails to pass continuing resolution, then
   a. the president has the right to raise the debt ceiling.
   b. federal agencies operate on the basis of the previous year's budget.
   c. the interest rate paid on the national debt automatically increases.
   d. the federal government shuts down.

3. Between 1998 and 2001, the federal budget was
   a. never in surplus.
   b. in surplus about as often as it was in deficit.
   c. in surplus.
   d. never in deficit.

4. The sum of past federal budget deficits is the
   a. GDP debt.
   b. trade debt plus GDP.
   c. national debt.
   d. Congressional debt.

5. To finance a federal budget deficit, the U.S. Treasury borrows by selling
   a. Treasury bills.
   b. Treasury notes.
   c. Treasury bonds.
   d. All of the above answers are correct.

6. Most of the U.S. national debt is owed to _____. Thus, a rising national debt implies that there will be a future redistribution of income and wealth in favor of _____.
   a. foreigners, foreigners
   b. other U.S. citizens, bondholders
   c. foreigners, those needing government services
   d. other U.S. citizens, those needing government services

7. Which of the following statements is *false*?
   a. The size of the national debt decreased steadily after World War II.
   b. The national debt increases in size whenever the federal government has a surplus budget.
   c. Currently, the size of the national debt is about the same size as it was during World War II.
   d. All of the answers above are correct.

8. Which of the following statements is *true*?
   a. Currently, the size of the national debt is about the same size as it was during World War II.
   b. The national debt increases in size whenever the federal government has a surplus budget.
   c. The size of the national debt decreased steadily after 1980.

Sample Quiz *continued*

d. The current U.S. national debt is over $15 trillion.

9. Compared to the United Kingdom, the national debt as a percentage of GDP in the United States is
   a. substantially larger.
   b. the same.
   c. slightly larger.
   d. substantially smaller.

10. The national debt is unlikely to cause national bankruptcy because the federal government can
    a. raise taxes.
    b. print money.
    c. refinance its debt.
    d. do all of the above.

11. In recent years, net interest on the national debt paid by the federal government as a percentage of GDP was equal to approximately
    a. 1 percent.
    b. 3 percent.
    c. 6 percent.
    d. 25 percent.

12. Which of the following U.S. Treasury securities represents ownership of the national debt?
    a. bonds owned by the banks and insurance companies
    b. bonds owned by the Social Security Administration
    c. bonds owned by private individuals
    d. All of the above answers are correct.

13. "Crowding out" refers to the situation in which
    a. borrowing by the federal government raises interest rates and causes firms to invest less.
    b. foreigners sell their bonds and purchase U.S. goods and services.
    c. borrowing by the federal government causes state and local governments to lower their taxes.
    d. increased federal taxes to balance the budget cause interest rates to increase and consumer credit to decrease.

14. The crowding-out effect can be
    a. zero.
    b. partial.
    c. complete.
    d. any of the answers are correct.

15. "Crowding in" refers to federal government deficits that
    a. are used for public infrastructure will offset any decline in business investment.
    b. reduce private business and consumption spending.
    c. reduce future rates of economic growth.
    d. all of the answers are correct.

16. If Congress fails to pass a budget before the fiscal year starts, then federal agencies may continue to operate only if Congress has passed a
    a. balanced budget amendment.
    b. deficit reduction plan.
    c. conference resolution.
    d. continuing resolution.

17. With regard to the national debt, to whom does the federal government owe money?
    a. taxpayers
    b. federal government workers
    c. the Federal Reserve system
    d. investors who buy U.S. Treasury bills, bonds, and notes

18. When measured as a percentage of GDP, the U.S. national debt reached its highest levels as a result of
    a. World War II.
    b. the Vietnam War.
    c. the Reagan defense buildup and tax cut.
    d. the Obama economic recovery program.

19. The national debt is unlikely to cause national bankruptcy because the
    a. national debt can be refinanced by issuing new bonds.
    b. interest on the public debt equals GDP.
    c. national debt cannot be shifted to future generations for repayment.
    d. federal government cannot refinance the outstanding national debt.

Sample Quiz *continued*

20. An increase in our federal government's budget deficit will likely
    a. increase the national debt.
    b. increase interest rates.
    c. decrease borrowing by households and businesses.
    d. be less effective in stimulating the economy than the spending multiplier implies because of crowding out.
    e. do all of the above.

Road Map
Macroeconomic Theory and Policy Issues

part 4

This road map feature helps you tie together material in the part as you travel the Economic Way of Thinking highway. The following are review questions listed by chapter from the previous part. The key concept in each question is given for emphasis, and each question or set of questions concludes with an interactive game to reinforce the concepts. Go to the Tucker website at www.cengage.com/economics/ tucker, select the chapter, and play the visual causation chain game designed to make learning fun. Enjoy the cheers when you are correct and suffer the jeers if you miss. The correct answers for the multiple choice questions are given in Appendix C of the text.

CHAPTER 8. THE KEYNESIAN MODEL

1. **Key Concept: Consumption function**
   The consumption function will shift for all of the following reasons except
   a. a change in a household's real assets.
   b. a change in interest rates.
   c. expectations of price changes.
   d. changes in a household's disposable incomes.
   e. changes in taxation policy.

 Causation Chain Game
   Movement along and Shifts in the Consumption Function—Exhibit 6

2. **Key Concept: Investment demand curve**
   Which of the following will increase investment spending?
   a. More optimistic business expectations
   b. An increase in interest rates
   c. An increase in business taxes
   d. A decrease in capacity utilization
   e. All of the answers above are correct.

 Causation Chain Game
   Movement along and Shifts in a Firm's Investment Demand—Exhibit 8

CHAPTER 9. THE KEYNESIAN MODEL IN ACTION

3. Key Concept: Spending multiplier

The ratio of the change in GDP to an initial change in aggregate expenditures (AE) is the

a. spending multiplier.
b. permanent income rate.
c. marginal expenditure rate.
d. marginal propensity to consume.

Causation Chain Game
The Multiplier Effect and Government Spending—Exhibit 4

CHAPTER 10. AGGREGATE DEMAND AND SUPPLY

4. Key Concept: Aggregate demand curve

Which of the following is *not* a reason for the downward slope of an aggregate demand curve?

a. real balances or wealth effect
b. real interest-rate effect
c. net exports effect
d. all of the above are reasons

Causation Chain Game
The Aggregate Demand Curve—Exhibit 1

5. Key Concept: Aggregate demand curve

Which of the following could *not* be expected to shift the aggregate demand curve?

a. net exports fall
b. consumption spending decreases
c. an increase in government spending
d. a change in real GDP

Causation Chain Game
A Shift in the Aggregate Demand Curve—Exhibit 3

6. Key Concept: Aggregate supply curve

The horizontal segment of the aggregate supply curve

a. shows that real GDP can increase only by affecting the economy's price level.
b. shows that real GDP can increase without affecting the economy's price level.
c. depicts a positive relationship between real GDP and the price level.

d. depicts a negative relationship between real GDP and the price level.
e. marks the full-employment level of real GDP.

Causation Chain Game
The Keynesian Horizontal Aggregate Supply Curve—Exhibit 4

7. **Key Concept: Aggregate supply curve**
According to classical theory, if the aggregate demand curve decreased and the economy experienced unemployment, then
a. the economy would remain in this condition indefinitely.
b. the government must increase spending to restore full employment.
c. prices and wages would fall quickly to restore full employment.
d. the supply of money would increase until the economy returned to full employment.

Causation Chain Game
The Classical Vertical Aggregate Supply Curve—Exhibit 5

8. **Key Concept: Aggregate supply curve**
If a new method for obtaining oil from dry oil fields is found, then we will see
a. the AS curve shift to the left.
b. a movement to the left along the AD curve.
c. the AD curve shift to the left.
d. the AD curve shift to the right.
e. the AS curve shift to the right.

Causation Chain Game
A Rightward Shift in the Aggregate Supply Curve—Exhibit 9

9. **Key Concept: Cost-push inflation**
Cost-push inflation occurs when the
a. aggregate demand curve shifts leftward while the aggregate supply curve is fixed.
b. aggregate supply curve shifts leftward while the aggregate demand curve is fixed.
c. aggregate demand curve shifts rightward while the aggregate supply curve is fixed.
d. aggregate supply curve shifts rightward.

Causation Chain Game
Cost-Push and Demand-Pull Inflation—Exhibit 11

10. **Key Concept: Demand-pull inflation**
Demand-pull inflation is caused by an
a. increase in aggregate demand.
b. decrease in aggregate demand.
c. increase in aggregate supply.
d. decrease in aggregate supply.

Causation Chain Game
Cost-Push and Demand-Pull Inflation—Exhibit 11

CHAPTER 11. FISCAL POLICY

11. Key Concept: Fiscal policy

Which of the following is an appropriate discretionary fiscal policy to use when the economy is in a recession?

a. increased government spending
b. higher taxes
c. a balanced-budget reduction in both spending and taxes
d. an expansion in the money supply

Causation Chain Game
Using Government Spending to Combat a Recession—Exhibit 2

12. Key Concept: Fiscal policy

If no fiscal policy changes are implemented to fight inflation, suppose the aggregate demand curve will exceed the current aggregate demand curve by $900 billion at any level of prices. Assuming the marginal propensity to consume is 0.90, this increase in aggregate demand could be prevented by

a. increasing government spending by $500 billion.
b. increasing government spending by $140 billion.
c. decreasing taxes by $40 billion.
d. increasing taxes by $100 billion.

Causation Chain Game
Using Fiscal Policy to Combat Inflation—Exhibit 6

13. Key Concept: Automatic stabilizers

Automatic stabilizers "lean against the prevailing wind" of the business cycle because

a. wages are controlled by the minimum wage law.
b. federal expenditures and tax revenues change as the level of real GDP changes.
c. the spending and tax multipliers are constant.
d. they include the power of special interests.

Causation Chain Game
Automatic Stabilizers—Exhibit 7

14. Key Concept: Supply-side economics

An advocate of supply-side fiscal policy would advocate which of the following?

a. subsidies to produce technological advances
b. reduction in regulation
c. reduction in resource prices
d. reduction in taxes
e. All of the answers above are correct.

Causation Chain Game
Keynesian Demand-Side versus Supply-Side Effects—Exhibit 8

CHAPTER 13. FEDERAL DEFICITS, SURPLUSES, AND THE NATIONAL DEBT

15. **Key Concept: Federal budget process**

    If Congress fails to pass a budget before the fiscal year starts, then federal agencies may continue to operate only if Congress has passed a
    a. balanced budget amendment.
    b. deficit reduction plan.
    c. conference resolution.
    d. continuing resolution.

Causation Chain Game

Major Steps in the Federal Budgetary Process—Exhibit 1

Money, Banking, and Monetary Policy

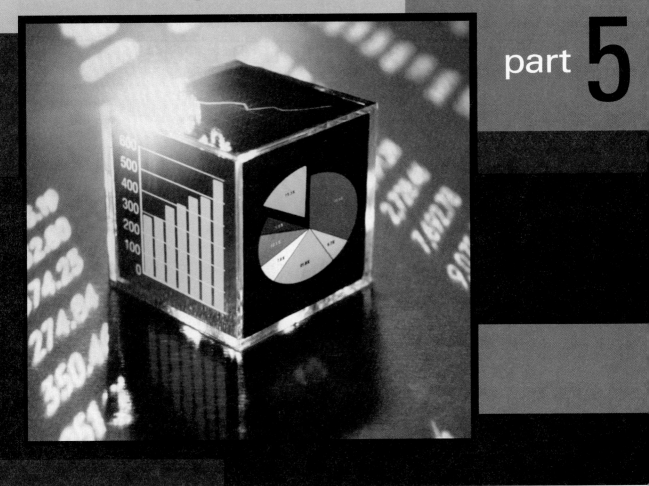

Students often find the material in these chapters the most interesting in their principles course because the topic is *money*. The first chapter begins the discussion of money with basic definitions and a description of the Federal Reserve System. Of special interest is a feature on the history of money in the colonies. The next chapter explains how the banking system and the Federal Reserve influence the supply of money. The following chapter compares different macroeconomic theories and concludes with a discussion of monetary policy in the Great Depression and the Great Recession. The final chapter in this part explores additional macro theories based on expectations.

chapter 14

Money and the Federal Reserve System

As the lyrics of the old song go, "Money makes the world go round, the world go round, the world go round." Recall the circular flow model presented in the chapter on GDP. Households exchange *money* for goods and services in the product markets, and firms exchange *money* for resources in the factor markets. In short, money affects the way an economy works. In the chapter on aggregate demand and supply and the chapter on fiscal policy presented earlier in the text, the AD-AS model was developed without explicitly discussing money. In this chapter, and throughout this part, money takes center stage.

Exactly what is money? The answer may surprise you. Imagine yourself on the small South Pacific island of Yap. You are surrounded by exotic fowl, crystal-clear lagoons, delicious fruits, and sunny skies. Now suppose while leisurely strolling along the beach one evening, you suddenly discover a beautiful bamboo hut for sale. As you will discover in this chapter, to pay for your dream hut, you must roll a 5-foot-diameter stone to the area of the island designated as the "bank."

We begin our discussion of money with the three functions money serves. Next, we identify the components of three different definitions of the money supply used in the United States. The remainder of the chapter describes the organization and services of the Federal Reserve System, our nation's central bank. Also, we discuss the Monetary Control Act of 1980 and its relationship to the savings and loan crisis of the 1980s and early 1990s that predated the banking crisis and Great Recession of 2007–2009. Beginning in this chapter and in the next three chapters, you will learn how the Federal Reserve System controls the stock of money in the economy. Then, using the AD-AS model, you will learn how variations in the stock of money in the economy affect total spending, unemployment, and prices.

- Why do nations use money?

- Is "plastic money" really money?

- What does a Federal Reserve bank do?

14-1 What Makes Money *Money*?

Can exchange occur in an economy without money? It certainly can, using a trading system called barter. Barter is the direct exchange of one good or service for another good or service, rather than for money. The problem with barter is that it requires a *coincidence of wants*. Imagine for a moment that dollars and coins are worthless. Farmer Brown needs shoes, so he takes his bushels of wheat to the shoe store and offers to barter wheat for shoes. Unfortunately, the store owner refuses to barter because she wants to trade shoes for pencils, toothpaste, and coffee. Undaunted, Farmer Brown spends more time and effort to find Mr. Jones, who has pencils, toothpaste, and coffee he will trade for bushels of wheat. Although Farmer Brown's luck has improved, he and Mr. Jones must agree on the terms of exchange. Exactly how many pounds of coffee, for example, is a bushel of wheat worth? Assuming this exchange is worked out, Farmer Brown must spend more time returning to the shoe store and negotiating the terms of an exchange of pencils, coffee, and toothpaste for shoes.

Barter

The direct exchange of one good or service for another good or service, rather than for money.

> **CONCLUSION:** *The use of money simplifies and therefore increases market transactions. Money also prevents wasting time that can be devoted to production, thereby promoting economic growth by increasing a nation's production possibilities.*

14-1a THE THREE FUNCTIONS OF MONEY

Suppose citizens of the planet of Starcom want to replace their barter system and must decide what to use for money. Assuming this planet is fortunate enough to have economists, they would explain that anything, regardless of its value, can serve as money if it conforms to the following definition. Money is anything that serves as a medium of exchange, unit of account, and store of value. Money is not limited to dimes, quarters, and dollar bills. Notice that "anything" meeting the three tests is a candidate to serve as money. This explains why precious metals, beaver skins, wampum (shells strung in belts), and cigarettes have all served as money. Let's discuss each of the three functions money serves.

Money

Anything that serves as a medium of exchange, unit of account, and store of value.

Money as a Medium of Exchange In a simple society, barter is a way for participants to exchange goods and services in order to satisfy wants. Barter, however, requires wasting time in the process of exchange that people could use for productive work. If the goal is to increase the volume of transactions and live in a modern economy, the most important function of money is to serve as

Medium of exchange

The primary function of money to be widely accepted in exchange for goods and services.

a medium of exchange. Medium of exchange is the primary function of money to be widely accepted in exchange for goods and services. Money removes the problem of coincidence of wants because everyone is willing to accept money in payment, rather than haggling over goods and services. You give up two $20 bills in exchange for a ticket to a rock concert. Because money serves as generalized purchasing power, all in society know that no one will refuse to trade their products for money. In short, money increases trade by providing a much more convenient method of exchange than a cumbersome barter system.

A fascinating question is whether people will find digital cash a more convenient means of payment. Each year more people avoid using checks, paper currency, or coins by transferring funds electronically from their accounts via various Internet-based and other systems. In fact, it is possible that widespread adoption of privately issued digital cash will ultimately replace government-issued currency. Vending and copy machines on many college campuses already accept plastic stored-value cards. Someday vending machines everywhere are likely to have smart card readers that accept electronic money.

Money as a Unit of Account

How does a wheat farmer know whether a bushel of wheat is worth one, two, or more pairs of shoes? How does a family compare its income to expenses or a business know whether it is making a profit? Government must be able to measure tax revenues collected and program expenditures made. And GDP is the *money* value of final goods and services used to compare the national output of the United States to, say, Japan's output. In each of these examples, money serves as a unit of account. Unit of account is the function of money to provide a common measurement of the relative value of goods and services. Without dollars, there is no common denominator. We must therefore decide if one pizza equals a box of pencils, 20 oranges equals one quart of milk, and so forth. Now let's compare the value of two items using money. If the price of one pizza is $20 and the price of a movie ticket is $10, then the value of one pizza equals two movie tickets. In the United States, the monetary unit is the dollar; in Japan, it is the yen; Mexico has its peso; and so on.

Unit of account

The function of money to provide a common measurement of the relative value of goods and services.

Money as a Store of Value

Can you put shrimp under your mattress for months and then exchange them for some product? No! Money, on the other hand, serves as a store of value in exchange for some item in the future. Store of value is the ability of money to hold value over time. You can bury money in your backyard or store it under your mattress for months or years and not worry about it spoiling. This also means you can save money and be confident that you can spend it in the future. However, recall from the chapter on inflation that hyperinflation can destroy money's store-of-value function and, in turn, its medium-of-exchange function.

Store of value

The ability of money to hold value over time.

CONCLUSION: *Money is a useful mechanism for transforming income in the present into future purchases.*

The key property of money is that it is completely *liquid*. This means that money is immediately available to spend in exchange for goods and services without any additional expense. Money is more liquid than real assets (real estate or gold) or paper assets (stocks or bonds). These assets also serve as stores of value, but liquidating (selling) them often involves expenses, such as brokerage fees, and time delays.

> **CONCLUSION:** *Money is the most liquid form of wealth because it can be spent directly in the marketplace.*

14-1b   ARE CREDIT CARDS MONEY?

Credit cards, such as Visa, MasterCard, and American Express, are often called "plastic money," but are these cards really money? Let's test credit cards for the three functions of money. First, because credit cards are widely accepted, they serve as a means of payment in an exchange for goods or services.

Second, the credit card statement, and not the card itself, serves as a unit of account. One of the advantages of credit cards is that you receive a statement listing the exact price in dollars paid for each item you charged. Your credit card statement clearly records the dollar amount you spent for gasoline, a dinner, or a trip.

But credit cards clearly fail to meet the store-of-value criterion and are therefore *not* money. The word *credit* means receiving money today to buy products in return for a promise to pay in the future. A credit card represents only a prearranged short-term loan up to a certain limit. If the credit card company goes out of business or for any reason decides not to honor your card, it is worthless. Hence, credit cards do not store value and are *not* money.

✔ CHECKPOINT

Are Debit Cards Money?

Debit cards are used to pay for purchases, and the money is automatically deducted from the user's bank account. Are debit cards money?

14-2   Other Desirable Properties of Money

Once something has passed the three basic requirements to serve as money, there are additional hurdles to clear. First, an important consideration is *scarcity*. Money must be scarce, but not too scarce. Sand, for example, could theoretically serve as money, but sand is a poor choice because people can easily gather a bucketful to pay their bills. A Picasso painting would also be undesirable as money. Because there are so few for circulation, people would have to resort to barter.

Counterfeiting threatens the scarcity of money. Advances in computer graphics, scanners, and color copiers were allowing counterfeiters to win their ongoing battle with the U.S. Secret Service. In response, new bills were issued with a polymer security thread running through them. The larger off-center portraits on the bills allow for a watermark next to the portrait that is visible from both sides against a light.

> **CONCLUSION:** *The supply of money must be great enough to meet ordinary transaction needs, but not be so plentiful that it becomes worthless.*

Why a Loan in Yap Is Hard to Roll Over

Applicable Concept: functions of money

On the tiny South Pacific island of Yap, life is easy, but the currency is hard as a rock. For nearly 2,000 years, the Yapese have used large stone wheels to pay for major purchases, such as land, canoes, and permission to marry. The people of Yap have been using stone money ever since a Yapese warrior named Anagumang used canoes to bring the huge stones over the sea in ancient times from limestone caverns on neighboring Palau. Inspired by the moon, he fashioned the stones into large circles, and the rest is history. The stone's value remained high because of the difficulty and hazards involved in obtaining them over the rough seas.

Yap is a U.S. trust territory, and the dollar is used in grocery stores and gas stations, but reliance on stone money continues. Buying property with stones is "much easier than buying it with U.S. dollars," says John Chodad, who purchased a building lot with a 30-inch stone wheel. "We don't know the value of the U.S. dollar."[1] However, stone wheels don't make good pocket money, so Yapese use other forms of currency, such as beer, for small transactions. Besides stone wheels and beer, the Yapese sometimes spend gaw, consisting of necklaces of stone beads strung together around a whale's tooth. They also buy things with yar, a currency made from large seashells, but these are small change.

Stone disks may change ownership during marriage, transfer of land title, or other exchanges. Yapese lean the stone wheels against their houses or prop up rows of them in village "banks." Most of the stones are smaller in diameter, but some are as much as 12 feet in diameter. Each has a hole in the center so that it can be slipped onto the trunk of a fallen betel-nut tree and carried. It takes 20 men to lift some wheels. Rather than risk a broken stone—or their backs—Yapese leave the larger stones where they are and make a mental accounting that the ownership has been transferred. There are some decided advantages to using massive stones for money. They are in short supply, difficult to steal, pose formidable obstacles to counterfeiting, and serve as a tourist attraction.

Analyze the Issue

1. Explain how Yap's large stones pass the three tests in the definition of money.
2. Briefly discuss Yap's large stones in terms of other desirable properties of money.

1. Art Pine, "Fixed Assets, Or: Why a Loan in Yap Is Hard to Roll Over," *The Wall Street Journal*, Mar. 29, 1984, p. 1.

Source: © Cengage Learning 2014

Second, money should be *portable* and *divisible*. That is, people should be able to reach into their pockets and make change to buy items at various prices. Statues of George Washington might be attractive money, but they would be difficult to carry and to use to make change. Finally, money must be *uniform*. An ounce of gold is an ounce of gold. The quality differences of beaver skins and seashells, on the other hand, complicate using these items for money. Each exchange would involve the extra trouble of buyers and sellers arguing over which skins or shells are better or worse.

14-3 What Stands behind Our Money?

Historically, early forms of money played two roles. If, for example, a ruler declared beans as money, you could spend them or sell them in the marketplace. Precious metals, tobacco, cows, and other tangible goods are examples of commodity money. Commodity money is anything that serves as money while having market value based on the material from which it is made. This means that money itself has intrinsic worth (the market value of the material). For example, money can be pure gold or silver, both of which are valuable for nonmoney uses, such as making jewelry and serving other industrial purposes.

Today, U.S. paper money and coins are no longer backed by gold or silver. Our paper money was exchangeable for gold or silver until 1934. As a result of the Great Depression, people rapidly tried to get rid of their paper money. The U.S. Treasury's stock of gold dropped so low that Congress passed a law in 1934 that prevented anyone from exchanging gold for $5 and larger bills. Later, in 1963, Congress removed the right to exchange $1 bills for silver. And in the mid-1960s, zinc, copper, and nickel replaced silver in coins.

The important consideration for money is acceptability. The acceptability of a dollar is due in no small degree to the fact that Uncle Sam decrees it to be fiat money. Fiat money is money accepted by law, and not because of its redeemability or intrinsic value. A dollar bill contains only about 3 cents worth of paper, printing inks, and other materials. A quarter contains maybe 10 cents worth of nickel and copper. Pull out a dollar bill and look at it closely. In the upper left corner on the front side is small print that proclaims, "THIS NOTE IS LEGAL TENDER FOR ALL DEBTS, PUBLIC AND PRIVATE." This means that your paper money is fiat money. Also notice that nowhere on the note is there any promise to redeem it for gold, silver, or anything else.

Commodity money

Anything that serves as money while having market value based on the material from which it is made.

Fiat money

Money accepted by law, and not because of its redeemability or intrinsic value.

> **CONCLUSION:** *An item's ability to serve as money does not depend on its own market value or the backing of precious metal.*

14-4 Money Supply Definitions

Now that you understand the basic definition of money, we turn to exactly what constitutes the money supply of the U.S. economy. The following sections examine the two basic methods used to measure the money supply, officially called M1 and M2.

14-4a M1: THE MOST NARROWLY DEFINED MONEY SUPPLY

M1 is the narrowest definition of the money supply. This money definition measures purchasing power immediately available to the public without borrowing or having to give notice. Specifically, M1 measures the currency and checkable

M1

The narrowest definition of the money supply. It includes currency and checkable deposits.

History of Money in the Colonies

The early colonists left behind their well-developed money system in Europe. North American Indians accepted wampum as money, which are beads of polished shells strung in belts. Soon, a group of settlers learned to counterfeit wampum, and it lost its value. As a result, the main method of trading with the Indians was to barter. Later, trade developed with the West Indies, and Spanish coins called "pieces of eight" were circulated widely. Colonists often cut these coins into pieces to make change. Half of a coin became known as "four bits." A quarter part of the coin was referred to as "two bits." The first English colony to mint its own coins was Massachusetts in 1652. A striking pine tree was engraved on these coins called shillings. Other coins such as a six-pence and three-pence were also produced at a mint in

Boston. Several other colonies followed by authorizing their own coin issues.

The first national coin of the United States was issued in 1787 when Congress approved a one-cent copper coin. One side was decorated with a chain of

---

deposits held by the public at a given time, such as a given day, month, or year. Expressed as a formula:

$$M1 = \text{currency} + \text{checkable deposits}$$

Exhibit 1 shows the components of M1 and M2 money supply definitions based on daily averages in 2011.

Currency

Money, including coins and paper money.

Currency   Currency includes coins and paper money, officially called Federal Reserve notes, that the public holds for immediate spending. The purpose of currency is to enable us to make small purchases. Currency represents 46 percent of M1.

Checkable Deposits   Most "big ticket" purchases are paid for with checks or credit cards (which are not money), rather than currency. Checks eliminate trips to the bank, and they are safer than cash. If lost or stolen, checks and credit cards can be replaced at little cost—money cannot. Exhibit 1 shows that a major share of M1 consists of checkable deposits. Checkable deposits are the total money in financial institutions that can be withdrawn "on demand" by writing a check. A checking account balance is a bookkeeping entry, often called a *demand deposit* because it can be converted into cash "on demand." Before the 1980s, only commercial banks could legally provide demand deposits. However, the law changed with the passage of the Depository Institutions Deregulation and Monetary Control Act of 1980. (This act will be discussed later in the chapter.) Today, checking accounts

Checkable deposits

The total money in financial institutions that can be withdrawn by writing a check.

13 links encircling the words "We Are One." The other side had a sundial, the noonday sun, and the Latin word *fugo*, meaning "time flies." Later, this coin became known as the Franklin cent, although there is no evidence that Benjamin Franklin played any role in its design.

In 1792, Congress established a mint in Philadelphia. It manufactured copper cents and half-cents about the size of today's quarters and nickels. In 1794, silver half-dimes and half-dollars increased the variety of available coins. The next year gold eagles ($10) and half-eagles ($5) appeared. The motto "E Pluribus Unum" ("out of many, one") was first used on the half-eagle in 1795. The next year America's first quarters and dimes were issued.

The first paper money in the Americas was printed in 1690. Massachusetts soldiers returned to the colony from fighting the French in Quebec, where they had unsuccessfully laid siege to the city. The colony had no precious metal to pay the soldiers. Hundreds of soldiers threatened mutiny, and the colony decided it must issue bills of credit, which were simply pieces of paper promising to pay the soldiers. Other colonies followed this example and printed their own paper money. Soon paper money was being widely circulated.

In 1775, the need to finance the American Revolution forced the Continental Congress to issue paper money called "continentals," but so much was issued that it rapidly lost its value. George Washington complained, "A wagon load of money will scarcely purchase a wagon load of provisions." This statement is today shortened to the phrase "not worth a continental."

are available from many different financial institutions, such as savings and loan associations, credit unions, and mutual savings banks. For example, many people hold deposits in negotiable order of withdrawal (NOW) accounts or automatic transfer of savings (ATS) accounts, which serve as interest-bearing checking accounts. NOW and ATS accounts permit depositors to spend their deposits without a trip to the bank to withdraw funds. In 2011, 54 percent of M1 was checkable deposits.

14-4b M2: ADDING NEAR MONIES TO M1

M2 is a broader measure of the money supply because it equals M1 plus *near monies*. Many economists consider M1 to be too narrow a measure because it does not include near money accounts that can be used to purchase goods and services. These include passbook savings accounts, money market accounts, mutual fund accounts, and time deposits of less than $100,000. Near monies are interest-bearing deposits easily converted into spendable funds. Written as a formula:

M2

The definition of the money supply that equals M1 plus near monies, such as savings deposits and small time deposits of less than $100,000.

$$M2 = M1 + near\ monies$$

rewritten as

$$M2 = M1 + savings\ deposits + small\ time\ deposits\ of\ less\ than\ \$100,000$$

EXHIBIT 1	Definitions of the Money Supply, 2011

Each of the two pie charts represents the money supply in 2011. M1, the most narrowly defined money supply, is equal to currency (coins and paper money) in circulation plus checkable deposits in financial institutions. M2 is a more broadly defined money supply, equal to M1 plus savings deposits and small time deposits of less than $100,000.

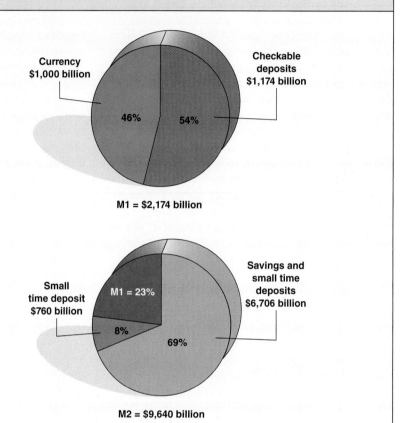

SOURCE: *Economic Report of the President*, 2012, http://www.gpo.gov/fdsys/pkg/ERP-2012/content-detail.htm1, Tables B-69 and B-70.

Savings Deposits   As shown in Exhibit 1, M1 was 23 percent of M2 in 2011, with savings deposits and small time deposits constituting the remainder of M2. Savings deposits are interest-bearing accounts that can be easily withdrawn. These deposits include passbook savings accounts, money market accounts, mutual fund accounts, and other types of interest-bearing deposits with commercial banks, mutual savings banks, savings and loan associations, and credit unions.

Small Time Deposits   There is a distinction between a *checkable deposit* and a *time deposit*. A time deposit is an interest-bearing account in a financial institution with guaranteed interest for a period of time. Certificates of deposit (CDs), for example, are deposits for a specified time, with a penalty charged for early withdrawal. Where is the line drawn between a small and a large time deposit? The answer is that time deposits of less than $100,000 are "small" and therefore are included in M2. In 2011, 8 percent of M2 was small time deposits.

CONCLUSION: *M1 is more liquid than M2.*

To simplify the discussion throughout the remainder of this text, we will be referring to M1 when we discuss the money supply. However, one can argue that M2, or another measurement of the money supply, may be the best definition. Actually, the boundary lines for any definition of money are somewhat arbitrary.

14-5 The Federal Reserve System

What controls the money supply in the United States? The answer is the Federal Reserve System, popularly called the "Fed." The Fed is the central banker for the nation and provides banking services to commercial banks, other financial institutions, and the federal government. The Fed regulates, supervises, and is responsible for policies concerning money. Congress and the president consult with the Fed to control the size of the money supply and thereby influence the economy's performance.

Other major nations have central banks, such as the Bank of England, the Bank of Japan, and the European Central Bank. The movement in the United States to establish a central banking system gained strength early in the 20th century as a series of bank failures resulted in The Panic of 1907. In that year, stock prices fell, many businesses and banks failed, and millions of depositors lost their savings. The prescription for preventing financial panic was for the government to establish more centralized control over banks. This desire for more safety in banking led to the creation of the Federal Reserve System by the Federal Reserve Act of 1913 during the administration of President Woodrow Wilson. No longer would the supply of money in the economy be determined by individual banks.

14-5a THE FED'S ORGANIZATIONAL CHART

The *Federal Reserve System* is an independent agency of the federal government. Congress is responsible for overseeing the Fed, but does not interfere with its day-to-day decisions. The chairman of the Fed reports to Congress twice each year and often coordinates its actions with the U.S. Treasury and the president. Although the Fed enjoys independent status, its independence can be revoked. If the Fed were to pursue policies contrary to the interests of the nation, Congress could abolish the Fed.

The Federal Reserve System consists of 12 central banks that service banks and other financial institutions within each of the Federal Reserve districts. Each Federal Reserve bank serves as a central banker for the private banks in its region. The United States is the only nation in the world to have 12 separate regional banks instead of a single central bank. In fact, the Fed's structure is the result of a compromise between the traditionalists, who favored a single central bank, and the populists, who distrusted concentration of financial power in the hands of a few. In addition, 25 Federal Reserve branch banks are located throughout the country. The map in Exhibit 2 shows the 12 Federal Reserve districts.

The organizational chart of the Federal Reserve System, given in Exhibit 3, shows that the Board of Governors, located in Washington, D.C., administers the system. The Board of Governors is made up of seven members, appointed by the president and confirmed by the U.S. Senate, who serve for one nonrenewable 14-year term. Their responsibility is to supervise and control the money

Federal Reserve System

The 12 Federal Reserve district banks that service banks and other financial institutions within each of the Federal Reserve districts; popularly called the "Fed."

Board of Governors of the Federal Reserve System

The seven members appointed by the president and confirmed by the U.S. Senate who serve for one nonrenewable 14-year term. Their responsibility is to supervise and control the money supply and the banking system of the United States.

Ben Bernanke, Chairman of the Board of Governors of the Federal Reserve System

EXHIBIT 2	The Twelve Federal Reserve Districts

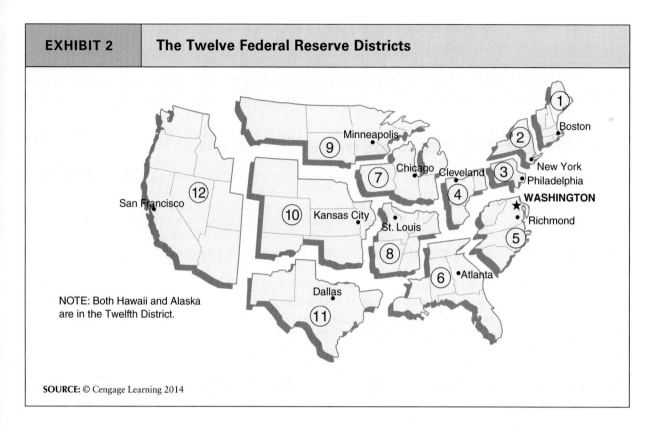

NOTE: Both Hawaii and Alaska are in the Twelfth District.

EXHIBIT 3	The Organization of the Federal Reserve System

The Federal Open Market Committee (FOMC) and the Federal Advisory Council assist the Federal Reserve System's Board of Governors. The 12 regional Federal Reserve district banks and their 25 branches implement broad policies affecting the money supply.

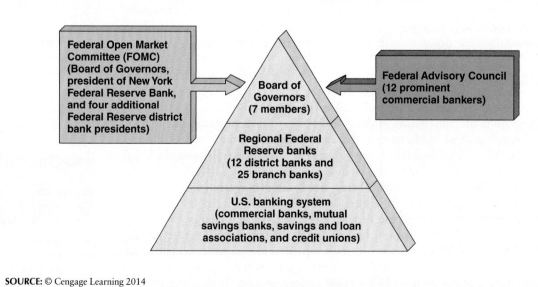

supply and the banking system of the United States. Fourteen-year terms for Fed governors create autonomy and insulate the Fed from short-term politics. These terms are staggered so that one term expires every two years. This staggering of terms prevents a president from stacking the board with members favoring the incumbent party's political interests. A president usually makes two appointments in a one-term presidency and four appointments in a two-term presidency. The president designates one member of the Board of Governors to serve as chairman for a four-year term. The chairman is the principal spokesperson for the Fed and has considerable power over policy decisions. In fact, it is often argued that the Fed's chairman is the most powerful individual in the United States next to the president. The current chairman is Ben Bernanke, who was appointed by former President George W. Bush and reappointed by President Barack Obama in 2010.

The Federal Reserve System receives no funding from Congress. This creates financial autonomy for the Fed by removing the fear of congressional review of its budget. Then where does the Fed get funds to operate? Recall from Exhibit 7 of the previous chapter that the Fed holds government securities issued by the U.S. Treasury. The Fed earns interest income from the government securities it holds and the loans it makes to depository institutions. Because the Fed returns any profits to the Treasury, it is motivated to adopt policies to promote the economy's well-being, rather than earning a profit. Moreover, the Board of Governors does not take orders from the president or any other politician. Thus, the Board of Governors is the independent, self-supporting authority of the Federal Reserve System.

On the left side of the organizational chart in Exhibit 3 is the very important Federal Open Market Committee (FOMC). The FOMC directs the buying and selling of U.S. government securities, which are major instruments for controlling the money supply. The FOMC consists of the seven members of the Board of Governors, the president of the New York Federal Reserve Bank, and the presidents of four other Federal Reserve district banks. The FOMC meets to discuss trends in inflation, unemployment, growth rates, and other macro data. FOMC members express their opinions on implementing various monetary policies and then issue policy statements known as *FOMC directives*. A directive, for example, might set the operation of the Fed to stimulate or restrain M1 in order to influence the economy. The next two chapters explain the tools of monetary policy in more detail.

As shown on the right side of the chart, the *Federal Advisory Council* consists of 12 prominent commercial bankers. Each of the 12 Federal Reserve district banks selects one member each year. The council meets periodically to advise the Board of Governors.

Finally, at the bottom of the organizational chart is the remainder of the Federal Reserve System, consisting of only about 3,000 member banks of the approximately 7,000 commercial banks in the United States. Although these 3,000 Fed member banks represent only about 40 percent of U.S. banks, they have about 70 percent of all U.S. bank deposits. A sure sign of Fed membership is the word *National* in a bank's name. The U.S. comptroller of the currency charters national banks, and they are required to be Fed members. Banks that do not have "National" in their title can also be Fed members. States can also charter banks, and these state banks have the option of joining the Federal Reserve. Less than 20 percent of state banks choose to join the Fed. Exhibit 4 shows the top 10 U.S. banks based on their assets.

Federal Open Market Committee (FOMC)

The Federal Reserve's committee that directs the buying and selling of U.S. government securities, which are major instruments for controlling the money supply. The FOMC consists of the seven members of the Federal Reserve's Board of Governors, the president of the New York Federal Reserve Bank, and the presidents of four other Federal Reserve district banks.

EXHIBIT 4	Top 10 Banks in the United States, 2011

The top 10 banks in the United States include JPMorgan Chase, Bank of America, and Wells Fargo.

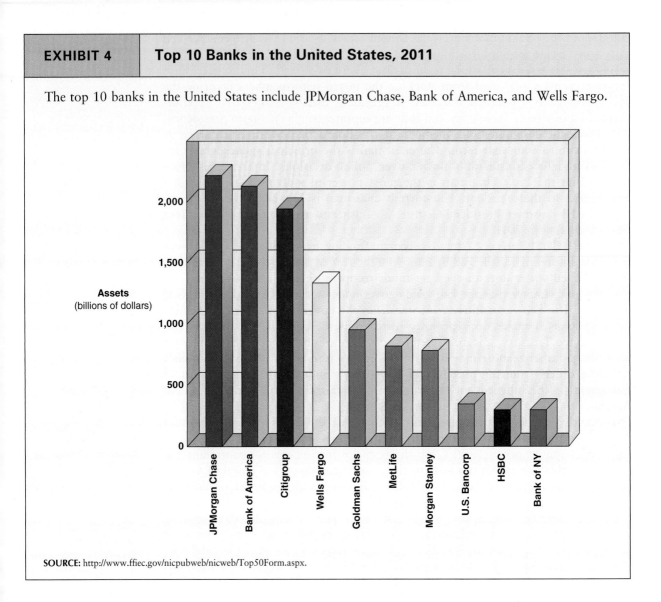

SOURCE: http://www.ffiec.gov/nicpubweb/nicweb/Top50Form.aspx.

Nonmember depository institutions, including many commercial banks, savings and loan associations (S&Ls), savings banks, and credit unions, are not official members of the Fed team. They are, however, influenced by and depend on the Fed for a variety of services, which we will now discuss.

14-6 What a Federal Reserve Bank Does

The typical bank customer never enters the doors of a Federal Reserve district bank or one of its branch banks. The reason is that the Fed does not offer the public checking accounts, savings accounts, or any of the services provided by commercial banks. Instead, the Federal Reserve serves as a "banker's bank." Following are brief descriptions of some of the principal functions of the Federal Reserve.

14-6a CONTROLLING THE MONEY SUPPLY

The primary role of the Fed is to control the nation's money supply. The mechanics of Fed control over the money supply are explained in the next two chapters. To most people, this is a wondrously mysterious process. So that you do not suffer in complete suspense, here is a sneak preview: The Fed has three policy tools, or levers, it can use to change the stock of money in the banking system. The potential macro outcome of changes in the money supply is to affect total spending and therefore real GDP, employment, and the price level.

14-6b CLEARING CHECKS

Because people and businesses use checks to pay for goods and services, check clearing is an important function. Suppose you live in Virginia and have a checking account with a bank in that state. While on vacation in California, you purchase tickets to Disneyland with a check for $200. Disneyland accepts your check and then deposits it in its business checking account in a California bank. This bank must collect payment for your check and does so by sending an electronic copy of your check to the Federal Reserve bank in San Francisco. From there, your check is sent to the Federal Reserve bank in Richmond. At each stop along its journey, the check earns a black stamp mark on the back. Finally, the process ends when $200 is subtracted from your personal checking account. Banks in which checks are deposited have their Fed accounts credited, and banks on which checks are written have their accounts debited. The Fed clearinghouse process is much speedier than depending on the movement of a check between commercial banks.

14-6c SUPERVISING AND REGULATING BANKS

The Fed examines banks' books, sets limits for loans, approves bank mergers, and works with the Federal Deposit Insurance Corporation (FDIC). The FDIC is a government agency established in 1933 that insures commercial bank deposits up to a limit if a bank fails. Congress created the FDIC in response to the huge number of bank failures during the Great Depression and set the insurance limit at $25,000. If the government provides a safety net, people are less likely to panic and withdraw their funds from banks during a period of economic uncertainty. When deposits are insured and a bank fails, the government stands ready to pay depositors or transfer their deposits to a solvent bank. Banks that are members of the Fed are members of the FDIC. State agencies supervise state-chartered banks that are not members of either the Federal Reserve System or the FDIC. To shore up confidence in the U.S. banking system in the wake of bank failures in 2008, the $700 billion U.S. financial industry rescue law raised the FDIC coverage of bank deposits to $250,000 per customer from $100,000.

Federal Deposit Insurance Corporation (FDIC)

A government agency established in 1933 to insure customer deposits up to a limit if a bank fails.

The 1946 film, **It's a Wonderful Life**, is based on a fractional reserve banking system without the FDIC.

14-6d MAINTAINING AND CIRCULATING CURRENCY

Recall that the M1 money supply consists of currency (coins and Federal Reserve notes) and checkable deposits. Note that the Fed does *not* print currency—it *maintains* and *circulates* money. All Federal Reserve notes are printed at the U.S. Bureau of Engraving and Printing's facilities in Washington, D.C., and Fort Worth, Texas. The Treasury mints and issues all coins. Coins are made at U.S. mints located in

Philadelphia and Denver. The bureau and the mints ship new notes and coins to the Federal Reserve banks for circulation. Much of this money is printed or minted simply to replace worn-out bills and coins. Another use of new currency is to meet public demand. Suppose it is the holiday season and banks need more paper money and coins to meet their customers' shopping needs. The Federal Reserve must be ready to ship extra money from its large vaults by armored truck.

14-6e PROTECTING CONSUMERS

Since 1968, the Federal Reserve has played a role in protecting consumers by enforcing statutes enacted by Congress. Perhaps the most important is the *Equal Credit Opportunity Act,* which prohibits discrimination based on race, color, gender, marital status, religion, or national origin in the extension of credit. It also gives married women the right to establish credit histories in their own names. The Federal Reserve receives and tries to resolve consumer complaints against banks.

In 2010, the Consumer Financial Protection Bureau (CFPB) was established. This is an independent bureau within the Federal Reserve that helps consumers make financial decisions. The goal of the CFPB is to promote fairness and make mortgages, credit cards, and other consumer financial services understandable. The objective is to let consumers see clearly the costs and features of loans. As a result, consumers will not be caught by hidden fees or sign loans they cannot afford.

Consumer Financial Protection Bureau (CFPB)

An independent bureau within the Federal Reserve that helps consumers make financial decisions.

14-6f MAINTAINING FEDERAL GOVERNMENT CHECKING ACCOUNTS AND GOLD

The Fed is also Uncle Sam's bank. The U.S. Treasury has the Fed handle its checking account. From this account, the federal government pays for such expenses as federal employees' salaries, Social Security, tax refunds, veterans' benefits, defense, and highways.

Finally, it is interesting to note that the New York Federal Reserve District Bank holds one of the oldest forms of money—*gold.* This gold belongs mainly to foreign governments and is one of the largest accumulations of this precious metal in the world. Viewing a Federal Reserve bank's vault is not something that most tourists typically have on their list of things to do, but I strongly recommend this tour.

The gold vault at the New York Federal Reserve Bank is nearly half the length of a football field and filled with steel and concrete walls several yards thick. Most cells contain the gold of only one nation, and only a few bank employees know the identities of the owners. When trade occurs between two countries, payment between the parties can be made by transferring gold bars from one compartment to another. Note that the Fed and the monetary system of the Yapese have a similarity. Recall from the Global Economics box that in Yap, large stone wheels are not moved; they just change ownership.

14-6g LENDER OF LAST RESORT

The Fed acts as the lender of last resort to prevent a banking crisis. For example, after the terrorist attacks in 2001, the Fed issued billions in loans to banks throughout the United States. And in 2008, several large banks collapsed and others were

on the verge. The Fed lent banks enough required reserve balances to meet their obligation to depositors.

14-7 The U.S. Banking Revolution

Prior to the 1980s, the U.S. banking system was simpler. It consisted of many commercial banks authorized by law to offer checking accounts. Then there were the other financial institutions, the so-called thrifts, which included S&Ls, mutual savings banks, and credit unions. The thrifts by law were permitted to accept only savings deposits with no checking privileges. The commercial banks, on the other hand, could not pay interest on checkable deposits. Moreover, a "maximum interest rate allowed by law" limited competition among commercial banks and other financial institutions. As will be explained momentarily, this relatively tranquil U.S. banking structure changed dramatically, and the stage was set for a fascinating banking "horror story."

14-7a THE MONETARY CONTROL ACT OF 1980

A significant law affecting the U.S. banking system is the Depository Institutions Deregulation and Monetary Control Act of 1980, commonly called the Monetary Control Act. This law gave the Federal Reserve System greater control over nonmember banks and made all financial institutions more competitive. The act's four major provisions are the following:

Monetary Control Act

A law, formally titled the Depository Institutions Deregulation and Monetary Control Act of 1980, that gave the Federal Reserve System greater control over nonmember banks and made all financial institutions more competitive.

1. *The authority of the Fed over nonmember depository institutions was increased.* Before the Monetary Control Act, less than half the banks in the United States were members of the Fed and subject to its direct control. Under the act's provisions, the Federal Reserve sets uniform reserve requirements for *all* commercial banks, including state and national banks, S&Ls, and credit unions with checking accounts.
2. *All depository institutions are able to borrow loan reserves from Federal Reserve banks.* This practice, called *discounting*, will be explained in the next chapter. Banks also have access to check clearing and other services of the Fed.
3. *The act allows commercial banks, thrifts, money market mutual funds, stock brokerage firms, and retailers to offer a wide variety of banking services.* For example, commercial banks and other financial institutions can pay unrestricted interest rates on checking accounts. Also, S&Ls and other financial institutions can offer checking accounts. Federal credit unions are authorized to make residential real estate loans, and other major corporations can offer traditional banking services.
4. *The act eliminated all interest rate ceilings.* Before this act, S&Ls were allowed to pay depositors a slightly higher interest rate on passbook savings deposits than those paid by commercial banks. The Monetary Control Act removed this advantage of S&Ls over other financial institutions competing for depositors.

Finally, the movement toward deregulation, which blurred the distinctions between financial institutions, continued in 1999 when the *Financial Services Modernization Act* was signed into law. This sweeping measure lifted Depression-era

The Wreck of Lincoln Savings and Loan
Applicable Concept: deposit insurance

The case of Lincoln Savings and Loan is a classic example of what went wrong during one of the worst financial crises in U.S. history prior to the banking crisis and Great Recession of 2007–2009. In 1984, the Securities and Exchange Commission charged Charles Keating, Jr., with fraud in an Ohio loan scam, but regulators later allowed him to buy Lincoln Savings and Loan in California. Keating hired a staff to carry out his wishes and paid them and his relatives millions. Keating was also generous with politicians in Washington, D.C. Allegedly, five U.S. senators received $1.5 million in campaign contributions from Keating to influence regulators.

Where did Keating's money come from? It came from Lincoln Savings depositors and, ultimately, from taxpayers because the federal government insures deposits of failed S&Ls. When Keating took over Lincoln, it was a healthy S&L with assets of $1.1 billion. But because of deregulation mandated by the Monetary Control Act and other legislation and the lack of enforcement of regulations under the new laws, many S&Ls plunged into high-risk, but potentially highly profitable, ventures. Keating therefore took Lincoln out of sound home mortgage loans and into speculation in Arizona hotels costing $500,000 per room to build, raw land for golf courses, shopping centers, junk bonds, and currency futures.

In 1987, after it was already too late, California regulators became alarmed at the way Lincoln operated and asked the FBI and the FSLIC to take over Lincoln. Keating responded by contacting his friends in Washington, and the regulatory process moved at a snail's pace. Years passed before the government finally closed Lincoln and informed the public that their deposits were not safe in this S&L. During the time regulators were deciding what action to take, it is estimated that Lincoln cost taxpayers another $1 billion. Ultimately, the collapse of Lincoln cost U.S. taxpayers about $3 billion, making it the most expensive S&L failure of all.

Keating and other S&L entrepreneurs say they did nothing wrong. After all, Congress and federal regulators encouraged, or did not discourage, S&Ls to compete by borrowing funds at high interest rates and making risky, but potentially highly profitable, investments. If oil prices and land values fall unexpectedly and loans fail, this is simply the way a market economy works and not the fault of risk-prone wheeler-dealers like Keating.

In 1993, a federal judge sentenced Keating to 12 1/2 years in prison for swindling small investors. The sentence ran concurrently with a 10-year state prison sentence. The judge also ordered Keating to pay $122.4 million in restitution to the government for losses caused by sham property sales. However, the government

has been unable to locate any significant assets. Keating served four years and nine months.

Analyze the Issue

Critics of federal banking policy argue that deposit insurance is a key reason for banking failures. The banks enjoy a "heads I win, tails the government loses" proposition. Several possible reforms of deposit insurance have been suggested. For example, the limit on insured deposits can be raised, reduced, or eliminated. Do you think a change in deposit insurance would prevent bank failures?

Source: © Cengage Learning 2014

barriers and allows banks, securities firms, and insurance companies to merge and sell each other's products.

14-7b THE SAVINGS AND LOAN CRISIS

Before the recent financial crisis discussed in the chapter on monetary policy, the savings and loan crisis of the 1980s and early 1990s was one of the worst U.S. financial crises since the Great Depression. After the Monetary Control Act removed interest rate ceilings on deposits, competition for customers forced S&Ls to pay higher interest rates on short-term deposits. Unlike the banks, however, S&Ls were earning their income from long-term mortgages at fixed interest rates below the rate required to keep or attract new deposits. The resulting losses enticed the S&Ls to forsake home mortgage loans, which they knew best, and seek high-interest, but riskier, commercial and consumer loans. Unfortunately, these risky higher-interest loans resulted in defaults and more losses. If conditions were not bad enough, lower oil prices depressed the oil-based state economies in Texas, Louisiana, and Oklahoma.

The Federal Savings and Loan Insurance Corporation (FSLIC) was the agency that insured deposits in S&Ls, similar to how the FDIC insures bank deposits. The magnitude of the losses exceeded the insurance fund's ability to pay depositors, and Congress placed the FSLIC's deposit-insurance fund under the FDIC's control. To close or sell ailing S&Ls and protect depositors, Congress enacted the Thrift Bailout Bill in 1989. One provision of this act created the Resolution Trust Corporation (RTC) to carry out a massive federal bailout of failed institutions. The RTC bought the assets and deposits of failed S&Ls and sold them to offset the cost borne by taxpayers. The RTC closed in 1995, and the ultimate cost to taxpayers totaled $125 billion!

Key Concepts

Barter
Money
Medium of exchange
Unit of account
Store of value
Commodity money
Fiat money

M1, M2
Currency
Checkable deposits
Federal Reserve System
Board of Governors of the
    Federal Reserve System

Federal Open Market Committee
    (FOMC)
Federal Deposit Insurance
    Corporation (FDIC)
Consumer Financial Bureau
    (CFPB)
Monetary Control Act

Summary

- **Money** can be anything that meets these three tests. Money must serve as (1) a medium of exchange, (2) a unit of account, and (3) a store of value. Money facilitates more efficient exchange than barter. Other desirable

properties of money include scarcity, portability, divisibility, and uniformity.
- **Medium of exchange** is the most important function of money. This means that money is widely accepted in payment for goods and services.

- **Unit of account** is another important function of money. Money is used to measure relative values by serving as a common yardstick for valuing goods and services.
- **Store of value** is the ability of money to hold its value over time. Money is said to be highly *liquid*, which means it is readily usable in exchange.
- **Credit cards** are not money. Credit cards represent a short-term loan and therefore fail as a store of value.
- **Commodity money** is money that has a marketable value, such as gold and silver. Today, the United States uses *fiat money*, which must be accepted by law, but is not convertible into gold, silver, or any commodity.
- **M1** is the narrowest definition of the money supply, which equals currency plus checkable deposits. **M2** is a broader definition of the money supply, which equals M1 plus *near monies*, such as savings deposits and small time deposits.
- The **Federal Reserve System**, our central bank, was established in 1913. The Fed consists of 12 Federal Reserve district banks with 25 branches. The *Board of Governors* is the Fed's governing body. The *Federal Open Market Committee* (FOMC) directs the buying and selling of U.S. government securities, which is a key method of controlling the money supply.
- **Basic Federal Reserve bank functions** are (1) controlling the money supply, (2) clearing checks, (3) supervising and regulating banking, (4) maintaining and circulating currency, (5) protecting consumers, and (6) maintaining the federal government's checking accounts and gold.

Definitions of Money Supply (M1 and M2)

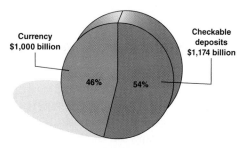

Currency $1,000 billion

Checkable deposits $1,174 billion

46%   54%

M1 = $2,174 billion

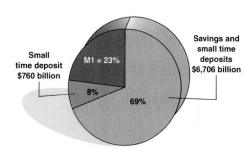

Small time deposit $760 billion

M1 = 23%

Savings and small time deposits $6,706 billion

8%   69%

M2 = $9,640 billion

SOURCE: *Economic Report of the President*, 2012, http://www.gpo.gov/fdsys/pkg/ERP-2012/content-detail.htm1, Tables B-69 and B-70.

- The **Monetary Control Act of 1980** revolutionized U.S. banking by expanding the authority of the Federal Reserve System to all financial institutions. In addition, this law increased competition by blurring the distinctions between commercial banks, thrift institutions, and even nonfinancial institutions.

Summary of Conclusion Statements

- The use of money simplifies and therefore increases market transactions. Money also prevents wasting time that can be devoted to production, thereby promoting economic growth by increasing a nation's production possibilities.
- Money is a useful mechanism for transforming income in the present into future purchases.
- Money is the most liquid form of wealth because it can be spent directly in the marketplace.

- The supply of money must be great enough to meet ordinary transaction needs, but not be so plentiful that it becomes worthless.
- An item's ability to serve as money does not depend on its own market value or the backing of precious metal.
- M1 is more liquid than M2.

Study Questions and Problems

1. Discuss this statement: "A man with a million dollars who is lost in the desert learns the meaning of money."

2. Could each of the following items potentially serve as money? Consider each as (1) a medium of exchange, (2) a unit of account, and (3) a store of value.
   a. Visa credit card
   b. Federal Reserve note
   c. Dog
   d. Beer mug

3. Consider each of the items in question 2 in terms of scarcity, portability, divisibility, and uniformity.

4. What backs the U.S. dollar? Include the distinction between commodity money and fiat money in your answer.

5. What are the components of the most narrowly defined money supply in the United States?

6. Distinguish between M1 and M2. What are near monies?

7. What is the major purpose of the Federal Reserve System? What is the major responsibility of the Board of Governors and the Federal Open Market Committee?

8. Should the Fed be independent or a government agency subordinate to Congress and the president?

9. Which banks must be insured by the FDIC? Which banks can choose not to be insured by the FDIC?

10. Briefly discuss the importance of the Depository Institutions Deregulation and Monetary Control Act of 1980.

For Online Exercises, go to the Tucker Web site at www.cengage.com/economics/tucker.

✓ CHECKPOINT ANSWER

Are Debit Cards Money?

Debit cards serve as a means of payment, and debit card statements serve as a unit of account. Finally, unlike credit cards, debit cards serve as a store of value because they are a means of accessing checkable deposits and not an extension of credit. If you said debit cards are money because they serve all three functions required for money, **YOU ARE CORRECT.**

Sample Quiz

For an explanation of the correct answers, visit the Tucker Web site at www.cengage.com/economics/tucker.

1. Buying a cup of coffee with a dollar bill represents the use of money as a
   a. medium of exchange.
   b. unit of account.
   c. store of value.
   d. All of the above answers are correct.

Sample Quiz *continued*

2. Comparing how many dollars it takes to attend college each year to annual earnings on a job represents the use of money as a
   a. medium of exchange.
   b. unit of account.
   c. store of value.
   d. store of coincidence.

3. Which of the following items does *not* provide a store of value?
   a. currency
   b. checkable deposits
   c. credit cards
   d. All of the above answers are correct.

4. Anything can be money if it acts as a
   a. unit of account.
   b. store of value.
   c. medium of exchange.
   d. All of the above answers must be correct.

5. The ease with which an asset can be converted into a medium of exchange is known as
   a. volatility.
   b. liquidity.
   c. currency.
   d. speculative exchange.

6. Which of the following items is included when computing M1?
   a. coins in circulation
   b. currency in circulation
   c. checking accounting entries
   d. All of the above answers are correct.

7. Which of the following statements is *true*?
   a. Money must be relatively "scarce" if it is to have value.
   b. Money must be divisible and portable.
   c. M1 is the narrowest definition of money.
   d. All of the above answers are correct.

8. M1 money includes all but which of the following?
   a. checkable deposits
   b. savings accounts
   c. paper money
   d. coins

9. Which of the following is counted as part of M2?
   a. currency
   b. checkable deposits at commercial banks
   c. money market funds
   d. All of the above answers are correct.

10. Which definition of the money supply includes credit cards?
    a. M1
    b. M2
    c. Both answers include credit card balances.
    d. Neither answer includes credit card balances.

11. With respect to controlling the money supply, the law requires the Fed to take orders from
    a. the president.
    b. the Speaker of the House.
    c. the Secretary of the Treasury.
    d. no one—the Fed is an independent agency.

12. Which of the following is *not* part of the Federal Reserve System?
    a. Council of Economic Advisors
    b. Board of Governors
    c. Federal Open Market Committee
    d. 12 Federal Reserve District Banks

13. The Fed's principal decision-making body, which directs buying and selling U.S. government securities, is the
    a. Federal Deposit Insurance Corporation.
    b. District Board of Governors.
    c. Federal Open Market Committee.
    d. Reserve Requirement Regulation Conference.

14. The major protection against a sudden mass attempt to withdraw cash from banks is the
    a. Federal Reserve.
    b. Consumer Protection Act.
    c. deposit insurance provided by the FDIC.
    d. gold and silver backing the dollar.

15. The Monetary Control Act of 1980
    a. created less competition among various financial institutions.

Sample Quiz *continued*

b. allowed fewer institutions to offer checking account services.

c. restricted savings and loan associations to long-term loans.

d. did none of the above.

16. Which of the following is a store of value?

a. federal reserve notes

b. debit card

c. passbook savings deposit

d. Each of the above answers is a store of value.

17. The difference between M1 and M2 is given by which of the following?

a. M1 includes currency, coins, gold, and silver, whereas M2 does not contain gold and silver.

b. M1 is made up of currency and checkable deposits, whereas M2 contains M1 plus savings deposits and small time deposits.

c. M1 is limited to checkable deposits, whereas M2 contains currency.

d. M1 includes only currency, whereas M2 contains M1 plus checkable deposits.

18. Which of the following is a desirable property of money?

a. scarcity

b. portability

c. divisibility

d. All of the above answers are correct.

19. The Federal Reserve System was founded in

a. 1913.

b. 1929.

c. 1933.

d. 1935.

20. The Monetary Control Act of 1980 extended the Fed's authority to

a. impose required reserve ratios on all depository institutions.

b. control the discount rate.

c. control the federal funds rate.

d. All of the above answers are correct.

Money Creation

It has been said that the most important person in Washington, D.C., is the chair of the Federal Reserve because he or she can influence the money supply and therefore the performance of the economy. This chapter builds on your knowledge of money and the Federal Reserve System gained in the previous chapter. You will discover that the Federal Reserve (the Fed) and the banks work together to determine the money supply. The chapter begins with a brief history of the evolution of banking. Then we examine the mechanics of how banks create money in a simplified system during a normal economy. This remarkable process depends on the ability of banks to amplify checkable deposits by generating a spiral of new loans and, in turn, deposits for new spending in the economy. Finally, the Fed's toolkit swings open, and we discuss the three tools used by the Fed to change the money supply.

A common misconception is that banks (including savings and loans and other depository institutions) accept deposits and make loans, and that's about the end of the story. But there is another very important chapter to tell. Banking transactions expand or contract the money supply. Without minting coins or using the printing presses to make paper money, your local bank and other banks can create money; that is, banks can increase the money supply (M1).

The reason people do not understand money creation is that they think the federal government controls the money supply by turning the printing presses on and off. As explained in the previous chapter, this notion is only partly true because money consists largely of bookkeeping entries (checkable deposits). Consequently, writing checks, using an automatic teller machine, and getting a loan affect the size of the checkable deposits component of the money supply.

In this chapter, you will learn to solve these economics puzzles:

- Exactly how is money created in the economy? That is, how does the money supply increase?
- What are the major tools the Federal Reserve uses to control the supply of money?
- Why is there nothing "federal" about the federal funds rate?

15-1 Money Creation Begins

In the Middle Ages, gold was the money of choice in most European nations. One of the problems with gold is that it is a heavy commodity, which makes it difficult to use in transactions or to hide from thieves. The medieval solution was to keep it safely deposited with the people who worked with gold, called *goldsmiths*. This demand for their services inspired goldsmith entrepreneurs to become the founders of modern-day banking.

The goldsmiths sat on their benches with ledgers close by and recorded the amounts of gold placed in their vaults. In fact, the word *bank* is derived from the Italian word for bench, which is *banco*. After assessing the purity of the gold, a goldsmith issued a receipt to the customer for the amount of gold deposited. In return, the goldsmith collected a service charge, just as you pay today for services at your bank. Anyone who possessed the receipt and presented it to the goldsmith could make a withdrawal for the amount of gold written on the receipt.

With these gold receipts in circulation, people began paying their debts with these pieces of paper, rather than actually exchanging gold. Thus, goldsmith receipts became paper money. At first, the goldsmiths were very conservative and issued receipts exactly equal to the amount of gold stored in their vaults. However, some shrewd goldsmiths observed that net withdrawals in any period were only a *fraction* of all the gold "on reserve." This observation produced a powerful idea. Goldsmiths discovered that they could make loans for more gold than they actually held in their vaults. As a result, goldsmiths made extra profit from interest on these loans, and borrowers had more money for spending in their hands.

15-2 How a Single Bank Creates Money

The medieval goldsmiths were the first to practice fractional reserve banking. Modern fractional reserve banking is a system in which banks keep only a percentage of their deposits on reserve as vault cash and deposits at the Fed. In a 100 percent reserve banking system, banks would be unable to create money by making loans. However, as you will learn momentarily, holding less than 100 percent on reserve allows banks to make loans, and in turn, these loans create money in the economy.

Fractional reserve banking

A system in which banks keep only a percentage of their deposits on reserve as vault cash and deposits at the Fed.

15-2a BANKER BOOKKEEPING

We begin our exploration of how the fractional reserve banking system operates in the United States by looking at the balance sheet of a single bank, Typical Bank. A balance sheet is a statement of the assets and liabilities of a bank at a given point in time. Balance sheets are called *T-accounts*. The hypothetical T-account of Typical Bank in Balance Sheet 1 lists only major categories and omits details to keep things simple.

Typical Bank

Balance Sheet 1

Assets		Liabilities	
Required reserves	$ 5 million	Checkable deposits	$50 million
Excess reserves	0		
Loans	45 million		
Total	$50 million	Total	$50 million

Note: The Fed requires the bank to keep 10 percent of its checkable deposits in reserves. Holding $5 million in required reserves, the bank has zero excess reserves and $45 million in loans to earn profit.

On the right side of the balance sheet are the bank's *liabilities*. Liabilities are the amounts the bank owes to others. In our example, the only liabilities are *checkable deposits*, or demand deposits. Note that checkable deposits are assets on the customers' personal balance sheets, but they are debt obligations of Typical Bank. If a depositor writes a check against his or her checking account, the bank must pay this amount. Therefore, checkable deposits are liabilities to the bank.

On the left side of the balance sheet, we see Typical Bank's *assets*. Assets are amounts the bank owns. In our example, these assets consist of required reserves, *excess reserves*, and *loans*. Required reserves are the minimum balance of reserves that the Fed requires a bank to hold in vault cash or on deposit with the Fed. Typical Bank will maximize profits by trying to keep only the minimum amount possible in required reserves.

The required reserve ratio determines the minimum required reserves. The required reserve ratio is the percentage of deposits that the Fed requires a bank to hold in vault cash or on deposit with the Fed rather than being loaned. Here we assume that the Fed's required reserve ratio is 10 percent. Thus, the bank must have required reserves of $5 million (10 percent of $50 million). This leaves Typical Bank with $45 million in loans that provide profit to the bank.

Exhibit 1 shows that the actual required reserve ratio depends on the level of a bank's checkable deposits. Note that the Fed requires a lower percentage for a smaller bank. In the real world, Typical Bank's required reserve ratio would be 3 percent if its checkable deposits were between $11.5 million and $71.0 million.

Required reserves

The minimum balance that the Fed requires a bank to hold in vault cash or on deposit with the Fed.

Required reserve ratio

The percentage of deposits that the Fed requires a bank to hold in vault cash or on deposit with the Fed.

EXHIBIT 1	Required Reserve Ratio of the Federal Reserve
Type of deposit	**Required reserve ratio**
Checkable deposits	
$11.75–$71.0 million	3%
Over $71.0 million	10

SOURCE: Federal Reserve Bank, *Reserve Requirements*, http://www.federalreserve.gov/monetarypolicy/reservereq.htm.

Typical Bank has zero excess reserves so far in our analysis. Excess reserves are potential loan balances of reserves held in vault cash or on deposit with the Fed in excess of required reserves. We will see shortly that excess reserves play a starring role in the banking system's ability to change the money supply. The relationship between reserves accounts can be expressed as follows:

Excess reserves

Potential loan balances held in vault cash or on deposit with the Fed in excess of required reserves.

$$\text{Total reserves} = \text{required reserves} + \text{excess reserves}$$

or

$$\text{Excess reserves} = \text{total reserves} - \text{required reserves}$$

The final entry on the asset side of Typical Bank's balance sheet is loans, which are interest-earning assets of the bank. Loans are bank assets because they represent outstanding credit payable to the bank. In a fractional reserve banking system, the bank uses balances not held in reserves to earn income. In our example, loan officers have written loans totaling $45 million. Finally, note that Typical Bank's assets equal its liabilities. As you will see momentarily, any change on one side of the T-account must be accompanied by an equal amount of change on the other side of the balance sheet.

15-2b STEP ONE: ACCEPTING A NEW DEPOSIT

You are now prepared to see how a bank creates money. Assume the required reserve ratio is 10 percent and one of Best National Bank's depositors, Brad Rich, takes $100,000 in cash from under his mattress and deposits it in his checking account. Balance Sheet 2 records this change by increasing the bank's checkable deposits on the liability side by $100,000. Brad's deposit is a liability of the bank because Brad could change his mind and withdraw his money. On the asset side, Brad's deposit increases assets because the bank has an extra $90,000 to lend after setting aside the proper amount of required reserves. Balance Sheet 2 shows that total reserves are divided between required reserves of $10,000 (10 percent of the deposit) and excess reserves of $90,000 (90 percent of the deposit). Thus, the bank's assets and liabilities remain equal when Brad makes his deposit.

Before proceeding, we must pause to make an important point. Depositing coins or paper currency in a bank has no initial effect on the money supply (M1). Recall from the previous chapter that M1 includes currency in circulation. Therefore, the transfer of $100,000 in cash from the mattress to the bank creates no money because M1 already counts this amount. Moreover, the money supply would *not* have increased had Brad Rich's initial $100,000 deposit been a check written on another bank. In this case, an increase in the assets and liabilities of Best National Bank by $100,000 would simply decrease the assets and liabilities of the other bank by $100,000. Recall that M1 also includes checkable deposits.

> **CONCLUSION:** *Transferring currency to a bank and moving deposits from one bank to another do not affect the money supply (M1).*

Best National Bank

Balance Sheet 2

Assets		Liabilities		Change in M1
Required reserves	+$ 10,000	Brad Rich account	+$100,000	0
Excess reserves	+ 90,000			
Total	$100,000	Total	$100,000	

Step 1: Brad Rich deposits $100,000 in cash, which increases checkable deposits. The Fed requires the bank to keep 10 percent of its new deposit in required reserves, so this account is credited with $10,000. The remaining 90 percent is excess reserves of $90,000. There is no effect on the money supply.

15-2c STEP TWO: MAKING A LOAN

So far, M1 has not changed, as shown in Balance Sheet 2, because Brad has simply taken $100,000 in currency and transferred it to a checkable deposit. Stated differently, the public holds the same $100,000 for spending, and only the form has changed from cash to a checkable deposit. In step two, the actual money creation process occurs. The profit motive provides the incentive for bank officials not to let $90,000 from a new deposit sit languishing in excess reserves. Instead, Best National Bank is eager to make loans and earn a profit by charging interest. Suppose, coincidentally, that Connie Jones walks in with a big smile, asking for a $90,000 loan to purchase equipment for her health spa. Connie has a fine credit record, so the bank accepts Connie's note (IOU) agreeing to repay the loan. Then the bank gives Connie a check for $90,000, which she deposits in her account with the bank. This increases the bank's liabilities by $90,000. As shown in Balance Sheet 3, three entries on the assets side have changed. First, the loan to Connie Jones boosts the loans account to $90,000. Second, the bank must increase required reserves by $9,000 because of the $90,000 increase in checkable deposits on the liabilities side. (Recall that required reserves are 10 percent of checkable deposits.) Required reserves are now $19,000. Third, transferring $9,000 from excess reserves to required reserves reduces the bank's excess reserves from $90,000 to $81,000. Total reserves remain at $100,000 in both Balance Sheet 2 and Balance Sheet 3.

Best National Bank

Balance Sheet 3

Assets		Liabilities		Change in M1
Required reserves	$ 19,000	Brad Rich account	$100,000	
Excess reserves	81,000	Connie Jones account	+90,000	+$90,000
Loans	+90,000			
Total	$190,000	Total	$190,000	

Step 2: The bank loans Connie Jones $90,000 by crediting her checking account with this amount. A corresponding $90,000 balance is added to the loan account. The result is an increase in the money supply of $90,000.

The corresponding entry on the liabilities side of the balance sheet is the bread and butter of money creation. Checkable deposits have increased by $90,000 to $190,000. The reason is that the bank issued a check in Connie's name drawn on a checking account in the bank. Thus, Best National Bank has performed money magic with this transaction. Look what happened to the $100,000 deposited by Brad Rich. It has generated a new $90,000 *loan*, which was added to checkable deposits and therefore increased the money supply by $90,000.

> **CONCLUSION:** *When a bank makes a loan, it creates deposits, and the money supply increases by the amount of the loan because the money supply includes checkable deposits.*

Before proceeding further, you need to pause and take particular notice of the impact of these transactions on the money supply. In step one, Brad's initial deposit did not change M1. But in step two, M1 increased by $90,000 when Best National Bank created money out of thin air by making the loan to Connie Jones. Now Connie has more money in her checking account than she did before, and no one else has less. Connie can now use this money to buy goods and services.

15-2d STEP THREE: CLEARING THE LOAN CHECK

Now Connie Jones can use her new money to purchase equipment for her spa. Suppose Connie buys equipment for her business from Better Health Spa and writes a check for $90,000 drawn on Best National Bank. The owner of Better Health Spa then deposits the check in the firm's account at Yazoo National Bank. Yazoo National will send the check to its Federal Reserve district bank for collection. Recall that each bank maintains required reserves at the Fed. The Fed clears the check by debiting the reserve account of Best National Bank and crediting the reserve account of Yazoo National Bank. The Fed then returns the check to Best National Bank, and this bank reduces Connie Jones's checking account by $90,000. As shown in Balance Sheet 4, Connie Jones's checking account falls to

Best National Bank			
Balance Sheet 4			
Assets		**Liabilities**	**Change in M1**
Required reserves	$ 10,000	Brad Rich account	$100,000	0
Excess reserves	0	Connie Jones account	0	
Loans	90,000			
Total	$100,000	Total	$100,000	

Step 3: Connie Jones pays Better Health Spa with a $90,000 check drawn on Best National Bank. Better Health Spa deposits the check in Yazoo National Bank, which collects from Best National Bank. The result is a debit to Connie's account and to her bank's reserves accounts.

zero, and Best National Bank's liabilities are reduced by $90,000. On the asset side of the balance sheet, required reserves decrease by $9,000, and excess reserves return to zero. Now that all the dust has settled, Best National Bank has required reserves of $10,000 and an IOU for $90,000. Note that this check-clearing process in step three has no effect on M1. The $90,000 increase in M1 created by Best National Bank's loan to Connie remains on deposit at Yazoo National Bank in Better Health Spa's checking account.

Finally, if Brad Rich withdraws $100,000 in cash from Best National Bank, the process described above operates in reverse. The result is a $90,000 decline (destruction) in the money supply.

15-3 Multiplier Expansion of Money by the Banking System

The process of money creation (loans) does not stop at the doors of Best National Bank. Just like the spending multiplier from the chapter on fiscal policy, there is a money multiplier process. Let's continue our story by following the effect on Yazoo National after Better Health Spa deposits $90,000 from Connie Jones. As shown in Balance Sheet 5, Yazoo National's checkable deposits increase by $90,000. Given a required reserve ratio of 10 percent, Yazoo National Bank must keep $9,000 in required reserves, and the remaining $81,000 goes into excess reserves.

Yazoo National Bank			
Balance Sheet 5			
Assets		**Liabilities**	
Required reserves	+$ 9,000	Better Health Spa account	+$90,000
Excess reserves	+ 81,000		
Total	$90,000	Total	$90,000

Note: Given a required reserve ratio of 10 percent, Better Health Spa's deposit of $90,000 from Connie Jones creates $81,000 in additional excess reserves that the bank can lend and thus create additional checkable deposits.

Yazoo National's loan officer now has $81,000 in additional excess reserves to lend and thus create additional checkable deposits, excess reserves, and eventually loans in other banks. Exhibit 2 presents the expansion of the money supply created when Brad Rich makes his initial $100,000 deposit, and then banks make loans that are deposited in other banks.

In Exhibit 2, we see that, lo and behold, an initial deposit of $100,000 in Best National Bank can eventually create a $900,000 increase in the money supply (ΔM1). This is because Brad Rich's initial $100,000 deposit eventually creates total excess reserves of $900,000 in the banking system as a whole. This was created by new loans and, in turn, new deposits in different banks. As this process continues, each bank accepts smaller and smaller increases in checkable deposits because 10 percent of each deposit is held as required reserves. Note that the initial $100,000 was from cash already counted in M1, and so it is not counted in the expansion of the money supply.

EXHIBIT 2	Expansion of the Money Supply			
Round	Bank	Increase in checkable deposits	Increase in required reserves	Increase in excess reserves
1	Best National Bank	$ 100,000	$ 10,000	$ 90,000
2	Yazoo National Bank	90,000	9,000	81,000
3	Bank A	81,000	8,100	72,900
4	Bank B	72,900	7,290	65,610
5	Bank C	65,610	6,561	59,049
6	Bank D	59,049	5,905	53,144
7	Bank E	53,144	5,314	47,830
.	.	.	.	.
.	.	.	.	.
.	.	.	.	.
Total all other banks		478,297	47,830	430,467
Total increase		$1,000,000	$100,000	$900,000 (ΔM1)

Note: A $100,000 cash deposit in Best National Bank creates $900,000 in new deposits in other banks. Each round creates excess reserves, which are loaned to a customer who deposits the loan check in another bank in the next round.

Source: © Cengage Learning 2014

15-3a THE MONEY MULTIPLIER

Fortunately, we do not need to calculate all the individual bank transactions listed in Exhibit 2 in order to derive the change in the money supply initiated by a deposit or withdrawal. Instead, we can use the money multiplier, or *deposit multiplier*. The money multiplier gives the *maximum* change in the money supply (checkable deposits) due to an initial change in the excess reserves held by banks.[1] The money multiplier is equal to 1 divided by the required reserve ratio. Expressed as a formula:

$$\text{Money multiplier (MM)} = \frac{1}{\text{required reserve ratio (RRR)}} = \frac{1}{1/10} = 10$$

The actual change in the money supply is computed by the following formula:

$$\textbf{Actual money supply change (ΔM1)} = \textbf{initial change in excess reserves (ER)}$$
$$\times \textbf{ money multiplier (MM)}$$

Money multiplier

The maximum change in the money supply (checkable deposits) due to an initial change in the excess reserves banks hold. The money multiplier is equal to 1 divided by the required reserve ratio.

---

[1] The money multiplier (MM) is the sum of the infinite geometric progression $1 + (1 - r) + (1 - r)^2 + (1 - r)^3 + \ldots + (1 - r)^\infty$, where r equals the required reserve ratio.

Symbolically, using the data in Exhibit 2,

$$\Delta M1 = \Delta ER \times MM$$

$$\$900,000 = \$90,000 \times 10$$

15-3b THE REAL-WORLD MONEY MULTIPLIER

In reality, for several reasons, the size of the money multiplier can be considerably smaller than our handy little formula indicates. First, Connie Jones, or any other customer along the money creation process, can decide to put a portion of the loan in her pocket, rather than writing a check to Better Health Spa for the full amount of the loan. Money outside the banking system in someone's wallet or purse or underneath the mattress is a cash leakage, which reduces the value of the money multiplier.

Second, the size of the money multiplier falls when banks do not use all their excess reserves to make loans. Perhaps a financial crisis causes many people to lose confidence in the banking system, and they make large deposit account withdrawals. As a result, banks hold their excess reserves. Or some banks can hold excess reserves because they lack enough "worthy" loan applications. This is the situation under the current credit crunch described in the You're the Economist feature in the next chapter. In short, banks are very cautious to make new loans because they are suffering from holding bad mortgage loans.

> **CONCLUSION:** *When banks decide to retain excess reserves, the money multiplier will be smaller.*

15-4 How Monetary Policy Creates Money

The previous chapter explained that the principal function of the Fed is to control the money supply using three policy tools, or levers. The Fed's use of these tools to influence the economy is more precisely called monetary policy. Monetary policy is the Federal Reserve's use of open market operations, changes in the discount rate, and changes in the required reserve ratio to change the money supply (M1). Using these three tools, or levers, of monetary policy, the Fed can limit or expand deposit creation by the banks and thereby change the money supply.

Monetary policy
The Federal Reserve's use of open market operations, changes in the discount rate, and changes in the required reserve ratio to change the money supply (M1).

15-4a OPEN MARKET OPERATIONS

You have seen how decisions of the public—including those of Brad Rich, Connie Jones, and Better Health Spa—worked through the banking system and increased M1. In this section, you will build on this foundation by learning how the Fed can expand or contract the money supply. We begin with the aggregated Balance Sheet 6 of the 12 Federal Reserve banks of the Federal Reserve System. Total assets of the Fed on June 6, 2012, were $2,854 billion. The majority of these assets ($1,664 billion) were held in U.S. government securities in the form of Treasury bills, Treasury notes, and Treasury bonds, and loans to banks were $5 billion. This contrasts with commercial banks, which hold most of their assets in loans. Finally, the other assets of the Fed include high-grade mortgage-backed securities purchased from banks in order to help stabilize the banking system during the recent financial crisis.

The major liability of the Fed was $1,068 billion worth of Federal Reserve notes—paper currency. This is in contrast to the major liability of commercial banks, which is checkable deposits. As explained in the previous chapter, the Fed issues, but does not actually print, Federal Reserve notes. Instead, the Fed decides how much to issue and then calls the Bureau of Engraving and Printing to order new batches of $10, $20, $50, and $100 bills, which the Fed sends to the banks in armored trucks.

Another important liability of the Fed is the deposits of banks and the U.S. Treasury totaling $1,622. The Fed therefore serves as a bank for these banks and the Treasury. Note that these bank deposits include the required reserve deposits discussed at the beginning of the chapter. Finally, total liabilities and net worth equaled total assets of $2,854 billion. Details of the balance sheet are omitted for simplicity.

Federal Reserve System

Balance Sheet 6

June 6, 2012
(billions of dollars)

Assets		Liabilities	
U.S. government securities	$1,664	Federal Reserve notes	$1,068
Loans to banks	5	Deposits	1,622
Other assets	1,185	Other liabilities and net worth	164
Total assets	$2,854	Total liabilities and net worth	$2,854

Source: Federal Reserve Board, *Factors Affecting Reserve Balances*, http://www.federalreserve.gov/releases/h41/Current/.

Recall the Federal Open Market Committee (FOMC) introduced in the previous chapter. The FOMC, as its name implies, determines the money supply through open market operations. Open market operations are the buying and selling of government securities by the Federal Reserve System. The New York Federal Reserve Bank's trading desk executes these orders. Suppose the FOMC decides to increase the money supply and instructs the New York Fed trading desk to *buy* $100,000 worth of 90-day U.S. Treasury bills (called T-bills).[2] The Fed contacts securities dealers in the private sector for competitive bids. Suppose the Fed accepts the lowest bid, buys $100,000 worth of

Open market operations

The buying and selling of government securities by the Federal Reserve System.

---

[2]The U.S. Treasury issues T-bills in minimum denominations of $10,000. These marketable obligations of the federal government mature in three months, six months, or one year and are used to finance the budget deficit, as explained in the chapter on this topic. The Treasury sells three-month bills at weekly auctions and six-month and one-year bills less often.

T-bills, and pays the dealer with a check drawn against itself. As shown in Balance Sheet 7, the Fed's assets increase by $100,000 worth of U.S. government IOUs. Once the securities dealer deposits the Fed's check in the firm's account at Best National Bank, the bank will send the $100,000 check back to the Fed. When the Fed receives the check, it will increase Best National's reserves account at the Fed by this amount. The Fed therefore increases its liabilities by $100,000, and M1 increases immediately by $100,000 because the security dealer's checking account increases at Best National Bank. Like a magician waving a magic wand, the Fed has created new money: the initial $100,000 checkable deposit and excess reserves for loans. Given a 10 percent reserve requirement, Best National Bank's required reserves increase by $10,000, and its excess reserves increase by $90,000. Therefore, the money supply will potentially increase by $1 million (the $100,000 initial increase in M1 when the Fed buys the security multiplied by the money multiplier of 10). Note that unlike the example shown previously in Exhibit 2 involving an initial $100,000 cash deposit already counted in M1, here the initial deposit was created by the Fed and therefore not already counted in M1. Expressed as a formula:

$$\text{Actual money supply change} = \text{initial checkable deposit (CD)}$$
$$+ \text{ (initial change in excess reserves}$$
$$\times \text{ money multiplier)}$$
$$\Delta M1 = \Delta CD + (\Delta ER \times MM)$$
$$\$1,000,000 = \$100,000 + (\$90,000 \times 10)$$

Federal Reserve Bank		
Balance Sheet 7		
Assets	**Liabilities**	**Initial change in M1**
U.S. government securities +$100,000	Reserves of Best National Bank +$100,000	+$100,000

Note: To increase the money supply, the Fed conducted open market operations by purchasing $100,000 in government securities. The Fed pays a securities dealer with a Fed check, which the dealer deposits in its bank. The initial change in the money supply is an increase of $100,000.

The process goes into reverse if the FOMC directs the New York Fed trading desk to *sell* U.S. government securities for the Fed's portfolio. As shown in Balance Sheet 8, the goal of the Fed is to decrease the money supply by selling, say, $100,000 in Treasury bonds from the asset side of its balance sheet. In this case, the Fed accepts the best offer from a securities dealer. Again, assume the securities dealer's $100,000 check payable to the Fed is written on the firm's account with Best National Bank. When the Fed accepts the check, it reduces the reserves recorded on the liabilities side of Balance Sheet 8, and Best National Bank reduces the checkable deposits account of the securities dealer. By subtracting $100,000 from Best National Bank's reserves, the Fed decreases M1 initially by $100,000. Again, the Fed has waved its magic wand and extinguished money in the banking system. Given a 10 percent reserve requirement, the money supply can potentially fall by $1 million (the $100,000 initial decrease in M1 when the Fed sells the security multiplied by the money multiplier of 10).

Federal Reserve Bank

Balance Sheet 8

Assets	Liabilities	Initial change in M1
U.S. government securities −$100,000	Reserves of Best National Bank −$100,000	−$100,000

Note: To decrease the money supply, the Fed conducted open market operations by selling $100,000 in government securities. The Fed accepts a securities dealer's check drawn on the dealer's bank. The initial change in the money supply is a decrease of $100,000.

Another way to study open market operations is to look at a typical day at the trading desk located at the Federal Reserve Bank of New York. The manager of the trading desk starts the day by studying estimates of excess reserves in the banking system. If excess reserves are low, few banks have funds to lend. High excess reserves mean many banks can make loans. After collecting this information and other data, the manager looks at the directive from the FOMC and formulates the day's "game plan." Then the manager makes conference calls to several members of the FOMC for approval. With their blessing, the manager has traders in the trading room call dealers who trade in government securities for price quotations. The open market operation has two alternative objectives: purchase or sell government securities.

CONCLUSION: *A purchase of government securities by the Fed injects reserves into the banking system and increases the money supply. A sale of government securities by the Fed reduces reserves in the banking system and decreases the money supply.*

Exhibit 3 illustrates the Federal Reserve's open market operations.

✔ CHECKPOINT

Who Has More Dollar Creation Power?

You find a $1,000 bill hidden beneath the floorboards in your house and decide to deposit it in your checking account. On the same day, the Fed decides to buy $1,000 in government securities from your bank. Assuming a 10 percent reserve requirement, which of these actions creates more money in the economy?

EXHIBIT 3	Open Market Operations

When the Fed buys government securities from dealers, it increases the reserves of the banks. Banks can use these reserves to make loans, which operate through the money multiplier to expand the money supply. When the Fed sells government securities to dealers, it decreases the reserves of the banks. Thus, the banks' capacity to lend diminishes, and as a consequence, the money supply decreases.

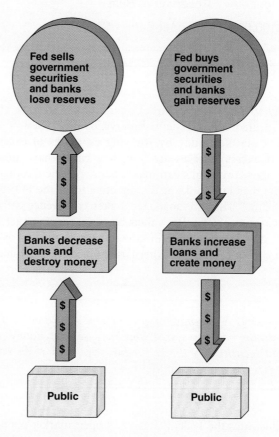

SOURCE: © Cengage Learning 2014

15-4b THE DISCOUNT RATE

So far, money creation in the banking system depends on excess reserves acquired from new checkable deposits. Actually, the Fed itself provides another option for banks to obtain reserves through its *discount window*. This is a department within each of the Federal Reserve district banks and not an actual window. Suppose Best National Bank has no excess reserves and

Brad Rich does not walk in with a deposit. Also assume the Fed does not purchase government securities and pay a dealer with a check deposited in Best National Bank. Now enter Connie Jones, who asks for a loan. In this situation, the bank has no money to lend, but it can borrow reserves from the Fed for a short period and pay the discount rate. The discount rate is the interest rate the Fed charges on loans of reserves to banks. All banks and other depository institutions have the privilege of occasionally borrowing at the Fed to cover reserve deficiencies. Changes in the discount rate often signal the Fed's monetary policy direction and therefore can affect the public's expectations about the economy. A lower discount rate encourages banks to borrow reserves and make loans.

Discount rate

The interest rate the Fed charges on loans of reserves to banks.

> **CONCLUSION:** *A higher discount rate discourages banks from borrowing reserves and making loans. If the Fed wants to expand the money supply, it reduces the discount rate. If the objective is to contract the money supply, the Fed raises the discount rate.*

Banks wanting to expand their reserves in order to seek profitable loan opportunities can also turn to the federal funds market. The federal funds market is a private market in which banks lend reserves to each other for less than 24 hours. The word *federal* does not mean it is a government market. It simply means this is an economy-wide or national market. In this market, a bank short of reserves can borrow some reserves from another bank. Using the interbank loan market, Best National Bank can borrow excess reserves from Yazoo National and pay the federal funds rate. The federal funds rate is the interest rate banks charge for overnight loans of reserves to other banks. Reserves borrowed in the federal funds market have no effect on the money supply because such borrowing simply moves reserves from one bank to another. Note that most banks borrow money to meet their reserve requirements primarily through the federal funds market and not the discount window. Also, the federal funds rate is a primary barometer of Fed policy reported in the media. The following You're The Economist provides further explanation of the federal funds rate.

Federal funds market

A private market in which banks lend reserves to each other for less than 24 hours.

Federal funds rate

The interest rate banks charge for overnight loans of reserves to other banks.

15-4c THE REQUIRED RESERVE RATIO

Under the Monetary Control Act of 1980, discussed in the preceding chapter, the Fed can set reserve requirements by law for all banks and savings and loan associations. By changing the required reserve ratio, the Fed can change banks' excess reserves and therefore banks' lending ability. This is potentially a powerful policy lever. Recall that the money multiplier equals 1 divided by the required reserve ratio. Suppose the Fed is concerned about inflation, so it wants to restrain the money supply and thereby dampen aggregate demand in the economy. If the Fed increases the required reserve ratio, the effect is to reduce excess reserves and generate a smaller change in the money supply because the money supply multiplier is smaller. For example, a required reserve ratio of 10 percent yields a money

How Does the FOMC Really Work?

Applicable Concept: monetary policy

The Federal Open Market Committee (FOMC), which is the Fed's most powerful monetary policy-making group, meets eight times a year at the Federal Reserve in Washington, D.C. Often it seems that the whole world is watching for the results. Before the meeting, board members are given three books prepared by the Fed's staff. The "Green Book" forecasts aggregate demand and various prices based on a variety of equations and the assumptions that monetary policy does or does not change. The "Blue Book" might discuss as many as three monetary policy options, the rationale for each option, and the impact of each option on the economy. There is also a "Beige Book," published

eight times per year, that gathers anecdotal information on current economic conditions obtained from interviews with key businesspersons, economists, bankers, and other sources.

The meeting begins at precisely 9 a.m. with a discussion of foreign currency operations and domestic open market operations illustrated with colorful graphics. Next, the staff presents their analysis of recent developments and forecasts for the economy laid out in the Green Book. Then each board member around the impressive 27-foot oval mahogany table expresses their views about the analyses, except for the chair, who may choose not to participate in this round. Now it's coffee time and everyone relaxes beneath a 23-foot ceiling with a 1,000-pound chandelier.

Lane V. Erickson/Shutterstock.com

After the coffee break, the staff discusses each policy option from the "Blue Book" without recommending a particular option. Generally, three options are presented. Option A is always a decline in interest rates, Option B is always no change in interest rates, and Option C is always an increase. After the staff presentation, board members politely discuss the policy options, but with an important difference. In this policy round, the

multiplier of 10 (1/0.10). If the Fed increases the ratio to 20 percent, the money multiplier falls to 5 (1/0.20).

> **CONCLUSION:** *There is an inverse relationship between the size of the required reserve ratio and the money multiplier.*

Raising the required reserve ratio can sharply reduce the lending power of banks. Consider an initial increase in excess reserves of $10 billion in the banking system when the required reserve ratio is 10 percent. The potential value of loans (deposits) is $100 billion ($10 billion of excess reserves × 10). Now assume the Fed raises the required reserve ratio to 20 percent. The potential value of loans (deposits) falls to $50 billion ($10 billion of excess reserves × 5).

chair goes first. He or she leads the discussion and advocates a policy decision. After other board members express their views, the chair summarizes the consensus and reads a draft of the Directive to be voted on. The Directive gives instructions to the Fed's staff on how to conduct open market operations until the next FOMC meeting. For example, the New York Fed's trading desk may be instructed to increase the money supply in the range of 1 to 5 percent and lower interest rates by buying 90-day U.S. Treasury bills. After discussion, board members vote on the Directive, with the chair voting first and the decision going to the majority. The chair is always expected to be on the winning side. The Directive is sent to the New York Fed's trading desk, and soon about four dozen bond dealers receive the Fed's call. If there is a change in policy, it will be announced at 2:15 that afternoon.

The Fed now communicates its changes in monetary policy by announcing changes in its targets for the federal funds rate. Recall that the Fed does not set this interest rate, but it can influence the rate through open market operations. If the Fed buys bonds, the supply of excess reserves in the banking system increases, and the rate falls. If the Fed sells bonds, the supply of excess reserves in the banking system decreases, and the rate increases. As a result, interest rates in general are influenced. In 2001, the Fed was trying to keep the economy out of recession, and it cut the federal funds rate 11 times, the most since the last recession in 1990–1991. The next chapter explains in more detail the link between changes in the interest rate and changes in other key macro measures. In 2002 and 2003, the Fed again cut the federal funds rate target to support economic recovery. Between 2004 and 2006, the Fed

became concerned about inflation and increased the federal funds rate 17 times. When measuring inflation, the Fed pays closest attention to the *core* CPI—the CPI excluding food and fuel because it is less volatile than the total CPI inflation rate. In 2007, the Fed changed its focus again because it became concerned that a housing slump and credit crunch would slow the economy, and it cut this key rate for the first time in four years. In 2008, the Fed continued cutting the federal funds rate until it reached a record low of almost zero in 2011.

Analyze the Issue

What happened at the last FOMC meeting? Visit http://www.federalreserve.gov/fomc/default.htm. To experience an FOMC meeting, visit http://www.frbsf.org/education/activies/chairman/index.html.

Source: © Cengage Learning 2014

CONCLUSION: *If the Fed wishes to increase the money supply, it decreases the required reserve ratio. If the objective is to decrease the money supply, the Fed increases the required reserve ratio. In reality, changing the required reserve ratio is considered a heavy-handed approach that is an infrequently used tool of monetary policy.*

The Fed used all three of its monetary policy tools to increase the money supply and battle the 1990–1991 recession. In the fall of 1990, the Fed recognized the economy was slipping into a recession, so it purchased federal government securities to inject new reserves into the banking system. The discount rate was lowered eight times between the end of 1990 and early 1992. In early 1992, the reserve requirement on demand deposits was also lowered from 12 percent to 10 percent. In 2002, the Fed responded to the 2001 recession by using open market purchases of securities to increase the money supply, and it decreased the discount rate numerous times. These responses by the Fed eased the negative effects of the terrorist attacks and the recession.

During the Great Recession of 2007–2009, the Fed again followed expansionary monetary policy and used open market purchases to sharply increase the money supply and decrease interest rates by dropping the federal funds rate to a historic low of about zero percent. Moreover, the Fed reduced its reserve requirement and dramatically expanded its scope in response to the loss in confidence among lenders and panic sweeping financial markets that resulted in the flow of credit falling sharply. Using Depression-era emergency powers, the Fed took the radical step of becoming a "lender of last resort" source of short-term loans for a wide range of institutions other than banks. For example, the Fed provided funds to bail out Fannie Mae (the Federal National Mortgage Association) and Freddie Mac (the Federal Home Mortgage Corporation), which backed about half of the nation's mortgage loans, and the Fed provided loans for AIG, the huge insurance firm, because it was simply too large to fail. For more details on monetary policy, read the You're the Economist titled "How Does the FOMC Really Work?"

Exhibit 4 presents a summary of the impact of monetary policy tools.

15-5 Monetary Policy Shortcomings

Monetary policy, like fiscal policy, has its limitations. The Fed's control over the money supply is imperfect for the following reasons.

EXHIBIT 4	The Effect of Monetary Policy Tools on the Money Supply		
Type of monetary policy	Monetary policy action	Mechanism	Change in the money supply
Expansionary	Open market operations purchase	Reserves increase	Increases
Contractionary	Open market operations sale	Reserves decrease	Decreases
Expansionary	Discount rate decreases	Borrowing reserves becomes cheaper	Increases
Contractionary	Discount rate increases	Borrowing reserves becomes costlier	Decreases
Expansionary	Required reserve ratio decreases	Money multiplier increases	Increases
Contractionary	Required reserve ratio increases	Money multiplier decreases	Decreases

SOURCE: © Cengage Learning 2014

15-5a MONEY MULTIPLIER INACCURACY

If the Fed is to manage the money supply, it must know the size of the money multiplier so that it can forecast the increase in the money supply resulting from a change in excess reserves. The value of the money multiplier, however, can be uncertain and subject to decisions independent of the Fed. As explained earlier in the chapter, the public's decision to hold cash and the willingness of banks to make loans affect the total expansion from an initial change in excess reserves. These decisions vary with conditions of prosperity and recession. When the business cycle is in an upturn, banks are very willing to use their excess reserves for making loans, and the money supply expands. During a downturn, bankers are less willing to use their excess reserves for making loans, and the money supply tends to contract.

15-5b WHICH MONEY DEFINITION SHOULD THE FED CONTROL?

As discussed in the previous chapter, there are different definitions of the money supply. What if the Fed masterfully controls M1, but the public transfers more of its deposits to M2? For example, banks can pay higher interest and attract more customers to invest in certificates of deposit. Consequently, the Fed might respond by focusing on M2 instead of M1. In fact, in recent years, the Fed has focused more on M2 than M1 because M2 more closely correlates with changes in GDP.

15-5c LAGS IN MONETARY POLICY VERSUS FISCAL POLICY

Fiscal policy does not happen instantaneously, and neither does monetary policy. Like fiscal policy, monetary policy is subject to time lags. First, an *inside lag* exists between the time a policy change is needed and the time the Fed identifies the problem and decides which policy tool to use. The inside lag is fairly short because financial data are available daily, data on inflation and unemployment monthly, and data on real GDP within three months. Once the Fed has the data, it can quickly decide which policy changes are needed and make appropriate adjustments. The inside lag for monetary policy is shorter than for fiscal policy because fiscal policy is usually the result of a long political budget process.

Second, there is an *outside lag* between the time a policy decision is made and the time the policy change has its effect on the economy. This lag refers to the length of time it takes the money multiplier or spending multiplier to have its full effect on aggregate demand and, in turn, employment, the price level, and real GDP.

Now it's time to answer an important question: Who is the hare and who is the tortoise in the race to the finish line of stabilizing the economy? In the popular version of this story, the hare is much faster, but goofs off along the way and eventually loses to the tortoise at the finish line. In our economics story, however, the Fed is the hare and wins easily over fiscal policy (the tortoise). Although computer model estimates differ widely, the total lag (inside plus outside lags) for monetary policy can be 3 to 12 months. In contrast, the total lag for fiscal policy is not less than a year, and a total lag of three years is quite possible.

Key Concepts

Fractional reserve banking	Money multiplier	Federal funds market
Required reserves	Monetary policy	Federal funds rate
Required reserve ratio	Open market operations	
Excess reserves	Discount rate	

Summary

- **Fractional reserve banking,** the basis of banking today, originated with the goldsmiths in the Middle Ages. Because depository institutions (banks) are not required to keep all their deposits in vault cash or with the Federal Reserve, banks create money by making loans.
- **Required reserves** are the minimum balance that the Fed requires a bank to hold in vault cash or on deposit with the Fed. The percentage of deposits that must be held as required reserves is called the **required reserve ratio.**
- **Excess reserves** exist when a bank has more reserves than required. Excess reserves allow a bank to create money by exchanging loans for deposits. The money supply is reduced when excess reserves are reduced and loans are repaid.
- The **money multiplier** is used to calculate the maximum change (positive or negative) in checkable deposits (money supply) due to a change in excess reserves. As a formula:

$$\text{Money multiplier} = \frac{1}{\text{required reserve ratio}}$$

The actual change is computed as

Money multiplier
$\times$ **initial change in excess reserves** $=$
money supply change

- **Monetary policy** is action taken by the Fed to change the money supply. The Fed uses three basic tools: (1) *open market operations*, (2) *changes in the discount rate*, and (3) *changes in the required reserve ratio.*
- **Open market operations** are the buying and selling of government securities by the Fed through its trading desk at the New York Federal Reserve Bank. **Buying government securities** creates extra bank reserves and loans, thereby *expanding* the money supply. **Selling government securities** reduces bank reserves and loans, thereby *contracting* the money supply.
- **Changes in the discount rate** occur when the Fed changes the rate of interest it charges on loans of reserves to banks. Lowering the discount rate makes it easier for banks to borrow reserves from the Fed and expands the money supply. Raising the discount rate discourages banks from borrowing reserves from the Fed and contracts the money supply.

Open Market Operations

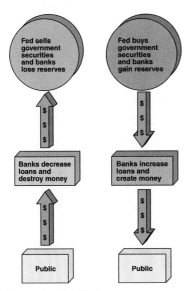

SOURCE: © Cengage Learning 2014

- Changes in the required reserve ratio and the size of the money multiplier are *inversely* related. Thus, if the Fed decreases the required reserve ratio, the money multiplier and money supply increase. If the Fed increases the required reserve ratio, the money multiplier and money supply decrease.
- **Monetary policy limitations** include the following: (1) The size or value of the money multiplier can vary. (2) The Fed might control M1, but the public can shift funds to the M2 money supply definition. (3) Time lags occur.

Summary of Conclusion Statements

- Transferring currency to a bank and moving deposits from one bank to another do not affect the money supply (M1).
- When a bank makes a loan, it creates deposits, and the money supply increases by the amount of the loan because the money supply includes checkable deposits.
- When banks decide to retain excess reserves, the money multiplier will be smaller.
- A purchase of government securities by the Fed injects reserves into the banking system and increases the money supply. A sale of government securities by the Fed reduces reserves in the banking system and decreases the money supply.
- A higher discount rate discourages banks from borrowing reserves and making loans. If the

Fed wants to expand the money supply, it reduces the discount rate. If the objective is to contract the money supply, the Fed raises the discount rate.
- There is an inverse relationship between the size of the required reserve ratio and the money multiplier.
- If the Fed wishes to increase the money supply, it decreases the required reserve ratio. If the objective is to decrease the money supply, the Fed increases the required reserve ratio. In reality, changing the required reserve ratio is considered a heavy-handed approach, so it is an infrequently used tool of monetary policy.

Study Questions and Problems

1. Relate Shakespeare's admonition "Neither a borrower nor a lender be" to the goldsmiths' evolutionary use of fractional reserve banking.

2. If you deposit a $20 bill into a checking account and your bank has a 10 percent reserve requirement, by how much will the bank's excess reserves rise?

3. Consider this statement: "Banks do not create money because this is the Fed's responsibility." Do you agree or disagree? Explain.

4. In what form does a bank hold its required reserves? Assume the Fed has a 20 percent required reserve ratio. What amount of checkable deposits can be supported by $10 million in required reserves?

5. Suppose you deposit your paycheck drawn on another bank. Explain the impact on the money supply.

6. Suppose you remove $1,000 from under your mattress and deposit it in First National Bank. Using a balance sheet, show the impact of your deposit on the bank's assets and liabilities. If the required reserve ratio is 10 percent, what is the maximum amount the bank can loan from this deposit?

7. Suppose it is the holiday season and you withdraw $1,000 from your account at First National Bank to purchase presents. Using a balance sheet, show the impact on this bank's assets and liabilities. If the required reserve ratio is 20 percent, what is the impact on the bank's loans?

8. Suppose the Federal Reserve's trading desk buys $500,000 in T-bills from a securities dealer who then deposits the Fed's check in Best National Bank. Use a balance sheet to show the impact on the bank's loans. Consider the money multiplier and assume the required reserve ratio is 10 percent. What is the maximum increase in the money supply that can result from this open market transaction?

9. Assume the required reserve ratio is 10 percent and a bank's excess reserves are $50 million. Explain why checkable deposits resulting from new loans based on excess reserves are not likely to generate the maximum of $500 million.

10. Briefly describe the effect on the money supply of the following monetary policies:
   a. The Fed purchases $20 million worth of U.S. Treasury bonds.
   b. The Fed increases the discount rate.
   c. The Fed decreases the discount rate.
   d. The Fed sells $40 million worth of U.S. T-bills.
   e. The Fed decreases the required reserve ratio.

11. What are some problems faced by the Fed in controlling the money supply?

For Online Exercises, go to the Tucker Web site at www.cengage.com/economics/tucker.

✔ CHECKPOINT ANSWER

Who Has More Dollar Creation Power?

Your action adds $1,000 to your bank's liabilities. Also, assets in the form of required reserves increase by $100 (0.10 × $1,000). This means excess reserves increase by $900, allowing the bank to make this amount of new loans. When the Fed buys $1,000 in government securities, the bank again receives $1,000 in reserves. But the Fed's transaction does not change the bank's liabilities; therefore, the full $1,000 can go into loans. Comparing the effect on the total money supply, the money multiplier effect shows a $9,000 addition to the money supply from your action and a $10,000 addition from the Fed's action. If you said the Fed's action creates more money, **YOU ARE CORRECT.**

Sample Quiz

For an explanation of the correct answers, visit the Tucker Web site at www.cengage.com/economics/tucker.

1. European banks began with which of the following?
   a. Monarchs were the first bankers, lending out cash to help the poor learn a craft.
   b. Churches were the first bankers, lending out cash to help the poor learn a craft.
   c. Goldsmiths were the first bankers, and the paper receipts they issued for gold held on deposit became valued as money.
   d. Fishermen were the first bankers, and the paper receipts they issued for fish they stored in the hulls of their ships became valued as money.

2. Which of the following does *not* appear on the asset side of a bank's balance sheet?
   a. required reserves
   b. checkable deposits
   c. loans
   d. excess reserves

3. Which of the following is *not* an interest bearing asset of commercial banks?
   a. required reserves
   b. securities
   c. loans
   d. All of the above are interest bearing assets of commercial banks.

4. Banks would be expected to minimize holding excess reserves because this practice is
   a. illegal.
   b. not profitable.
   c. technically difficult.
   d. subject to a stiff excess reserves tax.

5. Which of the following appears on the asset side of a bank's balance sheet?
   a. excess reserves
   b. loans
   c. required reserves
   d. None of the above answers are correct.
   e. All of the above answers are correct.

6. Assume a simplified banking system in which all banks are subject to a uniform reserve requirement of 20 percent and checkable deposits are the only form of money. A bank that received a new checkable deposit of $10,000 would be able to extend new loans up to a maximum of
   a. $2,000.
   b. $8,000.
   c. $9,000.
   d. $10,000.

7. If the required reserve ratio is a uniform 25 percent on all deposits, the money multiplier will be
   a. 4.00.
   b. 2.50.
   c. 0.40.
   d. 0.25.

8. Assume a simplified banking system subject to a 20 percent required reserve ratio. If there is an initial increase in excess reserves of $100,000, the money supply
   a. increases $100,000.
   b. increases $500,000.
   c. increases $600,000.
   d. decreases $500,000.

9. If the required reserve ratio decreases, the
   a. money multiplier increases.
   b. money multiplier decreases.
   c. amount of excess reserves the bank has decreases.
   d. money multiplier stays the same.

10. Decisions regarding purchases and sales of government securities by the Fed are made by the
    a. Federal Deposit Insurance Commission (FDIC).
    b. Discount Committee (DC).
    c. Federal Open Market Committee (FOMC).
    d. Federal Funds Committee (FFC).

Sample Quiz *continued*

11. The cost to a member bank of borrowing from the Federal Reserve is the
    a. reserve requirement.
    b. price of securities in the open market.
    c. discount rate.
    d. yield on government bonds.

12. Which of the following policy actions by the Fed would cause the money supply to decrease?
    a. an open market purchase of government securities
    b. a decrease in required reserve ratios
    c. an increase in the discount rate
    d. a decrease in the discount rate

13. The rate of interest charged by the Federal Reserve to member banks for reserves borrowed from the Fed is the
    a. federal funds rate.
    b. discount rate.
    c. repurchase rate.
    d. Q ceiling rate.

14. Which of the following actions by the Fed would increase the money supply?
    a. reducing the required reserve ratio
    b. selling government bonds in the open market
    c. increasing the discount rate
    d. None of the above answers are correct.

EXHIBIT 5	Lower Walloon National Bank	
Assets	**Liabilities**	
Reserves $10,000	Checkable $10,000 deposits	

SOURCE: © Cengage Learning 2014

15. In Exhibit 5, if the required reserve ratio is 20 percent for all banks and every bank in the banking system loans out all of its excess reserve., then a $10,000 deposit from Mr. Brown in checkable deposits could create for the entire banking system
    a. $8,000 worth of new money.
    b. $2,000 worth of new money.
    c. $10,000 worth of new money.
    d. $40,000 worth of new money.

16. The required reserve ratio for a bank is set by
    a. Congress.
    b. the bank itself.
    c. the Treasury Department.
    d. the banking system.
    e. the Federal Reserve.

17. Assume we have a simplified banking system in balance-sheet equilibrium. Also assume that all banks are subject to a uniform 10 percent reserve requirement and demand deposits are the only form of money. A commercial bank receiving a new demand deposit of $100 would be able to extend new loans in the amount of
    a. $10.
    b. $90.
    c. $100.
    d. $1,000.

18. A bank faces a required reserve ratio of 5 percent. If the bank has $200 million of checkable deposits and $15 million of total reserves, then how large are the bank's excess reserves?
    a. $0
    b. $5 million
    c. $10 million
    d. $15 million

19. A bank currently has checkable deposits of $100,000, reserves of $30,000, and loans of $70,000. If the required reserve ratio is lowered from 20 percent to 15 percent, this bank can increase its loans by
    a. $10,000.
    b. $15,000.
    c. $75,000.
    d. $5,000.
    e. $ 0.

Sample Quiz *continued*

20. When the Fed purchases government securities, it
    a. increases banks' reserves and makes possible an increase in the money supply.
    b. decreases banks' reserves and makes possible a decrease in the money supply.

c. automatically raises the discount rate.
d. uses discounting operations to influence margin requirements.
e. has no effect on either the money supply or the discount rate.

chapter 16

Monetary Policy

Vladimir Lenin, the first communist leader of the Soviet Union, once said the best way to destroy a nation is to destroy its money. Adolf Hitler had the same idea. During World War II, he planned to counterfeit British currency and drop it from planes flying over England. Both cases illustrate that the amount of money in circulation matters. A sudden increase in the quantity of money can render a nation's money valueless. As a consequence, people must resort to barter and waste time making direct exchanges of goods and services, rather than being productive.

The previous two chapters provided the prerequisites for understanding the market for money. You have learned two definitions for the money supply, how the banking system creates money, and how the Fed can control the money supply. Here you will begin by studying the demand for and the supply of money and how they interact to determine the rate of interest. Then we add to this story by linking changes in the money supply to the aggregate demand and aggregate supply model. Using this tool of analysis, you will understand how changes in the demand for money affect interest rates and, in turn, real GDP, employment, and prices.

The first half of this chapter explores how Keynesian economists view the relationship between monetary policy and the economy. The second half of the chapter presents the opposing view of the monetarists. This debate is a clash between two radically different perspectives over the channels through which monetary policy influences the economy. This ideologically charged confrontation is important to the United States' future and is still far from resolved. The chapter concludes with two You're the Economists that allow you to analyze the Keynesian and monetarist views applied to the current financial crisis and the Great Depression.

In this chapter, you will learn to solve these economics puzzles:

- Why do people wish to hold money balances?
- What is a monetary policy transmission mechanism?
- Why would a Nobel laureate economist suggest replacing the Federal Reserve with an intelligent horse?

16-1 The Keynesian View of the Role of Money

16-1a THE DEMAND FOR MONEY

Why do people hold (demand) currency and checkable deposits (M1), rather than put their money to work in stocks, bonds, real estate, or other nonmoney forms of wealth? Because money yields no direct return, people (including businesses) who hold cash or checking account balances incur an *opportunity cost* of forgone interest or profits on the amount of money held. So what are the benefits of holding money? Why would people hold money and thereby forgo earning interest payments? John Maynard Keynes, in his 1936 book *The General Theory of Employment, Interest, and Money*, gave three important motives for doing so: transactions demand, precautionary demand, and speculative demand.

Transactions Demand for Money   The first motive to hold money is the transactions demand. The transactions demand for money is the stock of money people hold to pay everyday predictable expenses. The desire to have "walking around money" to make quick and easy purchases is the principal reason for holding money. Students, for example, have a good idea of how much money they will spend on rent, groceries, utilities, gasoline, and other routine purchases. A business can also predict its payroll, utility bills, supply bills, and other routine expenses. Without enough cash, the public must suffer forgone interest and possibly withdrawal penalties as a result of converting their stocks, bonds, or certificates of deposit into currency or checkable deposits in order to make transactions.

Precautionary Demand for Money   In addition to holding money for ordinary expected purchases, people have a second motive to hold money, called the precautionary demand. The precautionary demand for money is the stock of money people hold to pay unpredictable expenses. This is the "mattress money" people hold to guard against those proverbial rainy days. For example, your car might break down, or your income may drop unexpectedly. Similarly, a business might experience unexpected repair expenses or lower-than-anticipated cash receipts from sales. Because of unforeseen events that could prevent people from paying their bills on time, people hold precautionary balances. This affords the peace of mind that unexpected payments can be made without having to cash in interest-bearing financial assets or to borrow.

Speculative Demand for Money   The third motive for holding money is the speculative demand. The speculative demand for money is the stock of money people hold to take advantage of expected future changes in the price of bonds, stocks, or other nonmoney financial assets. In addition to the transactions and precautionary motives, individuals and businesses demand "betting money" to speculate, or guess, whether the prices of alternative assets will rise or fall. This desire to take advantage of profit-making opportunities when the prices of nonmoney assets fall is the driving force behind the speculative demand. When the interest rate is high, people buy, say, Microsoft 30-year bonds because the opportunity cost of holding money is the high forgone interest earned on these nonmoney assets. When the interest rate is low, people hold more money because there is less opportunity cost in forgone interest earned on investing in bonds. Suppose the interest

Transactions demand for money

The stock of money people hold to pay everyday predictable expenses.

Precautionary demand for money

The stock of money people hold to pay unpredictable expenses.

Speculative demand for money

The stock of money people hold to take advantage of expected future changes in the price of bonds, stocks, or other nonmoney financial assets.

rate on Microsoft 30-year bonds is low. If so, people decide to hold more of their money in the bank and *speculate* that soon the interest rate will climb higher.

> **CONCLUSION:** *As the interest rate falls, the opportunity cost of holding money falls, and people increase their speculative balances.*

Demand for money curve

A curve representing the quantity of money that people hold at different possible interest rates, ceteris paribus.

The Demand for Money Curve   The three motives for holding money combine to create a demand for money curve, which represents the quantity of money people hold at different possible interest rates, ceteris paribus. As shown in Exhibit 1, people increase their money balances when interest rates fall. The reason is that many people move their money out of, for example, money market mutual funds and into checkable deposits (M1).

> **CONCLUSION:** *There is an inverse relationship between the quantity of money demanded and the interest rate.*

What determines the shape of the demand for money curve? Let's start with the transactions and the precautionary demands for money. These money balances are computed as a given proportion of real GDP. Suppose real GDP is $5,000 billion and people wish to hold, say, 10 percent for transactions and precautionary purposes. This means the first $500 billion read along the horizontal axis in Exhibit 1 are held to make purchases and handle unforeseen events.

Now consider the impact of changes in the interest rate on the speculative demand for money. As the interest rate falls, people add larger speculative balances to their transactions and precautionary balances. For example, when the rate is 4 percent per year, the total quantity of money demanded at point *A* is $1,000 billion, of which $500 billion are speculative balances. If the interest rate is 2 percent, the total quantity of money demanded increases to $1,500 billion at point *B*, of which $1,000 billion are speculative balances. Therefore, the demand for money curve, labeled "MD," looks much like any other demand curve.

> **CONCLUSION:** *The speculative demand for money at possible interest rates gives the demand for money curve its downward slope.*

16-1b THE EQUILIBRIUM INTEREST RATE

We are now ready to form the money market and determine the equilibrium interest rate by putting the demand for money and the supply of money together. In Exhibit 2, the money demand curve (MD) is identical to that in Exhibit 1. The supply of money curve (MS) is a vertical line because the $1,000 billion quantity of money supplied does not respond to changes in the interest rate. The reason is that our model assumes the Fed has used its tools to set the money supply at this quantity of money regardless of the interest rate.

EXHIBIT 1	The Demand for Money Curve

Assume the level of real GDP is $5,000 billion. Also assume households and businesses demand to hold 10 percent of real GDP ($500 billion) for transactions and precautionary balances. The speculative demand for money varies inversely with the interest rate. At an interest rate of 4 percent, the quantity of money demanded (M1) is $1,000 billion (point A), calculated as the sum of transactions and precautionary demand ($500 billion) and speculative demand ($500 billion). At a lower interest rate, a greater total quantity of money is demanded because the opportunity cost of holding money is lower.

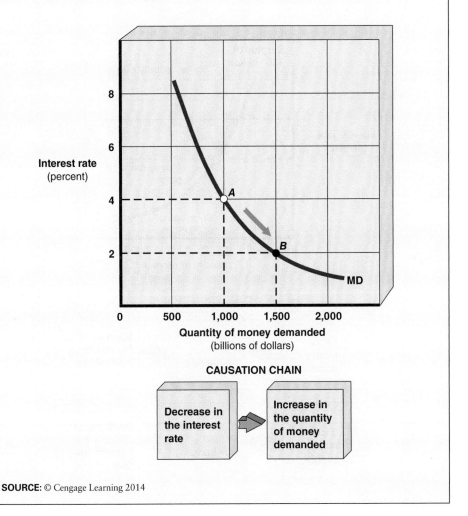

CAUSATION CHAIN

Decrease in the interest rate ⟹ Increase in the quantity of money demanded

SOURCE: © Cengage Learning 2014

At point *E*, the equilibrium interest rate is 8 percent, determined by the intersection of the demand for money curve and the vertical supply of money curve. People wish to hold exactly the amount of money in circulation, therefore, there is neither upward nor downward pressure on the interest rate.

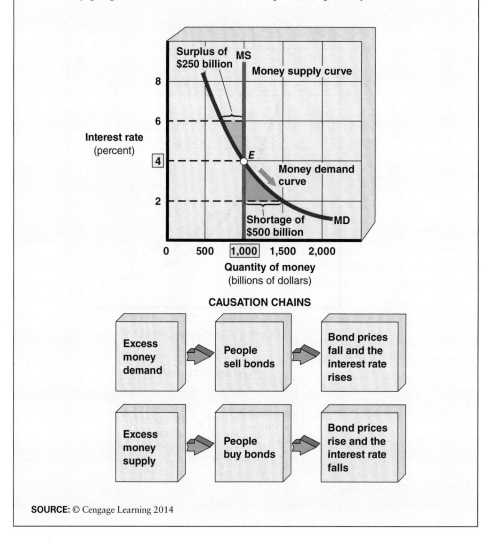

EXHIBIT 2   The Equilibrium Interest Rate

The money market consists of the demand for and the supply of money. The market demand curve represents the quantity of money people are willing to hold at various interest rates. The money supply curve is a vertical line at $1,000 billion, based on the assumption that this is the quantity of money supplied by the Fed. The equilibrium interest rate is 4 percent and occurs at the intersection of the money demand and money supply curves (point E). At any other interest rate, for example, 6 percent or 2 percent, the quantity of money people desire to hold does not equal the quantity available.

Excess Quantity of Money Demanded Suppose the interest rate in Exhibit 2 is 2 percent instead of 4 percent. Such a low opportunity cost of money means that people desire to hold a greater quantity of money than the quantity supplied. To eliminate this shortage of $500 billion, individuals and businesses adjust their asset portfolios. They seek more money by selling their bonds or other non-money assets. When many sell or try to sell their bonds, there is an increase in the supply of bonds for sale. Consequently, the price of bonds falls, and the interest rate rises. This rise in the interest rate ceases at the equilibrium interest rate of 4 percent because people are content with their portfolio of money and bonds at point E.

Here we need to pause and look at an example to understand what is happening. Suppose Apple pays 2 percent on its $1,000 30-year bonds. This means Apple pays a bondholder $20 in interest each year and promises to repay the original $1,000 price (face amount) at the end of 30 years. However, a holder of these bonds can sell them before maturity at a market-determined price. If bondholders desire to hold more money than is supplied, they will sell more of these bonds. Then the increase in the supply of bonds causes the price of bonds to fall to, say, $500. As a result, the interest rate rises to 4 percent ($20/$500).

Excess Quantity of Money Supplied   The story reverses for any rate of interest above 4 percent. Let's say the interest rate is 6 percent. In this case, people are holding more money than they wish. Stated differently, they wish to hold less money than is currently in circulation. In this case, the quantity of money demanded is $250 billion less than the quantity supplied. To correct this imbalance, people will move out of cash and checkable deposits by buying bonds. This increase in the demand for bonds will drive up the price of bonds and lower the interest rate. As the interest rate falls, the quantity of money demanded increases as people become more willing to hold money. Finally, the money market reaches equilibrium at point E, and people are content with their mix of money and bonds.

> **CONCLUSION:** *There is an inverse relationship between bond prices and the interest rate that enables the money market to achieve equilibrium.*

16-1c HOW MONETARY POLICY AFFECTS THE INTEREST RATE

Assuming a stationary demand for money, the equilibrium rate of interest changes in response to changes in monetary policy. As we learned in Exhibit 4 of the previous chapter, the Federal Reserve can alter the money supply through open market operations, changes in the required reserve ratio, or changes in the discount rate. In this section, you will see that the Fed's power to change the money supply can also alter the equilibrium rate of interest.

Increasing the Money Supply   Exhibit 3(a) shows how increasing the money supply will cause the equilibrium rate of interest to fall. Our analysis begins at point E_1, with the money supply at $1,000 billion, which is equal to the quantity of money demanded, and with the equilibrium interest rate at 6 percent. Now suppose the Fed increases the money supply to $1,500 billion by buying government securities in the open market. The impact of the Fed's expansionary monetary policy is to create a $500 billion surplus of money at the prevailing 6 percent interest rate.

How will people react to this excess money in their pockets or checking accounts? Money becomes a "hot potato," and people buy bonds. The rush to purchase bonds drives the price of bonds higher and the interest rate lower. As the

EXHIBIT 3	The Effect of Changes in the Money Supply

In part (a), the Federal Reserve increases the money supply from $1,000 billion ($MS_1$) to $1,500 billion ($MS_2$). At the initial interest rate of 6 percent (point E_1), there is an excess of $500 billion beyond the amount people wish to hold. They react by buying bonds, and the interest rate falls until it reaches a new lower equilibrium interest rate at 4 percent (point E_2).

The reverse happens in part (b). The Fed decreases the money supply from $1,500 billion ($MS_1$) to $1,000 billion ($MS_2$). Beginning at 4 percent (point E_1), people wish to hold $500 billion more than is available. This shortage disappears when people sell their bonds. As the price of bonds falls, the interest rate rises to the new higher equilibrium interest rate of 6 percent at point E_2.

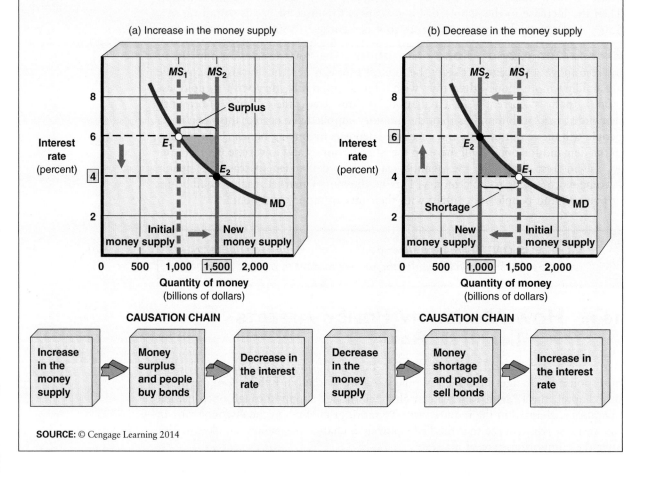

SOURCE: © Cengage Learning 2014

interest rate falls, people are *willing* to hold larger money balances. Or, stated differently, the quantity of money demanded increases until the new equilibrium at E_2 is reached. At the lower interest rate of 8 percent, the opportunity cost of holding money is also lower, and the imbalance between the money demand and money supply curves disappears.

Decreasing the Money Supply   Exhibit 3(b) illustrates how the Fed can put upward pressure on the interest rate with contractionary monetary policy. Beginning at point E_1, the money market is in equilibrium at an interest rate of

4 percent. This time the Fed shrinks the money supply by selling government securities through its trading desk, raising the required reserve ratio, or raising the discount rate. As a result, the money supply decreases from $1,500 billion to $1,000 billion. At the initial equilibrium interest rate of 4 percent, this decrease in the money supply causes a shortage of $500 billion.

Individuals and businesses wish to hold more money than is available. How can the public put more money in their pockets and checking accounts? They can sell their bonds for cash. This selling pressure lowers bond prices, causing the rate of interest to rise. At point E_2, the upward pressure on the interest rate stops. Once the equilibrium interest rate reaches 6 percent, people willingly hold the $1,000 billion money supply.

✓ CHECKPOINT

What Does the Money Supply Curve Look Like When the Fed Targets the Federal Funds Rate?

Suppose the Fed has a policy of adjusting the money supply to achieve interest rate targets. For example, the Fed might set a 6 percent target federal funds rate. If an increase in the demand for money boosts the federal funds rate above 6 percent, the Fed adjusts the money supply until the 6 percent interest rate is restored. Under such a monetary policy, is the supply of money curve vertical, horizontal, or upward sloping with respect to the federal funds rate?

16-1d HOW MONETARY POLICY AFFECTS PRICES, OUTPUT, AND EMPLOYMENT

The next step in our journey is to understand how monetary policy alters the macro economy. Here you should pause and study Exhibit 4. This exhibit illustrates the causation chain linking monetary policy and economic performance.

EXHIBIT 4	The Keynesian Monetary Policy Transmission Mechanism

Keynesians focus on how changes in the money supply affect interest rates and investment spending. In turn, aggregate demand shifts and affects prices, real GDP, and employment.

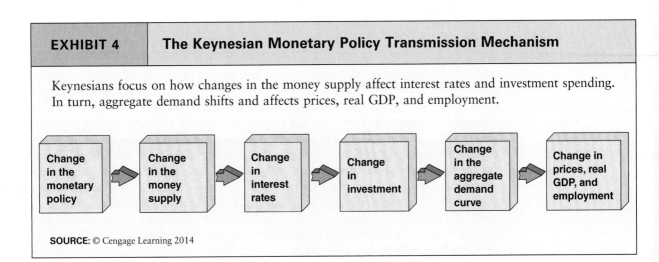

SOURCE: © Cengage Learning 2014

CONCLUSION: *In the Keynesian model, changes in the supply of money affect interest rates. In turn, interest rates affect investment spending, aggregate demand, and, finally, real GDP, employment, and prices.*

The Impact of Monetary Policy Using the AD-AS Model How do changes in the rate of interest affect aggregate demand? Begin with Exhibit 5(a), which is identical to Exhibit 3(a) and represents the money market. As explained earlier, we assume that the Fed increases the money supply from $1,000 billion ($MS_1$) to $1,500 billion ($MS_2$) and the equilibrium interest rate falls from 6 percent to 4 percent. In part (b), we can see that the falling rate of interest causes an increase in the quantity of investment spending from $800 billion to $850 billion per year. Stated another way, there is a movement downward along the *investment demand curve* (*I*), which you recall from the chapter on GDP is a component of total spending or aggregate demand. The investment demand curve shows the amount businesses spend for investment goods at different possible interest rates.

The classical economists believed that the interest rate alone determines the level of investment spending. Keynes disputed this idea. Instead, Keynes argued that the expectation of future profits is the primary factor determining investment and the interest rate is the financing cost of any investment proposal. Using a micro example to illustrate the investment decision-making process, suppose a consulting firm plans to purchase a new computer program for $1,000 that will be obsolete in a year. The firm anticipates the new software will increase its revenue by $1,100. Thus, assuming no taxes and other expenses, the expected rate of return or profit is 10 percent.

Now consider the impact of the cost of borrowing funds to finance the software investment. If the interest rate is less than 10 percent, the business will earn a profit, and it will make the investment expenditure to obtain the computer program. On the other hand, a rate of interest higher than 10 percent means the software investment will be a loss, so this purchase will not be made. The expected rate of the profit-interest rate-investment relationship follows this rule: *Businesses will undertake all investment projects for which the expected rate of profit equals or exceeds the interest rate.*

Exhibit 5(c) uses the fiscal policy aggregate demand and aggregate supply analysis developed earlier. Begin at point E_1, with a real GDP per year of $13 trillion and a price level of 210. Now consider the link to the change in the money supply. The increase in investment resulting from the fall in the interest rate works through the *spending multiplier* and shifts the aggregate demand curve rightward from AD_1 to AD_2. At the new equilibrium point, E_2, the level of real GDP rises from $13 trillion to $14 trillion, and full employment is achieved. In addition, the price level rises from 210 to 215. Exhibit 5(a) also demonstrates the effect of a contractionary monetary policy. In this case, assume the economy is initially at E_2 and the money supply shifts inward from MS_2 to MS_1, causing the equilibrium rate of interest to rise from 4 percent to 6 percent. The Fed's "tight" money policy causes the level of investment spending to fall from $850 billion to $800 billion, which, in turn, decreases the equilibrium level of real GDP per year from $14 trillion to $13 trillion. As a result, the unemployment rate rises, and the inflation rate falls because the price level falls from 215 to 210.

| EXHIBIT 5 | The Effect of Expansionary Monetary Policy on Aggregate Demand |

In part (a), the money supply is initially MS_1, and the equilibrium rate of interest is 6 percent. The equilibrium point in the money market changes from E_1 to E_2 when the Fed increases the money supply to MS_2. This causes the quantity of money people wish to hold to increase from \$1,000 billion to \$1,500 billion, and a new lower equilibrium interest rate is established at 4 percent.

The fall in the rate of interest shown in part (b) causes a movement downward along the investment demand curve from point A to point B. Thus, the quantity of investment spending per year increases from \$800 billion to \$850 billion.

In part (c), the investment component of the aggregate demand curve increases, causing this curve to shift outward from AD_1 to AD_2. As a result, the aggregate demand and supply equilibrium in the product market changes from E_1 to E_2, and the real GDP gap is eliminated. The price level also changes from 210 to 215.

SOURCE: © Cengage Learning 2014

16-2 The Monetarist View of the Role of Money

16-2a THE MONETARIST TRANSMISSION MECHANISM

Monetarism

The theory that changes in the money supply directly determine changes in prices, real GDP, and employment.

Monetarists believe Keynesians suffer from the delusion that monetary policy operates only indirectly, causing changes in the interest rate before affecting aggregate demand and then prices, real GDP, and employment. The opposing school of economic thought, called monetarism, challenges this view. Monetarism is the theory that changes in the money supply directly determine changes in prices, real GDP, and employment. Exhibit 6 illustrates the monetarist transmission mechanism. Comparison of this figure with Exhibit 4 shows that the monetarist model omits the Keynesian interest rate-investment linkage.

Equation of exchange

An accounting identity that states the money supply times the velocity of money equals total spending.

The Equation of Exchange Monetarists put the spotlight on the money supply. They argue that to predict the condition of the economy, you simply look at the money supply. If it expands too much, higher rates of inflation will be the forecast. If it contracts too much, unemployment lines will lengthen. Monetarism has its intellectual roots in classical economics, introduced in the chapter on aggregate demand and supply. Monetarists proudly wear *laissez faire* on their sleeves and believe the price system is the macro economy's best friend. To understand monetarism, we begin with the equation of exchange developed by the classical economists in the 19th century. The equation of exchange is an accounting identity that states the money supply times the velocity of money equals total spending. Expressed as a formula, the equation of exchange is written as

$$MV = PQ$$

Velocity of money

The average number of times per year a dollar of the money supply is spent on final goods and services.

Let's begin with the left side of the equation ($M \times V$). M is the money supply (more precisely M1) in circulation, and V represents the velocity of money. The velocity of money is the average number of times per year a dollar of the money supply is spent on final goods and services. Assume you have one crisp $20 bill

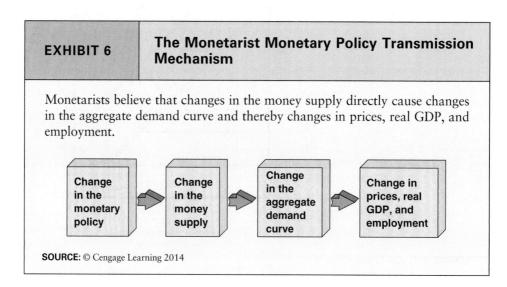

EXHIBIT 6	The Monetarist Monetary Policy Transmission Mechanism

Monetarists believe that changes in the money supply directly cause changes in the aggregate demand curve and thereby changes in prices, real GDP, and employment.

Change in the monetary policy → Change in the money supply → Change in the aggregate demand curve → Change in prices, real GDP, and employment

SOURCE: © Cengage Learning 2014

and this is the only money in an ultrasimple economy. Suppose you spend this money on a pizza and soda at Zeno's Pizza Hut. Once Mr. Zeno puts your money in his pocket, he decides to buy an economics book and learn how the views of Keynesians and monetarists differ. And so, Mr. Zeno buys the book at the Wise Professor Book Store for exactly $20. At this point, both Mr. Zeno and Ms. Wise have sold $20 worth of goods. Thus, a single $20 bill has financed $40 worth of total spending. And as long as this $20 bill passes from hand to hand during, say, one year, the value of sales will increase. For example, assume the $20 travels from hand to hand 5 times. This means the velocity of money is 5, and the equation of exchange is expressed as

$$\$20 \times 5 = \$100$$

The equation of exchange is an *identity*—true by definition—that expresses the fact that the value of what people spend is equal to, or exchanged for, what they buy. What people buy is nominal GDP, or $(P \times Q)$. Recall that nominal, or money, GDP is equal to the average selling price during the year (P) multiplied by the quantity of actual output of final goods and services (Q). In our simple economy, total spending equals $100. Note that the identity between MV and PQ does not say what happens to either P or Q if MV increases. Although we know by how much the total value of output (PQ) increases, we do not know whether the price level (P) or the quantity of output (Q) or both increase.

Consider a more realistic example. Suppose that nominal GDP last year was $5 trillion and M1 was $1 trillion. How many times did each dollar of the money supply have to be spent to generate this level of total spending in the economy? Using the equation of exchange,

$$M \times V = P \times Q$$
$$\$1 \text{ trillion} \times V = \$5 \text{ trillion}$$
$$V = 5$$

Thus, each dollar was spent an average of 5 times per year.

The Quantity Theory of Money   The equation of exchange is converted from an *identity* to a *theory* by making certain assumptions. The classical economists became the forerunners of modern-day monetarists by arguing that the velocity of money (V) and real output (Q) are fairly constant. The classical economists viewed V as constant because people's habits of holding a certain quantity of money, and therefore the number of times a dollar is spent, are slow to change. Recall from the chapter on aggregate demand and supply that classical economists believed in price and wage flexibility. Hence, they believed the economy would automatically adjust to long-run full-employment output (Q).

Because V and Q are constant by assumption, we have one of the oldest theories of inflation, called the quantity theory of money. The quantity theory of money states that changes in the money supply are directly related to changes in the price level. Monetary policy based on the quantity theory of money therefore directly affects the price level. To illustrate, we will modify the equation of exchange by putting a bar (–) over V and Q to indicate they are fixed or constant in value:

Quantity theory of money

The theory that changes in the money supply are directly related to changes in the price level.

$$M \times \overline{V} = P \times \overline{Q}$$

What if the money supply doubles? The price level also doubles. Or if the Fed cuts the money supply in half, then the price level is also cut in half. Meanwhile, real output of goods and services, Q, remains unchanged.

> **CONCLUSION:** *According to the quantity theory of money, any change in the money supply must lead to a proportional change in the price level.*

In short, monetarists say the cause of inflation is "too much money chasing too few goods." The quantity theory of money denies any role for nonmonetary factors, such as supply shocks from a hike in oil prices, which cause cost-push inflation [see Exhibit 11(a) in the chapter on aggregate demand and supply]. Moreover, this theory ignores the impact of fiscal policy changes in taxation and spending on the price level.

What do the data reveal about the link between changes in the money supply and changes in the rate of inflation? Although the relationship does not exist for all years, the evidence supports the general conclusion that sustained levels of higher growth in the money supply correspond to increases in the inflation rate. For example, when the money supply growth rate was low and averaged 2 percent between 1953 and 1962, the inflation rate averaged 1 percent. During 1973–1982, the money supply grew at a higher average rate of 7 percent, and the average inflation rate rose to 9 percent. More recently, between 1994 and 2007, the money supply increased at a lower average rate of 2 percent, and the average inflation rate dropped to 3 percent. After the Great Recession in 2007 through 2011, the average money supply growth rate increased sharply to 12 percent. If high growth rates of the money supply are sustained, the concern is that the inflation rate will rise.

Modern Monetarism   Today's monetarists have changed the assumptions of the classical quantity theory of money. The evidence indicates that velocity is not constant and the economy does not always operate at full employment. Although M and P are correlated, they do not change proportionally. *Monetarists argue that although velocity is not unchanging, it is nevertheless predictable.* Suppose the predicted velocity of money is 5 and the money supply increases by $100 billion this year. Monetarists would predict that nominal GDP will increase by about $500 billion ($\Delta M \times \hat{V}$). [The circumflex (^) indicates velocity is predicted.] If the economy is far below full employment, most of the rise in total spending will be in real output. If the economy is near full employment, much of the increase will be in rising prices.

Monetarists refute the Keynesian view that the rate of interest is so important. Instead, the monetarist view is often expressed in the famous single-minded statement that "money does matter." Instead of working through the rate of interest to affect investment and, in turn, the economy, changes in the money supply directly determine economic performance.

> **CONCLUSION:** *To avoid inflation and unemployment, the monetarists' prescription is to be sure that the money supply is at the proper level.*

Fixed Money Target Monetarism gained credibility in the late 1950s and 1960s, led by Professor Milton Friedman at the University of Chicago. The monetarists have an answer for how to make sure the economy grows at the right rate: Instead of risking policy errors, forget about the rate of interest and follow a steady, predictable monetary policy. Recall from the chapter on money creation that there are limitations on the Fed's ability to control the money supply because of the independent actions of households, firms, banks, and the U.S. Treasury. Monetarists would stop the Fed from tinkering with the money supply, missing the target, and making the economy worse, rather than better. Instead, they say the money supply should expand at the same rate as the potential growth rate in real GDP. That is, it should increase somewhere between 3 percent and 5 percent per year. The Fed should therefore pick a rate and stick to it, even if unexpected changes in velocity cause short periods of inflation or unemployment. This is called following a *monetary rule*. Monetarists argue that their "straitjacket" approach would reduce the intensity and duration of unemployment and inflation by eliminating the monetarists' public enemy number one—the Fed's discretion to change the money supply. A Keynesian once summarized the fixed money supply approach as "Don't do something, just stand there."

CONCLUSION: *Monetarists advocate that the Federal Reserve increase the money supply by a constant percentage each year.*

How Stable Is Velocity? How stable, or predictable, is the velocity of money? This is a critical question in the Keynesian-monetarist debate. Keynesians do not accept the monetarists' argument that over long periods of time, velocity is stable and predictable. Hence, a change in the money supply can lead to a much larger or smaller change in GDP than the monetarists would predict. As shown in Exhibit 7, Keynesians are quick to point out the turbulent variations in velocity. Velocity gyrated up and down during the 1980s, early 1990s, and years after 2001. Monetarists counter by pointing to the evidence that during the periods of 1960–1981 and 1993–2007, velocity generally rose along a quite predictable or steady annual rate trend line. Since 2007, velocity has declined.

Keynesians focus on short-run variations in V that accompany any long-run velocity growth rate. They therefore argue that following a monetary rule is folly. Suppose the money supply increases at a constant rate, but velocity is greater than expected. This means that total spending (aggregate demand) will be greater than predicted, causing inflation. Lower-than-predicted velocity results in unemployment because total spending is less than expected, which causes the economy to expand too little. The Keynesians believe that the Federal Reserve must be free to change the money supply to offset unexpected changes in velocity. Monetarists counter that the Fed *cannot* predict short-run variations in V, so its "quick-fix" changes in the money supply will often be wrong. This is why monetarists advocate that the Fed follow a monetary rule. Keynesians are willing to accept occasional policy errors and reject this idea in favor of maintaining Fed flexibility to change the money supply in order to affect interest rates, aggregate demand, and the economy.

EXHIBIT 7	The Velocity of Money, 1960–2011

The velocity of money (V) equals GDP divided by the supply of money (M1). Keynesians argue that velocity is not stable. During the 1980s, early 1990s, and years after 2001, velocity became quite unpredictable. Monetarists believe velocity is stable over the long term and point to the periods of 1960–1981 and 1993–2000. During these years, velocity rose along a predictable annual rate trend line.

SOURCE: *Economic Report of the President*, 1980 and 2012, http://www.gpo.gov/fdsys/pkg/ERP-2012/content-detail.htm1, Tables B-52, B-1, and B-69.

✓ CHECKPOINT

A Horse of Which Color?

A famous economist once proposed replacing the Fed with an intelligent horse. Each New Year's Day, the horse would stand in front of Fed headquarters to answer monetary policy questions. Reporters would ask, "What is going to happen to the money supply this year?" The horse would tap its hoof four times, and the next day headlines would read "Fed to Once Again Increase the Money Supply 4 Percent." Is this famous economist a Keynesian or a monetarist?

16-3 A Comparison of Macroeconomic Views

By now, your head is probably spinning with dueling schools of economic thought. The debate among the classicals, Keynesians, and monetarists can be quite confusing. This chapter has presented differences in monetary policy between these schools. To refresh your memory and complete the discussion, this section presents a brief review of key differences in fiscal policy introduced in earlier chapters. Exhibit 8 gives a thumbnail summary of the key differences between the three camps. Note the similarity between the classical and the monetarist schools.

16-3a CLASSICAL ECONOMICS

As discussed in the chapter on aggregate demand and supply, the dominant school of economic thought before the Great Depression was classical economics. Classical economics is the theory that free markets will restore full employment without government intervention. The basic theory of the classical economists, introduced by Adam Smith in *The Wealth of Nations* and followed by the 18th- and 19th-century economists, was that a market-directed economy will automatically correct itself to full employment. Consequently, there is no need for fiscal policy designed to restore full employment.

Recall that a key assumption of classical theory is that, given time to adjust, prices and wages will decrease to ensure the economy operates at full employment. A decrease in the aggregate demand curve causes a temporary surplus, which, in turn, causes businesses to cut prices, and, in turn, causes more goods to be purchased because of the real balances effect. As a result, wages adjust downward, and employment rises. Classical economists therefore view the economy as operating in the long run along a vertical aggregate supply curve originating at the full-employment real GDP.

Classical economics
The theory that free markets will restore full employment without government intervention.

16-3b KEYNESIAN ECONOMICS

The Great Depression challenged the classical prescription to wait until markets adjust and full employment is automatically restored. As the unemployment rate rose to 24.9 percent in 1933, people asked how long it would take for the market mechanism to adjust. John Maynard Keynes responded with his famous saying "In the long run we are all dead." Keynes, in his book *The General Theory*, attacked classical theory and in the process revolutionized macroeconomic thought.

As explained in the chapter on fiscal policy, using fiscal policy to affect aggregate demand is a cornerstone of Keynesian economics. Keynesian economics is the theory, first advanced by John Maynard Keynes, that the role of the federal government is to increase or decrease aggregate demand to achieve economic goals. While Keynesians believe monetary policy is often not very powerful, especially during a downturn, they regard fiscal policy as their "top banana." However, Keynesians recognize that one of the potential problems of fiscal policy is the *crowding-out effect*. As shown earlier in Exhibit 9 of the chapter on federal deficits and the national debt, financing a federal deficit by borrowing competes with private borrowers for funds. Given a fixed money supply, the extra demand from the federal government to finance its deficit causes the interest rate to rise. As a result, businesses cut back on investment spending and offset the expected increase in

Keynesian economics

The theory, first advanced by John Maynard Keynes, that the role of the federal government is to increase or decrease aggregate demand to achieve economic goals.

Did the Fed Cause the Great Recession?

Applicable Concept: monetarism

The story of the worst collapse of the housing market and the most serious financial crisis since the Great Depression is filled with villains and no action hero to sweep down from the sky and save the day. It is an Alice in Wonderland story with plenty of blame to go around: homeowners who bought a Trojan horse, rampant speculation, predatory lenders, slick Wall Street operators, greedy CEOs, lax regulators, and debatable Fed policy. Perhaps a phrase by Alan Greenspan, former Fed chairman, called "The Maestro," best described the bust of the housing market bubble when he said, "How do we know when irrational exuberance has unduly escalated asset values?"

The stage was set for the housing crisis by the Fed's response to the recession of 2001. The annual change in the money supply jumped sharply upward from –3.1 percent in 2000 to a 8.7 percent increase in 2001.[1] And, as shown in the above exhibit, the Fed decreased interest rates sharply after 2001 and kept them historically low in order to boost aggregate demand and prevent another recession. Then in 2004, Greenspan addressed the Credit Union Association and said, "American consumers might benefit if lenders provided greater mortgage product alternatives to the traditional fixed rate mortgage." And as if following the Fed chairman's advice, adjustable rate mortgages (ARMs) became the loan of choice for *subprime mortgage loan* borrowers who had poor or less than ideal credit scores. Mailboxes were stuffed with offers to borrow 100 percent or more of a home's value with zero down. Television shows advertised the idea that anyone could make it rich in real estate, and housing became a speculative game. Payments and "teaser" interest rates were held artificially low for the first few years of the loan and then would jump sharply upward. Forget worrying about not affording the home, your income would not be checked, following a "no document" lending practice. In fact, some loans were made to people who were no longer living. Thus,

Source: FRB Federal Open Market Committee, http://www.federalreserve.gov/fomc/fundsrate.htm.

using risky ARMs, banks lent billions of dollars to home buyers who could not pay the bank when the payments and interest rates rose.

Faced with accumulating portfolios of risky debt, banks and mortgage companies sold these risky mortgages to New York investment firms such as Bear Stearns (acquired by JPMorgan Chase with financial backing from the Fed) and Merrill Lynch, who pooled them with other securities. These packages, often called collateralized debt obligations, or CDOs, were sold to customers around

Subprime mortgage loan

A home loan made to borrowers with an above-average risk of default.

aggregate demand. The Keynesian view, however, is that the investment demand curve is not very sensitive to changes in the interest rate, and therefore, only a relatively small amount of investment spending will be crowded out. Thus, the decline in investment only slightly counteracts or offsets an increase in aggregate demand created by a deficit.

> **CONCLUSION:** *Keynesians view the shape of the investment demand curve as rather steep or vertical, so the crowding-out effect is insignificant.*

the world—a process called "securitization." And this securitization occurred with the blessing of ratings agencies such as Standard & Poor's which actually did not know how to evaluate the risk of these securities. With each of these transactions, large fees were collected, and in short, consummation of the deal was the criterion and not validity of the assessment of risk.

Expansion of the housing market bubble was based on an assumption by all the players that the party would never end and real estate prices would always go up. However, beginning in the summer of 2005, subprime foreclosures rose and home prices dropped as people's payments rose under their ARMs. Also, once the value of homes fell below the loan value, people could not refinance loans to get lower payments. When people walked away from their mortgages, Wall Street and foreign investors were stuck with bad loans in their CDOs to write off, CEOs were fired, and many real estate executives were indicted for mortgage fraud. As a result, lenders greatly tightened their lending standards to avoid further risky loans, and a credit crunch made home financing difficult to obtain.

In 2008, the Fed announced that it would allow Wall Street investment firms to receive emergency loans and exchange risky investments for Treasury securities. Also, the Housing and Economic Recovery Act of 2008 was passed that allowed some borrowers to refinance their mortgages with new fixed-rate loans backed by a federal guarantee, and it provided grants for state and local governments in the hardest-hit communities to buy foreclosed property. It also included a tax credit for first-time home buyers who buy housing that is unoccupied. And the Treasury Department was given authority to bail out or take over Fannie Mae and Freddie Mac, the troubled government-created firms that fund the vast majority of mortgage loans in the United States.

In addition, a massive $700 billion bailout plan was enacted in 2008 that gave the Treasury the authority under TARP (Troubled Assets Recovery Program) to buy and resell bad mortgage debt from financial institutions. But TARP changed its original purpose because it was very difficult to determine the price that the government should pay for the risky assets. Consequently, TARP changed its plan and spent over half of its funds to invest government capital into banks by buying preferred stock with a 5 percent rate of return, which is the equivalent of a loan to the bank. Also, the federal government decided to take partial ownership of private U.S. banks until they regain stability and increase lending. Participating banks must curtail executive bonuses and other perks. Meanwhile, the final price tag to the taxpayers for this financial crisis is unknowable.

> **Analyze the Issue**
>
> In support of the Fed's monetary policy prior to the deflation of the home prices bubble, one can argue that the reality is that increasing the money supply and low-interest rates were required to sustain expansion. Based on the monetarist school of thought, criticize the Fed's policy.

1. *Economic Report of the President 2012*, http://www.gpoaccess.gov/eop/, Table B-69.

Source: © Cengage Learning 2014

16-3c MONETARISM

Monetarists are iconoclasts because they attack the belief in the ability of either the Fed or the federal government to stabilize the economy. They argue that fiscal policy is an essentially useless tool that has little or no impact on output or employment because of a total crowding-out effect. Suppose the money supply remains fixed and the federal government borrows to finance its deficit. The intended goal is to increase aggregate demand and restore full employment. According to the monetarists, financing the deficit will drive up the interest rate and crowd out a substantial, not a small, amount of investment spending. The reason is that the

EXHIBIT 8	Comparison of Macroeconomic Theories		
Issue	**Classical**	**Keynesian**	**Monetarist**
	Adam Smith	**John Maynard Keynes**	**Milton Friedman**
Stability of economy	Stable in long run at full employment	Inherently unstable at less than full employment	Stable in long run at full employment
Price-wage flexibility	Yes	No	Yes
Velocity of money	Stable	Unstable	Predictable
Cause of inflation	Excess money supply	Excess aggregate demand	Excess money supply
Causes of unemployment	Short-run price and wage adjustment	Inadequate aggregate demand	Short-run price and wage adjustment
Effect of monetary policy	Changes aggregate demand and prices	Changes interest rate, which changes investment and real GDP	Changes aggregate demand and prices
Effect of fiscal policy	Not necessary	Spending multiplier changes aggregate demand	No effect because of crowding-out effect

Source: © Cengage Learning 2014

monetarists view the investment demand curve as sensitive to changes in the interest rate; therefore, greater amounts of investment spending will be crowded out. As a result, the net effect is no increase in aggregate demand and no reduction in unemployment.

> **CONCLUSION:** *Monetarists view the shape of the investment demand curve as less steep or relatively flat, so the crowding-out effect is significant.*

Monetary Policy during the Great Depression

Applicable Concept: Keynesians versus monetarists

Monetarists and Keynesians still debate the causes of the Great Depression. Monetarists Milton Friedman and Anna Schwartz, in their book *A Monetary History of the United States*, argued that the Great Depression was caused by the decline in the money supply, as shown in Exhibit 9(a).

During the 1920s, the money supply expanded steadily, and prices were generally stable. In response to the great stock market crash of 1929, bank failures, falling real GDP, and rising unemployment, the Fed changed its monetary policy. Through the Great Depression years from 1929 to 1933, M1 declined by 27 percent. Assuming velocity is relatively constant, how will a sharp reduction in the quantity of money in circulation affect the economy? Monetarists predict a reduction in prices, output, and employment. Between 1929 and 1933, the price level declined by 24 percent. In addition to deflation, real GDP was 27 percent lower in 1933 than in

1929. Unemployment rose from 3.2 percent in 1929 to 24.9 percent in 1933. Friedman and Schwartz argued that the ineptness of the Fed's monetary policy during the Great Depression caused the trough in the business cycle to be more severe and sustained.

The Great Depression was indeed not the Fed's finest hour. What should the Fed have done? Friedman and Schwartz argued that the Fed should have used open market operations to increase the money supply. Thus, they concluded that the Fed was to blame for not pursuing an expansionary policy, which would have reduced the severity and duration of the contraction. As shown in part (b), this was not the case for the Great Recession of 2007–2009. From the beginning, the Fed followed an expansionary policy and sharply increased the money supply.

Finally, although the emphasis here is monetary policy, parts (c) and (d) contrast fiscal policy during the two periods using the federal deficit as a percentage of GDP.

During the Great Depression, there was a slight budget surplus until 1931, when the budget turned into a slight budget deficit before reaching a deficit of 5.9 percent of GDP in 1934. In contrast, fiscal policy was more expansionary by running deficits from the beginning of the recession in 2007 to an estimated 10.6 percent of GDP in 2009.

Analyze the Issue

1. Explain why monetarists believe the Fed should have expanded the money supply during the Great Depression.
2. The Keynesians challenge the Friedman-Schwartz monetarists' monetary policy cure for the Great Depression. Use the AD-AS model to explain the Keynesian view. (Hint: Your answer must include the investment demand curve.)

Source: Milton Friedman and Anna J. Schwartz, *A Monetary History of the United States, 1867–1960* (Princeton, N.J.: Princeton University Press, 1963).

Although the monetarists do not trust the Federal Reserve to use discretionary monetary policy, they are quick to point out that only money is important. Changes in the money supply, the basic lever of monetary policy, have a powerful impact. Instead of ineffectual government deficit spending to cure unemployment, an increase in the money supply would definitely stimulate the economy based on the quantity theory of money. In short, changes in the money supply directly result in changes in real GDP.

EXHIBIT 9	The Great Depression Economic Data, 1929–1934 Compared to the Great Recession of 2007–2009

(a) Money supply 1929–34

(b) Money Supply 2007–09

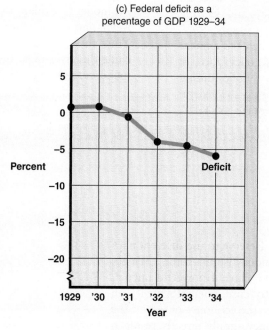

(c) Federal deficit as a percentage of GDP 1929–34

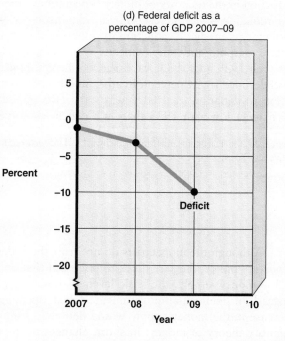

(d) Federal deficit as a percentage of GDP 2007–09

Key Concepts

Transactions demand for money
Precautionary demand for money
Speculative demand for money
Demand for money curve

Monetarism
Keynesian economics
Velocity of money
Quantity theory of money

Subprime mortgage loan
Classical economics
Equation of exchange

Summary

- The **demand for money** in the Keynesian view consists of three reasons why people hold money: (1) **Transactions demand** is money held to pay for everyday predictable expenses. (2) **Precautionary demand** is money held to pay unpredictable expenses. (3) **Speculative demand** is money held to take advantage of price changes in nonmoney assets.
- The **demand for money curve** shows the quantity of money people wish to hold at various rates of interest. As the interest rate rises, the quantity of money demanded is less than when the interest rate is lower.

Demand for Money Curve

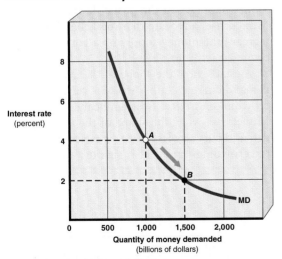

SOURCE: © Cengage Learning 2014

- The **equilibrium interest rate** is determined in the money market by the intersection of the demand for money and the supply of money curves. The money supply (M1), which is determined by the Fed, is represented by a vertical line.

The Equilibrium Interest Rate

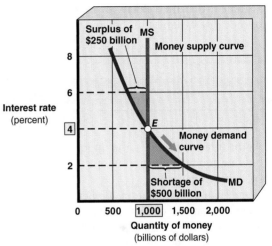

SOURCE: © Cengage Learning 2014

- An **excess quantity of money demanded** causes households and businesses to increase their money balances by selling bonds. This causes the price of bonds to fall, thus driving up the interest rate.
- An **excess quantity of money supplied** causes households and businesses to reduce their money balances by purchasing bonds. The effect is to cause the price of bonds to rise, and thereby, the rate of interest falls.
- The **Keynesian view of the monetary policy transmission mechanism** operates as follows: First, the Fed uses its policy tools to change the money supply. Second, changes in the money supply change the equilibrium interest rate, which affects investment spending. Finally, a change in investment changes aggregate demand and determines the level of prices, real GDP, and employment.
- **Monetarism** is the simpler view that changes in monetary policy directly change aggregate

demand, and thereby prices, real GDP, and employment. Thus, monetarists focus on the money supply, rather than on the rate of interest.

- The **equation of exchange** is an accounting identity that is the foundation of monetarism. The equation ($MV = PQ$) states that the money supply multiplied by the **velocity of money** is equal to the price level multiplied by real output. The velocity of money is the number of times each dollar is spent during a year. Keynesians view velocity as volatile, but monetarists disagree.
- The **quantity theory of money** is a monetarist argument that the velocity of money *(V)* and output *(Q)* variables in the equation of

exchange are relatively constant. Given this assumption, changes in the money supply yield proportional changes in the price level. The monetarist solution to inept Fed tinkering with the money supply that causes inflation or recession is to have the Fed simply pick a rate of growth in the money supply that is consistent with real GDP growth and stick to it.

- **Keynesians' and monetarists' views on fiscal policy** are also different. Keynesians believe the investment demand curve is relatively vertical, and monetarists view it as relatively flat. Monetarists assert that the *crowding-out effect* is large and, therefore, fiscal policy is ineffective. Keynesians argue that the crowding-out effect is small and that fiscal policy is effective.

Summary of Conclusion Statements

- As the interest rate falls, the opportunity cost of holding money falls, and people increase their speculative balances.
- There is an inverse relationship between the quantity of money demanded and the interest rate.
- The speculative demand for money at possible interest rates gives the demand for money curve its downward slope.
- There is an inverse relationship between bond prices and the interest rate that enables the money market to achieve equilibrium.
- In the Keynesian model, changes in the supply of money affect interest rates. In turn, interest rates affect investment spending, aggregate demand, and, finally, real GDP, employment, and prices.

- According to the quantity theory of money, any change in the money supply must lead to a proportional change in the price level.
- To avoid inflation and unemployment, the monetarists' prescription is to be sure that the money supply is at the proper level.
- Monetarists advocate that the Federal Reserve increase the money supply by a constant percentage each year.
- Keynesians view the shape of the investment demand curve as rather steep or vertical, so the crowding-out effect is insignificant.
- Monetarists view the shape of the investment demand curve as less steep or relatively flat, so the crowding-out effect is significant.

Study Questions and Problems

1. How much money do you keep in cash or checkable deposits on a typical day? Under the following conditions, would you increase or decrease your demand for money? Also identify whether the condition affects your transactions demand, precautionary demand, or speculative demand.

   a. Your salary doubles.
   b. The rate of interest on bonds and other assets falls.
   c. An automatic teller machine (ATM) is installed next door, and you have an ATM card.
   d. Bond prices are expected to rise.
   e. You are paid each week instead of monthly.

2. What are the basic motives for the transactions demand, precautionary demand, and speculative demand? Explain how these three demands are combined in a graph to show the total demand for money.

3. Suppose a bond pays annual interest of $80. Compute the interest rate per year that a bondholder can earn if the bond has a face value of $800, $1,000, and $2,000. State the conclusion drawn from your calculations.

EXHIBIT 10	Money Market	
Interest rate (percent)	Demand for money (billions of dollars)	Supply of money (billions of dollars)
8%	$100	$200
6	200	200
4	300	200
2	400	200
Source: © Cengage Learning 2014		

4. Using the demand and supply schedule for money shown in Exhibit 10, do the following:
   a. Graph the demand for money and the supply of money curves.
   b. Determine the equilibrium interest rate.
   c. Suppose the Fed increases the money supply by $100 billion. Show the effect in your graph, and describe the money market adjustment process to a new equilibrium interest rate. What is the new equilibrium rate of interest?

5. Assume you are the chair of the Federal Reserve Board of Governors and the condition of the economy is shown in Exhibit 5. Assume you are a Keynesian, and start at point E_1 in the money market and the product market. State the likely direction of change in the price level, real GDP, and employment caused by each of the following monetary policies:
   a. The Fed makes an open market sale of government bonds.
   b. The Fed reduces the required reserve ratio.
   c. The Fed increases the discount rate.

6. "A monetarist investigator might say that the sewer flow of 6,000 gallons an hour consisted of an average of 200 gallons in the sewer at any one time with a complete turnover of the water 30 times every hour."[1] Interpret this statement using the equation of exchange.

7. What is the quantity theory of money, and what does each term in the equation represent?

8. Exhibit 6 shows the monetarist monetary policy transmission mechanism. Assume the economy is in a recession. At each arrow, identify a reason why the transmission process could fail.

9. Explain the difference between the Keynesian and the monetarist views on how an increase in the money supply causes inflation.

10. Based on the quantity theory of money, what would be the impact of increasing the money supply by 25 percent?

11. Suppose the investment demand curve is a vertical line. Would the Keynesian or the monetarist view of the impact of monetary policy on investment spending be correct?

12. Why is the shape of the aggregate supply curve important to the Keynesian-monetarist controversy? (Hint: Review Exhibit 6 in the chapter on aggregate demand and supply.)

For Online Exercises, go to the Tucker Web site at www.cengage.com/economics/tucker.

[1]Werner Sichel and Peter Eckstein, *Basic Economic Concepts* (Chicago: Rand McNally, 1974), p. 344.

✓ CHECKPOINT ANSWERS

What Does the Money Supply Curve Look Like When the Fed Targets the Federal Funds Rate?

In Exhibit 11, consider the effect of a shift in the money demand curve from MD_1 to MD_2 when the Fed follows a federal funds rate target of 6 percent. The initial effects are an excess demand for money and upward pressure on the rate. Because the Fed sets the target at 6 percent, it will increase the money supply along the money supply curve, MS, and establish a new equilibrium at E_2. At the new equilibrium, the money supply has increased from $800 billion to $850 billion, and the rate is unchanged at 6 percent. Therefore, the money supply curve is traced by an infinite number of possible equilibrium points along the MS curve. If you said the money supply curve is horizontal when the Fed sets a federal funds rate target, **YOU ARE CORRECT**.

A Horse of Which Color?

The famous economist is Milton Friedman, who favors a monetary rule for the Fed. The horse is a sarcastic way of rejecting Keynesian activist policies that destabilize the economy. Friedman even argues that the Board of Governors of the Federal Reserve System should announce the growth rate

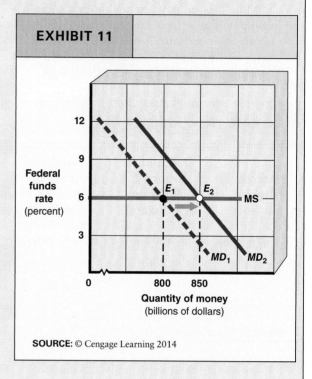

EXHIBIT 11

SOURCE: © Cengage Learning 2014

for the money supply each year and must resign if the target is missed. If you said the economist is a monetarist, **YOU ARE CORRECT**.

Sample Quiz

For an explanation of the correct answers, visit the Tucker Web site at www.cengage.com/economics/tucker.

1. The demand for money that households keep for emergency purposes is known as the
   a. precautionary demand.
   b. emergency demand.
   c. speculative demand.
   d. temporary demand.

2. The quantity of money held in response to interest rates is the

   a. transactions motive for holding money.
   b. precautionary motive for holding money.
   c. speculative motive for holding money.
   d. unit-of-account motive for holding money.

3. The speculative demand for money
   a. varies inversely with income.
   b. is only concerned with active money.

Sample Quiz *continued*

c. involves holding money for unexpected problems.

d. varies directly with the transactions demand for money.

e. varies inversely with the interest rate.

4. Other things being equal, the quantity of money that people wish to hold can be expected to

a. increase as the interest rate increases.

b. decrease as the interest rate increases.

c. decrease as real GDP increases.

d. None of the above answers are correct.

5. A decrease in the interest rate, other things being equal, causes a (an)

a. upward movement along the demand curve for money.

b. downward movement along the demand curve for money.

c. rightward shift of the demand curve for money.

d. leftward shift of the demand curve for money.

6. Which of the following statements is *true*?

a. The speculative demand for money at possible interest rates gives the demand for money curve its upward slope.

b. There is an inverse relationship between the quantity of money demanded and the interest rate.

c. According to the quantity theory of money, any change in the money supply will have no effect on the price level.

d. All of the above answers are correct.

7. In Exhibit 12, assume an equilibrium with an interest rate of 15 percent and the money supply at $100 billion. The Fed uses its policy tools to move the economy to a new equilibrium at E_2 with money supply of $150 billion and an interest rate of 10 percent. This change could be the result of a(an)

a. open market sale of securities by the Fed.

b. higher discount rate set by the Fed.

c. higher required reserve ratio set by the Fed.

d. open market purchase of securities by the Fed.

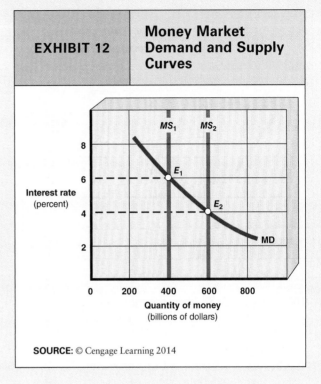

EXHIBIT 12   **Money Market Demand and Supply Curves**

SOURCE: © Cengage Learning 2014

8. According to Keynesians, an increase in the money supply will

a. decrease the interest rate, and increase investment, aggregate demand, prices, real GDP, and employment.

b. decrease the interest rate, and decrease investment, aggregate demand, prices, real GDP, and employment.

c. increase the interest rate and decrease investment, aggregate demand, prices, real GDP, and employment.

d. only increase prices.

9. While the classicists believed that both velocity and output are stable, Keynesians believe

a. velocity is stable, and output is variable.

b. velocity and output are both variable.

c. output is stable, and velocity is variable

d. the same as the classical economists that both output and velocity are stable.

Sample Quiz *continued*

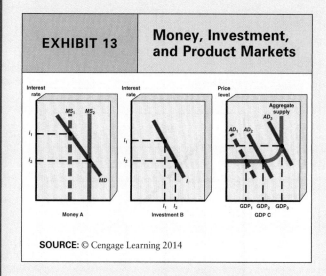

EXHIBIT 13 — **Money, Investment, and Product Markets**

SOURCE: © Cengage Learning 2014

10. In Exhibit 13, when the money supply increases from S_1 to S_2, the equilibrium interest rate
   a. remains unchanged.
   b. increases from i_2 to i_1, increasing investment spending from I_1 to I_2.
   c. increases from i_2 to i_1, decreasing investment spending from I_2 to I_1.
   d. decreases from i_1 to i_2, increasing investment spending from I_1 to I_2.

11. In Exhibit 13, if the interest rate falls from i_1 to i_2, investment spending will
   a. increase, and aggregate demand will shift from AD_1 to AD_2.
   b. decrease, and aggregate demand will shift from AD_2 to AD_1.
   c. remain the same, and aggregate demand will shift from AD_2 to AD_3.
   d. increase, and aggregate demand will shift from AD_2 to AD_1.

12. In Exhibit 13, a shift in aggregate demand from AD_1 to AD_2
   a. cannot raise real GDP because the economy is at full employment.
   b. cannot raise real GDP because the aggregate supply curve is upward sloping at GDP_2.
   c. will raise real GDP because the economy is operating below the full-employment level.
   d. will cause the interest rate to increase from i_2 to i_1.

13. The monetarist transmission mechanism through which monetary policy affects the price level, real GDP, and employment depends on the
   a. indirect impact of changes on the interest rate.
   b. indirect impact of changes on profit expectations.
   c. direct impact of changes in fiscal policy on aggregate demand.
   d. direct impact of changes in the money supply on aggregate demand.

14. The equation of exchange states
   a. $MV = PQ$.
   b. $MP = VQ$.
   c. $MP = V/Q$.
   d. $V = M/PQ$.

15. The quantity theory of money assumes that the velocity of money
   a. is constant.
   b. will rise if the money supply rises and fall if the money supply falls.
   c. will rise if the money supply rises, but will not change if the money supply falls.
   d. will fall if the money supply rises, and will rise if the money supply falls.

16. The transactions demand for money is the demand for money by households for
   a. rainy day spending.
   b. predictable spending purposes.
   c. liquidity purposes.
   d. investing purposes.

17. People react to an excess supply of money by
   a. selling bonds, thus driving up the interest rate.
   b. selling bonds, thus driving down the interest rate.
   c. buying bonds, thus driving up the interest rate.
   d. buying bonds, thus driving down the interest rate.

Sample Quiz *continued*

18. The belief that the velocity of money is *not* constant but is highly predictable is associated with the
    a. classical school.
    b. Keynesian school.
    c. supply-side school.
    d. rational expectations school.
    e. monetarist school.

19. The monetary rule is the view of the
    a. Keynesians that monetary policy is most important.
    b. monetarists that monetary policy is most important.
    c. classical economists that monetary policy is most important.
    d. monetarists that the Fed should expand the money supply at a constant rate.

20. Which of the following statements is *true*?
    a. Keynesians advocate increasing the money supply during economic recessions but decreasing the money supply during economic expansions.
    b. Monetarists advocate increasing the money supply by a constant rate year after year.
    c. Keynesians argue that the crowding-out effect is rather insignificant.
    d. Monetarists argue that the crowding-out effect is rather large.
    e. All of the above answers are correct.

16

Policy Disputes Using the Self-Correcting Aggregate Demand and Supply Model

In the appendix to the chapter on aggregate demand and supply, the classical self-correcting aggregate demand and supply model was explained without disagreement. Expansionary and contractionary fiscal policy was discussed in the chapter on fiscal policy, and this chapter explained monetary policy. In this appendix, we combine these topics and examine contrasting fiscal and monetary policies using the self-correcting model.

16A-1 The Classical versus Keynesian Views of Expansionary Policy

The Keynesian activist approach rejects classical nonintervention policy to stabilize the economy using discretionary fiscal policy or activist monetary policy. Exhibit A-1 illustrates opposing theories for restoring an economy in recession to full employment. In both parts (a) and (b), the economy starts with a real GDP of $8 trillion and a price level of 150 at macro equilibrium E_1. Since full-employment real GDP is $12 trillion, the recessionary gap equals $4 trillion. In part (a), the economy closes the gap through the self-correction process. The key classical assumption is that nominal wages are flexible and fall as a result of competition among unemployed workers for jobs. Over time, the result is that the short-term aggregate supply curve ($SRAS_1$) shifts rightward to $SRAS_2$ and the economy automatically adjusts to long-run macro full-employment equilibrium at E_2 with a price level of 100.

Part (b) illustrates the opposing Keynesian theory. This view argues that nominal wages are fixed in the short run. In contrast to the self-correction model, Keynesians advocate using discretionary fiscal policy in which the federal government manages the aggregate demand curve (AD) by increasing government spending or cutting taxes. Both of these policy options work through the multiplier process and increase AD_1 to AD_2. The result is that the economy achieves full employment at macro equilibrium point E_2, where the price level is 200.

Activist monetary policy can also stabilize the economy. The Federal Reserve can increase the money supply, which lowers the interest rate, and in response, business investment spending increases. As a result, AD_1 shifts to AD_2 in part (b) of Exhibit A-1, and full employment is restored at E_2.

Note that both approaches in parts (a) and (b) restore full-employment real GDP; however, the impact on the price level is quite different. If classical theory is correct, the price level falls from 150 to 100. In contrast, if Keynesian theory is correct, the price level rises from 150 to 200, resulting in a higher inflation rate.

EXHIBIT A-1	**Opposing Anti-recession Theories**

Part (a) illustrates classical theory, which advocates noninterventionist fiscal and monetary policy. The classical assumption is that nominal wages are flexible. At point E_1, unemployed workers compete for jobs, and the wage rate falls, causing the short-run aggregate supply curve to shift from $SRAS_1$ to $SRAS_2$. Full employment is therefore automatically restored at point E_2.

In part (b), Keynesian policy advocates interventionist fiscal and monetary policy. Discretionary fiscal policy increases government spending or cuts taxes to increase the aggregate demand curve from AD_1 to AD_2. Discretionary monetary policy would increase the money supply to increase AD_1 to AD_2.

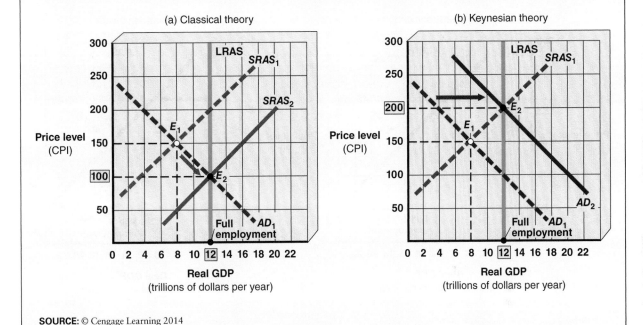

SOURCE: © Cengage Learning 2014

> **CONCLUSION:** *The classical approach to a recession is to let market forces shift the short-run aggregate supply curve rightward and restore the economy to full employment. The opposing Keynesian approach to cure a recession is to use discretionary fiscal and monetary policy to increase aggregate demand and achieve full-employment real GDP.*

16A-2 Classical versus Keynesian Views of Contractionary Policy

Exhibit A-2 shows alternative theories for closing an inflationary gap. The classical nonintervention policy relies on competition between firms in response to a shortage of labor. In parts (a) and (b), the economy is at macro equilibrium at point E_1, where the price level is 150 and real GDP is $16 trillion. There is an inflationary gap of $4 trillion greater than the potential real GDP of $12 trillion. In part (a),

EXHIBIT A-2	Opposing Anti-inflation Theories

In part (a), the classical assumption is that at point E_1, firms face a labor shortage and their competition for available workers drives up the nominal wage rate. Under a noninterventionist policy, the short-run aggregate supply curve shifts leftward from $SRAS_1$ to $SRAS_2$, and the economy is automatically restored to full employment at E_2.

Part (b) shows the effect of Keynesian contractionary policy. Discretionary fiscal policy decreases government spending or increases taxes to shift the aggregate demand curve leftward from AD_1 to AD_2. Discretionary monetary policy would decrease the money supply to decrease AD_1 to AD_2.

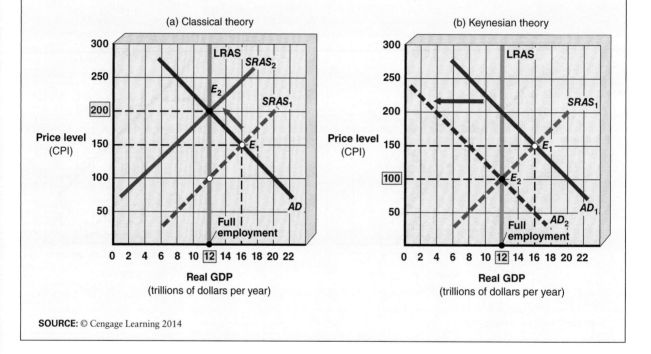

SOURCE: © Cengage Learning 2014

classical theory assumes flexible wages, so nominal wages rise, causing the $SRAS_1$ to shift upward to $SRAS_2$, and the economy reaches full-employment real GDP at point E_2 with a price level of 200.

In part (b), Keynesian contractionary policy aims at decreasing AD_1 to AD_2 using cuts in government spending or tax hikes. Working through the multiplier process, the inflationary gap is eliminated, and the economy moves from point E_1 to E_2, where the price level falls from 150 to 100 and full-employment real GDP of $12 trillion is achieved.

Monetary policy can also be used to shift the aggregate demand curve leftward. In this case, the Federal Reserve could follow a contractionary policy and decrease the money supply, resulting in a higher interest rate, and firms respond by decreasing their investment spending. Consequently, AD_1 decreases to AD_2, and full-employment real GDP is reached at E_2.

As shown in the previous exhibit, opposing theories have different impacts on the price level. In part (a) of Exhibit A-2, the classical approach leads to an increase in the price level from 150 to 200. In contrast, the Keynesian approach yields a decrease in the price level from 150 to 100.

> **CONCLUSION:** *The classical approach to an inflationary gap is to let market forces shift the short-run aggregate supply curve leftward and restore the economy to full employment. The opposing Keynesian approach to cure inflation uses discretionary fiscal and monetary policy to decrease aggregate demand and achieve full-employment real GDP.*

Summary

- The **Keynesian prescription for a recession** rejects the classical assumption that wages are flexible and will fall, causing the short-run aggregate supply curve to shift downward and restore full-employment GDP. Instead, Keynesians support expansionary fiscal and monetary policy to increase aggregate demand and return the economy to the natural rate of unemployment.

- The **Keynesian cure for inflation** also rejects the classical assumption that wages are flexible and will rise, causing the short-run aggregate supply curve to shift upward and restore full-employment GDP. In contrast, Keynesian theory advocates contractionary fiscal and monetary policy to decrease aggregate demand and achieve full-employment macro equilibrium.

Summary of Conclusion Statements

- The classical approach to a recession is to let market forces shift the short-run aggregate supply curve rightward and restore the economy to full employment. The opposing Keynesian approach to cure a recession is to use discretionary fiscal and monetary policy to increase aggregate demand and achieve full-employment real GDP.

- The classical approach to an inflationary gap is to let market forces shift the short-run aggregate supply curve leftward and restore the economy to full employment. The opposing Keynesian approach to cure inflation uses discretionary fiscal and monetary policy to decrease aggregate demand and achieve full-employment real GDP.

Sample Quiz

For an explanation of the correct answers, visit the Tucker Web site at www.cengage.com/economics/tucker.

1. Classical theory advocates _____ policy, and Keynesian theory advocates _____ policy.
   a. nonintervention; intervention
   b. active; nonstabilization
   c. fixed wages; flexible wages
   d. active; passive

2. If the economy is in short-run disequilibrium, an economist following classical theory would advocate that the Federal Reserve make appropriate changes in the
   a. money supply.
   b. reserve requirement.

Sample Quiz *continued*

   c. federal funds rate.

   d. None of the above answers is correct.

3. Assuming the economy is experiencing a recessionary gap, classical economists predict that
   a. wages will remain fixed.
   b. monetary policy should intervene.
   c. higher wages will shift the short-run aggregate supply curve leftward.
   d. lower wages will shift the short-run aggregate supply curve rightward.

4. Assume the economy is operating at a real GDP above full-employment real GDP. Keynesian economists would prescribe which of the following policies?
   a. nonintervention
   b. passive monetary policy
   c. contractionary
   d. expansionary

5. Assume the economy is experiencing an inflationary gap, Keynesian economists believe that
   a. flexible wages will restore full employment.
   b. the federal government should decrease spending to shift the aggregate demand curve leftward.
   c. the Federal Reserve should lower the interest rate.
   d. the federal government should increase spending to shift the aggregate demand curve rightward.

6. Assume the economy is in short-run equilibrium at a real GDP below its potential real GDP. According to Keynesian theory, which of the following policies should be followed?
   a. The Federal Reserve should increase the money supply.
   b. The federal government should increase spending.
   c. The federal government should do nothing because the economy will self correct to potential real GDP.
   d. All of the above answers are correct.

7. A policy to do nothing and allow the economy to self-correct or adjust without interference from the federal government is also called a (an) _____ policy.
   a. nonintervention
   b. active
   c. stabilization
   d. fixed rule

8. Assume the economy is experiencing a recessionary gap. Keynesian economists would support which of the following policies?
   a. nonstabilization
   b. expansionary
   c. nonintervention
   d. fixed wage

9. Assuming the economy is in a recession, Keynesian economists predict that
   a. wages will remain fixed.
   b. monetary policy will sell government securities.
   c. higher wages will shift the short-run aggregate supply curve leftward.
   d. lower wages will shift the short-run aggregate supply curve rightward.

10. Assume the economy is in short-run equilibrium at a real GDP above its potential real GDP. According to classical theory, which of the following policies should be followed?
   a. The Federal Reserve should use open market operations and buy U.S. government securities.
   b. The Federal Reserve should not follow a fixed rule.
   c. The federal government should cut taxes.
   d. Fiscal policy and monetary policy should *not* be activist.

11. Assume the economy is experiencing an inflationary gap, classical economists believe that
   a. flexible wages will restore full employment.
   b. the federal government should decrease spending to shift the aggregate demand curve leftward.

Sample Quiz *continued*

c. the Federal Reserve should lower the interest rate.

d. the federal government should increase spending to shift the aggregate demand curve rightward.

12. In part (a) of Exhibit A-3, the economy is initially in short-run equilibrium at real GDP level Y_1 and price level P_2. Classical theory argues
a. the federal government must shift AD_1 to AD_2 as shown in part (b).
b. the federal government must shift $SRAS_1$ to $SRAS_2$.
c. $SRAS_1$ will shift to $SRAS_2$ without government intervention.
d. AD_1 will shift to AD_2 without government intervention.

13. Assume that the economy depicted in part (a) of Exhibit A-3 is in short-run equilibrium with AD_1 and $SRAS_1$. If the economy is

left to correct itself according to classical theory
a. wages will fall as long as real GDP is above Y_p.
b. lower wages will result in a shift from $SRAS_1$ to $SRAS_2$.
c. long-run equilibrium will be established at Y_p and P_3.
d. All of the above will take place.

14. In part (b) of Exhibit A-3, the economy is initially in short-run equilibrium at real GDP level Y_1 and price level P_2. If the government decides to intervene, it would
a. increase taxes.
b. decrease the money supply.
c. increase the level of government spending for goods and services.
d. decrease the level of government spending for goods and services.

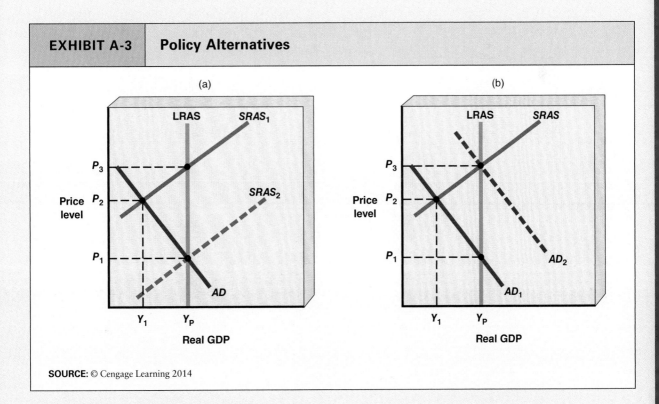

| EXHIBIT A-3 | Policy Alternatives |

Sample Quiz *continued*

15. Assume that the economy depicted in part (b) of Exhibit A-3 is in short-run equilibrium with AD_1 and $SRAS_1$. Keynesian theory argues
    a. nominal wages will fall as long as employment remains above the natural level of unemployment.

    b. lower wages will result in a shift from $SRAS_1$ to $SRAS_2$.
    c. long-run equilibrium will be established at Y_p and P_1.
    d. government intervention must shift AD_1 to AD_2.

chapter 17

The Phillips Curve and Expectations Theory

This chapter explores the Phillips curve, the expectations theory, and incomes policies (wage and price controls). The Phillips curve traces the relationship between two of the greatest problems of economies everywhere—inflation and unemployment. One of the most fascinating puzzles in economics is whether a stable trade-off exists between these two economic evils. If true, policymakers face a dilemma described by the old saying "Inside each solution there is another problem looking to work its way out." If policymakers reduce the unemployment rate, the inflation rate worsens. Or if they reduce the inflation rate, the unemployment rate rises. In the 1960s, most economists and policymakers thought the way to achieve a particular inflation-unemployment point on the Phillips curve menu was to use Keynesian demand-management policies.

Just as the reality of the Great Depression refuted classical theory, the Great Stagflations of the 1970s and early 1980s challenged the Phillips curve and Keynesian policies. To understand how varying rates of inflation can occur at the same rate of unemployment, we explore two competing ways of thinking called *adaptive expectations* and *rational expectations*. Both of these theories are attacks on the Keynesians who urge the government to interfere with the market economy in order to achieve full employment.

The chapter begins with a discussion of the Phillips curve that explains why both expectations camps believe there is no permanent inflation-unemployment trade-off. In the last part of this chapter, you will see what happens when policymakers fight inflation using policies to control wages and prices (incomes), rather than monetary and fiscal policies.

In this chapter, you will learn to solve these economics puzzles:

- Why might expansionary fiscal and monetary policies be useless in the long run?
- If the Fed is independent, why would the money supply increase before a presidential election?
- Can economic theory explain pop quizzes?
- Can wearing a button reduce inflation?

17-1 The Phillips Curve

In a celebrated article published in 1958, Australian economist A. W. Phillips of the London School of Economics plotted data on unemployment rates and the rate of change in wage rates between 1861 and 1957 in the United Kingdom.[1] Phillips showed there was a remarkably stable inverse relationship between changes in money wages and the unemployment rate. Economists have since extended this concept to the following definition of the Phillips curve. The Phillips curve is a curve showing an inverse relationship between the inflation rate and the unemployment rate. The reason it is acceptable to use the inflation rate, rather than the change in wages, is that wages are the main component of prices. At low rates of unemployment, labor has the market power to push up wages and, in turn, prices. When many workers are pounding the pavement eager for jobs, labor lacks bargaining power to ask for raises. As a result, the upward pressure on prices eases.

Phillips curve

A curve showing an inverse relationship between the inflation rate and the unemployment rate.

17-1a THE PHILLIPS CURVE IN THEORY

Exhibit 1 shows the relationship between the AD-AS model developed earlier and the Phillips curve. In part (a), we assume that the aggregate supply curve, AS, is stationary. Thus, points A–D represent possible equilibrium points depending on the location of the aggregate demand curve. As the aggregate demand curve increases from AD_1 to AD_4, real GDP rises from $6.0 trillion to $6.6 trillion, more workers are employed, and the price level (CPI) rises from 100 to 112. The astute reader will recognize from the chapter on aggregate demand and supply that we are discussing *demand-pull inflation*.

The inverse relationship between the price level and unemployment in part (a) determines the shape of the Phillips curve in part (b). Points A–D in both figures correspond. If the economy operates at point A, the annual rate of inflation is zero, and the unemployment rate is 8 percent. If the economy is at point B, the annual rate of inflation is 4 percent, and the unemployment rate is 5 percent. Similarly, points C and D correspond in both graphs. Note that below point A, the price level is below 100 and the economy experiences deflation.

> **CONCLUSION:** *Changes in aggregate demand cause a movement along a stationary Phillips curve.*

17-1b THE PHILLIPS CURVE IN PRACTICE

So far so good. If the world works this way, policymakers must choose from a menu of inflation rate and unemployment rate combinations along the Phillips curve. Do we want X percent less unemployment with an opportunity cost of Y percent more inflation? Early studies verified the Phillips curve for the U.S. economy in the 1960s. As shown in Exhibit 2, the data fit the Phillips curve very well. Based on this evidence, most economists, including Nobel laureates Paul Samuelson

---

[1]A. W. Phillips, "The Relation between Unemployment and the Rate of Change in Money Wage Rates in the United Kingdom, 1861–1957," *Economica* 25 (November 1958): 283–299.

EXHIBIT 1	The Theoretical Relationship between Changes in Aggregate Demand and the Phillips Curve

In part (a), the aggregate demand curve shifts upward, while the aggregate supply curve remains stationary. The result is a series of equilibrium points *A–D*. As aggregate demand rises along the *AS* curve, the price level (CPI), real GDP, and employment increase. Points *A–D* in parts (a) and (b) correspond. An increase in aggregate demand from AD_1 to AD_4 causes the unemployment rate to fall, but the inflation rate rises. Thus, the increase in aggregate demand results in a movement upward along the Phillips curve.

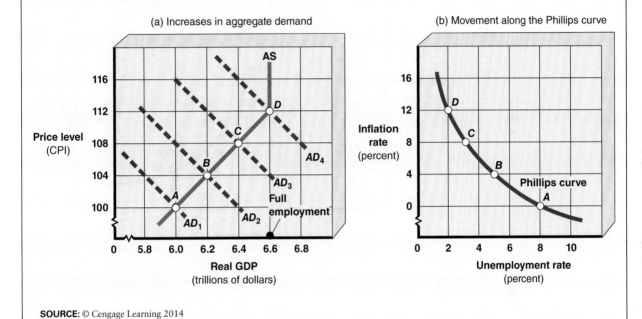

(a) Increases in aggregate demand

(b) Movement along the Phillips curve

(deceased) and Robert Solow of MIT, believed the Phillips curve was stable. Policymakers might choose low inflation and high unemployment, as in 1961. Or they may prefer higher inflation and lower unemployment, as, for example, in 1969. And the most popular way in the 1960s to reach a particular point on the Phillips curve was to fine-tune the economy using Keynesian demand-management policies.

Then, just as policymakers and economists became comfortable with the Phillips curve, the dream turned into a nightmare. As shown in Exhibit 3, the points for 1970–1990 show the Phillips curve in chaos. The pattern disappeared, and many points moved far above and to the right of the 1960s data. At higher unemployment rates, the corresponding inflation rate was much higher than the Phillips curve predicted. For example, look at 1975, 1979, 1980, and 1981. These data reflect bouts with stagflation, which occurred in the 1970s and early 1980s. Recall from Exhibit 12(a) in the chapter on aggregate demand and supply that *cost-push inflation* is the result of a leftward shift of the aggregate supply curve. In the Great Stagflations of 1973–1974 and 1979–1980, the influence of such "supply shocks" as soaring oil prices pushed up production costs and shifted

EXHIBIT 2	The Phillips Curve for the United States in the 1960s

The figure plots the inflation rate and unemployment rate combinations for the period 1960–1969. A freehand curve drawn through the points conforms very well to the Phillips curve.

SOURCE: *Economic Report of the President 2012*, http://www.gpoaccess.gov/eop/, Tables B-15 and B-64.

the economy's aggregate supply curve inward. Thus, the Phillips curve theory was in shambles as the nation simultaneously experienced both high inflation and high unemployment. Policymakers therefore turned their focus from the Phillips curve, based on trade-offs, to a "misery index," which added the inflation and unemployment rates.

17-2 The Long-Run Phillips Curve

The simple idea of a stable trade-off between unemployment and inflation was an overnight sensation in the 1960s. By the early 1970s, the Phillips curve was becoming a has-been. Because Keynesian demand-management policies generate the curve, it will come as no surprise that monetarists such as Milton Friedman and Edmund S. Phelps always believed the Phillips curve was just a transitory, short-run relationship. In the mid-1960s, they suggested that the unemployment rate and the rate of inflation are unrelated in the long run. As shown in Exhibit 4, the challengers argued that after a few years, the Phillips curve is a vertical line. As explained below, this monetarist view is also debatable.

EXHIBIT 3	Inflation and Unemployment Rates for the United States, 1970–1990

By 1990, the Phillips curve became unstable. Clearly, many points have been established upward and to the right. The inflation rate therefore can be much higher at any unemployment rate than the Phillips curve of the 1960s predicted.

SOURCE: *Economic Report of the President 2012*, http://www.gpoaccess.gov/eop/, Tables B-15 and B-64.

17-2a NATURAL RATE HYPOTHESIS

If the Phillips curve is vertical in the long run, there are profound implications for macroeconomic policy. Expansionary monetary and fiscal policies can, at best, produce a short-lived lowering of unemployment. This is the so-called natural rate hypothesis. The natural rate hypothesis argues that the economy will self-correct to the natural rate of unemployment. The long-run Phillips curve is therefore a vertical line at the natural rate of unemployment. Recall from the chapter on business cycles and unemployment that the natural rate of unemployment, or the full-employment unemployment rate, is equal to the sum of the frictional and structural

Natural rate hypothesis

The hypothesis that argues that the economy will self-correct to the natural rate of unemployment. The long-run Phillips curve is therefore a vertical line at the natural rate of unemployment.

EXHIBIT 4	The Short-Run and Long-Run Phillips Curves

Beginning at point *A*, the economy is operating at the 6 percent natural rate of unemployment. The actual and anticipated inflation rates are 3 percent. An increase in aggregate demand temporarily causes the inflation rate to rise to 6 percent. Under adaptive expectations theory, real wages fall, profits rise, and more workers are employed. The unemployment rate falls to 4 percent, and the economy moves along the short-run Phillips curve PC_1 to point *B*. Over time, workers demand and get nominal wage rate hikes, and profits fall. Workers lose their jobs, and the unemployment rate returns to 6 percent at point *C* on the short-run Phillips curve PC_2. This process will repeat each time expansionary policy attempts to reduce unemployment below the natural rate. The long-run Phillips curve is therefore a vertical line at the natural rate of unemployment. This suggests that Keynesian expansionary policies create only inflation over time.

Under rational expectations theory, workers do not rely only on recent experience. They adjust their nominal wages quickly in proportion to changes in prices. Expansionary policy will move the economy directly upward along the long-run Phillips curve.

SOURCE: © Cengage Learning 2014

unemployment rates. In Exhibit 4, the natural rate of unemployment is 6 percent. Two versions of expectations theory explain the natural rate model. We begin our analysis using *adaptive expectations theory* and then turn to the more recent *rational expectations theory*.

17-2b ADAPTIVE EXPECTATIONS THEORY

To explain the reasoning behind the natural rate hypothesis, let us begin in Exhibit 4 with the economy operating at point *A*, with a 3 percent inflation rate and a 6 percent unemployment rate. Assume the inflation rate has been 3 percent in recent years and this trend is expected to continue. Based on this recent 3 percent rise in the CPI, collective bargaining agreements call for hourly nominal or money wages of $10.00 this year and $10.30 next year. Now suppose an election is approaching and the president and Congress strive to make voters happy by reducing the unemployment rate to 4 percent. Or perhaps policymakers incorrectly believe 4 percent is the natural rate of unemployment. Regardless of the reason for setting this goal, suppose the new expansionary fiscal policy shifts the aggregate demand curve upward along the aggregate supply curve and the economy moves unexpectedly from point *A* this year to point *B* the next year.

Keynesians declare "mission accomplished" when the economy moves up the short-run Phillips curve PC_1 from point *A* to point *B*. This unexpected change brings good news to businesses. Based on an expected inflation rate of 3 percent, employers agreed to pay real wages of $10.00 at point *B*. However, if the inflation rate rises unexpectedly to 6 percent, real wages fall to $9.72 as prices rise.[2] With cheaper labor costs in real terms, profits increase, more workers are hired, real GDP expands, and the unemployment rate drops to 4 percent.

So far, Keynesians and monetarists agree that policymakers and businesses are running the race as though the hare and the workers are acting like the tortoise. But monetarists do not believe workers are caught flat-footed as time passes. Workers soon realize that higher prices have eroded their purchasing power. Consequently, they demand an extra 3 percent raise in the nominal wage rate so that their real wages can be restored to the level prior to the unexpected rise in the inflation rate from 3 to 6 percent. When workers get their raise to offset the higher cost of living, business profits decline, and some workers are laid off until the unemployment rate returns to 6 percent at point *C*. At point *C*, the unemployment rate is right back where it began before the government unsystematically changed its fiscal policy, but the inflation rate has risen from 3 to 6 percent. Keynesians, on the other hand, believe nominal wages are fixed because workers do not demand and get an extra 3 percent rise in nominal wages. In the Keynesian view, demand stimulus reduced unemployment in exchange for the higher inflation rate, and the economy remains at point *B* and does not automatically move in time to point *C*.

Our story describes a *wage-price spiral*, defined in the chapter on inflation, and we need a theory to explain how people form their inflationary expectations. The reason the economy moved from point *A* to point *B* is based on adaptive expectations theory. Adaptive expectations theory is the concept that people believe that the best indicator of the future is recent information. As a result, people

Adaptive expectations theory

The concept that people believe the best indicator of the future is recent information. As a result, people persistently underestimate inflation when it is accelerating and overestimate it while it is slowing down.

---

[2]Assume the price level at point *A* is 100 and the price level rises to 106 at point *B*. The real wage is computed as the nominal wage multiplied by the initial price level divided by the new price level. Thus, the real wage rate at point *B* is equal to $10.30 × (100/106) = $9.72. If the price level had risen to 103, as expected, the real wage at point *B* would have equaled $10.30 × (100/103) = $10.00.

persistently underestimate inflation when it is accelerating and overestimate it while it is slowing down. Adaptive expectations theory assumes ignorance of future events, including changes in fiscal and monetary policies. People learn from recent experience and gradually adjust their anticipated inflation rate to the actual inflation rate. This means that at point C, workers expect a higher rate of inflation at any unemployment rate because last year the actual rate of inflation was 6 percent. Unions therefore expect a 6 percent rate of inflation and are no longer satisfied with a contract with less than a 6 percent increase in the nominal wage rate; since anything less would mean a cut in real wages. Thus, workers *adapt* their expectations to 6 percent instead of 3 percent, and the short-run Phillips curve shifts outward from PC_1 to PC_2 in Exhibit 4. In other words, the economy moves from point A to point C on the vertical long-run Phillips curve. If policymakers follow a contractionary policy, adaptive expectations operate in reverse, and the inflation rate declines (see You're the Economist: The Political Business Cycle).

Suppose policymakers figure expansionary policy worked last time, so why not try it again? So they take another stab at creating jobs by stimulating aggregate demand. This time the economy will ride up the new short-run Phillips curve PC_2 from point C to point D, and the whole process will repeat. When the actual inflation rate rises from 6 to 9 percent, nominal wage increases will be a step slow in catching up with price hikes. In time, workers will demand and get a nominal wage hike, which restores their real wage rate, and the economy will reach point E. Faced with the new short-run Phillips curve PC_3, the government will cause an inflation rate of 12 percent at point F if it persists in trying to achieve 4 percent unemployment. Eventually, nominal wages will rise (reducing profits), some workers will lose their jobs, and the economy will move from point F to point G.

> **CONCLUSION:** *According to adaptive expectations theory, expansionary monetary and fiscal policies to reduce the unemployment rate are useless in the long run. After a short-run reduction in unemployment, the economy will self-correct to the natural rate of unemployment, but at a higher inflation rate. Thus, there is no long-run trade-off between inflation and unemployment.*

17-2c THE LONG-RUN PHILLIPS CURVE AND THE LABOR MARKET

We can now give one explanation for the tendency of the inflation-unemployment points shown earlier in Exhibit 3 to shift upward to the right in the 1970s and early 1980s. Demand stimulus policies in the 1960s caught people by surprise, and there was a movement upward along a short-run Phillips curve. As inflation worsened during the 1970s and the early 1980s, adaptive expectations caused the short-run Phillips curves to shift outward. As the inflation rate dropped sharply during the late 1980s, people's inflationary expectations adapted in the downward direction, and the short-run Phillips curve shifted inward. Moreover, as discussed in the chapter on business cycles and unemployment, economists estimated that the *natural rate of unemployment* increased from the 1960s to the 1980s. Recall that the natural rate of unemployment is the full-employment unemployment rate at which the economy operates at capacity

The Political Business Cycle

Applicable Concept: adaptive expectations

The basic ideal of Keynesian economics is that the government uses monetary and fiscal policies to stabilize the economy. On the other hand, the government may be diabolical and deliberately cause business cycles. The political business cycle is therefore Keynesianism in reverse. A political business cycle is a business cycle caused by policymakers to improve politicians' reelection chances.

A basic assumption of the political business cycle model is that democratic government causes business cycles. This theory views politics as, by nature, a short-run game. The rational self-interest goal of politicians is to maximize votes today and worry about tomorrow when tomorrow comes. This means a politician who faces an election must act now and not later. Voters are also short-sighted and want good news now, rather than promises of long-term solutions. If people want jobs, for example, the politicians who seek reelection will use expansionary policies to create jobs. The political process will therefore gladly force a lower unemployment rate now in exchange for a higher inflation rate in the future. The politician who commits the sin of truth and tells the voters a "quick fix" is harmful will probably taste defeat.

Given the realities of politics, politicians may find it easier to let the Fed stimulate the economy. Expansionary fiscal policy requires Congress to approve tax cuts or spending increases. Since members of Congress belong to opposing parties, each side has an incentive to prevent the other party from taking credit for legislation. Even if a bill eventually passes, it may be too late for the election. Fiscal policy takes considerable time to implement and actually affect the economy and, in turn, the voters.

If the Fed is independent, why would the Fed be willing to create political business cycles? Recall that the president appoints the Fed chair and members of the Board of Governors. Thus, the Fed is a semi-separate branch of government that often wishes to avoid conflict with Congress or the president. If the Fed is willing to stimulate aggregate demand before an election, incumbent politicians will benefit at the expense of their opponents. Once the election is over, the Fed will slow down the economy to reduce the inflation rate. Then the concern becomes recession until the next election looms and the Fed stimulates the economy again. Meanwhile, politicians can blame the Fed for driving up prices or starting the downturn.

Exhibit 5 reveals that the money supply has generally been on the rise before presidential elections. In 1964, 1968, 1972, 1976, 1980 (slight), 1988, 1992, and 2008, the money supply rose before the presidential election and then fell after the presidential election. The 1984, 1996, 2000, and 2004 elections were exceptions. Since this text was written in 2012, the money supply percentage change is not available for the election of 2012.

Analyze the Issue

Based on adaptive expectations theory, assume an expansionary monetary policy has moved the economy to point *C* in Exhibit 4. Now suppose the election is over and inflation concerns policymakers, so the Fed applies the brakes to monetary policy. Use this diagram to explain the short-run and long-run effects of a contractionary monetary policy.

(potential GDP). This means the vertical long-run Phillips curve intersecting each short-run Phillips curve shifted to the right. The explanation, in part, is because women and teenagers became a larger percentage of the labor force, and these groups of workers often experience higher rates of unemployment. It is also argued that the following measures might reduce the natural rate of unemployment: revising unemployment compensation, changing the minimum wage law, providing

Political business cycle

A business cycle caused by policymakers to improve politicians' reelection chances.

| EXHIBIT 5 | Money Supply Growth and Presidential Elections, 1960–2008 |

Since 1960, the money supply has often increased prior to presidential elections. The 1984, 1996, 2000, and 2004 elections were exceptions.

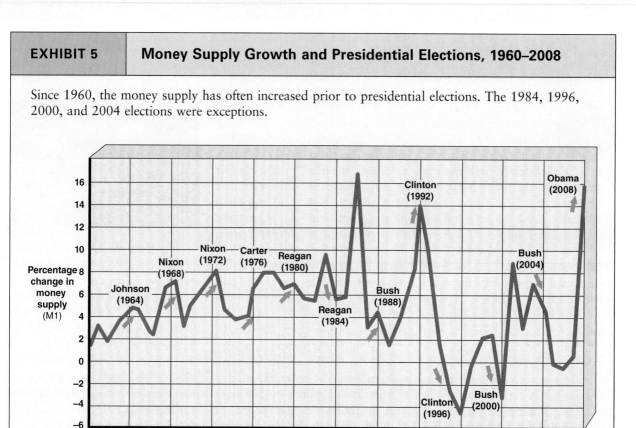

SOURCE: *Economic Report of the President 2012,* http://www.gpoaccess.gov/eop/, Tables B-69.

Rational expectations theory

The belief that people use all available information to predict the future, including the future impact of predictable expansionary monetary and fiscal policies. Predictable expansionary macroeconomic policies can therefore be negated by immediately flexible wages and prices when businesses and workers anticipate the effects of these policies on the economy.

better education and training, improving information on available jobs, removing discrimination, and reducing the monopoly power of unions and businesses.

17-3 The Theory of Rational Expectations

Whether expectations are formed "adaptively" or "rationally" is a hotly contested debate among economists. In the mid-1970s, Robert Lucas of the University of Chicago (1995 Nobel Laureate) is generally credited with introducing rational expectations theory, which is the competing view that adaptive expectations theory is too simplistic. Rational expectations theory is the belief that people use all available information to predict the future, including future monetary and fiscal policies. Hands-on discretionary macroeconomic policies intended to stabilize the economy can therefore be negated when businesses and workers anticipate the effects of these policies on the economy. According to the rational expectations hypothesis, people do not simply think inflation will be about the same next year as last year. Although everyone's crystal ball is clouded, people are intelligent and informed on how the economy works. They not only consider past price changes, but also consider how changes in the federal deficit or money supply will affect inflation next year. Suppose businesses and workers predict that a surge in the money supply or a tax cut will raise the actual inflation rate to, say, 6 percent. They will immediately raise their expectations of the inflation rate to 6 percent even though the most recent rate of inflation was 3 percent. In short, rational expectationists believe that both nominal wages and prices are flexible.

Let's reconsider the case in which the government is trying to reduce the unemployment rate. Begin at point A in Exhibit 4 and suppose policymakers strive to reduce unemployment using new expansionary policies to stimulate demand. Under rational expectations theory, workers are not caught napping. Workers will not simply wait until the actual inflation rate exceeds the expected inflation rate at point B and then ask for a raise. Although they may lack formal training in forecasting, workers are quite sophisticated in understanding the macro economy. They watch news on television; check economic data on the Internet; and read *The Wall Street Journal, Time*, the local newspapers, and AFL-CIO publications for information on government policies and future changes in prices. When new information becomes available, workers revise their expectations.

Because workers wisely use all relevant information to predict future changes, they anticipate that the aggregate demand curve is going to shift rightward, causing a rise in the price level and a fall in real wages. They know that unless they get wage hikes to match the price increases, they will be losers. Consequently, workers rationally raise their nominal wage demands without a time lag so that no gap between the actual and expected rates of inflation occurs. In fact, many collective bargaining agreements contain escalator clauses, providing automatic nominal wage increases as the price level rises. Assuming that workers correctly anticipate the inflation rate, real wages remain unchanged because nominal wages and prices rise proportionately. This means the temporary increase in profits, real GDP, and employment does *not* happen as predicted by adaptive expectationists. In short, rational expectationists refute the short-run Phillips curves drawn in Exhibit 4. There would be, for example, no decrease in unemployment from 6 percent (point A) to 4 percent (point B). Instead, the only movement in the inflation rate is directly from 3 percent (point A) to 6 percent (point C). This means higher anticipated inflation is added without delay to current nominal wages and prices, which generates a vertical Phillips curve along such points as A, C, E, and G.

CONCLUSION: *According to rational expectations theory, expansionary monetary and fiscal policies used to reduce unemployment are not only useless, but also harmful because the only result is higher inflation.*

On the brighter side, rational expectations theory argues that a credible "stay the course" contractionary fiscal and monetary policy can quickly cool inflation without increasing unemployment. Suppose the economy is at the natural rate of unemployment and the Fed decreases the money supply to lower the rate of inflation. Workers analyze available information on the future impact of the Fed's action from AFL-CIO economists and other sources. They are convinced that policymakers are committed to decreasing aggregate demand until the price level recedes. Armed with this analysis, workers are not surprised, and they reduce their nominal wages as prices fall. In this case, there is no short-run Phillips curve. Contrary to adaptive expectations, inflation can be cured without recession because workers are not caught off guard.

Keynesians reject rational expectations theory because they argue that prices and wages are "sticky" downward (see Exhibit 4 of the chapter on aggregate demand and supply). On the other hand, the classical economists believed that the economy automatically adjusts after short-run delays to full employment in the long run. But in the rational expectations model, not so! There is no short run. Nevertheless, because the theory of rational expectations is similar to the self-correction model of the classical economists, rational expectationists are called *new classical economists*.

> **CONCLUSION:** *According to rational expectations theory, flexible wages and prices adjust immediately to negated predictable monetary and fiscal policy changes, so the economy's self-correction mechanism will restore the natural rate of unemployment. Therefore, discretionary policies should be abandoned, and fixed-rule, stable policies to achieve constant money supply growth and a balanced federal budget are therefore the best way to lower the inflation rate.*

✓ CHECKPOINT

Does Rational Expectations Theory Work in the Classroom?

An economics professor is considering improving class attendance and preparation by giving pop quizzes. Two approaches are being considered: If rational expectations theory operates in the classroom, should the professor (1) give pop quizzes on days when homework is due or (2) keep the pop quizzes a secret and give them randomly?

17-4 Applying the AD-AS Model to the Great Expectations Debate

The distinction between adaptive expectations and rational expectations can be analyzed using the aggregate demand-aggregate supply model presented in Exhibit 6. Assume the economy is currently in equilibrium at point E_1, with a full-employment output of $6 trillion. Now suppose the Fed pursues an expansionary monetary policy designed to create jobs and further reduce unemployment. Hence, the aggregate demand curve shifts rightward from AD_1 to AD_2 along the short-run aggregate supply curve $SRAS_1$. Based on adaptive expectations theory, a monetarist urges the Fed to leave the economy alone. The monetarist's prediction is that the economy will move from equilibrium at E_1 to E_2, causing real GDP to rise from the potential GDP of $6 trillion to the GDP of $6.5 trillion. Recall from Exhibit 9 of the chapter on business cycles and unemployment that this condition in the

| EXHIBIT 6 | Adaptive Expectations versus Rational Expectations |

Suppose policymakers use expansionary policies to increase the aggregate demand curve from AD_1 to AD_2. Adaptive expectations theory argues that labor adjusts nominal wages sluggishly. As a result, the path of the economy is E_1 to E_2 to E_3 with a temporary increase in real GDP to $6.5 trillion and lower unemployment at point E_2. The theory of rational expectations is the competing view that the expansionary policy used to increase the aggregate demand curve from AD_1 to AD_2 is anticipated. Workers anticipate that the price level (CPI) will rise to 110, so they increase their nominal wages without a period of adjustment. As a result, the aggregate supply curve shifts from $SRAS_1$ to $SRAS_2$, causing the economy to move directly from equilibrium point E_1 to point E_3. The result of Keynesian expansionary policies under both theories is that inflation becomes worse and there is no effect on real GDP or employment.

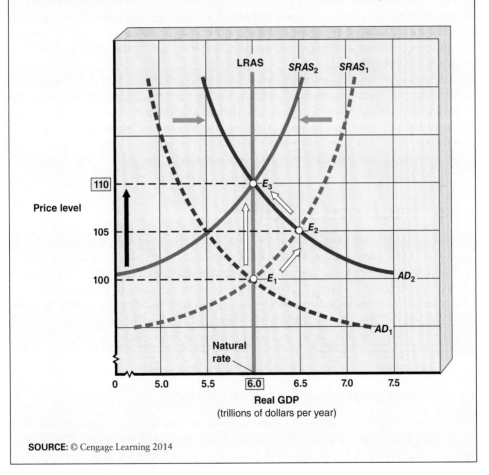

SOURCE: © Cengage Learning 2014

economy is a positive GDP gap of $0.5 trillion. In addition, the price level (CPI) increases from 100 to 105. Eventually, at equilibrium E_2, with unemployment below the natural rate, workers are no longer "caught off guard" and demand higher nominal wages to offset the rise in prices. As a result, production costs rise, causing the short-run aggregate supply curve to shift leftward from $SRAS_1$ to $SRAS_2$; therefore, a new equilibrium is established at E_3. This response drives up the unemployment rate to the natural rate as real output returns to the initial level of $6 trillion. However, Fed activism has not had a neutral effect on the price level because it has risen from the initial level of 100 to 110. The monetarist's prediction is therefore higher inflation and no impact on employment and real GDP in the long run.

A rational expectationist sees events differently. Most people are not "fooled." They are able to rationally predict the consequences of expansionary monetary policies. People anticipate that the economy will move from point E_1 to point E_3, the price level will rise from 100 to 110, and real GDP will not change. Consequently, businesses and workers do not stumble around in the dark, unable to see what the actual inflation rate is going to be. They know, or *anticipate*, that the inflation rate is going to rise 10 percent, and they react immediately by raising prices and wages 10 percent. Because prices and wages increase quickly and pro-portionately, rational expectations theory predicts a direct path of change in the economy's equilibrium from E_1 to E_3. Stated differently, if firms and workers for-mulate expectations rationally, any impact of stimulative monetary policy is nulli-fied. Under rational expectations theory, only *unanticipated* or *surprise* policies can influence output and employment. But monetary and fiscal policies based on surprises are not practical.

If workers foresee inflation and prevent erosion of their real wages by demanding and receiving nominal wage raises in advance, aggregate supply is the vertical curve, LRAS. When real wages remain unchanged, there is no incentive for businesses to alter production as prices rise. If rational expectations theory is correct, the economy does not enjoy the short-lived pleasure of lower unemploy-ment at point E_2, as predicted by adaptive expectations theory.

17-5 Incomes Policy

Suppose we accept the power of unions and businesses to raise wages and prices as inevitable. Let's also assume Milton Friedman is correct that discretionary mone-tary and fiscal policies are useless or counterproductive. Then what approach is left to fight inflation? There is another way, used in the past, which is a collection of regulatory policies called incomes policies. Incomes policies are federal govern-ment policies designed to affect the real incomes of workers by controlling nominal wages and prices. Such policies include presidential jawboning, wage-price guide-lines, and wage-price controls.

17-5a PRESIDENTIAL JAWBONING

The mildest form of incomes policies is jawboning. Jawboning is oratory intended to pressure unions and businesses to reduce wage and price increases. The govern-ment attempts to prevent or roll back wage and price hikes by appealing to labor and business leaders. The most spectacular success with this technique occurred in 1962. President John F. Kennedy called major U.S. steel manufacturers and con-vinced them to rescind their price increases. But President Kennedy jawboned with a club in hand. He threatened to sell government stockpiles of steel at lower prices.

Incomes policies
Federal government policies designed to affect the real incomes of workers by controlling nominal wages and prices. Such policies include presidential jawboning, wage-price guidelines, and wage-price controls.

Jawboning
Oratory intended to pressure unions and businesses to reduce wage and price increases.

The president also informed the firms that those failing to cooperate would lose government contracts to firms that would lower prices. President Lyndon Johnson followed Kennedy's example and jawboned even more. Then there was the "Blow the Whistle" program under President Richard Nixon. An official agency was established to monitor unwarranted price increases and publicly announce violators of the national interest.

Most economists argue that firms raise prices when changes in demand or cost make it profitable to do so. Jawboning may do a little good for a while, but over time, it is a blunt weapon against inflation.

17-5b WAGE AND PRICE GUIDELINES

A more formal policy to cool down the inflation rate is to establish wage and price guidelines. Wage and price guidelines are voluntary standards set by the government for "permissible" wage and price increases. The Truman and Eisenhower administrations made unsystematic attempts to discourage business and labor from raising prices and wages. But the first systematic wage and price guideline program was initiated during the Kennedy administration, and this approach was also used during the Johnson and Carter administrations. For example, the Carter administration asked labor unions to limit their wage increases to 7 percent. Violators were identified in hopes that adverse publicity would force the unions to comply. Without any enforcement mechanism, the dominant view among economists is that guidelines accomplish little against self-interest.

Wage and price guidelines

Voluntary standards set by the government for "permissible" wage and price increases.

17-5c WAGE AND PRICE CONTROLS

When guidelines have the force of law, the economy moves to a mandatory system of wage and price controls. Wage and price controls are legal restrictions on wage and price increases. Violations can result in fines and imprisonment. Once people believe wages and prices are under control by law, the good news is that they expect lower prices. The bad news is that controls are government interference with market supply and demand.

As discussed in Chapter 4, a ceiling price established below the equilibrium price will cause shortages in markets (see Exhibit 5 in Chapter 4). This usually means rationing of such scarce items as gasoline. When price is not allowed to serve as the rationing device, consumers must incur higher opportunity costs by waiting in long lines for gasoline. This happened in 1979, when the government imposed a price ceiling on gasoline. Another rationing device is government ration coupons that give the right to buy a good. Ration coupons were used for many goods during World War II. Shortages also lead to *black markets*, which are illegal markets for goods at unregulated prices. To enforce the system requires a government bureaucracy at taxpayers' expense.

Long lines for products, ration coupons, and black markets are not popular. This explains why wage and price controls appear primarily during war and rarely in peacetime. The United States has imposed wage and price controls during World War II; the Korean War and the Nixon administration hoped to combat high inflationary expectations built up during the Vietnam War. The inflation rate from 1969 to 1971 averaged 5.2 percent, an alarming rate in those days. The plan was to control inflation and then fight unemployment, which averaged 4.8 percent over the

Wage and price controls

Legal restrictions on wage and price increases. Violations can result in fines and imprisonment.

same period. The first phase of the attack was a 90-day freeze on wages and prices in August 1971. A 15-member Pay Board and a 7-member Price Commission administered the controls. For three months, businesses could not raise prices, wages were frozen, and landlords could not charge higher rents. The intent was to give inflationary expectations a shock treatment. Then the freeze lifted, and wage and price controls were established to limit increases between 1971 and 1974. The bottom line is that in 1971, the inflation rate was 4.4 percent. In 1973, the inflation rate climbed to 6.2 percent. When the experiment with controls ended in 1974, the inflation rate rose to 11 percent. During the same period, the unemployment rate remained between 5 and 6 percent. Obviously, controls did not slay the inflation dragon, although some economists have argued that controls made the dragon less fierce.

In 1968, the Council of Economic Advisors eloquently stated the opinion of most economists on wage and price controls:

> While such controls may be necessary under conditions of an all-out war, it would be folly to consider them as a solution to inflationary pressures that accompany high employment under any other circumstance. ... Although such controls may be unfortunately popular when they are in effect, the appeal quickly disappears once people live under them.[3]

The majority view is that controls destroy the efficient allocation of resources provided by the price system and intrude on economic freedom. Defenders of controls believe this is a small price to pay.

✓ CHECKPOINT

Can Wage and Price Controls Cure Stagflation?

Suppose war in the Persian Gulf destroys much of the world's oil reserves. As a result, the U.S. economy is experiencing a bout of stagflation. You are a member of Congress, and a bill is introduced to fight the problems of high inflation and high unemployment by imposing wage and price controls. Using the AD-AS model, will you vote in favor of controls to cure stagflation by freezing the price level? [Hint: Look at Exhibit 5 of Chapter 4 and Exhibit 12(a) in the chapter on aggregate demand and supply.]

17-6 How Different Macroeconomic Theories Attack Inflation

If incomes policies do not cure an overheated economy during peacetime, policymakers must decide which macroeconomic school "hat" to wear. Exhibit 7 gives a brief description of how four basic macroeconomic models deal with inflation. Recall the monetarist view presented in the previous chapter and supply-side economics explained in the chapter on fiscal policy.

---

[3]*Annual Report of the Council of Economic Advisors* (Washington, D.C.: Government Printing Office, 1968), p. 119.

EXHIBIT 7	How Different Macroeconomic Models Cure Inflation

School of thought
Monetarism

Milton Friedman

Inflation prescription
Monetarists see the cause of inflation as "too much money chasing too few goods," based on the quantity of money theory (MV = PQ). To cure inflation, they would cut the money supply and force the Fed to stick to a fixed money supply growth rate. In the short run, the unemployment rate will rise, but in the long run, it self-corrects to the natural rate.

School of thought
Keynesianism

John Maynard Keynes

Inflation prescription
Keynesians believe in using contractionary fiscal and monetary policies to cool an over-heated economy. To decrease aggregate demand, they advocate that the government use tax hikes and/or spending cuts. The Fed should reduce the money supply and cause the rate of interest to rise. The opportunity cost of reducing inflation is greater unemployment. Keynesians also believe that incomes policies are effective.

School of thought
Supply-side economics

Arthur Laffer

Inflation prescription
Supply-siders view the cause of inflation as "not enough goods." Their approach is to increase aggregate supply through cuts in marginal tax rates, government regulations, and import bar-riers. The effect provides incentives to work, invest, and expand production capacity. Thus, both the inflation rate and the unemployment rate fall.

School of thought
New classical school

Robert Lucas

Inflation prescription
The theory of rational expectations asserts that the public must be convinced that policymakers will stick to restrictive and persistent fiscal and monetary policies. If policymakers have credibility, the inflation rate will be anticipated and will quickly fall without a rise in unemployment.

Source: © Cengage Learning 2014

Ford's Whip Inflation Now (WIN) Button

Applicable Concept: incomes policies

The most interesting historical artifact of the fight against inflation is gathering dust in the White House attic. In October 1974, President Gerald Ford proposed the "WIN" button to a joint session of Congress. The idea was that Americans would wear their "Whip Inflation Now" buttons, and this would break the wage-price spiral. The WIN button represented an appeal to patriotism that would discourage businesses and labor from raising prices and wages.

The logical question is, What circumstances drove the president of the United States to use a button against inflation? We will begin the story in 1971, when the Nixon administration approved wage and price controls to cool inflationary expectations. Beginning in 1972, bad crops caused food prices to soar, and the OPEC oil embargo boosted the price of crude oil. These supply shocks boosted the inflation rate from 3.2 percent in 1972 to 6.2 percent in 1973. Clearly, the wage and price control program was falling apart before controls ended in 1974.

Following the demand-management prescription against inflation, the Fed raised the discount rate in late 1973. Federal Reserve Chair Arthur Burns stated that the Fed must follow a contractionary monetary policy for years to come. Despite the Fed's restrictive policy, the inflation rate rose to an annual rate of about 14 percent in early 1974. By late 1974, the unemployment rate had risen to 6 percent, but policymakers remained committed to anti-inflation policies. The Fed raised the discount rate again in the fall of 1974, and President Ford called an economic summit meeting. The outcome of the summit was a resolve to stick to the battle plan and beat inflation before turning to the worsening unemployment problem. Aiming for public support, President Ford unveiled the WIN button, accompanied by a tax surcharge and federal spending ceiling proposals. While the fight against inflation preoccupied policymakers, the unemployment rate rose from 5.6 percent in 1974 to 8.5 percent in 1975. The percentage change in real GDP between 1974 and 1975 was –0.6 percent, and recession suddenly replaced inflation as the number one enemy. In response, Congress approved a $22.8 billion tax cut bill in 1975, and the Fed increased the money supply. In 1974, the inflation rate was 11.0 percent, and in 1975, the inflation rate was still at the high rate of 9.1 percent.

What caused this puzzling twist in stabilization policy to deal with stagflation? Many economists

© Bettmann/CORBIS

explain this turn of events by the absence of a conceptual framework to understand the effects of supply shocks on the aggregate supply curve. Instead, policymakers tried to shift the aggregate demand curve back and forth while asking people to wear a WIN button.

Analyze the Issue

Assume the economy is in equilibrium at full employment and the public anticipates restrictive monetary and fiscal policies, including WIN buttons, which decrease aggregate demand in order to combat inflation. Use the AD-AS model depicted in Exhibit 6 to explain the new classical predictions of the impact on the price level, real GDP, and the unemployment rate.

Key Concepts

Phillips curve	Political business cycle	Jawboning
Natural rate hypothesis	Rational expectations theory	Wage and price guidelines
Adaptive expectations theory	Incomes policies	Wage and price controls

Summary

- The **Phillips curve** shows a stable inverse relationship between the inflation rate and the unemployment rate. If policymakers reduce inflation, unemployment increases, and vice versa. During the 1960s, the curve closely fit the inflation and unemployment rates in the United States. Since 1970, the Phillips curve has not conformed to the stable inflation-unemployment trade-off pattern of the 1960s.

The Phillips Curve for the United States in the 1960s

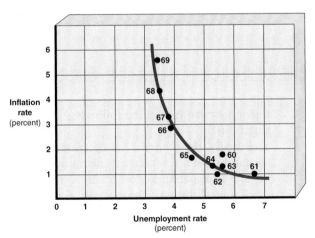

SOURCE: *Economic Report of the President 2012*, http://www.gpoaccess .gov/eop/, Tables B-15 and B-64.

- The **natural rate hypothesis** argues that the economy self-corrects to the natural rate of unemployment. Over time, changes in the rate of inflation are fully anticipated, and prices and wages rise or fall proportionately. As a result, the long-run Phillips curve is a vertical line at the natural rate of unemployment. Thus, Keynesian demand-management policies ultimately cause only higher or lower inflation, and the natural rate of unemployment remains unchanged.

- **Adaptive expectations theory** is the proposition that people base their economic forecasts on recent past information, rather than future information. Once the government causes the inflation rate to rise or fall, people adapt their inflationary expectations to the current inflation rate. The result is a short-run Phillips curve that intersects the vertical long-run Phillips curve. Over time, the economy self-corrects to the natural rate of unemployment.

- The **political business cycle** is created by the incentive for politicians to manipulate the economy to get reelected. Using expansionary policies, officeholders can stimulate the economy before an election. Unemployment falls, and the price level rises. After the election, the strategy is to contract the economy to fight inflation and unemployment rises.

- **Rational expectations theory** argues that it is naive to believe that people change their inflationary expectations based only on the current inflation rate. Rational expectationists belong to the new classical school. Assuming the impact of government policy is predictable, people immediately anticipate higher or lower inflation. Workers quickly change their nominal wages as businesses change prices. Consequently, inflation worsens or improves, and unemployment remains unchanged at the natural rate. Thus, there is no short-run Phillips curve, and the vertical long-run Phillips curve is identical to adaptive expectations theory.

- **Incomes policies** are a variety of federal government programs aimed at directly controlling wages and prices. Incomes policies include jawboning, wage-price guidelines, and wage-price controls. Over time, incomes policies tend to be ineffective.

- **Wage and price controls** are legal restrictions on wages and prices. Most economists do not favor wage and price controls in peacetime.

Such controls are expensive to administer, destroy efficiency, and intrude on economic freedom.

Summary of Conclusion Statements

- Changes in aggregate demand cause a movement along a stationary Phillips curve.
- According to adaptive expectations theory, expansionary monetary and fiscal policies to reduce the unemployment rate are useless in the long run. After a short-run reduction in unemployment, the economy will self-correct to the natural rate of unemployment, but at a higher inflation rate. Thus, there is no long-run trade-off between inflation and unemployment.
- According to rational expectations theory, expansionary monetary and fiscal policies used to reduce unemployment are not only useless, but also harmful because the only result is higher inflation.
- According to rational expectations theory, flexible wages and prices adjust immediately to negate predictable monetary and fiscal policy changes, so the economy's self-correction mechanism will restore the natural rate of unemployment. Therefore, discretionary policies should be abandoned, and fixed-rule, stable policies to achieve constant money supply growth and a balanced federal budget are the best way to lower the inflation rate.

Study Questions and Problems

1. What is a Phillips curve? Assuming the economy's aggregate supply curve is stable, how would an increase in aggregate demand affect the unemployment rate and the inflation rate?

2. What were the inflation rate and the unemployment rate last year? Do these rates lie on a Phillips curve?

3. What happened in the 1970s and early 1980s to cast doubt on the Phillips curve?

4. Suppose you flipped an honest coin ten times and heads came up eight times. You are about to toss the coin another ten times. Using adaptive expectations, how many heads do you expect? Based on rational expectations, how many heads do you expect?

5. According to adaptive expectations, what happens to the inflation rate and the unemployment rate in the following situations?
   a. Initially, the economy is operating at the natural rate of 6 percent unemployment. The anticipated rate of inflation is 6 percent, and the actual rate is also 6 percent.
   b. In the next period, there is an unexpected rise in the inflation rate to 10 percent.
   c. In the next period, there is an unexpected rise in the inflation rate to 12 percent.

6. Explain what happens under adaptive expectations theory when monetary and fiscal policymakers use expansionary policy to achieve an unemployment rate below the natural rate.

7. Keynesians believe monetary and fiscal policymakers should stabilize the business cycle. Compare the political business cycle to Keynesian policy objectives.

8. Use Exhibit 8 to answer the questions that follow.
   a. Which points represent the natural unemployment rate?
   b. Which points represent an unemployment rate below the natural unemployment rate?
   c. Which points represent an unemployment rate above the natural unemployment rate?
   d. Explain points A and D on the graph.
   e. Explain points B and C on the graph.
   f. Explain points E and F on the graph.
   g. Why is curve PC_2 to the right of curve PC_1?

9. Based on rational expectations theory, what happens to the inflation rate and the unemployment rate in the following situations?
   a. Initially, the economy is operating at the natural unemployment rate of 4 percent, and the inflation rate is also 4 percent. People correctly anticipate that an increase in the money supply will increase the inflation rate to 6 percent next year.
   b. In the next period, people correctly forecast that a tax cut will cause the inflation rate to rise to 8 percent.
   c. In the next period, they anticipate that the Fed's hike in the discount rate will cause the inflation rate to fall to 4 percent.

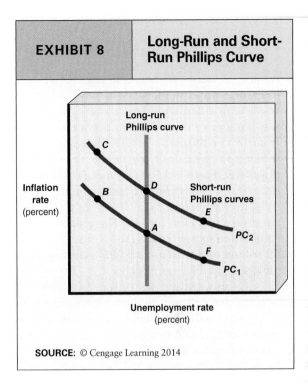

EXHIBIT 8 · **Long-Run and Short-Run Phillips Curve**

SOURCE: © Cengage Learning 2014

For Online Exercises, go to the Tucker Web site at www.cengage.com/economics/tucker.

Can Wage and Price Controls Cure Stagflation?

Assume the economy begins in equilibrium at E_1 in Exhibit 9 and an oil shock causes the economy to move to a new equilibrium at E_2. Without wage and price controls, the price level increases from 150 to 200, and real GDP decreases from $4 trillion to $3 trillion. Now assume laws keep the price level frozen at 150. This means firms cannot raise prices to meet higher costs, so under controls, they are forced to lay off more workers and cut production even further. The economy's equilibrium moves from E_2 to E_3, and real GDP is $2 trillion, rather than $3 trillion, causing unemployment to climb even higher.

Using wage and price controls to fight inflation would cause an even more severe decrease in real GDP; therefore, unemployment is greater than would otherwise be the case. If you voted *no* on the wage and price controls bill because it causes greater shortages and a deeper recession, **YOU ARE CORRECT.**

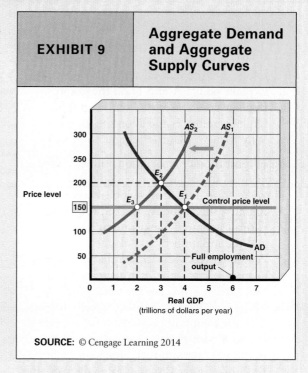

| EXHIBIT 9 | Aggregate Demand and Aggregate Supply Curves |

SOURCE: © Cengage Learning 2014

Sample Quiz

For an explanation of the correct answers, visit the Tucker Web site at www.cengage.com/economics/tucker.

1. The Phillips curve relates the inflation rate to
   a. the unemployment rate.
   b. GDP.
   c. disposable personal income.
   d. the interest rate.

2. On a Phillips curve diagram, an increase in the rate of inflation, other things being equal, is represented by a(an)
   a. upward movement along the Phillips curve.
   b. downward movement along the Phillips curve.
   c. upward shift of the Phillips curve.
   d. downward shift of the Phillips curve.

3. Economists began to lose confidence in the Phillips curve during the
   a. 1930s.
   b. 1960s.
   c. 1970s.
   d. 1980s.

4. The Phillips curve
   a. was relatively well-defined during the 1960s.
   b. demonstrates how to achieve stable economic growth.
   c. shows the trade-off between deficits and inflation.
   d. helps to stimulate entrepreneurial profits.

Sample Quiz *continued*

5. If the long-run Phillips curve is vertical, then any government policy designed to lower
   a. unemployment will not change the unemployment rate and only increase the inflation rate.
   b. unemployment will work, leaving the inflation rate unchanged.
   c. inflation will cause employment to rise.
   d. unemployment will work, causing the inflation rate to fall.

6. The natural rate hypothesis argues that the economy will
   a. self-correct to the natural rate of inflation.
   b. require expansionary fiscal policy to reach the natural rate of unemployment.
   c. self-correct to the natural rate of unemployment.
   d. require expansionary monetary policy to reach the natural rate of unemployment.

7. The long-run Phillips curve is a(an) _____ line at the natural rate of unemployment.
   a. horizontal
   b. vertical
   c. upward-sloping
   d. downward-sloping

8. Under the natural rate hypothesis, expansionary monetary and fiscal policies can at *best* produce a
   a. permanent change in the long-run Phillips curve.
   b. short-run change in the unemployment rate.
   c. long-run change in the unemployment rate.
   d. permanent change in the unemployment rate.

9. The hypothesis that people believe that the *best* indicator of the future is the recent past is
   a. rational expectations.
   b. adaptive expectations.
   c. lagged expectations.
   d. trend expectations.

10. Under adaptive expectations theory, people expect the rate of inflation this year to be
    a. zero, regardless of the rate last year.
    b. the same as last year.

c. the rate based on predictable fiscal policies.
d. All of the answers are correct.

11. According to adaptive expectations theory, expansionary monetary and fiscal policies to reduce the unemployment rate are
    a. useless in the long run.
    b. useless in the short run.
    c. ineffective on the price level.
    d. None of the answers are correct.

12. "Preannounced, stable policies to achieve a low and constant money supply growth and a balanced federal budget are therefore the *best* way to lower the inflation rate." This statement best illustrates
    a. Keynesian theory.
    b. rational expectations theory.
    c. incomes policy.
    d. supply-side theory.

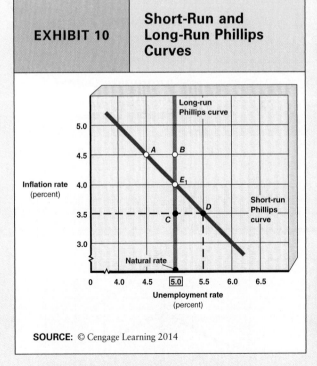

EXHIBIT 10	Short-Run and Long-Run Phillips Curves

SOURCE: © Cengage Learning 2014

13. Suppose the economy in Exhibit 10 is at point E_1, and the Fed increases the money supply. If people have adaptive expectations, then the economy will move

---

a. to point A in the short run and point B in the long run.

Sample Quiz *continued*

c. from 100 to 105 initially and then eventually back to 100.

d. from 100 to 105 initially and then eventually to 110.

20. As shown in Exhibit 11, if people behave according to rational expectations theory, an increase in the aggregate demand curve from AD_1 to AD_2 will cause the economy to move

a. directly from E_1 to E_3 and then remain at E_3.

b. directly from E_1 to E_2 and then remain at E_2.

c. from E_1 to E_2 initially and then eventually back to E_1.

d. from E_1 to E_2 initially and then eventually to E_3.

Road Map
Money, Banking, and Monetary Policy

This road map feature helps you tie together material in the part as you travel the Economic Way of Thinking highway. The following are review questions listed by chapter from the previous part. The key concept in each question is given for emphasis, and each question or set of questions concludes with an interactive game to reinforce the concepts. Go to the Tucker Web site at www.cengage.com/economics/tucker, select the chapter, and play the visual causation chain game designed to make learning fun. Enjoy the cheers when you are correct and suffer the jeers if you miss. For an explanation of the correct answers, please visit the tutorial at academic.cengage.com/economics/tucker.

CHAPTER 14. MONEY AND THE FEDERAL RESERVE SYSTEM

1. **Key Concept: Money supply definitions**
   Suppose you transfer $1,000 from your checking account to your savings account. How does this action affect the M1 and M2 money supplies?
   a. M1 and M2 are both unchanged.
   b. M1 falls by $1,000, and M2 rises by $1,000.
   c. M1 is unchanged, and M2 rises by $1,000.
   d. M1 falls by $1,000, and M2 is unchanged.

2. **Key Concept: Federal Reserve System**
   Which of the following groups oversees and administers the Federal Reserve System?
   a. House of Representatives
   b. President's Council of Economic Advisors
   c. U.S. Treasury Department
   d. None of the above because the Fed is an independent agency

3. **Key Concept: Monetary Control Act**
   The Monetary Control Act of 1980
   a. allowed savings and loan associations to offer checking accounts.
   b. allowed more institutions to offer checking account services.
   c. created greater competition among various financial institutions.
   d. did all of the above.
   e. did none of the above.

CHAPTER 15. MONEY CREATION

4. Key Concept: Open market operations
When the Fed sells government securities, it
a. lowers the cost of borrowing from the Fed, encouraging banks to make loans to the general public.
b. raises the cost of borrowing from the Fed, discouraging banks from making loans to the general public.
c. increases the amount of excess reserves that banks hold, encouraging them to make loans to the general public.
d. increases the amount of excess reserves that banks hold, discouraging them from making loans to the general public.
e. decreases the amount of excess reserves that banks hold, discouraging them from making loans to the general public.

5. Key Concept: Open market operations
When the Fed buys government securities, it
a. lowers the cost of borrowing from the Fed, encouraging banks to make loans to the general public.
b. raises the cost of borrowing from the Fed, discouraging banks from making loans to the general public.
c. increases the amount of excess reserves that banks hold, encouraging them to make loans to the general public.
d. increases the amount of excess reserves that banks hold, discouraging them from making loans to the general public.
e. decreases the amount of excess reserves that banks hold, discouraging them from making loans to the general public.

CHAPTER 16. MONETARY POLICY

6. Key Concept: Money demand curve
In a two-asset economy with money and T-bills, the quantity of money that people will want to hold, other things being equal, can be expected to
a. decrease as real GDP increases.
b. increase as the interest rate decreases.
c. increase as the interest rate increases.
d. do all of the above.

Causation Chain Game
The Demand for Money Curve—Exhibit 1

7. Key Concept: Equilibrium interest rate
Assume the Fed decreases the money supply and the demand for money curve is fixed. In response, people will
a. sell bonds, thus driving up the interest rate.
b. buy bonds, thus driving down the interest rate.
c. buy bonds, thus driving up the interest rate.
d. sell bonds, thus driving down the interest rate.

8. **Key Concept: Equilibrium interest rate**

Assume a fixed demand for money curve and the Fed increases the money supply. In response, people will
a. sell bonds, thus driving up the interest rate.
b. sell bonds, thus driving down the interest rate.
c. buy bonds, thus driving up the interest rate.
d. buy bonds, thus driving down the interest rate.

Causation Chain Game
The Equilibrium Interest Rate—Exhibit 2

9. **Key Concept: Change in money supply**

Assume the demand for money curve is stationary and the Fed increases the money supply. The result is that people
a. increase the supply of bonds, thus driving up the interest rate.
b. increase the supply of bonds, thus driving down the interest rate.
c. increase the demand for bonds, thus driving up the interest rate.
d. increase the demand for bonds, thus driving down the interest rate.

10. **Key Concept: Change in money supply**

Assume a fixed demand for money curve and the Fed decreases the money supply. In response, people will
a. sell bonds, thus driving up the interest rate.
b. sell bonds, thus driving down the interest rate.
c. buy bonds, thus driving up the interest rate.
d. buy bonds, thus driving down the interest rate.

Causation Chain Game
The Effect of Changes in the Money Supply—Exhibit 3

11. **Key Concept: Keynesian transmission mechanism**

The Keynesian cause-and-effect sequence predicts that a decrease in the money supply will cause interest rates to
a. fall, boosting investment and shifting the AD curve rightward, leading to an increase in real GDP.
b. fall, boosting investment and shifting the AD curve rightward, leading to a decrease in real GDP.
c. rise, cutting investment and shifting the AD curve rightward, leading to an increase in real GDP.
d. rise, boosting investment and shifting the AD curve rightward, leading to an increase in real GDP.
e. rise, cutting investment and shifting the AD curve leftward, leading to a decrease in real GDP.

Causation Chain Game
The Keynesian Monetary Policy Transmission Mechanism—Exhibit 4

12. **Key Concept: Monetarists transmission mechanism**

Most monetarists favor
a. frequent changes in the growth rate of the money supply to avoid inflation.

b. placing the Federal Reserve under the Treasury.

c. a steady, gradual shrinkage of the money supply.

d. a constant increase in the money supply year after year equal to the potential annual growth rate in real GDP.

Causation Chain Game
The Monetarist Policy Transmission Mechanism—Exhibit 6

CHAPTER 17. THE PHILLIPS CURVE AND EXPECTATIONS THEORY

13. **Key Concept: Adaptive expectations**
According to adaptive expectations theory, expansionary monetary and fiscal policies to reduce the unemployment rate are

a. useless in the long run.

b. useless in the short run.

c. ineffective on the price level.

d. none of the above.

14. **Key Concept: Rational expectations**
The belief that the government can do absolutely nothing in either the short run or the long run to reduce the unemployment rate, because people will anticipate the government's actions, is held by the

a. rational expectations school.

b. neo-Keynesian school.

c. classical school.

d. supply-side school.

e. Keynesian school.

Causation Chain Game
The Short-Run and Long-Run Phillips Curve—Exhibit 4

The International Economy

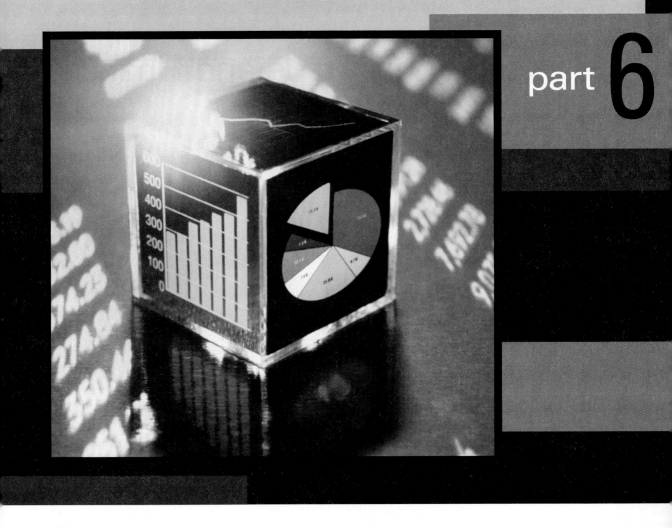

T he final part of this text is devoted to global topics. The first chapter explains the importance of free trade and the mechanics of trade bookkeeping and exchange rates. Here you will find a feature on the birth of the euro. The second chapter takes a historical look at the theoretical debate over capitalism and the transition of Cuba, Russia, and China toward this system. The final chapter provides comparisons of advanced and developing countries. The chapter concludes with the fascinating economic success story of Hong Kong.

chapter 18

International Trade and Finance

Just imagine your life without world trade. For openers, you could not eat bananas from Honduras or chocolate from Nigerian cocoa beans. Nor could you sip French wine, Colombian coffee, or Indian tea. Also forget about driving a Japanese motorcycle or automobile. In addition, you could not buy Italian shoes and most DVDs, televisions, fax machines, and personal computers because they are foreign-made. Taking your vacation in London would also be ruled out if there were no world trade. And the list goes on and on, so the point is clear. World trade is important because it gives consumers more power by expanding their choices. Today, the speed of transportation and communication means producers must compete on a global basis for the favor of consumers.

Trade is often highly controversial. Regardless of whether it is a World Trade Organization (WTO) meeting or a G8 summit meeting, trade talks face protesters in the streets complaining that globalization has triggered a crisis in the world, such as global warming, poverty, soaring oil prices, or food shortages. And in the United States, outsourcing jobs to lower-paid workers overseas continues to be a hotly debated issue.

The first part of this chapter explains the theoretical reason why countries should specialize in producing certain goods and then trade them for imports. Also, you will study arguments for and against the United States protecting itself from "unfair" trade practices by other countries. In the second part of the chapter, you will learn how nations pay each other for world trade. Here you will explore international bookkeeping and discover how supply and demand forces determine that, for example, 1 dollar is worth 100 yen.

In this chapter, you will learn to solve these economics puzzles:

- How does Babe Ruth's decision not to remain a pitcher illustrate an important principle in global trade?

- Is there a valid argument for trade protectionism?

- Should the United States return to the gold standard?

18-1 Why Nations Need Trade

The United States leads the world in imports while also being one of the top exporters in the world. Exhibit 1 reveals which regions are our major trading partners (exports plus imports). Leading the list of nations is Canada, our largest trading partner, followed by China, Mexico, and Japan. Leading U.S. exports are chemicals, machinery, agricultural products, computers, automobiles, and airplanes. Major imports include petroleum, cars, trucks, clothing, and electronics. Why does a nation even bother to trade with the rest of the world? Does it seem strange for the United States to import goods it could produce for itself? Indeed, why doesn't the United States become self-sufficient by growing all its own food, including bananas, sugar, and coffee, making all its own cars, and prohibiting sales of all foreign goods? This section explains why specialization and trade are a nation's keys to a higher standard of living.

18-1a The Production Possibilities Curve Revisited

Consider a world with only two countries—the United States and Japan. To keep the illustration simple, also assume *both* countries produce only two goods—grain and steel. Accordingly, we can construct in Exhibit 2 a *production possibilities*

EXHIBIT 1	U.S. Trading Partners, 2011

In 2011, Canada, China, Mexico, and Japan accounted for over 40 percent of U.S. trade (exports plus imports).

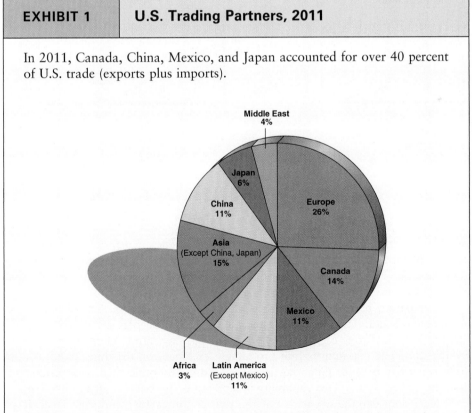

SOURCE: Bureau of Economic Analysis, *U.S. International Transactions by Area,* http://www.bea.gov/international/index.htm, Table 12.

EXHIBIT 2	The Benefits of Specialization and Trade

As shown in part (a), assume the United States chooses point *B* on its production possibilities curve, *PPC*U.S.. Without trade, the United States produces and consumes 60 tons of grain and 20 tons of steel. In part (b), assume Japan also operates along its production possibilities curve, *PPC*Japan, at point *E*. Without trade, Japan produces and consumes 30 tons of grain and 10 tons of steel.

Now assume the United States specializes in producing grain at point *A* and imports 20 tons of Japanese steel in exchange for 30 tons of grain. Through specialization and trade, the United States moves to consumption possibility point *B′*, outside its production possibilities curve. Japan also moves to a higher standard of living at consumption possibility point *E′*, outside its production possibilities curve.

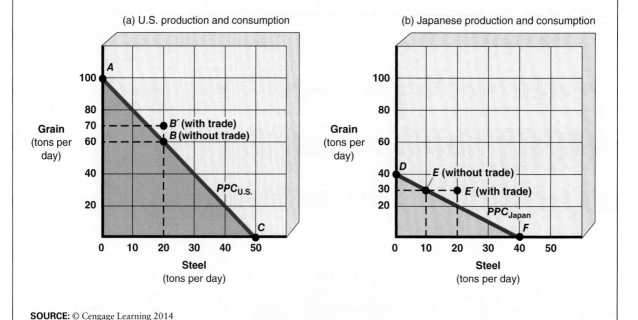

SOURCE: © Cengage Learning 2014

curve for each country. We will also set aside the *law of increasing opportunity costs*, explained in Chapter 2, and assume workers are equally suited to producing grain or steel. This assumption transforms the bowed-out shape of the production possibilities curve into a straight line.

Comparing parts (a) and (b) of Exhibit 2 shows that the United States can produce more grain than Japan. If the United States devotes all its resources to this purpose, 100 tons of grain are produced per day, represented by point *A* in Exhibit 2(a). The maximum grain production of Japan, on the other hand, is only 40 tons per day because Japan has less labor, land, and other factors of production than the United States. This capability is represented by point *D* in Exhibit 2(b).

Now consider the capacities of the two countries for producing steel. If all their respective resources are devoted to this output, the United States produces 50 tons per day (point *C*), and Japan produces only 40 tons per day (point *F*). Again, the greater potential maximum steel output of the United States reflects its greater resources. Both countries are also capable of producing other combinations of grain and steel along their respective production possibilities curves, such as point *B* for the United States and point *E* for Japan.

18-1b SPECIALIZATION WITHOUT TRADE

Assuming no world trade, the production possibilities curve for each country also defines its *consumption possibilities*. Stated another way, we assume that both countries are *self-sufficient* because without imports, they must consume only the combination chosen along their production possibilities curve. Under the assumption of self-sufficiency, suppose the United States prefers to produce and consume 60 tons of grain and 20 tons of steel per day (point *B*). Also assume Japan chooses to produce and consume 30 tons of grain and 10 tons of steel (point *E*). Exhibit 3 lists data corresponding to points *B* and *E* and shows that the total world output is 90 tons of grain and 30 tons of steel.

Now suppose the United States specializes by producing and consuming at point *A*, rather than point *B*. Suppose also that Japan specializes by producing and consuming at point *F*, rather than point *E*. As shown in Exhibit 3, specialization in each country increases total world output per day by 10 tons of grain and 10 tons of steel. Because this extra world output has the potential for making both countries better off, why wouldn't the United States and Japan specialize and produce at points *A* and *F*, respectively? The reason is that although production at these points is clearly possible, neither country wants to consume these combinations of output. The United States prefers to consume less grain and more steel at point *B* compared to point *A*. Japan, on the other hand, prefers to consume more grain and less steel at point *E*, rather than point *F*.

EXHIBIT 3	Effect of Specialization without Trade on World Output	
	Grain production (tons per day)	**Steel production (tons per day)**
Before specialization		
United States (at point *B*)	60	20
Japan (at point *E*)	30	10
Total world output	90	30
After specialization		
United States (at point *A*)	100	0
Japan (at point *F*)	0	40
Total world output	100	40

SOURCE: © Cengage Learning 2014

> **CONCLUSION:** *When countries specialize, total world output increases, and therefore, the potential for greater total world consumption also increases.*

18-1c SPECIALIZATION WITH TRADE

Now let's return to Exhibit 2 and demonstrate how world trade benefits countries. Suppose the United States agrees to specialize in grain production at point *A* and to import 20 tons of Japanese steel in exchange for 30 tons of its grain output. Does the United States gain from trade? The answer is Yes. At point *A*, the United States produces 100 tons of grain per day. Subtracting the 30 tons of grain traded to Japan leaves the United States with 70 tons of its own grain production to consume. In return for grain, Japan unloads 20 tons of steel on U.S. shores. Hence, specialization and trade allow the United States to move from point *A* to point *B′*, which is a consumption possibility *outside* its production possibilities curve in Exhibit 2(a). At point *B′*, the United States consumes the same amount of steel and 10 more tons of grain compared to point *B* (without trade).

Japan also has an incentive to specialize by moving its production mix from point *E* to point *F*. With trade, Japan's consumption will be at point *E′*. At point *E′*, Japan has as much grain to consume as it had at point *E*, plus 10 more tons of steel. After trading 20 tons of the 40 tons of steel produced at point *F* for grain, Japan can still consume 20 tons of steel from its production, rather than only 10 tons of steel at point *E*. Thus, point *E′* is a consumption possibility that lies *outside* Japan's production possibilities curve.

> **CONCLUSION:** *Global trade allows a country to consume a combination of goods that exceeds its production possibilities curve.*

18-2 Absolute and Comparative Advantage

Why did the United States decide to produce and export grain instead of steel? Why did Japan choose to produce and export steel rather than grain? Here you study the economic principle that determines specialization and trade. These concepts are absolute advantage and comparative advantage. Absolute advantage is the ability of a country to produce more of a good using the same or fewer resources as another country. Comparative advantage is the ability of a country to produce a good at a lower opportunity cost than another country.

Perhaps a non-economic example will clarify the difference between absolute advantage and comparative advantage. When Babe Ruth played for the New York Yankees, he was the best hitter and the best pitcher not only on the team, but also in all of major league baseball. In fact, before Ruth was traded to the Yankees and switched to the outfield, he was the best left-handed pitcher in the American League for a few seasons with the Boston Red Sox. His final record was 94–46. In other words, he had an *absolute advantage* in both hitting and throwing the baseball. Stated differently, Babe Ruth could produce the same home runs as any

Absolute advantage

The ability of a country to produce a good at a lower opportunity cost than another country.

Comparative advantage

The ability of a country to produce a good at a lower opportunity cost than another country.

other teammate with fewer times at bat. The problem was that if he pitched, he would bat fewer times because pitchers need rest after pitching. The coaches decided that the Babe had a *comparative advantage* in hitting. A few pitchers on the team could pitch almost as well as the Babe, but no one could touch his hitting. In terms of opportunity costs, the Yankees would lose fewer games if the Babe specialized in hitting.

18-2a ABSOLUTE ADVANTAGE

So far in our grain versus steel example, a country's production and trade decisions have not considered how much labor, land, or capital either the United States or Japan uses to produce a ton of grain or steel. For example, Japan might have an absolute advantage in producing *both* grain and steel. In our example, compared to the United States, Japan might use fewer resources per ton to produce grain and steel. Maybe the Japanese work harder or are more skilled. In short, the Japanese may be more productive producers, but their absolute advantage does not matter in specialization and world trade decisions. If Japan has a comparative advantage in steel, it should specialize in steel even if, compared to the United States, it can produce both grain and steel with fewer resources.

> **CONCLUSION:** *Specialization and trade are based on opportunity costs (comparative advantage) and not an absolute advantage.*

18-2b COMPARATIVE ADVANTAGE

Engaging in world trade permits countries to escape the prison of their own production possibilities curves by producing bread, cars, or whatever goods they make best. The decision of the United States to specialize in and export grain and the decision of Japan to specialize in and export steel are based on comparative advantage. Continuing our example from Exhibit 2, we can calculate opportunity costs for the two countries and use comparative advantage to determine which country should specialize in grain and which should specialize in steel. For the United States, the opportunity cost of producing 50 tons of steel is 100 tons of grain not produced, so 1 ton of steel costs 2 tons of grain. For Japan, the opportunity cost of producing 40 tons of steel is 40 tons of grain, so 1 ton of steel costs 1 ton of grain. Japan's steel is therefore cheaper in terms of grain forgone. This means Japan has a comparative advantage in steel production because it must give up less grain to produce steel than the United States. Stated differently, the opportunity cost of steel production is lower in Japan than in the United States.

The other side of the coin is to measure the cost of grain in terms of steel. For the United States, the opportunity cost of producing 100 tons of grain is 50 tons of steel not produced. This means 1 ton of grain costs 1/2 ton of steel. For Japan, the opportunity cost of producing 40 tons of grain is 40 tons of steel, so 1 ton of grain costs 1 ton of steel. The United States has a comparative advantage in grain because its opportunity cost in terms of steel forgone is lower. Thus, the United States should specialize in grain because it is more efficient in grain production. Japan, on the other hand, is relatively more efficient at producing steel and should specialize in this product.

> **CONCLUSION:** *Comparative advantage refers to the relative opportunity costs between different countries of producing the same goods. World output and consumption are maximized when each country specializes in producing and trading goods for which it has a comparative advantage.*

✓ CHECKPOINT

Do Nations with an Advantage Always Trade?

Comparing labor productivity, suppose the United States has an absolute advantage over Costa Rica in the production of calculators and towels. In the United States, a worker can produce 4 calculators or 400 towels in 10 hours. In Costa Rica, a worker can produce 1 calculator or 100 towels in the same amount of time. Under these conditions, are specialization and trade advantageous?

18-3 Free Trade versus Protectionism

Free trade

The flow of goods between countries without restrictions or special taxes.

In theory, global trade should be based on comparative advantage and free trade. Free trade is the flow of goods between countries without restrictions or special taxes. In practice, despite the advice of economists, to some degree, every nation protects its own domestic producers from foreign competition. Behind these barriers to trade are special interest groups whose jobs and incomes are threatened, so they clamor to the government for protectionism. Protectionism is the government's use of embargoes, tariffs, quotas, and other restrictions to protect domestic producers from foreign competition.

Protectionism

The government's use of embargoes, tariffs, quotas, and other restrictions to protect domestic producers from foreign competition.

18-3a EMBARGO

Embargo

A law that bars trade with another country.

Embargoes are the strongest limit on trade. An embargo is a law that bars trade with another country. For example, the United States and other nations in the world imposed an arms embargo on Iraq in response to its invasion of Kuwait in 1990. The United States also maintains embargoes against Iran, Cuba, and North Korea.

18-3b TARIFF

Tariff

A tax on an import.

Tariffs are the most popular and visible measures used to discourage trade. A tariff is a tax on an import. Tariffs are also called customs duties. Suppose the United States imposes a tariff of 2.9 percent on autos. If a foreign car costs $40,000, the amount of the tariff equals $1,160 ($40,000 × 0.029), and the U.S. price, including the tariff, is $41,160. The current U.S. tariff code specifies tariffs on nearly 70 percent of U.S. imports. A tariff can be based on weight, volume, or number of units,

EXHIBIT 4	The Average Tariff Rate, 1930–2011

Under the Smoot-Hawley Act of 1930, the average tariff rate peaked at 20 percent. Since the GATT in 1947 and other trade agreements, tariffs have declined to less than 5 percent.

SOURCES: *Economic Report of the President 1989*, http://www.gpoaccess.gov/eop/, p. 151; United States International Trade Commission, *The Economic Effect of Significant U.S. Import Restraints*, June 2002, p. 146, http://www.USITC.gov/, and *Trade Profiles*, http://stat.wto.org/CountryProfiles/US_e.htm.

or it can be *ad valorem* (figured as a percentage of the price). The average U.S. tariff is less than 5 percent, but individual tariffs vary widely. Tariffs are imposed to reduce imports by raising import prices and to generate revenues for the U.S. Treasury. Exhibit 4 shows the trend of the average tariff rate since 1930.

During the worldwide depression of the 1930s, when one nation raised its tariffs to protect its industries, other nations retaliated by raising their tariffs. Under the Smoot-Hawley tariffs of the 1930s, the average tariff in the United States reached a peak of 20 percent. Durable imports, which were one-third of imports, were subject to an unbelievable tariff rate of 60 percent. In 1947, most of the world's industrialized nations mutually agreed to end the tariff wars by signing the *General Agreement on Tariffs and Trade (GATT)*. Since then, GATT nations have met periodically to negotiate lower tariff rates. GATT agreements have significantly reduced tariffs over the years among member nations. In the 1994 *Uruguay round*, member nations signed a GATT agreement that decreased tariffs and reduced other trade barriers. The most divisive element of this agreement was the creation in 1995 of the Geneva-based World Trade Organization (WTO) to enforce rulings in global trade disputes. The WTO has 155 members and a standing appellate body to render final decisions regarding disputes between WTO members. Critics fear that the WTO might be far more likely to rule in favor of other countries in their trade disputes with the United States. Some people argue that the WTO is unaccountable, and these critics reject free trade and globalization.

To illustrate an interesting case, the United States imposed tariffs in 2002 on steel imports to protect jobs in the struggling U.S. steel industry against foreign

World Trade Organization (WTO)

An international organization of member countries that oversees international trade agreements and rules on trade disputes.

competition. The WTO ruled these tariffs were illegal, and countries in Europe and Asia prepared a list of retaliatory tariffs. These levies targeted products such as citrus fruit grown in Florida and apparel produced in southern states crucial to President Bush's reelection. Meanwhile, U.S. automakers and other steel-consuming industries complained because the tariffs increased their costs. Facing these threats, the United States removed the tariffs on steel imports in 2003. It is interesting to compare this case to the Global Economics feature titled "World Trade Slips on Banana Peel."

18-3c QUOTA

Quota

A limit on the quantity of a good that may be imported in a given time period.

Another way to limit foreign competition is to impose a quota. A quota is a limit on the quantity of a good that may be imported in a given time period. For example, the United States may allow 10 million tons of sugar to be imported over a one-year period. Once this quantity is reached, no more sugar can be imported for the year. About 12 percent of U.S. imports are subject to import quotas. Examples include import quotas on sugar, dairy products, textiles, steel, and even ice cream. Quotas can limit imports from all foreign suppliers or from specific countries. In 2005, for example, global quotas were lifted from Chinese imports. The United States and other European countries demanded quotas to protect their countries from Chinese textiles. Critics argue that, like all barriers to trade, quotas invite nations to retaliate with their own measures to restrict trade, and consumers are harmed by higher prices because of the lack of competition from lower-priced imports. In addition to embargoes, tariffs, and quotas, some nations use subtler measures to discourage trade, such as setting up an overwhelming number of bureaucratic steps that must be taken in order to import a product.

18-4 Arguments for Protection

Free trade provides consumers with lower prices and larger quantities of goods from which to choose. Thus, removing import barriers might save each family a few hundred dollars a year. The problem, however, is that imports could cost some workers their jobs and thousands of dollars per year from lost income. Thus, it is no wonder that in spite of the greater total benefits from free trade to consumers, trade barriers exist. The reason is primarily because workers and owners from import-competing firms have more at stake than consumers, so they go to Washington and lobby for protection. The following are some of the most popular arguments for protection. These arguments have strong political or emotional appeal, but weak support from economists.

18-4a INFANT INDUSTRY ARGUMENT

As the name suggests, the *infant industry argument* is that a new domestic industry needs protection because it is not yet ready to compete with established foreign competitors. An infant industry is in a formative stage and must bear high start-up costs to train an entire workforce, develop new technology, establish marketing channels, and reach economies of scale. With time to grow and protection, an infant industry can reduce costs and "catch up" with established foreign firms.

Economists ask where one draws the arbitrary line between an "infant" and a "grown-up" industry. It is also difficult to make a convincing case for protecting an infant industry in a developed country, such as the United States, where industries are well established. The infant industry argument, however, may have some validity for less-developed countries. Yet, even for these countries, there is a danger. Once protection is granted, the new industry will not experience the competitive pressures necessary to encourage reasonably quick growth and participation in world trade. Also, once an industry is given protection, it is difficult to take it away.

18-4b NATIONAL SECURITY ARGUMENT

Another common argument is that defense-related industries must be protected with embargoes, tariffs, and quotas to ensure national security. By protecting critical defense industries, a nation will not be dependent on foreign countries for the essential defense-related goods it needs to defend protect itself in wartime. The *national defense argument* has been used to protect a long list of industries, including petrochemicals, munitions, steel, and rubber.

This argument gained validity during the War of 1812. Great Britain, the main trading partner of the United States, became an enemy that blockaded our coast. Today, this argument makes less sense for the United States. The government stockpiles missiles, sophisticated electronics, petroleum, and most goods needed in wartime.

18-4c EMPLOYMENT ARGUMENT

The *employment argument* suggests that restricting imports increases domestic jobs in protected industries. According to this protectionist argument, the sale of an imported good comes at the expense of its domestically produced counterpart. Lower domestic output therefore leads to higher domestic unemployment than would otherwise be the case.

It is true that protectionism can increase output and save jobs in some industries at home. Ignored, however, are the higher prices paid by consumers because protectionism reduces competition between domestic goods and imported goods. In addition, there are employment reduction effects to consider. For example, suppose a strict quota is imposed on steel imported into our nation. Reduced foreign competition allows U.S. steelmakers to charge higher prices for their steel. As a result, prices rise and sales fall for cars and other products using steel, causing production and employment to fall in these industries. Thus, the import quota on steel may save jobs in the steel industry, but at the expense of more jobs lost in the steel-consuming industries. Also, by selling U.S. imports, foreigners earn dollars that they can use to buy U.S. exports. Import quotas cause foreigners to have fewer dollars to spend on U.S. exports, resulting in a decrease in employment in U.S. export industries. In short, protectionism may cause a net reduction in the nation's total employment.

18-4d CHEAP FOREIGN LABOR ARGUMENT

Another often heard popular claim is the *cheap labor argument*. It goes something like this: "How can we compete with such unfair competition? Labor costs $10 an hour in the United States, and firms in many developing countries pay only $1 an

World Trade Slips on Banana Peel
Applicable Concept: protectionism

Growing bananas for European markets was a multibillion-dollar bright spot for Latin America's struggling economies. In fact, about half of this region's banana exports traditionally were sold to Europe. Then, in 1993, the European Union (EU) adopted a package of quotas and tariffs aimed at cutting Europe's banana imports from Latin America. The purpose of these restrictions was to give trade preference to 66 banana-growing former colonies of European nations in Africa, the Caribbean, and the Pacific. Ignored was the fact that growers in Latin America grow higher-quality bananas at half the cost of EU-favored growers because of their low labor costs and flat tropical land near port cities.

In 1999, the World Trade Organization (WTO) ruled that the EU was discriminating in favor of European companies importing the fruit and the WTO imposed $191.4 million per year in punitive tariffs on European goods. This was the first time in the four years the WTO had been in existence that such retaliation had been approved and only the second time going back to its predecessor, the General Agreement

on Tariffs and Trade. When the EU failed to comply with the WTO findings, the United States enforced its WTO rights by imposing increased duties on EU imports, including goods ranging from cashmere sweaters and Italian handbags to sheep's milk cheese, British biscuits, and German coffeemakers. The effect of the U.S. sanctions was to double the wholesale prices of these items. Denmark and the Netherlands were exempt from the U.S. tariffs because they were the only nations that voted against the EU banana rules.

hour. Without protection against outsourcing our jobs, U.S. wages will be driven down, and our standard of living will fall."

A major flaw in this argument is that it neglects the reason for the difference in the wage rates between countries. A U.S. worker has more education, training, capital, and access to advanced technology. Therefore, if U.S. workers produce more output per hour than workers in another country, U.S. workers will earn higher wages without a competitive disadvantage. Suppose textile workers in the United States are paid $10 per hour. If a U.S. worker takes 1 hour to produce a rug, the labor cost per rug is $10. Now suppose a worker in India earns $1 per hour, but requires 20 hours to produce a rug on a handloom. In this case, the labor cost per rug is $20. Although the wage rate is 10 times higher in the United States, U.S. productivity is 20 times higher because a U.S. worker can produce 20 rugs in 20 hours, while the worker in India produces only 1 rug in the same amount of time.

Sometimes U.S. companies move their operations to foreign countries where labor is cheaper. Such moves are not always successful because the savings from paying foreign workers a lower wage rate are offset by lower productivity. Other disadvantages of foreign operations include greater transportation costs to U.S. markets and political instability.

Critics charged that the United States was pushing the case for political reasons. American companies, including Chiquita Brands International and Dole Food Company, grow most of their bananas in Latin America. With America's trade deficit running at a record level, U.S. trade experts also argued that the United States had little choice but to act against the EU for failing to abide by the WTO's ruling. Moreover, with increasing voices in the United States questioning the wisdom of globalization, it was important that the WTO prove that it could arbitrate these disputes.

In 2001, it appeared that the banana dispute might be resolved. The EU agreed to increase market access for U.S. banana distributors, and the United States lifted its retaliatory duties on EU products. The agreement also provided that the United States could reimpose the duties if the EU did not complete its phased-in reductions in restrictions on banana imports.

But the banana story just kept "slipping along."

European Union anti-fraud officials say that illegal banana trafficking is proving more lucrative than that in cocaine. A recently exposed scheme saw Italian banana importers use false licenses to pay greatly reduced customs duties on non-quota fruit. The fraud netted smugglers hundreds of millions of euros over a two-year period.

Source: © Cengage Learning 2014

In 2004, Latin American growers again complained that the EU was discriminating against their bananas in favor of producers from African, Caribbean, and Pacific countries. Under the 2001 WTO ruling, the EU was compelled to replace its complex quota and tariff system on bananas with a tariff-only regime. So the EU placed a 176 euro tariff per ton on Latin American suppliers to get into the EU market, while bananas from African and Caribbean countries could export up to 775,000 tons duty-free. The banana war continued in 2008 when a WTO dispute panel ruled for the third time that the EU tariff/quota banana regime was unfair. Finally, the EU initiated a deal agreed to in 2009 that might end this longest trade battle in history. The EU will gradually cut the import tariff on bananas from Latin America in stages until 2017. Also, the banana producing countries from African, Caribbean, and Pacific countries will receive financial aid to help them adjust to stiffer competition.

Analyze the Issue

Make an argument in favor of the European import restrictions. Make an argument against this plan.

18-5 Free Trade Agreements

The trend in recent years has been for nations to negotiate a reduction in trade barriers. In 1993, Congress approved the *North American Free Trade Agreement (NAFTA)*, which linked the United States to its first- and third-largest trading partners, Canada and Mexico. Under NAFTA, which became effective January 1, 1994, tariffs were phased out, and other impediments to trade and investment were eliminated among the three nations. For example, elimination of trade restrictions allows the United States to supply Mexico with more U.S. goods and to boost U.S. jobs. On the other hand, NAFTA was expected to raise Mexico's wages and standard of living by increasing Mexican exports to the United States. Note that NAFTA made no changes in restrictions on labor movement, and workers must enter the United States under a limited immigration quota or illegally. The success of NAFTA remains controversial. At the conclusion of this chapter, we will use data to examine its impact.

The United States and other countries are considering other free trade agreements. In Europe, 27 nations have joined the *European Union (EU)*, which is dedicated to removing all trade barriers within Europe, thereby creating a single European economy almost as large as the U.S. economy. See the Birth of the Euro boxed feature in this chapter.

Birth of the Euro

In 1958, several European nations formed a Common Market to eliminate trade restrictions among member countries. The Common Market called for gradual removal of tariffs and import quotas on goods traded among member nations. Later the name was changed to the *European Economic Community (EEC)*, and it is now called the *European Union (EU)*. This organization established a common system of tariffs for imports from nonmember nations and created common policies for economic matters of joint concern, such as agriculture and transportation. The EU now comprises the 27 nations listed in the following table.

In 1999, 11 European countries, joined later by Greece, followed the United States as an example and united in the *European Economic and Monetary Union (EMU)*. In the United States, 50 states are linked with a common currency, and the Federal Reserve serves as the central bank by conducting monetary policy for the nation. Among the states, trade, labor, and investment enjoy freedom of movement. In 2002, the EMU

Matt Trommer/Shutterstock.com

members replaced their national currencies with a single currency, the euro. The objective was to remove exchange rate fluctuations that impede cross-border transactions. This is why the U.S. Congress created a national currency in 1863 to replace state and private bank currencies.

The EU faces many unanswered questions. Unlike the states of the United States, the EU's member nations do not share a common language or governments. This makes maintaining common macro policies difficult,

The *Asian-Pacific Economic Cooperation (APEC)* was formed in 1989 and today has 21 member nations, including China, Hong Kong, Russia, Japan, and Mexico. This organization is based on a nonbinding agreement to reduce trade barriers between member nations.

In 2003, trade ministers from 34 nations met in Miami to create a plan for the world's largest free-trade area that would tear down trade barriers from Alaska to Argentina. The Free Trade Area of the Americas (FTAA) would span the Western Hemisphere except Cuba. In 2005, the *Central American Free Trade Agreement (CAFTA)* extended the free trade zone to six Central American countries that signed, including Costa Rica, Guatemala, El Salvador, Honduras, Nicaragua, and Dominican Republic. The success or failure of CAFTA will have an impact on future negotiation for FTAA.

Critics are concerned that regional free-trade accords will make global agreements increasingly difficult to achieve. Some fear that trading blocs may erect new barriers, creating "Fortress North America," "Fortress Europe," and similar impediments to the worldwide reduction of trade barriers.

Balance of payments
A bookkeeping record of all the international transactions between a country and other countries during a given period of time.

18-6 The Balance of Payments

When trade occurs between the United States and other nations, many types of financial transactions are recorded in a summary called the balance of payments. The balance of payments is a bookkeeping record of all the international transactions between a country and other countries during a given period of time.

and in recent years, Greece and several other members have experienced financial crises. France, for example, might seek to control inflation, while Germany has reducing unemployment as its highest priority. Coordinating monetary policy among EU nations is also difficult. Although the EU has established the *European Central Bank* headquartered in Frankfurt, Germany, with sole authority over the supply of euros, the central banks of member nations still function. But these national central banks operate similar to the district banks of the Federal Reserve System in the United States. Only time will tell whether EU nations will perform better with a single currency than with separate national currencies. Currently, the United Kingdom, Denmark, and Sweden still use their own currencies.

European Union (EU) Members

Austria	Finland	Latvia	Romania
Belgium	France	Lithuania	Slovenia
Bulgaria	Germany	Luxembourg	Spain
Cyprus	Greece	Malta	Sweden
Czech Republic	Hungary	Netherlands	United Kingdom
Denmark	Ireland	Poland	
Estonia	Italy	Portugal	

This summary is the best way to understand interactions between economies because it records the value of a nation's spending inflows and outflows made by individuals, firms, and governments. Exhibit 5 presents a simplified U.S. balance of payments for 2011.

Note the pluses and minuses in the table. A transaction that is a payment to the United States is entered as a positive amount. A payment by the United States to another country is entered with a minus sign. As our discussion unfolds, you will learn that the balance of payments provides much useful information.

18-6a CURRENT ACCOUNT

The first section of the balance of payments is the *current account*, which includes trade in goods and services. The most widely reported part of the current account is the balance of trade, also called the trade balance. The balance of trade is the value of a nation's imports subtracted from its exports, and it can be expressed in terms of goods, services, or goods and services. The balance of trade most often reported is in terms of goods and services. As shown in lines 1–4, the United States had a *balance of trade deficit* of −$560 billion in 2011. A trade deficit occurs when the value of a country's imports exceeds the value of its exports. When a nation has a trade deficit, it is called an *unfavorable balance of trade* because more is spent for imports than is earned from

Balance of trade

The value of a nation's imports subtracted from its exports. Balance of trade can be expressed in terms of goods, services, or goods and services.

EXHIBIT 5	U.S. Balance of Payments, 2011 (billions of dollars)	
Type of transaction		
Current account		
1. Goods exports		$ +1,497
2. Goods imports		−2,236
3. Service exports		+608
4. Service imports		−429
Trade balance (lines 1–4)		−560
5. Investment income (net)		+221
6. Unilateral transfers (net)		−135
Current account balance (lines 1–6)		−474
Capital account		
7. U.S. capital inflow		+784
8. U.S. capital outflow		−396
Capital account balance (lines 7–8)		+388
9. Statistical discrepancy		+86
Net balance (lines 1–9)		0

SOURCE: Bureau of Economic Analysis, click on "Detailed Estimates" for *U.S. International Transactions*, http://www.bea.gov/international/index.htm, Table 1.

exports. Recall that net exports can have a positive (favorable) or negative (unfavorable) effect on GDP = $C + I + G + (X - M)$.

Exhibit 6 charts the annual balance of trade for the United States from 1975 through 2011. Observe that the United States experienced a *balance of trade surplus* in 1975. A trade surplus arises when the value of a country's exports is greater than the value of its imports. This is called a *favorable balance of trade* because the United States earned more from exports than it spent for imports. Since 1975, however, sizable trade deficits have occurred. These trade deficits have attracted much attention because, in part, they reflect the popularity of foreign goods and the lack of competitiveness of goods "Made in U.S.A." Between 2005 and 2008, the U.S. trade deficits reached record-breaking levels of about $700 billion due in part to the rising price of oil imports. During this period, the price per barrel grew steadily until it reached a peak in 2008, and the U.S. trade deficit with OPEC countries doubled while our trade deficit with China tripled. After 2008, oil import prices plunged sharply from a high of $134 per barrel in 2008 to $82 per barrel in 2010, and U. S. trade deficits with OPEC countries fell. Also, U.S. trade deficits with China remained constant at $262 billion between 2008 and 2010. These

| EXHIBIT 6 | U.S. Balance of Trade, 1975–2011 (billions of dollars) |

Since 1975, the United States has experienced trade deficits in which the value of goods and services imports has exceeded the value of goods and services exports. These trade deficits attract much attention because, in part, they reflect the popularity of foreign goods in the United States. During the recession in 2001, the U.S. trade deficit narrowed briefly before continuing an upward trend. The deficit grew to an all-time high of about $700 billion between 2005 and 2008 before declining to $500 billion in 2010 and $560 billion in 2011.

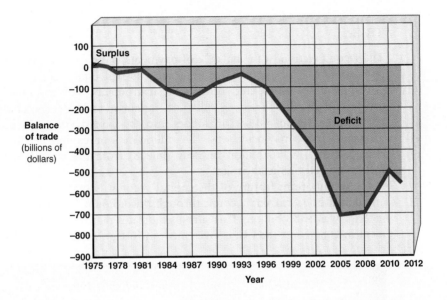

SOURCE: Bureau of Economic Analysis, *International U.S. International Transactions Accounts*, http://www.bea.gov/international/index.htm, Table 1.

factors contributed to the fall in the U.S. balance of trade in 2010. In 2011, the U.S. trade deficit rose again to $560 billion because of higher oil prices and a trade deficit with China.

Lines 3–6 of the current account in Exhibit 5 list ways other than trade of goods that move dollars back and forth between the United States and other countries. Services include insurance, banking, transportation, and tourism. For example, a Japanese tourist who pays a hotel bill in Hawaii buys an export of services, which is a plus, or credit, to our current account (line 3). Similarly, an American visitor to foreign lands buys an import of services, which is a minus, or debit, to our services and therefore a minus to our current account (line 4). Income flowing back from U.S. investments abroad, such as plants, real estate, and securities, is a payment for use of the services of U.S. capital. Foreign countries also receive income flowing from the services of their capital owned in the United States. In 2011, line 5 of the table reports a net investment income flow of $221 billion to the United States.

Finally, we consider line 6, unilateral transfers. This category includes gifts made by our government, charitable organizations, or private individuals to other governments or private parties elsewhere in the world. For example, this item includes U.S. foreign aid to other nations. Similar unilateral transfers into the United States must be subtracted to determine the *net* unilateral transfers. Net unilateral transfers for the United States were −$135 billion in 2011.

Adding lines 1–6 gives the current account balance deficit of −$474 billion in 2011. This deficit means that foreigners sent us more goods, services, investment income, and transfers than we sent to them. Because the current account balance includes more than goods and services, it is a broader measure than the trade balance. Since 1982, the trend in the current account balance has followed the swing into the red shown by the trade balance in Exhibit 6.

18-6b CAPITAL ACCOUNT

The second section of the balance of payments is the *capital account*, which records payment flows for financial capital, such as real estate, corporate stocks, bonds, government securities, and other debt instruments. For example, when Chinese investors buy U.S. Treasury bills or Japanese investors purchase farmland in Hawaii, there is an inflow of dollars into the United States. As Exhibit 5 shows, foreigners made payments of $784 billion to our capital account (line 7). This exceeded the −$396 billion outflow (line 8) from the United States to purchase foreign-owned financial capital.

An important feature of the capital account is that the United States finances any deficit in its current account through this account. The capital account balance in 2011 was $388 billion. This surplus indicates that there was more foreign investment in U.S. assets than U.S. investment in foreign assets during this year.

> **CONCLUSION:** *A current account deficit is financed by a capital account surplus.*

The current account deficit should equal the capital account surplus, but line 9 in the exhibit reveals that the balance of payments is not perfect. The capital account balance does not exactly offset the current account balance. Hence, a credit amount is simply recorded as a statistical discrepancy; therefore, the balance of payments always balances, or equals zero.

18-6c THE INTERNATIONAL DEBT OF THE UNITED STATES

If each nation's balance of payments is always zero, why is there so much talk about a U.S. balance-of-payments problem? The problem is with the *composition* of the balance of payments. Suppose the United States runs a $500 billion deficit in its current account. This means that the current account deficit must be financed by a net annual capital inflow in the capital account of $500 billion. That is, foreign lenders, such as banks and businesses, must purchase U.S. assets and grant loans to the United States that on balance equal $500 billion. For example, a Chinese bank could buy U.S. Treasury bonds. Recall from Exhibit 7 in the chapter on federal deficits and the national debt that the portion of the national debt owed to lenders outside the United States is called *external debt*.

| EXHIBIT 7 | **U.S. Balance of Trade with Selected Countries, 2011 (billions of dollars)** |

The United States has its greatest trade deficits with China, Mexico, and Germany.

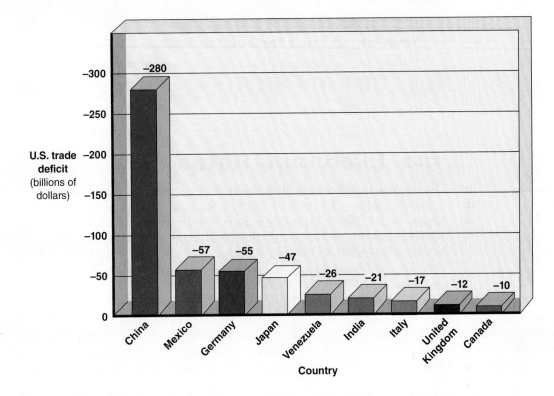

SOURCE: Bureau of Economic Analysis, *U.S. International Transactions by Area*, http://www.bea.gov/international/index.htm, Table 12.

In 1984, the United States became a net debtor for the first time in about 70 years. This means that investments in the United States accumulated by foreigners—stocks, bonds, real estate, and so forth—exceeded the stock of foreign assets owned by the United States. In fact, during the decade of the 1980s, the United States moved from being the world's largest creditor nation to being the largest debtor nation.

Exhibit 7 shows that the United States has its largest trade deficits with China, Mexico, Germany, and Japan, respectively. The concern over continuing trade deficits and the rising international debt that accompanies them is that the United States is artificially enjoying a higher standard of living. When the United States continues to purchase more goods and services abroad than it exports, it might find itself "enjoying now and paying later." Suppose the Chinese and other foreigners decide not to make new U.S. investments and loans. In this case, the United States will be forced to eliminate its trade deficit by bringing exports and imports into balance. In fact, if other countries not only refuse to provide new capital inflows, but also decide to liquidate their investments, the United States would be forced to run a trade surplus. Stated differently, we would be forced to tighten our belts and accept a lower standard of living. How a change in foreign willingness to purchase U.S. assets also affects the international value of the dollar is the topic to which we now turn.

✔ CHECKPOINT

Should Everyone Keep a Balance of Payments?

Nations keep balances of payments and calculate accounts such as their trade deficit or surplus. If nations need these accounts, the 50 states should also maintain balances of payments to manage their economies. Or should they? What about cities?

18-7 Exchange Rates

Each transaction recorded in the balance of payments requires an exchange of one country's currency for that of another. Suppose you buy a Japanese car made in Japan, say, a Mazda. Mazda wants to be paid in yen and not dollars, so dollars must be traded for yen. On the other hand, suppose Pink Panther Airline Company in France purchases an airplane from Boeing in the United States. Pink Panther has euros to pay the bill, but Boeing wants dollars. Consequently, euros must be exchanged for dollars.

Exchange rate

The number of units of one nation's currency that equals one unit of another nation's currency.

The critical question for Mazda, Pink Panther, Boeing, and everyone involved in world trade is, "What is the exchange rate?" The exchange rate is the number of units of one nation's currency that equals one unit of another nation's currency. For example, assume 1.81 dollars can be exchanged for 1 British pound. This means the exchange rate is 1.81 dollars = 1 pound. Alternatively, the exchange rate can be expressed as a reciprocal. Dividing 1 British pound by 1.81 dollars gives 0.552 pounds per dollar. Now suppose you are visiting England and want to buy a T-shirt with a price tag of 10 pounds. Knowing the exchange rate tells you the T-shirt costs $18.10 (10 pounds × $1.81/pound).

CONCLUSION: *An exchange rate can be expressed as a reciprocal.*

18-7a SUPPLY AND DEMAND FOR FOREIGN EXCHANGE

The exchange rate for dollars, or any nation's currency floats, which means it is determined by global forces of supply and demand. For example, consider the exchange rate of yen to dollars, shown in Exhibit 8. Like the price and the quantity of any good traded in markets, the quantity of dollars exchanged is measured on the horizontal axis, and the price per unit is measured on the vertical axis. In this case, the price per unit is the value of the U.S. dollar expressed as the number of yen per dollar.

The demand for dollars in the world currency market comes from Japanese individuals, corporations, and governments that want to buy U.S. exports. Because

---

| EXHIBIT 8 | The Supply of and Demand for Dollars |

The number of Japanese yen per dollar in the foreign exchange market is determined by the demand for dollars by Japanese citizens and the supply of dollars by U.S. citizens. The equilibrium exchange rate is 100 yen per dollar, and the equilibrium quantity is $300 million per day.

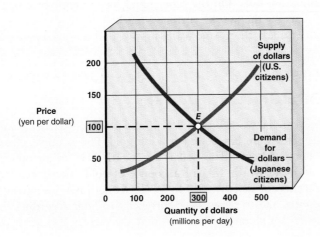

SOURCE: © Cengage Learning 2014

---

the Japanese buyers must pay for U.S. exports with dollars, they *demand* to exchange their yen for dollars. As expected, the demand curve for dollars or any foreign currency is downward sloping. A decline in the number of yen per dollar means that one yen buys a larger portion of a dollar. This means U.S. goods and investment opportunities are less expensive to Japanese buyers because they must pay fewer yen for each dollar. Thus, as the yen price of dollars decreases, the quantity of dollars demanded by the Japanese to purchase Fords, stocks, land, and other U.S. products and investments increases. For example, suppose a CD recording of the hottest rock group has a $20 price tag. If the exchange rate is 200 yen to the dollar, a Japanese importer would pay 4,000 yen. If the price of dollars to Japanese buyers falls to 100 yen each, the same $20 CD will cost Japanese importers only 2,000 yen. This lower price causes Japanese buyers to increase their orders, which, in turn, increases the quantity of dollars demanded.

The supply curve of dollars is upward sloping. This curve shows the amount of dollars offered for exchange at various yen prices per dollar in the world currency exchange market. Similar to the demand for dollars, the supply of dollars in this market flows from individuals, corporations, and governments in the United States that want to buy Mazdas, stocks, land, and other products and investments from Japan. Because U.S. citizens must pay for the Japanese goods and services in yen, they must exchange dollars for yen. An example will illustrate why the supply curve of dollars slopes upward. Suppose a Nikon camera sells for 100,000 yen in Tokyo and the exchange rate is 100 yen per dollar or 0.01 dollar per yen ($1/100 yen). Therefore, the camera costs an American tourist $1,000. Now assume the exchange rate rises to 250 yen per dollar or 0.004 dollar per yen ($1/250 yen).

The camera will now cost the American buyer only $400. Because the prices of the Nikon camera and other Japanese products fall when the number of yen per dollar rises, Americans respond by purchasing more Japanese imports, which, in turn, increases the quantity of dollars supplied.

The foreign exchange market in Exhibit 8 is in equilibrium at an exchange rate of 100 yen for $1. As you learned in Chapter 3, if the exchange rate is above equilibrium, there will be a surplus of dollars in the world currency market. Citizens of the United States are supplying more dollars than the Japanese demand, and the exchange rate falls. On the other hand, below equilibrium, there will be a shortage of dollars in the world currency market. In this case, the Japanese are demanding more dollars than Americans supply, and the exchange rate rises.

18-7b SHIFTS IN SUPPLY AND DEMAND FOR FOREIGN EXCHANGE

For most of the years between World War II and 1971, currency exchange rates were *fixed*. Exchange rates were based primarily on gold. For example, the German mark was fixed at about 25 cents. The dollar was worth 1/35 of an ounce of gold, and 4 German marks were worth 1/35 of an ounce of gold. Therefore, 1 dollar equaled 4 marks, or 25 cents equaled 1 mark. In 1971, Western nations agreed to stop fixing their exchange rates and to allow their currencies to *float* according to the forces of supply and demand. Exhibit 9 illustrates that these rates can fluctuate widely. For

EXHIBIT 9	Changes in the Yen-per-Dollar Exchange Rate, 1980–2011

Today, most economies are on a system of flexible exchange rates. As the demand and supply curves for currencies change, exchange rates change. In 1980, 1 dollar was worth about 230 Japanese yen. By 2011, the exchange rate had dropped to a post-war low of 80 yen per dollar.

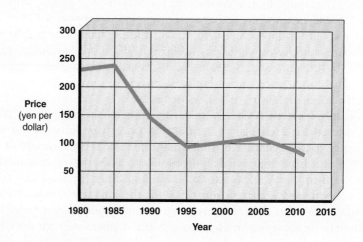

SOURCE: FRED Economic Data, http://research.stlouisfed.org/fred2/series/AEXJUS.

example, in 1980, 1 dollar was worth about 230 Japanese yen. After gyrating up and down over the years, the exchange rate hit a postwar low of 80 yen per dollar in 2011.

Recall from Chapter 3 that the equilibrium price for products changes in response to shifts in the supply and demand curves. The same supply and demand analysis applies to equilibrium exchange rates for foreign currency. There are four important sources of shifts in the supply and demand curves for foreign exchange. Let's consider each in turn.

Tastes and Preferences   Exhibit 10(a) illustrates one important factor that causes the demand for foreign currencies to shift. Suppose the Japanese lose their "taste" for tobacco, U.S. government bonds, and other U.S. products and

EXHIBIT 10	Changes in the Supply and Demand Curves for Dollars

In part (a), U.S. exports become less popular in Japan. This change in tastes for U.S. products and investments decreases the demand for dollars, and the demand curve shifts leftward from D_1 to D_2. As a result, the equilibrium exchange rate falls from 150 yen to the dollar at E_1 to 100 yen to the dollar at E_2.

Part (b) assumes U.S. citizens are influenced by the "Buy American" idea. In this case, our demand for Japanese imports decreases, and U.S. citizens supply fewer dollars to the foreign currency market. The result is that the supply curve shifts leftward from S_1 to S_2, and the equilibrium exchange rate rises from 100 yen per dollar at E_1 to 150 yen per dollar at E_2.

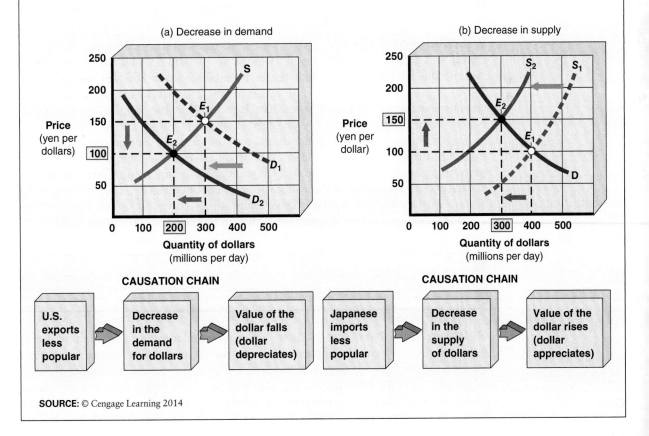

SOURCE: © Cengage Learning 2014

Depreciation of currency

A fall in the price of one currency relative to another.

investment opportunities. This decline in the popularity of U.S. products in Japan decreases the demand for dollars at each possible exchange rate, and the demand curve shifts leftward from D_1 to D_2. This change causes the equilibrium exchange rate to fall from 150 yen to the dollar at E_1 to 100 yen to the dollar at E_2. Because the number of yen to the dollar declines, the dollar is said to *depreciate* or become *weaker*. Depreciation of currency is a fall in the price of one currency relative to another.

What happens to the exchange rate if the "Buy American" idea changes our tastes and the demand for Japanese imports decreases? In this case, U.S. citizens supply fewer dollars at any possible exchange rate, and the supply curve in Exhibit 10(b) shifts leftward from S_1 to S_2. As a result, the equilibrium exchange rate rises from 100 yen to the dollar at E_1 to 150 yen to the dollar at E_2. Because the number of yen per dollar rises, the dollar is said to *appreciate* or become *stronger*. Appreciation of currency is a rise in the price of one currency relative to another.

Appreciation of currency

A rise in the price of one currency relative to another.

Relative Incomes   Assume income in the United States rises, while income in Japan remains unchanged. As a result, U.S. citizens buy more domestic products and more Japanese imports. The results are a rightward shift in the supply curve for dollars and a decrease in the equilibrium exchange rate. Paradoxically, growth of U.S. income leads to the dollar depreciating, or becoming weaker, against the Japanese yen.

> **CONCLUSION:** *An expansion in relative U.S. income causes a depreciation of the dollar.*

Relative Price Levels   Now we consider a more complex case in which a change in a factor causes a change in both the supply and demand curves for dollars. Assume the foreign exchange rate begins in equilibrium at 100 yen per dollar, as shown at point E_1 in Exhibit 11. Now assume the price level increases in Japan, but remains constant in the United States. The Japanese therefore want to buy more U.S. exports because they have become cheaper relative to Japanese products. This willingness of the Japanese to buy U.S. goods and services shifts the demand curve for dollars rightward from D_1 to D_2. In addition, U.S. products are cheaper for U.S. citizens compared to Japanese imports. As a result, the willingness to import from Japan is reduced at each exchange rate, which means the supply curve of dollars decreases from S_1 to S_2. The result of the shifts in both the demand and supply curves for dollars is to establish a new equilibrium at point E_2, and the exchange rate reaches 200 yen per dollar.

> **CONCLUSION:** *A rise in a trading partner's relative price level causes the dollar to appreciate.*

Relative Real Interest Rates   Changes in relative real (inflation-adjusted) interest rates can have an important effect on the exchange rate. Suppose real interest rates in the United States rise, while those in Japan remain constant. To take advantage of more attractive yields, Japanese investors buy an increased amount of bonds and other interest-bearing securities issued by private and government borrowers in the United States. This change increases the demand for dollars,

EXHIBIT 11	The Impact of Relative Price Level Changes on Exchange Rates

Begin at E_1, with the exchange rate equal to 100 yen per dollar. Assume prices in Japan rise relative to those in the United States. As a result, the demand for dollars increases, and the supply of dollars decreases. The new equilibrium is at E_2 when the dollar appreciates (rises in value) to 200 yen per dollar.

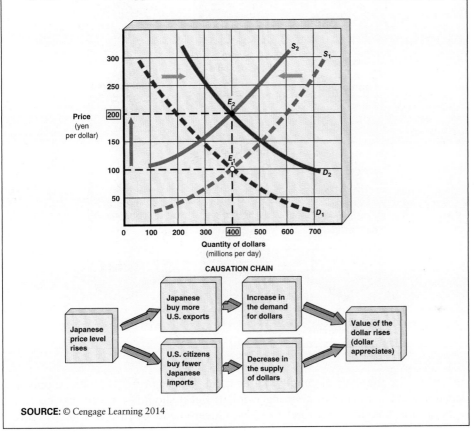

which increases the equilibrium exchange rate of yen to the dollar, causing the dollar to appreciate (or the yen to depreciate).

There can also be an effect on the supply of dollars. When real interest rates rise in the United States, our citizens purchase fewer Japanese securities. Hence, they offer fewer dollars at each possible exchange rate, and the supply curve for dollars shifts leftward. As a result, the equilibrium exchange rate increases, and the dollar appreciates from changes in both the demand for and supply of dollars.

18-7c THE IMPACT OF EXCHANGE RATE FLUCTUATIONS

Now it is time to stop for a minute and draw some important conclusions. As you have just learned, exchange rates between most major currencies are flexible. Instead of being pegged to gold or another fixed standard, their value floats as

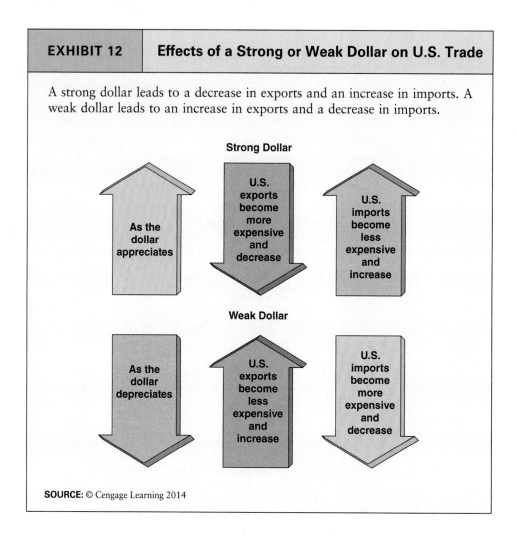

EXHIBIT 12   **Effects of a Strong or Weak Dollar on U.S. Trade**

A strong dollar leads to a decrease in exports and an increase in imports. A weak dollar leads to an increase in exports and a decrease in imports.

Strong Dollar

As the dollar appreciates

U.S. exports become more expensive and decrease

U.S. imports become less expensive and increase

Weak Dollar

As the dollar depreciates

U.S. exports become less expensive and increase

U.S. imports become more expensive and decrease

SOURCE: © Cengage Learning 2014

determined by the laws of supply and demand. Consequently, shifts in supply and demand create a weaker or a stronger dollar. But it should be noted that exchange rates do not fluctuate with total freedom. Governments often buy and sell currencies to prevent wide swings in exchange rates. In summary, the strength or weakness of any nation's currency has a profound impact on its economy.

A weak dollar is a "mixed blessing." Ironically, a weak dollar makes U.S. producers happy. Because foreigners pay less of their currency for dollars, this means U.S. producers can sell their less expensive exports to foreign buyers. As export sales rise, jobs are created in the United States. On the other hand, a weak dollar makes foreign producers and domestic consumers unhappy because the prices of Japanese cars, French wine, and Italian shoes are higher. As U.S. imports fall, jobs are lost in foreign countries.

CONCLUSION: *When the dollar is weak, or depreciates, U.S. goods and services cost foreign consumers less, so they buy more U.S. exports. At the same time, a weak dollar means foreign goods and services cost U.S. consumers more, so they buy fewer imports.*

EXHIBIT 13	U.S. Trade Balances with Mexico, 1993–2011			
Year	U.S. Exports to Mexico (billions of dollars)	U.S. Imports from Mexico (billions of dollars)	Exchange Rate (pesos per dollar)	U.S. Trade Surplus (+) or Deficit (−) (billions of dollars)
1993	$ 52	$ 48	3.12	$ +4
1995	55	71	6.45	−16
1997	82	97	7.92	−15
1999	101	120	9.55	−19
2001	118	143	9.34	−25
2003	115	152	10.79	−37
2005	143	188	10.89	−45
2007	161	231	10.93	−70
2009	152	193	13.50	−41
2011	224	281	12.43	−57

SOURCES: Bureau of Economic Analysis, *U.S. International Transactions by Area*, http://www.bea.gov/international.index.htm, Table 12 and FRED Economic Data, http://research.stlouisfed.org/fred2/data/AEXMXUS.txt.

A strong dollar is also a "mixed blessing." A strong dollar makes our major trading partners happy. When U.S. buyers pay fewer dollars for foreign currency, means the prices of Japanese cars, French wine, and Italian shoes are lower. A strong dollar, contrary to the implication of the term, makes U.S. producers unhappy because their exports are more expensive and related jobs decline. Conversely, a strong dollar makes foreign producers happy because the prices of their goods and services are lower, causing U.S. imports to rise. Exhibit 12 summarizes the weak versus strong dollar effects.

CONCLUSION: *When the dollar is strong, or appreciates, U.S. goods and services cost foreign consumers more, so they buy fewer U.S. exports. At the same time, a strong dollar means foreign goods and services cost U.S. consumers less, so they buy more foreign imports.*

Finally, as promised earlier in this chapter, we return to the discussion of NAFTA in order to illustrate the impact of this free trade agreement and the effect of a strong dollar. Recall that in January 1994, NAFTA began a gradual phaseout of tariffs and other trade barriers. Exhibit 13 provides trade data for the United States and Mexico for the years surrounding NAFTA. As the exhibit shows, both exports and imports of goods and services increased sharply after NAFTA. On the

Return to the Yellow Brick Road?
Applicable Concept: exchange rates

Gold is always a fascinating story: *The Wonderful Wizard of Oz* was first published in 1900, and this children's tale has been interpreted as an allegory for political and economic events of the 1890s. For example, the Yellow Brick Road represents the gold standard, Oz in the title is an abbreviation for ounce, Dorothy is the naive public, Emerald City symbolizes Washington, D.C., the Tin Woodman represents the industrial worker, the Scarecrow is the farmer, and the Cyclone is a metaphor for a political revolution. In the end, Dorothy discovers magical powers in her *silver* shoes (changed to ruby in the 1939 film) to find her way home and not the fallacy of the Yellow Brick Road. Although the author of the story, L. Frank Baum, never stated it was his intention, it can be argued that the issue of the story concerns the election of 1896. Democratic presidential nominee William Jennings Bryan (the Cowardly Lion) supported fixing the value of the dollar to both gold and silver (bimetallism), but Republican William McKinley (the Wicked Witch) advocated using only the gold standard. Since McKinley won, the United States remained on the Yellow Brick Road.[1]

The United States adopted the gold standard in 1873, and until the 1930s, most industrial countries were on the gold standard. The gold standard served as an international monetary system in which currencies were defined or pegged in terms of gold. Under the gold standard, a nation with a balance of payments deficit was required to ship gold to other

nations to finance the deficit. Hence, a large excess of imports over exports meant a corresponding outflow of gold from a nation. As a result, that nation's money supply decreased, which, in turn, reduced the aggregate demand for goods and services. Lower domestic demand led to falling prices, lower production, and fewer jobs. In contrast, a nation with a balance of payments surplus would experience an inflow of gold and the opposite effects. In this case, the nation's money supply increased, and its aggregate demand for goods and services rose. Higher aggregate spending, in turn, boosted employment and the price level. In short, the gold standard meant that governments could not control their money supplies and thereby conduct monetary policy.

The gold standard worked fairly well as a fixed exchange rate system so long as nations did not face sudden or severe swings in flows from their stocks of gold. The Great Depression marked the beginning of the end of the gold standard. Nations faced with trade deficits and high unemployment began going off the gold standard, rather than contracting their money supplies by following the gold standard.

In 1933, President Franklin D. Roosevelt took the United States off the gold standard and ordered all 1933 gold double eagle coins already manufactured to be melted down and not circulated. Through a long twisted story worthy of a Sherlock Holmes mystery novel involving the Smithsonian Institution, the former king of Egypt, the Treasury Department,

other hand, a small U.S. trade surplus of $4 billion with Mexico in 1993 turned into a huge trade deficit of $57 billion in 2011.

Before blaming this trade deficit entirely on NAFTA, you must note that the exchange rate rose from 3.12 to 12.43 pesos per dollar. Since 1995, the peso was devalued, and the stronger dollar has put the price of U.S. goods out of reach for many Mexican consumers. This is one reason U.S. exports to Mexico have been lower than they would have been otherwise. At the same time, Mexican goods became less expensive for U.S. consumers, so U.S. imports from Mexico have risen.

the Justice Department, the U.S. Mint, and a long list of intriguing supporting characters, one 1933 double eagle surfaced and was sold for $7.59 million in 2002. This was double the previous record for a coin.

Once the Allies felt certain they would win World War II, the finance ministers of Western nations met in 1944 at Bretton Woods, New Hampshire, to establish a new international monetary system. The new system was based on fixed exchange rates and an international central bank called the *International Monetary Fund (IMF)*. The IMF makes loans to countries faced with short-term balance-of-payments problems. Under this system, nations were expected to maintain fixed exchange rates within a narrow range. In the 1960s and early 1970s, the Bretton Woods system became strained as conditions changed. In the 1960s, inflation rates in the United States rose relative to those in other countries, causing U.S. exports to become more expensive and U.S. imports to become less expensive. This situation increased the supply of dollars abroad and caused an increasing surplus of dollars, thus putting downward pressure on the exchange rate. Monetary authorities in the United States worried that central banks would demand gold for their dollars, the U.S. gold stock would diminish sharply, and the declining money supply would adversely affect the economy.

Something had to give, and it did. In August 1971, President Richard Nixon announced that the United States would no longer honor its obligation to sell gold at $35 an ounce. By 1973, the gold standard was dead, and most of our trading partners were letting the forces of supply and demand determine exchange rates.

Today, some people advocate returning to the gold standard. These gold buffs do not trust the government to control the money supply without the discipline of a gold standard. They argue that if governments have the freedom to print money, political pressures will sooner or later cause them to increase the money supply too much and let inflation rage.

One argument against the gold standard is that no one can control the supply of gold. Big gold discoveries can cause inflation and have done so in the past. On the other hand, slow growth in the stock of mined gold can lead to slow economic growth and a loss of jobs. Governments therefore are unlikely to return to the gold standard because it would mean turning monetary policy over to uncontrollable swings in the stock of gold.

Analyze the Issue

Return to Exhibit 8, and assume the equilibrium exchange rate is 150 yen per dollar and the equilibrium quantity is $300 million. Redraw this figure, and place a horizontal line through the equilibrium exchange rate to represent a fixed exchange rate. Now use this figure to explain why a country would abandon the gold standard.

---

1. Bradley A. Hansen, "The Fable of the Allegory," *Journal of Economic Education*, Summer 2002, pp. 254–264.

Source: © Cengage Learning 2014

Key Concepts

Absolute advantage	Tariff	Balance of trade
Comparative advantage	World Trade Organization	Exchange rate
Free trade	(WTO)	Depreciation of currency
Protectionism	Quota	Appreciation of currency
Embargo	Balance of payments	

Summary

- **Comparative advantage** is a principle that allows nations to gain from trade. Comparative advantage means that each nation *specializes* in a product for which its opportunity cost is lower in terms of the production of another product, and then nations trade. When nations follow this principle, they gain. The reason is that world output increases, and each nation ends up with a higher standard of living by consuming more goods and services than would be possible without specialization and trade.

Comparative Advantage

(a) U.S. production and consumption

(b) Japanese production and consumption

SOURCE: © Cengage Learning 2014

- **Free trade** benefits a nation as a whole, but individuals may lose jobs and incomes because of the competition from foreign goods and services.
- **Protectionism** is a government's use of embargoes, tariffs, quotas, and other methods to impose barriers intended to both reduce imports and protect

particular domestic industries. *Embargoes* prohibit the import or export of particular goods. *Tariffs* discourage imports by making them more expensive. *Quotas* limit the quantity of imports or exports of certain goods. These trade barriers often result primarily from domestic groups that exert political pressure on government in order to gain from these barriers.

- The **balance of payments** is a summary bookkeeping record of all the international transactions a country makes during a year. It is divided into different accounts, including the *current account*, the *capital account*, and the *statistical discrepancy*. The current account summarizes all transactions in currently produced goods and services. The overall balance of payments is always zero after an adjustment for the statistical discrepancy.

- The **balance of trade** measures only goods (not services) that a nation exports and imports. A balance of trade can be in deficit or in surplus. The balance of trade is the most widely reported and largest part of the current account. Since 1975, the United States has experienced balance of trade deficits.

Balance of Trade

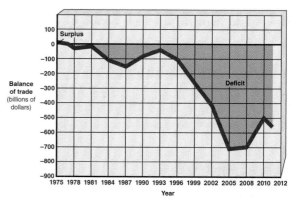

SOURCE: Bureau of Economic Analysis, *International U.S. International Transactions Accounts*, http://www.bea.gov/international/index.htm, Table 1.

- An **exchange rate** is the price of one nation's currency in terms of another nation's currency. Foreigners who wish to purchase U.S. goods, services, and financial assets demand dollars. The supply of dollars reflects the desire of U.S. citizens to purchase foreign goods, services, and financial assets. The intersection of the supply and demand curves for dollars determines the number of units of a foreign currency per dollar.

Exchange Rate

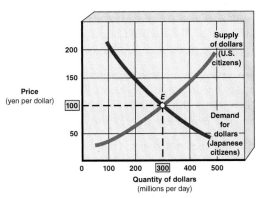

SOURCE: © Cengage Learning 2014

- **Shifts in supply and demand for foreign exchange** result from changes in such factors as tastes, relative price levels, relative real interest rates, and relative income levels.
- **Depreciation of currency** occurs when one currency becomes worth fewer units of another currency. If a currency depreciates, it becomes weaker. Depreciation of a nation's currency increases its exports and decreases its imports.
- **Appreciation of currency** occurs when one currency becomes worth more units of another currency. If a currency appreciates, it becomes stronger. Appreciation of a nation's currency decreases its exports and increases its imports.

Summary of Conclusion Statements

- When countries specialize, total world output increases, and therefore, the potential for greater total world consumption also increases.
- Global trade allows a country to consume a combination of goods that exceeds its production possibilities curve.
- Specialization and trade are based on opportunity costs (comparative advantage) and not on absolute advantage.
- Comparative advantage refers to the relative opportunity costs between different countries of producing the same goods. World output and consumption are maximized when each country specializes in producing and trading goods for which it has a comparative advantage.
- A current account deficit is financed by a capital account surplus.

- An exchange rate can be expressed as a reciprocal.
- An expansion in relative U.S. income causes a depreciation of the dollar.
- A rise in a trading partner's relative price level causes the dollar to appreciate.
- When the dollar is weak, or depreciates, U.S. goods and services cost foreign consumers less, so they buy more U.S. exports. At the same time, a weak dollar means foreign goods and services cost U.S. consumers more, so they buy fewer imports.
- When the dollar is strong, or appreciates, U.S. goods and services cost foreign consumers more, so they buy fewer U.S. exports. At the same time, a strong dollar means foreign goods and services cost U.S. consumers less, so they buy more foreign imports.

Study Questions and Problems

1. The countries of Alpha and Beta produce diamonds and pearls. The production possibilities schedule below describes their potential output in tons per year:

Points on production possibilities curve	Alpha		Beta	
	Diamonds	Pearls	Diamonds	Pearls
A	150	0	90	0
B	100	25	60	60
C	50	50	30	120
D	0	75	0	180

Using the data in the table, answer the following questions:

a. What is the opportunity cost of diamonds for each country?

b. What is the opportunity cost of pearls for each country?

c. In which good does Alpha have a comparative advantage?

d. In which good does Beta have a comparative advantage?

e. Suppose Alpha is producing and consuming at point B on its production possibilities curve and Beta is producing and consuming at point C on its production possibilities curve. Use a table such as Exhibit 3 to explain why both nations would benefit if they specialized.

f. Draw a graph, and use it to explain how Alpha and Beta benefit if they specialize and Alpha agrees to trade 50 tons of diamonds to Beta and Alpha receives 50 tons of pearls in exchange.

2. Bill can paint either two walls or one window frame in one hour. In the same time, Frank can paint either three walls or two window frames. To minimize the time spent painting, who should specialize in painting walls, and who should specialize in painting window frames?

3. Consider this statement: "The principles of specialization and trade according to comparative advantage among nations also apply to states in the United States." Do you agree or disagree? Explain.

4. Would the U.S. government gain any advantage from using tariffs or quotas to restrict imports?

5. Suppose the United States passed a law stating that we would not purchase imports from any country that imposed any trade restrictions on our exports. Who would benefit and who would lose from such retaliation?

6. Now consider question 5 in terms of the law's impact on domestic producers that export goods. Does this policy adversely affect domestic producers that export goods?

7. Consider this statement: "Unrestricted foreign trade costs domestic jobs." Do you agree or disagree? Explain.

8. Do you support a constitutional amendment to prohibit the federal government from imposing any trade barriers, such as tariffs and quotas, except in case of war or national emergency? Why or why not?

9. Discuss this statement: "Because each nation's balance of payments equals zero, it follows that there is actually no significance to a balance of payments deficit or surplus."

10. For each of the following situations, indicate the direction of the shift in the supply curve or the demand curve for dollars, the factor causing the change, and the resulting movement of the equilibrium exchange rate for the dollar in terms of foreign currency:

a. American-made cars become more popular overseas.

b. The United States experiences a recession, while other nations enjoy economic growth.

c. Inflation rates accelerate in the United States, while inflation rates remain constant in other nations.

d. Real interest rates in the United States rise, while real interest rates abroad remain constant.

e. The Japanese put quotas and high tariffs on all imports from the United States.

f. Tourism from the United States increases sharply because of a fare war among airlines.

11. The following table summarizes the supply and the demand for euros:

	U.S. Dollars per Euro				
	$0.05	$0.10	$0.15	$0.20	$0.25
Quantity demanded (per day)	500	400	300	200	100
Quantity supplied (per day)	100	200	300	400	500

Using the above table:
a. Graph the supply and demand curves for euros.
b. Determine the equilibrium exchange rate.
c. Determine what the effect of a fixed exchange rate at $0.10 per euro would be.

For Online Exercises, go to the Tucker Web site at www.cengage.com/economics/tucker.

✓ CHECKPOINT ANSWERS

Do Nations with an Advantage Always Trade?

In the United States, the opportunity cost of producing 1 calculator is 100 towels. In Costa Rica, the opportunity cost of producing 1 calculator is 100 towels. If you said because the opportunity cost is the same for each nation, specialization and trade would not boost total output and therefore Costa Rica would not trade these products, **YOU ARE CORRECT.**

Should Everyone Keep a Balance of Payments?

The principal purpose of the balance of payments is to keep track of payments of national currencies. Because states and cities within the same nation use the same national currency, payments for goods and services traded between these parties do not represent a loss (outflow) or gain (inflow). If you said only nations need to use the balance of payments to account for flows of foreign currency across national boundaries, **YOU ARE CORRECT.**

Sample Quiz

For an explanation of the correct answers, visit the Tucker Web site at www.cengage.com/economics/tucker.

1. The theory of comparative advantage suggests that a (an)
   a. industrialized country should not import.
   b. country that is not competitive should import everything.
   c. country specialize in producing goods or services for which it has a lower opportunity cost.
   d. None of the above answers are correct.

2. Assume the United States can use a given amount of its resources to produce either 20 airplanes or 8 automobiles and Japan can employ the same amount of its resources to

Sample Quiz *continued*

produce either 20 airplanes or 10 automobiles. The United States should specialize in
a. airplanes.
b. automobiles.
c. both goods.
d. neither good.

EXHIBIT 14	Potatoes and Wheat Output (tons per day)	
Country	Potatoes	Wheat
United States	4	2
Ireland	3	1

SOURCE: © Cengage Learning 2014

3. In Exhibit 14, the United States has an absolute advantage in producing
   a. potatoes.
   b. wheat.
   c. both potatoes and wheat.
   d. neither potatoes nor wheat.

4. In Exhibit 14, Ireland's opportunity cost of producing one unit of wheat is
   a. 1/3 ton of potatoes.
   b. 3 tons of potatoes.
   c. either a or b.
   d. neither a nor b.

5. In Exhibit 14, the United States has a comparative advantage in producing
   a. potatoes.
   b. wheat.
   c. both potatoes and wheat.
   d. neither potatoes nor wheat.

6. If each nation in Exhibit 14 specializes in producing the good for which it has a comparative advantage, then
   a. Ireland would produce neither potatoes nor wheat.
   b. the United States would produce both potatoes and wheat.
   c. the United States would produce potatoes.
   d. Ireland would produce potatoes.

7. A tariff is a
   a. tax on an exported product.
   b. limit on the number of goods that can be exported.
   c. limit on the number of goods that can be imported.
   d. tax on an imported product.
   e. subsidy on an imported product.

8. The principal objective of the WTO is to
   a. reduce the level of all tariffs.
   b. establish fair prices for all goods traded internationally.
   c. prevent the trading of services across nations' borders.
   d. encourage countries to establish quotas.

9. Which of the following is *not* an argument used in favor of protectionism?
   a. to protect an "infant" industry
   b. to protect domestic jobs
   c. to preserve national security
   d. to protect against "unfair" competition because of cheap foreign labor
   e. to reduce prices paid by domestic consumers

10. The main explanation for why the cheap foreign labor argument is a poor reason for restricting international trade is that
    a. workers who get paid less tend to have lower productivity than those who get paid more.
    b. all firms and workers gain when there are no restrictions on international trade.
    c. infant industries such as steel and automobiles need to be protected.
    d. specialization and free trade usually raise the prices of all the traded goods, so that the workers can get paid more.

11. The account that records a nation's foreign economic transactions is called the
    a. trade account.
    b. T account.
    c. exchange market.
    d. balance of payments.

12. Expenditures for services such as tourism, income for foreign investment, and foreign gifts are tabulated in the
    a. current account.
    b. capital account.

Sample Quiz *continued*

c. official reserve account.

d. goods account.

13. Suppose a German bank purchases a U.S. Treasury bond. This transaction would be recorded in the
   a. capital account.
   b. current account.
   c. goods trade balance.
   d. unilateral transfers.

14. Exhibit 15 shows a situation in which
   a. both the dollar and the pound have depreciated.
   b. both the dollar and the pound have appreciated.
   c. the dollar has depreciated and the pound has appreciated.
   d. the dollar has appreciated and the pound has depreciated.

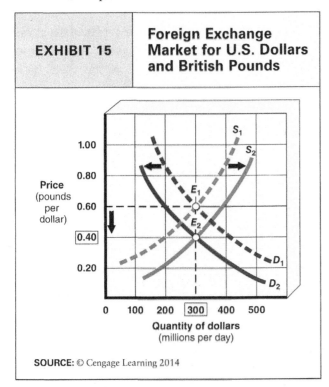

EXHIBIT 15 — **Foreign Exchange Market for U.S. Dollars and British Pounds**

SOURCE: © Cengage Learning 2014

15. Which of the following could cause the dollar-pound exchange rate to change as shown in Exhibit 15?
   a. American goods become more popular in Great Britain.

b. British incomes rise, while U.S. incomes remain unchanged.

c. The U.S. price level rises, while the British price level remains unchanged.

d. The U.S. real interest rate rises, while the British real interest rate remains unchanged.

16. A country that has a lower opportunity cost of producing a good
   a. has a comparative advantage.
   b. can produce the good using fewer resources than another country.
   c. requires fewer labor hours to produce the good.
   d. All of the above answers are correct.

17. If one country can produce a good with fewer resources than another country, this is called
   a. specialization.
   b. geographic advantage.
   c. comparative advantage.
   d. absolute advantage.

18. One big difference between tariffs and quotas is that tariffs
   a. raise the price of a good while quotas lower it.
   b. generate tax revenues while quotas do not.
   c. stimulate international trade while quotas inhibit it.
   d. hurt domestic producers while quotas help them.

19. Which of the following is *not* included in the current account?
   a. exports of goods
   b. imports of goods
   c. U.S. capital inflow and outflow
   d. unilateral transfers

20. A shift of the U.S. demand curve for Mexican pesos to the left and a decrease in the peso price per dollar would result from
   a. an increase in the U.S. inflation rate relative to the rate in Mexico.
   b. a change in U.S. consumers' tastes away from Mexican products and toward products made in South Korea, India, and Taiwan.
   c. U.S. buyers perceiving that domestically-produced products are of a lower quality than products made in Mexico.
   d. All of the above answers are correct.

Globally Free Markets for the Twenty-First Century?

Year after year in Washington, . . . debates seem to come down to an old, tired argument: on one side, those who want more government regardless of the cost; on the other, those who want less government, regardless of the need.

—PRESIDENT GEORGE W. BUSH, ADDRESS OF THE PRESIDENT TO THE JOINT

SESSION OF CONGRESS, FEBRUARY 27, 2001

Well, this quotation is a little bit dated, but it is right on the mark. More government or less government: that has been the debate throughout the last century, as well as throughout this textbook. As we shall see, however, the world has recently embraced a direction decidedly in favor of globally free markets—markets characterized by minimal government involvement. But what about the future?

The title of this chapter ends with a question mark. Although the direction of change has been clear, there is no reason to expect that free markets will work for all countries and all times. There is also no reason to assume that the transition to free markets will go smoothly for all nations or that a return to policies of the past will not occur. Indeed, several countries, especially Latin American ones, have begun to shift to the left. Let's examine the trends.

Markets

Throughout this book, there have been repeated references to demand and supply and the workings of markets in general. There have also been repeated references to government intervention in the economy. The proper role for government versus the proper role for the marketplace has prompted heated discussion among economists and politicians for decades. The respective roles for government and market have been the focal point for the ViewPoint sections throughout this text. In terms of economic philosophy and in U.S. terminology, those who favor a limited role for government are generally referred to as economic conservatives, whereas those who favor a greater role for government are regarded as economic liberals. **The conservative view maintains that free markets are efficient and they provide the proper incentives for economic prosperity and growth to occur.** Market failures are believed to be minimal, and government interference in properly functioning markets can only create inefficiencies and restrict growth. Limiting the government's role as much as possible is best.

This conservative view was evident in the discussion of supply-side policy in Chapter 15. Supply-side economists favor reductions in government regulations, taxes, domestic programs, and transfers. Their view is that the marketplace works efficiently; we must untie the hands of businesses and consumers to enable them to make their own private decisions, and the economy will be better as a result.

Liberals, on the other hand, see the marketplace as imperfect and market failures as serious. In their view, markets are not necessarily equitable, and sometimes not even efficient. Furthermore, society has goals, such as environmental protection, care for the poor and elderly, and economic stabilization, that cannot be met by the marketplace operating freely on its own. Liberals believe that the government must intervene in markets to achieve these goals.

Most economies have some combination of markets and government involvement. Some countries are more heavily capitalist, whereas some are predominantly socialist. Under capitalism, the private sector (individuals and private business) makes economic decisions via the marketplace and owns the means of production (factories, equipment, and land). Under socialism, by contrast, the public sector (the government) makes economic decisions and owns and controls the means of production. Under capitalism, consumers and producers interact through the marketplace, responding to market-determined prices. Under socialism, the government has a more prominent role in determining which goods will be produced, how they will be produced, and what their prices will be.

Keep in mind that capitalism and socialism refer to economic systems. They imply nothing about political systems, such as democracy and communism. Certainly, a socialist economy may exist under either communism (Vietnam) or democracy (Chile); and a capitalist economy may exist under communism (Hong Kong) or democracy (the United States). In this text, we are focusing our attention on economic systems.

The movement toward free markets has been a recent global phenomenon, the direction entailing different circumstances in different parts of the globe. We will consider each of the three major regions of the world in turn. We will define the Western industrialized world as the industrialized capitalist countries of the world, including the United States, Canada, most of Western Europe, and other countries (including Japan) that have achieved high economic performance through predominantly stable market conditions. We will define the formerly socialist industrialized world as the industrialized ex-socialist countries of Eastern Europe. These countries include the former Soviet Union and much of the rest of Eastern and Central Europe. Finally, the less-developed world encompasses all of the less-developed countries (LDCs), including most countries of Africa, Asia, and Latin America. These countries are often referred to as Third World countries.

Capitalism

An economic system wherein the economic decisions are made by the private sector via the marketplace and the means of production are owned by the private sector.

Socialism

An economic system wherein the economic decisions are made by the public (government) sector and the means of production are owned by the public sector.

Western industrialized world

The industrialized capitalist countries of the world.

Formerly socialist industrialized world

The industrialized ex-socialist countries of Eastern and Central Europe.

Less-developed world

The less-developed countries of the world.

One more term should be clarified. Economists often refer to the changes taking place in the formerly socialist and less-developed countries as liberalism (or sometimes neo-liberalism). This term is confusing, because it refers to a movement toward markets with *less* government intervention, rather than the traditional liberal philosophy we have described. Do not confuse the words *liberal* and *liberalism*. The first implies government involvement in the economy; the latter implies change toward free markets.

The Western Industrialized World: Economic Growth

Conservative Republicans controlled the U.S. presidency for the 12 years from 1981 to 1992. And although a Democrat became president in 1993, conservative Republicans took control of both houses of Congress in 1994. A conservative Republican once again took the presidential office in 2001, with an administration that includes conservatives from prior Republican administrations. President George W. Bush's views toward tax policy, education, health care, the environment, Social Security, and government regulation reflect the familiar undercurrent of supply-side economics and a philosophy of free markets with a minimal economic role for government.

This conservative framework has not been unique to the United States. Many of the larger democracies of the Western industrialized world, including Britain, France, and Germany, have taken on a conservative philosophy that has resulted in restricted government involvement in their economies and more focus on free markets. Domestic social programs have declined, and economic growth is driving Western Europe in the new century.

Note that Japan is often included with the Western industrialized countries, despite the fact that it is an eastern (Asian) country.

ECONOMIC GROWTH RATES

Recall that economic growth is defined as a sustained increase in production. One standard measure of economic growth is the annual growth rate of GDP, averaged over a period of several years. (An alternative measure, the growth rate of GDP per capita, was used in Chapter 7.) Table 17-1 displays average annual GDP growth rates for the Western industrialized nations for the time periods 1990–2000 and 2000–2005 (the latest year for which data are available for all countries). As revealed by these data, these growth rates for 2000–2005 range from less than 1 percent to 5 percent per year. In almost all countries, average annual growth rates are slower during the period 2000–2005 than they were over 1990–2000. This is also the case for the United States, with average annual growth rates of 3.5 percent from 1990–2000 and 2.8 percent from 2000–2005. During the more recent time period, the United States has grown faster than most of the Western industrialized world.

The increase in GDP that underlies the growth rates in Table 17-1, on page 408, can be discussed in the framework of aggregate supply (in the short run) and production possibilities (in the long run).

AGGREGATE SUPPLY AND PRODUCTION POSSIBILITIES

Supply-side philosophies are based on the idea that reductions in government regulations, programs, taxes, and transfers create incentives for greater productivity, thereby increasing aggregate supply. This forward shift in the aggregate

---

Liberalism (or neo-liberalism)

A movement toward freer (more capitalist) markets. This is another term for *economic reform* or *economic transition*.

Economic growth

A sustained increase in production, represented by an outward shift of the production possibilities curve. An increase in GDP (or GDP per capita) over an extended time period.

EconNews

"Is More Spending on Infrastructure the Key to Economic Growth?"

The full debate is available under the Productivity and Growth category.

http://econapps.swlearning.com

TABLE 17-1	AVERAGE ANNUAL ECONOMIC GROWTH RATES, WESTERN INDUSTRIALIZED COUNTRIES AND JAPAN, 1990–2000 AND 2000–2005

Country	Average Annual Growth of GDP (%) 1990–2000	Average Annual Growth of GDP (%) 2000–2005
Austria	2.4	1.3
Belgium	2.1	1.5
Canada	3.1	2.6
Denmark	2.5	1.5
Finland	2.6	2.4
France	2.0	1.5
Germany	1.8	0.7
Greece	2.2	4.2
Ireland	7.5	5.0
Italy	1.6	0.7
Japan	1.3	1.3
Netherlands	2.9	0.6
Norway	4.0	1.7
Portugal	2.7	0.3
Spain	2.6	3.1
Sweden	2.2	2.2
Switzerland	1.0	0.9
United Kingdom	2.7	2.3
United States	3.5	2.8

Source: World Bank, *World Development Indicators 2007*, http://www.worldbank.org.

supply curve would be associated with an increase in gross domestic product. Supply-side policies and their effects were discussed in Chapter 15. Figure 17-1 summarizes the desired effects of supply-side policy.

Supply-side policies are intended to increase GDP, but a sustained expansion of GDP requires additional policies that create long-term changes. These fundamental changes can be analyzed in the context of the production possibilities curve discussed in Chapter 1.

Recall that the production possibilities curve shows the alternative combinations of the maximum amounts of output that an economy can produce if all of its resources and technology are fully and efficiently utilized. The economy can achieve higher levels of production if the production possibilities curve shifts outward over time. We have defined economic growth as a sustained expansion of output. The factors that cause this outward shift in production possibilities include an increase in the quantity or quality of society's resources or an improvement in technology. These factors can generate a sustained expansion of output—that is, economic growth.

POLICIES TO ACHIEVE ECONOMIC GROWTH

The production possibilities curve from Chapter 1 is repeated in Figure 17-2. Let's consider four specific examples of the factors contributing to economic growth. These are an increase in capital, an improvement in labor productivity, an improvement in technology, and a decrease in unnecessary regulation. As we examine these dynamics, we can consider government policy with respect to each of them.

FIGURE 17-1	**EFFECTS OF SUPPLY-SIDE POLICY ON THE MACROECONOMY**

Supply-side policy is designed to cause an increase in aggregate supply, as shown by the shift of the aggregate supply curve AS to AS'. The result is an increase in GDP to GDP' and a reduction in the average price level from P to P'.

FIGURE 17-2	**PRODUCTION POSSIBILITIES CURVE WITH ECONOMIC GROWTH**

Points A through F show alternative combinations of bread and roses that the economy can produce. More of both bread and roses can be produced when the production possibilities curve shifts outward as a result of economic growth.

An Increase in Capital

Economic growth can occur if there is a sustained increase in the quantity of physical capital: that is, an increase in our nation's stock of factories, equipment, machinery, and the like. This increase in capital is made possible by an increase in investment, and investment is made possible by saving—either private saving by households and businesses or public saving through government taxes.

Savings rate

Total savings divided by gross domestic product.

High investment activity necessitates a high **savings rate**, which is defined here as total savings divided by total GDP. The current U.S. savings rate is around 15 percent. The U.S. savings rate is tied with Portugal and the United Kingdom as the lowest in the Western industrialized world. Norway, Switzerland, and Japan have the highest savings rates. These savings rates are displayed in Table 17-2. The relatively low rate of the United States concerns many economists.

Some expect the U.S. savings rate to increase in the twenty-first century as the baby-boomer generation grows older, enjoying higher incomes and finishing their payments for houses and education for their children. However, government savings and dissavings will play a role as well. When the government spends less than it brings in through tax revenue, it engages in saving. When it spends more than its tax revenue, it engages in dissaving. The temporary spate of budget surpluses at the turn of the century encouraged those who sought a higher U.S. savings rate. However, the more recent major tax cuts of the Bush administration, coupled with greatly increased expenditures on the military, imply continued government dissaving for the foreseeable future.

Numerous efforts and proposals have been made to increase the national savings rate through supply-side policy. These efforts and proposals have been

TABLE 17-2	SAVINGS RATES FOR THE WESTERN INDUSTRIALIZED COUNTRIES,* 2004	
	Country	**Savings Rate**
	Austria	24%
	Belgium	24%
	Canada	23%
	Denmark	23%
	Finland	24%
	France	19%
	Germany	21%
	Greece	18%
	Ireland	23%
	Italy	19%
	Japan	27%
	Netherlands	23%
	Norway	33%
	Portugal	15%
	Spain	23%
	Sweden	24%
	Switzerland	29%
	United Kingdom	15%
	United States	15%

*Calculated as total savings divided by GDP.

Source: World Bank, *World Development Indicators 2006,* http://www.worldbank.org.

aimed at increasing incentives for households and businesses to save and invest. The 1981 tax law accelerated tax write-offs for new investment by businesses, greatly reducing corporate income taxes. The 1981 and subsequent tax laws provided tax breaks to households placing income into individual retirement accounts (IRAs) and 401(k) accounts. The capital gains tax has been reduced. As discussed in Chapter 16 on taxes, a **capital gain** is the net income earned when one sells an asset at a higher price than was paid for the asset. Taxes on dividends, received by shareholders, have also been reduced. The latter two tax cuts have been very controversial because while the Bush administration states that the cuts contribute to economic growth, the vast majority of the tax benefits accrue to the wealthiest Americans, the ones who are more likely to have these types of investment income.

Finally, there have been repeated proposals for a **consumption tax** to replace our current personal income tax. Like a national sales tax, a consumption tax taxes only the share of household income that is spent on consumer goods and services; it does not tax the portion of income that is saved. Although the goal is to provide greater incentives for saving, this tax would place the greatest burden on low-income individuals, who by necessity must spend virtually all of their incomes on consumption. This would represent a very regressive tax (recall that the definition of a regressive tax is one that takes a larger percent of income from lower-income people).

If these types of policies prove successful in increasing savings, we would expect to see an expansion in investment in our nation's stock of physical capital. The expansion of our nation's factories, equipment, and machinery would result in an expansion of gross domestic product—that is, in economic growth.

Although most of the conservative emphasis has been on providing incentives for increased private saving and investment, liberal interest in increasing government investment should not be overlooked. The government can play an important role by investing in highways and mass transit, as well as schools and health care facilities. Since all of these forms of investment can improve the business environment, as well as the productivity of workers, they can enhance both the physical and human capital of our nation.

An Improvement in Labor Productivity

Labor productivity is defined as total output per average work hour, calculated as gross domestic product divided by the number of work hours performed in the economy. Annual U.S. labor productivity growth, which lagged in the 1970s and 1980s, has now increased to much higher levels. For example, U.S. value added per worker in manufacturing was $47,276 in the early 1980s, but $81,353 in the last decade.[1] **Labor productivity hinges on the type and amount of capital and technology used in conjunction with labor, and these, of course, have improved in recent years.** Keep in mind, however, that labor productivity also depends on human capital. Human capital includes the skills and abilities of people. Once again, government support for training programs, education, health, and nutrition all remain important for ensuring high levels of human capital.

An Improvement in Technology

Technology can be thought of as ways of using available resources to produce output. Improvements in technology enable us to produce more output, given our limited resources. These improvements are embodied in new and more efficient machines, new products, and new methods of production.

Capital gains

The net income received when an asset is bought at a particular price and sold at a higher price.

Consumption tax

A hypothetical tax on the portion of income that is spent on consumer goods and services, as opposed to income that goes into savings.

EconNews

"Working Longer and Harder"

Find out which country is the most productive by reading this article under the Labor Markets category.

http://econapps. swlearning.com

Labor productivity

Total output per average work hour, calculated as GDP divided by the number of work hours.

Technology

Ways of using available resources to produce output.

Technological advance depends on research and development (R&D). Some 4,484 scientists and engineers are engaged in R&D per each million people in the United States, placing it seventh among the countries of the world. Finland has the highest number of researchers, with 7,992 for each million people in the country. The numbers for the top seven countries are shown in Table 17-3.

Government policies can again be used to encourage research and development. The government can increase university funding available for research and offer tax breaks for businesses that engage in research and development. The government can also provide patent protection to developers of new products. A **patent** is a government grant of exclusive rights to use or sell a new technology for a period of time. Without patents, other businesses might copy the new technology or product, thereby creating profits for themselves at the expense of the developer. Without patents, businesses have little incentive to develop new products. Patents have been extremely important in areas such as pharmaceuticals, communications technology, and consumer goods. Recently, patent applications filed by U.S. residents exceeded 200,000 per year. In comparison, Japan has over 371,000 patent applications per year.

Nowhere has technological advance been more prominent than in the area of computers. Indeed, investment in information technology, including computers, software, communications networks, and Internet infrastructure, has contributed to a large share of economic growth in recent years. Table 17-4 shows data for many of the top countries in terms of number of personal computers (PCs) and Internet users. We see that surprisingly (as least to your author) Estonia in Eastern Europe has the highest number of PCs per 1,000 population (921). The United States has the fifth largest number of personal computers per 1,000 population (749). New Zealand has the largest number of Internet users per 1,000 population (788). The United States ranks sixth in terms of Internet users per 1,000 people (630). Computer technology helps businesses in the United States and other countries to produce more and better products at the same or lower costs of production. It has also been a major factor in improving labor productivity.

A Decrease in Regulation

The government regulates business in a variety of ways, including protections for consumers of pharmaceuticals, food, and manufactured goods; safeguards for workers in industry; and protection of the environment. In light of recent

Patent

A government grant of exclusive rights to use or sell a new technology or product for a period of time.

TABLE 17-3	NUMBER OF RESEARCHERS IN RESEARCH AND DEVELOPMENT (PER MILLION POPULATION), TOP SEVEN COUNTRIES IN ORDER, 1996 TO 2004*	
Country		**Researchers per Million Population**
Finland		7,992
Sweden		5,416
Japan		5,287
Denmark		5,016
Singapore		4,745
Norway		4,587
United States		4,484

*Most recent available year.
Source: World Bank, *World Development Indicators 2006,* http://www.worldbank.org.

TABLE 17-4	NUMBER OF PERSONAL COMPUTERS AND NUMBER OF INTERNET USERS (PER THOUSAND POPULATION), 2004	
Country	PCs	Internet Users
Australia	682	646
Canada	700	626
Denmark	656	696
Estonia	921	497
Finland	481	629
Israel	741	471
Netherlands	682	614
New Zealand	474	788
North Korea	545	657
Singapore	763	571
Sweden	763	756
Switzerland	826	474
United Kingdom	599	628
United States	749	630

Source: World Bank, *World Development Indicators 2006,* http://www.worldbank.org.

deaths caused by unsafe tires and certain pharmaceutical drugs, the necessity for wisely developed government regulations is clear. On the other hand, unwise and unnecessary regulation merely increases business costs and decreases output. Therefore, cutting unwise regulation is a desirable policy and is conducive to economic growth. The problem, of course, is recognizing which regulations are harmful and which are beneficial.

Generally speaking, economic conservatives prefer less government regulation, whereas economic liberals prefer more. The supply-side policies since the early 1980s include widespread cuts in government regulations. Environmental protection is a good case in point. President Ronald Reagan and President George H. W. Bush greatly reduced government regulations in this area. Many of President Bill Clinton's proposed regulations met a hostile Congress and were not passed. President George W. Bush has continued the trend toward less environmental regulation and a more industry friendly environmental policy. Although this policy may provide some short-run benefit to the economy through a reduction in the compliance costs of business and a resulting increase in aggregate supply, the long-run costs might outweigh this benefit. Just as an increase in productive resources will shift the production possibilities curve outward over time, a decrease in our natural resources caused by environmental damage and resource depletion will shift the curve inward. The capacity of our nation to produce and grow will be compromised, and the quality of life of our citizens will decline.

As suggested in Chapter 3 on the environment, environmental protection is a global necessity. Deforestation and the burning of fossil fuels contribute to global warming and loss of precious biodiversity. Acid rain destroys crops, waterways, and capital structures across countries. Use of certain chemicals destroys the ozone layer. Air and water pollution know no boundaries.

In the final days of his administration, President Clinton considered but ultimately decided against an executive order that would have protected nearly 60 million acres of U.S. forested area by prohibiting oil exploration in Alaska's

Arctic National Wildlife Refuge. President George W. Bush's plan for oil exploration in this refuge was a central part of his energy policy. Similarly, President Bush refused to sign the 1997 Kyoto Accord, approved by President Clinton, which forces industrial nations to reduce greenhouse gases. This treaty is seen as critical to reducing the problem of global warming and is discussed in more detail in Chapter 3 on the environment. Other global environmental issues are discussed in that chapter as well.

IMPLICATIONS OF GROWTH FOR THE TWENTY-FIRST CENTURY

The market-oriented growth policies of the Western industrialized world are likely to persist for at least the near future. However, there may be a cyclical movement of philosophy from a restricted government role to an expanded government role and back again, as dissatisfaction with the drawbacks of either extreme becomes evident. In the United States, post-World War II economic growth did little to mitigate extremely high poverty rates. The war on poverty and the civil rights movement of the 1960s addressed the needs of the population to which the prosperity of the 1950s did not trickle down. Yet, the policies of the 1960s and 1970s brought forth a conservative backlash as many politicians (and Supreme Court justices) in the 1980s, 1990s, and early 2000s sought to reverse years of affirmative action and antipoverty policies. In the twenty-first century, concern for the people left behind from the prosperity of worldwide economic growth may well again precipitate a greater call for government response.

The Formerly Socialist Industrialized World: Economic Transition

The recent changes in Eastern Europe are nothing short of revolutionary. The Cold War ended. Germany is reunified, and the Berlin Wall is down. The Soviet Union no longer exists; it has been divided into some 16 independent nations (the largest of which is Russia). And finally, the former socialist economies of Eastern and Central Europe are now undergoing an economic transition toward capitalism.

Economic transition

A shift in policies and institutions that move economies from socialism toward capitalism.

This transition has achieved varied levels of success, as evidenced by diverse economic growth rates. Table 17-5 displays the variation in growth rates for countries of the formerly socialist industrialized world over the period 1990–2000 and 2000–2005. These growth rates are fascinating! First, about two-thirds of the average annual growth rates for the time period 1990–2000 are negative. This means that GDP declined on average each year during the time period. Nevertheless, all of these growth rates turned positive over the time period 2000–2005. Sometimes, the reversal is incredible. For example, Tajikistan had the largest negative growth rate (–10.4%) from 1990–2000, but close to the highest average annual growth rate (9.7 percent) over 2000–2005! Other countries with very high growth rates from 2000–2005 include Armenia, Azerbaijan, Kazakhstan, the Ukraine, and Estonia. (Recall the high number of PCs in Estonia—this has likely played an important role.) Russia's negative average annual growth rate from 1990–2000 (–4.7%) reversed to a positive rate in 2000–2005 (6.2%). **Note that the reversal from negative to positive growth rates for the formerly socialist industrialized countries is in stark contrast to the Western industrialized countries, which generally had lower growth rates in the more recent time period.**

TABLE 17-5	AVERAGE ANNUAL ECONOMIC GROWTH RATES, FORMERLY SOCIALIST INDUSTRIALIZED COUNTRIES, 1990–2000 AND 2000–2005

Country	Average Annual Growth of GDP (%), 1990–2000	Average Annual Growth of GDP (%), 2000–2005
Albania	3.5	5.3
Armenia	−1.9	12.3
Azerbaijan	−6.3	12.7
Belarus	−1.7	7.6
Bosnia & Herzegovina	N/A[a]	5.1
Bulgaria	−1.8	5.0
Croatia	0.6	4.4
Czech Republic	1.1	3.5
Estonia	0.2	7.0[b]
Georgia	−7.2	7.4
Hungary	1.6	4.0
Kazakhstan	−4.1	10.1
Kyrgyzstan	−4.1	4.0
Latvia	−1.6	7.9
Lithuania	−2.7	7.8
Macedonia	−0.8	1.7
Moldova	−9.6	7.0
Poland	4.6	3.1
Romania	−0.6	5.8
Russia	−4.7	6.2
Serbia & Montenegro[c]	1.5	5.3
Slovak Republic	1.9	4.9
Slovenia	2.7	3.4
Tajikistan	−10.4	9.7
Turkmenistan	−4.8	N/A
Ukraine	−9.3	8.0
Uzbekistan	−0.2	5.3

[a]N/A = Not available.
[b]2000–2004
[c]At the time of publication, Montenegro had just voted to form a country separate from Serbia.
Source: World Bank, *World Development Indicators 2007*, http://www.worldbank.org.

The most prominent elements of the transition to capitalism have been the movement toward market-determined prices and the process of privatization, as well as the development of entrepreneurship. Russia has experienced some of the difficulties inherent in the transition process. Nevertheless, in terms of entrepreneurship, there is no question that everyday Russian citizens have embraced entrepreneurial activities; whether in the form of kiosks lining the streets of Moscow's famous Arbat and metro stops, babushkas selling homemade fast foods and household articles at every metro stop, teenagers selling gasoline along highways near the long lines at gas stations, professionals moonlighting as translators and drivers, and residents seeking Western partners in Russian joint ventures.[2] Problems in Russia have been more evident in the areas of prices and privatization.

MARKET-DETERMINED PRICES

Recall the efficiencies associated with market-determined prices. Demand and supply equate so that shortages and surpluses are eliminated. (It is when the government intervenes by setting rental ceilings in housing or price supports in agriculture, for example, that we end up with shortages or surpluses.) In a free market, the high prices of scarce goods encourage consumers to be frugal in their use of the goods and encourage suppliers to expand production of the goods. Shortages do not result. On the other hand, the low prices of plentiful goods encourage consumers to use the goods more extensively and encourage suppliers to produce fewer of these goods and shift production away from these goods and toward a greater number of goods more desirable to consumers. Surpluses are thus prevented.

Under pure socialism, the government sets the prices of goods and services. Prices had traditionally been set artificially low in the socialist economies of Eastern Europe. For example, consumers had been able to afford basic items of food, clothing, and gasoline. **Artificially low prices operate like price ceilings, however, and shortages are the result.** So, although people could afford to purchase needed items, these goods were often unavailable in stores. People would expend considerable time and energy standing in long lines and leaving their jobs to rush to stores whenever new supplies arrived.

These shortages are largely relics of the past. Prices of most items have been allowed to rise to market-determined levels in most Eastern European countries. In other words, decontrol of prices has occurred. Governments no longer set prices. However, because wages have not always risen as rapidly as prices, the purchasing power of consumers has declined. Supplies are now plentiful, but many people cannot afford the goods. **Inflation is always a short run effect of extensive price decontrol.**

Decontrol of prices

Removal of government controls on prices.

Price decontrol in Russia was abrupt. Within days, prices on 80 to 90 percent of wholesale and retail goods were decontrolled.[3] The rise in prices of so many goods and services naturally caused a sudden rise in the average price level. The inflation rate soared, peaking at approximately 1,353 percent per year at the height of price decontrol in 1992. Inflation has since subsided but is still considered to be a serious problem. (The average annual inflation rate over 1990–2000 was 72 percent and 17 percent over 2000–2005. This is still high, but no way near the problem it was previously.)

PRIVATIZATION

Privatization

The transfer of government-owned enterprises or responsibilities to the private sector.

Privatization refers to the sale of government enterprises to the private sector. Throughout Eastern Europe, governments have owned everything from industry and businesses to agricultural land, energy facilities, agricultural marketing boards, and transportation networks. The process of privatization presumes that private ownership of the means of production enhances efficiency and growth.

Once again, Russia presents an interesting example of this process of privatization. The Russian privatization program started in April 1992 with the sale of municipally owned shops. At the same time, the government began the process whereby state and collective farms converted to private ownership. In June, the government began to convert large- and medium-sized firms into shareholding companies (meaning that individuals may own shares in the company). Finally, in October the government began to issue to all Russian citizens a voucher that can be used to purchase shares in such companies.[4] (Your author even managed to purchase a voucher, a "piece of Russia," in a secondary market to a secondary market—that is, a hallway outside of an auction site.)

The Russian privatization program has not been without difficulty. First, different elements of the Russian government have disagreed greatly over the pace of privatization. Second, small businesses, mostly shops and services, have been sold off more rapidly than larger enterprises. The largest enterprises are far more difficult to privatize. Third, machinery and equipment in many Russian enterprises were outmoded and in poor repair. Productivity in these enterprises was very low. As privatized businesses became more profit oriented, and as government subsidies to these businesses declined, many firms went bankrupt, resulting in worker layoffs. **Unemployment is always a short run result of extensive privatization.** Fourth, Russian enterprises tended to be monopolies. Before the transition, Soviet planners had categorized industry into 7,664 "product groups." Of these product groups, 77 percent were produced by single firms.[5] Even as these government-owned monopolies became privatized, there remained the problems associated with monopoly that were discussed in Chapter 11. Finally, nearly 15 percent of Russia's industries were defense related. Since the end of the Cold War, Russian demand for defense-related products has been low.[6] All of this suggests that Russia will continue to face hurdles in the forms of privatization, demonopolization, and defense conversion. Despite all this, Russia has now successfully established many small- and median-sized private firms. With over 8.5 million such firms, Russia has more than any other country except China and Indonesia.

EFFECTS OF THE TRANSITION

The objectives of the transition from socialism to capitalism throughout the formerly socialist industrialized world are greater efficiency and growth. But this transition has posed many problems for people. Inflation has made it difficult for consumers to afford basic necessities. Farmers have been hard hit by increases in the prices of inputs such as fertilizer, and the prices that they receive for their food products often still remain artificially low. Workers have been laid off in defense industries, government jobs, and privatized businesses, and other workers frequently have not been paid. Corruption is often widespread, and organized crime is sometimes rampant. Whereas many people have struggled to make do in light of these difficulties, others have profited from liberalization, creating blatant inequality. Alcoholism and suicide rates in some countries have been rising, and life expectancies have even declined. A quotation from a young Russian woman studying in the United States summarizes some of these difficulties.

> The situation in Russia is very difficult for the ordinary citizen. My father recently lost his government job, though he was soon hired into a different job. My mother, who works at a bank, did not lose her job but she was not paid for seven months. Imagine, a bank with all that money, and my mother not being paid! Lost jobs and non-payment of wages are common. People get by by moonlighting. Old women beg or sell homemade food, used clothing, or anything that anyone will buy. Pensions are often very small, as low as $30 per month or less. This will buy maybe a loaf of bread and a bottle of milk each day, plus a little bit of meat each week. With wages falling behind prices, it now takes about seven days of work at a typical wage to purchase a tube of mascara, and two months of work to purchase a good pair of shoes. Twenty rubles will buy a bottle of bad vodka. Many people drink. In the meanwhile, middle-aged men flaunt their wealth and drive their Mercedes, Audis, and BMWs. It is easy to recognize the Mafia.[7]

THE TWENTY-FIRST CENTURY?

The twenty-first century is a question mark. Although policies of liberalization will undoubtedly continue, the struggles and dissatisfactions of ordinary people may slow down or change the nature of the transition. In some countries, the transition may even be reversed. In Russia, the rise in power of politicians who wish to return to the policies of the past exemplifies the dissatisfaction of people with the current political and economic situation. Opinion polls show that large shares of the population wish to return to the "old days," when they were provided with housing, jobs, child care, and health care. In other formerly socialist countries, some policies of liberalization have been reversed and some socialist-leaning politicians have been elected. In still other Eastern European countries, significant minorities favor the return to socialist economies.

One of the critical issues in the transition to freer-market economies in Eastern and Central Europe is a safety net for people. Under socialism, governments had guaranteed jobs, housing, child care, and medical coverage for all citizens. As ordinary citizens now experience a loss of jobs and purchasing power, governments must ensure that people's basic needs are met. Otherwise, the transition will proceed neither smoothly nor successfully.

Safety net

Government programs, such as housing, nutrition, and health care, to maintain the well-being of people.

The Less-Developed World: Economic Reform

Much of the less-developed world is undergoing a process referred to as economic reform. This means that developing countries are adopting policies that move their economies toward freer markets; or to use another word, they are engaged in liberalism. The economic growth rates reported in Chapter 7 indicate much variation in the success of less-developed countries in increasing GDP per capita. The economic reforms predominant in the 1990s and 2000s have their roots in the international debt crisis of the 1980s. And that crisis has its roots in the world economic conditions of the 1970s.

Economic reform

Change in policies and institutions that moves economies to freer (more capitalist) markets.

THE 1970s: OIL CRISIS

The most significant economic events of the 1970s revolved around oil: the restriction of oil supplies by the Organization of Petroleum Exporting Countries (OPEC), the Arab oil embargo in 1973–1974, and the Iranian Revolution in 1979. These events restricted oil supplies to the West and sent world oil prices skyrocketing. The OPEC countries; including several countries in the Middle East; as well as Nigeria, Libya, Algeria, and Gabon in Africa; Venezuela and Ecuador in South America; and Indonesia in Southeast Asia; received massive increases in their *earnings* from oil exports. However, the non-oil-exporting countries, including most less-developed countries (LDCs), suffered huge increases in their *spending* for oil imports. The effects of the oil shocks were threefold.

First, the OPEC nations began a process of "recycling" their oil revenue; that is, they deposited much of their oil revenue in U.S. and European financial institutions. These petrodollars (so named because petroleum prices are denominated in dollars) greatly enhanced the lending capacity of these Western commercial banks and other financial institutions. Second, many less-developed countries began to borrow heavily. The non-oil-exporting LDCs borrowed to finance their oil imports; while several of the oil-exporting LDCs, such as Mexico, borrowed to develop their oil sectors and diversify their economies. Some LDCs borrowed in order to finance economic development, while others had other purposes in mind (as we shall see). At the time, the cost of borrowing was low because interest rates were low and the lending capacity of the Western financial institutions was high.

Petrodollars

Money earned from the sale of petroleum. (Petroleum prices are denominated in dollars.)

Commercial banks were quite willing and able to lend. Third and finally, the rising oil prices of the decade triggered worldwide inflation. (This was described as an example of cost-push inflation in Chapter 15.) This inflation set the stage for the events of the 1980s.

THE 1980s: DEBT CRISIS

The 1980s began with great concern in the United States over the inflation that was largely generated by the escalating oil prices. In 1981, the Federal Reserve engaged in **contractionary monetary policy** (recall the discussion in Chapter 15 on macro policy in the early 1980s). The consequences of this were several. (1) Inflation was brought under control, but at the expense of skyrocketing interest rates and consequent U.S. recession that later spread worldwide. (2) Rising interest rates meant that interest payments by LDC borrowers increased as well. (3) Rising interest rates in the United States had a secondary effect of pushing up the value of the dollar. The rising dollar made LDC payments for oil imports even more difficult because oil is valued in dollars. It also made repaying predominantly dollar-denominated debt more difficult for the LDCs. Less-developed-country **international debt** was now a full-blown crisis.

By 1988, the less-developed countries had borrowed more than a trillion dollars, and the amount was increasing. They borrowed for a variety of reasons, including those related to the oil market, which we've noted. Many LDCs also borrowed for other laudable purposes, including investment in infrastructure and industry and development of agricultural and export sectors. In many LDCs, however, borrowed funds were grossly misused. Banks had so much lending capacity that they neglected to take adequate care in who they lent to and for what purpose. Countless stories tell of funds that were squandered on grandiose but inefficient government projects, on luxury goods for the rich, and on the coffers of wealthy businesspeople and government officials. For example, Tyler Bridges, then a writer for the *Washington Post*, examined Venezuela's use of borrowed funds in the mid-1980s. He wrote:

> I discovered that the government hadn't kept track of where the money had gone, though various sources indicated that only a portion of the money was invested in projects fostering long-term growth. . . . [In one example,] thanks in part to a presidential decree requiring that every public bathroom and elevator have an attendant, public-sector employment tripled from 1974–1984.[8]

Another problem was that of capital flight. **Capital flight** is a process whereby borrowed funds are reinvested in financial markets or real estate abroad. Corrupt government officials or businesspeople with access to borrowed funds often invested these funds overseas, rather than using them for local projects. Capital flowed outward, profits and interest earnings accrued to wealthy investors, and LDCs failed to benefit from the borrowed money. When governments fail to invest borrowed funds productively, this naturally hampers the ability of borrowing countries to repay their debt. As an analogy, when you borrow money to finance your education, you are making yourself more productive (recall the discussion of an investment in human capital), and this means that you will eventually earn more money with which to repay your loan. When borrowed funds are used unproductively, the ability to repay becomes tenuous. In the case of LDC borrowing, the fault may lie with an inefficient or corrupt government, but it is the residents of the borrowing countries who then bear the burden of the debt.

The enormous burden of the debt becomes clear when we carefully consider the process by which a country tries to pay off its debt. First, the amount of money

Contractionary monetary policy

Reductions in the nation's money supply that serve to raise interest rates and reduce aggregate demand.

International debt

The amount of money owed by one country to a foreign country or institution.

Capital flight

A process whereby less-developed (or other) countries invest funds in foreign countries.

that must be paid on the debt each year (interest payment plus repayment of principal) may represent a very large expenditure. Since the income of LDCs is generally low, the demands on this limited income represent a bewildering array of choices in a typical low-income country trying desperately to develop. Large expenditures must go to satisfying the basic consumption needs of people: food, shelter, and medical care. Government expenditures are also necessary for a variety of social services, public education, and infrastructure. With a population at the margin of subsistence and with a driving need for development, any expenditures diverted toward repaying the debt will directly harm the well-being of people. This state of affairs explains a commonly made observation: "In poor countries, the debt crisis has a child's face." **The reallocation of spending toward repaying the debt has harmed the well-being of people, the most vulnerable of whom are typically the very young.**

In addition to finding money to repay the debt, there is the problem of the form that this money must take. **Debt repayment must be made in the form of the currency initially borrowed; thus, repayment must typically be in U.S. dollars or in the currency of other major countries.** We'll refer to this currency as "hard currency," meaning that it is widely accepted throughout the world. LDCs have very limited means of obtaining hard currency with which to make their payments. They may earn foreign currency through their exports to other countries. Typically, these export earnings are very limited, and they declined for many LDCs over the 1980s as a consequence of the U.S. and worldwide recession. (Do you recall the problem of LDC declining terms of trade discussed in Chapter 7?) A country may also acquire foreign currency through foreign investment by other countries and through international assistance. A final option, and one that has been increasingly chosen by LDC governments, is to continually borrow to repay past debts. Obviously, the latter results in a vicious cycle of continuous borrowing in which LDCs have little hope of becoming debt free.

In a country with limited opportunity to earn hard currency, such currency must be carefully spent. When that currency must be used for debt repayment, it cannot be used for other important activities such as the purchase of foreign capital or technology or the import of important food and energy products. Yet, perhaps the most dire implications of debt repayment take place in the long term. Countries that are desperate for hard currency earnings to repay their debt will undertake overall development policies that are quite different from the ones they might otherwise undertake. **Countries under pressure to acquire export earnings may feel forced to expand patterns of export cropping that can worsen the income distribution, use up limited resources, harm food security, and cause environmental problems.** They may succumb to pressures to encourage indiscriminate foreign investment that may not be the most conducive to their overall development objectives. They may emphasize industrial over agricultural sector development. Under more ideal conditions, a country might well pursue very different, and more beneficial, paths to development. (These were discussed in more detail in Chapter 7.)

THE 1990s: ECONOMIC REFORM

The final phase of the debt crisis occurred as many countries were forced by their inability to meet payment schedules to seek financial assistance from the International Monetary Fund (IMF). IMF assistance is helpful, but it has typically involved conditionality, forcing countries to undertake the economic reforms referred to earlier (often called "austerity measures") as a condition for assistance.

International Monetary Fund (IMF)

An international organization, largely funded by Western industrialized countries, that provides conditional loans and financial assistance to needy countries.

Conditionality

The obligation to meet certain requirements in exchange for financial assistance.

In other words, there were "strings attached" to the assistance. These reforms include requirements that governments reduce their spending and privatize government enterprises. Governments are also required to allow food and other prices to rise to market levels and to reduce their controls on foreign trade and investment. In other words, they must move toward freer markets, reducing the government's role in the economy and allowing the market to determine prices. Some countries have voluntarily adopted economic reforms, but most others have had these reforms imposed on them. Some of these reforms have created tremendous hardship for governments and residents alike. One African leader expressed his frustration this way:

> *You do not talk of "austerity" to a [person] who has not tasted food for days, who can conceive of no more ecstatic pleasure than to have a few drops of water to wet his [or her] lips and tongue. . . . Enforced increases in food prices are meaningless mutterings to the mother brushing the flies off her baby's eyes, watching [the child] starve to death by the minute because there is no food or milk or water.*[9]

THE TWENTY-FIRST CENTURY?

Less-developed countries have had mixed reactions to economic reforms. In many countries, such as Nigeria and other African countries, privatization has resulted in massive layoffs of public-sector employees. The private sector has not yet been able to restore employment adequately in these countries. In other countries as diverse as Kenya, Indonesia, and Mexico, rising food prices were met with riots or demonstrations by urban consumers. In still other countries such as Chile, economic reforms have created rapid economic growth and national prosperity despite the fact that large segments of the population have remained abysmally poor. **One thing that is clear is that less developed countries undergoing economic reform, just as formerly socialist industrialized countries undergoing economic transition, need a safety net to protect those citizens harmed by the changing economy.**

Many third world residents are rejecting the notion that economic reform, along with capitalism and a market-based economy, will ultimately benefit the poor. They are turning toward modified versions of socialism in reaction to the failures of conservative economic policy. This is especially true in Latin America, where many socialist presidents have recently been elected (often with overwhelming victories). Some examples are Chile, Bolivia, Ecuador, Brazil, Nicaragua, and Venezuela. The Bush administration has vigorously opposed President Hugo Chavez of Venezuela, despite the fact that the United States imports much of its oil from Venezuela. As Chavez began his new six-year term as president in 2006, he pledged to nationalize (take government ownership of) companies in the telecommunications and electricity industries. Bolivia has very recently nationalized its petroleum and natural gas sector, and Chile has pledged itself to be an alternative economic model for the third world. The newly elected president of Ecuador, Rafael Correa, vowed to put Ecuador's poor ahead of foreign debt payments as he was sworn into power in January 2007. In all of these cases, however, it is important to keep in mind that the shift has not been to *pure* socialism, with complete government control over the economy. Most property has remained in the hands of the private sector and most prices remain market determined.

Mexico provides a very interesting example. After approximately 70 years of rule by the moderate to conservative PRI party, the citizens of Mexico elected the conservative PAN party's candidate Vicente Fox for the presidency in 2000. (The three major political parties in Mexico are usually referred to by their initials.) In 2006, residents went again to the polls, giving a very narrow victory to the new PAN party candidate, Felipe Calderon. (He won by less than 150,000 votes, which was approximately one-half of 1 percent of the total vote.) His socialist rival, Manuel Lopez Obrador, claimed that the vote count was dishonest and called for massive demonstrations. As this text goes to press, most Mexicans seem to accept the election of Calderon, though the elections have certainly raised the aspirations of both liberal and conservative Mexicans alike.

Once again, in all of these examples, it is important to keep in mind that we are seeing neither a total shift to socialism nor a total shift to capitalism. Just as countries such as Vietnam and Cuba are adopting aspects of capitalism in the context of socialist economies, countries such as Chile and Venezuela are adopting aspects of socialism in the context of capitalist economies. In other words, the world is neither moving toward pure capitalism nor pure socialism, but rather somewhere in-between. While this may be reassuring to some, it still remains to be seen how the less-developed countries and the formerly socialist industrialized countries (as well as the Western industrialized countries, for that matter) will react to the failures of capitalism and socialism. Will they push forward with even more conservative policies, hoping that benefits will trickle down to the poor? Or will they react like the Latin American examples and seek policies to soften, or even nullify, the market-oriented policies of economic transition and reform? Just as the title to this chapter ends with a question mark, so too does this final paragraph.

ViewPoint

CONSERVATIVE VERSUS LIBERAL

This chapter has examined a conservative movement throughout the world toward capitalism and globally freer markets. Economists vary in their views of this movement. Market economies often lead to efficiency and growth, but issues of equity may be neglected. If this is the case, and if governments fail to provide adequate programs for the poor and the unemployed, the benefits of a market economy will fail to trickle down to the needy. In the new millennium, the disparity between the rich and the poor may become greater. Liberals tend to be more concerned than conservatives about this equity issue.

On the other hand, if socialist interventions go so far as to reduce the usefulness of the price system and the incentives of the marketplace, economies may stagnate and fail to grow.

Conservatives tend to be more concerned than liberals about these issues of incentives and efficiency.

The ideal economy will seek a balance between conservative and liberal. After all, the efficiencies of the marketplace mean little if shares of the population fail to benefit from them. Similarly, the equity achieved by more socialist economies cannot provide maximum benefits if inefficiencies prevent economic growth and productivity.

Just where is the balance between conservative and liberal? You have studied this contrast throughout the course, whether the issue is agriculture, housing, health care, or the environment. You now have the information and insight you need to analyze this issue by yourself and to come to the policy conclusions that make sense to you.

Summary

The Western industrialized world, the formerly socialist industrialized world, and the less-developed world have all embarked on a movement toward freer markets for their economies. Much of the Western industrialized world has embraced conservative economic policies in the hope of generating economic growth. Most formerly socialist industrialized countries are experiencing a revolutionary transition from socialism to capitalism. And finally, large numbers of less-developed countries have adopted economic reform policies, voluntarily or involuntarily, that are designed to make their economies more market oriented. Both socialism and capitalism have their successes and failures, and the long-term outcomes of these economic systems remain to be seen.

Discussion and Action Questions

1. Are you an economic liberal or conservative? What is your view of government social programs, taxes, and regulation of business?

2. Consider the U.S. supply-side policies and proposals of the 2000s, such as reductions in taxes and environmental regulations. Do you expect these policies to achieve efficiency and economic growth? Do you expect the benefits of these policies to trickle down to all?

3. What do you think about some of the specific conservative tax policies and proposals, such as replacing the personal income tax with a consumption tax and reducing the capital gains and dividends tax? Do you think these would be effective in creating economic growth? How do you feel about the effect they would have on U.S. income distribution?

4. How might the U.S. government encourage greater research and development? How would R&D benefit the economy?

5. Suppose that the government of a formerly socialist country decontrols prices and permits them to rise to market levels. How can the government assist low-income consumers who might be unable to afford higher food and other prices?

6. Assume that the process of privatization continues successfully in Russia. Would all the problems of Russian industry by solved? What other policies may be necessary?

7. Use the Central Intelligence Agency (CIA) *World Factbook* at http://www.cia.gov/cia/publications/factbook/index.html to look up the current economic situation in any one of the formerly socialist industrialized countries. Has GDP been increasing or decreasing? How high is the inflation rate? How do some of the standards of living (life expectancy, infant mortality rate, and so on) compare with those presented in Chapter 7 for less-developed countries?

8. How have international conditions outside the control of less-developed countries exacerbated the problem of international debt? Do you believe it is right for the IMF to stipulate conditions when providing financial assistance to debt-ridden less-developed countries?

9. Go to the International Monetary Fund (IMF) Web site at http://www.imfsite.org. It provides links to countless statistics, reports, and other global information, including the transformation of countries to capitalism.

10. Go again to the International Monetary Fund (IMF) Web site (http://www.imfsite.org) and click "Conditionality" to learn more about the history, role, operation, and effectiveness of IMF conditionality (in the IMF view).

11. Use the World Bank Web site (http://www.worldbank.org) to look up debt information on a less-developed country of your choice. Look for the debt service ratio, which is the ratio between debt service (annual repayment of debt plus interest) and export earnings and which is written as Total Debt Service/Exports. This ratio is the best indicator of the debt burden of an individual country.

12. Go to the home page of the World Bank at http://www.worldbank.org to discover the wealth of information on worldwide economic and social indicators, including information on savings rates, standards of living, and international debt. To obtain data quickly, click a country of your choice to obtain the most recently available data.

13. What type of safety net is necessary for residents of formerly socialist and less-developed countries as they move toward market economies?

14. Do you believe that the global movement toward freer markets will continue well into the twenty-first century, or will it reverse itself? Why?

Notes

1. Value added refers to the additional value placed on the manufactured product (by each worker in this case). The World Bank reports these numbers for the most recent year available during 1980–1984 and 1990–2004 (World Bank, *World Development Indicators 2006*, http://www.

world bank.org). Unless otherwise indicated, this
or the 2007 version is the source for other data in
this chapter.

2. Jacqueline Brux and Jacques Foust, "Doing Business
in the Russian Economy in Transition" (paper presented at the Midwest Economic Association
meetings, Chicago, Illinois, March 1994).

3. U.S. Department of Commerce, Business
Information Service for the Newly Independent
States (BISNIS), International Trade Administra-
tion, *Commercial Overview of Russia*, Moscow,
January 28, 1993.

4. "Russia Reborn," *The Economist,* December 5, 1992.

5. Ibid.

6. U.S. Department of Commerce, *Commercial
Overview of Russia*, op cit.

7. Yana S. Yurgelyanis, in a conversation with the
author.

8. Tyler Bridges, "Before Bailing Them Out, Plug the
Leaks," *Washington Post National Weekly Edition,*
March 22–April 7, 1989.

9. Bread for the World Institute, *Africa: Crisis to
Opportunity,* 1995, http://www.bread.org.

index

chapter **19**

Economies in Transition

The inherent vice of capitalism is the unequal sharing of blessings. The inherent virtue of communism is the equal sharing of miseries.

—Winston Churchill

The emergence of the market system in Russia, China, and other countries continues while leaders of these countries who were devoted followers of Marxist ideology now say they believe that capitalism, private property, and profit are ideas superior to the communist system. The failure of communism and the transformation toward a market system is personified by the success of McDonald's in Russia and Wal-Mart in China. Today, Russia and other countries continue to experience economic problems during their restructuring, but the commitment to free-market reforms remains. In contrast, in 2009, the media reported the news that the United States was nationalizing banks and General Motors. And in 2011 and 2012, a protest movement called Occupy Wall Street spread across the United States. The anticapitalist slogan of the protests was "We are the 99 percent." The main issues protested were inequity between the wealthiest 1 percent and the rest of the population and corrupt influence of corporations on government. What caused these astonishing turn of events?

To understand how the pieces of the global economic puzzle fit together, this chapter begins with a discussion of the three basic types of economies. Then you will examine the pros and cons of the "isms"—capitalism, socialism, and communism. Here you will explore the worldwide clash between the ideas of Adam Smith and Karl Marx and study their current influence on economic systems. Finally, you will examine economic reforms in Cuba, Russia, and China.

In this chapter, you will learn to solve these economics puzzles:

- Why did drivers in the former Soviet Union remove the windshield wipers and side mirrors whenever they parked their cars?

- What did Adam Smith mean when he said that an "invisible hand" promotes the public interest?

- If the Soviet Union was foolish to run its economy on five-year plans, why do universities, businesses, and governments in a capitalistic economy bother to plan?

19-1 Basic Types of Economic Systems

North Korea and South Korea share the same language and historical background. However, South Korea today is a modern economy and people starve in North Korea. This difference relates to their differing economic systems. An economic system consists of the organizations and methods used to determine what goods and services are produced, how they are produced, and for whom they are produced. As explained earlier in Chapter 2, scarcity forces each economic system to decide what combination of goods to produce, how to produce such goods, and who gets the output once it is produced. The decision-making process involves interaction among many aspects of a nation's culture, such as its laws, form of government, ethics, religions, and customs. Economist Robert L. Heilbroner established a simple way to look at the basic methods society can employ. Each economic system can be classified into one of three basic types: (1) *traditional*, (2) *command*, or (3) *market*.

> **Economic system**
>
> The organizations and methods used to determine what goods and services are produced, how they are produced, and for whom they are produced.

19-1a THE TRADITIONAL ECONOMY

Why does England have a king or queen? Tradition is the answer. Historically, the traditional economy has been a common system for making economic decisions. The traditional economy is a system that answers the What, How, and For Whom questions the way they have always been answered. People in this type of society learn that copying the previous generation allows them to feel accepted. Anyone who changes ways of doing things asks for trouble from others. This is because people in such a society believe that what was good yesterday, and years ago, must still be a good idea today.

Although most traditional economies have changed to keep pace with modern economic trends, traditional systems are used today, for example, by the Ainu of Canada, the native people of Brazil's rain forest, and the Amish of Pennsylvania. In these societies, the way past generations decided what crops are planted, how they are harvested, and to whom they are distributed remains unchanged over time. People perform their jobs in the manner established by their ancestors. The Amish are well known for rejecting tractors and using horse-drawn plows. Interestingly, the Amish reject Social Security because their society voluntarily redistributes wealth to members who are needy.

> **Traditional economy**
>
> An economic system that answers the What, How, and For Whom questions the way they have always have been answered.

19-1b THE TRADITIONAL ECONOMY'S STRENGTHS AND WEAKNESSES

The benefit of the traditional approach is that it minimizes friction among members because relatively little is disputed. Consequently, people in this system may cooperate more freely with one another. In today's industrial world, the Amish and other traditional economies appear very satisfied with their relatively uncomplicated systems. However, critics argue that the traditional system restricts individual initiative and therefore does not lead to the production of advanced goods, new technology, and economic growth.

19-1c THE COMMAND ECONOMY

In a command economy, a dictator or group of central planners makes economic decisions for society. In this system, the What, How, and For Whom questions are answered by a dictator or planners with central authority. The former Soviet Union

> **Command economy**
>
> An economic system that answers the What, How, and For Whom questions by a dictator or central authority.

in the past and Cuba and North Korea today are examples of nations with command economies using national economic plans implemented through powerful government committees. Politically selected committees decide on everything, including the number, color, size, quality, and price of autos, brooms, sweaters, and tanks. The state owns the factors of production and dictates answers to the three basic economic questions. The authorities might decide to produce modern weapons instead of schools, or they might decide to devote resources to building huge monuments like the pyramids, built by the rulers of ancient Egypt to honor their dead kings and queens.

In the old Soviet economy, for example, the three basic economic questions were answered by a central planning agency called the *Gosplan*. Following the policies of the political authority (the Politburo), the Gosplan set production quotas and prices for farms, factories, mines, housing construction, medical care, and other producing units. What should the cows be fed? If it is hay, how much land can be used to grow it? How much milk should the cows give? How many people will be dairy farmers? What wages should a dairy farmer earn? Should milk be given to everyone, to a few, or to people chosen by the leaders? If there was a shortage of goods in the shops, then goods would be rationed through queuing. The Gosplan tried to make all these decisions. Today, in Russia and the other former Soviet republics, the Gosplan is a distant memory of the discarded Soviet command system.

The pyramid shown in Exhibit 1 represents the command economy. At the top of the pyramid is a supremely powerful group of central planners, such as the old Soviet Gosplan. That agency established production targets and prices for goods and services. Then the Gosplan transmitted this information to a second layer of specialized state planning agencies. One of these specialized government bureaucracies purchased raw materials, another agency established fashion trends, another set prices, and another government bureaucracy made decisions based on employment and wages.

Production objectives were transmitted from the upper authority layers to the individual producing units, represented by the third layer of the pyramid in Exhibit 1. These producers supplied goods and services to the consumers, as commanded by the central authorities. The bottom portion of the pyramid illustrates the distribution, according to the master plan, of output to consuming units of individuals and households.

19-1d THE COMMAND ECONOMY'S STRENGTHS AND WEAKNESSES

Believe it or not, the command system can be defended. Proponents argue that economic change occurs much faster in a command system than in a traditional economy. This is one reason those dissatisfied with a traditional society might advocate establishment of a command system. The central authorities can ignore custom and order new ways of doing things. Another reason for adopting a command economy is the controversial belief that the government will provide economic security and equity. It is alleged that central authorities ensure that everyone is provided food, clothing, shelter, and medical care regardless of their ability to contribute to society.

The absolute power of central authorities to make right decisions is also the power to be absolutely wrong. Often the planners do not set production goals accurately, and either shortages or surpluses of goods and services are the result. For example, at one point, the planners miscalculated and produced too few windshield wipers and side mirrors for Soviet cars. Faced with shortages of these parts, Soviet drivers removed windshield wipers and side mirrors whenever they parked their cars to prevent theft. On the other hand, the Gosplan allocated some collective

EXHIBIT 1	The Command Economy Pyramid

The principal feature of a command economy is the central planning board at the top, which transmits economic decisions down to the various producing and consuming units below. This process begins with an overall plan from a supreme planning board, such as the old Soviet Gosplan. The Gosplan established production targets and was the ultimate authority over a layer of specialized planning agencies, which authorized capital expansion, raw material purchases, prices, wages, and all other production decisions for individual producing units. Finally, the factories, farms, mines, and other producers distributed the specified output to consumers according to the approved master plan.

SOURCE: © Cengage Learning 2014

farms far more fertilizer than they could use. To receive the same amount of fertilizer again the next year, farmers simply burned the excess fertilizer. As a result of such decision-making errors, people waited in long lines or stole goods. How does any decision-making group really know how many windshield wipers to produce each year and how much workers making them should earn?

Because profit is not the motive of producers in a command economy, quality and variety of goods also suffer. If the Gosplan ordered a state enterprise to produce 400,000 side mirrors for cars, for example, producers had little incentive to make the extra effort required to create a quality product in a variety of styles. The easiest way to meet the goal was to produce a low-quality product in one style regardless of consumer demand.

Exhibit 2 illustrates how the pricing policy of central planners causes shortages. The demand curve for side mirrors conforms to the law of demand. At lower prices in rubles, the quantity demanded increases. The supply curve is fixed at 400,000 side mirrors because it is set by the central planners and is therefore unresponsive to price variations.

Suppose one of the principal goals of the command economy is to keep the price low. To reach this goal, the central planners set the price of side mirrors at 20 rubles, which is below the equilibrium price of 40 rubles. At 20 rubles, more people can afford a side mirror than at the equilibrium price set by an uncontrolled

EXHIBIT 2	Central Planners Fixing Prices

The central planners' goal is to keep prices low, so they set the price of a side mirror for a car at 20 rubles, which is below the market-determined equilibrium price of 40 rubles. At the set price, however, the quantity demanded is 800,000 side mirrors per year. Also set by the planners, the quantity supplied is 400,000 per year. Thus, the shortage at the government-established price is 400,000 side mirrors per year. As a result, long lines form to buy side mirrors, and black markets appear.

marketplace. The consequence of this lower price set by the planners is a shortage. The quantity demanded at 20 rubles is 800,000 side mirrors, and the quantity supplied is only 400,000 mirrors. Thus, the model explains why side mirrors disappeared from stores long before many who were willing to buy them could do so.

The same graphical analysis applies to centrally planned rental prices for apartments. The central planners in the former Soviet Union set rents below the equilibrium rental prices for apartments. As the model predicts, low rents resulted in a shortage of housing. Meanwhile, the planners promised that improvements in housing would come in time.

> **CONCLUSION:** *When central planners set prices below equilibrium for goods and services, they create shortages, which mean long lines, empty shelves, and black markets.*[1]

19-1e THE MARKET ECONOMY AND THE IDEAS OF ADAM SMITH

In a market economy, neither customs nor a single person or group of central planners answers the three basic economic questions facing society. The market economy is an economic system that answers the What, How, and For Whom questions using prices determined by the interaction of the forces of supply and demand. One of the first people to explain the power of a market economy was the Scottish economist Adam Smith. In the same year that the American colonies declared their political independence in 1776, Smith's *An Inquiry into the Nature and Causes of the Wealth of Nations* presented the blueprint for employing markets to improve economic performance. Smith spent over ten years observing the real world and writing about how nations could best improve their material well-being. He concluded that the answer was to use free markets because this mechanism provides the incentive for everyone to follow his or her *self-interest*.

Adam Smith is the *father of modern economics*. He intended to write a book that would influence popular opinion, and unlike many famous works, his book was an immediate success. The basic philosophy of his book is "the best government is the least government." This belief is known as *laissez-faire*, a French expression meaning "allow to act." As Smith stated, the role of the government should be limited to providing national defense, providing education, maintaining infrastructure, enforcing contracts, and little else. Smith also advocated free trade among nations and rejected the idea that nations should impose trade barriers.

During Smith's lifetime, European nations such as England, France, and Spain intervened to control economic activities. In *The Wealth of Nations*, he argued that economic freedoms are "natural rights" necessary for the dignity of humankind. He believed that free competition among people who follow their self-interest would best benefit society because markets free of government interference produce the greatest output of goods and services possible. As noted above, Smith was an advocate of free international trade and asked the question implied in the full title of his book: Why are some nations richer than others? He explained that the source of any nation's wealth is not really the amount of gold or silver it owns. This was an idea popular during Smith's time called *mercantilism*. Instead, he argued that it is the ability of people to produce products and trade in free markets that creates a nation's wealth.

The importance of markets is that they harness the power of self-interest to answer the What, How, and For Whom questions. Without central planning, markets coordinate the actions of millions of consumers and producers. Smith said that the market economy seemed to be controlled by an invisible hand. The *invisible hand* is a phrase that expresses the belief that the best interests of a society are served when individual consumers and producers compete to achieve their own private interests. Guided by an invisible hand, producers must compete with one another to win consumers'

Market economy

An economic system that answers the What, How, and For Whom questions using prices determined by the interaction of the forces of supply and demand.

Adam Smith (1723–1790) The father of modern economics who wrote *The Wealth of Nations*, published in 1776.

Invisible hand

A phrase that expresses the belief that the best interests of a society are served when individual consumers and producers compete to achieve their own private interests.

---

[1] Recall from Exhibit 5 in Chapter 4 that a black market is an illegal market that emerges when a price ceiling is imposed in a free market.

money. The *profit motive* in a competitive marketplace provides profits as a reward for efficient producers, while losses punish inefficient producers. Smith saw profit as the necessary driving force in an individualistic market system. The profit motive leads the butcher, the baker, and other producers to answer the What, How, and For Whom questions at the lowest prices. Consumers also compete with one another to purchase the best goods at the lowest price. Competition automatically regulates the economy and provides more goods and services than a system in which government attempts to accomplish the same task in the *public interest*. In Smith's own words:

> Every individual necessarily labours to render the annual revenue of the society as great as he can. He generally, indeed, neither intends to promote the public interest, nor knows how much he is promoting it. By … directing that industry in such a manner as its produce may be of the greatest value, he intends only his own gain, and he is in this, as in many other cases, led by an invisible hand to promote an end which was no part of his intention. Nor is it always the worse for the society that it was no part of it. By pursuing his own interest he frequently promotes that of the society more effectually than when he really intends to promote it.[2]

19-1f   THE MARKET ECONOMY'S STRENGTHS AND WEAKNESSES

In a market system, if consumers want Sudoku puzzles, they can buy them because sellers seek to profit from the sale of Sudoku puzzles. No single person or central planning board makes a formal decision to shift resources and tell firms how to produce what many might view as a frivolous product. Because no central body or set of customs interferes, the market system provides a wide variety of goods and services that buyers and sellers exchange at the lowest prices.

> **CONCLUSION:** *A market economy answers the What to produce and How to produce questions very effectively.*

Those who attack the market economy point out the market failure problems of lack of competition, externalities, public goods, and income inequality, discussed in Chapter 4. For example, critics contend that competition among buyers and sellers results in people who are very wealthy and people who are very poor. In a market economy, output is divided in favor of people who earn higher incomes and own property. Some people will dine on caviar in fine restaurants, while others will wander the streets and beg for food and shelter. Supporters of the market system argue that this inequality of income must exist to give people incentives or rewards for the value of their contributions to others.

19-1g   THE MIXED ECONOMY

In the real world, no nation is a pure traditional, command, or market economy. Even primitive tribes employ a few markets in their system. For example, members of a tribe may exchange shells for animal skins. In China, the government allows many private

---

[2]Adam Smith, *An Inquiry into the Nature and Causes of the Wealth of Nations* (1776; reprint, New York: Random House, 1937), p. 423.

shops and farms to operate in free markets. Although the United States is best described as a market economy, it is also a blend of the other two systems. As mentioned earlier, the Amish operate a well-known traditional economy in our nation. The draft during wartime is an example of a command economy in which the government obtains involuntary labor. In addition, taxes "commanded" from taxpayers fund government programs, such as national defense and Social Security. If the economic systems of most nations do not perfectly fit one of the basic definitions, what term best describes their economies? A more appropriate description is that most countries employ a blend of the basic types of economic systems, broadly called a mixed economy. A mixed economy is a system that answers the What, How, and For Whom questions through a mixture of traditional, command, and market systems.

> **Mixed economy**
>
> An economic system that answers the What, How, and For Whom questions through a mixture of traditional, command, and market systems.

The traditional, command, and market economies can exist in a wide variety of political situations. For instance, the United States and Japan are politically "free" societies in which the market system flourishes. But China uses the market system to a limited degree in spite of its lack of political freedom. Moreover, some of the Western democracies engage in central economic planning. French officials representing government, business, and labor meet annually to discuss economic goals for industry for the next five-year period, but compliance is voluntary. In Japan, a government agency called the *Ministry of Economy, Trade and Industry (METI)* engages in long-term planning. One of the goals of the METI is to encourage exports so that Japan can earn the foreign currencies it needs to pay for oil and other resources.

19-2 The "ISMS"

What type of economic system will a society choose to answer the What, How, and For Whom questions? We could call most economies "mixed," but this would be too imprecise. In the real world, economic systems are labeled with various forms of the popular "isms"—capitalism, socialism, and communism, which are based on the basic types of systems.

19-2a CAPITALISM

The popular term for the market economy discussed previously is capitalism. Capitalism is an economic system characterized by private ownership of resources and markets. *Capitalism* is also called the *free enterprise system*. Regardless of its political system, a capitalist economic system must possess two characteristics: (1) private ownership of resources and (2) decentralized decision making using markets.

> **Capitalism**
>
> An economic system characterized by private ownership of resources and markets.

Private Ownership   Ownership of resources determines to a great degree who makes the What, How, and For Whom decisions. In a capitalist system, resources are primarily *privately* owned and controlled by individuals and firms, rather than having property rights be *publicly* held by government on behalf of society. In the United States, most capital resources are privately owned, but the term *capitalism* is somewhat confusing because it stresses private ownership of factories, raw materials, farms, and other forms of *capital* even though public ownership of land exists as well.

Decentralized Decision Making   This characteristic of capitalism allows buyers and sellers to exchange goods in markets without government involvement. A capitalist system operates on the principle of consumer sovereignty. Consumer sovereignty is the freedom of consumers to cast their dollar votes to buy, or not to buy, at

> **Consumer sovereignty**
>
> The freedom of consumers to cast their dollar votes to buy, or not to buy, at prices determined in competitive markets.

prices determined in competitive markets. As a result, consumer spending determines what goods and services firms produce. In a capitalist system, most allocative decisions are coordinated by consumers and producers interacting through markets and making their own decisions guided by Adam Smith's "invisible hand." Friedrich Hayek, an Austrian economist who was a 1974 recipient of the Nobel Prize and author of *The Road to Serfdom*, argued that political and economic freedoms are inseparable.

In the real world, many U.S. markets are not perfectly open or free markets with the consumer as sovereign. For example, consumers cannot buy illegal drugs or body organs. In Chapter 4, you learned that the U.S. government sets minimum prices (support prices) for wheat, milk, cheese, and other products. These markets are free only if the market price is above the support price. Similarly, the minimum wage law forces employers to pay a wage above some dollar amount per hour regardless of market conditions.

> **CONCLUSION:** *No nation in the world precisely fits the two criteria for capitalism; however, the United States comes close.*

19-2b   CAPITALISM'S STRENGTHS AND WEAKNESSES

One of the major strengths of capitalism is its capacity to achieve *economic efficiency* because competition and the profit motive force production at the lowest cost. Another strength of pure capitalism is *economic freedom* because economic power is widely dispersed. Individual consumers, producers, and workers are free to make decisions based on their own self-interest. Economist Milton Friedman makes a related point: Private ownership limits the power of government to deny goods, services, or jobs to its adversaries.

Critics of capitalism cite several shortcomings. First, capitalism tends toward an unequal distribution of income. This inequality of income among citizens results for several reasons. Private ownership of capital and the other factors of production can cause these factors to become concentrated in the hands of a few individuals or firms. Also, people do not have equal labor skills, and the marketplace rewards those with greater skills. These inequalities may be perpetuated because the rich can provide better education, legal aid, political platforms, and wealth to their heirs. Second, pure capitalism is criticized for its failure to protect the environment. The pursuit of profit and self-interest can take precedence over damage or pollution to the air, rivers, lakes, and streams. Recall the graphical model used in Chapter 4 to illustrate the socially unacceptable impact of producers who pollute the environment.

19-2c   SOCIALISM

Socialism

An economic system characterized by government ownership of resources and centralized decision making.

The idea of socialism has existed for thousands of years. Its basis is the command system. Socialism is an economic system characterized by government ownership of resources and centralized decision making. Socialism is also called *command socialism*. Under a socialist economy, a command system owns and controls in the *public interest* the major industries, such as steel, electricity, and agriculture. However, some free markets can exist in farming, retail trade, and certain service areas. Just as no pure capitalist system exists in the real world, none of the socialist countries in the world today practices pure socialism. In fact, there are as many variants of socialism as there are countries called socialist.

Before discussing socialism further, you must realize that socialism is an economic system, and politics should not be confused with economics. Great Britain, France, and Italy have representative democracies, but many of their major industries are or have been nationalized. In the United States, the federal government owns and operates the Tennessee Valley Authority (TVA), the National Aeronautics and Space Administration (NASA), and the U.S. Postal Service, while at the same time allowing private utilities and mail service firms to operate.

19-2d THE IDEAS OF KARL MARX

Despite the transition to capitalism in Russia and Eastern Europe, socialism still prevails in China, Cuba, and many less-developed countries. The theory for socialism and *communism* can be traced to Karl Marx. Marx was a 19th-century German philosopher, revolutionary, and economist. Unlike other economists of the time who followed Adam Smith, Marx rejected the concept of a society operating through private interest and profit.

Karl Marx was born in Germany, the son of a lawyer. In 1841, after receiving a doctorate in philosophy from Berlin University, he turned to journalism and became interested in radical politics. In 1843, Marx married the daughter of a wealthy family and moved to Paris, but his political activities forced him to leave Paris for England. From the age of 31, he lived and wrote his books in London. In London, Marx lived an impoverished life while he and his lifelong friend Friedrich Engels wrote *The Communist Manifesto*, published in 1848. A massive work followed, titled *Das Kapital*, which was published in three volumes between 1867 and 1894. These two works made Karl Marx the most influential economist in the history of socialism. In fact, he devoted his entire life to a revolt against capitalism. As Marx read *The Wealth of Nations*, he saw profits as unjust payments to owners of firms—the capitalists. Marx predicted that the market system would destroy itself because wealthy owners would go too far and exploit workers because unrelenting greed for profits would lead the owners to pay starvation wages. Moreover, the owners would force laborers to work in unsafe conditions, and many would not have a job at all.

Marx believed that private ownership and exploitation would produce a nation driven by a class struggle between a few "haves" and many "have-nots." As he stated in *The Communist Manifesto*, "The history of all existing society is the history of class struggle. Freeman and slave, patrician and plebeian, lord and serf, guildmaster and journeyman, in a word, oppressor and oppressed."[3] In Marx's vision, capitalists were the modern-day oppressors, and the workers were the oppressed proletariat. Someday, Marx predicted, the workers would rise up in a spontaneous bloody revolution against a system benefiting only the owners of capital. Marx believed communism to be the ideal system, which would evolve in stages from capitalism through socialism. Communism is a stateless, classless economic system in which all the factors of production are owned by the workers and people share in production according to their needs. This is the highest form of socialism toward which the revolution should strive.

Under communism, no private property exists to encourage self-interest. There is no struggle between classes of people, and everyone cooperates. In fact, there is no reason to commit crime, and police, lawyers, and courts are unnecessary. Strangely, Marx surpassed Adam Smith in advocating a system with little central government. Marx believed that those who work hard, or are more skilled, will be public spirited. Any "haves" will give voluntarily to "have-nots" until everyone has exactly the same

Karl Marx (1818–1883) His criticism of capitalism advanced communism. He wrote *The Communist Manifesto* and *Das Kapital*.

Communism

A stateless, classless economic system in which all the factors of production are owned by the workers and people share in production according to their needs. In Marx's view, this is the highest form of socialism toward which the revolution should strive.

---

[3]Karl Marx and Friedrich Engels, *The Communist Manifesto* (New York: International Press, 1848), p. 31.

material well-being. In Marx's own words, people would be motivated by the principle "from each according to his ability, to each according to his need." World peace would evolve as nation after nation accepted cooperation and rejected profits and competition. Under the idealized society of communism, there would be no state. No central authority would be necessary to pursue the interests of the people.

Today, we call the economic systems that existed in the former Soviet Union and Eastern Europe, and still exist in Cuba and other countries, *communist*. However, the definition of *socialism* given in this chapter more accurately describes their real-world economic systems. Actually, no nation has achieved the ideal communist society described by Marx, nor has capitalism self-destructed as he predicted. The 1917 communist revolution in Russia did not fit Marx's theory. At that time, Russia was an underdeveloped country, rather than an industrial country filled with greedy capitalists who exploited workers.

19-2e CHARACTERISTICS OF SOCIALISM

Regardless of a society's political system, a socialist economy has two basic characteristics: (1) public ownership and (2) centralized decision making.

Public Ownership   Under socialism, the government owns most of the factors of production, including factories, farms, mines, and natural resources. Agriculture in the old Soviet Union illustrates how even this real-world socialist country deviated from total public ownership. In the Soviet Union, there were three rather distinct forms of agriculture: state farms, collective farms, and private plots. In both the state farm and collective farm sectors, central planning authorities determined prices and outputs. In contrast, the government allowed those holding small private plots on peasant farms to operate primarily in free markets that determined price and output levels. Reforms now allow farmers to buy land, tractors, trucks, and other resources from the state. If these reforms continue, they will dramatically end the collectiviation of agriculture begun under Josef Stalin.

Centralized Decision Making   Instead of the pursuit of *private interest*, the motivation of pure socialism is the *public interest* of the whole society. For instance, a factory manager cannot decide to raise or lower prices to obtain maximum profits for the factory. Regardless of inventory levels or the opportunity to raise prices, the planners will not permit this action. Instead of exploiting the ups and downs of the market, the goal of the socialist system is to make centralized decisions that protect workers and consumers from decentralized market decisions. Critics argue that the main objective of this centralization is to perpetuate the personal dictatorships of leaders such as Stalin in the old Soviet Union and Fidel Castro in Cuba.

Before the open market reforms, Soviet planners altered earnings to attract workers into certain occupations and achieve planned goals. For example, if space projects needed more engineers, then the state raised the earnings of engineers until the target number of people entered the engineering profession. As shown earlier in Exhibit 2, central planners in the Soviet Union also manipulated consumer prices. If consumers desired more cars than were available, the authorities increased the price of cars. If people wished to purchase less of an item than was available, planners lowered prices. The problem was that this decision process took time. And while the market awaited its orders from the Soviet planners, excess inventories of some items accumulated, and consumers stood in line for cheap products that never seemed to be available. There was an old Soviet saying, "If you see a line, get in it. Whatever it is, it's scarce, and you will not see it tomorrow."

The Soviet factory system did not adhere completely to the command system. The government rewarded successful managers with bonuses that could be substantial. Better apartments, nice vacations, and medals were incentives for outstanding performance. Under economic reforms, plant managers now make decisions based on profitability instead of centralized controls.

✔ CHECKPOINT

To Plan or Not to Plan—That Is the Question

You make plans. You planned to go to college. You plan which career to follow. You plan to get married, and so on. Businesses plan. They plan to hire employees, expand their plants, increase profits, and so forth. Because individuals and businesses plan in a market economy, there is really no difference between our system and a command economy. Or is there?

19-2f SOCIALISM'S STRENGTHS AND WEAKNESSES

Proponents of the socialism model argue that this system is superior in achieving an equitable distribution of income. This is because government ownership of capital and other resources prevents a few individuals or groups from acquiring a disproportionate share of the nation's wealth. Also, supporters argue that rapid economic growth is achieved when planners have the power to direct more resources to producing capital goods and fewer resources to producing consumer goods (see Exhibit 5 in Chapter 2).

National goals may seem to be easily formulated and pursued under state directives, but there are problems. For example, proponents of such an economy can claim there is no unemployment because the government assigns all workers a job and allocates resources to complete their production goals. However, economic inefficiency results because the government often uses many workers to perform work requiring only one or two workers. Critics also point out that the absence of the profit motive discourages entrepreneurship and innovation and thus suppresses economic growth.

Socialism is particularly vulnerable to the charge that it ignores the goal of economic freedom and instead creates a privileged class of government bureaucrats who assume the role of "capitalists." Central planners are the key translators of information about consumer preferences and production capabilities flowing to millions of economic units. This complex and cumbersome process is subject to errors and is unresponsive to the wants of the majority of the population. Critics also question whether the distribution of income under socialism is more equitable than under capitalism. In the socialist system, "perks" for government officials, nepotism, and the illegal use of markets create disparities in income.

19-3 Comparing Economic Systems

In reality, all nations operate economic systems that blend capitalism and socialism. Exhibit 3 presents a continuum that attempts to place countries between the two extremes of pure socialism on the left and pure capitalism on the right. Economies characterized by a high degree of both private ownership and market allocation are

EXHIBIT 3	A Classification of Economic Systems

No nation has an economic system that is pure socialism or pure capitalism. All nations mix government ownership and reliance on markets. North Korea and Cuba are closest to pure socialism, while Hong Kong comes closest to pure capitalism. Other real-world economies are placed between these two extremes on the basis of their use of government ownership versus markets.

Cuba

China, Russia

United States, Canada, Western Europe, Japan

Pure socialism

Pure capitalism

North Korea

France, Sweden, Israel

Mexico, Latin America

Hong Kong

SOURCE: © Cengage Learning 2014

closest to pure capitalism. Hong Kong, Japan, the United States, and Canada fall at the capitalism end of the line. Conversely, economies characterized by much government ownership of resources and central planning are closest to pure socialism. North Korea and Cuba fall close to the pure socialism end of the spectrum, with China and Russia further away from pure socialism.

19-4 Economies in Transition

By the early 1990s, the centrally planned economies in the old Soviet Union and Eastern Europe had collapsed. After more than 70 years in the Soviet Union and over 40 years in Eastern Europe and China, the failed communist economies made a startling switch to embrace capitalism. Faced with severe shortages of food, housing, cars, and other consumer goods, communism could no longer claim better living standards for its citizens. The following is a brief discussion of reforms aimed at introducing market power into the economic systems of Cuba, Russia, and China.

19-4a CUBA

Cuba is a landscape of crumbling once-elegant buildings that often experiences daily power blackouts, fuel shortages, housing shortages, food shortages, and other economic hardships. But regardless of its economics woes, Cuba remains wedded to the communist system. Nevertheless, the collapse of Soviet bloc aid coupled with the effects of the U.S. trade embargo have forced Fidel Castro and the country's new leader, Raul Castro, die-hard Marxists, to reluctantly adopt limited free market reforms. To earn foreign exchange, the dollar has been legalized, and the Cuban government has poured capital into tourism by building several new state-owned hotels and restoring historic sections of Havana. Interestingly, Cuba operates special medical tourist hospitals that treat foreigners and diplomats while excluding Cubans. Cuba has also set up quasi-state enterprises that accept only hard currency. Because few Cubans have dollars or other hard currency, many are earning it by turning to illegal schemes, such as driving gypsy cabs, engaging in prostitution, or selling Cuba's famous cigars and coffee on the black market. Other Cubans have abandoned state jobs and opened small businesses under these new rules. For example, spare rooms in houses can be rented, and artisans can sell their work to tourists. In addition, state farm enterprises have been organized into worker-owned units, and the government allows farmers to sell produce left over after they have met the state's quota. As a result of this free market, some farmers have become venture capitalists, and more food, and a greater variety of food, have become available. In 2008, a series of changes opened access to cell phones, computers, and DVD players. Cubans are now also allowed to patronize tourist hotels. However, such luxuries are prohibitive for most Cubans. And in 2009, to improve its woeful transportation system, Cuban owners of classic American cars were recruited by the government to apply for taxi licenses and set their own fares subject to price floors.

In spite of the private enterprise reforms, Cuba remains essentially a communist system. Workers receive free education, housing, health care, low state salaries in pesos, and rations of staples, such as a monthly allowance of rice, beans, and milk. Profits from hotels and shops go directly into the central bank and help finance Castro's government. The state also discourages private enterprises by taxing them heavily on expected earnings, rather than on actual sales. In addition, there are highly restrictive regulations. For example, restaurants in Havana are limited to 12 seats and cannot expand regardless of demand. And Cuba has halted new licenses for some types of self-employment, including jewelers, mousetrap makers, and magicians or clowns. Currently, Hugo Chavez, president of Venezuela, is using his country's tremendous oil reserves to throw Cuba an economic lifeline, and counter the U.S. embargo against Cuba.

19-4b RUSSIA

In 1991, communist rule ended in Russia. To function efficiently, markets must offer incentives, so workers, the public, and even foreign investors were permitted to buy state property. This meant individuals could own the factors of production and earn profits. Such market incentives were a dagger thrust into the heart of a system previously devoted to rejecting capitalism. A key reform for Russia was to allow supply and demand to set higher prices for basic consumer goods. As shown earlier in Exhibit 2, without central planners, when prices rise to their equilibrium level, the quantity supplied increases and the quantity demanded decreases. At the beginning of 1992, the Russian government removed direct government price controls on most market goods. As the model predicts, average prices rose, leaping 1,735 percent in 1992, and a greater variety of goods started appearing on the shelves. Although workers had to pay more for basic consumer goods, they could at least find goods to buy.

Since 1992, Russia has established an independent central bank and implemented anti-inflationary monetary policies. Cities throughout Russia now have restaurants, megamalls, decent hotels, and streets choked with foreign cars. Russian entrepreneurial spirit and acceptance of it in society is in an embryonic stage, and corruption, including the legal system, is a frequent way of life. Although Russia is far from a successful market economy, the nation is struggling to achieve an amazing economic transition. Russian privatization plans are being implemented, and steps are continuing to create a dynamic economy embracing capitalism. And *Forbes* magazine reports that about 100 billionaires reside in Russia.

China's Quest for Free Market Reform

Applicable Concept: comparative economic systems

For more than 2,000 years, China had a "self-reliance" policy that caused its economy to lag far behind advanced economies. After 1949, the communists under Chairman Mao Zedong abolished private property, executed landlords, and put farmers to work in collectives where members shared equally. These reforms are referred to as *The Great Leap Forward*, which in reality became *The Great Leap Backward*. Without the self-interest motive, communal property created low incentives to work that resulted in widespread famine and millions of deaths. After the death of Mao Zedong in 1976, China adopted new economic reforms that are continuing to transform one of the poorest economies in the world into one of the fastest growing. Under this reform system, households operate in a mixed world of state controls and free markets. A two-track pricing system still exists for some key goods and services, such as coal, petroleum, steel, transportation, and agriculture.

The rural economy is central to China's economic reforms. In the past, when farmers worked collectively in people's communes, the government told the farmers what to produce and how much to produce. They could sell their products only to the state at a price fixed by the government, rather than in markets. A so-called

household contract responsibility system was created as a reform to assign land owned by the state to farmers. The farmers must pay an annual share of their profits to the government, and the state does not cover losses. Farmers, however, have the authority to decide what to produce and the price at which to sell in open markets. As a result, both farmers and consumers are noticeably better off because everyone can find and afford more food.

As farming productivity rose sharply, fewer farmers were needed to work on the land, and this surplus

19-4c THE PEOPLE'S REPUBLIC OF CHINA

Unlike Russia, China has sought economic reform under the direction of its Communist Party. Fundamental economic reforms began in China after the death of Mao Zedong in 1976. Much of this reform was due to the leadership of Deng Xiaoping. Mao was devoted to the egalitarian ideal of communist ideology. Under his rule, thoughts of self-interest were counterrevolutionary, and photographs of Marx, Lenin, and Mao hung on every street corner and in every office and factory. Deng shifted priorities by increasing production of consumer goods and steering China toward becoming a global economic power. And the results have been dramatic. International trade expanded from less than 1 percent of U.S. trade in 1975 to 11 percent in 2011, and the label "Made in China" is common throughout the world. China joined the WTO in 2001 and agreed to open some markets closed to foreigners. China's real GDP growth rate averaged over 10 percent between 2001 and 2011, making it the world's fastest-growing economy.

To make China an industrial power in the 21st century, Chinese planners introduced a two-tier system for industry and agriculture in 1978. Each farm and state enterprise was given a contract to produce a quota. Any amount produced over the quota could be sold in an open market. The Chinese government also encouraged the formation labor moved into emerging township and village non-state enterprises. These enterprises were mostly in light industry and owned collectively by townships or villages. As a result, the composition of rural output has changed. When the reforms began in the late 1970s, farming accounted for 70 percent of the total output and industry for 20 percent. Currently, the structure of the economy has changed dramatically. In 2011, agriculture accounted for only 10 percent of GDP and industry's share had risen to 47 percent.[1]

A 1993 article in *The Boston Globe* provides an interesting observation on China's economic transformation:

> Stuffing the genie back into the bottle might prove difficult. The flood of money has created a bubble, particularly in stocks and property, making some people in China very rich, very fast. The China Daily, China's official English-language newspaper, recently heralded the existence of 1 million millionaires.... These millionaires, many of whom just five years ago were still wearing Mao outfits and following the party's socialist dictates, now sport stylish Western-style suits with the label ostentatiously left on the cuff.[2]

China's controversial womb police have spent decades attempting to control the nation's population according to China's one-child policy. They have succeeded remarkably well, and the country has solved its population problem. China's population will actually decline in 2040, according to U.N. projections.

At the 16th Communist Party Congress in 2003, President Hu Jintao and Communist Party leaders announced another turning point and a new starting point in China's reform process. A key debate concerned reforms that would move China closer to capitalism, including the first-ever guarantee of private property under communist rule. In 2011, Forbes reported that China had over 100 billionaires. And Rupert Hoogewerf, CEO of the *Hurun Report*, says China's recent surge in mega-wealth is "comparable to the U.S. at the end of the 19th century, when you had the Rockefellers and Carnegies."

Analyze the Issue

1. Why would China abandon the goal of income equality and shift from a centrally planned system to a more market-oriented economy?
2. Which groups in China are likely to resist the reforms?

---

1. The World Bank, *Key Development Data & Statistics*, http://web.worldbank.org/.
2. Maggie Farley, "China's Economic Boom Energizing Inflation," *Boston Globe*, Aug. 13, 1993, p. 1A.

Source: © Cengage Learning 2014

of nonstate enterprises owned jointly by managers and their workforces and special economic zones open to foreign investment. In other words, a blend of capitalism and socialism would provide the incentives needed to increase output. As Deng Xiaoping explained, "It doesn't matter whether the cat is black or white as long as it catches mice." These reforms worked, leading to huge increases in farm and industrial output in the 1980s. In fact, some peasant farmers became the wealthiest people in China. After Deng's death in the mid-1990s, leadership of China passed to leaders who continued the policy of free market reforms. Today, forests of glossy skyscrapers, expressways, upscale apartments, and enormous shopping malls in Beijing, Shanghai, and other cities attest to the market-oriented reforms begun years ago. And life in China's fast lane now includes the opportunity of dining at Kentucky Fried Chicken and McDonald's restaurants located in cities throughout the country. Disney is scheduled to open its theme park in 2015, and China is estimated to overtake the United States in total theme park visits by 2020. Also, despite government censorship, China has the largest number of Internet users in the world. (See "Global Economics: China's Quest for Free Market Reform.")

Today, China is a huge nation transforming itself swiftly into a powerful player in the global economy. U.S. exporters are overjoyed at the prospect of selling products to over a billion Chinese consumers. For example, swarms of bicyclists once synonymous with urban China are being pushed off the road by consumers who now can afford cars and trucks. Rolls-Royce and Bentley, the ultra-luxury cars, have expanded into China, and it is estimated that by 2030, China will have more cars on the road than the United States. Also, more Chinese are traveling by air. Consequently, the Chinese are buying more Boeing airplanes and American-made cars. The other side of the coin is the threat of what goods the industrious Chinese workers, with increasing training and foreign investment, might produce and sell abroad. For example, China manufactures most of the world's copiers, microwave ovens, DVD players, and shoes. A ballooning U.S. trade deficit with China is often cited as evidence that China is not playing fair, and the political rhetoric has intensified on both sides of the issue. Other countries fear that China will eliminate their export business with the United States. Moreover, there is concern that lowering trade barriers under free trade agreements will increase Chinese imports into domestic markets and eliminate jobs. In 2007, one Chinese-made product after another was removed from U.S. shelves, for example, lethal pet food, toxic toothpaste, and other contaminated products. This prompted calls for more stringent safety regulations for imports.

Currently, China's leaders are dealing with an economy that is experiencing overheating. Factories suffer electricity shortages, while ports and railways cannot handle all the cargo flowing in and out of the country. China is consuming huge quantities of crude oil, copper, steel, and aluminum. Moreover, there is discontent over labor issues, pollution, and income inequality. While some people dig through trash bins, there are now wealthy private business owners. Despite the unease, China remains a market of great profit and promise and a target for protectionists as it continues its transition from a communist command economy to capitalism. And the debate continues over whether China, a socialist economy, is a strategic trading partner or an emerging economic colossus that will dominate the world economy.

19-5 Privatization versus Nationalization

Privatization

The process of turning a government enterprise into a private enterprise.

Nationalization

The act of transforming a private enterprise's assets into government ownership.

The above discussions of Cuba, Russia, and China provide examples of privatization. Privatization is the process of turning a government enterprise into a private enterprise. It is the opposite of nationalization, which is the act of transforming a private enterprise's assets into government ownership. The motives for nationalization are political as well as economic. Proponents believe that government ownership enables the state on behalf of the people to exercise more effective control and equitable redistribution of wealth and income. Critics argue that government ownership suppresses incentives, entrepreneurship, and private investment that are essential for an enterprise to prosper. During a financial crisis, the argument in favor of nationalization is that a brief period of nationalization is needed to prevent the largest corporations and banks from a downward spiral that affects the entire economy. This is the "too big to fail" argument.

In recent years, Venezuelan president Hugo Chavez has received much press coverage for nationalizing a list of industries, including oil, cement, steel, and ordering the army to take over all rice processing and packaging plants. Chavez stated in a 2007 speech in Caracas, "We're heading toward socialism, and nothing and no one can prevent it."

The United States also has a history of nationalization—most of which was temporary. But one that has endured: Amtrak is a government-owned corporation created in 1971 after railroads had petitioned repeatedly to abandon unprofitable passenger service. As discussed at the conclusion of the chapter on money and the Federal

Reserve System, the Resolution Trust Corporation (RTC) was established in 1989 to take over more than 1,000 failed savings and loans institutions with bad loans and foreclosed homes. After fulfilling its mission to sell the assets of these S&Ls, the RTC was closed in 1995. The recent financial crisis has generated several nationalizations that only in the future will it be known if they are temporary. General Motors provides a prime case. With GM facing bankruptcy in 2009, the U.S. government replaced the CEO and took a 60 percent controlling share, with Canada a 12.5 percent share, the United Auto Workers (UAW) 17.5 percent, and bondholders ending up with the remaining 10 percent. Existing stockholders were given zero shares. Will GM emerge to become successful and nationalization given credit, or will the reverse be the result?

Key Concepts

Economic system
Traditional economy
Command economy
Market economy

Invisible hand
Mixed economy
Capitalism
Consumer sovereignty

Socialism
Communism
Privatization
Nationalization

Summary

- An **economic system** is the set of established procedures by which a society answers the What, How, and For Whom to produce questions.
- **Three basic types of economic systems** are the traditional, command, and market systems. The **traditional system** makes decisions according to custom, and the **command system**, shown in the figure below, answers the three economic questions through some powerful central authority. In contrast, the **market system** uses the impersonal mechanism of the interaction of buyers and sellers in markets to answer the What, How, and For Whom questions.

Command Economy

SOURCE: © Cengage Learning 2014

- **Capitalism** is an economic system in which the factors of production are privately owned and

economic choices are made by consumers and firms in markets. As prescribed by Adam Smith, government plays an extremely limited role, and self-interest is the driving force, held in check, or regulated, by competition.
- **Consumer sovereignty** is the freedom of consumers to determine the types and quantities of products that are produced in an economy by choosing to buy or not to buy.
- **Socialism** is an economic system in which the government owns the factors of production. The central authorities make the myriad of society's economic decisions according to a national plan. The collective good, or public interest, is the intended guiding force behind the central planners' decisions.
- **Communism** is an economic system envisioned by Karl Marx to be an ideal society in which the workers own all the factors of production. Marx believed that workers who work hard will be public spirited and voluntarily redistribute income to those who are less productive. Such a communist nation described by Marx does not exist.
- **Privatization** is the process of turning a government enterprise into a private enterprise. It is the opposite of **nationalization**, which is the act of transforming a private enterprise's assets into government ownership.

Summary of Conclusion Statements

- When central planners set prices below equilibrium for goods and services, they create shortages, which mean long lines, empty shelves, and black markets.

- A market economy answers the What to produce and How to produce questions very effectively.
- No nation in the world precisely fits the two criteria for capitalism; however, the United States comes close.

Study Questions and Problems

1. Give an example of how a nation's culture affects its economic system.
2. Explain the advantages and disadvantages of any two of the three basic types of economic systems.
3. Suppose a national program of free housing for the elderly is paid for by a sizable increase in income taxes. Explain a trade-off that might occur between economic security and efficiency.
4. "The schools are not in the business of pleasing parents and students, and they cannot be allowed to set their own agendas. Their agendas are set by politicians, administrators, and various constituencies that hold the keys to political power. The public system is built to see to it that the schools do what their government wants them to do—that they conform to the higher-order values their governors seek to impose."[4] Relate this statement to Exhibit 1.
5. Suppose you are a farmer. Explain why you would be motivated to work in traditional, command, and market economies.
6. Karl Marx believed the market system was doomed. Why do you think he was right or wrong?
7. If all real-world economies are mixed economies, why is the U.S. economy described as capitalist, while the Cuban economy is described as communist?
8. Suppose you are a factory manager. Describe how you might reach production goals under a system of pure capitalism and under a system of pure socialism.

For Online Exercises, go the Tucker Web site at www.cengage.com/economics/tucker.

✓ CHECKPOINT ANSWER

To Plan or Not to Plan—That Is the Question

When an individual or a business plans in a market economy, other individuals are free to make and follow their own plans. Suppose Hewlett-Packard decides to produce X number of laser printers and sell them at a certain price. The decision does not prohibit IBM from producing Y number of laser printers and selling them for less than Hewlett-Packard's printers. If either firm makes a mistake, only that firm suffers, and other industries are, for the most part, unaffected. Under a command system, a central economic plan would be made for all laser printer manufacturers. If the central planners order the wrong quantity or quality, there could be major harm to other industries and society. If you said there is a major difference between individual planning and central planning for all society, **YOU ARE CORRECT.**

---

[4]John Chubb and Terry More, *Politics, Markets, and the Nation's Public Schools* (Washington, D.C.: Brookings Institution, 1990), p. 38.

Sample Quiz

For an explanation of the correct answers, visit the Tucker Web site at www.cengage.com/economics/tucker.

1. An economic system is the organizations and methods used to determine
   a. what goods and services are produced.
   b. how goods and services are produced.
   c. for whom goods and services are produced.
   d. All of the above answers are correct.

2. In a command economy, the basic economic questions are answered by
   a. central authority.
   b. individual buyers and sellers.
   c. traditional methods.
   d. None of the above answers are correct.

3. Adam Smith was an advocate of
   a. mercantilism.
   b. a nation maximizing its stock of gold.
   c. unrestricted or free trade.
   d. the "visible hand" of public interest.

4. In Adam Smith's competitive market economy, the question of what goods to produce is determined by the
   a. "invisible hand" of the price system.
   b. "invisible hand" of government.
   c. "invisible hand" of public interest.
   d. "visible hand" of laws and regulations.

5. Adam Smith wrote that the
   a. economic problems of 18th-century England were caused by free markets.
   b. government should control the economy.
   c. pursuit of private self-interest promotes the public interest in a market economy.
   d. public or collective interest is not promoted by people pursuing their self-interest.

6. Which of the following is a criticism of capitalism?
   a. unequal distribution of income
   b. failure to protect the environment
   c. exploitation of workers
   d. All of the above answers are correct.

7. Which of the following statements is *true*?
   a. The doctrine of *laissez-faire* advocates an economic system with extensive government intervention and little individual decision making.

   b. In capitalism, income is distributed on the basis of need.
   c. Adam Smith was the father of socialism.
   d. Most real-world economies are mixed economic systems.

8. Which of the following is a strength of a command-based economic system?
   a. Goods can be allocated based on need rather than willingness and ability to pay.
   b. Producers have strong incentives to innovate because successful innovators are rewarded with higher profit.
   c. Consumers can transmit their preference for product quality and variety by way of their "dollar votes" cast in the marketplace.
   d. Because price is freely set based on supply and demand, there are few shortages or surpluses.

9. The term *socialism* refers to which of the following?
   a. a religion centered on community interaction
   b. an economic system characterized by private ownership of resources and decentralized market-price allocation
   c. an economic system characterized by government ownership of resources and centralized allocation
   d. an economic system characterized by voluntary allocation

10. Karl Marx was a (an)
    a. 19th-century German philosopher.
    b. 18th-century Russian economist.
    c. 14th-century Polish banker.
    d. 19th-century Russian journalist.

11. Karl Marx published
    a. *Das Kapital.*
    b. *General Theory of Communism.*
    c. *The Wealth of Nations.*
    d. *The Capitalist Manifesto.*

12. In Marx's ideal communist society, the state
    a. actively promotes income incentives.
    b. follows the doctrine of *laissez-faire.*
    c. owns resources and conducts planning.
    d. does not exist.

Sample Quiz *continued*

13. According to Adam Smith, the "invisible hand" refers to which of the following?
    a. The "best interests of society" (public interest) will occur as an outcome of the market process coordinating the self-interested interactions of buyers and sellers (private interest).
    b. Government interference in markets to prevent greed.
    c. Bribes and graft that interfere with the market process.
    d. The "best interest of society" (public interest) will occur as an outcome of careful guidance by government authorities in allocating scarce good and services according to private interest.

14. A principal feature of a command economy is that _____.
    a. production decisions are made by profit-maximizing firms.
    b. there is a central planning board at the top, which transmits economic decisions down to the various producing and consuming units below.
    c. consumers are allowed to determine that is produced based on their demand for goods and services.
    d. regulatory agencies constrain the most egregious forms of market power in a market system of allocation.

15. Which nation achieved the ideal communist society as described by Marx?
    a. Castro's Cuba
    b. Mao's China
    c. Stalin's Soviet Union
    d. No nation has achieved Marx's vision of a communist society.

16. Adam Smith's book, *The Wealth of Nations*, was published at the time of the
    a. War of 1812.
    b. U.S. Declaration of Independence.
    c. U.S. Civil War.
    d. Great Depression.

17. Which of the following economies is an example of a mixed system?
    a. United States
    b. United Kingdom
    c. Sweden
    d. All of the above answers are correct.

18. Property rights allowing individuals to own goods, services, and factors of production are *most* important in
    a. socialistic economies.
    b. planned economies.
    c. capitalist economies.
    d. command economies.

19. Which of the following is a *correct* characterization of socialism?
    a. Tradition answers the basic economic questions.
    b. Markets are used exclusively to answer the basic economic questions.
    c. Central planning is used to answer the basic economic questions.
    d. Government ownership of many resources and centralized decision-making answers the basic economic questions.

20. Which of the following statements is *true*?
    a. The United States today comes closer to the socialist form of economic organization than it does to capitalism.
    b. When central planners set prices above equilibrium for goods and services, they create shortages.
    c. According to Karl Marx, under capitalism, workers would be exploited and would revolt against the owners of capital.
    d. Adam Smith argued that government's role in society would be to do absolutely nothing.

chapter 20

Growth and the Less-Developed Countries

How would your life be different if you lived in Rwanda or Haiti instead of the United States? It is unlikely that anyone in your family would have a telephone or a car. You surely would not own a personal computer or an iPod. You would not have new clothes or be enrolled in a college or university studying economics. You would not be going out to restaurants or movies. You would be fortunate to have shoes and one full meal each day. You would receive little or no medical care and live in unsanitary surroundings. Hunger, disease, and squalor would engulf you. In fact, the World Bank estimates that over 20 percent of people in developing countries survive on less than $1.25 per day. It is exceedingly difficult for Americans to grasp that one-fifth of the world's population lives at such a meager subsistence level. This chapter's important task is unraveling the secrets of economic growth and development. Why do some countries prosper while others decline?

At different times in history, Egypt, China, Italy, and Greece were highly developed by the standards of their time. On the other hand, at one time, the United States was a struggling, relatively poor country on the path to becoming a rich country. Its growth came in three stages: First, was the agricultural stage. Then came the manufacturing stage when industries such as railroads, steel, and automobiles were driving forces toward economic growth. And, finally, there has been a shift toward service industries. This is the U.S. success story, but it is not the only road countries can follow to lift themselves from the misery of poverty.

In this chapter, you will learn to solve these economics puzzles:

- Is there a difference between economic growth and economic development?
- Why are some countries rich and others poor?
- Is trade a better "engine of growth" than foreign aid and loans?

20-1 Comparing Developed and Less-Developed Countries

Income disparity exists not only among families within the United States, but also among nations. In this section, the great inequality of income between the families of nations will be used to classify nations as rich or poor.

20-1a CLASSIFYING COUNTRIES BY GDP PER CAPITA

GDP per capita

The value of final goods produced (GDP) divided by the total population.

Industrially advanced countries (IACs)

High-income nations that have market economies based on large stocks of technologically advanced capital and well-educated labor. The United States, Canada, Australia, New Zealand, Japan, and most of the countries of Western Europe are IACs.

Less-developed countries (LDCs)

Nations without large stocks of technologically advanced capital and well-educated labor. LDCs are economies based on agriculture, such as most countries of Africa, Asia, and Latin America.

There are about 196 countries in the world. Exhibit 1 shows a ranking of selected countries from high to low GDP per capita. GDP per capita is the value of final goods produced (GDP) divided by the total population. Although any system of defining rich versus poor countries is arbitrary, GDP per capita or average GDP is a fundamental measure of a country's economic well-being. At the top of the income ladder are 27 developed countries called the industrially advanced countries (IACs). Industrially advanced countries are high-income nations that have market economies based on large stocks of technologically advanced capital and well-educated labor. The United States, Canada, Australia, New Zealand, Japan, and most of the countries of Western Europe are IACs. Excluded from the IACs are countries with high incomes whose economies are based on oil under the sand, and not on widespread industrial development. The United Arab Emirates is an example of such a country.

Countries of the world other than IACs are classified as underdeveloped or less-developed countries (LDCs). Less-developed countries are nations without large stocks of technologically advanced capital and well-educated labor. Their economies are based on agriculture, as in most countries of Africa, Asia, and Latin America. Most of the world's population live in LDCs and share widespread poverty.

A closer examination of Exhibit 1 reveals that the differences in living standards between the IACs and LDCs are enormous. For example, the GDP per capita in the United States was $48,387 greater than the average income of $605 in Rwanda. Stated differently, the 2011 average income in the United States was about 80 times larger than the average income in Rwanda. What a difference! Imagine trying to live on only $605 a year in the United States. You probably would not survive.

Exhibit 2 compares GDP per capita for IACs to LDCs by regions of the world for 2011. The average citizen in the IACs enjoyed an income of $48,231, which was 41 times that of the average citizen in Sub-Saharan Africa ($48,231/$1,188). Sub-Saharan Africa includes countries such as Nigeria, Angola, Congo, Sudan, and Zimbabwe. The exhibit also reveals that the greatest concentrations of world poverty are located in the rural areas of East Asia and the Pacific and Sub-Saharan Africa. These regions have many countries characterized by bleak and pervasive poverty, but there are notable exceptions, nicknamed the "Four Tigers" of East Asia—Hong Kong, Singapore, South Korea, and Taiwan. These Pacific Rim countries are newly industrialized economies, which we discuss at the end of this chapter.

EXHIBIT 1	Annual GDP per Capita for Selected Countries, 2011		
Country	**GDP per capita**	**Country**	**GDP per capita**
Industrially Advanced Countries (IACs)			
Luxembourg	$113,533	Japan	45,920
Norway	97,255	France	44,008
Switzerland	81,161	Germany	43,742
Australia	65,477	United Kingdom	38,592
Denmark	59,928	New Zealand	36,648
Sweden	56,956	Spain	36,360
Canada	50,435	Italy	36,267
Netherlands	50,355	Hong Kong	34,049
Austria	49,809	Israel	31,986
Finland	49,350	Greece	27,073
Singapore	49,271	South Korea	22,778
United States	48,387	Portugal	22,413
Ireland	47,531	Taiwan	20,100
Belgium	46,878		
Less-Developed Countries (LDCs)			
Chile	14,278	Iraq	3,513
Russia	12,993	Indonesia	3,509
Brazil	12,789	Georgia	3,210
Venezuela	10,610	Egypt	2,970
Turkey	10,522	India	1,389
Mexico	10,153	Vietnam	1,374
Romania	8,863	Pakistan	1,201
Panama	8,514	Haiti	738
South Africa	8,066	Bangladesh	678
Iran	6,360	Rwanda	605
China	5,414	Mozambique	583
Thailand	5,394	Ethiopia	360
Ukraine	3,621		

SOURCE: International Monetary Fund, *World Economic Outlook Database*, http://www.imf.org/external/ns/cs.aspx?id=28.

EXHIBIT 2	Average GDP per Capita for IACs and LDCs by Region, 2011

This exhibit shows average GDP per capita by regions of the world for 2011. The differences between the rich, industrially advanced countries (IACs) and the poor, less-developed countries (LDCs) in the various regions of the world are enormous. For example, the average citizen in the IACs had an income 41 times that of the average citizen in the LDCs of Sub-Saharan Africa.

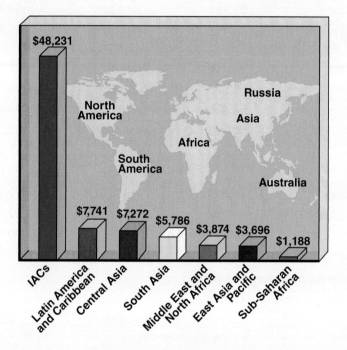

SOURCE: World Bank Group, *Key Development Data & Statistics*, http://data.worldbank.org/country.

20-1b PROBLEMS WITH GDP PER CAPITA COMPARISONS

Several problems are associated with using GDP per capita to compare rich versus poor countries. First, there is a measurement problem because countries tabulate GDP with differing degrees of accuracy. LDCs in general do not use sophisticated methods of gathering and processing GDP and population data. For example, in countries whose economies are based largely on agriculture, a family is more likely to produce goods and services outside the price system. In LDCs, families often grow their own food, make their own clothes, and build their own homes. Estimating the value of this output at market prices is difficult.

CONCLUSION: *LDCs' GDP per capita is subject to greater measurement errors than data for IACs.*

Second, GDP per capita comparisons among countries can be misleading because they ignore the relative income distribution. Some countries have very high per capita incomes, yet most of the income goes to just a few wealthy families. The United Arab Emirates' GDP per capita is higher than that of several IACs. However, the United Arab Emirates earns its income from oil exports, and its income is actually distributed disproportionately to a relatively small number of wealthy families.

> **CONCLUSION:** *GDP per capita comparisons among nations can be misleading because GDP per capita does not measure income distribution.*

Third, GDP per capita comparisons between nations are subject to conversion problems. Making these data comparisons requires converting one nation's currency, say, Japan's yen, into a common currency, the U.S. dollar. Because, as explained in the chapter on international trade and finance, the value of a country's currency can rise or fall for many reasons, the true value of a nation's output can be distorted. For example, during a given year, one government might maintain an artificially high exchange rate and another government might not.

> **CONCLUSION:** *A conversion problem may widen or narrow the GDP per capita gap between nations because the fluctuations in exchange rates do not reflect actual differences in the value of goods and services produced.*

20-1c QUALITY-OF-LIFE MEASURES OF DEVELOPMENT

GDP per capita measures market transactions, but this measure does not give a complete picture of differences in living standards among nations. Exhibit 3 presents other selected socioeconomic indicators of the quality of life. These are variables such as life expectancy at birth, infant mortality rate, literacy rate, per capita energy consumption, and economic freedom ranking. Take a close look at the statistics in Exhibit 3. These data reflect the dimensions of poverty in many of the LDCs. For example, a person born in Japan has a life expectancy that is much longer than a person born in Mozambique, and the infant mortality rate is dramatically higher in Mozambique. Per capita energy consumption measures the use of nonhuman energy to perform work. In IACs, most work is done by machines, and in LDCs, virtually all work is done by people. For example, the average American uses 7,075 kilograms of (oil-equivalent) energy per year, while the average person in Mozambique uses only 416 kilograms. Finally, it is interesting to note that GDP per capita and other quality-of-life indicators are related to the ranking in economic freedom.

How good an indicator of the quality of life is GDP per capita? Exhibit 3 reflects the principle that lower GDP per capita is highly correlated with measures of the quality of life.

> **CONCLUSION:** *In general, GDP per capita is highly correlated with alternative measures of quality of life.*

EXHIBIT 3	Quality-of-Life Indicators for Selected Countries, 2011					
Country	(1) GDP per Capita	(2) Life Expectancy at Birth (years)	(3) Infant Mortality Rate[1]	(4) Literacy Rate[2]	(5) Per Capita Energy Consumption[3]	(6) Economic Freedom Rank[4]
United States	$48,387	79	8	99%	7,075	10
Japan	45,920	83	3	99	3,713	22
Mexico	10,153	77	17	93	1,646	75
China	5,414	74	18	94	1,598	92
India	1,389	66	63	63	545	94
Bangladesh	678	68	48	56	175	103
Mozambique	583	50	135	55	416	128

[1]Per 1,000 live births.

[2]Percentage age 15 and over who can read and write.

[3]Kilograms of oil equivalent.

[4]The Fraser Institute.

SOURCES: The CIA World Factbook, https://www.cia.gov/library/publications/the-world-factbook/index.html, World Bank Group, *Key Development Data & Statistics*, http://data.worldbank.org/country, The Fraser Institute, http://www.freetheworld.com.

20-2 Economic Growth and Development around the World

Economic growth and development are major goals of IACs and LDCs. People all over the world strive for a higher quality of life for their generation and future generations. However, growth is closer to a life-or-death situation for many LDCs, such as Bangladesh and Mozambique.

Economic growth and economic development are somewhat different, but related, concepts. As shown in Exhibit 4, recall from Chapter 2 that economic growth is the ability of an economy to produce greater levels of output, represented by an outward shift of its production possibilities curve (PPC). Thus, economic growth is defined on a *quantitative* basis using the percentage change in GDP per capita. When a nation's GDP rises more rapidly than its population, GDP per capita rises, and the nation experiences economic growth. Conversely, if GDP expands less than the population of a nation, GDP per capita falls, and the nation experiences negative economic growth.

Economic development is a broader concept that is more *qualitative* in nature. Economic development encompasses improvement in the quality of life, including economic growth in the production of goods and services. In short, continuous economic growth is necessary for economic development, but economic growth is not the only consideration. For example, as explained earlier, GDP per capita does not measure the distribution of income or the political environment that provides the

---

EXHIBIT 4	Economic Growth

The economy begins with the capacity to produce combinations along production possibilities curve PPC_1. Growth in the resource base or technological advance shifts the production possibilities curve outward from PPC_1 to PPC_2. Points along PPC_2 represent new production possibilities that were previously impossible. The distance that the curve shifts represents an increase in the nation's productive capacity.

SOURCE: © Cengage Learning 2014

---

legal, monetary, education, and transportation structures necessary for economic growth.

Economic growth and development involve a complex process that is determined by several interrelated factors. Like the performance of an NBA basketball team, success depends on the joint effort of team players, and one or two weak players can greatly reduce overall performance. However, there is no precise formula for winning. If your team has a player like former NBA great Michael Jordan, it can win even with a few weak players. The remainder of this section examines the key factors, or players, that operate together to produce a nation's economic well-being.

20-2a ENDOWMENT OF NATURAL RESOURCES

Most of the LDCs have comparatively limited bases of natural resources, including mineral deposits and arable land resources. In these countries, most of the available land is used for agricultural production, and clearing tropical forests to obtain more land can cause soil erosion. Also, tropical climates prevail in Central and South America, Africa, the Indian subcontinent, and Southeast Asia. The hot, humid climate in these regions is conducive to weed and insect infestations that plague agriculture.

Although a narrow base of resources does pose a barrier to economic growth and development, no single conclusion can be drawn. For example, how have Hong Kong, Japan, and Israel achieved high standards of living in spite of limited natural resource bases? Each has practically no minerals, little fertile land, and no domestic sources of energy. Nonetheless, these economies have become prosperous. In contrast, Argentina, Venezuela, and Brazil have abundant fertile land and minerals. Yet these and other countries have been growing slowly or not at all. Venezuela, for example, is one of the most oil-rich countries in the world. Ghana, Kenya, and Bolivia are also resource-rich countries that are poor, with little or no economic growth.

> **CONCLUSION:** *Natural resource endowment can promote economic growth, but a country can develop without a large natural resource base.*

20-2b INVESTMENT IN HUMAN RESOURCES

A low level of human capital can also present a barrier to economic growth and development. Recall that human capital is the education, training, experience, and health that improve the knowledge and skills of workers to produce goods and services. In most of the LDCs, investment in human capital is much less than in the IACs. Look back at column (4) in Exhibit 3. Consider how the literacy rate falls for the poorer countries. A country with a lower literacy rate has less ability to educate its labor force and create a basic foundation for economic growth. In fact, often the skills of workers in the poor countries are suited primarily to agriculture, rather than being appropriate for a wide range of industries and economic growth. Further complicating matters is a "brain drain" problem because the best educated and trained workers of poor countries pursue their education in wealthier countries. Column (2) of Exhibit 3 also gives a measure of health among countries with varying levels of GDP per capita. As the GDP per capita falls, the life expectancy at birth falls. Thus, richer countries have the advantage of a better educated and healthier workforce.

> **CONCLUSION:** *Investment in human capital generally results in increases in GDP per capita.*

Thus far, the discussion has been about the quality of labor. We must also talk about the quantity of labor because productivity is related to both the quality and quantity of labor. Overpopulation is a problem for LDCs. In a nutshell, here is why: Other factors held constant, population (labor force) growth can increase a country's GDP. Yet rapid population growth can convert an expanding GDP into a GDP per capita that is stagnant, slow growing, or negative. Stated another way, there is no gain if an increase in output is more than matched by an increase in the number of mouths that must be fed. Suppose the GDP of an LDC grows at, say, 3 percent per year. If there is no growth in population, GDP per capita also grows at 3 percent per year. But what if the population also grows at 3 percent per year? The result is that GDP per capita remains unchanged. If population growth is instead only 1 percent per year, GDP per capita rises 2 percent per year. Obstacles to population control are great and include strong religious and sociocultural arguments against birth control programs.

> **CONCLUSION:** *Rapid population growth combined with low human capital investment explains why many countries are LDCs.*

✓ CHECKPOINT

Does Rapid Growth Mean a Country Is Catching Up?

Suppose country Alpha has a production possibilities curve closer to the origin than the curve for country Beta. Now assume Alpha experiences a 3 percent growth rate in GDP for 10 years and Beta experiences a 6 percent growth rate in GDP for 10 years. At the end of five years, which of the following is the best prediction for the standard of living? (1) Alpha's residents are better off. (2) Beta's residents are better off. (3) Which country's residents are better off cannot be determined.

20-2c ACCUMULATION OF CAPITAL

It did not take long for Robinson Crusoe stranded on a deserted island, to invest in a net in order to catch more fish than he could catch with his hands. Similarly, farmers working with modern tractors can cultivate more acres than farmers working with horse-drawn plows. Recall from Chapter 1 that capital in economics means factories, tractors, trucks, roads, computers, irrigation systems, electricity-generating facilities, and other human-made goods used to produce goods and services.

LDCs suffer from a critical shortage of capital. A family in Somalia owns little in the way of tools except a wooden plow. To make matters worse, roads are terrible, there are few plants generating electricity, and telephone lines are scarce. As shown in Exhibit 5, recall from Chapter 2 that a high-investment country can shift its production possibilities curve outward, but investment in capital goods is not a "free lunch." When more resources are used to produce more factories and machines, there is an opportunity cost of fewer resources available for the production of current consumer goods. This means that LDCs are often caught in a vicious circle of poverty. A vicious circle of poverty is the trap in which countries are poor and cannot afford to save. And low savings translate into low investment. Low investment results in low productivity, which, in turn, keeps incomes low. Any savings that do exist among higher-income persons in poor LDCs are often invested in IACs. This phenomenon is often called "capital flight." These wealthy individuals are afraid to save in their own countries because they fear that their governments may be overthrown and their savings could be lost.

Vicious circle of poverty

The trap in which countries are poor because they cannot afford to save and invest, but they cannot save and invest because they are poor.

EXHIBIT 5	Alpha's and Beta's Present and Future Production Possibilities Curves

In part (a), each year Alpha produces only enough capital (K_a) to replace existing capital that is worn out. Without greater capital and assuming other resources remain fixed, Alpha is unable to shift its production possibilities curve outward. In part (b), each year Beta produces K_b capital, which is more than the amount required to replenish its depreciated capital. In 2010, this expanded capital provides Beta with the extra production capacity to shift its production possibilities curve to the right. If Beta chooses point B on its curve, it has the production capacity to increase the amount of consumer goods from C_b to C_c without producing fewer capital goods.

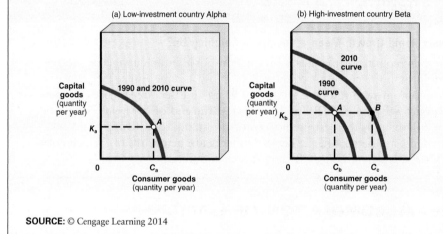

SOURCE: © Cengage Learning 2014

The United States and other nations have attempted to provide LDCs with foreign aid so that they might grow. These countries desperately need more factories and infrastructure. Infrastructure is capital goods usually provided by the government, including highways, bridges, waste and water systems, and airports. Unfortunately, the amount of capital given to the LDCs is relatively small, and as explained above, workers in the LDCs lack the skills necessary to use the most modern forms of capital. More specifically, LDCs face a major obstacle to capital accumulation because of the lack of entrepreneurs to assume the risks of capital formation.

Infrastructure

Capital goods usually provided by the government, including highways, bridges, waste and water systems, and airports.

> **CONCLUSION:** *There is a significant positive relationship between investment and economic growth and development.*

20-2d TECHNOLOGICAL PROGRESS

As explained earlier in Chapter 2, holding natural resources, labor, and capital constant, advancing the body of knowledge applied to production shifts the production possibilities curve of a country. In fact, technological advances have been at the heart of economic growth and development in recent history. During the last 250 years, brainpower has invented new power-driven machines, advanced communication devices, new energy sources, and countless ways to produce more output with the same resources. How have innovative products improved your productivity? Consider, to name just a few products, the impact of personal computers, word processing software, cell phone photography, the iPhone, and the Internet. In contrast, in many poor countries, waterwheels still bring water to the surface, cloth is woven on handlooms, and oxcarts are the major means of transportation. Consequently, large inputs of human effort are used relative to capital resources.

The United States and other IACs have provided the world with an abundant accumulation of technological knowledge that might be adopted by those LDCs without the resources to undertake the required cost of research and development. However, the results of this transfer process have been mixed. For example, countries such as China, Hong Kong, Singapore, Taiwan, South Korea, and Japan have surely achieved rapid growth in part from the benefit of technological borrowing. Currently, Russia and other Eastern European nations are attempting to apply existing technological knowledge to boost their rates of growth.

The other side of the coin is that much available technology is not suited to LDCs. The old saying "You need to learn to walk before you can run" often applies to the LDCs. For example, small farms of most LDCs are not suited for much of the agricultural technology developed for IACs' large farms. And how many factories in the LDCs are ready to use the most modern robotics in the production process? Stated differently, LDCs need appropriate technology, rather than necessarily the latest technology.

> **CONCLUSION:** *Many LDCs continue to experience low growth rates even though IACs have developed advanced technologies that the world can utilize.*

20-2e POLITICAL ENVIRONMENT

The discussion above leads to the generalization that in order for LDCs to achieve economic growth and development, they must wisely use natural resources, invest in human and physical capital, and adopt advanced technology. This list of policies is not complete. LDC governments must also create a political environment favorable to economic growth. All too often a large part of the problem in poor countries is that resources are wasted as a result of war and political instability. Political leaders must not be corrupt and/or incompetent. Instead of following policies that favor a small elite ruling class, LDC governments must adopt appropriate domestic and international economic policies, discussed under the following three headings of law and order, infrastructure, and international trade.

Law and Order A basic governmental function is to establish domestic law and order. This function includes many areas, such as a stable legal system, stable money and prices, competitive markets, and private ownership of property. In particular, expropriation of private property rights among LDCs is a barrier to growth. Well-defined private property rights have fostered economic growth in the IACs because this institutional policy has encouraged an entrepreneurial class. Private ownership provides individuals with the incentive to save money and invest in businesses. A stable political environment that ensures private ownership of profits also provides an incentive for individuals in other countries to invest in developing poor countries.

Infrastructure   Assuming an LDC government maintains law and order and the price system is used to allocate goods and services, it is vital that wise decisions be made concerning infrastructure. Indeed, inadequate infrastructure is one of the greatest problems of LDCs. Without such public goods as roads, schools, bridges, and public health and sanitation services, poor countries are unable to generate the substantial external benefits that are an important ingredient in economic growth and development. From the viewpoint of individual firms, government must provide infrastructure because these public goods projects are too costly for a firm to undertake.

International Trade   In general, LDCs can benefit from an expanding volume of trade. This is the theory behind the North American Free Trade Agreement (NAFTA), the General Agreement on Tariffs and Trade (GATT), and the World Trade Organization (WTO) discussed in the chapter on international trade and finance. As explained earlier in this chapter, policies such as tariffs and quotas restrain international trade and thereby inhibit economic growth and development. These trade policies are antigrowth because they restrict the ability of people in one country to trade with people in other countries. Similarly, a country that fixes the exchange rate of its own currency above the market-determined exchange rate makes that country's exports less attractive to foreigners. This means, in turn, that domestic citizens sell less of their goods to foreigners and earn less foreign currency with which to buy imports.

CONCLUSION: *Exchange rate controls artificially set by government above the market exchange rates reduce the volume of both exports and imports (international trade).*

Exhibit 6 summarizes the key factors explained above that determine the economic growth and development of countries. Analysis of this exhibit reveals that economic growth and development are the result of a multidimensional process. This means that it is difficult for countries to break the poverty barrier because they must follow various avenues and improve many factors in order to increase their economic well-being. But it is important to remember that lack of one or more key factors, such as natural resources, does not necessarily keep an LDC in the trap of underdevelopment.

CONCLUSION: *There is no single strategy for economic growth and development.*

EXHIBIT 6	Key Categories That Determine Economic Growth and Development

There are five basic categories that interact to determine the economic growth and development of countries: natural resources, human resources, capital, technological progress, and the political environment. The exhibit also indicates important factors that influence investment in human resources, capital, technological advances, and the political environment. LDCs are faced with a formidable task. Because economic growth and development are multidimensional, LDCs must improve many factors in order to achieve economic progress.

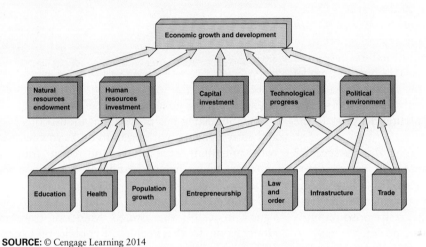

SOURCE: © Cengage Learning 2014

20-3 The Helping Hand of Advanced Countries

How can poor countries escape the vicious circle of poverty? Low GDP per capita leads to low savings and investment, which lead, in turn, to low growth. Although there is no easy way for poor countries to become richer, the United States and other advanced countries can be an instrument of growth. The necessary funds can come from the LDCs' own domestic savings, or it can come from external sources that include foreign private investment, foreign aid, and foreign loans.

Exhibit 7 illustrates how external funds can shift a country's production possibilities curve outward. Here you should look back and review Exhibit 5. Suppose country Alpha is trapped in poverty and produces only enough capital (K_a) to replace the existing capital being worn out. Alpha's consumption level is at C_a, corresponding to point A on production possibilities curve PPC_1. Because C_a is at the subsistence level, Alpha cannot save and invest by substituting

Hong Kong: A Leaping Pacific Rim Tiger

Applicable Concept: newly industrialized economies

As the map shows, the Pacific Rim economies are located along an arc extending from Japan and South Korea in the north to New Zealand in the south. The Four Tigers of East Asia are Hong Kong, Singapore, South Korea, and Taiwan. These "miracle economies" have often experienced higher economic growth rates, lower inflation rates, and lower unemployment rates than many long-established advanced countries.

Hong Kong is a great success story. When Adam Smith published his famous book, *The Wealth of Nations*, in 1776, Hong Kong was little more than a small, barren rock island void of natural resources except fish. Today, Hong Kong is a bustling model of free enterprise in spite of the fact that 7 million inhabitants are crowded into only about 400 square miles—one of the highest population densities in the world.

What is the reason for Hong Kong's success? Following the doctrine of Adam Smith, this economy is a paragon of *laissez-faire*. Hong Kong has among the lowest individual and corporate income tax rates in the world and almost no legal restrictions on business. It has no capital gains tax, no interest tax, no sales tax, and no withholding tax. Hong Kong has become the largest banking center in the Pacific region after Tokyo. International trade is also largely unrestricted, and Hong Kong depends to a large extent on trade through its magnificent harbor for its economic success. Tariffs on imported goods are low, and Hong Kong is known as a safe-haven

zhu difeng/Shutterstock.com

warehouse and trading center, with little or no interference from the government.

Hong Kong has proved that industrious people and entrepreneurs working hard on a crowded island with minimum regulations and open trade can improve their living standard without natural resources. Nevertheless, Hong Kong faces economic and political uncertainty. Under a 99-year lease signed in 1898, the United Kingdom transferred Hong Kong to the People's Republic of China in 1997. Will China allow Hong Kong to continue to follow Adam Smith's *laissez-faire* philosophy, resulting in high growth rates, or will Hong Kong change direction? It is anyone's guess. So far, China has not tampered with Hong Kong's *laissez-faire* economy, and its economic freedom ranking is higher than any other country in the world.[1]

capital for current consumption and move upward along PPC_1. This inability to increase capital means Alpha cannot use internal sources of funds to increase its production possibilities curve in the future. There is a way out of the trap using external sources. Now assume Alpha receives an inflow of funds from abroad and buys capital goods that increase its rate of investment from K_a to K_b. At K_b, the rate of capital formation exceeds the value of capital depreciated, and Alpha's production possibilities curve shifts rightward to PPC_2. Economic growth made possible by external investment means Alpha can improve its standard of living by increasing its consumption level from C_a at point A on PPC_1 to C_b at point B on PPC_2.

Recessions in the United States affect the global economy, and Hong Kong is no exception. Hong Kong's GDP growth depends heavily on exports. If, for example, U.S. consumers cut back on purchasing electronic devices, then Hong Kong's growth rate declines. After an 8 percent growth rate in 2000, the falloff in global demand triggered by the 2001 recession in the United States slowed Hong Kong's real GDP growth rate to only 0.5 percent. Between 2004 and 2007, Hong Kong's growth rate recovered to an average of 7.3 percent, and this East Asian tiger was leaping forward and roaring again. However, as a result of the recent financial crisis, Hong Kong slipped into recession in 2011 with a growth rate of –3 percent. But in 2010, Hong Kong became a "leaping Tiger" with a roaring 7 percent growth rate and a 5 percent rate in 2011. The following map compares 2011 data for the Four Tigers of East Asia.

Singapore
GDP per capita: $49,271
GDP growth: 5%
People: 5.3 million
Literacy: 95%

Hong Kong
GDP per capita: $34,049
GDP growth: 6.8%
People: 7.1 million
Literacy: 97%

Taiwan
GDP per capita: $20,100
GDP growth: 4%
People: 23.3 million
Literacy: 96%

South Korea
GDP per capita: $22,778
GDP growth: 4%
People: 48.9 million
Literacy: 99%

Analyze the Issue

One of the keys to Hong Kong's success is its free trade policy. Why is this so important for a developing country? What would be the effect of Hong Kong attempting to protect its domestic industries by raising tariffs and following other protectionist trade policies?

<hr>

1. Frazer Institute, http://www.freetheworld.com/.

Source: © Cengage Learning 2014

20-3a FOREIGN PRIVATE INVESTMENT

Many countries' development benefits from private-sector foreign investment from private investors. For example, Microsoft might finance construction of a plant in the Philippines to manufacture software, or Bank of America may make loans to the government of Haiti. These large multinational corporations and commercial banks supply scarce capital to the LDCs. A multinational corporation is a firm with headquarters in one country and one or more branch plants in other countries. Multinational firms often seek new investment opportunities in LDCs because these poor countries offer abundant supplies of low-wage labor and raw materials. But the political environment in the LDCs must be conducive to investment. Multinational corporations often become the largest employers, largest taxpayers, and largest exporters in the LDCs.

EXHIBIT 7	The Effect of External Financing on an LDC's Production Possibilities Curve

The poor country of Alpha is initially operating at point A on production possibilities curve PPC_1, with only enough capital (K_a) to replace depreciation. If C_a is the consumption level of subsistence, Alpha's economy cannot grow by reducing consumption. An inflow of external funds from abroad permits the LDC to increase its capital from K_a to K_b and its production possibilities curve shifts outward to PPC_2. At PPC_2, Alpha is able to increase its production of consumer goods from C_a to C_b.

SOURCE: © Cengage Learning 2014

20-3b FOREIGN AID

About 1 percent of the U.S. federal budget is spent on foreign aid. Foreign aid is the transfer of money or resources from one government to another with no repayment required. These transfers may be made as outright grants, technical assistance, or food supplies. Foreign aid flows from country to country through governments and voluntary agencies, such as the Red Cross, CARE, and Church World Relief. The United States distributes most of its official development assistance through the Agency for International Development (AID), established in 1961. The AID is the agency of the U.S. State Department that is in charge of U.S. aid to foreign countries.

One reason that countries such as the United States provide foreign aid to LDCs is the belief that it is a moral responsibility of richer countries to share their wealth with poorer countries. A second reason is that it is in the best economic interest of the IACs to help the LDCs. When these countries become more prosperous, the IACs have more markets for their exports, and thereby all countries benefit from trade.

The LDCs often complain that foreign aid comes with too many economic and political strings attached. Loans are often offered on a "take it or leave it" basis, tied to policies other than basic trade policies, such as human rights, politics, or the military. Consequently, many LDCs argue for "trade, not aid." If the IACs would simply buy more goods from the LDCs, the LDCs could use their gains in export earnings to purchase more capital and other resources needed for growth. Many people in the United States believe that most foreign aid is a waste of money because it is misused by the recipient countries. This belief has caused Congress to grow increasingly reluctant to send taxpayers' money abroad except in the clearest cases of need or for reasons of national security.

20-3c FOREIGN LOANS

A third source of external funds that can be used to finance LDCs' domestic investment is loans from abroad. Governments, international organizations, and private banks all make loans to LDCs. Like foreign private investment and foreign aid, loans give LDCs the opportunity to shift their production possibilities curves outward. There are various types of loan sources for LDCs. Bilateral loans are made directly from one country to another. The principal agent for official U.S. bilateral loans is the U.S. Agency for International Development, introduced earlier.

One prominent multilateral lending agency is the World Bank. The 188-member World Bank is the lending agency affiliated with the United Nations that makes long-term low-interest loans and provides technical assistance to LDCs. Loans are made only after a planning period lasting a year or more. The World Bank was established in 1944 by major nations meeting in Bretton Woods, New Hampshire. Its first charge was to assist with reconstruction after World War II. Today, the World Bank is located in Washington, D.C., and its main purpose is to channel funds from rich countries to poor countries. Voting shares are in proportion to the money provided by the members. The World Bank makes "last resort" loans to LDCs that are limited to financing basic infrastructure projects, such as schools, health centers, dams, irrigation systems, and transportation facilities, for which private financing is not available. In addition, the World Bank helps LDCs get loans from private lenders by insuring the loans. Thus, the poor countries are able to complete projects and use the economic returns to pay off the lender with interest.

The World Bank is not the only multilateral lending agency making loans to LDCs. The World Bank's partner institution is the International Monetary Fund (IMF). The International Monetary Fund is the lending agency that makes short-term conditional low-interest loans to developing countries. The IMF was also established at Bretton Woods in 1944. Its purpose is to help countries overcome short-run financial difficulties. Typically, the IMF makes conditional loans that require the debtor countries to implement fiscal and monetary policies that will alleviate balance-of-payments deficit problems and promote noninflationary economic growth. The 186-member IMF is not a charitable institution. It operates like a credit union with funding quotas that earn interest on the loans. The United States is the IMF's largest shareholder and thus has effective veto power over IMF decisions.

The IMF has performed a major role in providing short-term loans to developing countries and to economies making the transition to capitalism. In the late 1990s, the IMF provided multibillion-dollar bailouts to Russia, several Asian countries, Brazil, and other countries experiencing economic turmoil. In recent years, the IMF and some of the EU countries made rescue loans to debt-plagued Greece with the condition of deep cutbacks in government spending and tax hikes. Critics argue that as long as governments believe the IMF will bail them out, they will fail to correct their own problems. IMF supporters counter that if the IMF does not intervene, troubled economies will default on outstanding loans and cause a worldwide ripple effect. Critics respond that a flood of low-cost short-term loans from the IMF encourages bad government policies and excessive risk taking by banks. Consequently, a bailout in a crisis generates new financial crises and reduces world economic growth.

World Bank
The lending agency that makes long-term low-interest loans and provides technical assistance to less-developed countries.

International Monetary Fund (IMF)
The lending agency that makes short-term conditional low-interest loans to developing countries.

✓ CHECKPOINT

Is the Minimum Wage an Antipoverty Solution for Poor Countries?

Imagine you are an economic adviser to the president of a poor LDC. The president is seeking policies to promote economic growth and a higher standard of living for citizens of this country. You are asked whether adopting a minimum wage equal to the average of the IACs' average hourly wages would achieve these goals. Recall the discussion of the minimum wage from Chapter 4 and evaluate this policy.

Key Concepts

GDP per capita
Industrially advanced countries
   (IACs)
Less-developed countries
   (LDCs)

Vicious circle of poverty
Infrastructure
Foreign aid
Agency for International
   Development (AID)

World Bank
International Monetary Fund
   (IMF)

Summary

- **GDP per capita** provides a general index of a country's standard of living. Countries with low GDP per capita and slow growth in GDP per capita are less able to satisfy basic needs for food, shelter, clothing, education, and health.
- **Industrially advanced countries (IACs)** are countries with high GDP per capita, and output is produced by technologically advanced capital. Countries that have high incomes without widespread industrial development, such as the oil-rich Arab countries, are not included in the IAC list.
- **Less-developed countries (LDCs)** are countries with low production per person. In these countries, output is produced without large amounts of technologically advanced capital and well-educated labor. The LDCs account for about three-fourths of the world's population.
- The **Four Tigers of the Pacific Rim** are Hong Kong, Singapore, South Korea, and Taiwan. These newly industrialized countries have achieved high growth rates and standards of living.
- **GDP per capita comparisons** are subject to four problems: (1) the accuracy of LDC data is

questionable, (2) GDP per capita ignores income distribution, (3) fluctuations in exchange rates affect GDP per capita gaps between countries, and (4) there is no adjustment for cost-of-living differences between countries.
- **Economic growth** and **economic development** are related, but somewhat different concepts. Economic growth is measured quantitatively by GDP per capita, while economic development is a broader concept. In addition to GDP per capita, economic development includes quality-of-life measures, such as life expectancy at birth, adult literacy rate, and per capita energy consumption. Economic growth and development are the result of a complex process that is determined by five major factors: (1) natural resources, (2) human resources, (3) capital, (4) technological progress, and (5) the political environment. There is no single correct strategy for economic development, and a lack of strength in one or more of the five areas does not prevent growth.
- The **vicious circle of poverty** is a trap in which an LDC is too poor to save and therefore it

cannot invest and shift its production possibilities curve outward. As a result, the LDC remains poor. One way for a poor country to gain savings, invest, and grow is to use funds from external sources such as foreign private investment, foreign aid, and foreign loans.

Summary of Conclusion Statements

- LDCs' GDP per capita is subject to greater measurement errors than data for IACs.
- GDP per capita comparisons among nations can be misleading because GDP per capita does not measure income distribution.
- A conversion problem may widen or narrow the GDP per capita gap between nations because the fluctuations in exchange rates do not reflect actual differences in the value of goods and services produced.
- In general, GDP per capita is highly correlated with alternative measures of quality of life.
- Natural resource endowment can promote economic growth, but a country can develop without a large natural resource base.
- Investment in human capital generally results in increases in GDP per capita.

- Rapid population growth combined with low human capital investment explains why many countries are LDCs.
- There is a significant positive relationship between investment and economic growth and development.
- Many LDCs continue to experience low growth rates even though IACs have developed advanced technologies that the world can utilize.
- Exchange rate controls artificially set by government above the market exchange rates reduce the volume of both exports and imports (international trade).
- There is no single strategy for economic growth and development.

Study Questions and Problems

1. What is the difference between industrially advanced countries (IACs) and less-developed countries (LDCs)? List five IACs and five LDCs.

2. Explain why GDP per capita comparisons among nations are not a perfect measure of differences in economic well-being.

3. Assume you are given the following data for country Alpha and country Beta:

Country	GDP per capita
Alpha	$25,000
Beta	15,000

a. Based on the GDP per capita data given above, in which country would you prefer to live?

b. Now assume you are given the following additional quality-of-life data. In which country would you prefer to reside?

Country	Life Expectancy at Birth (years)	Daily per Capita Calorie Supply	Per Capita Energy Consumption*
Alpha	65	2,500	3,000
Beta	70	3,000	4,000

*Kilograms of oil equivalent.

4. What is the difference between economic development and economic growth? Give examples of how each of these concepts can be measured.

5. Do you agree with the argument that the rich nations are getting richer and the poor nations are getting poorer? Is this an oversimplification? Explain.

6. Explain why it is so difficult for poor LDCs to generate investment in capital in order to increase productivity and growth and therefore improve their standard of living.

7. Why is the quest for economic growth and development complicated?

8. Indicate whether each of the following is associated with a high or low level of economic growth and development:

	High	Low
a. Overpopulation	___	___
b. Highly skilled labor	___	___
c. High savings rate	___	___
d. Political stability	___	___
e. Low capital accumulation	___	___
f. Advanced technology	___	___
g. Highly developed infrastructure	___	___
h. High proportion of agriculture	___	___
i. High degree of income inequality	___	___

9. Without external financing from foreign private investment, foreign aid, and foreign loans, poor countries are caught in the vicious circle of poverty. Explain. How does external financing help poor countries achieve economic growth and development?

10. What are some of the problems for LDCs of accepting foreign aid?

11. Why would an LDC argue for "trade, not aid"?

12. Explain the differences among the Agency for International Development (AID), the World Bank, and the International Monetary Fund (IMF).

For Online Exercises, go to the Tucker Web site at www.cengage.com/economics/tucker.

✓ CHECKPOINT ANSWERS

Does Rapid Growth Mean a Country Is Catching Up?

GDP growth alone does not measure the standard of living. You must also consider population. Even though Beta experienced a greater GDP growth rate, its GDP per capita might be less than Alpha's because its population growth rate is greater. Of course, the reverse is also possible, but without population data, we cannot say. If you said which country's people are better off cannot be determined because the GDP must be divided by the population to measure the average standard of living, **YOU ARE CORRECT.**

Is the Minimum Wage an Antipoverty Solution for Poor Countries?

An important source of foreign investment for LDCs is multinational corporations that locate plants and other facilities in these countries. LDCs compete with each other for the economic growth and development benefits that these multinational corporations can provide. For an LDC to win the competition, it must offer political stability, adequate infrastructure, a favorable business climate, and a cheap labor force. If you said you would not support the president's proposal to raise the minimum wage because it would place the LDC at a competitive disadvantage in the labor market, thereby reducing foreign private investment and growth, **YOU ARE CORRECT.**

Sample Quiz

For an explanation of the correct answers, visit the Tucker Web site at www.cengage.com/economics/tucker.

1. Which of the following is a problem when comparing GDP per capita between nations?
   a. GDP per capita fails to measure income distribution.
   b. Fluctuations in exchange rates affect differences in GDP per capita.
   c. GDP per capita is subject to greater measurement errors for LDCs compared to IACs.
   d. All of the above answers are correct.

2. GDP per capita is a relatively good measurement of
   a. the distribution of income.
   b. purchasing power.
   c. household production.
   d. the standard of living.

3. Which of the following is infrastructure?
   a. police
   b. training and education
   c. highways.
   d. All of the answers above answers are correct.

4. Which of the following statements explains the vicious circle of poverty?
   a. By investing in education and infrastructure at the same time, the country can overcome the problems of poverty.
   b. Poverty arises out of the lack of investment, but countries cannot invest because they are poor.
   c. A nation can shift its production possibilities curve inward by shifting more resources into the production of capital goods.
   d. A nation can shift its production possibilities curve outward by shifting more resources into the production of consumer goods.

5. Which of the following is *not* a characteristic of *most* less-developed countries?
   a. inadequate human capital
   b. inadequate capital goods
   c. high population growth rate
   d. inadequate water supplies
   e. high productivity

6. Compared to IACs, LDCs are often characterized by
   a. lower life expectancy.
   b. lower adult literacy.
   c. lower per capita energy consumption.
   d. All of the above answers are correct.

7. Real GDP per capita and other alternative measures of the quality of life are
   a. independent.
   b. directly correlated.
   c. poorly correlated.
   d. inversely related.

8. Economic development encompasses which of the following measures?
   a. economic growth
   b. the political environment
   c. education
   d. All of the above answers are correct.

9. Which of the following is a characteristic of an LDC?
   a. capital flight
   b. vicious circle of poverty
   c. lack of entrepreneurs
   d. All of the above answers are correct.

10. Economic growth and development in LDCs are low because many of them lack
    a. savings.
    b. infrastructure.
    c. a political environment favorable to growth.
    d. All of the above answers are correct.

11. Which of the following is a *true* statement?
    a. The LDC classification is of questionable accuracy.
    b. GDP per capita ignores the degree of income distribution.
    c. GDP per capita is affected by exchange rate changes.
    d. GDP per capita does not account for the difference in the cost of living among nations.
    e. All of the above answers are correct.

Sample Quiz *continued*

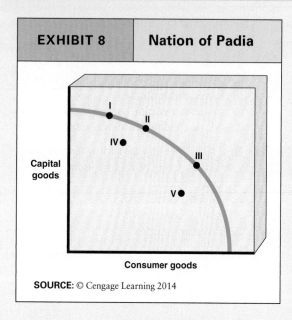

EXHIBIT 8 | **Nation of Padia**

Capital goods

Consumer goods

SOURCE: © Cengage Learning 2014

12. Exhibit 8 shows the production possibilities curve of the nation of Padia. Based only on this information, which point would produce the highest rate of growth?
   a. I
   b. II
   c. III
   d. IV
   e. V

13. Exhibit 8 shows the production possibilities curve of the nation of Padia. Based only on this information, the point which would produce the lowest rate of growth would be
   a. I
   b. II
   c. III
   d. IV
   e. V

14. Which of the following is in charge of U.S. aid to foreign countries?
   a. Agency for International Development (AID)
   b. World Bank
   c. International Monetary Fund (IMF)
   d. New International Economic Order (NIEO)

15. Which of the following makes long-term low-interest loans to LDCs?
   a. Agency for International Development (AID)
   b. World Bank
   c. International Monetary Fund (IMF)
   d. New International Economic Order (NIEO)

16. Which of the following makes short-term conditional low-interest loans to LDCs?
   a. World Bank
   b. Agency for International Development (AID)
   c. Agency for International Finance (AIF)
   d. International Monetary Fund (IMF)

17. Which of the following is *not* an example of a country's infrastructure?
   a. transportation system
   b. communications system
   c. political system
   d. educational system

18. Which of the following *best* defines the vicious circle of poverty?
   a. Countries are poor because they cannot afford to save and invest.
   b. Countries are poor because of high population growth.
   c. Countries are poor because of lack of education and training for workers.
   d. Countries are poor because of poor international credit.

19. If a country's population grows at the same rate as its real GDP, then real per capita GDP
   a. grows at an increasing rate.
   b. grows at a constant rate.
   c. doesn't change.
   d. decreases at a decreasing rate.

20. In order for Ethiopia to increase its future economic growth, it must choose a point that is
   a. below its production possibilities curve.
   b. further along on its production possibilities curve toward the capital goods axis.
   c. further along on its production possibilities curve toward the consumption goods axis.
   d. above its production possibilities curve.

APPENDIX 1

Evaluating a Tax Policy

Economics includes cost/benefit analysis of various options to arrive at better decisions. The realm of tax policy provides us with an opportunity to balance the benefits of a particular tax (the Tax Revenue) against the costs of a tax (the Deadweight Loss)

Definition of 'Deadweight Loss'

The costs to society created by market inefficiency. Mainly used in economics, deadweight loss can be applied to any deficiency caused by an inefficient allocation of resources. Price ceilings (such as price controls and rent controls), price floors (such as minimum wage and living wage laws) and taxation are all said to create deadweight losses. Deadweight loss occurs when supply and demand are not in equilibrium. (Princeton)

Investopedia explains 'Deadweight Loss'

Minimum wage and living wage laws can create a deadweight loss by causing employers to overpay for employees and preventing low-skilled workers from securing jobs. Price ceilings and rent controls can also create deadweight losses by discouraging production and decreasing the supply of goods, services or housing below what consumers truly demand. Consumers experience shortages and producers earn less than they would otherwise. Taxes are also said to create a deadweight loss because they prevent people from engaging in purchases they would otherwise make because the final price of the product will be above the equilibrium market price.

Comparing Dead Weight Loss to Tax Revenue

Dead Weight Loss = damage done to Industry
Tax Revenue = new tax revenue raised by new tax
TR = Difference in price paid v selling price * Quantity
Tax Revenue = (dPt -sPt) * Qt

Industry Revenue = Price * Quantity
Industry Revenue before tax = Pe * Qe
Industry Revenue after tax = sPt * Qt
IRev before - IRev after = Dead Weight Loss

The price that demanders pay includes the tax
dPt
Pe
The suppliers get every dollar the demanders pay.
sPt
The amount the suppliers receive has been reduced by the tax

Without a Tax, the selling price and the price paid are the same.

Qt   Qe

When a tax is imposed, the incidence of taxation falls in such a way that reduces the quantity supplied and quantity demanded.

Industry Before Tax   MINUS   Industry After the Tax   Equals the Dead Weight loss

Pe

sPt

Qe   Qt

Dead Weight Loss

• The damage to the market which is caused by taxation
• The loss of sales
• The loss of production
• The loss of jobs
• The loss of revenue
• The loss of the benefit of the product or service

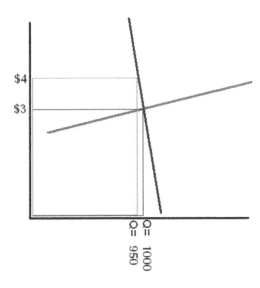

Compare Tax Revenue to Dead Weight Loss

Before the tax was passed this market enjoyed $3 prices and 1000 units were produced and consumed each month. After the $1.05 tax was passed the price jumped to $4 and the number of units decreased to 950. The Tax Revenue is $997.50 ($1.05 * 950) and the deadweight loss is $197.50

Incidence of taxation
- The ultimate payer of a tax
- The group who actually bears the burden of a tax
- Incidence of taxation tends to fall on those who have the least power and options – the group who has the most inelastic curve
- Example: Who really pays the Yacht Tax?
- What about a luxury tax, cigarette tax, salt,

The following schedule indicates the Quantity Demanded and Quantity Supplied at various prices in the market for lemonade. Use the schedule to answer the following questions.

Price	Qs	Qd
55¢	850	1250
62¢	875	1240
70¢	900	1210
78¢	925	1190
85¢	950	1180
92¢	980	1080
$0.93	984	1070
$0.94	988	1060
$0.95	992	1050
$0.96	995	1040
$0.97	997	1030
$0.98	998	1020
$0.99	999	1010
$1.00	1000	1000
$1.01	1001	990
$1.02	1011	980
$1.03	1021	970
$1.04	1031	960
$1.05	1041	950
$1.06	1050	940
$1.07	1060	930
$1.08	1070	920
$1.09	1080	910
$1.10	1090	900
$1.11	1100	891
$1.12	1110	883
$1.13	1120	875
$1.14	1130	862
$1.15	1140	850

1) What is the current Equilibrium Price and Quantity? (No Taxation Initially)
   a. How much do buyers pay?
   b. How much do sellers receive?
   c. How many units are bought and sold?
   d. What is the total revenue? (Size of the lemonade market)
2) Which is relatively more elastic, supply or demand, in this market?

3) To whom would you expect the incidence of taxation to fall?
   a. Completely absorbed by seller
   b. Completely paid for by buyer
   c. Shared equally between buyers and sellers
   d. Shared, but majority of the tax would be paid by sellers
   e. Shared, but majority of the tax would be paid by buyers
4) Now suppose the government imposes a 10¢ per unit tax on this lemonade market. The tax will prevent the market from reaching equilibrium. What are the answers to these questions now?
   a. How much do buyers pay?
   b. How much do sellers receive?
   c. How many units are bought and sold?
   d. What is the total revenue? (Size of the taxed lemonade market)
5) Compare the total revenue of the lemonade industry before and after the tax. What is the deadweight loss of the tax?
6) What is the total tax revenue raised by the 10¢ tax?
7) Which is greater, the tax revenue or the deadweight loss?
8) Do you support this tax? What might be more efficient?

Consider the graphs for the four markets below. Which market would you predict will suffer the greatest deadweight loss due to taxation? Which market(s) appear to generate a greater tax revenue compared to the associated deadweight loss?

APPENDIX 2

Building Theories to Explain Everyday Life: From Observations to Questions to Theories to Predictions

Introduction In this chapter, we build theories to explain everyday life. Some of the things we seek to explain are the birth rates in various countries, one's ethical code, burglary, segregated neighborhoods, cheating on an exam, house prices and school districts, and more.

21-1 A DIFFERENT KIND OF CHAPTER

This chapter differs from others in this text in two fundamental ways: in your experience and in its content.

First, this chapter offers a different experience. Think about a new house that took eight months to build. You see the house for the first time on the day it is completed. You look at the outside, then walk into the house, go into every room, touch the various surfaces—the freshly painted walls, the granite countertop in the kitchen, the shiny new hardwood floor.

How different would it be to watch the house being built from day to day? You would see the land being cleared, the excavation dug, the concrete laid, the house framed, plumbing and wiring put in, the walls painted.

These are two very different experiences: the view of a completed house and the building of a home. Which experience is more like yours in reading this text so far? It is probably like the first—viewing the completed house. The text has presented various complete theories, such as the theory of supply and demand. Then we discussed certain things within those theories. That is how the material in most economics principles texts is presented, and it is an important part of your economic education.

Also important is another part of your economic education: seeing the process that leads to the completed theory—seeing how the house is built. If contractors build houses, economists build theories. It is time for you to see the nitty-gritty process of how economists go about doing what they do. That is the experience of this chapter.

Building an economic theory is a five-step process:

1. It starts with economists making an observation or having a thought.
2. This leads to a question.
3. The economist then builds a theory to try to answer the question.
4. Next, if the theory has been built correctly, predictions pour forth, based on the theory.
5. Finally, the theory is tested; data are gathered and analyzed.

In this chapter, we present only the first four steps. We leave the last step—testing the theory—to a course you might take in statistics or econometrics.

This chapter also differs from others in its content. Most other chapters have contained discussions of fairly standard economic topics: supply and demand, market structures, labor markets, and the like. In this chapter, we include everyday experiences and topics: the ethical code in small towns and large cities, punctuality and office hours, family size, and so on. We chose these topics for three reasons, two of which are that most people are familiar with them from their own everyday life experiences and no specialized knowledge is needed to discuss them.

The third reason is to show that economic thinking, concepts, and theorizing can often extend to places that most people would not have guessed. To noneconomists, economic thinking and concepts can be readily applied to business firms, inflation, unemployment, markets, interest rates, and monetary policy. But rarely do they think that economic thinking and concepts can be applied to topics such as dating, ethical codes, or family size. Why are economists extending themselves into the domains of the sociologist, psychologist, and anthropologist? It's sort of like a baseball player telling a football player how to play football. Stick to baseball!

It's been said that economics is becoming an imperialist social science; that is, it is spreading out into other fields. It is going where it has not gone before—into sociology, history, political science, anthropology, psychology, and law. In any of these fields today, you will see the imprint of economists. For economic imperialists (those who venture into other fields), economics isn't so much a field of study as it is a method of analysis. Economics is not just a list of topics (unemployment, inflation, firms, monetary policy, and so on) but rather a set of tools that can be applied to a whole host of phenomena. This set of tools is relevant not only to studying markets and the economy but also to social and political environments. This, the imperialist viewpoint, is presented in this chapter. In that sense, this chapter presents a different perspective (from that of other chapters) of the practitioners of economics today.

21-2 THE PROCESS

As explained, the process of building a theory consists of five steps. Here are the first four, stated in slightly more formal terms:

1. Observation or thought
2. Question based on observation
3. Building a theory to answer the question
4. Making predictions based on the theory

We begin with our first of many observations.

21-3 OBSERVATION 1: THE BIRTH RATES IN VARIOUS COUNTRIES ARE DIFFERENT

You observe that the birth rate is not the same in all countries. In some countries it is 1.4 children per couple, and in other countries it is 2.7.

21-3a The Question

Why are the birth rates different in various countries?

21-3b The Theory

The proposed theory is based on the opportunity cost for a woman of having a child. To illustrate, consider two women, A and B. Woman A lives in a rather poor country and has few opportunities to earn income. If she were to work, she would earn $10 a day. Woman B lives in a relatively rich country and has numerous opportunities to earn income. If she were to work, she would earn $400 a day.

Each woman is considering having a child. Each woman intends, if she has a child, to take off two years from work to have and care for the child. For woman A, the opportunity cost of having the child is $10 a day for two years: $5,200. For woman B, the opportunity cost of having the child is $400 a day for two years: $208,000.[1]

21-3c The Predictions

PREDICTION 1. Our first prediction is very general: The higher the opportunity cost for a woman to have a child, the fewer children she will have.

PREDICTION 2. If women in rich countries have greater opportunities to earn income and women in poorer countries have fewer, then women in rich countries will have fewer children than women in poor countries.

PREDICTION 3. Within a rich country, women who have the greatest opportunity to earn income will have fewer children than those who have poor opportunities to earn income. A more specific prediction is that a woman who goes to medical school and becomes a physician will have fewer children than a woman who becomes a schoolteacher. Stated slightly differently, women physicians are predicted to have fewer children, on average, than women schoolteachers.

21-3d A Detour: The Issue of Falsifiability (Refutability)

A good theory should have the virtue of falsifiability. In other words, not only must a theory predict things that we should observe *if it is right*, but it should also predict things that we should observe *if it is wrong*. A theory is falsifiable, or refutable, if it can be falsified or refuted; it can be shown to be wrong if it is indeed wrong. Consider the last specific prediction: Women physicians will have fewer children, on average, than women

---

1. After computing the two dollar amounts, we could, to put things on an even more solid basis, adjust each for the cost of living in each country. For instance, the cost of living may be lower in the poor country than in the rich country, so that $1 buys more in the poor country than in the rich country. Still, it would probably be the case that one woman's opportunity cost of having children was different from another's. It is this relative relationship that matters for our example.

schoolteachers. If we collect the data on women having children and find that women physicians, on average, have more children or the same number of children as women schoolteachers, we know that the theory is false (refuted). That is what we want in a theory: the ability to know not only when it is right but also when it is wrong.

A theory can also be not falsifiable, or not refutable. Consider this theory: Everything that happens to you happens because of the specific time and day you were born. In other words, if a person was born on September 21, 1992, at 9:01:33 a.m. Eastern time, then everything that happens to the person happens because of being born at that specific time. So, if the person goes to a specific college, takes a specific major, and eats a bologna sandwich for lunch one day—all this happens because of being born at that specific time.

We cannot falsify or refute this theory. No matter what a person does or doesn't do—go to college X or go to college Y, eat a bologna sandwich or eat a BLT sandwich—is supposedly a consequence of being born on a certain day and time. The theory predicts nothing that, if it happens, can falsify or refute the model. So there is no way to know whether what is being said is true or false. There is no way to judge or evaluate the theory. In effect, the theory is saying, "Accept what I say as true because I say it is true."

Instead, it would be better if the theory were to say, "Don't accept what I say as true because I say it is true. Here is what I propose: If you see X, Y, or Z, then what I have said is true. If you see A, B, or C, what I have said is false." Scientists strive to build theories that can be falsified or refuted. They seek to build theories that are capable of telling them not only when they are right but also when they are wrong.

Self-Test

Answers to Self-Test questions are in Answer to Self-Test Questions at the back of the book.

1. What does it mean to say that a theory is falsifiable?

2. What is the five-step process to building a theory?

3. Women in some countries have more children than women in other countries because they have a stronger preference for having children. Would an economist be likely to use different preferences to explain differences in behavior? Why or why not?

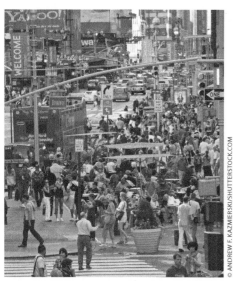
© ANDREW F. KAZMIERSKI/SHUTTERSTOCK.COM

21-4 OBSERVATION/THOUGHT 2: THE ETHICAL CODE OF PEOPLE WHO LIVE IN A SMALL TOWN IS DIFFERENT FROM THAT OF PEOPLE WHO LIVE IN A LARGE CITY

Bob lives and works in New York City but recently visited a small town in the Midwest for two weeks. When he returned to New York City, he told all his friends and coworkers how friendly, decent, and honest the people seemed to be in the small town. Bob suspects, based on his limited observation, that the people in small towns might have a slightly better ethical code than those who live in large cities.

21-4a The Question

Do small town people have a somewhat different (better?) ethical code than big city people?

21-4b **The Theory**

The theory has to do with what percentage of the population an individual represents. If a person lives in a town of 1,000 persons, she is 1/1,000th of the population. If the person lives in a city of 5 million persons, she is 1/5,000,000th of the population. According to the theory, the larger a percentage of the population that a person is, the more likely it is that the person will treat others as he or she wants to be treated. Why? The larger a percentage of the population a person is, the more likely it is that the person will keep meeting those he initially gets to know.

For example, if John lives in a town of 200 people, he can be fairly sure of knowing most, if not all, of the town folk. He also knows that he has a good chance of running into the same people over and over again; after all, that's what happens in a small town. He might see Melanie in the grocery store or at the post office or getting her car fixed. He might run into Kevin at the park or at a restaurant. In other words, in a small town the probability of running into the same people over and over again is higher than in a large city.

That fact makes it fairly costly to treat people poorly—to lie to them, to cheat them, to take advantage of them. If you treat them poorly one day (that is, not treat them as you want to be treated), you could very well run into them the next day. (And they will probably have a few choice words for you.) Of course, even if you don't run into them the next day, word gets around in a small town. If you cheat Jack on Saturday, and he tells Joanne on Sunday, then Joanne might be wary of you on Monday.

Things might be different in a big city, where one person is a smaller percentage of the population. In a big city, you don't have as great a chance of meeting the same people over and over again. You might cheat Jack on Saturday, and he might tell Joanne on Sunday, but are you really going to run into Joanne on Monday? After all, it's a big city. Simply put, treating someone poorly in a big city may come with lower costs (fewer negative consequences) than treating someone badly in a small town.

21-4c **The Predictions**

PREDICTION 1. The owner of a car repair shop in a small town will be more careful not to overcharge customers than the owner of a car repair shop in a large city.

PREDICTION 2. No matter the size of the town or city, people are more likely to treat others as they want to be treated in a setting of small numbers that they frequent often than in a large numbers setting that they rarely frequent. Again, consider John who lives and works in New York City. He works in lower Manhattan at a small office with 10 people. In his work life, he works in a very small town. It is as if he is back in that small town in the Midwest, except that the town is smaller. He is a larger percentage of the office population than he is of the city. The theory predicts that he will more likely adopt the treat-others-as-you-want-to-be-treated principle in the office than he will outside the office. Generalizing the prediction, people will have a higher ethical code with those they work with (and see every day) than with those they rarely meet or are only mildly acquainted with.

PREDICTION 3. If a person treats coworkers (whom she sees every day) poorly, the theory predicts that she treats others worse (i.e., those she doesn't see regularly or have as much chance of later running into).

© ROBERT KNESCHKE/SHUTTERSTOCK.COM

21-5 OBSERVATION/THOUGHT 3: THE CLOSER THE DOLLAR TUITION THE STUDENT PAYS IS TO THE EQUILIBRIUM TUITION, THE MORE ON TIME AND RESPONSIVE UNIVERSITY INSTRUCTORS WILL BE FOR OFFICE HOURS

21-5a The Question

When the gap between student tuition and the equilibrium tuition is small, will instructors be on time more often for, and more responsive in, office hours than instructors who teach at universities where the gap is large?

21-5b The Theory

For most four-year traditional universities (both private and public), the tuition the student is charged is not the same as the equilibrium tuition. Often, the student tuition is below the equilibrium tuition. For example, the equilibrium tuition at a private university might be $60,000 a year, and the student is charged $40,000. Or the equilibrium tuition at a public university might be $55,000 a year, and the student is charged $20,000. Openings in universities (for first-year students) are not fully rationed by dollar price (tuition). They are rationed by a combination of dollar price, high school grades, standardized test scores, and so on. In other words, to be admitted to a university, a student may need a grade point of average of at least 3.00 and an SAT score of at least 1,800.

If most four-year traditional universities are charging students less than the equilibrium tuition, then a dollar gap must exist between what a student pays and the equilibrium tuition. If the equilibrium tuition is $60,000 and the student tuition is $40,000, the gap is $20,000. Does this gap matter to the behavior of university instructors when holding their office hours? According to our theory, it does.

Exhibit 1 shows the demand to attend two universities, A and B. The supply of openings at each university is assumed to be the same: 3,000. Because the demand to attend university A is higher than it is to attend university B, the equilibrium tuitions are $50,000 at university A and $40,000 at university B. However, the tuition charged students at each university is the same: $30,000. At this tuition, the gap (between the equilibrium tuition and student tuition) and the shortage (between students applying and openings) are both greater at university A than B. The shortage at university A at the $30,000 tuition is 2,200 students because, at this tuition, 5,200 students want to attend the university but only 3,000 can be admitted. At the same tuition, the shortage at university B is 1,000 students; 4,000 students want to attend but only 3,000 can be admitted.

Will the sizes of the gap and of the shortage affect how punctual and responsive an instructor will be at office hours?

The theory predicts that it will: The bigger the gap, the more the demand (to attend the university) has to fall before there is no shortage. In Exhibit 1, the demand to attend university A would have to shift leftward by enough to go through point X before there is no shortage of openings. The demand to attend university B would also have to shift leftward to go through point X, but *not as much*. The demand (curve) to attend university B is closer to point X than the demand (curve) to attend university A is to point X.

The Gap Between Equilibrium Tuition and Student Tuition

The supply of openings at each of two universities, A and B. The demand to attend university A is higher than the demand to attend university B, as shown by the respective demand curves. The equilibrium tuitions are $50,000 at university A and $40,000 at B. However, at each university the student pays

$30,000. The gap between the equilibrium tuition at university A and the student tuition is $20,000; at B, the gap is $10,000. At university A, the shortage of openings at the student tuition ($30,000) is 2,200 students: 5,200 students want to be admitted but only 3,000 will be admitted. At university B, the shortage at the student tuition ($30,000) is 1,000: 4,000 students want to be admitted, but only 3,000

will be admitted. The demand to attend university A has to fall more to go through point X in this exhibit (where there is no shortage of openings at the student tuition) than the demand to attend university B has to fall. This fact gives the instructors at A more room to advance demand-reducing behavior than the instructors at B.

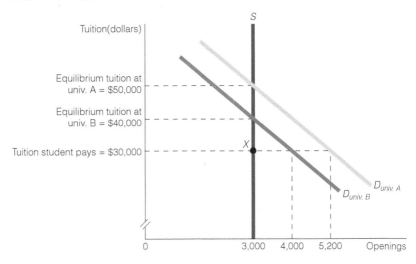

© CENGAGE LEARNING 2014

What does this mean for the instructors at each university? The instructors at university A have more room to take *demand-reducing actions* than the instructors at university B. Such actions might include showing up late for office hours and not being responsive during office hours, things that students (as customers of the university) do not like. If word gets around that instructors don't regularly meet their office hours at a given university, demand to attend that university may decrease. (Books and websites address the college experience at various colleges in the country.)

Of course, why would an instructor not be punctual for office hours and not be responsive during them? We doubt that any instructor plans to be this way. Instructors might be on the other side of the university campus just before office hours and/or might be feeling a little hurried or overwhelmed on a particular day. The theory simply states that the cost of not hurrying to office hours or of being less responsive is lower for the instructor at a university with a big gap than for the instructor at a university with a small gap. At the big-gap university, many other students are willing to take the place of a student who leaves; at the small-gap college, there aren't as many.

21-5c **The Predictions**

PREDICTION 1. University instructors who work at big-gap universities will be less nearly punctual for office hours and less responsive during office hours than university instructors who work at small-gap universities or no-gap colleges.

PREDICTION 2. The bigger the gap, the more flexibility instructors have to teach their courses the way they want to teach it. To illustrate, suppose the instructor wants to do X, Y, and Z in the course, and students prefer the instructor to do A, B, and C. How will the course be taught? The bigger the gap, the more likely the instructor will teach X, Y, and Z (even if it isn't what the students want) and not be adversely affected by the students who leave. That's because with a big gap between equilibrium and student tuition, there is a big shortage of openings at the university. Having students go elsewhere because they don't like how the instructor teaches the course (the papers he assigns, the material she goes over, the large number of readings she assigns) doesn't adversely affect the instructor because so many other students want to take their places.

21-6 OBSERVATION/THOUGHT 4: CRIMINALS ARE NOT RATIONAL

Some people say that criminals are not rational. They are not like regular people, who think in terms of the costs and benefits of their actions. Who, in their right minds, would commit a crime—whether it is burglary, kidnapping, arson, or murder?

21-6a The Question

Are criminals rational? Does their behavior respond to changes in costs and benefits?

21-6b The Theory

We build a theory, based on a rational criminal, holding that criminals think and act in terms of costs and benefits. The theory posits that criminals have two equations in mind (and might not be aware of them). The first equation relates to the benefits of committing a criminal act—let's say a burglary. The benefit equation is:

$$EB = Ps \times \text{Loot}$$

where EB is the expected benefits of burglary, Ps is the probability of successfully burglarizing a house (getting into and out of a house with the goods), and Loot is the dollar take.

The cost equation looks like this:

$$EC = [Pp \times (I + F)] + AC$$

where EC is the expected costs of burglary, Pp is the probability of imprisonment, I is the income the criminal gives up if caught and imprisoned, F is the dollar value the criminal puts on freedom (how much the person would pay to stay out of prison), and AC is the anguish cost of committing a burglary.

An economist would say that criminals simply substitute various values into the equations and then determine whether the expected benefits of the criminal act are greater than, less than, or equal to the expected costs. If the expected benefits are greater than the expected costs, they commit the crime. If the expected benefits are less, they do not commit the crime. And if the expected benefits equal the expected costs, they flip a coin. Heads, commit the crime; tails, don't commit the crime.

Suppose the values are as follows:

$$Ps = 80 \text{ percent}$$

$$Loot = \$400,000$$

$$Pp = 30 \text{ percent}$$

$$I = \$80,000$$

$$F = \$42,000$$

$$AC = \$3,000$$

Substituting these numbers for the variables into our two equations, we find that the expected benefits equal $320,000, and the expected costs equal $39,600. With these numbers, the person goes ahead and commits the crime.

21-6c The Predictions

PREDICTION 1. If people put more locks on their doors and install more security devices in their homes, the probability of success (Ps) will fall, lowering the benefits of burglary. And lowering the benefits of burglary will lead to fewer burglaries.

PREDICTION 2. If more police are on the streets, the probability of being arrested after committing a crime will rise, and the probability of being imprisoned (Pp) will likely rise too. Thus, the costs of committing a burglary will rise, and fewer burglaries will be committed.

PREDICTION 3. During a recession, incomes usually fall, and unemployment usually rises. Thus, the income one forfeits is usually lower during a recession than during boom times. Lower foregone income (I) will lower the cost of burglary and thus will lead to more burglaries.

PREDICTION 4. If prison became more severe (hard labor), a person would pay more to stay out of prison (F). Paying more to stay out of prison will raise the cost of burglary, and fewer burglaries will be committed.

21-6d A Detour: Does Evidence Prove a Theory Correct?

Suppose a theory predicts that all swans will be white. You and others go out into the field to test the theory, looking for swans. So far, you and others have found and counted 4,324 swans—all white. Does this prove that the theory predicting that all swans are white is correct? No. The reason is simple: We can't be sure that all the existing swans have been found and counted. Perhaps there are 5,000 swans in total, and only 4,324 have been found, have been counted, and are white.

So evidence of white swans does not prove the swan theory correct. The best evidence can do is give us a reason not to reject a theory. We cannot say, "The evidence proves the theory correct." It is more accurate to say, "The evidence fails to reject the theory." In other words, given the amassed evidence so far, none of it is inconsistent with the predictions of the theory. On the other hand, any evidence that is inconsistent with the theory—such as finding a black swan—is reason enough to say, "The evidence rejects the theory."

21-6e Another Detour: After You Have One Theory That Explains and Predicts, Search for Another

Suppose another planet, somewhere in the universe, has living beings that resemble human beings on earth. These beings speak a language, read and write, do mathematics, raise families, and do all the things we do. However, half the beings on the planet are blue in color, and half are green. In the neighborhoods on the planet, blue beings live only with blue beings, and green beings live only with green beings. Asked to explain why only completely segregated neighborhoods exist on the planet, you think the explanation has something to do with color discrimination. You put forth a discrimination theory holding that the beings of one color (either green or blue) are discriminating against the beings of the other color. Perhaps green beings have gotten into positions of power and passed laws that prevent blue beings from living in neighborhoods where green beings reside.

You test your theory by seeking out evidence of discrimination. You find that green beings have, in fact, passed laws prohibiting blue persons from living in the same neighborhoods with green persons. Does it follow, then, that discrimination—and discrimination alone—explains the completely segregated neighborhoods? Perhaps not. To illustrate, suppose we advance a nondiscrimination theory for the segregated neighborhoods. This theory is based on the work of Thomas Schelling, the winner of the Nobel Prize in Economic Science in 2005.[2]

We start with 200 persons, 100 of whom are blue and 100 of whom are green. Each person (no matter which color) prefers to live in an integrated neighborhood. However, no person wants to live in a neighborhood where he or she is a minority of less than 30 percent.

Now suppose that there are two neighborhoods, A and B, and that their populations are as follows:

Neighborhood A	Neighborhood B
70 blue persons	70 green persons
30 green persons	30 blue persons

Obviously, the two neighborhoods are integrated; blue and green people live in each. Also, the two neighborhoods are satisfactory to everyone living in them. No person in either neighborhood falls into a minority that is less than 30 percent of the population.

Then, for work-related reasons, one green person moves from A to B, and one blue person moves from B to A. The neighborhoods now look this way:

Neighborhood A	Neighborhood B
71 blue persons	71 green persons
29 green persons	29 blue persons

Green persons have fallen to a 29 percent minority in A, and blue persons have fallen to a 29 percent minority in B. Although both green and blue persons prefer integrated neighborhoods to segregated neighborhoods, they do not want to become a minority of less than 30 percent. So, green persons are likely to move from A to B, and blue persons are likely to move from B to A. If another green person and another blue person move, we get the following:

Neighborhood A	Neighborhood B
72 blue persons	72 green persons
28 green persons	28 blue persons

---

2. See *Micromotives and Macrobehavior* by Thomas C. Schelling (New York: W.W. Norton & Company, 1978).

In neighborhood A, blue persons are becoming a bigger majority, and green persons are becoming a smaller minority. In B, green persons are becoming a bigger majority, and blue persons are becoming a smaller minority.

Where will the movement end? The neighborhoods will be in equilibrium when things look like this:

Neighborhood A	Neighborhood B
100 blue persons	100 green persons

The neighborhoods are completely segregated. Blue people live with other blue people, and green people live with other green people. There are no blue-green neighborhoods at all.

Although this is an equilibrium setting, all blue and green persons would prefer to live in integrated neighborhoods. But no one wants to a live in an integrated neighborhood as a minority of less than 30 percent minority. Therefore, after a move by one green person and one blue person, we end up with complete segregation.

Now, as the creator of the color discrimination theory, you had no idea of this process that ended with the segregated neighborhoods. What would you think if you came across the two segregated neighborhoods, not knowing how they came to be that way? You might think that color discrimination was the cause.

Does it follow that segregated neighborhoods can be caused only by one thing or another, but never by two? No. Sometimes multiple causes are behind what we observe, and each cause, by itself, is sufficient to bring about what we see. When trying to explain why neighborhoods are segregated, color discrimination, encased in law, could be enough to explain the segregated neighborhoods. But even in the absence of discrimination, segregated neighborhoods could arise, even when paradoxically everyone prefers to live in an integrated neighborhood.

The lesson is that a single-cause theory that predicts well (i.e., accurately) does not necessarily rule out other possible causes. Specifically, the lesson for the theory builder is that after you have developed one theory to explain something (segregated neighborhoods, dating relationships, ethical codes, inflation, or unemployment), try to build another theory to explain the very same effect. If it, too, predicts well, and the predictions of one theory are not the opposite of the predictions of the other, then we probably have a multiple-cause explanation.

21-6f A Final Detour: Why Prediction Is So Important, or Why Good-Sounding Stories Are Not Enough

Sometimes we want to believe some theories over others, especially when the theory seems to confirm what we already believe. The theory seems to say, "See, you were right all along." Accepting a theory that tells us we were right all along is easier than accepting one that says, "You were wrong all along."

To illustrate, Smith has always believed that people who are on welfare are lazy and unmotivated. Contrary to Smith, Jones believes that people who are on welfare have had unfortunate things happen; they've lost a job or gotten sick and were unable to work, and so on.

Two economists present two different theories on welfare. The first theory seems to confirm the description of welfare recipients as lazy and unmotivated. The second theory describes welfare recipients in terms of job loss, sickness, and other causes beyond their control. Smith ends up believing the first theory because it seems to confirm what she has always believed. Jones ends up believing the second theory because it seems to confirm what he has always believed.

Do we accept theories because they seem to confirm what we have always believed or want to believe? Sure, people do it all the time. But what both Smith and Jones should be asking of the economists is "What are your predictions? Do the data support your predictions? What are the predictions of the lazy-unmotivated-person theory of welfare?" If the predictions are X, Y, and Z, then the question is whether the evidence is consistent with X, Y, and Z. If it is, then we now have reason to accept the lazy-unmotivated-person theory of welfare, no matter what you might have believed before. The same goes for the beyond-their-control theory of welfare. If that theory predicts A, B, and C, then the question is whether the evidence is consistent with A, B, and C. If so, then there is now reason to accept that theory, no matter what you might have believed before.

By accepting theories simply because they confirm our beliefs, or because they sound right, or because we want them to be right, we do ourselves a disservice. We need to push theories and theorists to the limit and ask them for more than a "good" or "believable" story or explanation. We need to ask for the predictions. If the theory has no predictions, then it might be nothing more than a fictional account of what someone thinks explains something. Then we must ask for the evidence that leads us to say one of two things: The evidence either (1) fails to reject the theory or (2) rejects the theory.

Self-Test

1. Consider Jack, who attends his son's high school football games and professional football games too. At which games is Jack more likely to be well behaved? Why?

2. Kidnappers can't be rational because no rational person would be a kidnapper. Comment.

3. Can evidence prove a theory is correct?

21-7 OBSERVATION 5: MORE STUDENTS WEAR BASEBALL CAPS IN CLASS ON EXAM DAYS THAN ON OTHER DAYS

21-7a The Question

What purpose does wearing a baseball cap in class on exam days serve that it doesn't serve on other days?

21-7b The Theory

A baseball cap can shield your eyes. A student may want to shield his eyes from the view of the instructor who is administering an exam if he plans to glance over to his neighbor's test. So, on exam day, wearing a baseball cap in class serves a purpose it doesn't serve any other day: It helps a student pick up answers from his neighbors without anyone seeing. It makes one's cheating invisible to others.

21-7c The Predictions

PREDICTION 1. A smaller percentage of students will be wearing baseball caps when those students are taking an essay exam than when taking a multiple-choice exam.

PREDICTION 2. A smaller percentage of students will be wearing baseball caps when a lecture is being given than when an exam is being taken.

PREDICTION 3. Instructors are likely to notice anything that stands out on exam day as being different from other days. In nonclassroom environments, more males than females seem to wear baseball caps. This practice gives males a better chance than females of wearing a baseball cap in class without tipping the instructor into thinking something is out of the ordinary. Thus, males wearing baseball caps on exam day are less likely to be noticed than females wearing them. Females, then, have one less thing they can use to help them cheat than males, and so we can expect them to cheat less. Specific prediction: On a multiple-choice exams, a larger percentage of the cheaters in the class will be male than female.

PREDICTION 4. Sooner or later, instructors figure out that a baseball cap can be used for shielding one's eyes when looking at another person's exam paper. At that time, they will either tell students that they can't wear baseball caps in class on exam days or perhaps closely watch students wearing baseball caps. After all, when instructors figure out the purpose of the ball cap on exam day, it then becomes a signal to the instructor that the wearer may try to cheat on the exam. The baseball cap is then like a neon sign that reads: "Watch me. I am about to cheat on this exam." Specific prediction: On exam day, instructors will look more often at the students wearing baseball caps than at other students. They will also patrol the class on exam day by walking more often near students wearing baseball caps than other students.

PREDICTION 5. When the instructor is giving a lecture in class, a student wearing a baseball cap will often have to look down to write notes. When looking down, the bill of the baseball cap is pointed downward at a certain angle. On exam day, the student wearing a baseball cap always has to look downward in order to write answers, and again, the bill of the cap will be at a certain angle. However, if the student intends to cheat, the angle is likely to be greater on exam day than on a lecture day, when the student is taking notes. That's because the student has more of a reason to shield the eyes on exam day. The greater slope (greater angle) of the bill on exam day is indicative of doing something more than just writing. It is indicative of writing and glancing left and right. So, specific prediction: Students with baseball caps in class on exam days and lecture days will likely be cheating if the bill of their baseball caps is more sloped (at a greater angle) on exam days.

PREDICTION 6. Students who wear baseball caps backward on lecture days but frontward on exam days are probably cheating on exam days.

21-8 OBSERVATION 6: HOUSES IN "GOOD" SCHOOL DISTRICTS ARE OFTEN MORE EXPENSIVE THAN COMPARABLE HOUSES IN "BAD" SCHOOL DISTRICTS

21-8a The Question
Why are comparable houses (same square footage, size of lot, etc.) often priced differently?

21-8b The Theory
Suppose school districts could be ranked on a scale from 1 to 10, with 10 being the best and 1 the worst. Two houses, A and B, are alike in every way except that house A is located in a school district ranked 5 and house B is in a school district ranked 10. Currently, the

prices of both houses are the same. Which one would you buy if you had children starting school soon? Most people would choose the house in the number 10 school district—house B.

Why? Being in a higher-ranked school district is something that people with children consider to be a good (something from which they derive utility). So, a utility-maximizing couple would prefer to get more rather than less utility for a given amount of money spent on a house. Better to spend $250,000 for a house and get 10,000 utils of utility than to spend $250,000 for a house and get 9,000 utils of utility.

But the real question is, if people get more utility from house B than from house A (because it's located in a better school district), would the prices of the houses really be the same? The answer is no. If house B has something that people value that house A does not have, then the demand for house B will be higher. And a higher demand in the face of a given supply means a higher price. In other words, the house with something more—in this case, a higher-ranked school district—will end up priced higher than the house with less—a lower-ranked school district.

The conclusion: When a person buys a house in a highly ranked school district, part of the purchase price represents what one must pay to be in the highly ranked school district. In other words, the benefits of being in the higher-ranked school district are incorporated into the price of the house. You might be able to break down the price of the house this way: (1) land = $100,000; (2) materials and labor to build the house = $200,000; (3) price paid to be located in a higher-ranked school district = $70,000. Total price = $370,000.

21-8c **The Predictions**

PREDICTION 1. Houses with ocean views will sell for higher prices than comparable houses with no view. You will pay for the view.

PREDICTION 2. Houses located in major metropolitan areas (where there are many things to do) will sell for higher prices than comparable houses in small towns. You will pay for having the opportunity to do a lot of things.

PREDICTION 3. Houses located in cities with clean air will sell for higher prices than comparable houses located in cities with dirty air. You will pay for the cleaner air.

PREDICTION 4. If a major professional sports team were to move to a city that previously did not have a major professional sports team, house prices in the city would rise. You will pay for the sports team. (This prediction is similar to prediction 2, except that it is more specific.)

PREDICTION 5. People will pay (donate money) to meet the president of the United States. Think of the president first as a human being and second as a unique human being. Of the billions of human beings, there is only one president at a time. Now think of the president of the United States and other human beings as you would think of two houses that were comparable in every way except that one had an ocean view and the other didn't. People will pay more for the house with the view. The president is similar to a house with an ocean view, whereas most people are similar to a house without a view. The president has something—the presidency—that *all* others do not. Although people might not be willing to pay to meet just an average, everyday human being, they would be willing to pay to meet a unique human being (the one and only president of the United States).

21-9 OBSERVATION/THOUGHT 7: ARE PEOPLE BETTER OFF WITH OR WITHOUT HEALTH CARE VOUCHERS?

Suppose 100,000 persons do not have health insurance of any kind. Congress passes legislation that mandates a $200 health care voucher per month for each person. With the vouchers, which can be used only to purchase health care, each person can have up to $200 worth of health care a month, or $2,400 of health care a year. For example, Jack doesn't have any health insurance. If he were to get hurt and need medical attention, he could simply go to a doctor or hospital, get the attention needed, and pay for the services rendered (up to $200 a month or $2,400 a year) with the vouchers.

21-9a **The Question**

Will the 100,000 persons purchase more health care with the vouchers than without them? The obvious answer to this question seems to be yes, but is it necessarily correct?

21-9b **The Theory**

Jack is one of the 100,000 persons currently without health insurance. He earns $3,200 a month and spends each month's income the following way:

- Food = $1,000.
- Rent = $2,000.
- Savings for future health care expenses = $200.

Now suppose Jack receives the $200-a-month health care voucher. He can now reorder his expenditures this way:

- Food = $1,000
- Rent = $2,000
- Health care voucher = $200
- Entertainment = $200

Because of the voucher, $200 is freed up for Jack to do other things—if he wants to. He decides to spend the $200 that he had been saving each month on entertainment.

Of course, he doesn't have to spend the money on entertainment. He could spend it on books, clothes, more food, more health care, a higher rent, or even cocaine, gambling, or alcohol. Fact is, we know some things about him but don't know other things about him. We don't know how he will spend the freed-up $200. What we do know is that it will be spent for whatever is *next* on his list of things to buy. If more health care is next on his list, then instead of buying only $200 worth of health care a month (when he didn't have the voucher), he can now buy $400 worth. But if what is next on his list is, say, clothes, then the health care voucher is not financing more health care for Jack, but rather more clothes.

Our theory essentially says this: A monetary gift (of, say, $200 in cash) or an in-kind gift (a $200 voucher that can be used only to purchase health care) will end up going for whatever is next on the recipient's list to purchase.

21-9c **The Predictions**

PREDICTION 1. A mother has two children. She gives both of them gifts of money and in-kind. The theory predicts that she will give more gifts to the child whose next-on-the-list is more acceptable to her. An example: A mother says child 1 is more trustworthy when it comes to spending money than child 2. In the eyes of the mother, what's next on child 1's list is superior to what's next on child 2's list. (Starkly, suppose that what's next on child 1's list are more books and DVDs and that what's next on child 2's list are more cigarettes.)

PREDICTION 2. If each of two candidates running for office says that she will do X, Y, and Z if elected, people will be more willing to vote for the candidate they more nearly agree with in terms of what comes next. To illustrate, suppose A and B are running against each other for U.S. senator from some state. Both say they will vote for reduced taxes, more spending on education, and strong pollution standards. How does a voter who wants all three things decide whom to vote for? If the voter is equally convinced that both candidates are true to their word, she will think in terms of what's next—what will the candidate do if elected? If, for the voter, A's what's next is thought to be better than B's what's next, then the voter votes for A.

How could we test to see whether this prediction is correct? Perhaps the voter who speaks of a candidate as "trustworthy" is thinking in terms of what's next. The more the voter agrees with the candidate's next thing to do, the more trustworthy the voter believes the candidate is. We would predict, then, that the voter will vote for the candidate who seems more trustworthy.

21-10 OBSERVATION 8: PEOPLE WHO GIVE TO OTHERS OFTEN COMPLAIN THAT THEY END UP GIVING TOO MUCH

21-10a **The Question**

Why don't people simply stop giving at the efficient point of giving—when the marginal benefits of giving equal the marginal costs?

21-10b **The Theory**[3]

Suppose person G is a gift giver (he gives gifts to person R) and person R is the gift recipient. The utility for G is specified the following way:

$$U_G = f(\text{Goods A–Z}, U_R)$$

where U_G represents the utility of person G, goods A–Z are various goods that give person G utility, and U_R is the utility of the gift recipient (stemming from receiving G's gifts). Because U_R is included in person G's utility function in a positive way, every time R's utility rises, so does G's utility. In other words, when G gives a gift to R, this gift benefits not only R but also G. Person G likes seeing R happy and benefits more as R becomes happier. To make this point more concrete, think of a mother giving gifts to her children (the recipients). Giving

---

3. This theory is based on a theory first put forth by Wilson E. Schmidt, in "Charitable Exploitation," *Public Choice* 10 (Spring 1969), pp. 103–104. The theory is also discussed in *The New World of Economics*, 5th ed., by Richard B. McKenzie and Gordon Tullock.

the gifts to her children makes her children happy, and when the mother sees her children happy, she gains some utility. She says, "I am happy when my children are happy."

Now consider R's utility function:

$$U_R = f(\text{Goods A–Z})$$

In this case, U_G is not included in the utility function of the gift recipient. Person R is unaffected by the utility that G receives.

Now consider what we mean by a gift. In this theory, a gift is anything that one person gives (without seeking payment in return) to another person that benefits the other person. It could be money, a specific good (such as a computer, car, or item of clothing), or something as simple as a back rub. It could be doing the dishes for someone, going to the store to pick up something, and so on. Simply put, we define a gift broadly. Don't think only in terms of a birthday or holiday gift; think in terms of anything that someone wants and that gives the person utility or satisfaction.

Exhibit 2(a) shows the marginal benefits and marginal costs to person G of giving gifts to person R. The marginal benefits (*MB*) curve is downward sloping, indicating that the law of diminishing marginal utility (benefits) holds for gift giving. The marginal costs (*MC*) curve is horizontal, indicating the constant marginal cost of gift giving. Obviously, the efficient (or optimum) number of gifts, according to G, is 10, where *MB* = *MC*. The area under the *MB* curve and above the *MC* curve out to 10 gifts represents the net gains to G of giving gifts. This is the shaded blue area.

Now it would be preferable for R to receive 11 gifts, rather than 10, but how can R get G to give 11 gifts if 10 is the efficient number of gifts for G to give? As shown in Exhibit 2(b), moving from the 10th to the 11th gift presents G with a net loss because, for the 11th gift, marginal benefits are less than marginal costs. The green area represents the net loss.

Perhaps R can get G to give 11 instead of 10 gifts by presenting G with an *all-or-nothing deal* that takes the efficient option (10 gifts) off the table. In other words, suppose R suggests to G that only two options are available for choosing: either zero gifts or 11 gifts. In other words, instead of letting G choose from three options—0, 10, and 11—G may choose between only two options: 0 or 11. In other words, R is saying to G, "Either give me 11 gifts, or I will not accept any gifts from you."

Will limiting G to only two options—0 or 11—force G to give R 11 gifts? Yes. G now has to calculate what he receives in net gains by giving zero gifts with what he receives in net gains if he receives 11 gifts. Obviously, if he gives zero gifts, he receives no net gains. But if he gives 11 gifts, he receives net gains on the first 10 gifts and a net loss on the 11th. If the net gains on gifts 1–10 are greater than the net loss on the 11th gift, then it is better to give 11 gifts than to give none.

In dollar terms, let's say the blue area in Exhibit 2(b) is worth $500 and the green area in the exhibit is worth $20. Subtracting the net loss on the 11th gift from the net gain of $500 on the first 10 gifts, we are left with $480 in net gains. Person G must therefore compare the $480 in net gains of giving 11 gifts to R to the net gains (zero) he would receive if he gives R zero gifts. In other words, because the blue area (the gains) is greater than the green area (the losses), it is better for G to go with 11 gifts than with zero. Conclusion: By presenting G with an all-or-nothing deal (all = 11 and nothing = 0), R is able to push G beyond his efficient level of gift giving and benefit by receiving more gifts.

In the extreme, how far can R push G? A quick glance at Exhibit 2(c) shows the answer. When the blue area (gains) equals the green area (losses), G will become indifferent between giving R 20 gifts and giving R zero gifts. In other words, the most gifts R can get G to give is 20. Given the option of giving, say, 21 or zero gifts, G will choose zero gifts.

EXHIBIT 2

Giving and Receiving Gifts

(a) The marginal benefits and marginal cost for the gift giver (person G) of giving gifts to gift recipient (person R). The efficient or optimum number of gifts for G to give is 10, where the marginal benefits of giving gifts equals the marginal costs of giving gifts. (b) G's net gain of giving 10 gifts (blue area) and G's net loss of giving an 11th gift. If person R presents G with an all-or-nothing deal ("Give me 11 gifts or give me nothing"), person G will likely give 11 gifts because the net gain on gifts 1–10 is greater than the net loss on the 11th gift. (c) How far can person R push G into giving more than the efficient number of gifts (10)? The answer is 20 gifts, at which point the net gain on gifts 1–10 for G equals the net loss on gifts 11–20. G will not give R a 21st gift. (d) Unless R makes the all-or-nothing request of G in a subtle, nonconfrontational way, R is not likely to benefit. That's because G could find that he receives fewer benefits per gift giving to R. This results in the *MB* curve of giving gifts shifting to the left, from MB_1 to MB_2 and the new efficient number of gifts being 5 instead of 10.

(a)

(b)

(C)

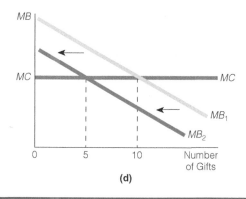

(d)

© CENGAGE LEARNING 2014

A question arises: Suppose R makes the all-or-nothing deal to G in a rude, demanding way. Might this cause G to rethink giving gifts to R at all? Person R would have to be wary of this effect because if G reacts too negatively to the all-or-nothing deal, G's marginal benefits curve (of giving gifts to R) may shift leftward by enough to decrease the efficient number of gifts. This effect is shown in Exhibit 2(d) by a leftward shift in the marginal benefits curve from MB_1 to MB_2. As a result, G will now want to give fewer gifts to R than before the all-or-nothing demand. The new efficient number of gifts is 5 instead of 10.

21-10c **The Predictions**

PREDICTION 1. Gift givers will have less reason to move beyond their efficient number of gifts as the number of persons they can give gifts to increases. In other words, an all-or-nothing deal (from a gift recipient to a gift giver) has less chance of working if the gift giver can substitute one recipient for another. To illustrate, G gives gifts to person R1. R1 tries to get G to give more gifts than the efficient number by presenting G with an all-or-nothing deal. G has potential recipients waiting in the wings and simply replaces R1 with R2 and then gives R2 the efficient number of gifts. Specific prediction: A recipient (an R person) who can't be replaced easily is more likely to push G beyond the efficient number of gifts than a recipient who can be replaced easily.

To illustrate, consider two relationships:

1. A mother-daughter relationship, where the mother has only the one daughter

2. A relationship between two friends

In each relationship are two persons: an R and a G. In the mother-daughter relationship, the mother is the gift giver (G), and the daughter is the gift recipient. The mother (G) gives the efficient number of gifts to the daughter. The daughter tries to push the mother to give more. The daughter gives the mother an all-or-nothing deal. Can the mother replace the daughter with another daughter? No; she has only the one daughter.

Now consider the relationship between two friends, G and R. G gives R the efficient number of gifts. R tries to push G beyond the efficient number. G can more easily find another friend to give gifts to than the mother can find another daughter. Specific prediction: A G–person will give more gifts, beyond the efficient number of gifts, to an R-person who cannot be replaced than to an R-person who can be replaced. In short, the mother is more likely to give in to the daughter's requests than the G-friend will give in to the R-friend's requests.

PREDICTION 2. Recipients in dating relationships will be less likely to push for more than the efficient number of gifts than recipients in a marriage. To illustrate, A and B are dating, and A is the gift giver and B is the gift recipient (the taker). B, the taker, will be less likely to push A beyond the efficient number of gifts when dating than if they were married. In other words, the theory predicts that, if A and B marry, B will be a bigger taker in the marriage with A than in the dating relationship. That's because it is harder to replace a spouse than to replace a boyfriend or girlfriend. In other words, divorce is a costlier proposition than simply breaking up.

PREDICTION 3. Smith wants to buy X, Y, and Z from a company. Buying X, Y, and Z maximizes Smith's net gains. The company presents Smith with an all-or-nothing deal: Either buy W, X, Y, and Z or buy nothing. In other words, it's a package deal or nothing. Smith takes a net loss on buying W, but the net loss on W is smaller than the sum of net gains on X + Y + Z. Smith chooses to buy the company's package. Specific prediction: Package deals often contain something that the customer would have preferred not to have purchased. For example, Smith buys a package of 40 cable channels from his cable television provider. He says he would have preferred buying only 30 because he never watches anything on 10 of the 40 channels.

Self-Test

1. Identify two observations that are inconsistent with the baseball-cap-wearing theory of cheating on an exam.

2. Ocean views (from a house) are not free. Do you agree or disagree? Explain your answer.

3. What does it mean if you are included in another person's utility function in a positive way?

Office Hours

"Can Anyone Build a Theory?"

STUDENT:

I always thought that building theories was the purview of people who are well educated in a particular subject. For example, only those with a PhD in economics should build economic theories, and only those with a doctorate in sociology should build sociological theories. Am I wrong about this?

INSTRUCTOR:

There is no clear line of demarcation between who should and who should not try to build a theory. The purpose of this chapter is to give you the details of how to build and evaluate a theory. On this subject, consider what Richard Feynman (1918–1988), a Nobel Laureate in Physics, said about how theorists start to build theories. He said that the first part of building a theory is to "guess" how things work.

STUDENT:

But anyone can guess about why things are as they are. Isn't there a big difference between my guessing about physical laws and Richard Feynman guessing about laws? Aren't his guesses more likely to turn out right than mine?

INSTRUCTOR:

Yes, probably so, but that's not the point. The point is that theory building starts with a guess—albeit sometimes an educated guess—as to the way things are. Then from the guess, we "unravel," in Feynman's words, the "the consequences of the guess." And finally we compare those consequences to experience. In other words, the evaluation part of the scientific method process comes at the end, when we compare the consequences of the guess, or the predictions of the theory, that we have built with real-world experience, observation, or data.

STUDENT:

In other words, anyone can build a theory, but not everyone's theory is going to be consistent with experience-observation-data. Many theories will be rejected by the evidence.

INSTRUCTOR:

Yes, that's correct. But if you want to get a feel for theorizing, try to build your own theories to explain something you are interested in. Once you have done so, be sure to logically deduce the theory's predictions. Then ask yourself whether the theory's predictions are accurate. Do you actually observe those things that are consistent with the theory?

POINTS TO REMEMBER

1. At the heart of building a theory is the motivation to explain something. (In this chapter, we've tried to explain why the birth rate is higher in some countries than in others, what might explain the burglary rate, why neighborhoods might be segregated, and so on.)
2. Building a theory differs from evaluating a theory. Guesswork plays a part in building a theory; when evaluating a theory, evidence matters. Simply put, the evidence either rejects or fails to reject the predictions of the theory.

Chapter Summary

WHAT A THEORY IS AND IS NOT

- A theory is not perfectly descriptive of reality.
- Theories should not judged by how they sound or by whether they say the things we want to hear. Theories should be judged according to how well they explain things and how consistently and accurately they predict.

THE BIRTH RATES IN VARIOUS COUNTRIES

- The question was: Why do birth rates differ in various countries?
- A key part of answering the question was to consider the opportunity cost for a woman of having a child. The higher the opportunity cost for a woman of having children (in

terms of the wage she would not earn if she took off time to have and raise a child), the fewer children she would have; the lower the opportunity cost of having children, the more children she would have.

THE ISSUE OF FALSIFIABILITY (REFUTABILITY)

- A good theory should have the virtue of falsifiability; that is, a theory must not only predict things that you should observe if it is right but it should also predict things that you should observe if it is wrong.
- Scientists strive to build theories that can be falsified or refuted. They seek to build theories that are capable of telling them not only when they are right but also when they are wrong too.

ETHICAL CODES AND TOWN SIZE

- The question was: Do people who live in small towns have a somewhat different (better?) ethical code than those who live in large cities?
- The theory argues that the larger a percentage of the population that a person is, the more likely the person will treat others as he or she wants to be treated. That's because, as a larger percentage of the population, the person is more likely to have to meet again and again with people he or she initially meets.

STUDENT TUITION AND EQUILIBRIUM TUITION

- The question was: Will instructors who teach at universities with a small gap between student tuition and the equilibrium tuition be on time more often for office hours and more responsive during those hours than instructors at universities with a larger gap?
- For most four-year traditional public and private universities, the tuition the student pays is below the equilibrium tuition. The larger the gap between the student tuition and the equilibrium tuition, the greater the shortage of spots at the university and the more demand for the university can fall without completely eliminating the shortage at the university. Therefore, the larger the gap, the more room instructors have to take demand-reducing actions at the university without any consequences. One of these demand-reducing actions might be not being on time for office hours or not being as responsive as possible during office hours.

CRIMINALS AND RATIONALITY

- The questions were: Are criminals rational? Does their behavior respond to changes in costs and benefits?
- We built a simple theory based on two equations: One related to the expected benefits of committing a criminal act (specifically, burglary), and one related to the expected costs of committing the criminal act. We hypothesized that individuals would commit criminal acts only when the expected benefits outweighed the expected costs. Changes in variables

on the cost side and on the benefits side of the theory were then changed, and predictions materialized as to whether the crime rate (burglary rate) would rise or fall.

- If the predictions are consistent with reality, then we can argue that criminals are rational.

DOES EVIDENCE PROVE A THEORY IS CORRECT?

- If evidence is consistent with a theory's predictions, we state that the evidence fails to reject the theory. We do not say that the evidence proves the theory is correct.
- If evidence is inconsistent with a theory's predictions, we state that the evidence rejects the theory.

BASEBALL CAPS IN CLASS AND EXAM DAYS

- The question was: What purpose does wearing a baseball cap in class on exam days serve that it doesn't serve on other days?
- One of the things that a baseball cap can do is shield one's eyes. If students want to cheat on a multiple-choice test, it is a good idea to shield their eyes from the view of the instructor. A baseball cap can help meet this objective.

HOUSE PRICES AND SCHOOL DISTRICTS

- The question was: Why are comparable houses often priced differently?
- If two houses are alike in every way except that one is located in a good school district and the other in a bad school district, we would expect that the one located in a good school district would be priced higher. Individuals pay for the good school district in terms of house prices.

HEALTH CARE AND VOUCHERS

- The question was: Will individuals purchase more health care with health care vouchers than without them?
- A monetary or in-kind gift will end up going for whatever is next on the recipient's list to purchase. For example, suppose Smith is currently spending $200 on X and $300 on Y. Someone gives Smith $100. Smith may spend the $100 on X, on Y, or on a combination of the two, or he may spend it on Z. The monetary gift goes for whatever is next on his list to purchase.

GIVING

- The question here was: Will a person who is giving gifts to another person stop giving gifts at the point at which the marginal benefits of giving gifts equals the marginal costs of giving gifts?
- Both marginal benefits and marginal costs accompany each gift a gift giver gives to a gift recipient. The efficient number of gifts that the gift giver wants to give is the number at which marginal benefits of giving a gift equal its marginal

costs. As a result, the gift giver maximizes net gains from giving gifts. However, if the gift recipient presents the gift giver with an all-or-nothing demand that takes the efficient number of gifts off the table, the gift giver could end up giving the gift recipient more than the efficient number of gifts. How many more depends on net gains on the efficient number of gifts compared with the net losses on the gifts beyond the efficient number.

Video Questions and Problems

For video tutorials and answers, visit www.cengagebrain.com and search Arnold.

1. No theory is perfectly descriptive of reality. Explain.
2. The size town in which you live can affect how you behave. Explain.
3. The larger the shortage at a university, the greater freedom instructors have to teach their courses the way they want to teach them. Do you agree or disagree? Explain your answer.
4. There is a limit to how many gifts a gift giver will give to a gift recipient. Do you agree or disagree? Explain and diagrammatically represent your answer.
5. People can pay for good weather, good school districts, and good views indirectly as opposed to directly. Do you agree or disagree? Explain your answer.

Questions and Problems

1. Why is it better for theories to be judged by how accurately they predict than by how they sound to us?
2. What role does opportunity cost play in the theory that birth rates are likely to be higher in some countries than others?
3. What does it mean to say that a theory is falsifiable or refutable?
4. A person is more likely to lose his temper with a friend than with his boss. Do you agree or disagree? Explain your answer.
5. One prediction made in the chapter was that "the owner of a car repair shop in a small town will be more careful not to overcharge customers than the owner of a car repair shop in a large city." Why?
6. Put forth two observations that are inconsistent with the cost-benefit theory of burglary discussed in the chapter.
7. What does the difference between the equilibrium tuition and the student tuition have to do with instructors holding office hours?
8. For an economist, is it preferable to assume that criminals are rational or to build a theory based on a rational criminal and then check the evidence? Explain your answer.
9. Segregated neighborhoods of blue and green people can be the result of the people of each color preferring a certain type of integration over segregation. What specifically is the certain type of integration?
10. The quality of the school district can affect house prices in that district. If this is true, what should we observe?
11. A man asks his brother for $400 to buy a television set. His brother gives him the money, and the man buys a television set. Is it guaranteed that the brother's $400 went to buy the television set? Why or why not?
12. People will often make charitable donations to religious organizations, but not to gangs. Why?
13. Under what condition might persons buy more of something than the efficient amount for them to buy?
14. Do the following: (1) Make an observation; (2) identify a question based on the observation; (3) put forth a theory to answer the question; (4) identify at least two predictions based on the theory.

Working with Numbers and Graphs

1. Diagrammatically represent what happens to the efficient number of gifts that a gift giver wants to give to a gift recipient as the marginal cost of giving gifts declines.
2. Diagrammatically represent what happens to the efficient number of gifts a gift giver wants to give to a gift recipient as the marginal benefits of giving gifts declines.

APPENDIX 3

1

♦♦♦

JOSEPH E. STIGLITZ

ANYONE WHO THINKS OF academic knowledge as dry and irrelevant simply hasn't studied economics. And anyone who thinks of economics as an impartial discipline, plodding on modestly without controversy, simply hasn't heard of Joseph Stiglitz, winner of the 2001 Sveriges Riksbank Prize in Economic Sciences in Memory of Alfred Nobel. After Stiglitz left Stanford University to serve as a senior vice-president and chief economist of the World Bank, his appointment came to a premature end when, in 2000, he published an article excoriating the International Monetary Fund (IMF). Stiglitz, a "neo-Keynesian," targeted the IMF because it had imposed harsh austerity on the East Asian economies after a real estate bubble there collapsed. Even though many economists agreed with Stiglitz's criticisms, so notorious did the article become that the leadership of the World Bank pressured him to leave. After accepting a new post at Columbia University, Stiglitz continued to write and speak about the failures of neoliberal economics, which encourages smaller government, the deregulation of finance, and the privatizing of public services like health care and education.

Stiglitz, a prolific author, has written, co-written, or edited 26 books so far. The selection that follows is an excerpt from his best-selling book *The Price of Inequality: How Today's Divided Society Endangers Our Future* (2012). There he makes the case that neoliberal reforms starting with Ronald Regan have produced a growing inequality that has swelled the ranks of the working poor and undermined the middle class. Stiglitz maintains that this long-term trend has dimmed the prospects for our full recovery from the collapse of 2008. After decades of lost buying power, the middle class has simply become too weak to generate the consumer spending needed for robust economic growth. Cash-strapped families no longer possess the resources to invest in their businesses or in better schooling for their children. Combined with tax cuts for the wealthiest, beginning under George W. Bush, the decline in middle class earnings has meant lower tax revenue for government, a swelling of the national debt, and a neglect of roads, public property, and other social goods. Finally, income inequality makes the economic future more volatile, increasing the frequency of booms and busts and causing more severe collapses. Stiglitz is confident, however, that these problems can be rectified if our society is willing to take the steps he recommends: curbing the power of the financiers, raising taxes on the wealthiest 1% and

"Rent Seeking and the Making of an Unequal Society," The Price of Inequality: How Today's Divided Society Endangers Our Future (New York: W. W. Norton, 2012), 28–51, 312–20.

on the big corporations, strengthening unions and citizens' rights, and reinvesting in public education, infrastructure, the environment, and sustainable technology.

Rent Seeking and the Making of an Unequal Society

American inequality didn't just happen. It was created. Market forces played a role, but it was not market forces alone. In a sense, that should be obvious: economic laws are universal, but our growing inequality—especially the amounts seized by the upper 1 percent—is a distinctly American "achievement." That outsize inequality is not predestined offers reason for hope, but in reality it is likely to get worse. The forces that have been at play in creating these outcomes are self-reinforcing.

By understanding the origins of inequality, we can better grasp the costs and benefits of reducing it. The simple thesis of this chapter is that even though market forces help shape the degree of inequality, government policies shape those market forces. Much of the inequality that exists today is a result of government policy, both what the government does and what it does not do. Government has the power to move money from the top to the bottom and the middle, or vice versa.

… America's current level of inequality is unusual. Compared with other countries and compared with what it was in the past even in the United States, it's unusually large, and it has been increasing unusually fast. It used to be said that watching for changes in inequality was like watching grass grow: it's hard to see the changes in any short span of time. But that's not true now.

Even what's been happening in this recession is unusual. Typically, when the economy weakens, wages and employment adjust slowly, so as sales fall, profits fall more than proportionately. But in this recession the share of wages has actually fallen, and many firms are making good profits.[1]

Addressing inequality is of necessity multifaceted—we have to rein in the excesses at the top, strengthen the middle, and help those at the bottom. Each goal requires a program of its own. But to construct such programs, we have to have a better understanding of what has given rise to each facet of this unusual inequality.

Distinct as the inequality we face today is, inequality itself is not something new. The concentration of economic and political power was in many ways more extreme in the precapitalist societies of the West. At that time, religion both explained and justified the inequality: those at the top of society were there because of divine right. To question that was to question the social order, or even to question God's will.

However, for modern economists and political scientists, as also for the ancient Greeks, this inequality was not a matter of a preordained social order.

Power—often military power—was at the origin of these inequities. Militarism was about economics: the conquerors had the right to extract as much as they could from the conquered. In antiquity, natural philosophy in general saw no wrong in treating other humans as means for the ends of others. As the ancient Greek historian Thucydides famously said, "right, as the world goes, is only in question between equals in power, while the strong do what they can and the weak suffer what they must."[2]

Those with power used that power to strengthen their economic and political positions, or at the very least to maintain them.[3] They also attempted to shape thinking, to make acceptable differences in income that would otherwise be odious.

As the notion of divine right became rejected in the early nation-states, those with power sought other bases for defending their positions. With the Renaissance and the Enlightenment, which emphasized the dignity of the individual, and with the Industrial Revolution, which led to the emergence of a vast urban underclass, it became imperative to find new justifications for inequality, especially as critics of the system, like Marx, talked about exploitation.[4]

The theory that came to dominate, beginning in the second half of the nineteenth century—and still does—was called "marginal productivity theory"; those with higher productivities earned higher incomes that reflected their greater contribution to society. Competitive markets, working through the laws of supply and demand, determine the value of each individual's contributions. If someone has a scarce and valuable skill, the market will reward him amply, because of his greater contribution to output. If he has no skills, his income will be low. Technology, of course, determines the productivity of different skills: in a primitive agriculture economy, physical strength and endurance is what mattered; in a modern hi-tech economy, brainpower is of more relevance.

Technology and scarcity, working through the ordinary laws of supply and demand, play a role in shaping today's inequality, but something else is at work, and that something else is government. A major theme of [my argument] is that inequality is the result of political forces as much as of economic ones. In a modern economy government sets and enforces the rules of the game—what is fair competition, and what actions are deemed anticompetitive and illegal, who gets what in the event of bankruptcy, when a debtor can't pay all that he owes, what are fraudulent practices and forbidden. Government also gives away resources (both openly and less transparently) and, through taxes and social expenditures, modifies the distribution of income that emerges from the market, shaped as it is by technology and politics.

Finally, government alters the dynamics of wealth by, for instance, taxing inheritances and providing free public education. Inequality is determined not just by how much the market pays a skilled worker relative to an unskilled worker, but also by the level of skills that an individual has acquired. In the absence of government support, many children of the poor would not be able to afford basic health care and nutrition, let alone the education required to acquire the skills necessary for enhanced productivity and high wages. Government can affect the extent to which an individual's education and inherited wealth depends on that of his parents. More formally, economists say that inequality depends on the distribution of "endowments," of financial and human capital.

3

The way the American government performs these functions determines the extent of inequality in our society. In each of these arenas there are subtle decisions that benefit some group at the expense of others. The effect of each decision may be small, but the cumulative effect of large numbers of decisions, made to benefit those at the top, can be very significant.

Competitive forces should limit outsize profits, but if governments do not ensure that markets are competitive, there can be large monopoly profits. Competitive forces should also limit disproportionate executive compensation, but in modern corporations, the CEO has enormous power—including the power to set his own compensation, subject, of course, to his board—but in many corporations, he even has considerable power to appoint the board, and with a stacked board, there is little check. Shareholders have minimal say. Some countries have better "corporate governance laws," the laws that circumscribe the power of the CEO, for instance, by insisting that there be independent members in the board or that shareholders have a say in pay. If the country does not have good corporate governance laws that are effectively enforced, CEOs can pay themselves outsize bonuses.

Progressive tax and expenditure policies (which tax the rich more than the poor and provide systems of good social protection) can limit the extent of inequality. By contrast, programs that give away a country's resources to the rich and well connected can increase inequality.

Our political system has increasingly been working in ways that increase the inequality of outcomes and reduce equality of opportunity. This should not come as a surprise: we have a political system that gives inordinate power to those at the top, and they have used that power not only to limit the extent of redistribution but also to shape the rules of the game in their favor, and to extract from the public what can only be called large "gifts." Economists have a name for these activities: they call them rent seeking, getting income not as a reward to creating wealth but by grabbing a larger share of the wealth that would otherwise have been produced without their effort. (We'll give a fuller definition of the concept of rent seeking later in the chapter.) Those at the top have learned how to suck out money from the rest in ways that the rest are hardly aware of—that is their true innovation.

Jean-Baptiste Colbert, the adviser to King Louis XIV of France, reportedly said, "The art of taxation consists in so plucking the goose as to obtain the largest amount of feathers with the least possible amount of hissing." So, too, for the art of rent seeking.

To put it baldly, there are two ways to become wealthy: to create wealth or to take wealth away from others. The former adds to society. The latter typically subtracts from it, for in the process of taking it away, wealth gets destroyed. A monopolist who overcharges for his product takes money from those whom he is overcharging and at the same time destroys value. To get his monopoly price, he has to restrict production.

Unfortunately, even genuine wealth creators often are not satisfied with the wealth that their innovation or entrepreneurship has reaped. Some eventually turn to abusive practices like monopoly pricing or other forms of rent extraction to garner even more riches. To take just one example, the railroad barons of the nineteenth century provided an important service in constructing the railroads, but much of their wealth was the result of their political influence—getting large government land grants on either side of the railway. Today, over a century after the railroad barons dominated the economy, much of the wealth at the top in the United States—and some of the suffering at the bottom—stems from wealth transfers instead of wealth creation.

Of course, not all the inequality in our society is a result of rent seeking, or of government's tilting the rules of the game in favor of those at the top. Markets matter, as do social forces (like discrimination).

GENERAL PRINCIPLES

Adam Smith's Invisible Hand and Inequality

Adam Smith, the father of modern economics, argued that the private pursuit of self-interest would lead, as if by an invisible hand, to the well-being of all.[5] In the aftermath of the financial crisis [of 2008–09], no one today would argue that the bankers' pursuit of their self-interest has led to the well-being of all. At most, it led to *the bankers'* well-being, with the rest of society bearing the cost. It wasn't even what economists call a zero-sum game, where what one person gains exactly equals what the others lose. It was a negative-sum game, where the gains to winners are less than the losses to the losers. What the rest of society lost was far, far greater than what the bankers gained.

There is a simple reason for why financiers' pursuit of *their* interests turned out to be disastrous for the rest of society: the bankers' incentives were not well aligned with social returns. When markets work well—in the way that Adam Smith hypothesized—it is because private returns and social benefits are well aligned, that is, because private rewards and social contributions are equal, as had been assumed by marginal productivity theory. In that theory, the social contribution of each worker is exactly equal to the private compensation. People with higher productivity—a larger social contribution—get higher pay.

Adam Smith himself was aware of one of the circumstances in which private and social returns differ. As he explained, "People of the same trade seldom meet together, even for merriment and diversion, but the conversation ends in a conspiracy against the public, or in some contrivance to raise prices."[6] Markets by themselves often fail to produce efficient and desirable outcomes, and there is a role for government in correcting these market failures, that is, designing policies (taxes and regulations) that bring private incentives and social returns into alignment. (Of course, there are often disagreements about the best way of doing it. But few today believe in unfettered financial markets—their failures impose too great a cost on the rest of society—or that firms should be allowed to despoil the environment without restriction.) When government does its job well, the returns received by, say, a worker or an investor are in fact equal to the benefits to society that his actions contribute. When these are not aligned, we say there is a market failure, that is, markets fail to produce efficient outcomes. Private rewards and social returns are not well aligned when competition is

5

imperfect; when there are "externalities" (where one party's actions can have large negative or positive effects on others for which he does not pay or reap the benefit); when there exist imperfections or asymmetries of information (where someone knows something relevant to a market trade that someone else doesn't know); or where risk markets or other markets are absent (one can't, for instance, buy insurance against many of the most important risks that one faces). Since one or more of these conditions exist in virtually every market, there is in fact little presumption that markets are in general efficient. This means that there is an enormous potential role for government to correct these market failures.

Government never corrects market failures perfectly, but it does a better job in some countries than in others. Only if the government does a reasonably good job of correcting the most important market failures will the economy prosper. Good financial regulation helped the United States—and the world—avoid a major crisis for four decades after the Great Depression. Deregulation in the 1980s led to scores of financial crises in the succeeding three decades, of which America's crisis in 2008–09 was only the worst.[7] But those governmental failures were no accident: the financial sector used its political muscle to make sure that the market failures were *not* corrected, and that the sector's private rewards remained well in excess of their social contributions—one of the factors contributing to the bloated financial sector and to the high levels of inequality at the top.

Shaping Markets

We'll describe below some of the ways that private financial firms act to ensure that markets *don't work well*. For instance, as Smith noted, there are incentives for firms to work to reduce market competition. Moreover, firms also strive to make sure that there are no strong laws prohibiting them from engaging in anticompetitive behavior or, when there are such laws, that they are not effectively enforced. The focus of businesspeople is, of course, not to enhance societal well-being broadly understood, or even to make markets more competitive: their objective is simply to make markets work *for them*, to make them more profitable. But the consequence is often a less efficient economy marked by greater inequality. For now, one example will suffice. When markets are competitive, profits above the normal return to capital cannot be sustained. That is so because if a firm makes greater profits than that on a sale, rivals will attempt to steal the customer by lowering prices. As firms compete vigorously, prices fall to the point that profits (above the normal return to capital) are driven down to zero, a disaster for those seeking big profits. In business school we teach students how to recognize, and create, barriers to competition—including barriers to entry—that help ensure that profits won't be eroded. Indeed, as we shall shortly see, some of the most important innovations in business in the last three decades have centered not on making the economy more efficient but on how better to ensure monopoly power or how better to circumvent government regulations intended to align social returns and private rewards.

Making markets less transparent is a favorite tool. The more transparent markets are, the more competitive they are likely to be. Bankers know this.

That's why banks have been fighting to keep their business in writing derivatives, the risky products that were at the center of AIG's collapse,[8] in the shadows of the "over the counter" market. In that market, it's difficult for customers to know whether they're getting a good deal. Everything is negotiated, as opposed to how things work in more open and transparent modern markets. And since the sellers are trading constantly, and buyers enter only episodically, sellers have more information than buyers, and they use that information to their advantage. This means that on average, sellers (the writers of the derivatives, the banks) can extract more money out of their customers. Well-designed open auctions, by contrast, ensure that goods go to those who value them the most, a hallmark of efficiency. There are publicly available prices for guiding decisions.

While lack of transparency results in more profits for the bankers, it leads to lower economic performance. Without good information, capital markets can't exercise any discipline. Money won't go to where returns are highest, or to the bank that does the best job of managing money. No one can know the true financial position of a bank or other financial institution today—and shadowy derivative transactions are part of the reason. One would have hoped that the recent crisis might have forced change, but the bankers resisted. They resisted demands, for instance, for more transparency in derivatives and for regulations that would restrict anticompetitive practices. These rent-seeking activities were worth tens of billions of dollars in profits. Although they didn't win every battle, they won often enough that the problems are still with us. In late October 2011, for instance, a major American financial firm[9] went bankrupt (the eighth-largest bankruptcy on record), partly because of complex derivatives. Evidently the market hadn't seen through these transactions, at least not in a timely way.

Moving Money from the Bottom of the Pyramid to the Top

One of the ways that those at the top make money is by taking advantage of their market and political power to favor themselves, to increase their own income, at the expense of the rest.

The financial sector has developed expertise in a wide variety of forms of rent seeking itself. We've already mentioned some, but there are many others: taking advantage of asymmetries of information (selling securities that they had designed to fail, but knowing that buyers didn't know that);[10] taking excessive risk—with the government holding a lifeline, bailing them out and assuming the losses, the knowledge of which, incidentally, allows them to borrow at a lower interest rate than they otherwise could; and getting money from the Federal Reserve at low interest rates, now almost zero.

But the form of rent seeking that is most egregious—and that has been most perfected in recent years—has been the ability of those in the financial sector to take advantage of the poor and uninformed, as they made enormous amounts of money by preying upon these groups with predatory lending and abusive credit card practices.[11] Each poor person might have only a little, but there are so many poor that a little from each amounts to a great deal. Any sense of social justice—or any concern about overall efficiency—would have led government to prohibit

7

these activities. After all, considerable amounts of resources were used up in the process of moving money from the poor to the rich, which is why it's a negative-sum game. But government didn't put an end to these kind of activities, not even when, around 2007, it became increasingly apparent what was going on. The reason was obvious. The financial sector had invested heavily in lobbying and campaign contributions, and the investments had paid off.

I mention the financial sector partly because it has contributed so powerfully to our society's current level of inequality.[12] The financial sector's role in creating the crisis in 2008–09 is apparent to all. Not even those who work in the sector deny it, though each believes that some other part of the financial sector is really to blame. Much of what I have said about the financial sector, though, could be said about other players in the economy that have had a hand in creating current inequities.

Modern capitalism has become a complex game, and those who win at it have to have more than a little smarts. But those who win at it often possess less admirable characteristics as well: the ability to skirt the law, or to shape the law in their own favor; the willingness to take advantage of others, even the poor; and to play *unfair* when necessary.[13] As one of the successful players in this game put it, the old adage "Win or lose, what matters is how you play the game" is rubbish. *All that matters is whether you win or lose.* The market provides a simple way of showing that—the amount of money that you have.

Winning in the game of rent seeking has made fortunes for many of those at the top, but it is not the only means by which they obtain and preserve their wealth. The tax system also plays a key role, as we'll see later. Those at the top have managed to design a tax system in which they pay less than their fair share—they pay a lower fraction of their income than do those who are much poorer. We call such tax systems regressive.

And while regressive taxes and rent seeking (which takes money from the rest of society and redistributes it to the top) are at the core of growing inequality, especially at the top, broader forces exert particular influence on two other aspects of American inequality—the hollowing out of the middle class and the increase in poverty. Laws governing corporations interact with the norms of behavior that guide the leaders of those corporations and determine how returns are shared among top management and other stakeholders (workers, shareholders, and bondholders). Macroeconomic policies determine the tightness of the labor market—the level of unemployment, and thus how market forces operate to change the share of workers. If monetary authorities act to keep unemployment high (even if because of fear of inflation), then wages will be restrained. Strong unions have helped to reduce inequality, whereas weaker unions have made it easier for CEOs, sometimes working with market forces that they have helped shape, to increase it. In each arena—the strength of unions, the effectiveness of corporate governance, the conduct of monetary policy—politics is central.

Of course, market forces, the balancing of, say, the demand and supply for skilled workers, affected as it is by changes in technology and education, play an important role as well, even if those forces are partially shaped by politics. But instead of these market forces and politics balancing each other out, with the political process dampening the increase in inequality in periods when market forces might have led to growing disparities, instead of government *tempering* the excesses of the market, in America today the two have been working together to increase income and wealth disparities.

RENT SEEKING

Earlier, we labeled as *rent seeking* many of the ways by which our current political process helps the rich at the expense of the rest of us. Rent seeking takes many forms: hidden and open transfers and subsidies from the government, laws that make the marketplace less competitive, lax enforcement of existing competition laws, and statutes that allow corporations to take advantage of others or to pass costs on to the rest of society. The term "rent" was originally used to describe the returns to land, since the owner of land receives these payments by virtue of his ownership and not because of anything he *does*. This stands in contrast to the situation of workers, for example, whose wages are compensation for the *effort* they provide. The term "rent" then was extended to include monopoly profits, or monopoly rents, the income that one receives simply from the control of a monopoly. Eventually the term was expanded still further to include the returns on similar ownership claims. If the government gave a company the exclusive right to import a limited amount (a quota) of a good, such as sugar, then the extra return generated as a result of the ownership of those rights was called a "quota-rent."

Countries rich in natural resource are infamous for rent-seeking activities. It's far easier to get rich in these countries by gaining access to resources at favorable terms than by producing wealth. This is often a negative-sum game, which is one of the reasons why, on average, such countries have grown more slowly than comparable countries without the bounty of such resources.[14]

Even more disturbing, one might have thought that an abundance of resources could be used to help the poor, to ensure access to education and health care for all. Taxing work and savings can weaken incentives; in contrast, taxing the "rents" on land, oil, or other natural resources won't make them disappear. The resources will still be there to be taken out, if not today, then tomorrow. There are no adverse incentive effects. That means that, in principle, there should be ample revenues to finance both social expenditures and public investments—in, say, health and education. Yet, among the countries with the greatest inequality are those with the most natural resources. Evidently, a few within these countries are better at rent seeking than others (usually those with political power), and they ensure that the benefits of the resources accrue largely to themselves. In Venezuela, the richest oil producer in Latin America, half of the country lived in poverty prior to the rise of Hugo Chavez—and it is precisely this type of poverty in the midst of riches that gives rise to leaders like him.[15]

Rent-seeking behavior is not just endemic in the resource-rich countries of the Middle East, Africa, and Latin America. It has also become endemic in modern economies, including our own. In those economies, it takes many forms, some of which are closely akin to those in the oil-rich countries: getting state assets (such as oil or minerals) at below fair-market prices. It's not hard to become wealthy if the government sells you for $500 million a mine that's worth $1 billion.

Another form of rent seeking is the flip side: selling to government products at *above* market prices (noncompetitive procurement). The drug companies and military contractors excel in this form of rent seeking. Open government subsidies (as in agriculture) or hidden subsidies (trade restrictions that reduce competition or subsidies hidden in the tax system) are other ways of getting rents from the public.

Not all rent seeking uses government to extract money from ordinary citizens. The private sector can excel on its own, extracting rents from the public, for instance, through monopolistic practices and exploiting those who are less informed and educated, exemplified by the banks' predatory lending. CEOs can use their control of the corporation to garner for themselves a larger fraction of the firms' revenues. Here, though, the government too plays a role, by not doing what it should: by not stopping these activities, by not making them illegal, or by not enforcing laws that exist. Effective enforcement of competition laws can circumscribe monopoly profits; effective laws on predatory lending and credit card abuses can limit the extent of bank exploitation; well-designed corporate governance laws can limit the extent to which corporate officials appropriate for themselves firm revenues.

By looking at those at the top of the wealth distribution, we can get a feel for the nature of this aspect of America's inequality. Few are inventors who have reshaped technology, or scientists who have reshaped our understandings of the laws of nature. Think of Alan Turing, whose genius provided the mathematics underlying the modern computer. Or of Einstein. Or of the discoverers of the laser (in which Charles Townes played a central role)[16] or John Bardeen, Walter Brattain, and William Shockley, the inventors of transistors.[17] Or of Watson and Crick, who unraveled the mysteries of DNA, upon which rests so much of modern medicine. None of them, who made such large contributions to our well-being, are among those most rewarded by our economic system.

Instead, many of the individuals at the top of the wealth distribution are, in one way or another, geniuses at business. Some might claim, for instance, that Steve Jobs or the innovators of search engines or social media were, in their way, geniuses. Jobs was number 110 on the *Forbes* list of the world's wealthiest billionaires before his death, and Mark Zuckerberg was 52. But many of these "geniuses" built their business empires on the shoulders of giants, such as Tim Berners-Lee, the inventor of the World Wide Web, who has never appeared on the *Forbes* list. Berners-Lee could have become a billionaire but chose not to—he made his idea available freely; which greatly speeded up the development of the Internet.[18]

A closer look at the successes of those at the top of the wealth distribution shows that more than a small part of their genius resides in devising better ways of exploiting market power and other market imperfections—and, in many cases, finding better ways of ensuring that politics works for them rather than for society more generally.

We've already commented on financiers, who make up a significant portion of the top 1 or 0.1 percent. While some gained their wealth by producing value, others did so in no small part by one of the myriad forms of rent seeking that we described earlier. At the top, in addition to the financiers, whom we have already discussed,[19] are the monopolists and their descendants who, through one mechanism or another, have succeeded in achieving and sustaining market dominance. After the railroad barons of the nineteenth century came John D. Rockefeller and Standard Oil. The end of the twentieth century saw Bill Gates and Microsoft's domination of the PC software industry.

Internationally, there is the case of Carlos Slim, a Mexican businessman who was ranked by *Forbes* as the wealthiest person in the world in 2011.[20] Thanks to his dominance of the telephone industry in Mexico, Slim is able to charge prices that are a multiple of those in more competitive markets. He made his breakthrough when he was able to acquire a large share in Mexico's telecommunications system after the country privatized it,[21] a strategy that lies behind many of the world's great fortunes. As we've seen, it's easy to get rich by getting a state asset at a deep discount. Many of Russia's current oligarchs, for example, obtained their initial wealth by buying state assets at below-market prices and then ensuring continuing profits through monopoly power. (In America most of our government giveaways tend to be more subtle. We design rules for, say, selling government assets that are in effect partial giveaways, but less transparently so than what Russia did.)[22]

... [A]nother important group of the very wealthy [are] corporate CEOs, such as Stephen Hemsley from UnitedHealth Group, who received $102 million in 2010, and Edward Mueller from Qwest Communications (now CenturyLink, after a merger in 2011), who made $65.8 million.[23] CEOs have successfully garnered a larger and larger fraction of corporate revenues.[24] As we'll explain later, it is not a sudden increase in their productivity that allowed these CEOs to amass such riches in the last couple of decades but rather an enhanced ability to take more from the corporation that they are supposed to be serving, and weaker qualms about, and enhanced public toleration of, doing so.

A final large group of rent seekers consists of the top-flight lawyers, including those who became wealthy by helping others engage in their rent seeking in ways that skirt the law but do not (usually) land them in prison. They help write the complex tax laws in which loopholes are put, so their clients can avoid taxes, and they then design the complex deals to take advantage of these loopholes. They helped design the complex and nontransparent derivatives market. They help design the contractual arrangements that generate monopoly power; seemingly within the law. And for all this assistance in making our markets work not the way markets should but as instruments for the benefit of those at the top, they get amply rewarded.[25]

Monopoly Rents: Creating Sustainable Monopolies

To economists large fortunes pose a problem. The laws of competition, as I have noted, say that profits (beyond the normal return to capital) are supposed to be driven to zero, and quickly. But if profits are zero, how can fortunes be built? Niches in which there isn't competition, for one reason or another, offer one avenue.[26] But that goes only a little way to explaining sustainable excessive profits (beyond the competitive level). Success will attract entry, and profits will quickly disappear. The real key to success is to make sure that there won't ever be competition—or at least there won't be competition for a long enough time that one can make a monopoly killing in the meanwhile. The simplest way to a sustainable monopoly is getting the government to give you one. From the seventeenth century to the nineteenth, the British granted the East India Company a monopoly on trade with India.

There are other ways to get government-sanctioned monopolies. Patents typically give an inventor a monopoly over that innovation for a temporary period, but the details of patent law can extend the length of the patent, reduce entry of new firms, and enhance monopoly power. America's patent laws have been doing exactly that. They are designed not to maximize the pace of innovation but rather to maximize rents.[27]

Even without a government grant of monopoly, firms can create entry barriers. A variety of practices discourage entry, such as maintaining excess capacity, so that an entrant knows that, should he enter, the incumbent firm can increase production, lowering prices to the point that entry would be unprofitable.[28] In the Middle Ages, guilds successfully restricted competition. Many professions have continued that tradition. Although they argue that they are simply trying to maintain standards, restrictions on entry (limiting the number of places at medical school or restricting migration of trained personnel from abroad) help keep incomes high.[29]

At the turn of the previous century, concern about the monopolies that formed the basis of many of the fortunes of that period, including Rockefeller's, grew so great that under the trust-busting president Theodore Roosevelt, America passed a slew of laws to break up monopolies and prevent some of these practices. In the years that followed, numerous monopolies were broken up—in oil, cigarettes, and many other industries.[30] And yet today, as we look around the American economy, we can see many sectors, including some that are central to its functioning, where one or a few firms dominate—such as Microsoft in PC operating systems, or AT&T, Verizon, T-Mobile, and Sprint in telecommunications.

Three factors contributed to this increased monopolization of markets. First, there was a battle over ideas about the role that government should take in ensuring competition. Chicago school economists (like Milton Friedman and George Stigler) who believe in free and unfettered markets[31] argued that markets are naturally competitive[32] and that seemingly anticompetitive practices really enhance efficiency. A massive program to "educate"[33] people, and especially judges, regarding these new doctrines of law and economics, partly sponsored by right-wing foundations like the Olin Foundation, was successful. The timing was ironic: American courts were buying into notions that markets were "naturally" competitive and placing a high burden of proof on anyone claiming otherwise just as the economics discipline was exploring theories that explain why markets often were *not* competitive, even when there were seemingly many firms. For instance, a new and powerful branch of economics called game theory explained how collusive behavior could be maintained tacitly over extended periods of time. Meanwhile, new theories of imperfect and asymmetric information showed how information imperfections impaired competition, and new evidence substantiated the relevance and importance of these theories.

The influence of the Chicago school should not be underestimated. Even when there are blatant infractions—like predatory pricing, where a firm lowers its price to force out a competitor and then uses its monopoly power to raise prices—they've been hard to prosecute.[34] Chicago school economics argues that markets are presumptively competitive and efficient. If entry were easy, the dominant firm would gain nothing from driving out a rival, because the firm that is forced out would be quickly replaced by another firm. But in reality entry is not so easy, and predatory behavior does occur.

A second factor giving rise to increased monopoly is related to changes in our economy. The creation of monopoly power was easier in some of the new growth industries. Many of these sectors were marked by what are called network externalities. An obvious example is the computer operating system: just as it's very convenient for everyone to speak the same language, it's very convenient for everyone to use the same operating system. Increasing interconnectivity across the world naturally leads to standardization. Those with a monopoly over the standard that is chosen benefit.

As we have noted, competition naturally works against the accumulation of market power. When there are large monopoly profits, competitors work to get a share. That's where the third factor that has increased monopoly power in the United States comes in: businesses found new ways of resisting entry, of reducing competitive pressures. Microsoft provides the example par excellence. Because it enjoyed a near-monopoly on PC operating systems, it stood to lose a lot if alternative technologies undermined its monopoly. The development of the Internet and the web browser to access it represented just such a threat. Netscape brought the browser to the market, building on government-funded research.[35] Microsoft decided to squelch this potential competitor. It offered its own product, Internet Explorer, but the product couldn't compete in the open market. The company decided to use its monopoly power in PC operating systems to make sure that the playing field was not level. It deployed a strategy known as FUD (fear, uncertainty, and doubt), creating anxiety about compatibility among users by programming error messages that would randomly appear if Netscape was installed on a Windows computer. The company also did not provide the disclosures necessary for full compatibility as new versions of Windows were developed. And most cleverly, it offered Internet Explorer at a zero price—free, bundled in as part of its operating system. It's hard to compete with a zero price. Netscape was doomed.[36]

It was obvious that selling something at a zero price was not a profit-maximizing strategy—in the short run. But Microsoft had a vision for the long run: the maintenance of its monopoly. For that, it was willing to make short-run sacrifices. It succeeded, but so blatant were its methods that courts and tribunals throughout the world charged it with engaging in anticompetitive practices. And yet, in the end, Microsoft won—for it realized that in a network economy, a monopoly position, once attained, is hard to break. Given Microsoft's dominance of the operating system market, it had the incentives and capabilities to dominate in a host of other applications.[37]

No wonder, then, that Microsoft's profits have been so enormous—an average of $7 billion per year over the last quarter century, $14 billion over the past ten years, increasing in 2011 to $23 billion[38]—and reaping wealth for those who bought shares early enough. The conventional wisdom has it that in spite of its dominant position and huge resources, Microsoft has not been a real innovator. It did not develop the first widely used word processor, the first spreadsheet, the first browser, the first media player, or the first dominant search engine. Innovation lay elsewhere. This is consistent with theory and historical evidence: monopolists are not good innovators.[39]

Looking at the U.S. economy, we see in many sectors large numbers of firms, and therefore infer that there must be competition. But that's not always the case. Take the example of banks. While there are hundreds of banks, the big four share between them almost half of the country's banking assets,[40] a marked increase from the degree of concentration fifteen years ago. In most smaller communities, there are at most one or two. When competition is so limited, prices are likely to be far in excess of competitive levels.[41] That's why the sector enjoys profits estimated to be more than $115 billion a year, much of which is passed along to its top officials and other bankers—helping create one of the major sources of inequality at the top.[42] In some products, such as over-the-counter credit default swaps (CDSes), four or five very large banks totally dominate, and such market concentration always gives rise to the worry that they collude, albeit tacitly. (But sometimes the collusion is not even tacit—it is explicit. The banks set a critical rate, called the London Interbank Offered Rate, or Libor. Mortgages and many financial products are linked to Libor. It appears that the banks worked to rig the rate, enabling them to make still more money from others who were unaware of these shenanigans.)

Of course, even when laws that prohibit monopolistic practices are on the books, these have to be enforced. Particularly given the narrative created by the Chicago school of economics, there is a tendency not to interfere with the "free" workings of the market, even when the outcome is anticompetitive. And there are good political reasons not to take too strong a position: after all, it's antibusiness—and not good for campaign contributions—to be too tough on, say, Microsoft.[43]

Politics: Getting to Set the Rules and Pick the Referee

It's one thing to win in a "fair" game. It's quite another to be able to write the rules of the game—and to write them in ways that enhance one's prospects of winning. And it's even worse if you can choose your own referees. In many areas today, regulatory agencies are responsible for oversight of a sector (writing and enforcing rules and regulations)—the Federal Communications Commission (FCC) in telecom; the Securities and Exchange Commission (SEC) in securities; and the Federal Reserve in many areas of banking. The problem is that leaders in these sectors use their political influence to get people appointed to the regulatory agencies who are sympathetic to their perspectives.

Economists refer to this as "regulatory capture."[44] Sometimes the capture is associated with pecuniary incentives: those on the regulatory commission come from and return to the sector that they are supposed to regulate. Their incentives and those of the industry are well aligned, even if their incentives are not well aligned with those of the rest of society. If those on the regulatory commission serve the sector well, they get well rewarded in their post-government career.

Sometimes, however, the capture is not just motivated by money. Instead, the mindset of regulators is captured by those whom they regulate. This is called "cognitive capture," and it is more of a sociological phenomenon. While neither Alan Greenspan nor Tim Geithner actually worked for a big bank before coming to the Federal Reserve, there was a natural affinity, and they may have come to share the same mindset. In the bankers' mindset—despite the mess that the bankers had made—there was no need to impose stringent conditions on the banks in the bailout.

The bankers have unleashed enormous numbers of lobbyists to persuade any and all who play a role in regulation that they should not be regulated—an estimated 2.5 for every U.S. representative.[45] But persuasion is easier if the target of your efforts begins from a sympathetic position. That is why banks and their lobbyists work so strenuously to ensure that the government appoints regulators who have already been "captured" in one way or another. The bankers try to veto anyone who does not share their belief. I saw this firsthand during the Clinton administration, when potential names for the Fed were floated, some even from the banking community. If any of the potential nominees deviated from the party line that markets are self-regulating and that the banks could manage their own risk—there arose a hue and cry so great that the name wouldn't be put forward or, if it was put forward, that it wouldn't be approved.[46]

Government Munificence

We've seen how monopolies—whether government granted or government "sanctioned," through inadequate enforcement of competition laws—have built the fortunes of many of the world's wealthiest people. But there is another way to get rich. You can simply arrange for the government to hand you cash. This can happen in myriad ways. A little-noticed change in legislation, for example, can reap billions of dollars. This was the case when the government extended a much-needed Medicare drug benefit in 2003.[47] A provision in the law that prohibited government from bargaining for prices on drugs was, in effect, a gift of some $50 billion or more per year to the pharmaceutical companies.[48] More generally, government procurement—paying prices well above costs—is a standard form of government munificence.

Sometimes gifts are hidden in obscure provisions of legislation. A provision of one of the key bills deregulating the financial derivative market—ensuring that no regulator could touch it, no matter how great the peril to which it exposed the economy—also gave derivatives claims "seniority" in the event of bankruptcy. If a bank went under, the claims on the derivatives would be paid off before workers, suppliers, or other creditors saw any money—even if the derivatives had pushed the firm into bankruptcy in the first place.[49] (The derivatives market played a central role in the 2008–09 crisis and was responsible for the $150 billion bailout of AIG.)

15

There are other ways that the banking sector has benefited from government munificence, evident most clearly in the aftermath of the Great Recession. When the Federal Reserve (which can be thought of as one branch of the government) lends unlimited amounts of money to banks at near-zero interest rates, and allows them to lend the money back to the government (or to foreign governments) at much higher interest rates, it is simply giving them a hidden gift worth billions and billions of dollars.

These are not the only ways that governments spur the creation of enormous personal wealth. Many countries, including the United States, control vast amounts of natural resources like oil, gas, and mining concessions. If the government grants you the right to extract these resources for free, it doesn't take a genius to make a fortune. That is, of course, what the U.S. government did in the nineteenth century, when anyone could stake a claim to natural resources. Today, the government doesn't typically give away its resources; more often it requires a payment, but a payment that is far less than it should be. This is just a less transparent way of giving away money. If the value of the oil under a particular piece of land is $100 million after paying the extraction costs, and the government requires a payment of only $50 million, the government has, in effect, given away $50 million.

It doesn't have to be this way, but powerful interests ensure that it is. In the Clinton administration, we tried to make the mining companies pay more for the resources they take out of public lands than the nominal amounts that they do. Not surprisingly, the mining companies—and the congressmen to whom they make generous contributions—opposed these measures, and successfully so. They argued that the policy would impede growth. But the fact of the matter is that, with an auction, companies will bid to get the mining rights so long as the value of the resources is greater than the cost of extraction, and if they win the bid, they will extract the resources. Auctions don't impede growth; they just make sure that the public gets paid appropriately for what is theirs. Modern auction theory has shown how changing the design of the auction can generate much more revenue for the government. These theories were tested out in the auction of the spectrum used for telecommunications beginning in the 1990s, and they worked remarkably well, generating billions for the government.

Sometimes government munificence, instead of handing over resources for pennies on the dollar, takes the form of rewriting the rules to boost profits. An easy way to do this is to protect firms from foreign competition. Tariffs, taxes paid by companies abroad but not by domestic firms, are in effect a gift to domestic producers. The firms demanding protection from foreign competition always provide a rationale, suggesting that society as a whole is the beneficiary and that any benefits that accrue to the companies themselves are incidental. This is self-serving, of course, and while there are instances in which such pleas contain some truth, the widespread abuse of the argument makes it hard to take seriously. Because tariffs put foreign producers at a disadvantage, they enable domestic firms to raise their prices and increase their profits. In some cases, there may be some incidental benefits such as higher domestic employment and the opportunity for companies to invest in R&D that will increase productivity and competitiveness. But just as often, tariffs protect old and tired industries that have lost their competitiveness and are not likely to regain it, or occasionally those that have made bad bets on new technologies and would like to postpone facing competition.

The ethanol subsidy offers an example of this phenomenon. A plan to reduce our dependence on oil by replacing it with the energy of the sun embedded in one of America's great products, its corn, seemed irresistible. But converting plant energy into a form that can provide energy for cars instead of people is hugely expensive. It is also easier to do with some plants than others. So successful has Brazil's research on sugar-based ethanol been that in order for America to compete, for years it had to tax Brazilian sugar-based ethanol 54 cents a gallon.[50] Forty years after the introduction of the subsidy, it was still in place to support an infant technology that seemingly would not grow up. When oil prices fell after the 2008 recession, many ethanol plants went bankrupt, even with massive subsidies.[51] It wasn't until the end of 2011 that the subsidy and tariff were allowed to expire.

The persistence of such distortionary subsidies stems from a single source: politics. The main—and for a long while, effectively the only—*direct* beneficiary of these subsidies were the corn-ethanol producers, dominated by the megafirm Archer Daniels Midland (ADM). Like so many other executives, those at ADM seemed to be better at managing politics than at innovation. They contributed generously to both parties, so that as much as those in Congress might rail against such corporate largesse, lawmakers were slow to touch the ethanol subsidies.[52] As we've noted, firms almost always argue that the true beneficiaries of any largesse they receive lie elsewhere. In this case, ethanol advocates argued that the real beneficiaries were America's corn farmers. But that was, for the most part, not the case, especially in the early days of the subsidy.[53]

Of course, why American corn farmers, who were already the recipients of massive government handouts, receiving almost half of their income from Washington rather than from the "soil," should receive still further assistance is hard to understand, and hard to reconcile with principles of a free-market economy. (In fact, the vast preponderance of government money subsidizing agriculture does not go, as many believe, to poor farmers or even family farms. The design of the program reveals its true objective: to redistribute money from the rest of us to the rich and corporate farms.)[54]

Sadly, government munificence toward corporations does not end with the few examples we have given, but to describe each and every instance of government approved rent seeking would require another book.[55]

NOTES

1. That's one of the reasons that good stock market performance is no longer a good indicator of a healthy economy. Stocks can do well because wages are low and the Fed, worried about the economy, keeps interest rates at near zero.

2. Thucydides, *The Peloponnesian War*, trans. Richard Crawley (New York: Modern Library, 1951), p. 331 (book 5.89).

3. That's why the cases where those in power voluntarily give some of it up are so interesting. In some of them, it's because those in power have an understanding of their own long-term interests—and the long-term interests of those they are supposed to serve. That was the case, e.g., when the king of Bhutan, in 2007, insisted on converting his country into a constitutional monarchy. He had to persuade his citizens that that was the right course for them. The elites of nineteenth-century countries that extended education must have known that there was a risk that this would over the long run weaken their dominance of the political franchise; yet the short-term economic advantages of having a more educated workplace seem to have dominated the long-term political consequences. See François Bourguignon and Sébastien Dessus, "Equity and Development: Political Economy Considerations," pt. 1 of *No Growth without Equity?* ed. Santiago Levy and Michael Walton (New York: Palgrave Macmillan, 2009). Daron Acemoglu and James Robinson theorize that democratization is a way for ruling elites to commit to future redistribution, and thus avoid the extreme of revolution when faced with social unrest. If there is not sufficient strength in the rebellion, repression or temporary reform (or transfers) might suffice. Acemoglu and Robinson, *Economic Origins of Dictatorship and Democracy* (Cambridge: Cambridge University Press, 2006).

4. See Karl Polyani, *The Great Transformation* (New York: Rinehart, 1944). One of the theories developed in response to Marx was that of Nassau Senior, the first holder of the Drummond Chair at Oxford University, who argued that the return capitalists earned was compensation for their "abstinence" (i.e., saving, or *not consuming*).

5. The formalization of this idea is called the "first welfare theorem of economics." It asserts that under certain conditions—when markets work well—no one can be made better-off without making someone else worse-off. But, as we shall explain shortly, there are many instances in which markets do not work well. A recent popular analysis is Kaushik Basu, *Beyond the Invisible Hand: Groundwork for a New Economics* (Princeton: Princeton University Press, 2011). Basu uses the metaphor of a magic show to describe the way the discussion of economics on the political right draws attention to the conclusion of this theorem—that markets are efficient—and away from the very special and unrealistic conditions under which the conclusion holds—perfect markets. Like a good magician, a free-market economist succeeds by drawing spectators' attention to what he wants them to see—the rabbit jumping out of the hat—while distracting their attention from other things—how the rabbit got into the hat in the first place.

6. Adam Smith, *The Wealth of Nations* (1776; New York: P. F. Collier, 1902), p. 207.

7. See Carmen Reinhart and Kenneth Rogoff, *This Time Is Different: Eight Centuries of Financial Folly* (Princeton: Princeton University Press, 2009).

8. A derivative is just a financial instrument the return to which is *derived* on the basis of something else, e.g., the performance of a stock or the price of oil or the value of a bond. A few banks have profited enormously by keeping this market nontransparent, garnering for themselves an amount widely estimated at more than $20 billion a year.

9. On October 31, 2011, MF Global Holdings, a brokerage firm run by Jon Corzine, filed for bankruptcy protection in New York. It was the eighth-largest corporate bankruptcy in U.S. history and the biggest failure by a securities firm since Lehman Brothers Holdings Inc. filed for Chapter 11 in September 2008.

10. While there may be some debate about when taking advantage of information asymmetries is unethical (reflected in the maxim "caveat emptor," putting the

obligation on the buyer to beware of the possibility of information asymmetries), there is no doubt that the banks stepped over the line. ...

11. This predatory behavior took a number of forms. One way was to charge *very* high interest rates, sometimes obfuscated by fees. The abolition of usury laws (which limit the interest rates lenders can charge) provided lenders greater scope for charging exorbitant interest rates; and lenders found ways of circumventing whatever regulations there were. Rent-a-Center claimed to be renting furniture; it was really selling furniture and simultaneously lending money—at extraordinarily high interest rates. Many states tried to circumscribe its activities, but it used its political influence (it had senior ex-politicians, including a former leader of the Republicans in the House of Representatives, on its board) to try to get federal preemption (whereby weaker federal rules preempt the rights of states to regulate). In 2006 Rent-a-Center (with nationwide revenues in excess of $2 billion) was successfully sued by the state of California for deceptive business practices. See http://oag.ca.gov/news/press_release?id=1391. Credit cards and payday loans provided other venues for predatory practices. Among many discussions, see, e.g., Robert Faris, "Payday Lending: A Business Model That Encourages Chronic Borrowing," *Economic Development Quarterly* 17, no. 1 (February 2003): 8–32; James H. Carr and Lopa Kolluri, *Predatory Lending: An Overview* (Washington, DC: Fannie Mae Foundation, 2001).

12. A well-performing financial sector is absolutely essential for a well-performing economy. It allocates capital, manages risk, and runs the payments mechanism. As I explain in *Freefall* (New York: Norton, 2010), in the run-up to the 2008–09 crisis, it did not perform these functions well. Part of the reason is that it was focused more on circumventing regulations and exploitive activities, like predatory lending. The negative-sum nature is reflected in the immense losses in the real estate sector. The financial sector likes to claim that it has been highly innovative, and that these innovations are at the root of the economy's overall success. But as Paul Volcker, former chairman of the Federal Reserve, pointed out, there is little evidence of any significant effect of these innovations on economic growth or societal well-being (with the exception of the ATM machine). But even if the financial sector had contributed slightly to the country's growth in the years before the crisis, the losses associated with the crisis more than offset any of these gains.

13. A recent study has shown that people of higher status/income have fewer qualms about breaking the rules, are more likely to be driven by self-interest, more likely to cheat, and more likely to behave in other ways that would generally be viewed as unethical. Paul K. Piff, Daniel M. Stancato, Stephane Cote, Rodolfo Menoza-Denton, and Dacher Keltner, "Higher Social Class Predicts Increased Unethical Behavior," *Proceedings of the National Academy of Sciences*, February 27, 2012. While what is "unfair" or "unethical" depends on "norms," and there may be disagreements about what is or is not fair, the experiment focused on situations where there would be broad consensus on what was fair or ethical. Similarly, much of the financial sector behavior that I criticize ... violates virtually any sense of "fairness" or "ethics."

14. This problem has come to be called the "natural resource curse." There are other reasons that such countries have not done well: managing natural resources can be difficult (prices fluctuate and exchange rates can become overvalued). For a recent review of some of the problems and how they can be addressed see *Escaping the Resource Curse*, ed. M. Humphreys, J. Sachs, and J. E. Stiglitz (New York: Columbia University Press, 2007). See also, e.g., Michael Ross, *The Oil Curse: How Petroleum*

Wealth Shapes the Development of Nations (Princeton: Princeton University Press, 2012); and idem, *Timber Booms and Institutional Breakdown in Southeast Asia* (New York: Cambridge University Press, 2001).

15. According to World Bank Indicators, 50 percent of the population was living under the national poverty line in 1998 before Chavez took office in 1999.

16. He shared the 1964 Nobel Prize in Physics with the Soviet scientists Nikolay Basov and Aleksandr Prokhorov for "fundamental work in the field of quantum electronics, which has led to the construction of oscillators and amplifiers based on the maser-laser principle."

17. They received the 1956 Nobel Prize in Physics "for their researches on semiconductors and their discovery of the transistor effect."

18. The World Wide Web Consortium he founded decided that its standards should be based on royalty-free technology, so that they could easily be adopted by anyone. Like Jobs, Bill Gates is often heralded as an innovator, but even though the adoption of his products is nearly universal now, that is due more to his business acumen—and near-monopoly of the market—than to the uniqueness of the technology he sells.

19. Bakija et al. found (p. 3) that "executives, managers, supervisors, and financial professionals account for about 60 percent of the top 0.1 percent of income earners in recent years, and can account for 70 percent of the increase in the share of national income going to the top 0.1 percent of the income distribution between 1979 and 2005." The composition of the top 1 percent in 2005 was 31 percent "Executives, managers, supervisors (non-finance)"; 15.7 percent "Medical," 13.9 percent "Financial professionals, including management," and 8.4 percent "Lawyers." The share of finance almost doubled over the period, rising from 7.7 percent in 1979 to 13.9 percent in 2005. (Nonfinance executives and medical fell slightly; lawyers increased marginally.) These statistics are based on an income measure that *excludes* capital gains. This is very important because about half of all capital gains accrue to the top 0.1 percent. For the top 400 income earners, 60 percent of their income is in the form of capital gains. J. Bakija, A. Cole, and B. T. Hein, "Jobs and Income Growth of Top Earners and the Causes of Changing Income Inequality: Evidence from U.S. Tax Return Data." See also comments by C. Rampell, "The Top 1%: Executives, Doctors and Bankers" *New York Times*, October 17, 2011, available at http://economix.blogs.nytimes.com/2011/10/17/the-top-1-executives-doctors-and-bankers/; and Laura D'Andrea Tyson, "Tackling Income Inequality," *New York Times*, November 18, 2011, available at http://economix.blogs.nytimes.com/2011/11/18/tackling-income-inequality/.

20. See Forbes World's Billionaires list at http://www.forbes.com/wealth/billionaires/; ranking is from 2011.

21. Slim's Grupo Carso, France Telecom, and Southwestern Bell paid $1.7 billion in December 1990 to acquire "a controlling 20.4 percent stake in Telmex, which includes 51 percent of the votes in the company." See Keith Bradsher, "Regulatory Pitfall in Telmex Sale," *New York Times*, December 7, 1990, available at http://www.nytimes.com/1990/12/27/business/talking-deals-regulatory-pitfall-in-telmex-sale.html?scp=1&sq=telmex%20southwestern%20bell%201990&st=cse (accessed March 3, 2012).

22. In the midnineties, Russia borrowed large amounts of money from the private sector, putting up shares in its oil and natural resource companies as collateral. But it was all a ruse to turn over state assets to the oligarchs. This was called "loans for shares." See Chrystia Freeland, *Sale of the Century: Russia's Wild Ride from Communism to Capitalism*

(New York: Crown Business, 2000). A variety of specious arguments are often put forward for these privatizations. Most recently, Greece has been pushed to privatize, as a condition for getting assistance from Europe and the IMF. For a discussion of privatization and the arguments used for it … and *J. E. Stiglitz, The Price of Inequality: How Today's Divided Society Endangers Our Future* (New York: Norton, 2012), and J. E. Stiglitz, *Globalization and Its Discontents* (New York: Norton, 2002). Not every country and not every privatization has suffered from transferring state assets to private parties at below fair market prices. Many believe that the privatizations in the UK under Margaret Thatcher, with shares publicly floated and with the number of shares any one person or company could buy strictly limited, were conducted deliberately in a manner to avoid such outcomes.

23. See Forbes America's Highest Paid Chief Executives 2011, available at http://www.forbes.com/lists/2011/12/ceo-compensation-11_land.html.

24. This is obviously a controversial claim: the CEOs might argue that in fact they receive but a small fraction of what they contribute to shareholder value. But … the so-called incentive structures are poorly designed, providing little link between that part of the increase in market value that is attributable to the efforts of the CEO and that which is the result of broader market forces—lower costs of inputs or higher stock market prices in general. Some studies have suggested, moreover, that once total compensation is taken into account (including adjustments of bonuses when the stock market doesn't do well), there is little relationship between firm performance and compensation. For a broader discussion of this issue, see J. E. Stiglitz, *Roaring Nineties* (New York: W. W. Norton, 2003); and especially Lucian Bebchuk and Jesse Fried, *Pay without Performance: The Unfulfilled Promise of Executive Compensation* (Cambridge: Harvard University Press, 2004).

25. Still one more group is real estate moguls, who benefit from special provisions of the tax code and often get rents as a result of local government variances in zoning laws.

26. These are sometimes called natural monopolies. They include the examples given earlier where network externalities are very large.

27. The advocates of stronger intellectual property rights, of course, claim otherwise. Interestingly, in the United States many of the most innovative firms, those in Silicon Valley, have been among those opposing certain proposals by those in the drug and entertainment industries to strengthen intellectual property rights. Recent revisions of patent law arguably gave large corporations an advantage over new firms, illustrating the fact … that there are strong distributive consequences of any legal framework. For a discussion of how our current intellectual property framework may actually inhibit innovation, see J. E. Stiglitz, *Making Globalization Work* (New York: Norton, 2006), and Claude Henry and J. E. Stiglitz, "Intellectual Property, Dissemination of Innovation, and Sustainable Development," *Global Policy* 1, no. 1 (October 2010): 237–51.

28. See, e.g., A. Dixit, "The Role of Investment in Entry-Deterrence," *Economic Journal* 90, no. 357 (March 1980): 95–106; and J. Tirole and D. Fudenberg, "The Fat Cat Effect, the Puppy Dog Ploy and the Lean and Hungry Look," *American Economic Review* 74 (1984): 361–68. The practices Microsoft used to rid itself of its rivals (described below) also helped prevent entry of new competitors.

29. It's clear that one wants standards; one doesn't want to be operated on by an unqualified doctor. But, for instance, the supply of qualified doctors could have been increased simply by increasing the number of places in medical school.

30. In 1890 Congress passed the Sherman Anti-Trust Act, and its enforcement speeded up in the twentieth century. In 1911 the Supreme Court ordered the dissolution of the Standard Oil Company and the American Tobacco Company, which brought down the two powerful industrial trusts. In 1984 the Court broke up AT&T's monopoly following *United States v. AT&T*. See Charles R. Geisst, *Monopolies in America: Empire Builders and Their Enemies from Jay Gould to Bill Gates* (New York: Oxford University Press, 2000).

31. The term "Chicago school" is often applied to this group of economists, partially because the high priest of this religion, Milton Friedman (and many of his acolytes), taught at the University of Chicago. But it should be understood that many at that great university are not devotees of this school of thought, and that there are many devotees in other universities around the world. The term has, however, become a commonly used shorthand.

32. One group even went so far as to argue that markets will behave competitively even if there is only one firm, so long as there is potential competition. This argument played an important role in airline deregulation, where it was contended that even if there was only one airline on a given route, it would be disciplined from charging monopoly prices by the threat of entry. Both theory and experience have shown that this argument is wrong, so long as there are sunk costs (costs that won't be recovered if a firm enters and subsequently leaves), no matter how small those costs. See Joseph Farrell, "How Effective Is Potential Competition?," *Economics Letters* 20, no. 1 (1986): 67–70; J. E. Stiglitz, "Technological Change, Sunk Costs, and Competition," *Brookings Papers on Economic Activity* 3 (1987), pp. 883–947; and P. Dasgupta and J. E. Stiglitz, "Potential Competition, Actual Competition, and Economic Welfare," *European Economic Review* 32, nos. 2–3 (March 1988): 569–77.

33. For discussion and examples of conservative foundations' contribution to the Chicago school law and economics programs, see Alliance for Justice, *Justice for Sale: Short-changing the Public Interest for Private Gain* (Washington, DC: Alliance for Justice, 1993).

34. The Department of Justice brought a case against American Airlines in the early years of this century. I thought the evidence that American Airlines had engaged in predatory behavior was especially compelling, but the judge didn't need to look at the evidence: the Supreme Court had ruled that there was just too strong a presumption *against* the existence of predatory pricing to make prosecution possible.

35. One of Netscape's founders, Marc Andreessen, was part of the team at the University of Illinois at Urbana-Champaign that developed Mosaic, the first widely used web browser, which was a project of the university's National Center for Supercomputing Applications (one of the original sites of the National Science Foundation's Supercomputer Centers Program). See the website of the NCSA, http://www.ncsa.illinois.edu/Projects/mosaic.html (accessed March 3, 2012); and John Markoff, "New Venture in Cyberspace by Silicon Graphics Founder," *New York Times*, May 7, 1994, available at http://www.nytimes.com/1994/05/07/business/new-venture-in-cyberspace-by-silicon-graphics-founder.html?ref=marcandreessen (accessed March 3, 2012).

36. For an overview of the Microsoft case, see Geisst, *Monopolies in America*.

37. See Steven C. Salop and R. Craig Romaine, "Preserving Monopoly: Economic Analysis, Legal Standards, and Microsoft," *George Mason Law Review* 4, no. 7 (1999): 617–1055.

38. See Microsoft's annual report.

39. As the late Oxford professor and Nobel Prize winner John Hicks said, "The best of all monopoly profits is a quiet life." J. R. Hicks, "Annual Survey of Economic Theory: The Theory of Monopoly," *Econometrica* 1, no. 8 (1935). Kenneth Arrow pointed out that because monopolists restrict production, the saving they get from reducing costs is diminished. See Arrow, "Economic Welfare and the Allocation of Resources for Invention," in *The Rate and Direction of Inventive Activity: Economic and Social Factors* (Princeton: Princeton University Press, 1962), pp. 609–26. Monopolies, of course, don't last forever: new technologies and the open-source movement are already beginning to challenge Microsoft's dominance.

40. Calculated by total assets of commercial banks, as of September 3, 2011. See FDIC Statistics on Banking, available at http://www2.fdic.gov/SDI/SOB/index.asp; and Federal Reserve Statistical Release Large Commercial Banks, available at http://www.federalreserve.gov/releases/lbr/current/default.htm.

41. Moreover, banks don't compete on price for the services they offer. If you want to do a merger or acquisition, every major bank charges the same percentage fee. When takeovers were hundreds of millions of dollars, the resulting charges were large; when they became billions, charges became astronomical, for essentially the same amount of work by the same number of people.

42. From 2010 Q4 to 2011 Q3 (the most recently available year), FDIC-insured institutions made an aggregate profit of $115 billion. ... But these numbers don't really capture the magnitude of bank profits, since they are the profits after paying out the mega-bonuses to the executives, which can push compensation at some firms above 50 percent of revenues after other costs have been taken out, i.e., the "true" profits may be as much as double the above number. The *profits and bonuses* of the banking sector exceed 1 percent of the country's entire national output. Such numbers lead many to conclude that the financial sector, which is supposed to be the servant of the rest of the economy, has become its master.

43. Microsoft tried to exert political influence through a variety of channels. It has made campaign contributions of $13,516,304 from 1999 to present. See campaignmoney.com, compiled from campaign finance reports and data disclosed by Federal Election Commission, lists of contribution available at http://www.campaignmoney.com/Microsoft.asp?pg=88 (accessed March 6, 2012). The remedies put forward by President Bush's Justice Department in response to Microsoft's conviction on anticompetitive behavior were mild and did not effectively curtail its market power. See, e.g., Andrew Chin's account of the outcome of *United States v. Microsoft Corp.*: "Decoding Microsoft: A First Principles Approach," *Wake Forest Law Review* 40, no. 1 (2005):1–157. In the case of antitrust laws, there's a partial remedy for the absence of effective public enforcement: private antitrust action (which was introduced because of worries about the willingness of public authorities to take enforcement action).

44. The late Nobel Prize–winning economist George Stigler wrote extensively about this. See, e.g., Stigler, "The Economic Theory of Regulation," *Bell Journal of Economics* 11 (1971): 3–21.

45. Data from the OpenSecrets.org, a website of the Center for Responsive Politics, counting lobbyists for commercial banks, finance, and credit companies. When all lobbyists are counted in the finance, insurance, and real estate industries, the number balloons to nearly five per congressman. See http://www.opensecrets.org/lobby/indus.php?id=F&year=a (accessed March 24, 2012).

46. The latest instance was the veto by the Senate Banking Committee chairman of the nomination of Nobel Prize–winning economist Peter Diamond. Diamond would have provided a critical voice on some of the doctrines that prevail among some of the governors. (Diamond was first nominated to the Fed by President Obama in April 2010; he was renominated in September and again in January 2011, after Senate Republicans blocked a floor vote on his confirmation. On June 5, 2011, Diamond withdrew his nomination, ending a fourteen-month nomination effort resisted by Senator Richard Shelby of Alabama, who, with party colleagues repeatedly criticized Diamond for supporting the central bank's monetary stimulus. Diamond responded that his opponents failed to appreciate that understanding the determinants of unemployment is essential to effective monetary policy.)

47. The Medicare Prescription Drug, Improvement, and Modernization Act of 2003.

48. The economist Dean Baker's research shows that $332 billion could be saved between 2006 and 2013 (around $50 billion a year) in the most conservative high-cost scenario, if Medicare were allowed to negotiate prices; in the middle-cost scenario, $563 billion could be saved for the same budget window. See Baker, *The Savings from an Efficient Medicare Prescription Drug Plan* (Washington, DC: Center for Economic and Policy Research, January 2006).

49. It is estimated that four banks in the United States take home a windfall of some $20 billion a year in derivatives.

50. The market for ethanol was distorted in other ways—such as ethanol requirements and subsidies for gasoline refiners who blended gasoline with ethanol—most of which came from America's corn producers. See the 2010 CBO study "Using Biofuel Tax Credits to Achieve Energy and Environmental Policy Goals," available at http://www.cbo.gov/sites/default/files/cbofiles/ftpdocs/114xx/doc11477/07-14-biofuels.pdf (accessed March 2, 2012); and "The Global Dynamics of Biofuel," Brazil Institute Special Report, April 2007, issue no. 3, available at http://www.wilsoncenter.org/sites/default/files/Brazil_SR_e3.pdf (accessed March 2, 2012).

51. Congress finally allowed the subsidy to expire at the end of 2011.

52. Famously, ADM was fined a then record $100 million for lysine price fixing in 1997, a result of a lengthy federal investigation that also led to convictions and prison time for three executives. (This became a book by Kurt Eichenwald and then a 2009 movie starring Matt Damon, *The Informant.*)

53. In the early days of corn-based ethanol, this was flatly wrong: the demand for corn by ethanol producers was so low that the corn farmers received almost no benefit from the subsidy. Because usage of corn for ethanol production was such a small fraction of global supply, it had a negligible effect on corn prices. ADM and other ethanol producers were the true beneficiaries.

54. The U.S. government paid a total of $261.9 billion for agriculture subsidies from 1995 to 2010. According to USDA, 63 percent of farms do not receive any payments. Among those payments, a large chunk (62 percent in 2009) goes to large-scale commercial farms (with gross annual sales of $250,000 or more). Between 1995 and 2010, the top 10 percent of farms received $30,751 average per year, while the bottom 80 percent of farms received $587 average per year. See USDA Economic Research Service, "Farm Income and Cost: Farms Receiving Government Payments," available at http://www.ers.usda.gov/Briefing/FarmIncome/govtpayby-farmtype.htm; Environmental Working Group, Farm Subsidy Database, available at http://farm.ewg.org/region.php.

55. And indeed, many books have been written on the subject. See, e.g., Glenn Parker, *Congress and the Rent-Seeking Society* (Ann Arbor: University of Michigan Press, 1996).

QUESTIONS FOR MAKING CONNECTIONS
WITHIN THE READING

1. Writing at a time when most Americans praise free markets uncritically, Stiglitz challenges a number of beliefs about the wisdom of the "invisible hand." He argues, for example, that competition tends to drive profits down, not up. He suggests that manufacturers typically try to protect profit margins by banding together to create monopolies. He alleges that investors often destroy wealth instead of increasing it. He even claims that "markets by themselves often fail to produce efficient and desirable outcomes." Choose one argument that challenges our current common sense about free markets and explain Stiglitz's reasoning. Consider as well the role he appears to think that markets should be allowed to play.

2. Why does Stiglitz see rent seeking as destructive? Who benefits from rent seeking? What are its economic consequences, and why? What does he see as its impact on society, and what is the relationship between economics and social life in general? Why is Stiglitz skeptical about the power of the market to correct itself? Would it be fair to say that the problem of rent seeking can be solved only by political means—that is, through government intervention? Why has government failed to intervene, and what steps does Stiglitz recommend to restore a balance between outcomes and opportunities?

3. Early in his argument about inequality Stiglitz includes a short historical overview, beginning with the once widespread belief that wealth and poverty are divinely ordained. Once a "vast urban underclass" had arisen in the wake of the Industrial Revolution, "it became imperative," Stiglitz writes, "to find new justifications for inequality." What justifications have become the most compelling ones in our time? Is Stiglitz opposed to inequality, or does he regard it as a problem that society will never fully solve? Does he regard it as a problem at all?

QUESTIONS FOR WRITING

1. What does Stiglitz see as the purpose of wealth? Although he never explicitly develops an answer to that question, his entire argument implies a set of commitments about the purposes that wealth-creation should serve. Does he believe that the purpose of wealth is to lift the wealth-creators above the rest? Does he believe that wealth should offer a reward to the hardest-working, while poverty should serve as punishment to motivate lazy people? Or does he see wealth as a means for improving our society as a whole?

Does Stiglitz believe that a society's wealth belongs in some sense to all its members? On what grounds does he argue that the government should redistribute wealth?

2. Ordinarily, we experience the economy in terms of our own jobs, annual earnings, debts, expenses, and so on. Unless we are trained economists, we tend not to understand these matters as the effects of a system—a system of the kind that Stiglitz describes. Drawing on Stiglitz, make an argument about the difference between our personal experience of day-to-day finances and the systemic perspective that economics provides. What are the blind spots in our experience? How does the narrowness of personal life help to conceal larger commonalities and differences? What elements of your experience are overlooked by the focus on the economy as a system?

QUESTIONS FOR MAKING CONNECTIONS
BETWEEN READINGS

1. Bringing Stiglitz together with Maggie Nelson's "Great to Watch," consider the relationship between the arts and inequality. Nelson never refers to economics, and Stiglitz never mentions the world of art, but this question asks you to explore possible connections between them. In what ways does the art world challenge the values of a market society? In what ways does it reinforce social distinctions between "high" and "low" culture—between the cultural "haves" and "have nots"? Does the violence of the avant-garde liberate or intimidate? Consider what Nelson tells us about the trend among artists to respond to middle class "banality" by inflicting on their audience an experience of "brutal, sensory overload." What relation does this strategy establish between artists and their public? In what other areas of life, aside from art, is "sensory overload" a problem?

2. The conflict between Microsoft and Google, as chronicled by Tim Wu in "Father and Son," might be described as a textbook case of dueling monopolies—two companies vying to control an ever larger share of their industries. How might Stiglitz describe the conflict between these two giants? To what extent do their activities qualify as genuine rent seeking—completely, or, to some degree, or not at all? Would it be fair to describe Google as engaged in a struggle against monopoly—to describe it, in other words, as a hero of equality and freedom? Or is Google simply trying to protect a monopoly of its own? In what ways does Wu's narrative complicate Stiglitz's analysis? Does it prove or disprove the claim that markets sometimes fail to make life better for most members of society?

Answers to Odd-Numbered Study Questions and Problems*

Chapter 1 Introducing the Economic Way of Thinking

1. A poor nation with many people who lack food, clothing, and shelter certainly experiences wants beyond the availability of goods and services to satisfy these unfulfilled wants. On the other hand, no wealthy nation has all the resources necessary to produce everything everyone in the nation wishes to have. Even if you had $1 million and were completely satisfied with your share of goods and services, other desires would be unfulfilled. There is never enough time to accomplish all the things that you can imagine would be worthwhile.

3. Macroeconomics applies an overview perspective to an economy by examining economywide variables, such as inflation, unemployment, and growth of the economy. Microeconomics examines individual economic units, such as the market for corn, gasoline, or ostrich eggs.

5. The real world is full of complexities that make it difficult to understand and predict the relationships between variables. For example, the relationship between changes in the price of gasoline and changes in consumption of gasoline requires abstraction from the reality that such variables as the fuel economy of cars and weather conditions often change at the same time as the price of gasoline.

7. The two events are associated, and the first event (cut in military spending) is the cause of the second event (higher unemployment in the defense industry). The point is that association does not necessarily mean causation, but it might.

Appendix to Chapter 1 Applying Graphs to Economics

1. a. The probability of living is *inversely* related to age. This model could be affected by improvements in diet, better health care, reductions in hazards to health in the workplace, or changes in the speed limit.

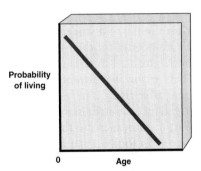

b. Annual income and years of formal education are *directly* related. This relationship might be influenced by changes in such human characteristics as intelligence, motivation, ability, and family background. An example of an institutional change that could affect this relationship over a number of years is the draft.

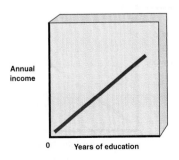

---

*Note: Answers to even-numbered questions are in the Instructor's Manual.

c. Inches of snow and sales of bathing suits are *inversely* related. The weather forecast and the price of travel to sunny vacation spots can affect this relationship.

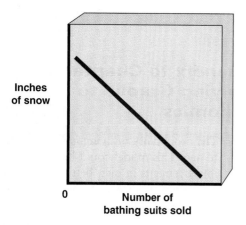

d. Most alumni and students will argue that the number of football games won is *directly* related to the athletic budget. They reason that winning football games is great advertising and results in increased attendance, contributions, and enrollment that, in turn, increase the athletic budget. Success in football can also be related to other factors, such as school size, age and type of institution, number and income of alumni, and quality of the faculty and administrators.

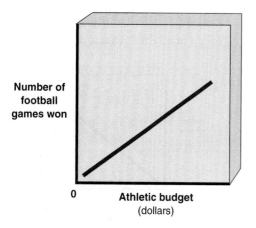

Chapter 2 Production Possibilities, Opportunity Cost, and Economic Growth

1. Because the wants of individuals and society exceed the goods and services available to satisfy these desires, choices must be made. The consumption possibilities of an individual with a fixed income are limited, and as a result, additional consumption of one item necessarily precludes an expenditure on another next-best choice. The forgone alternative is called the opportunity cost, and this concept also applies to societal decisions. If society allocates resources to the production of guns, then those same resources cannot be used at the same time to make butter.

3. Regardless of the price of a lunch, economic resources-land, labor, and capital-are used to produce the lunch. These scarce resources are no longer available to produce other goods and services.

5. Using marginal analysis, students weigh the benefits of attending college against the costs. There is an incentive to attend college when the benefits (improved job opportunities, income, intellectual improvement, social life, and so on) outweigh the opportunity costs.

7.

Flower boxes	Opportunity cost (pies forgone)
0	
1	4 (30 − 26)
2	5 (26 − 21)
3	6 (21 − 15)
4	7 (15 − 8)
5	8 (8 − 0)

9. Movements along the curve are efficient points and conform to the well-known "free lunch" statement. However, inefficient points are exceptions because it is possible to produce more of one output without producing less of another output.

11.

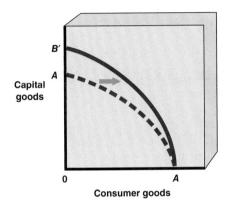

Chapter 3 Market Demand and Supply

1. If people buy a good or service because they associate higher quality with higher price, this is a violation of the ceteris paribus assumption. An increase in the quantity demanded results only from a decrease in price. Quality and other nonprice determinants of demand, such as tastes and preferences and the price of related goods, are held constant in the model.

3. a. Demand for cars decreases; oil and cars are *complements*.
   b. Demand for insulation increases; oil and home insulation are *substitutes*.
   c. Demand for coal increases; oil and coal are *substitutes*.
   d. Demand for tires decreases; oil and tires are *complements*.

5. One reason that the demand curve for word processing software shifted to the right might be that people desire new, higher-quality output features. The supply curve can shift to the right when new technology makes it possible to offer more software for sale at different prices.

7. a. Demand shifts to the right.
   b. Supply shifts to the left.
   c. Supply shifts to the right.
   d. Demand shifts to the right.
   e. Demand shifts to the right.
   f. Supply of corn shifts to the left.

9. a. The supply of Blu-ray disc players shifts rightward.
   b. The demand for Blu-ray disc players is unaffected.
   c. The equilibrium price falls, and the equilibrium quantity increases.
   d. The demand for Blu-ray discs increases because of the fall in the price of Blu-ray disc players (a complementary good).

11. The number of seats (quantity supplied) remains constant, but the demand curve shifts because tastes and preferences change according to the importance of each game. Although demand changes, the price is a fixed amount, and to manage a shortage, colleges and universities use amount of contributions, number of years as a contributor, or some other rationing device.

Appendix to Chapter 3 Consumer Surplus, Producer Surplus, and Market Efficiency

1. $50

3.

Price	$30	$15
Consumer surplus	$80	$105
Producer surplus	$25	$5
Total surplus	$105	$110

The lower price results in higher total surplus because in this case the rise in consumer surplus exceeds fall in producer surplus.

Chapter 4 Markets in Action

1.

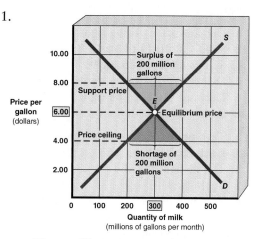

Price per gallon (dollars)

Quantity of milk (millions of gallons per month)

a. The equilibrium price is $6.00 per gallon, and the equilibrium quantity is 300 million gallons per month. The price system will restore the market's $6.00 per gallon price because either a surplus will drive prices down or a shortage will drive prices up.

b. The support price results in a persistent surplus of 200 million gallons of milk per month, which the government purchases with taxpayers' money. Consequently, taxpayers who do not drink milk are still paying for milk. The purpose of the support price is to bolster the incomes of dairy farmers.

c. The ceiling price will result in a persistent shortage of 200 million gallons of milk per month, but 200 million gallons are purchased by consumers at the low price of $4.00 per gallon. The shortage places a burden on the government to ration milk in order to be fair and to prevent black markets. The government's goal is to keep the price of milk below the equilibrium price of $6.00 per gallon, which would be set by a free market.

3. The labor market can be divided into two separate markets, one for skilled union workers and one for unskilled workers. If the minimum wage is above the equilibrium wage rate and is raised, the effect will be to increase the demand for, and the wage of, skilled union workers because the two groups are substitutes.

5. The equilibrium price rises.

7. The government can reduce emissions by (a) regulations that require smoke-abatement equipment or (b) imposing pollution taxes that shift supply leftward.

9. Pure public goods are not produced in sufficient quantities by private markets because there is no feasible method to exclude free riders.

Chapter 5 Gross Domestic Product

1. a. final service
   b. final good
   c. intermediate good
   d. intermediate good

3. 3 million pounds of food
   $\times$ $1 per pound   = $3 million
   50,000 shirts $\times$ $20 per shirt   = 1 million
   20 houses $\times$ $50,000 per house = 1 million
   50,000 hours of medical
       services $\times$ $20 per hour   = 1 million
   1 automobile plant
       $\times$ $1 million per plant   = 1 million
   2 tanks $\times$ $500,000 per tank   = 1 million
   Total value of output   = $8 million

5. Capital is not excluded from being a final good. A final good is a finished good purchased by an ultimate user and not for resale. The ultimate user is the warehouse, so the sale would be included in GDP and there would be no double-counting problem.

7. Using the expenditure approach, net exports are exports minus imports. If the expenditures by foreigners for U.S. products exceed the expenditures by U.S. citizens for foreign products, net exports will be a positive contribution to GDP. If foreigners spend less for U.S. products than U.S. citizens spend for foreign products, GDP is reduced.

9. NI = GDP − depreciation
   $4,007 = $4,486 − $479

   The depreciation charge is not a measure of newly produced output. It is an estimate, subject to error, of the value of capital worn out in the production of final goods and services. Errors in the capital consumption allowance overstate or understate GDP.

11. When the price level is rising, nominal GDP overstates the rate of change between years. Dividing nominal GDP by the GDP chain price index results in real GDP by removing the distortion from inflation. Comparison of real GDP changes between years reflects only changes in the market value of all final products and not changes in the price level.

13. GDP does not tell the mix of output in two nations, say, between military and consumer goods. GDP also does not reveal whether GDP is more equally distributed in one nation compared to another.

Chapter 6 Business Cycles and Unemployment

1. The generally accepted theory of business cycles is that they are the result of changes in the level of total spending, or aggregate demand. Total spending includes spending for final goods by households, businesses, government, and foreign buyers. Expressed as a formula, $GDP = C + I + G + (X − M)$.

3. Civilian unemployment rate

$$= \frac{unemployed}{civilian\ labor\ force} \times 100$$

where the civilian labor force = unemployed + employed. Therefore,

$$8.3\% = \frac{10\ million\ persons}{120\ million\ persons} \times 100$$

5. The official unemployment rate is overstated when respondents to the BLS falsely report that they are seeking employment. The unemployment rate is understated when *discouraged workers* who want to work have given up searching for a job.

7. Structural unemployment occurs when those seeking jobs do not possess the skills necessary to fill the available jobs. Cyclical unemployment is caused by a recession (deficient total spending). In this case, there are not enough available jobs.

9. The increasing participation of women and teenagers in the labor force has increased the rate of unemployment. Women take more time out of the labor force than do men for childbearing and child rearing.

11. The GDP gap is the difference between potential real GDP and actual real GDP. Because potential real GDP is estimated on the basis of the full-employment rate of unemployment, the GDP gap measures the cost of *cyclical* unemployment in terms of real GDP.

Chapter 7 Inflation

1. This statement is incorrect. The price of a single good or service can rise while the average price of all goods and services falls. In short, the inflation rate rises when the average price of consumer goods and services rises.

3. First, the CPI is based on a typical market basket purchased by the urban family. Any group not buying the same market basket, such as retired persons, is not experiencing the price changes measured by changes in the CPI. Second, the CPI fails to adjust for quality changes. Third, the CPI ignores the law of demand and the substitution effect as prices of products change.

5. If the percentage increase in the CPI exceeds the salary increase, a person's purchasing power declines in a given year.

7. The loan is advantageous to you because the real interest rate is −5 percent (5 percent nominal interest rate minus 10 percent inflation). In one year, you must repay $105. If prices rise by 10 percent during the year, the real value of the $105 will be only $95. Therefore, you have borrowed $100 worth of purchasing power and are repaying $95 worth of purchasing power.

9. At full employment, the economy operates at full capacity and produces the maximum output of goods and services. As buyers try to outbid one another for the fixed supply of goods and services, prices rise rapidly.

11. If buyers think prices will be higher tomorrow, they may buy products today and cause demand-pull inflation. If businesses believe prices for inputs will be higher in the future, many will raise prices today and cause cost-push inflation.

Chapter 8 The Keynesian Model

1. Classical economists argued that underconsumption and unemployment could not exist in the long run because of price-wage flexibility. Unsold merchandise would force firms to compete and lower product prices, and unemployed workers would accept a lower wage rate.

3. Consumers have only two options for any extra disposable income they receive. The MPC and MPS must add up to one because the portion of extra income that is not spent must be saved.

5. a. The consumption schedule downshifts, and the saving schedule downshifts.
   b. The consumption schedule upshifts, and the saving schedule downshifts.
   c. The consumption schedule downshifts, and the saving schedule upshifts.
   d. The consumption schedule downshifts, and the saving schedule downshifts.
   e. Both the consumption and the saving schedules downshift.

7. Changes in the nonincome determinants of the consumption and saving schedules tend to offset each other, and people are reluctant to change their consumption and saving habits. On the other hand, Keynes considered the volatility of businesses' decisions to invest as a major cause of the business cycle. The potentially unstable determinants of investment spending include expectations, technological change, the stock of capital goods, and business taxes.

9. a.

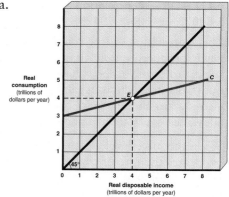

b. The autonomous consumption is $3 trillion where real disposable income is 0. The MPC = 0.25 because each $1 trillion increase in real disposable income results in a $0.25 trillion increase in consumption. Since MPS = (1 − MPC), MPS = (1 − 0.25) = 0.75.

c. The break-even income of real disposable income equals $4 trillion where the C line intersects the 45° line.

d. At $2 trillion real GDP on the 45° line, consumption is $3.5 trillion, so dissavings is $1.5 trillion. At $7 trillion real GDP on the 45° line, consumption is $4.75 trillion, so savings is $2.5 trillion.

Chapter 9 The Keynesian Model in Action

1.

Employment, Output, Consumption, and Unplanned Inventory			
Possible levels of employment (millions)	Real GDP (output) equals disposable income (billions of dollars)	Consumption (billions of dollars)	Unplanned inventory (billions of dollars)
40	325	300	−75
45	375	325	−50
50	425	350	−25
55	475	375	0
60	525	400	25
65	575	425	50
70	625	450	75

a. Answers are given in the above table.

b. $MPC = \dfrac{\text{change in consumption}}{\text{change in disposable income}}$

$= \dfrac{\$25 \text{ billion}}{\$50 \text{ billion}} = \dfrac{1}{2} = 0.50$

since $MPS = 1 - MPC = 1 - 0.50 = 0.50$

c. At an employment level of 40 million workers, $75 million in unplanned inventory investment encourages businesses to expand output, and GDP increases toward the equilibrium real GDP of $475 billion.

3.

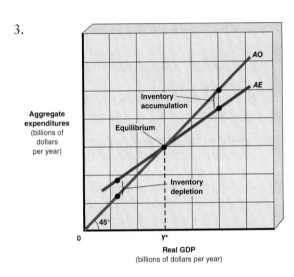

Aggregate expenditures (billions of dollars per year)

Real GDP (billions of dollars per year)

The aggregate expenditures (AE) line intersects the aggregate output (AO) line at the equilibrium level of real GDP, Y^*. Below Y^*, an unplanned inventory depletion causes businesses to expand output, which pushes the economy toward equilibrium output. Above Y^*, an unintended inventory accumulation pushes the economy toward Y^* by pressuring businesses to reduce production.

5. $\text{Multiplier} = \dfrac{1}{1 - MPC} = \dfrac{1}{MPS}$

The greater the MPC, the smaller the MPS and the greater the size of the multiplier.

a. 1, 1.5, 10

b. $Y = M \times I = 5 \times \$10 \text{ billion} = \$50 \text{ billion}$

c. $Y = M \times I = 3 \times \$10 \text{ billion} = \$30 \text{ billion}$

7. a.

Round	Component of total spending	New consumption spending (billions of dollars)
1	Investment	$100
2	Consumption	75
3	Consumption	56
4	Consumption	42
	Total spending	$273

b. The spending multiplier is

$$\dfrac{1}{(1 - MPC)} = \dfrac{1}{(1 - 0.75)} = \dfrac{1}{0.25} = 4$$

Therefore, change in investment spending × spending multiplier = change in aggregate spending ($100 billion × 4 = $400 billion). Note: This problem demonstrates how useful the spending multiplier formula is because it avoids working through individual steps in the multiplier process.

9. Spending multiplier

$$= \dfrac{\text{change in GDP}}{\text{change in government spending}} = \dfrac{\Delta Y}{\Delta G}$$

Since $MPC = 0.75$,

$$\text{Spending multiplier} = \dfrac{1}{(1 - MPC)} = \dfrac{1}{0.25} = 4$$

rewritten as

$$4 = \dfrac{\$100 \text{ billion}}{\Delta G}$$

Therefore,

$$\Delta G = \dfrac{\$100 \text{ billion}}{4} = \$25 \text{ billion}$$

Given that the MPC is 0.75, this means households spend only $18.75 billion of the additional $25 billion of disposable income from the tax cut. Therefore,

$\Delta C \times$ spending multiplier = change in GDP

$18.75 billion $\times$ 4 = $75 billion

Because GDP must increase by $100 billion, a tax cut of $25 billion would not be enough to restore full-employment GDP.

Chapter 10 Aggregate Demand and Supply

1. There are three reasons why the aggregate demand curve is downward sloping:
   a. The *real balances effect* means that a lower price level increases the purchasing power of money and other financial assets. The result is an increase in consumption, which increases the quantity of real GDP demanded.
   b. The *interest-rate effect* assumes a fixed money supply, and, therefore, a lower price level reduces the demand for borrowing and the interest rate. The lower rate of interest increases spending for consumption and investment.
   c. The *net exports effect* encourages foreign customers to buy more of an economy's domestic exports relative to its domestic purchases of imports when the price level falls. An increase in net exports increases aggregate expenditures.
   Rationales for the downward-sloping demand curve for an individual market are the income effect, the substitution effect, and the law of diminishing marginal utility, which are quite different from the three effects that determine the aggregate demand curve.

3. a. A leftward shift occurs because of a decrease in the consumption schedule.
   b. A rightward shift occurs because of an increase in autonomous investment spending.
   c. A rightward shift occurs because of an increase in government spending.
   d. A rightward shift occurs because of an increase in net exports.

5. This statement may not be correct. The equilibrium GDP is not necessarily the same as the full-employment GDP. Equilibrium GDP refers to the equality between the aggregate demand and the aggregate supply curves, which does not necessarily equal the full capacity of the economy to produce goods and services.

7. a. leftward because of an increase in resource prices
   b. rightward because of a decrease in resource prices
   c. rightward because technological change reduces the cost of production
   d. leftward because an increase in taxes means the price must cover the tax at each possible quantity supplied

9. a. Aggregate demand increases.
   b. Aggregate supply increases.
   c. Aggregate demand decreases.
   d. Aggregate supply decreases.
   e. Aggregate demand decreases along the classical range.
   f. Aggregate demand increases along the Keynesian range.

11. Assuming the aggregate supply curve remains constant, a rightward shift of the aggregate demand curve from AD_1 to AD_2 in the upward-sloping or the vertical range of the aggregate supply curve causes the price level to rise from P_1 to P_2. In addition to demand-pull inflation, the level of real GDP increases from Q_1 to Q_2 and provides the economy with new jobs. In the classical range, inflation is the only undesirable result, and real GDP remains unaffected at Q_2.

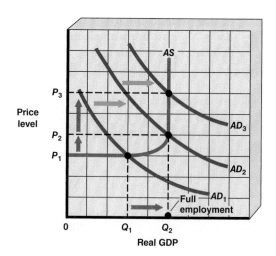

Appendix to Chapter 10 The Self-Correcting Aggregate Demand and Supply Model

1. a.–c.

3.

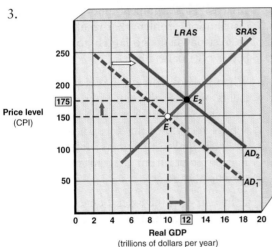

5. Nominal incomes of workers in the short run are fixed. In response to the fall in aggregate demand, firms' profits decline, and they cut output and employment. As a result, the economy moves downward along SRAS to temporary equilibrium at E_2. When workers lower their nominal incomes because of competition from unemployed workers, the short-run aggregate supply curve shifts rightward to E_3 and returns to long-run equilibrium. Profits rise and firms increase output and employment while the price level falls.

Chapter 11 Fiscal Policy

1. *Expansionary* fiscal policy refers to increasing government spending and/or decreasing taxes in order to increase aggregate demand and eliminate a GDP gap. *Contractionary* fiscal policy is designed to cool inflation by decreasing aggregate demand. This result is accomplished by decreasing government spending and/or increasing taxes.

3. a. contractionary fiscal policy
   b. contractionary fiscal policy
   c. expansionary fiscal policy

5. The spending multiplier is

$$\frac{1}{1 - MPC} = \frac{1}{0.25} = \frac{1}{1/4} = 4$$

The spending multiplier (SM) times the change in government spending ($\triangle G$) equals the change in aggregate demand ($\triangle AD$). Therefore,

$$\triangle G \times SM = \triangle AD$$
$$\triangle G \times 4 = \$500 \text{ billion}$$
$$\triangle G = \$125 \text{ billion}$$

The government must increase government spending by $125 billion in order to eliminate the GDP gap.

7. The tax multiplier equals the spending multiplier minus 1. Thus, the impact of the expansion in government spending exceeds the impact of an equal amount of tax cut.

9. As a supply-side economist, you would argue that the location of the aggregate supply curve is related to the tax rates. Ceteris paribus, if the tax rates are cut, there will be strong incentives for workers to supply more work, households to save more, and businesses to invest more in capital goods. Thus, cutting tax rates shifts the aggregate supply curve rightward, the level of real GDP rises, and the price level falls.

11. a. rightward shift in the aggregate demand curve
    b. leftward shift in the aggregate demand curve

c. rightward shift in the aggregate supply curve

d. rightward shift in the aggregate demand curve

e. leftward shift in the aggregate supply curve

Chapter 12 The Public Sector

1. Transfer payments account for the difference between total government expenditures, or outlays, and total government spending. Transfers do not "use up" resources; they reallocate purchasing power by collecting taxes from one group and paying benefits to other groups.

3. The primary sources are individual income taxes at the federal level, sales and excise taxes at the state level, and property taxes at the local level.

5. The marginal tax rate is the percentage of additional income paid in taxes. The average tax rate is the amount of taxes paid as a percentage of income.

7. a. more than $6,000
   b. less than $6,000
   c. $6,000

9. Sales tax paid as a percentage of income:
   10%
   7%
   6%
   4%
   Because the sales tax paid as a percentage of income falls as income rises, the tax is regressive.

11. A profit-maximizing firm follows the marginal rule that units will be produced so long as the marginal benefit exceeds or equals the marginal cost. Dollars can measure the intensity of benefits in relation to costs. A "one-person, one-vote" system does not necessarily measure benefits in proportion to the dollar value of benefits among individual voters. Thus, a majority of voters can approve projects for which costs exceed benefits and reject projects for which benefits exceed costs.

Chapter 13 Federal Deficits, Surpluses, and the National Debt

1. The national debt is the sum of past federal budget deficits. When budget deficits are large, the national debt increases at a rapid rate. When budget deficits are small, the national debt increases at a lower rate.

3. The statement makes the argument that most of the debt is internal national debt that one U.S. citizen owes to another U.S. citizen. Suppose the federal government finances a deficit by having the Treasury sell government bonds to one group of U.S. citizens, thereby increasing the national debt. When the bonds mature, the government can pay the interest and principal by issuing new government bonds (rolling over the debt) to another group of U.S. citizens. This argument ignores the income distribution problem that results because interest payments go largely to those who are better off financially.

5. When the government makes interest payments on internally held debt, the money remains in the hands of U.S. citizens. External debt is very different. Repayment of interest and principal to foreigners withdraws purchasing power from U.S. citizens in favor of citizens abroad.

7. a. In year one, the federal deficit begins at $50 billion, and the U.S. Treasury issues $50 billion worth of bonds to finance the deficit.
   b. The next year the federal government must pay interest of $5 billion to service the debt ($50 billion bonds × 0.10 interest rate). Adding the interest payment to the $100 billion spent for goods and services yields a $105 billion expenditure in year two.
   c. For the second year, the deficit is $55 billion ($105 billion in expenditures − $50 billion in taxes), and the U.S. Treasury borrows this amount by issuing new bonds. The new national debt is $105 billion, consisting of the $50 billion in bonds issued in the first year and the $55 billion in bonds issued in the second year.

9. During a depression, tax hikes and/or expenditure cuts would only reduce aggregate demand and, in turn, real GDP, jobs, and income. Because the economy is operating in the Keynesian segment of the aggregate demand curve, this fiscal policy would have no impact on the price level.

11. This answer should be logical and supported by a thoughtful explanation. For example, the federal deficit might be the result of a recession and you argue that the deficit is correct fiscal policy. When the recession ends, the deficit will decline. Other arguments include some combinations of cutting spending or increasing taxes.

Chapter 14 Money and the Federal Reserve System

1. Money is worthless in and of itself. The value of money is to serve as a medium of exchange, a unit of account, and a store of value.

3. a. The quantity of credit cards can be controlled. Credit cards are portable, divisible, and uniform in quality.
   b. The quantity of Federal Reserve notes is controlled by the U.S. government. These notes are portable, divisible, and uniform in quality.
   c. The quantity of dogs is difficult to control. Dogs are not very portable or divisible, and they are certainly not uniform.
   d. The quantity of beer mugs can be controlled. Beer mugs are not very portable or divisible, but they could be made fairly uniform.

5. The narrowest definition of money in the United States is M1. M1 = currency (coins + paper bills) + checkable deposits.

7. The Fed's most important function is to regulate the U.S. money supply. The *Board of Governors* is composed of seven persons who have the responsibility to supervise and control the money supply and the U.S. banking system. The *Federal Open Market Committee (FOMC)* controls the money supply by directing the buying and selling of U.S. government securities.

9. Banks that belong to the Fed must join the FDIC. Banks chartered by the states may affiliate with the FDIC. There are relatively few nonmember, noninsured state banks.

Chapter 15 Money Creation

1. At first, the goldsmiths followed Shakespeare's advice and gave receipts only for gold on deposit in their vaults. They then realized that at any given time new deposits were coming in that could offset old deposits people were drawing down. The conclusion is that banking does not require a 100 percent required reserve ratio. Therefore, loans can be made, which stimulate the economy.

3. Banks can and do create money by granting loans to borrowers. These loans are deposited in customers' checking accounts, and, therefore, banks are participants in the money supply creation process.

5. There is no impact on the money supply. A check deposited in bank *A*, drawn on bank *B*, increases deposits, reserves, and lending at bank *A*. However, bank *B* experiences an equal reduction in deposits, reserves, and lending.

7.

First National Bank

Balance Sheet

Assets		Liabilities	
Reserves	−$1,000	Checkable deposits	−$1,000
Required	−$100		
Excess	−$900		
Total assets	−$1,000	Total liabilities	−$1,000

Negative excess reserves mean that loans must be reduced by $1,000.

9. Some customers may hold cash, rather than writing a check for the full amount of the loan. Some banks may hold excess reserves, rather than using these funds to make loans.

11. The decision of the public to hold cash and the willingness of banks to use excess reserves for loans affect the money multiplier. Variations in the money multiplier can cause unexpected changes in the money supply. Nonbanks can make loans and offer other financial services that are not under the direct control of the Federal Reserve. Finally, the public can decide to transfer funds from M1 to M2 or other definitions of the money supply.

Chapter 16 Monetary Policy

1. a. Transactions and precautionary balances increase.
   b. Speculative balances decrease.
   c. Transactions and precautionary balances decrease.
   d. Speculative balances increase.
   e. Transactions and precautionary balances decrease.

3.

Bond price	Interest rate
$ 800	10%
1,000	8
2,000	44

There is an inverse relationship between the price of a bond and the interest rate.

5. a. The price level declines slightly. Real GDP and employment fall substantially.
   b. The price level, real GDP, and employment rise.
   c. The price level declines slightly. Real GDP and employment fall substantially.

7. In the monetarist view, the velocity of money, V, and the output, Q, variables in the equation of exchange are constant. Therefore, the quantity theory of money is stated as

$$M \times V = P \times Q$$

Given this equation, changes in the money supply, M1, yield proportionate changes in the price level, P.

9. In the Keynesian view, an increase in the money supply decreases the interest rate and causes investment spending, which increases aggregate demand through the multiplier effect and causes demand-pull inflation. In the monetarist view, money supply growth gives people more money to spend. This direct increase in aggregate demand causes demand-pull inflation.

11. Under such conditions, the Keynesian view is correct. The Fed would have no influence on investment because changes in the interest rate failed to alter the quantity of investment goods demanded.

Chapter 17 The Phillips Curve and Expectations Theory

1. The Phillips curve is an inverse relationship between the inflation rate and the unemployment rate. The increase in aggregate demand would cause the inflation rate to increase and the unemployment rate to decrease.

3. In the 1970s and early 1980s, the economy experienced supply shocks from skyrocketing oil and food prices. The result was a leftward shift in the aggregate supply curve and stagflation.

5. a. The inflation rate is 6 percent, and the unemployment rate is 6 percent.
   b. The inflation rate rises to 10 percent, and the employment rate falls in the short run. In the long run, the unemployment rate returns to 6 percent.
   c. The inflation rate rises to 12 percent, and the unemployment rate falls in the short run. In the long run, the unemployment rate returns to 6 percent.

7. The economy is stimulated prior to an election, and there is a boom. After the election, the strategy is to contract the economy, causing recession until the next election approaches. Thus, political policies are counter to Keynesian policies because political policies cause the business cycle instead of stabilizing it.

9. a. Both prices and nominal wages will rise immediately, causing the inflation rate to

rise from 4 percent to 6 percent. The unemployment rate remains unchanged at the 4 percent natural rate.

b. Both prices and nominal wages will rise immediately, causing the inflation rate to rise from 6 percent to 8 percent. The unemployment rate remains unchanged at the 4 percent natural rate.

c. Both prices and nominal wages will fall immediately, causing the inflation rate to fall from 8 percent to 4 percent. The unemployment rate remains unchanged at the 4 percent natural rate.

Chapter 18 International Trade and Finance

1. a. In Alpha, the opportunity cost of producing 1 ton of diamonds is 1/2 ton of pearls. In Beta, the opportunity cost of producing 1 ton of diamonds is 2 tons of pearls.

   b. In Alpha, the opportunity cost of producing 1 ton of pearls is 2 tons of diamonds. In Beta, the opportunity cost of producing 1 ton of pearls is 1/2 ton of diamonds.

   c. Because Alpha can produce diamonds at a lower opportunity cost than Beta can, Alpha has a comparative advantage in the production of diamonds.

   d. Because Beta can produce pearls at a lower opportunity cost than Alpha can, Beta has a comparative advantage in the production of pearls.

   e.

	Diamonds (tons per year)	Pearls (tons per year)
Before specialization		
Alpha (at point B)	100	25
Beta (at point C)	30	120
Total output	130	145
After specialization		
Alpha (at point A)	150	0
Beta (at point D)	0	180
Total output	150	180

As shown in the above table, specialization in each country increases total world output per year by 20 tons of diamonds and 35 tons of pearls.

f.

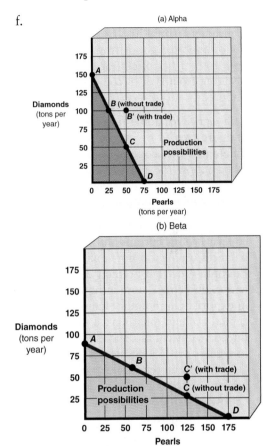

Without trade, Alpha produces and consumes 100 tons of diamonds and 25 tons of pearls at point *B* on its production possibilities curve. Without trade, Beta produces and consumes 30 tons of diamonds and 120 tons of pearls (point *C*). Now assume Alpha specializes in producing diamonds at point *A* and imports 50 tons of pearls in exchange for 50 tons of diamonds. Through specialization and trade, Alpha moves its consumption possibility to point *B'*, outside its production possibilities curve.

3. The principle of specialization and trade according to comparative advantage applies to both nations and states in the United States. For example, Florida grows oranges, and

Idaho grows potatoes. Trade between these states, just like trade between nations, increases the consumption possibilities.

5. U.S. industries (and their workers) that compete with restricted imports would benefit. Consumers would lose from the reduced supply of imported goods from which to choose and from higher prices for domestic products, resulting from lack of competition from imports.

7. Although some domestic jobs may be lost, new ones are created by international trade. Stated differently, the economy as a whole gains when nations specialize and trade according to the law of comparative advantage, but imports will cost jobs in some specific industries.

9. Although each nation's balance of payments equals zero, its current and capital account balances usually do not equal zero. For example, a current account deficit means a nation purchased more in imports than it sold in exports. On the other hand, this nation's capital account must have a surplus to offset the current account deficit. This means that foreigners are buying more domestic capital (capital inflow) than domestic citizens are buying foreign capital (capital outflow). Thus, net ownership of domestic capital stock is in favor of foreigners.

11. a.

b. $0.15 per euro
c. An excess quantity of 200 million euros would be demanded.

Chapter 19 Economies in Transition

1. Americans prefer large cars and canned soup. Europeans predominantly buy small cars and dry soup. The role of women and minorities in the workplace is an excellent example of how culture relates to the labor factor of production.

3. Such a program would provide additional economic security for the elderly, but higher taxes could reduce the incentive to work, and economic efficiency might be reduced.

5. In a traditional agricultural system, a benefit would be that members of society would cooperate by helping to build barns, harvest, and so on. Under the command system, worrying about errors and crop failures would be minimized because the state makes the decisions and everyone in society has a basic income. In a market economy, a bumper crop would mean large profits and the capacity to improve one's standard of living.

7. Because most economies are mixed systems, this term is too broad to be very descriptive. The terms *capitalism* and *communism* are more definitive concerning the role of private ownership, market allocations, and decentralized decision making. Embracing a market-oriented system means a transfer of power from the command bureaucracy to consumers. Markets are incompatible with the principle that socialist citizens are supposed to be concerned with the collective interest.

Chapter 20 Growth and the Less-Developed Countries

1. The difference between IACs and LDCs is based on GDP per capita. This classification is somewhat arbitrary. A country with a high GDP per capita and narrow industrial development based on oil, such as the United Arab Emirates, is excluded from the IAC list. There are 27 economies listed in the text as IACs, including Switzerland, Japan, the United States, Singapore, and Hong Kong. The

	1949	1950	1951	1952	1953	1954	1955	1956	1957	1958
1. Gross domestic product	267.2	293.7	339.3	358.3	379.3	380.4	414.7	437.4	461.1	467.2
2. Personal consumption expenditures	178.5	192.2	205.5	219.5	233.1	240.0	258.8	271.7	286.9	296.2
3. Gross private domestic investment	36.9	54.1	60.2	54.0	56.4	53.8	69.0	72.0	70.5	64.5
4. Government consumption expenditures and gross investment	46.6	46.7	68.1	83.6	90.5	86.1	86.4	91.4	99.7	106.0
5. Net exports	5.2	0.7	2.5	1.2	−0.7	0.4	0.5	2.4	4.1	0.5
6. National income	237.5	263.9	303.8	321.3	338.6	338.7	372.0	394.9	413.3	415.6
7. Personal income	207.0	228.9	257.9	275.2	291.7	294.3	316.0	339.5	358.5	368.9
8. Disposable personal income	190.2	209.9	230.8	243.2	258.4	264.1	283.1	302.9	319.7	330.4
9. Real gross domestic product (in 2005 dollars)	1,843.1	2,004.2	2,159.3	2,242.0	2,345.2	2,330.4	2,498.2	2,547.6	2,598.8	2,575.4
10. Percent change in real GDP	−0.5	8.7	7.7	3.8	4.6	−0.6	7.2	2.0	2.0	−0.9
11. Consumer price index (1982–84 = 100)	23.8	24.1	26.0	26.5	26.7	26.9	26.8	27.2	28.1	28.9
12. Rate of inflation (percent)	−1.2	1.3	7.9	1.9	0.8	0.7	−0.4	1.5	3.3	2.8
13. Civilian unemployment rate (percent)	5.9	5.3	3.3	3.0	2.9	5.5	4.4	4.1	4.3	6.8
14. Supply of money, M1 (in billions of dollars)	111.2	116.2	122.7	127.4	128.8	132.3	135.2	136.9	135.9	141.1
15. Percent change in M1	−0.3	4.5	5.6	3.8	1.1	2.7	2.2	1.3	−0.7	3.8
16. Prime rate charged by banks	2.0	2.1	2.6	3.0	3.2	3.1	3.2	3.8	4.2	3.8
17. Federal budget surplus or deficit (in billions of dollars)	0.6	−3.1	6.1	−1.5	−6.5	−1.2	−3.0	3.9	3.4	−2.8
18. Federal debt (in billions of dollars)	252.6	256.9	255.3	259.1	266.0	270.8	274.4	272.7	272.3	279.7

(Continued)

U.S. Gross Domestic Product (in billions of dollars) and Related Statistics (Continued)

	1959	1960	1961	1962	1963	1964	1965	1966	1967	1968
1. Gross domestic product	506.6	526.4	544.8	585.7	617.8	663.6	719.1	787.7	832.4	909.8
2. Personal consumption expenditures	317.7	331.8	342.2	363.3	382.7	411.5	443.8	480.9	507.8	558.0
3. Gross private domestic investment	78.5	78.9	78.2	88.1	93.8	102.1	118.2	131.3	128.6	141.2
4. Government consumption expenditures and gross investment	110.0	111.5	119.5	130.1	136.4	143.2	151.4	171.6	192.5	209.3
5. Net exports	0.4	4.2	4.9	4.1	4.9	6.9	5.6	3.9	3.6	1.4
6. National income	453.5	473.9	490.7	528.9	559.7	601.4	652.2	701.1	750.4	821.2
7. Personal income	392.3	411.3	428.8	456.4	479.5	514.3	555.5	603.8	648.1	711.7
8. Disposable personal income	350.1	365.2	381.6	404.9	525.0	462.3	497.8	537.4	575.1	624.7
9. Real gross domestic product (in 2005 dollars)	2,760.1	2,828.5	2,894.4	3,069.8	3,204.0	3,389.4	3,607.0	3,842.1	3,939.2	4,129.9
10. Percent change in real GDP	7.2	2.5	2.3	6.1	4.4	5.8	6.4	6.5	2.5	4.8
11. Consumer price index (1982–84 = 100)	29.1	29.6	29.9	30.2	30.6	31.0	31.5	32.4	33.4	34.8
12. Rate of inflation (percent)	0.7	1.7	1.0	1.0	1.3	1.3	1.6	2.9	3.1	4.2
13. Civilian unemployment rate (percent)	5.5	5.5	6.7	5.5	5.7	5.2	4.5	3.8	3.8	3.6
14. Supply of money, M1 (in billions of dollars)	140.0	140.7	145.2	147.8	153.3	160.3	167.9	172.0	183.3	197.4
15. Percent change in M1	−0.8	0.5	3.2	1.8	3.7	4.6	4.7	2.5	6.6	7.7
16. Prime rate charged by banks	4.5	4.8	4.5	4.5	4.5	4.5	4.5	5.6	5.6	6.3
17. Federal budget surplus or deficit (in billions of dollars)	−12.8	0.3	−3.3	−7.1	−4.8	−5.9	−1.4	−3.7	−8.6	−25.2
18. Federal debt (in billions of dollars)	287.5	290.5	292.6	302.9	310.3	316.1	322.3	328.5	340.4	368.7

	1969	1970	1971	1972	1973	1974	1975	1976	1977	1978
1. Gross domestic product	984.4	1,038.3	1,126.8	1,237.9	1,382.3	1,499.5	1,637.7	1,824.6	2,030.1	2,293.8
2. Personal consumption expenditures	605.1	648.3	701.6	770.2	852.0	932.9	1,033.8	1,151.3	1,277.8	1,427.6
3. Gross private domestic investment	156.4	152.4	178.2	207.6	244.5	249.4	230.2	292.0	361.3	438.0
4. Government consumption expenditures and gross investment	221.4	233.7	246.4	263.4	281.7	317.9	357.7	383.0	414.7	453.6
5. Net exports	1.4	4.0	0.6	−3.4	4.1	−0.8	16.0	−1.6	−23.1	−25.4
6. National income	888.5	929.5	1,005.6	1,110.3	1,246.1	1,341.5	1,444.0	1,609.8	1,797.4	2,027.9
7. Personal income	778.3	838.6	903.1	992.6	1,110.5	1,222.7	1,334.9	1,474.7	1,632.5	1,836.7
8. Disposable personal income	673.8	735.5	801.4	869.0	978.1	1,071.7	1,187.3	1,302.3	1,435.0	1,607.3
9. Real gross domestic product (in 2005 dollars)	4,258.2	4,266.3	4,409.5	4,643.8	4,912.8	4,885.7	4,875.4	5,136.9	5,373.1	5,672.8
10. Percent change in real GDP	3.1	0.2	3.4	5.3	5.8	−0.6	−0.2	5.4	4.6	5.6
11. Consumer price index (1982–84 = 100)	36.7	38.8	40.5	41.8	44.4	49.3	53.8	56.9	60.6	65.2
12. Rate of inflation (percent)	5.5	5.7	4.4	3.2	6.2	11.0	9.1	5.8	6.5	7.6
13. Civilian unemployment rate	3.5	4.9	5.9	5.6	4.9	5.6	8.5	7.7	7.1	6.1
14. Supply of money, M1 (in billions of dollars)	203.9	214.4	228.3	249.2	262.9	274.2	287.1	306.2	330.9	357.3
15. Percent change in M1	3.3	5.1	6.5	9.2	5.5	4.3	4.7	6.7	8.1	8.0
16. Prime rate charged by banks	8.0	7.9	5.7	5.3	8.0	10.8	7.9	6.8	6.8	9.1
17. Federal budget surplus or deficit (in billions of dollars)	3.2	−2.8	−23.0	−23.4	−14.9	−6.1	−53.2	−73.7	−53.7	−59.2
18. Federal debt (in billions of dollars)	365.8	380.9	408.2	435.9	466.3	483.9	541.9	629.0	706.4	776.6

(Continued)

U.S. Gross Domestic Product (in billions of dollars) and Related Statistics (Continued)

	1979	1980	1981	1982	1983	1984	1985	1986	1987	1988
1. Gross domestic product	2,562.2	2,788.1	3,126.8	3,253.2	3,534.6	3,930.9	4,217.5	4,460.1	4,736.4	5,100.4
2. Personal consumption expenditures	1,591.2	1,755.8	1,939.5	2,075.5	2,288.6	2,501.1	2,717.6	2,896.7	3,097.0	3,350.1
3. Gross private domestic investment	492.9	479.3	572.4	517.2	564.3	735.6	736.2	746.5	785.0	821.6
4. Government consumption expenditures and gross investment	500.7	566.1	627.5	680.4	733.4	796.9	878.9	949.3	999.4	1,038.9
5. Net exports	−22.5	−13.1	−12.5	−20.0	−51.7	−102.7	−115.2	−132.5	−145.0	−110.1
6. National income	2,248.3	2,433.0	2,729.8	2,851.4	3,070.9	3,461.3	3,696.3	3,871.5	4,150.0	4,522.3
7. Personal income	2,059.5	2,301.5	2,582.3	2,766.8	2,952.2	3,268.9	3,496.7	3,696.0	3,924.4	4,231.2
8. Disposable personal income	1,790.9	2,002.7	2,237.1	2,412.7	2,599.8	2,891.5	3,079.3	3,258.8	3,435.3	3,726.3
9. Real gross domestic product (in 2005 dollars)	5,850.1	5,834.0	5,982.1	5,865.9	6,130.9	6,571.5	6,843.4	7,080.5	7,307.0	7,607.4
10. Percent change in real GDP	3.1	−0.3	2.5	−1.9	4.5	7.2	4.1	3.5	3.2	4.1
11. Consumer price index (1982–84 = 100)	72.6	82.4	90.9	96.5	99.6	103.9	107.6	109.6	113.6	118.3
12. Rate of inflation (percent)	11.3	13.5	10.3	6.2	3.2	4.3	3.6	1.9	3.6	4.1
13. Civilian unemployment rate	5.8	7.1	7.6	9.7	9.6	7.5	7.2	7.0	6.2	5.5
14. Supply of money, M1 (in billions of dollars)	381.8	408.5	436.7	474.8	521.4	551.6	619.8	724.7	750.2	786.7
15. Percent change in M1	6.9	7.0	6.9	8.7	9.8	5.8	12.4	16.9	3.5	4.9
16. Prime rate charged by banks	12.7	15.3	18.9	14.9	10.8	12.0	9.9	8.3	8.2	9.3
17. Federal budget surplus or deficit (in billions of dollars)	−40.7	−73.8	−79.0	−128.0	−207.8	−185.4	−212.3	−221.2	−149.7	−155.2
18. Federal debt (in billions of dollars)	829.5	909.1	994.8	1,137.3	1,371.7	1,564.6	1,817.4	2,120.5	2,346.0	2,601.1

	1989	1990	1991	1992	1993	1994	1995	1996	1997	1998
1. Gross domestic product	5,482.1	5,800.5	5,992.1	6,342.3	6,667.4	7,085.2	7,414.7	7,838.5	8,332.4	8,793.5
2. Personal consumption expenditures	3,594.5	3,835.5	3,980.1	4,236.9	4,483.6	4,750.8	4,967.3	5,273.6	5,570.6	5,918.5
3. Gross private domestic investment	874.9	861.0	802.9	864.8	953.3	1,097.3	1,144.0	1,240.2	1,388.7	1,510.8
4. Government consumption expenditures and gross investment	1,100.6	1,181.7	1,236.1	1,273.5	1,294.8	1,329.8	1,374.0	1,421.0	1,474.4	1,526.1
5. Net exports	−87.9	−77.6	−27.0	−32.8	−64.4	−92.7	−90.7	−96.3	−101.4	−161.8
6. National income	4,800.5	5,059.5	5,217.9	5,517.1	5,784.7	6,181.3	6,522.3	6,931.7	7,406.0	7,875.6
7. Personal income	4,557.5	4,846.7	5,031.5	5,347.3	5,568.1	5,874.8	6,200.9	6,591.6	7,000.7	7,525.4
8. Disposable personal income	3,991.4	4,254.0	4,444.9	4,736.7	4,921.6	5,184.3	5,457.0	5,759.6	6,074.6	6,498.9
9. Real gross domestic product (in 2005 dollars)	7,879.2	8,027.1	8,008.3	8,280.0	8,516.2	8,863.1	9,086.0	9,425.8	9,845.9	10,274.7
10. Percent change in real GDP	3.6	1.9	−0.2	3.4	2.9	4.1	2.5	3.7	4.5	4.4
11. Consumer price index (1982–84 = 100)	124.0	130.7	136.2	140.3	144.5	148.2	152.4	156.9	160.5	163.0
12. Rate of inflation (percent)	4.8	5.4	4.2	3.0	3.0	2.6	2.8	3.0	2.3	1.6
13. Civilian unemployment rate	5.3	5.6	6.8	7.5	6.9	6.1	5.6	5.4	4.9	4.5
14. Supply of money, M1 (in billions of dollars)	792.9	824.7	897.0	1,024.9	1,129.8	1,150.8	1,127.5	1,081.4	1,072.5	1,095.7
15. Percent change in M1	0.8	4.0	8.8	14.3	10.2	1.9	−2.0	−4.1	−.08	2.2
16. Prime rate charged by banks	10.9	10.0	8.5	6.3	6.0	7.2	8.8	8.3	8.4	8.4
17. Federal budget surplus or deficit (in billions of dollars)	−152.6	−221.0	−269.2	−290.3	−255.1	−203.2	−164.0	−107.4	−21.9	69.3
18. Federal debt (in billions of dollars)	2,867.8	3,206.3	3,598.2	4,001.8	4,351.0	4,643.3	4,920.6	5,181.5	5,369.2	5,478.2

(Continued)

U.S. Gross Domestic Product (in billions of dollars) and Related Statistics *(Continued)*

	1999	2000	2001	2002	2003	2004	2005	2006
1. Gross domestic product	9,353.5	9,951.5	10,286.2	10,642.3	11,142.2	11,853.3	12,623.0	13,377.2
2. Personal consumption expenditures	6,342.8	6,830.4	7,148.8	7,439.2	7,804.1	8,270.6	8,803.5	9,301.0
3. Gross private domestic investment	1,641.5	1,772.2	1,661.9	1,647.0	1,729.7	1,968.6	2,172.3	2,327.1
4. Government consumption expenditures and gross investment	1,631.3	1,731.0	1,846.4	1,983.3	2,112.6	2,232.8	2,369.9	2,518.4
5. Net exports	−262.1	−382.1	−371.0	−427.2	−504.1	−618.7	−722.7	−769.3
6. National income	8,358.0	8,938.9	9,185.2	9,408.5	9,840.2	10,534.0	11,237.8	12,031.2
7. Personal income	7,910.8	8,559.4	8,883.3	9,060.1	9,378.1	9,9937.2	10,485.9	11,268.1
8. Disposable personal income	6,803.3	7,327.2	7,648.5	8,009.7	8,377.8	8,889.4	9,277.3	9,915.7
9. Real gross domestic product (in 2005 dollars)	10,770.7	11,216.4	11,337.5	11,543.1	11,836.4	12,246.9	12,623.0	12,958.5
10. Percent change in real GDP	4.8	4.1	1.1	1.8	2.5	3.5	3.1	2.7
11. Consumer price index (1982–84 = 100)	166.6	172.2	177.1	179.9	184.0	188.9	195.3	201.6
12. Rate of inflation (percent)	2.2	3.4	2.8	1.6	2.3	2.7	3.4	3.2
13. Civilian unemployment rate	4.2	4.0	4.7	5.8	6.0	5.5	5.1	4.6
14. Supply of money, M1 (in billions of dollars)	1,122.4	1,087.8	1,182.8	1,220.6	1,307.0	1,376.7	1,375.0	1,367.2
15. Percent change in M1	2.4	−3.1	8.7	3.2	7.1	5.3	−0.1	−0.6
16. Prime rate charged by banks	8.0	9.2	6.9	4.7	4.1	4.3	6.2	8.0
17. Federal budget surplus or deficit (in billions of dollars)	125.6	236.2	128.2	−157.8	−377.6	−412.7	−318.3	−248.2
18. Federal debt (in billions of dollars)	5,605.5	5,628.7	5,769.9	6,198.4	6,760.0	7,354.7	7,905.3	8,451.4

	2007	2008	2009	2010	2011
1. Gross domestic product	14,028.7	14,291.5	13,939.0	14,526.5	15,094.0
2. Personal consumption expenditures	9,772.3	10,035.5	9,866.1	10,245.5	10,726.0
3. Gross private domestic investment	2,295.2	2,087.6	1,546.8	1,795.1	1,916.2
4. Government consumption expenditures and gross investment	2,674.2	2,878.1	2,917.5	3,002.8	3,030.6
5. Net exports	−713.1	−709.7	−391.5	−516.9	−578.7
6. National income	12,396.4	12,609.1	12,147.6	12,840.1	13,437.3
7. Personal income	11,912.3	12,460.2	11,930.2	12,373.5	13,005.3
8. Disposable personal income	10,423.6	11,024.5	10,788.8	11,179.7	11,604.9
9. Real gross domestic product (in 2005 dollars)	13,206.4	13,161.9	12,703.1	13,088.0	13,315.1
10. Percentage change in real GDP	1.9	−0.3	−3.5	3.0	1.7
11. Consumer price index (1982–84 = 100)	207.3	215.3	214.5	218.0	224.9
12. Rate of inflation (percent)	2.8	3.8	−0.4	1.6	3.2
13. Civilian unemployment rate	4.6	5.8	9.3	9.6	8.9
14. Supply of money, M1 (in billions of dollars)	1,375.4	1,606.9	1,697.8	1,840.3	2,173.9
15. Percent change in M1	0.6	16.8	5.7	8.4	18.1
16. Prime rate charged by banks	8.1	5.1	3.3	3.3	3.3
17. Federal budget surplus or deficit (in billions of dollars)	−160.7	−458.6	−1,412.7	−1,293.5	−1,299.6
18. Federal debt (in billions)	8,950.7	11,875.9	13,528.8	14,764.2	16,350.9

Glossary

A

Ability-to-pay principle The concept that those who have higher incomes can afford to pay a greater proportion of their income in taxes, regardless of benefits received.

Absolute advantage The ability of a country to produce a good using the same or fewer resources than another country.

Adaptive expectations theory The concept that people believe the best indicator of the future is recent information. As a result, people persistently underestimate inflation when it is accelerating and overestimate it while it is slowing down.

Adjustable-rate mortgage (ARM) A home loan that adjusts the nominal interest rate to changes in an index rate, such as rates on Treasury securities.

Agency for International Development (AID) The agency of the U.S. State Department that is in charge of U.S. aid to foreign countries.

Aggregate demand curve (AD) The curve that shows the level of real gross domestic product (GDP) purchased by households, businesses, government, and foreigners (net exports) at different possible price levels during a time period, ceteris paribus.

Aggregate expenditures function (AE) The function that represents total spending in an economy at a given level of real disposable income.

Aggregate expenditures model The model that determines the equilibrium level of real GDP by the intersection of the aggregate expenditures and aggregate output (and income) curves.

Aggregate supply curve (AS) The curve that shows the level of real GDP produced at different possible price levels during a time period, ceteris paribus.

Appreciation of currency A rise in the price of one currency relative to another.

Arbitrage The practice of earning a profit by buying a good at a low price and reselling the good at a higher price.

Automatic stabilizers Federal expenditures and tax revenues that automatically change levels in order to stabilize an economic expansion or contraction; sometimes referred to as *nondiscretionary fiscal policy*.

Autonomous consumption Consumption that is independent of the level of income (disposable income or real GDP).

Autonomous expenditure Spending that does not vary with the current level of income (disposable income or real GDP).

Average fixed cost (AFC) Total fixed cost divided by the quantity of output produced.

Average tax rate The tax divided by the income.

Average total cost (ATC) Total cost divided by the quantity of output produced.

Average variable cost (AVC) Total variable cost divided by the quantity of output produced.

B

Balance of payments A bookkeeping record of all the international transactions between a country and other countries during a given period of time.

Balance of trade The value of a nation's imports subtracted from its exports. Balance of trade can be expressed in terms of goods, services, or goods and services.

Balanced budget multiplier An equal change in government spending and taxes, which changes aggregate demand by the amount of the change in government spending.

Barrier to entry Any obstacle that makes it difficult for a new firm to enter.

Barter The direct exchange of one good or service for another good or service, rather than for money.

Base year A year chosen as a reference point for comparison with some earlier or later year.

Benefit-cost analysis The comparison of the additional rewards and costs of an economic alternative.

Benefits-received principle The concept that those who benefit from government expenditures should pay the taxes that finance their benefits.

Board of Governors of the Federal Reserve System The seven members appointed by the president and confirmed by the U.S. Senate who serve for one nonrenewable 14-year term. Their responsibility is to supervise and control the money supply and the banking system of the United States.

Budget deficit A budget in which government expenditures exceed government revenues in a given time period.

Budget line A line that represents all combinations of two goods that a consumer can purchase with a fixed amount of money given the price of each good.

Budget surplus A budget in which government revenues exceed government expenditures in a given time period.

Business cycle Alternating periods of economic growth and contraction, which can be measured by changes in real GDP.

C

Capital A human-made good used to produce other goods and services.

Capitalism An economic system characterized by private ownership of resources and markets.

Cartel A group of firms that formally agree to reduce competition by coordinating the price and output of a product.

Celler-Kefauver Act A 1950 amendment to the Clayton Act that prohibits one firm from merging with a competitor by purchasing its physical assets if the effect is to substantially lessen competition.

Ceteris paribus A Latin phrase that means while certain variables change, "all other things remain unchanged."

Change in demand An increase or a decrease in the quantity demanded at each possible price. An increase in demand is a rightward shift in the entire demand curve. A decrease in demand is a leftward shift in the entire demand curve.

Change in quantity demanded A movement between points along a stationary demand curve, ceteris paribus.

Change in quantity supplied A movement between points along a stationary supply curve, ceteris paribus.

Change in supply An increase or a decrease in the quantity supplied at each possible price. An increase in supply is a rightward shift in the entire supply curve. A decrease in supply is a leftward shift in the entire supply curve.

Checkable deposits The total money in financial institutions that can be withdrawn by writing a check.

Circular flow model A diagram showing the exchange of money, products and resources between households and businesses.

Civilian labor force The number of people 16 years of age and older who are employed or who are actively seeking a job, excluding members of the armed forces, homemakers, discouraged workers, and other persons not in the labor force.

Classical economics The theory that free markets will restore full employment without government intervention.

Classical economists A group of economists whose theory dominated economic thinking from the 1770s to the Great Depression. They believed recessions would naturally cure themselves because the price system would automatically restore full employment.

Classical range The vertical segment of the aggregate supply curve, which represents an economy at full-employment output.

Clayton Act A 1914 amendment that strengthens the Sherman Act by making it illegal for firms to engage in certain anticompetitive business practices.

Coase Theorem The proposition that private market negotiations can achieve social efficiency regardless of the initial definition of property rights.

Coincident indicators Variables that change at the same time real GDP changes.

Collective bargaining The process of negotiating labor contracts between the union and management concerning wages and working conditions.

Command economy An economic system that answers the What, How, and For Whom questions by a dictator or central authority.

Command-and-control regulations Government regulations that set an environmental goal and dictate how the goal will be achieved.

Commodity money Anything that serves as money while having market value based on the material from which it is made.

Communism A stateless, classless economic system in which all the factors of production are owned by the workers and people share in production according to their needs. In Marx's view, this is the highest form of socialism toward which the revolution should strive.

Comparable worth The principle that employees who work for the same employer must be paid the same wage when their jobs, even if different, require similar levels of education, training, experience, and responsibility. A nonmarket wage-setting process is used to evaluate and compensate jobs according to point scores assigned to different jobs.

Comparative advantage The ability of a country to produce a good at a lower opportunity cost than another country.

Complementary good A good that is jointly consumed with another good. As a result, there is an inverse relationship between a price change for one good and the demand for its "go together" good.

Conglomerate merger A merger between firms in unrelated markets.

Constant-cost industry An industry in which the expansion of industry output by the entry of new firms has no effect on the individual firm's cost curve.

Constant returns to scale A situation in which the long-run average cost curve does not change as the firm increases output.

Consumer equilibrium A condition in which total utility cannot increase by spending more of a given budget on one good and spending less on another good.

Consumer Financial Protection Bureau (CFPB) An independent bureau within the Federal Reserve that helps consumers make financial decisions.

Consumer price index (CPI) An index that measures changes in the average prices of consumer goods and services.

Consumer sovereignty The freedom of consumers to cast their dollar votes to buy, or not to buy, at prices determined in competitive markets.

Consumer surplus The value of the difference between the price consumers are willing to pay for a product on the demand curve and the price actually paid for it.

Consumption function The graph or table that shows the amount households spend for goods and services at different levels of income (disposable income or real GDP).

Cost-push inflation A rise in the general price level resulting from an increase in the cost of production that causes the aggregate supply curve to shift leftward.

Cross-elasticity of demand The ratio of the percentage change in quantity demanded for a good or service to a given percentage change in the price of another good or service.

Crowding-in effect An increase in private-sector spending as a result of federal budget deficits financed by U.S. Treasury borrowing. At less than full employment, consumers hold more Treasury securities, and this additional wealth causes them to spend more. Business investment spending increases because of optimistic profit expectations.

Crowding-out effect A reduction in private-sector spending as a result of federal budget deficits financed by U.S. Treasury borrowing. When federal government borrowing increases interest rates, the result is lower consumption by households and lower investment spending by businesses.

Currency Money, including coins and paper money.

Cyclical unemployment Unemployment caused by the lack of jobs during a recession.

D

Deadweight loss The net loss of consumer and producer surplus from underproduction or overproduction of a product.

Debt ceiling A legislated legal limit on the national debt.

Decreasing-cost industry An industry in which the expansion of industry output by the entry of new firms decreases the individual firm's cost curves (cost curve shifts downward).

Deflation A decrease in the general (average) price level of goods and services in the economy.

Demand A curve or schedule showing the various quantities of a product consumers are willing to purchase at possible prices during a specified period of time, ceteris paribus.

Demand curve for labor A curve showing the different quantities of labor employers are willing to hire at different wage rates in a given time period, ceteris paribus. It is equal to the marginal revenue product of labor.

Demand for money curve A curve representing the quantity of money that people hold at different possible interest rates, ceteris paribus.

Demand-pull inflation A rise in the general price level resulting from an excess of total spending (demand) caused by a rightward shift in the aggregate demand curve.

Depreciation of currency A fall in the price of one currency relative to another.

Deregulation The elimination or phasing out of government restrictions on economic activity.

Derived demand The demand for labor and other factors of production that depends on the consumer demand for the final goods and services the factors produce.

Direct relationship A positive association between two variables. When one variable increases, the other variable increases, and when one variable decreases, the other variable decreases.

Discount rate The interest rate the Fed charges on loans of reserves to banks.

Discouraged worker A person who wants to work, but who has given up searching for work because he or she believes there will be no job offers.

Discretionary fiscal policy The deliberate use of changes in government spending or taxes to alter aggregate demand and stabilize the economy.

Diseconomies of scale A situation in which the long-run average cost curve rises as the firm increases output.

Disinflation A reduction in the rate of inflation.

Disposable personal income (DI) The amount of income that households actually have to spend or save after payment of personal taxes.

Dissaving The amount by which personal consumption expenditures exceed disposable income.

E

Economic growth The ability of an economy to produce greater levels of output, represented by an outward shift of its production possibilities curve. Also, an expansion in national output measured by the annual percentage increase in a nation's GDP.

Economic profit Total revenue minus explicit and implicit costs.

Economic system The organizations and methods used to determine what goods and services are produced, how they are produced, and for whom they are produced.

Economics The study of how society chooses to allocate its scarce resources to the production of goods and services in order to satisfy unlimited wants.

Economies of scale A situation in which the long-run average cost curve declines as the firm increases output.

Effluent tax A tax on a pollutant.

Elastic demand A condition in which the percentage change in quantity demanded is greater than the percentage change in price.

Embargo A law that bars trade with another country.

Emissions trading Trading that allows firms to buy and sell the right to pollute.

Entrepreneurship The creative ability of individuals to seek profits by taking risks and combining resources to produce innovative products.

Equation of exchange An accounting identity that states the money supply times the velocity of money equals total spending.

Equilibrium A market condition that occurs at any price at which the quantity demanded and the quantity supplied are equal.

Excess reserves Potential loan balances held in vault cash or on deposit with the Fed in excess of required reserves.

Exchange rate The number of units of one nation's currency that equals one unit of another nation's currency.

Expansion An upturn in the business cycle during which real GDP rises. Also called a *recovery*.

Expenditure approach The national income accounting method that measures GDP by adding all the spending for final goods during a period of time.

Explicit costs Payments to nonowners of a firm for their resources.

External national debt The portion of the national debt owed to foreign citizens.

Externality A cost or benefit imposed on people other than the consumers and producers of a good or service.

F

Federal Deposit Insurance Corporation (FDIC) A government agency established in 1933 to insure customer deposits up to a specified limit if a bank fails.

Federal funds market A private market in which banks lend reserves to each other for less than 24 hours.

Federal funds rate The interest rate banks charge for overnight loans of reserves to other banks.

Federal Open Market Committee (FOMC) The Federal Reserve's committee that directs the buying and selling of U.S. government securities, which are major instruments for controlling the money supply. The FOMC consists of the seven members of the Federal Reserve's Board of Governors, the president of the New York Federal Reserve Bank, and the presidents of four other Federal Reserve district banks.

Federal Reserve System The 12 Federal Reserve district banks that service banks and other financial institutions within each of the Federal Reserve districts; popularly called the Fed.

Federal Trade Commission Act The federal act that in 1914 established the Federal Trade Commission (FTC) to investigate unfair competitive practices of firms.

Fiat money Money accepted by law and not because of its tangible value.

Final goods Finished goods and services produced for the ultimate user.

Fiscal policy The use of government spending and taxes to influence the nation's output, employment, and price level.

Fixed input Any resource for which the quantity cannot change during the period of time under consideration.

Flow The rate of change in a quantity during a given period of time, such as dollars per year. For example, income and consumption are flows that occur per week, per month, or per year.

Foreign aid The transfer of money or resources from one government to another with no repayment required.

Fractional reserve banking A system in which banks keep only a percentage of their deposits on reserve as vault cash and deposits at the Fed.

Free trade The flow of goods between countries without restrictions or special taxes.

Free rider An individual who enjoys benefits without paying the costs.

Free-rider problem The problem that if some individuals benefit, while others pay, few will be willing to pay for improvement of the environment or other public goods. As a result, these goods are underproduced.

Frictional unemployment Temporary unemployment caused by the time required of workers to move from one job to another.

Full employment The situation in which an economy operates at an unemployment rate equal to the sum of the frictional and structural unemployment rates. Also called the *natural rate of unemployment*.

G

Game theory A model of the strategic moves and countermoves of rivals.

GDP chain price index A measure that compares changes in the prices of all final goods during a given year to the prices of those goods in a base year.

GDP gap The difference between full-employment real GDP and actual real GDP.

GDP per capita The value of final goods produced (GDP) divided by the total population.

Government expenditures Federal, state, and local government outlays for goods and services, including transfer payments.

Government failure Government intervention or lack of intervention that fails to correct market failure.

Gross domestic product (GDP) The market value of all final goods and services produced in a nation during a period of time, usually a year.

H

Horizontal merger A merger of firms that compete in the same market.

Hot spot problem For emissions that do not disperse uniformly, emissions may be higher in locations where firms buy permits that allow them to increase emissions.

Human capital The accumulation of education, training, experience, and health that enables a worker to enter an occupation and be productive.

Hyperinflation An extremely rapid rise in the general price level.

I

Implicit costs The opportunity costs of using resources owned by a firm.

Incentive-based regulations Government regulations that set an environmental goal, but are flexible as to how buyers and sellers achieve the goal.

Income approach The national income accounting method that measures GDP by adding all incomes, including compensation of employees, rents, net interest, and profits.

Income effect The change in quantity demanded of a good or service caused by a change in real income (purchasing power).

Income elasticity of demand The ratio of the percentage change in quantity demanded for a good or service to a given percentage change in income.

Incomes policies Federal government policies designed to affect the real incomes of workers by controlling nominal wages and prices. Such policies include presidential jawboning, wage-price guidelines, and wage-price controls.

Increasing-cost industry An industry in which the expansion of industry output by the entry of new firms increases the individual firm's cost curves (cost curves shifts upward).

Independent relationship A zero association between two variables. When one variable changes, the other variable remains unchanged.

Indifference curve A curve showing the different quantity combinations of two goods that produce the same satisfaction or total utility to a consumer.

Indifference map A selection of indifference curves with each curve representing a different level of satisfaction or total utility.

Indirect business taxes Taxes levied as a percentage of the prices of goods sold and therefore collected as part of the firm's revenue. Examples include general sales taxes, excise taxes, and customs duties.

Industrially advanced countries (IACs) High-income nations that have market economies based on large stocks of technologically advanced capital and well-educated labor. The United States, Canada, Australia, New Zealand, Japan, and most of the countries of Western Europe are IACs.

Inelastic demand A condition in which the percentage change in quantity demanded is less than the percentage change in price.

Inferior good Any good for which there is an inverse relationship between changes in income and its demand curve.

Inflation An increase in the general (average) price level of goods and services in the economy.

Inflationary gap The amount by which aggregate expenditures exceed the amount required to achieve full-employment equilibrium.

Infrastructure Capital goods usually provided by the government, including highways, bridges, waste and water systems, and airports.

In-kind transfers Government payments in the form of goods and services, rather than cash, including such government programs as food stamps, Medicaid, and housing.

Interest-rate effect The impact on total spending (real GDP) caused by the direct relationship between the price level and the interest rate.

Intermediate goods Goods and services used as inputs for the production of final goods.

Intermediate range The rising segment of the aggregate supply curve, which represents an economy as it approaches full-employment output.

Internal national debt The portion of the national debt owed to a nation's own citizens.

International Monetary Fund (IMF) The lending agency that makes short-term conditional low-interest loans to developing countries.

Inverse relationship A negative association between two variables. When one variable increases, the other variable decreases, and when one variable decreases, the other variable increases.

Investment The accumulation of capital, such as factories, machines, and inventories, that is used to produce goods and services.

Investment demand curve The graph that shows the amount businesses spend for investment goods at different possible rates of interest.

Invisible hand A phrase that expresses the belief that the best interests of a society are served when individual consumers and producers compete to achieve their own private interests.

J

Jawboning Oratory intended to pressure unions and businesses to reduce wage and price increases.

K

Keynes, John Maynard A British economist (1883–1946) whose influential work offered an explanation of the Great Depression and suggested, as a cure, that the government should play an active role in the economy.

Keynesian economics The theory, first advanced by John Maynard Keynes, that the role of the federal government is to increase or decrease aggregate demand to achieve economic goals.

Keynesian range The horizontal segment of the aggregate supply curve, which represents an economy in a severe recession.

Kinked demand curve A demand curve facing an oligopolist that assumes rivals will match a price decrease, but ignore a price increase.

L

Labor The mental and physical capacity of workers to produce goods and services.

Laffer curve A graph depicting the relationship between tax rates and total tax revenues.

Lagging indicators Variables that change after real GDP changes.

Land Any natural resource provided by nature that is used to produce goods and services.

Law of demand The principle that there is an inverse relationship between the price of a good and the quantity buyers are willing to purchase in a defined time period, ceteris paribus.

Law of diminishing marginal utility The principle that the extra satisfaction of a good or service declines as people consume more in a given period.

Law of diminishing returns The principle that beyond some point the marginal product decreases as additional units of a variable factor are added to a fixed factor.

Law of increasing opportunity costs The principle that the opportunity cost increases as production of one output expands.

Law of supply The principle that there is a direct relationship between the price of a good and the quantity sellers are willing and able to offer for sale in a defined time period, ceteris paribus.

Leading indicators Variables that change before real GDP changes.

Less-developed countries (LDCs) Nations without large stocks of technologically advanced capital and well-educated labor. LDCs are economies based on agriculture, such as most countries of Africa, Asia, and Latin America.

Long run A period of time so long that all inputs are variable.

Long-run aggregate supply curve (LRAS) The curve that shows the level of real GDP produced at different possible price levels during a time period in which nominal incomes change by the same percentage as the price level.

Long-run average cost curve (LRAC) The curve that traces the lowest cost per unit at which a firm can produce any level of output when the firm can build a plant of any desired plant size.

Lorenz curve A graph of the actual cumulative distribution of income compared to a perfectly equal cumulative distribution of income.

M

M1 The narrowest definition of the money supply. It includes currency and checkable deposits.

M2 The definition of the money supply that equals M1 plus near monies, such as savings deposits and small time deposits of less than $100,000.

Macroeconomics The branch of economics that studies decision making for the economy as a whole.

Marginal analysis An examination of the effects of additions to or subtractions from a current situation.

Marginal-average rule The rule states that when marginal cost is below average cost, average cost falls. When marginal cost is above average cost, average cost rises. When marginal cost equals average cost, average cost is at its minimum point.

Marginal cost (MC) The change in total cost when one additional unit of output is produced.

Marginal cost pricing A system of pricing in which the price charged equals the marginal cost of the last unit produced.

Marginal factor cost (MFC) The additional total cost resulting from a one-unit increase in the quantity of a factor.

Marginal product The change in total output produced by adding one unit of a variable input, with all other inputs used being held constant.

Marginal propensity to consume (MPC) The change in consumption spending resulting from a given change in income (real disposable income or real GDP).

Marginal propensity to save (MPS) The change in saving resulting from a given change in income (real disposable income or real GDP).

Marginal rate of substitution (MRS) The rate at which the consumer is willing to substitute one good for another good with no change in total utility. The MRS equals the slope of an indifference curve at any point on the curve.

Marginal revenue (MR) The change in total revenue from the sale of one additional unit of output.

Marginal revenue product (MRP) The increase in a firm's total revenue resulting from hiring an additional unit of labor or other variable resource.

Marginal tax rate The fraction of additional income paid in taxes.

Marginal utility The change in total utility from one additional unit of a good or service.

Market Any arrangement in which buyers and sellers interact to determine the price and quantity of goods and services exchanged.

Market economy An economic system that answers the What, How, and For Whom questions using prices determined by the interaction of the forces of supply and demand.

Market failure A situation in which market equilibrium results in too few or too many resources being used in the production of a good or service. This inefficiency may justify government intervention.

Market structure A classification system for the key traits of a market, including the number of firms, the similarity of the products they sell, and the ease of entry into and exit from the market.

Means test A requirement that a family's income not exceed a certain level to be eligible for public assistance.

Medium of exchange The primary function of money to be widely accepted in exchange for goods and services.

Microeconomics The branch of economics that studies decision making by a single individual, household, firm, industry, or level of government.

Mixed economy An economic system than answers the What, How, and For Whom questions through a mixture of traditional, command, and market systems.

Model A simplified description of reality used to understand and predict the relationship between variables.

Monetarism The theory that changes in the money supply directly determine changes in prices, real GDP, and employment.

Monetary Control Act A law, formally titled the Depository Institutions Deregulation and Monetary Control Act of 1980, that gave the Federal Reserve System greater control over nonmember banks and made all financial institutions more competitive.

Monetary policy The Federal Reserve's use of open market operations, changes in the discount rate, and changes in the required reserve ratio to change the money supply (M1).

Money Anything that serves as a medium of exchange, unit of account, and store of value.

Money multiplier The maximum change in the money supply (checkable deposits) due to an initial change in the excess reserves banks hold. The money multiplier is equal to 1 divided by the required reserve ratio.

Monopolistic competition A market structure characterized by (1) many small sellers, (2) a differentiated product, and (3) easy market entry and exit.

Monopoly A market structure characterized by (1) a single seller, (2) a unique product, and (3) impossible entry into the market.

Monopsony A labor market in which a single firm hires labor.

Mutual interdependence A condition in which an action by one firm may cause a reaction from other firms.

N

National debt The total amount owed by the federal government to owners of government securities.

National income (NI) The total income earned by resource owners, including wages, rents, interest, and profits. NI is calculated as GDP minus depreciation of the capital worn out in producing output.

Nationalization The act of transforming a private enterprise's assets to government ownership.

Natural monopoly An industry in which the long-run average cost of production declines throughout the entire market. As a result, a single firm can supply the entire market demand at a lower cost than two or more smaller firms.

Natural rate hypothesis The concept that the economy will self-correct to the natural rate of unemployment. The long-run Phillips curve is therefore a vertical line at the natural rate of unemployment.

Negative income tax (NIT) A plan under which families below a certain break-even level of income would receive cash payments that decrease as their incomes increase.

Net exports effect The impact on total spending (real GDP) caused by the inverse relationship between the price level and the net exports of an economy.

Net public debt National debt minus all government inter-agency borrowing.

Network good A good that increases in value to each user as the total number of users increases. As a result, a firm can achieve economics of scale. Examples include Facebook and Match.com.

New-source bias Bias that occurs when regulations provide an incentive to keep assets past the efficient point.

Nominal GDP The value of all final goods based on the prices existing during the time period of production.

Nominal income The actual number of dollars received over a period of time.

Nominal interest rate The actual rate of interest without adjustment for the inflation rate.

Nonprice competition The situation in which a firm competes using advertising, packaging, product development, better quality, and better service, rather than lower prices.

Normal good Any good for which there is a direct relationship between changes in income and its demand curve.

Normal profit The minimum profit necessary to keep a firm in operation. A firm that earns normal profit earns total revenue equal to its total opportunity cost.

Normative economics An analysis based on value judgment.

O

Offset Reduction in an existing pollution source to counteract pollution from a new source.

Offshoring Work for a company performed by the company's employees located in another country.

Oligopoly A market structure characterized by (1) few large sellers, (2) either a homogeneous or a differentiated product, and (3) difficult market entry.

Open market operations The buying and selling of government securities by the Federal Reserve System.

Opportunity cost The best alternative sacrificed for a chosen alternative.

Outsourcing The practice of a company having its work done by another company in another country.

P

Peak The phase of the business cycle in which real GDP reaches its maximum after rising during a recovery.

Per se rule The antitrust doctrine that the existence of monopoly alone is illegal, regardless of whether or not the monopoly engages in illegal business practices.

Perfect competition A market structure characterized by (1) a large number of small firms, (2) a homogeneous product, and (3) very easy entry into or exit from the market. Perfect competition is also referred to as *pure competition*.

Perfectly competitive firm's short-run supply curve The firm's marginal cost curve above the minimum point on its average variable cost curve.

Perfectly competitive industry's long-run supply curve The curve that shows the quantities supplied by the industry at different equilibrium prices after firms complete their entry and exit.

Perfectly competitive industry's short-run supply curve The supply curve derived from the horizontal summation of the marginal cost curves of all firms in the industry above the minimum point of each firm's average variable cost curve.

Perfectly elastic demand A condition in which a small percentage change in price brings about an infinite percentage change in quantity demanded.

Perfectly inelastic demand A condition in which the quantity demanded does not change as the price changes.

Personal income (PI) The total income received by households that is available for consumption, saving, and payment of personal taxes.

Phillips curve A curve showing an inverse relationship between the inflation rate and the unemployment rate.

Political business cycle A business cycle caused by policymakers to improve politician's reelection chances.

Positive economics An analysis limited to statements that are verifiable.

Poverty line The level of income below which a person or a family is to be considered poor.

Precautionary demand for money The stock of money people hold to pay unpredictable expenses.

Predatory pricing The practice of one or more firms temporarily reducing prices in order to eliminate competition and then raising prices.

Price ceiling A legally established maximum price a seller can charge.

Price discrimination The practice of a seller charging different prices for the same product that are not justified by cost differences.

Price elasticity of demand The ratio of the percentage change in the quantity demanded of a product to a percentage change in its price.

Price elasticity of supply The ratio of the percentage change in the quantity supplied of a product to the percentage change in its price.

Price floor A legally established minimum price a seller can be paid.

Price leadership A pricing strategy in which a dominant firm sets the price for an industry and the other firms follow.

Price maker A firm that faces a downward-sloping demand curve and therefore it can choose among price and output combinations along the demand curve.

Price system A mechanism that uses the forces of supply and demand to create an equilibrium through rising and falling prices.

Price taker A seller that has no control over the price of the product it sells.

Privatization The process of turning a government enterprise into a private enterprise.

Private benefits and costs Benefits and costs to the decision maker, ignoring benefits and costs to third parties. Third parties are people outside the market transaction who are affected by the product.

Producer surplus The value of the difference between the actual selling price of a product and the price producers are willing to sell it for on the supply curve.

Product differentiation The process of creating real or apparent differences between goods and services.

Production function The relationship between the maximum amounts of output that a firm can produce and various quantities of inputs.

Production possibilities curve A curve that shows the maximum combinations of two outputs an economy can produce in a given period of time with its available resources and technology.

Progressive tax A tax that charges a higher percentage of income as income rises.

Proportional tax A tax that charges the same percentage of income, regardless of the size of income. Also called a *flat-rate tax* or simply a *flat tax*.

Protectionism The government's use of embargoes, tariffs, quotas, and other restrictions to protect domestic producers from foreign competition.

Public choice theory The analysis of the government's decision-making process for allocating resources.

Public good A good or service with two properties: (1) users collectively consume benefits, and (2) there is no way to bar people who do not pay (free riders) from consuming the good or service.

Q

Quantity theory of money The theory that changes in the money supply are directly related to changes in the price level.

Quota A limit on the quantity of a good that may be imported in a given time period.

R

Rational expectations theory The belief that people use all available information to predict the future, including the future impact of predictable monetary and fiscal policies.

Predictable expansionary macroeconomic policies can therefore be negated by immediately flexible wages and prices when businesses and workers anticipate the effects of these policies on the economy.

Rational ignorance The voter's choice to remain uninformed because the marginal cost of obtaining information is higher than the marginal benefit from knowing it.

Real balances effect The impact on total spending (real GDP) caused by the inverse relationship between the price level and the real value of financial assets with fixed nominal value.

Real GDP The value of all final goods produced during a given time period based on the prices existing in a selected base year.

Real income The actual number of dollars received (nominal income) adjusted for changes in the CPI.

Real interest rate The nominal rate of interest minus the inflation rate.

Recession A downturn in the business cycle during which real GDP declines. Also called a *contraction*.

Recessionary gap The amount by which aggregate expenditures fall short of the amount required to achieve full-employment equilibrium.

Regressive tax A tax that charges a lower percentage of income as income rises.

Required reserve ratio The percentage of deposits that the Federal Reserve requires a bank to hold in vault cash or on deposit with the Fed.

Required reserves The minimum balance that the Federal Reserve requires a bank to hold in vault cash or on deposit with the Fed.

Resources The basic categories of inputs used to produce goods and services. Resources are also called *factors of production*. Economists divide resources into three categories: land, labor, and capital.

Robinson-Patman Act A 1936 amendment to the Clayton Act that strengthens the Clayton Act against price discrimination.

Rule of reason The antitrust doctrine that the existence of monopoly alone is not illegal unless the monopoly engages in illegal business practices.

S

Saving The part of disposable income households do not spend for consumer goods and services.

Say's Law The theory that supply creates its own demand.

Scarcity The condition in which human wants are forever greater than the available supply of time, goods, and resources.

Sherman Act The federal antitrust law enacted in 1890 that prohibits monopolization and conspiracies to restrain trade.

Short run A period of time so short that there is at least one fixed input.

Short-run aggregate supply curve (SRAS) The curve that shows the level of real GDP produced at different possible price levels during a time period in which nominal incomes do not change in response to changes in the price level.

Shortage A market condition existing at any price where the quantity supplied is less than the quantity demanded.

Slope The ratio of the change in the variable on the vertical axis (the rise or fall) to the change in the variable on the horizontal axis (the run).

Social benefits and costs The sum of benefits to everyone in society, including both private benefits and external benefits. Social costs are the sum of costs to everyone in society, including both private costs and external costs.

Socialism An economic system characterized by government ownership of resources and centralized decision making.

Speculative demand for money The stock of money people hold to take advantage of expected future changes in the price of bonds, stocks, or other nonmoney financial assets.

Spending multiplier (SM) The ratio of the change in aggregate demand (total spending) resulting from an initial change in any component of aggregate expenditures or aggregate demand, including consumption, investment, government spending, and net exports. As a formula, the spending multiplier equals $1/(1 - MPC)$ or $1/MPS$.

Stagflation The condition that occurs when an economy experiences the twin maladies of high unemployment and rapid inflation simultaneously.

Stock A quantity measured at one point in time. For example, an inventory or the amount of money in a checking account.

Store of value The ability of money to hold value over time.

Structural unemployment Unemployment caused by a mismatch of the skills of workers out of work and the skills required for existing job opportunities.

Subprime mortgage loan A home loan made to borrowers with an above-average risk of default.

Substitute good A good that competes with another good for consumer purchases. As a result, there is a direct relationship between a price change for one good and the demand for its "competitor" good.

Substitution effect The change in quantity demanded of a good or service caused by a change in its price relative to substitutes.

Supply A curve or schedule showing the various quantities of a product sellers are willing to produce and offer for sale at possible prices during a specified period of time, ceteris paribus.

Supply curve of labor A curve showing the different quantities of labor workers are willing to offer employers at different wage rates in a given time period, ceteris paribus.

Supply-side fiscal policy A fiscal policy that emphasizes government policies that increase aggregate supply in order to achieve long-run growth in real output, full employment, and a lower price level.

Surplus A market condition existing at any price where the quantity supplied is greater than the quantity demanded.

Sustainability Meeting the needs of the present generation without compromising the ability of future generations to meet their needs.

T

Tariff A tax on an import.

Tax incidence The share of a tax ultimately paid by consumers and sellers.

Tax multiplier The change in aggregate demand (total spending or total expenditures) resulting from an initial change in taxes. As a formula, the tax multiplier equals 1 − spending multiplier.

Technology The body of knowledge applied to how goods are produced.

Total cost (TC) The sum of total fixed cost and total variable cost at each level of output.

Total fixed cost (TFC) Costs that do not vary as output varies and that must be paid even if output is zero. These are payments that the firm must make in the short run, regardless of the level of output.

Total revenue The total number of dollars a firm earns from the sale of a good or service, which is equal to its price multiplied by the quantity demanded.

Total utility The amount of satisfaction received from all the units of a good or service consumed.

Total variable cost (TVC) Costs that are zero when output is zero and vary as output varies.

Traditional economy An economic system that answers the What, How, and For Whom questions the way they always have been answered.

Tragedy of the Commons Individuals will use an open access resource to the point of exhaustion, basing their use on private benefits while disregarding external costs to others.

Transactions costs The costs of negotiating and enforcing a contract.

Transactions demand for money The stock of money people hold to pay everyday predictable expenses.

Transfer payment A government payment to individuals not in exchange for goods or services currently produced.

Trough The phase of the business cycle in which real GDP reaches its minimum after falling during a recession.

Trust A combination or cartel consisting of firms that place their assets in the custody of a board of trustees.

U

Unemployment compensation The government insurance program that pays income for a short time period to unemployed workers.

Unemployment rate The percentage of people in the civilian labor force who are without jobs and are actively seeking jobs.

Unit of account The function of money to provide a common measurement of the relative value of goods and services.

Unitary elastic demand A condition in which the percentage change in quantity demanded is equal to the percentage change in price.

Utility The satisfaction, or pleasure, that people receive from consuming a good or service.

V

Variable input Any resource for which the quantity can change during the period of time under consideration.

Velocity of money The average number of times per year a dollar of the money supply is spent on final goods and services.

Vertical merger A merger of a firm with its suppliers.

Vicious circle of poverty The trap in which countries are poor because they cannot afford to save and invest, but they cannot save and invest because they are poor.

W

Wage and price controls Legal restrictions on wage and price increases. Violations can result in fines and imprisonment.

Wage and price guidelines Voluntary standards set by the government for "permissible" wage and price increases.

Wage-price spiral A situation that occurs when increases in nominal wage rates are passed on in higher prices, which, in turn, result in even higher nominal wage rates and prices.

Wealth The value of the stock of assets owned at some point in time.

Wealth effect A shift in the consumption function casued by a change in the value of real and financial assets.

World Bank The lending agency that makes long-term low-interest loans and provides technical assistance to less-developed countries.

World Trade Organization (WTO) An international organization of member countries that oversees international trade agreements and rules on trade disputes.

Index

Chapter 9 The Keynesian Model in Action

1. c   2. c   3. a   4. d   5. c   6. a   7. c
8. a   9. b   10. b   11. a   12. d   13. d
14. a   15. b   16. d   17. b   18. c   19. d
20. d

Chapter 10 Aggregate Demand and Supply

1. c   2. e   3. a   4. b   5. a   6. a   7. d
8. a   9. c   10. b   11. c   12. c   13. d
14. b   15. b   16. a   17. a   18. e   19. c
20. c

Appendix 10 The Self-Correcting Aggregate Demand and Supply Model

1. c   2. e   3. a   4. d   5. b   6. a   7. d
8. d   9. b   10. b   11. b   12. a   13. b
14. b   15. b   16. a   17. a   18. c   19. d
20. c

Chapter 11 Fiscal Policy

1. c   2. c   3. d   4. a   5. d   6. d   7. d
8. a   9. c   10. c   11. b   12. a   13. d
14. d   15. d   16. b   17. a   18. c   19. b
20. a

Chapter 12 The Public Sector

1. a   2. a   3. a   4. a   5. b   6. d   7. c   8. a
9. a   10. b   11. c   12. c   13. b   14. d
15. b   16. d   17. a   18. c   19. d   20. b

Chapter 13 Federal Deficits, Surpluses, and the National Debt

1. a   2. d   3. c   4. c   5. d   6. b   7. d
8. d   9. c   10. d   11. a   12. d   13. a

14. d   15. a   16. d   17. d   18. a   19. a
20. e

Chapter 14 Money and the Federal Reserve System

1. a   2. b   3. c   4. d   5. b   6. d   7. d
8. b   9. d   10. d   11. d   12. a   13. c
14. c   15. d   16. d   17. b   18. d   19. a
20. a

Chapter 15 Money Creation

1. c   2. b   3. a   4. b   5. e   6. b   7. a
8. b   9. a   10. c   11. c   12. c   13. b
14. a   15. d   16. e   17. b   18. b   19. b
20. a

Chapter 16 Monetary Policy

1. a   2. c   3. e   4. b   5. b   6. b   7. d
8. a   9. b   10. d   11. a   12. c   13. d
14. b   15. a   16. b   17. d   18. e   19. d
20. e

Appendix 16 Policy Disputes Using the Self-Correcting Aggregate Demand and Supply Model

1. a   2. d   3. a   4. c   5. b   6. b   7. a
8. b   9. a   10. d   11. a   12. c   13. b
14. c   15. d

Chapter 17 The Phillips Curve and Expectations Theory

1. a   2. a   3. c   4. a   5. a   6. c   7. b
8. b   9. b   10. b   11. a   12. b   13. a
14. b   15. d   16. d   17. d   18. d   19. b
20. a

Chapter 18 International Trade and Finance

1. c   2. a   3. c   4. b   5. b   6. d   7. d
8. a   9. e   10. a   11. d   12. a   13. a
14. c   15. c   16. a   17. d   18. b   19. c
20. b

Chapter 20 Growth and the Less-Developed Countries

1. d   2. d   3. c   4. b   5. e   6. d   7. b   8. d
9. d   10. d   11. e   12. a   13. e   14. a
15. b   16. b   17. c   18. a   19. c   20. b

Chapter 19 Economies in Transition

1. d   2. a   3. c   4. a   5. c   6. d   7. d
8. a   9. c   10. a   11. a   12. d   13. a
14. b   15. d   16. b   17. d   18. c   19. d   20. c

Appendix C

Answers to Road Map Questions

Part 1

1. e   2. c   3. c   4. d   5. a   6. e   7. d
8. d   9. d   10. b

Part 2

1. b   2. c   3. a   4. a   5. d   6. d   7. d
8. c   9. c   10. c   11. b   12. a   13. c

Part 3

1. e   2. a   3. a   4. c   5. c   6. b   7. b
8. d   9. a   10. a   11. c   12. d

Part 4

1. d   2. a   3. a   4. d   5. d   6. b   7. c
8. e   9. b   10. a   11. a   12. d   13. b
14. e   15. d

Part 5

1. d   2. d   3. d   4. e   5. c   6. b   7. a
8. d   9. d   10. a   11. e   12. d   13. a
14. a

Part 6

1. d   2. d   3. b   4. e   5. e   6. c   7. d   8. e
9. b   10. d

Appendix

D

U.S. Gross Domestic Product and Related Statistics

U.S. Gross Domestic Product (in billions of dollars) and Related Statistics

	1929	1930	1931	1932	1933	1934	1935	1936	1937	1938
1. Gross domestic product	103.6	91.2	76.5	58.7	56.4	66.0	73.3	83.8	91.9	86.1
2. Personal consumption expenditures	77.4	70.1	60.7	48.7	45.9	51.5	55.9	62.2	66.8	64.3
3. Gross private domestic investment	16.5	10.8	5.9	1.3	1.7	3.7	6.7	8.6	12.2	7.1
4. Government consumption expenditures and gross investment	9.4	10.0	9.9	8.7	8.7	10.5	10.9	13.1	12.8	13.8
5. Net exports	0.4	0.3	0.0	0.0	0.1	0.3	-0.2	-0.1	0.1	1.0
6. National income	93.9	82.9	67.4	51.1	48.8	58.1	66.0	74.7	83.3	76.6
7. Personal income	84.9	76.1	65.2	49.9	46.8	53.7	60.3	68.6	74.1	68.4
8. Disposable personal income	83.2	74.6	64.2	49.1	46.0	52.8	59.3	67.3	72.2	66.5
9. Real gross domestic product (in 2005 dollars)	976.1	892.0	834.2	725.2	715.8	793.7	864.2	977.0	1,027.1	991.8
10. Percent change in real GDP	—	-8.6	-6.5	-13.1	-1.3	10.9	8.9	13.1	5.1	-3.4
11. Consumer price index (1982–84 = 100)	17.1	16.7	15.2	13.7	13.0	13.4	13.7	13.9	14.4	14.1
12. Rate of inflation (percent)	0.0	-2.3	-9.0	-9.9	-5.1	3.1	2.2	1.5	3.6	-2.1
13. Civilian unemployment rate (percent)	3.2	8.7	15.9	23.6	24.9	21.7	20.1	16.9	14.3	19.0
14. Supply of money, M1 (in billions of dollars)	26.4	26.6	21.9	20.4	19.8	23.1	27.0	31.0	29.6	31.8
15. Percent change in M1	—	-0.1	-17.7	-6.8	-2.9	16.7	16.9	14.8	-4.5	7.4
16. Prime rate charged by banks	5.5	1.5	1.5	1.5	1.5	1.5	1.5	1.5	1.5	1.5
17. Federal budget surplus or deficit (in billions of dollars)	0.7	0.7	-0.5	-2.7	-2.6	-3.6	-2.8	-4.3	-2.2	-1.0
18. Federal debt (in billions of dollars)	16.9	16.2	16.8	19.5	22.5	27.1	28.7	33.8	36.4	37.2

(Continued)

U.S. Gross Domestic Product (in billions of dollars) and Related Statistics *(Continued)*

	1939	1940	1941	1942	1943	1944	1945	1946	1947	1948
1. Gross domestic product	92.2	101.4	126.7	161.9	198.6	219.8	223.0	222.2	244.1	269.1
2. Personal consumption expenditures	67.2	71.3	81.1	89.0	99.9	108.7	102.0	144.3	162.0	175.0
3. Gross private domestic investment	9.3	13.6	18.1	10.4	6.1	7.8	10.8	31.1	35.0	48.1
4. Government consumption xpenditures and gross investment	14.8	15.0	26.5	62.7	94.8	105.3	93.0	39.6	36.3	40.5
5. Net exports	0.8	1.5	1.0	−0.3	−2.2	−2.0	−0.8	7.2	10.8	5.5
6. National income	82.0	90.5	115.8	149.5	184.2	198.0	198.3	198.6	216.3	242.6
7. Personal income	72.9	78.4	96.0	123.4	152.1	166.0	171.6	178.6	190.9	209.7
8. Disposable personal income	71.4	76.8	93.7	118.5	135.4	148.3	152.2	161.4	171.1	190.5
9. Real gross domestic product (in 2005 dollars)	1,071.9	1,165.9	1,365.0	1,616.8	1,881.5	2,033.5	2,010.7	1,790.7	1,774.6	1,852.7
10. Percent change in real GDP	8.1	8.8	17.1	18.5	16.4	8.1	−1.1	−10.9	−0.9	4.4
11. Consumer price index (1982–84 = 100)	13.9	14.0	14.7	16.3	17.3	17.6	18.0	19.5	22.3	24.1
12. Rate of inflation (percent)	−1.4	0.7	5.0	10.9	6.1	1.7	2.3	8.3	14.4	8.1
13. Civilian unemployment rate (percent)	17.2	14.6	9.9	4.7	1.9	1.2	1.9	3.9	3.9	3.8
14. Supply of money, M1 (in billions of dollars)	36.2	42.3	48.6	62.9	79.6	90.4	102.3	101.0	113.1	111.5
15. Percent change in M1	13.8	16.9	14.9	29.4	26.6	13.6	13.2	7.5	2.8	−1.4
16. Prime rate charged by banks	1.5	1.5	1.5	1.5	1.5	1.5	1.5	1.5	1.5	1.7
17. Federal budget surplus or deficit (in billions of dollars)	−3.9	−2.9	−4.9	−20.5	−54.6	−47.6	−47.6	−15.9	4.0	11.8
18. Federal debt (in billions of dollars)	48.2	50.7	57.5	79.2	142.6	204.1	260.1	271.0	257.1	252.0